ASSET ALLOCATION

CFA® Program Curriculum
2025 • LEVEL III CORE • VOLUME 1

WILEY

CONTENTS

Contents

How to Use the CFA Program Curriculum

The CFA® Program exams measure your mastery of the core knowledge, skills, and abilities required to succeed as an investment professional. These core competencies are the basis for the Candidate Body of Knowledge (CBOK™). The CBOK consists of four components:

> A broad outline that lists the major CFA Program topic areas (www .cfainstitute.org/programs/cfa/curriculum/cbok/cbok)

> Topic area weights that indicate the relative exam weightings of the top-level topic areas (www.cfainstitute.org/en/programs/cfa/curriculum)

> Learning outcome statements (LOS) that advise candidates about the specific knowledge, skills, and abilities they should acquire from curriculum content covering a topic area: LOS are provided at the beginning of each block of related content and the specific lesson that covers them. We encourage you to review the information about the LOS on our website (www.cfainstitute.org/programs/cfa/curriculum/study-sessions), including the descriptions of LOS "command words" on the candidate resources page at www.cfainstitute.org/-/media/documents/support/programs/cfa-and -cipm-los-command-words.ashx.

> The CFA Program curriculum that candidates receive access to upon exam registration

Therefore, the key to your success on the CFA exams is studying and understanding the CBOK. You can learn more about the CBOK on our website: www.cfainstitute .org/programs/cfa/curriculum/cbok.

The curriculum, including the practice questions, is the basis for all exam questions. The curriculum is selected or developed specifically to provide candidates with the knowledge, skills, and abilities reflected in the CBOK.

CFA INSTITUTE LEARNING ECOSYSTEM (LES)

Your exam registration fee includes access to the CFA Institute Learning Ecosystem (LES). This digital learning platform provides access, even offline, to all the curriculum content and practice questions. The LES is organized as a series of learning modules consisting of short online lessons and associated practice questions. This tool is your source for all study materials, including practice questions and mock exams. The LES is the primary method by which CFA Institute delivers your curriculum experience. Here, candidates will find additional practice questions to test their knowledge. Some questions in the LES provide a unique interactive experience.

DESIGNING YOUR PERSONAL STUDY PROGRAM

An orderly, systematic approach to exam preparation is critical. You should dedicate a consistent block of time every week to reading and studying. Review the LOS both before and after you study curriculum content to ensure you can demonstrate the knowledge, skills, and abilities described by the LOS and the assigned reading. Use the LOS as a self-check to track your progress and highlight areas of weakness for later review.

Successful candidates report an average of more than 300 hours preparing for each exam. Your preparation time will vary based on your prior education and experience, and you will likely spend more time on some topics than on others.

ERRATA

The curriculum development process is rigorous and involves multiple rounds of reviews by content experts. Despite our efforts to produce a curriculum that is free of errors, in some instances, we must make corrections. Curriculum errata are periodically updated and posted by exam level and test date on the Curriculum Errata webpage (www.cfainstitute.org/en/programs/submit-errata). If you believe you have found an error in the curriculum, you can submit your concerns through our curriculum errata reporting process found at the bottom of the Curriculum Errata webpage.

OTHER FEEDBACK

Please send any comments or suggestions to info@cfainstitute.org, and we will review your feedback thoughtfully.

Asset Allocation

1

Capital Market Expectations, Part 1: Framework and Macro Considerations

by Christopher D. Piros, PhD, CFA (USA).

LEARNING OUTCOMES

Mastery	The candidate should be able to:
☐	discuss the role of, and a framework for, capital market expectations in the portfolio management process
☐	discuss challenges in developing capital market forecasts
☐	explain how exogenous shocks may affect economic growth trends
☐	discuss the application of economic growth trend analysis to the formulation of capital market expectations
☐	compare major approaches to economic forecasting
☐	discuss how business cycles affect short- and long-term expectations
☐	explain the relationship of inflation to the business cycle and the implications of inflation for cash, bonds, equity, and real estate returns
☐	discuss the effects of monetary and fiscal policy on business cycles
☐	interpret the shape of the yield curve as an economic predictor and discuss the relationship between the yield curve and fiscal and monetary policy
☐	identify and interpret macroeconomic, interest rate, and exchange rate linkages between economies

Parts of this reading have been adapted from a former Capital Market Expectations reading authored by John P. Calverley, Alan M. Meder, CPA, CFA, Brian D. Singer, CFA, and Renato Staub, PhD

1   INTRODUCTION & FRAMEWORK FOR DEVELOPING CAPITAL MARKET EXPECTATIONS

☐ | discuss the role of, and a framework for, capital market expectations in the portfolio management process

A noted investment authority has written that the "fundamental law of investing is the uncertainty of the future."[1] Investors have no choice but to forecast elements of the future because nearly all investment decisions look toward it. Specifically, investment decisions incorporate the decision maker's expectations concerning factors and events believed to affect investment values. The decision maker integrates these views into expectations about the risk and return prospects of individual assets and groups of assets.

This reading's focus is **capital market expectations (CME)** expectations concerning the risk and return prospects of asset classes, however broadly or narrowly the investor defines those asset classes. Capital market expectations are an essential input to formulating a strategic asset allocation. For example, if an investor's investment policy statement specifies and defines eight permissible asset classes, the investor will need to have formulated long-term expectations concerning each of those asset classes. The investor may also act on short-term expectations. Insights into capital markets gleaned during CME setting should also help in formulating the expectations concerning individual assets that are needed in security selection and valuation.

This is the first of two readings on capital market expectations. A central theme of both readings is that a disciplined approach to setting expectations will be rewarded. With that in mind, Sections 1 and 2 of this reading present a general framework for developing capital market expectations and alert the reader to the range of problems and pitfalls that await investors and analysts in this arena. Sections 3–11 focus on the use of macroeconomic analysis in setting expectations. The second of the two CME readings builds on this foundation to address setting expectations for specific asset classes: equities, fixed income, real estate, and currencies. Various analytical tools are reviewed as needed throughout both readings.

Framework and Challenges

In this section, we provide a guide to collecting, organizing, combining, and interpreting investment information. After outlining the process, we turn to a discussion of typical problems and challenges to formulating the most informed judgments possible.

Before laying out the framework, we must be clear about what it needs to accomplish. The ultimate objective is to develop a set of projections with which to make informed investment decisions, specifically asset allocation decisions. As obvious as this goal may seem, it has important implications.

Asset allocation is the primary determinant of long-run portfolio performance.[2] The projections underlying these decisions are among the most important determinants of whether investors achieve their long-term goals. It thus follows that it is vital to get the long-run *level* of returns (approximately) right. Until the late 1990s, it was standard practice for institutional investors to extrapolate historical return

---

1 Peter L. Bernstein in the foreword to Rapaport and Mauboussin (2001), p. xiii.
2 See Brinson, Hood, and Beebower (1986) and Ibbotson and Kaplan (2000).

data into forecasts. At the height of the technology bubble,[3] this practice led many to project double-digit portfolio returns into the indefinite future. Such inflated projections allowed institutions to underfund their obligations and/or set unrealistic goals, many of which have had to be scaled back. Since that time, most institutions have adopted explicitly forward-looking methods of the type(s) discussed in our two CME readings, and return projections have declined sharply. Indeed, as of the beginning of 2018, consensus rate of return projections seemed to imply that US private foundations, which must distribute at least 5% of assets annually, could struggle to prudently generate long-run returns sufficient to cover their required distributions, their expenses, and inflation. To reiterate, projecting a realistic overall level of returns has to be a top priority.

As appealing as it is to think we could project asset returns with precision, that idea is unrealistic. Even the most sophisticated methods are likely to be subject to frustratingly large forecast errors over relevant horizons. We should, of course, seek to limit our forecast errors. We should not, however, put undue emphasis on the precision of projections for individual asset classes. Far more important objectives are to ensure internal consistency across asset classes (**cross-sectional consistency**) and over various time horizons (**intertemporal consistency**). This emphasis stems once again from the primary use of the projections—asset allocation decisions. Inconsistency across asset classes is likely to result in portfolios with poor risk–return characteristics over any horizon, whereas intertemporal inconsistency is likely to distort the connection between portfolio decisions and investment horizon.

Our discussion adopts the perspective of an analyst or team responsible for developing projections to be used by the firm's investment professionals in advising and/or managing portfolios for its clients. As the setting of explicit capital market expectations has become both more common and more sophisticated, many asset managers have adopted this centralized approach, enabling them to leverage the requisite expertise and deliver more consistent advice to all their clients.

A Framework for Developing Capital Market Expectations

The following is a framework for a disciplined approach to setting CME.

1. *Specify the set of expectations needed, including the time horizon(s) to which they apply.* This step requires the analyst to formulate an explicit list of the asset classes and investment horizon(s) for which projections are needed.

2. *Research the historical record.* Most forecasts have some connection to the past. For many markets, the historical record contains useful information on the asset's investment characteristics, suggesting at least some possible ranges for future results. Beyond the raw historical facts, the analyst should seek to identify and understand the factors that affect asset class returns.

3. *Specify the method(s) and/or model(s) to be used and their information requirements.* The analyst or team responsible for developing CME should be explicit about the method(s) and/or model(s) that will be used and should be able to justify the selection.

4. *Determine the best sources for information needs.* The analyst or team must identify those sources that provide the most accurate and timely information tailored to their needs.

---

3 Explosive growth of the internet in the late 1990s was accompanied by soaring valuations for virtually any internet-related investment. The NASDAQ composite index, which was very heavily weighted in technology stocks, nearly quintupled from 1997 to early 2000, then gave up all of those gains by mid-2002. A variety of names have been given to this episode including the tech or technology bubble.

5. *Interpret the current investment environment using the selected data and methods, applying experience and judgment.* Care should be taken to apply a common set of assumptions, compatible methodologies, and consistent judgments in order to ensure mutually consistent projections across asset classes and over time horizons.

6. *Provide the set of expectations needed, documenting conclusions.* The projections should be accompanied by the reasoning and assumptions behind them.

7. *Monitor actual outcomes and compare them with expectations, providing feedback to improve the expectations-setting process.* The most effective practice is likely to synchronize this step with the expectations-setting process, monitoring and reviewing outcomes on the same cycle as the projections are updated, although several cycles may be required to validate conclusions.

The first step in the CME framework requires the analyst to define the universe of asset classes for which she will develop expectations. The universe should include all of the asset classes that will typically be accorded a distinct allocation in client portfolios. To put it another way, the universe needs to reflect the key dimensions of decision making in the firm's investment process. On the other hand, the universe should be as small as possible because even pared down to minimum needs, the expectations-setting process can be quite challenging.

Steps 2 and 3 in the process involve understanding the historical performance of the asset classes and researching their return drivers. The information that needs to be collected mirrors considerations that defined the universe of assets in step 1. The more granular the classification of assets, the more granular the breakdown of information will need to be to support the investment process. Except in the simplest of cases, the analyst will need to slice the data in multiple dimensions. Among these are the following:

- Geography: global, regional, domestic versus non-domestic, economic blocs (e.g., the European Union), individual countries;
- Major asset classes: equity, fixed-income, real assets;
- Sub-asset classes:
  - Equities: styles, sizes, sectors, industries;
  - Fixed income: maturities, credit quality, securitization, fixed versus floating, nominal or inflation-protected;
  - Real assets: real estate, commodities, timber.

How each analyst approaches this task depends on the hierarchy of decisions in their investment process. One firm may prioritize segmenting the global equity market by Global Industry Classification Standard (GIC) sector, with geographic distinctions accorded secondary consideration, while another firm prioritizes decisions with respect to geography considering sector breakdowns as secondary.[4]

In Step 3, the analyst needs to be sensitive to the fact that both the effectiveness of forecasting approaches and relationships among variables are related to the investor's time horizon. As an example, a discounted cash flow approach to setting equity market expectations is usually considered to be most appropriate to long-range forecasting. If forecasts are also to be made for shorter, finite horizons, intertemporal consistency dictates that the method used for those projections must be calibrated so that its projections converge to the long-range forecast as the horizon extends.

---

4 There is extensive literature on the relative importance of country versus industry factors in global equity markets. Marcelo, Quiros, and Martins (2013) summarized the evidence as "vast and contradictory."

Executing the fourth step—determining the best information sources—requires researching the quality of alternative data sources and striving to fully understand the data. Using flawed or misunderstood data is a recipe for faulty analysis. Furthermore, analysts should be alert to new, superior data sources. Large, commercially available databases and reputable financial publications are likely the best avenue for obtaining widely disseminated information covering the broad spectrum of asset classes and geographies. Trade publications, academic studies, government and central bank reports, corporate filings, and broker/dealer and third-party research often provide more specialized information. Appropriate data frequencies must be selected. Daily series are of more use for setting shorter-term expectations. Monthly, quarterly, or annual data series are useful for setting longer-term CME.

The first four steps lay the foundation for the heart of the process: the fifth and sixth steps. Monitoring and interpreting the economic and market environment and assessing the implications for relevant investments are activities the analyst should be doing every day. In essence, step five could be labelled "implement your investment/research process" and step six could be labelled "at designated times, synthesize, document, and defend your views." Perhaps what most distinguishes these steps from the day-to-day investment process is that the analyst must make simultaneous projections for all asset classes and all designated, concrete horizons.

Finally, in step 7 we use experience to improve the expectations-setting process. We measure our previously formed expectations against actual results to assess the level of accuracy the process is delivering. Generally, good forecasts are:

- unbiased, objective, and well researched;
- efficient, in the sense of minimizing the size of forecast errors; and
- internally consistent, both cross-sectionally and intertemporally.

Although it is important to monitor outcomes for ways in which our forecasting process can be improved, our ability to assess the accuracy of our forecasts may be severely limited. A standard rule of thumb in statistics is that we need at least 30 observations to meaningfully test a hypothesis. Quantitative evaluation of forecast errors in real time may be of limited value in refining a process that is already reasonably well constructed (i.e., not subject to obvious gross errors). Hence, the most valuable part of the feedback loop will often be qualitative and judgmental.

EXAMPLE 1

Capital Market Expectations Setting: Information Requirements

---

1. Consider two investment strategists charged with developing capital market expectations for their firms, John Pearson and Michael Wu. Pearson works for a bank trust department that runs US balanced separately managed accounts (SMAs) for high-net-worth individuals. These accounts' mandates restrict investments to US equities, US investment-grade fixed-income instruments, and prime US money market instruments. The investment objective is long-term capital growth and income. In contrast, Wu works for

a large Hong Kong SAR–based, internationally focused asset manager that uses the following types of assets within its investment process:

Equities	Fixed Income	Alternative Investments
Asian equities	Eurozone sovereign	Eastern European venture capital
Eurozone	US government	New Zealand timber
US large-cap		US commercial real estate
US small-cap		
Canadian large-cap		

Wu's firm runs SMAs with generally long-term time horizons and global tactical asset allocation (GTAA) programs. Compare and contrast the information and knowledge requirements of Pearson and Wu.

Guideline Answer:

Pearson's in-depth information requirements relate to US equity and fixed-income markets. By contrast, Wu's information requirements relate not only to US and non-US equity and fixed-income markets but also to three alternative investment types with non-public markets, located on three different continents. Wu has a more urgent need to be current on political, social, economic, and trading-oriented operational details worldwide than Pearson. Given their respective investment time horizons, Pearson's focus is on the long term whereas Wu needs to focus not only on the long term but also on near-term disequilibria among markets (for GTAA decisions). One challenge that Pearson has in US fixed-income markets that Wu does not face is the need to cover corporate and municipal as well as government debt securities. Nevertheless, Wu's overall information and knowledge requirements are clearly more demanding than Pearson's.

2   CHALLENGES IN FORECASTING

☐ | discuss challenges in developing capital market forecasts

A range of problems can frustrate analysts' expectations-setting efforts. Expectations reflecting faulty analysis or assumptions may cause a portfolio manager to construct a portfolio that is inappropriate for the client. At the least, the portfolio manager may incur the costs of changing portfolio composition without any offsetting benefits. The following sections provide guidance on points that warrant special caution. The discussion focuses on problems in the use of data and on analyst mistakes and biases.

Limitations of Economic Data

The analyst needs to understand the definition, construction, timeliness, and accuracy of any data used, including any biases. The time lag with which economic data are collected, processed, and disseminated can impede their use because data that are not timely may be of little value in assessing current conditions. Some economic data may be reported with a lag as short as one week, whereas other important data may be reported with a lag of more than a quarter. The International Monetary Fund sometimes reports data for developing economies with a lag of two years or more. Older data increase the uncertainty concerning the current state of the economy with respect to that variable.

Furthermore, one or more official revisions to initial data values are common. Sometimes these revisions are substantial, which may give rise to significantly different inferences. Often only the most recent data point is revised. Other series are subject to periodic "benchmark revisions" that simultaneously revise all or a portion of the historical data series. In either case—routine updating of the most recent release or benchmark revision—the analyst must be aware that using revised data as if it were known at the time to which it applies often suggests strong historical relationships that are unreliable for forecasting.

Definitions and calculation methods change too. For example, the US Bureau of Labor Statistics (BLS) made significant changes to the Consumer Price Index for All Urban Consumers (CPI-U) in 1983 (treatment of owner-occupied housing) and again in 1991 (regression-based product quality adjustments). Analysts should also be aware that suppliers of economic and financial indexes periodically **re-base** these indexes, meaning that the specific period used as the base of the index is changed. Analysts should take care to avoid inadvertently mixing data relating to different base periods. Exhibit 1 illustrates the impact of re-basing a time series: Statistics Denmark announced that beginning January 2016, the Danish Consumer Price Index (CPI) was revised and the new base year is 2015. The CPI series based on the old base was no longer published, and the new series was computed back to 1980 retrospectively, such that the CPI took a value of 100.00 on 31 August 2015.

Exhibit 1: Danish CPI before and after Re-Basement (31 August 2015 = 100)

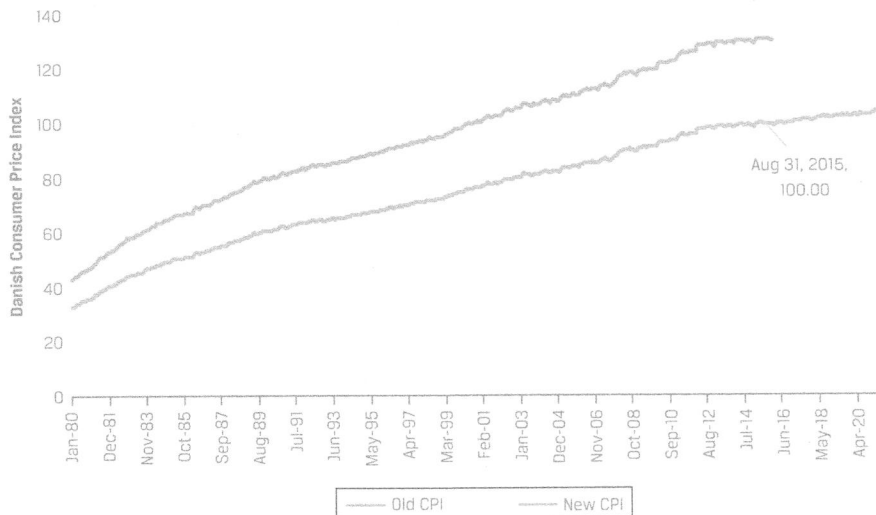

Sources: Statistics Denmark; Bloomberg

Data Measurement Errors and Biases

Analysts need to be aware of possible biases and/or errors in data series, including the following:

- Transcription errors. These are errors in gathering and recording data.

- Survivorship bias. This bias arises when a data series reflects only entities that survived to the end of the period. Without correction, statistics from such data can be misleading. Data on alternative assets such as hedge funds are notorious for survivorship bias.

- Appraisal (smoothed) data. For certain assets without liquid public markets, notably but not only real estate, appraisal data are used in lieu of transaction data. Appraised values tend to be less volatile than market-determined values. As a result, measured volatilities are biased downward and correlations with other assets tend to be understated.

The Limitations of Historical Estimates

Although history is often a helpful guide, the past should not be extrapolated uncritically. There are two primary issues with respect to using historical data. First, the data may not be representative of the future period for which an analyst needs to forecast. Second, even if the data are representative of the future, statistics calculated from that data may be poor estimates of the desired metrics. Both of these issues can be addressed to some extent by imposing structure (that is, a model) on how data is presumed to have been generated in the past and how it is expected to be generated in the future.

Changes in technological, political, legal, and regulatory environments; disruptions such as wars and other calamities; and changes in policy stances can all alter risk–return relationships. Such shifts are known as changes in **regime** (the governing set of relationships) and give rise to the statistical problem of **nonstationarity** (meaning, informally, that different parts of a data series reflect different underlying statistical properties). Statistical tools are available to help identify and model such changes or turning points.

A practical approach for an analyst to decide whether to use the whole of a long data series or only part of it involves answering two questions.

1. Is there any reason to believe that the entirety of the sample period is no longer relevant? In other words, has there been a fundamental regime change (such as political, economic, market, or asset class structure) during the sample period?

2. Do the data support the hypothesis that such a change has occurred?

If the answer to both questions is yes, the analyst should use only that part of the time series that appears relevant to the present. Alternatively, he may apply statistical techniques that account for regime changes in the past data as well as the possibility of subsequent regime changes. Example 2 illustrates examples of changes in regime.

EXAMPLE 2

Regimes and the Relevance of Historical Bond Returns

In the 1970s, oil price shocks combined with accommodative monetary policy by the US Federal Reserve fueled sharply rising inflation. In 1980, the Fed abruptly shifted to an aggressively tight stance. After the initial shock of sharply higher interest rates, US bond yields trended downward for roughly 35 years as the Fed kept downward pressure on inflation. Throughout the 1980s and 1990s, the Fed eased monetary policy in the aftermath of the technology bubble. Then, switching to an extraordinarily expansionary policy in the midst of the 2008–2009 global financial crisis, the Fed reduced its policy rate to 0% in December 2008. Subsequently, it aggressively bought Treasury bonds and mortgage-backed securities. The Fed finally raised its policy rate target in December 2015 and continued hiking it up until it reached 2.5% at the end of 2018. In October 2017, it stopped rolling over maturing bonds, allowing its balance sheet to shrink, albeit very slowly. After the outbreak of COVID-19, the Fed once again cut its policy rate target, to 0%–0.25% in March 2020. It can be argued that bond returns from the 1970s through 2021 reflect at least three distinct regimes: the inflationary 1970s, with accommodative Fed policy; the 1980–2008 period of disinflationary policy and secularly falling yields; and the unprecedented 2009–21 period of zero interest rates and explosive liquidity provision. The years after the 2008-09 global financial crisis were dominated by multiple waves of central bank asset buying, not only in the United States but also globally. The most recent wave of asset purchases (quantitative easing, or QE) came after the outbreak of COVID-19. Exhibit 2 illustrates how QE by the Fed, the European Central Bank, and the Bank of Japan drove long-term government yields lower—even to negative territory in some cases.

Exhibit 2: Effects of QE on Long-Term Government Yield

Source: Bloomberg.

As of mid-2021, nominal interest rates were still negative in some developed markets, and major central banks including the Fed were aiming to "normalize" policy over the next few years. There is ample reason to believe that future bond returns will reflect a regime like none before.

In general, the analyst should use the longest data history for which there is reasonable assurance of stationarity. This guideline follows from the fact that sample statistics from a longer history are more precise than those with fewer observations.

Although it is tempting to assume that using higher-frequency data (e.g., monthly rather than annual observations) will also provide more-precise estimates, this assumption is not necessarily true. Although higher-frequency data improve the precision of sample variances, covariances, and correlations, they do *not* improve the precision of the sample mean.

When many variables are considered, a large number of observations may be a statistical necessity. For example, to calculate a sample covariance matrix, the number of observations must exceed the number of variables (assets). Otherwise, some asset combinations (i.e., portfolios) will spuriously appear to have zero volatility. This problem arises frequently in investment analysis, and a remedy is available. Covariance matrices are routinely estimated even for huge numbers of assets by assuming that returns are driven by a smaller set of common factors plus uncorrelated asset-specific components.

As the frequency of observations increases, the likelihood increases that data may be asynchronous (i.e., not simultaneous or concurrent in time) across variables. This means that data points for different variables may not reflect exactly the same period even though they are labeled as if they do. For example, daily data from different countries are typically asynchronous because of time zone differences. Asynchronicity can be a significant problem for daily, and perhaps even weekly data, because it distorts measured correlations and induces lead–lag relationships that might not exist if the data were measured synchronously. Lower-frequency data (e.g., monthly or quarterly) are less susceptible to asynchrony, although it can still arise. For example, two series that are released and labeled as monthly could reflect data collected at different times of the month.

As a final note on historical data, some care should be taken with respect to whether data are normally distributed. Historical asset returns, in particular, routinely exhibit skewness and "fat tails," which cause them to fail formal tests of normality. The cost in terms of analytical complexity of accounting for non-normality, however, can be quite high. As a practical matter, the added complexity is often not worth the cost.[5]

Ex Post Risk Can Be a Biased Measure of Ex Ante Risk

In interpreting historical prices and returns over a given sample period, the analyst needs to evaluate whether asset prices reflected the possibility of a very negative event that did not materialize during the period. This phenomenon is often referred to as the "peso problem." Looking backward, we are likely to underestimate *ex ante* risk and overestimate *ex ante* anticipated returns. The key point is that high *ex post* returns that reflect fears of adverse events that did not materialize provide a poor estimate of *ex ante* expected returns.

THE ARGENTINE PESO DEVALUATIONS

Starting in 1992, the Argentine peso (ARS) was pegged to the US dollar at a 1:1 ratio, and the ARS/USD exchange rate remained fixed at 1.0 until the Argentine great depression of 1998–2002, which was characterized by bank runs, riots, and sovereign debt default. In January 2002, the government decided to abandon the fixed exchange rate policy and devalued the peso to a rate of 1.4 ARS/USD. The currency was allowed to fluctuate freely, and the peso further depreciated to 3.8 ARS/USD by June 2001. Over the following years, additional default waves took place, and Argentina suffered from elevated inflation, fluctuating around

---

5 See Chapter 5 of Stewart, Piros, and Heisler (forthcoming 2019) for discussion of the effect of alternative probability distributions on asset allocation decisions.

20%–40%, with fiscal imbalances over the 2010s. The 2018 Argentine monetary crisis led to a further severe devaluation of the peso, trading at a rate of 18.6 ARS/USD at the end of 2017 but closing the year at 37.7.

The opposite situation is also a problem, especially for risk measures that consider only the subset of worst-case outcomes (e.g., value at risk, or VaR). If our data series includes even one observation of a rare event, we may substantially overstate the likelihood of such events happening in the future. Within a finite sample, the observed frequency of this bad outcome will far exceed its true probability. As a simple example, there were 22 trading days in March 2020, the month of the COVID-19-related market panic. On 16 March, the price of Facebook (now named as Meta Platforms) stock closed down −14.3%. The second worst day in the same month was 12 March, with the stock price down −9.3%. Based on this sample, the (interpolated) daily 5% VaR on Facebook stock was 13.4%. That is, an investor in Facebook shares would expect to lose at least 13.4% once every 20 days. Note that the stock did not experience any such loss over the subsequent 19 months.

Biases in Analysts' Methods

Analysts naturally search for relationships that will help in developing better capital market expectations. Among the preventable biases that the analyst may introduce are the following:

- Data-mining bias arises from repeatedly searching a dataset until a statistically significant pattern emerges. It is almost inevitable that some relationship will appear. Such patterns cannot be expected to have predictive value. Lack of an explicit economic rationale for a variable's usefulness is a warning sign of a data-mining problem: no story, no future.[6] Of course, the analyst must be wary of inventing the story after discovering the relationship and bear in mind that correlation does not imply causation.
- Time-period bias relates to results that are period specific. Research findings often turn out to be sensitive to the selection of specific starting and/or ending dates.

SMALL-CAP OUTPERFORMANCE AND TIME-PERIOD BIAS

Evidence suggesting that small-cap stocks outperform large-cap stocks over time (the so-called small firm effect) is very sensitive to the choice of sample period. From 1926 through 1974, US small-cap stocks outperformed large caps by 0.43% per year, but if we skip the Great Depression and start in 1932, the differential becomes 3.49% per year. Similarly, small caps outperformed by 4.5% per year from 2000 through 2010 but underperformed by −2.8% per year from 2010 through 2020.[7]

How might analysts avoid using an irrelevant variable in a forecasting model? The analyst should scrutinize the variable selection process for data-mining bias and be able to provide an economic rationale for the variable's usefulness in a forecasting model. A further practical check is to examine the forecasting relationship out of sample (i.e., on data that was not used to estimate the relationship).

---

6 See McQueen and Thorley (1999).

7 Source: Ibbotson Associates database (Morningstar). Returns calculated by the author.

The Failure to Account for Conditioning Information

The discussion of regimes introduced the notion that assets' risk and return characteristics vary with the economic and market environment. That fact explains why economic analysis is important in expectation setting. The analyst should not ignore relevant information or analysis in formulating expectations. Unconditional forecasts, which dilute this information by averaging over environments, can lead to misperception of prospective risk and return. Example 3 illustrates how an analyst may use conditioning information.

EXAMPLE 3

Incorporating Conditioning Information

Noah Sota uses the CAPM to set capital market expectations. He estimates that one asset class has a beta of 0.8 in economic expansions and 1.2 in recessions. The expected return on the market is 12% in an expansion and 4% in a recession. The risk-free rate is assumed to be constant at 2%. Expansion and recession are equally likely. Sota aims to calculate the unconditional expected return for the asset class.

The conditional expected returns on the asset are 10% = 2% + 0.8 × (12% − 2%) in an expansion and 4.4% = 2% + 1.2 × (4% − 2%) in a recession. Weighting by the probabilities of expansion and recession, the unconditional expected return is 7.2% = [(0.5 × 10%) + (0.5 × 4.4%)].

EXAMPLE 4

Ignoring Conditioning Information

1. Following on from the scenario in Example 3, one of Noah Sota's colleagues suggests an alternative approach to calculate the unconditional expected return for the asset class. His method is to calculate the unconditional beta to be used in the CAPM formula, 1.0 = (0.5 × 0.8) + (0.5 × 1.2). He then works out the unconditional expected return on the market portfolio, 8% = (0.5 × 12%) + (0.5 × 4%). Finally, using the unconditional beta and the unconditional market return, he calculates the unconditional expected return on the asset class as 8.0% = 2.0% + 1.0 × (8% − 2%).

Explain why the alternative approach is right or wrong.

Guideline Answer:

The approach suggested by Sota's colleague is wrong. It ignores the fact that the market excess return and the asset's beta vary with the business cycle. The expected return of 8% calculated this way would overestimate the (unconditional) expected return on this asset class. Such a return forecast would ignore the fact that the beta differs for expansion (0.8) and recession (1.2).

Misinterpretation of Correlations

When a variable *A* is found to be significantly correlated with another variable *B*, there are at least four possible explanations: (1) A predicts B, (2) B predicts A, (3) a third variable C predicts both A and B, or (4) the relationship is spurious. The observed correlation alone does not allow us to distinguish among these situations. Consequently, correlation relationships should not be used in a predictive model without investigating the underlying linkages.

Although apparently significant correlations can be spurious, it is also true that lack of a strong correlation can be misleading. A negligible measured correlation may reflect a strong but *nonlinear* relationship. Analysts should explore this possibility if they have a solid reason for believing a relationship exists.

Psychological Biases

The behavioral finance literature documents a long and growing list of psychological biases that can affect investment decisions. Only a few of the more prominent ones that could undermine the analyst's ability to make accurate and unbiased forecasts are outlined here. Furthermore, note that the literature contains various names and definitions of behavioral biases, which are not necessarily mutually exclusive.

- Anchoring bias is the tendency to give disproportionate weight to the first information received or first number envisioned, which is then adjusted. Such adjustment is often insufficient, and approximations are consequently biased. Analysts can try to avoid anchoring bias by consciously attempting to avoid premature conclusions.

- Status quo bias reflects the tendency for forecasts to perpetuate recent observations—that is, to avoid making changes and preserve the status quo, and/or to accept a default option. This bias may reflect greater pain from errors of commission (making a change) than from errors of omission (doing nothing). Status quo bias can be mitigated by disciplined effort to avoid "anchoring" on the status quo.

- Confirmation bias is the tendency to seek and overweight evidence or information that confirms one's existing or preferred beliefs and to discount evidence that contradicts those beliefs. This bias can be mitigated by examining all evidence with equal rigor and/or debating with a knowledgeable person capable of arguing against one's own views.

- Overconfidence bias is unwarranted confidence in one's own intuitive reasoning, judgment, knowledge, and/or ability. This bias may lead an analyst to overestimate the accuracy of her forecasts and/or fail to consider a sufficiently broad range of possible outcomes or scenarios. Analysts may not only fail to fully account for uncertainty about which they are aware (sometimes described as "known unknowns") but they also are very likely to ignore the possibility of uncertainties about which they are not even aware (sometimes described as "unknown unknowns").

- Prudence bias reflects the tendency to temper forecasts so that they do not appear extreme or the tendency to be overly cautious in forecasting. In decision-making contexts, one may be too cautious when making decisions that could damage one's career or reputation. This bias can be mitigated by conscious effort to identify plausible scenarios that would give rise to more extreme outcomes and to give greater weight to such scenarios in the forecast.

- Availability bias is the tendency to be overly influenced by events that have left a strong impression and/or for which it is easy to recall an example. Recent events may likewise be overemphasized. The effect of this bias can be mitigated by attempting to base conclusions on objective evidence and analytical procedures.

EXAMPLE 5

Biases in Forecasting and Decision Making

1. Cynthia Casey is a London-based investment adviser with a clientele of ultra-high-net-worth individuals in the UK, the US, and the EU. Within the equity portion of her portfolios, she rarely deviates significantly from the country weightings of the MSCI World Index, even though more often than not she tilts the allocation in the right direction. Hence, she can claim a good tactical track record despite having added little value in terms of return through tactical allocation. Because most investors have an implicit "home bias," her European clients tend to view their portfolios as significantly overweight the US (nearly 50% of the World index) and are happy because the US market outperformed the MSCI World ex-US Index by about 8% per year over the 10 years ending 31 December 2020. Conversely, her US clients are unhappy because Casey persistently projected US outperformance but maintained what they instinctively perceive as a significant underweight in the United States. Citing year-to-date performance as of 31 December 2020—US performance was up 21%, while World ex-US performance was up 8%, largely lagging behind the United States, with 8 of 15 European markets actually down in local currencies—Casey's US clients are pressuring her to aggressively increase allocations to US equities. Although experience has taught her to be wary of chasing a strong market, Casey vividly remembers losing clients in the late 1990s because she doubted that the explosive rally in technology stocks would be sustained. With that in mind, she has looked for and found a rationale for a bullish view on US stocks—very robust year-to-date earnings growth.

   What psychological biases are Casey and her clients exhibiting?

   Guideline Answer:

   Casey's clients are implicitly anchoring their expectations on the performance of their respective domestic markets. In pressing Casey to increase the allocation to US stocks based on recent outperformance, her US clients are clearly projecting continuation of the trend, a status quo bias. Casey herself is exhibiting several biases. Prudence bias is apparent in the fact that she has a good record of projecting the correct direction of relative performance among markets but has not translated that into reallocations large enough to add meaningful value. We cannot assess whether that bias affects the magnitude of her forecasts, the extent to which she responds to the opportunities, or both. Losing clients when she doubted the sustainability of the late 1990s technology rally made a very strong impression on Casey, so much so that she has apparently convinced herself to look for a reason to believe the recent relative performance trends will persist. This is indicative of availability bias. Searching for evidence to support a favored view (continued strength of the US market) is a clear sign of confirmation bias, whereas finding support for that view in the recent strength of earnings growth reflects status quo bias.

Model Uncertainty

The analyst usually encounters at least three kinds of uncertainty in conducting an analysis. **Model uncertainty** pertains to whether a selected model is structurally and/or conceptually correct. **Parameter uncertainty** arises because a quantitative model's parameters are invariably estimated with error. **Input uncertainty** concerns whether the inputs are correct. Any or all of these may give rise to erroneous forecasts and/or cause the unwary analyst to overestimate the accuracy and reliability of his forecasts.

The effects of parameter uncertainty can be mitigated through due attention to estimation errors. Input uncertainty arises primarily from the need to proxy for an unobservable variable such as "the market portfolio" in the CAPM. Whether or not this is a serious issue depends on the context. It is a problem if the analyst wants to test the validity of the underlying theory or identify "anomalies" relative to the model. It is less of an issue if the analyst is merely focused on useful empirical relationships rather than proof of concept/theory. Model uncertainty is potentially the most serious issue because the wrong model may lead an analyst to fundamentally flawed conclusions.

Our discussion of the limitations of historical data touched on a model that led many investors far astray in the late 1990s. Up to that point, the implicit model used by many, if not most, institutional investors for setting long-term equity expectations was, "The *ex ante* expected return is, was, and always will be a constant number μ, and the best estimate of that number is the mean over the longest sample available." As the market soared in the late 1990s, the historical estimate of μ rose steadily, leading investors to shift more heavily into equities, which fueled further price appreciation and more reallocation toward equities, and so on, until the technology bubble burst. Ironically, belief in the sanctity of historical estimates coincided with the diametrically opposed notion that the "new economy" made historical economic and market relationships obsolete. There seemed to be no limits to growth or to valuations, at least in some segments of the market. But, of course, there were. This description of the technology bubble illustrates the breakdown of a particular forecasting model. It is not a literal description of anyone's thought process. For various reasons, however—competitive pressures, status quo/availability/prudence biases—many investors acted *as if* they were following the model.

Another flawed model unraveled during the global financial crisis of 2007–2009. One component of that model was the notion that housing price declines are geographically isolated events: There was no risk of a nationwide housing slump. A second component involved "originate to sell" loan pipelines: businesses that made loans with the intention of immediately selling them to investors and therefore had very little incentive to vet loan quality. A third component was the notion that the macro risk of an ever-growing supply of increasingly poor-quality mortgages could be diversified away by progressive layers of securitization. End investors were implicitly sold the notion that the securities were low risk because numerous computer simulations showed that the "micro" risk of individual loans was well diversified. The macro risk of a housing crisis, however, was not reflected in prices and yields—until, of course, the model proved to be flawed. The scenario highlighted here provides another illustration of a particular model breaking down. In this case, it was a flawed model of risk and diversification, and its breakdown was one of many aspects of the financial crisis.

ECONOMIC AND MARKET ANALYSIS: THE ROLE OF ECONOMIC ANALYSIS AND ANALYSIS OF ECONOMIC GROWTH: EXOGENOUS SHOCKS TO GROWTH

3

☐ | explain how exogenous shocks may affect economic growth trends

The previous section outlined various pitfalls in forecasting. Each of these is important. Yet they pale in comparison to a fundamental mistake: losing sight of the fact that investment outcomes are inherently linked to the economy. The technology bubble and the global financial crisis offer two extreme illustrations of the consequences of falling into this trap. Less dramatic, but still consequential, instances of this mistake regularly contribute to the differential investment performance that separates "winners" and "losers." The remainder of this reading is dedicated to effective incorporation of economic and market analysis into capital market expectations.

The Role of Economic Analysis

History has shown that there is a direct yet variable relationship among actual realized asset returns, expectations for future asset returns, and economic activity. Analysts need to be familiar with the historical relationships that empirical research has uncovered concerning the direction, strength, and lead–lag relationships between economic variables and capital market returns.

The analyst who understands which economic variables may be most relevant to the current economic environment has a competitive advantage, as does the analyst who can discern or forecast changes in acceleration and deceleration of a trend.

Economic output has both cyclical and trend growth components. Trend growth is of obvious relevance for setting long-term return expectations for asset classes such as equities. Cyclical variation affects variables such as corporate profits and interest rates, which are directly related to asset class returns and risk. In the following sections, we address trend growth, business cycles, the role of monetary and fiscal policies, and international interactions.

Analysis of Economic Growth

The economic growth trend is the long-term average growth path of GDP around which the economy experiences semi-regular business cycles. The analyst needs to understand and analyze both the trend and the cycles. Though each could exist without the other, they are related.

It might seem that trends are inherently easier to forecast than cycles. After all, trends are about long-term averages, whereas cycles are about shorter-term movements and turning points. The assumption that trends are easier to forecast would be true if trend growth rates were constant. But trend growth rates do change, which is what makes forecasting them relevant for investment analysis. Some changes are fairly easy to forecast because they are driven by slowly evolving and easily observable factors such as demographics. Trend changes that arise from significant "exogeneous shocks" to underlying economic and/or market relationships are not only impossible to foresee but also difficult to identify, assess, and quantify until the change is well-established and retrospectively revealed in the data. Virtually by definition, the effect of truly exogenous shocks on the level and/or growth rate of the economy will not have been built into asset prices in advance—although the risk of such events will likely have been reflected in prices to some degree.

Exogenous Shocks to Growth

Shocks arise from various sources. Some are purely domestic. Others are transmitted from other parts of the globe. Some are negative for potential growth, while others enhance it. Significant shocks typically arise from the following:

- Policy changes. Elements of pro-growth government policies include sound fiscal policy, minimal intrusion on the private sector, encouraging competition within the private sector, support for infrastructure and human capital development, and sound tax policies. Any significant, unexpected change in these policies that is likely to persist will change the expected trend rate of growth. The overhaul of US business taxes at the end of 2017, although not entirely unexpected, was intended to be a pro-growth change in policy. On the other hand, standard economic arguments indicate that erecting trade barriers will diminish trend growth.

- New products and technologies. Creation and assimilation of new products, markets, and technologies enhances potential growth. Consider the printing press, steam engine, telegraph and telephone, railroad, automobile, airplane, transistor, random-access memory (RAM), integrated circuits, internet, wireless communication (radio, TV, smartphone), rockets, and satellites, to name just a few.

- Geopolitics. Geopolitical conflict has the potential to reduce growth by diverting resources to less economically productive uses (e.g., accumulating and maintaining weapons, discouraging beneficial trade). The fall of the Berlin wall, which triggered German reunification and a "peace dividend" for governments as they cut defense spending, was a growth-enhancing geopolitical shock. Interestingly, geopolitical tensions (e.g., the space race) can also spur innovation that results in growth-enhancing technologies.

- Natural disasters. Natural disasters destroy productive capacity. In the short run, a disaster is likely to reduce growth, but it may actually enhance long-run growth if old capacity is replaced with more efficient facilities.

- Natural resources/critical inputs. Discovery of new natural resources or of new ways to recover them (e.g., fracking) can be expected to enhance potential growth, directly via production of those resources and indirectly by reducing the cost of production for other products. Conversely, sustained reduction in the supply of important resources diminishes growth (e.g., the OPEC oil shock in 1973).

- Financial crises. The financial system allows the economy to channel resources to their most efficient use. Financial crises arise when market participants lose confidence in others' ability (or willingness) to meet their obligations and cease to provide funding—first to specific counterparties and then more broadly as potential losses cascade through the system. As discussed in Example 6, a financial crisis may affect both the level of output and the trend growth rate.

Trend Growth after a Financial Crisis

An extensive study of growth and debt dynamics in the wake of the 2007–2009 global financial crisis identified three types of crises:

- Type 1: A persistent (permanent, one-time) decline in the level of output, but the subsequent trend rate of growth is unchanged.
- Type 2: No persistent decline in the level of output, but the subsequent trend rate of growth is reduced.
- Type 3: Both a persistent decline in the level of output and a reduction in the subsequent trend rate of growth.

The eurozone experienced a sharp, apparently permanent drop in output after the global financial crisis, and subsequent growth was markedly lower than before the crisis, suggesting a Type 3 crisis.

The eurozone's stagnant growth may be traced to structural problems in conjunction with policy missteps. Structural issues included rigid labor markets, a relatively rapid aging of the population, legal and regulatory barriers, cultural differences among countries, use of a common currency in dissimilar economies, and lack of a unified fiscal policy. In terms of policy response, the European Central Bank was slow to cut rates, was slow to expand its balance sheet, and failed to sustain that expansion. Insolvent banks were allowed to remain operational, thwarting deleveraging of the financial system. In part as the result of a lack of fiscal integration that would have facilitated cross-country transfers, several countries were forced to adopt drastic budget cuts that magnified the impact on their particular economies, the differential impact across countries, and the consequences of structural impediments.

Note: See Buttiglione, Lane, Reichlin, and Reinhart (2014).

It should be clear that any of the shocks listed would likely constitute a "regime change" as discussed earlier.

Impact of Exogenous Shocks on Trend Growth

1. Philippe Leblanc, an analyst focusing on economic forecasting, recently read about a discovery by scientists at a major university that may allow the efficiency of solar panels to double every two to three years, a result similar to Moore's Law with respect to computer chips. In further reading, he found new research at Tsinghua University that may rapidly increase the distance over which electricity can be transmitted.

What implications should Leblanc draw with regard to growth trends if either, or both, of these developments come to fruition? What government policy changes might offset the impact?

Guideline Answer:

Either of these developments would be expected to increase trend growth. They would be especially powerful together. Rapid increases in solar panel efficiency would drive down the cost of energy over time, especially in areas with long days and intense sunlight. The closer to the equator, the larger the potential effect. The developments would also make it increasingly possible to bring large-scale power production to remote areas, thereby expanding the range and scale of economically viable businesses in those areas. Extending the range of electrical transmission would allow moving lower-cost energy (regardless of how it is generated) to where it is most efficiently used. A variety of government actions could undermine the pro-growth nature of these developments; for example, tariffs on solar panels, restrictions on electrical transmission lines, subsidies to support less efficient energy sources, failure to protect intellectual property rights, or prohibition on transfer of technology.

4   APPLYING GROWTH ANALYSIS TO CAPITAL MARKET EXPECTATIONS

> ☐ | discuss the application of economic growth trend analysis to the formulation of capital market expectations

The expected trend rate of economic growth is a key consideration in a variety of contexts. First, it is an important input to discounted cash flow models of expected return. The trend growth rate imposes discipline on forecasts of fundamental metrics such as earnings because these must be kept consistent with aggregate long-run growth at the trend rate. Second, a country with a higher trend rate of growth may offer equity investors a particularly good return if that growth has not already been priced into the market. Third, a higher trend rate of growth in the economy allows actual growth to be faster before accelerating inflation becomes a significant concern. This fact is especially important in projecting the likely path of monetary policy and bond yields. Fourth, theory implies, and empirical evidence confirms, that the average level of real government bond yields is linked to the trend growth rate. Faster trend growth implies higher average real yields.

Most countries have had periods of faster and slower trend growth during their development. Emerging countries often experience rapid growth as they catch up with the leading industrial countries, but the more developed they become, the more likely it is that their growth will slow.

A Decomposition of GDP Growth and Its Use in Forecasting

The simplest way to analyze an economy's aggregate trend growth is to split it into the following components:

- growth from labor inputs, consisting of

  - growth in potential labor force size and
  - growth in actual labor force participation, plus
- growth from labor productivity, consisting of

  - growth from increasing capital inputs and
  - growth in total factor productivity.

Labor input encompasses both the number of workers and the average number of hours they work. Growth in the potential labor force size is driven by demographics such as the population's age distribution, net migration, and workplace norms such as the length of the work week. All of these factors tend to change slowly, making growth in the potential labor force relatively predictable. Trends in net migration and workplace norms, however, may change abruptly in response to sudden structural changes, such as changes in government policies.

Labor force participation primarily reflects labor versus leisure decisions by workers. All else the same, we should expect labor force participation to decline (or at least grow more slowly) as a country becomes more affluent. On the other hand, rising real wages tend to attract workers back into the labor force. Social norms and government policies also play a large role.

Growth in labor productivity comes from investment in additional capital per worker ("capital deepening") and from increases in **total factor productivity** (TFP), which is often taken to be synonymous with technological improvement.[8] Government policy (e.g., regulations) can also influence TFP. In historical analyses, TFP is often measured as a "residual"—that is, output growth that is not accounted for by the other factors.

The trend rate of growth in mature, developed markets is generally fairly stable. As a result, extrapolating past trends in the components outlined in the foregoing can be expected to provide a reasonable initial estimate of the future growth trend. This forecast should then be adjusted to reflect observable information indicating how future patterns are likely to differ from past patterns. This same approach can be applied to less developed markets. It must be recognized, however, that these economies are likely to be undergoing rapid structural changes that may require the analyst to make more significant adjustments relative to past trends.

Anchoring Asset Returns to Trend Growth

Both theory and empirical evidence indicate that the average level of real (nominal) default-free bond yields is linked to the trend rate of real (nominal) growth.[9] To put it another way, bond yields will be pulled toward this level over time. Thus, the trend rate of growth provides an important anchor for estimating bond returns over horizons long enough for this reversion to prevail over cyclical and short-term forces. Intertemporal consistency demands that this anchor be factored into forecasts even for shorter horizons.

The trend growth rate also provides an anchor for long-run equity appreciation.[10] We can express the aggregate market value of equity, V^e, as the product of three factors: the level of nominal GDP, the share of profits in the economy, S^k (earnings/GDP), and the P/E ratio (PE).

$$V_t^e = \text{GDP}_t \times S_t^k \times PE_t$$

It is clear that over long periods, capital's share of income cannot continually increase or decrease. The same is true for the P/E multiple applied to earnings. As a result, in the long run, the growth rate of the total value of equity in an economy is linked to the growth rate of GDP. Over finite horizons, the way in which the share of capital and the P/E multiple are expected to change will also affect the forecast of the total value of equity, as well as its corresponding growth rate over that period.

---

8 Total factor productivity captures a variety of effects, such as the impact of adding not just *more* physical capital (i.e., "capital deepening") but *better* capital, as well as the impact of increasingly skilled labor (i.e., increases in "human capital"). Earlier readings provide a more granular breakdown of the drivers/components of growth.

9 With regard to nominal yields and growth, it is assumed that inflation is sufficiently well behaved.

10 See Stewart, Piros, and Heisler (forthcoming 2019) for more thorough development of these arguments.

This argument applies to the capital appreciation component of equity returns. It does not supply a way to estimate the other component: the dividend yield. An estimate for the dividend yield (annual dividends/market value) can be obtained by noting that the dividend yield equals the dividend payout ratio (dividends/profit) divided by the profit multiple (market value/profit). The analyst may set any two of these three ratios and infer the third.

EXAMPLE 8

Long-Run Equity Returns and Economic Growth

In January 2000, Alena Bjornsdottir, CFA, was updating her firm's projections for US equity returns. The firm had always used the historical average return with little adjustment. Alena was aware that historical averages are subject to large sampling errors and was especially concerned about this fact because of the sequence of very high returns in the late 1990s, as well as over the past few years partly due to very low levels of interest rates. She decided to examine whether US equity returns since World War II had been consistent with economic growth. For the period 1946–2020, the continuously compounded (i.e., logarithmic) return was 10.7% per annum, which reflected the following components:

Real GDP Growth	Inflation	EPS/GDP (Chg)	P/E (Chg)	Dividend Yield
2.9%	3.5%	0.00%	0.9%	3.4%

1. What conclusion was Alena likely to have drawn from this analysis?

   Guideline Answer:

   Alena is likely have concluded that the post-war stock return exceeded what would have been consistent with growth of the economy. In particular, the rising P/E added 0.9% of "extra" return per year for 74 years, adding 67% (= 74 × 0.9%) to the cumulative, continuously compounded return and leaving the market 95% (exp[67%] = 1.95) above "fair value."

2. If she believed that in the long run that the US labor input would grow by 0.9% per annum and labor productivity by 1.5%, that inflation would be 2.1%, that the dividend yield would be 2.25%, and that there would be no further growth in P/E, what is likely to have been her baseline projection for continuously compounded long-term US equity returns?

   Guideline Answer:

   Her baseline projection is likely to have been 6.75% = 0.9% + 1.5% + 2.1% + 2.25%.

3. In light of her analysis, how might she have adjusted her baseline projection?

   Guideline Answer:

   She is likely to have adjusted her projection downward to some degree to reflect the likelihood that the effect of the P/E would decline toward zero over time. Assuming, for example, that this would occur over 30 years would imply reducing the baseline projection by 2.2% = (67%/30) per year.

Studies have shown that countries with higher economic growth rates do not reliably generate higher equity market returns.[11] A partial explanation is likely to be that the higher growth rate was already reflected in market prices. The sources of growth may be a second factor. Stock market returns ultimately reflect the rate of return on invested capital. If the capital stock is growing rapidly, the rate of return on invested capital may be driven down. Both of these explanations are consistent with the arguments outlined earlier. High growth need not translate one-for-one into higher return unless it can be expected to continue forever. Declining return on investment essentially means that either GDP growth slows or profits decline as a share of GDP, or both. And, of course, valuation multiples do matter.

APPROACHES TO ECONOMIC FORECASTING

5

☐ | compare major approaches to economic forecasting

Whereas the trend growth rate is a long-term average and reflects only the supply side of the economy, most macroeconomic forecasting focuses on short- to intermediate-term fluctuations around the trend—that is, the business cycle. These fluctuations are usually ascribed primarily to shifts in aggregate demand, although shifts in the short-term aggregate supply curve also play a role.

Before discussing the business cycle, we outline the main approaches available for tracking and projecting these movements. There are at least three distinct approaches:

- Econometric models: the most formal and mathematical.
- Indicators: variables that lead, lag, or coincide with turns in the economy.
- Checklists: subjective integration of the answers to relevant questions.

These approaches are not mutually exclusive. Indeed, thorough analysis is likely to incorporate elements of all three.

Econometric Modeling

Econometrics is the application of statistical methods to model relationships among economic variables. **Structural models** specify functional relationships among variables based on economic theory. The functional form and parameters of these models are derived from the underlying theory. **Reduced-form models** have a looser connection to theory. As the name suggests, some such models are simply more-compact representations of underlying structural models. At the other end of the spectrum are models that are essentially data driven, with only a heuristic rationale for selection of variables and/or functional forms.

Econometric models vary from small models with a handful of equations to large, complex models with hundreds of equations. They are all used in essentially the same way, however. The estimated system of equations is used to forecast the future values of economic variables, with the forecaster supplying values for the exogenous variables. For example, such a model may require the forecaster to enter exchange rates, interest rates, commodity prices, and/or policy variables. The model then uses the estimated past relationships to forecast the future. It is important to consider that

---

11 Joachim Klement, "What's Growth Got to Do with It? Equity Returns and Economic Growth," *Journal of Investing* Summer 2015 is one such study covering 44 countries.

the forecaster's future values for the exogenous variables are themselves subject to estimation error. This fact will increase the variability of potential forecast errors of the endogenous variables beyond what results from errors in the estimated parameter values. The analyst should examine a realistic range of values for the exogenous variables to assess the forecast's sensitivity to these inputs.

Econometric models are widely regarded as very useful for simulating the effects of changes in key variables. The great merit of the econometric approach is that it constrains the forecaster to a certain degree of consistency and also challenges the modeler to reassess prior views based on what the model concludes. It does have important limitations, however. Econometric models require the user to find adequate measures for the real-world activities and relationships to be modeled. These measures may be unavailable. Variables may also be measured with error. Relationships among the variables may change over time because of changes in economic structure and/or because the model may have been based on faulty assumptions as to how the world works. As a result, the econometric model may be mis-specified. In practice, therefore, skillful econometric modelers monitor the model's recent forecasts for signs of systematic errors. Persistent forecast errors should ideally lead to a complete overhaul of the model. In practice, however, a more pragmatic approach is often adopted: Past forecast errors are incorporated into the model as an additional explanatory variable.

Economic Indicators

Economic indicators are economic statistics published by official agencies and/or private organizations. These indicators contain information on an economy's recent past activity or its current or future position in the business cycle. Lagging economic indicators and coincident indicators reflect recent past and current economic activity, respectively. A **leading economic indicator** (LEI) moves ahead of the business cycle by a fairly consistent time interval. Most analysts focus primarily on leading indicators because they purport to provide information about upcoming changes in economic activity, inflation, interest rates, and security prices.

Leading indicator–based analysis is the simplest forecasting approach to use because it requires following only a limited number of statistics. It also has the advantage of not requiring the analyst to make assumptions about the path of exogenous variables. Analysts use both individual LEIs and composite LEIs, reflecting a collection of economic data releases combined to give an overall reading. The OECD composite LEI for each country or region is based on five to nine variables such as share prices, manufacturing metrics, inflation, interest rates, and monetary data that exhibit cyclical fluctuations similar to GDP, with peaks and troughs occurring six to nine months earlier with reasonable consistency. Individual LEIs can also be combined into a so-called **diffusion index**, which measures how many indicators are pointing up and how many down. For example, if 7 out of 10 are pointing upward, then the odds are that the economy is accelerating.

One of the drawbacks of the (composite) leading indicator methodology is that the entire history may be revised each month. As a result, the most recently published historical indicator series will almost certainly appear to have fit past business cycles (i.e., GDP) better than it actually did in real time. This distortion is known as "look ahead" bias. Correspondingly, the LEI may be less reliable in predicting the current/ next cycle than history suggests.

Business cycle indicators have been published for decades. A new methodology for tracking the business cycle, known generically as "nowcasting," emerged in the United States in the wake of the global financial crisis. The best-known of these forecasts, the Federal Reserve Bank of Atlanta's "GDPNow," was first published on 1 May 2014 for the second quarter of that year. The objective is to forecast GDP for the current quarter (which will not be released until after quarter-end) based on data as it is released throughout the quarter. To do this, the Atlanta Fed attempts to use the same methodology and data as will be used by the Bureau of Economic Analysis (BEA) to estimate GDP, replacing data that has not yet been released with forecasts based on the data already observed. As the quarter progresses, more of the actual data will have been observed, and GDPNow should, at least on average, converge to what will be released by the BEA.

BEA RELEASES OF ESTIMATES

The BEA releases a sequence of three GDP estimates for each quarter. The first, labeled the "advance" estimate, is released four weeks after the end of the quarter and tends to have the greatest market impact. The "preliminary" estimate is released a month later, and the "final" estimate comes at the end of the following quarter. The Atlanta Fed's GDPNow is actually a forecast of the BEA's advance estimate, not of the final GDP release. Exhibit 3 compares the history of Atlanta Fed's GDPNow model forecast with the actual GDP change.

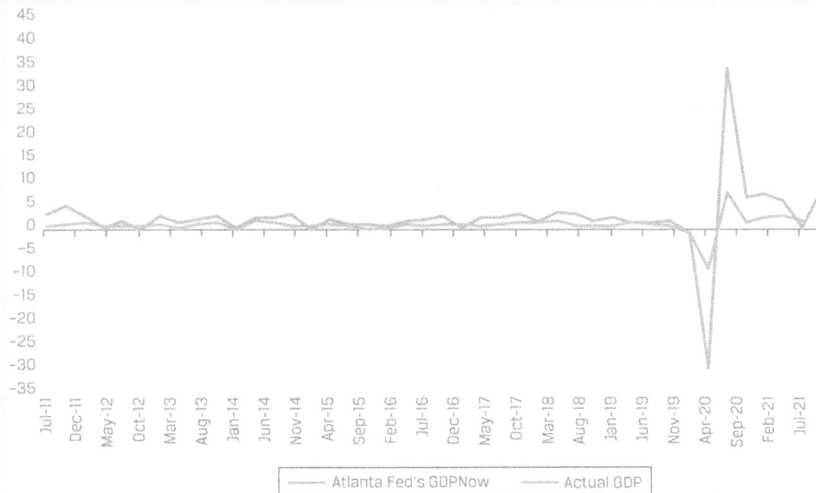

Exhibit 3: GDPNow Model Forecast vs. Actual GDP Change

Sources: Federal Reserve Economic Data; St. Louis Fed.

It remains to be seen how useful nowcasting will be for investment analysts. It has a couple of clear advantages: It is updated in real time, and it is focused directly on a variable of primary interest (GDP and its components). Nowcasting is not designed to be predictive of anything beyond the end of the current quarter, however. In addition, it tends to be very volatile until a significant portion of the data for the quarter has been observed, at which point it may have lost some of its usefulness as a guide for investment decisions.

Checklist Approach

Formally or informally, many forecasters consider a whole range of economic data to assess the economy's future position. Checklist assessments are straightforward but time-consuming because they require continually monitoring the widest possible range of data. The data may then be extrapolated into forecasts via objective statistical methods, such as time-series analysis, or via more subjective or judgmental means. An analyst may then assess whether the measures are in an equilibrium state or nearer to an extreme reading.

The subjectivity of the checklist approach is perhaps its main weakness. The checklist's strength is its flexibility. It allows the forecaster to quickly take into account changes in economic structure by changing the variables or the weights assigned to variables within the analysis.

Economic Forecasting Approaches: Summary of Strengths and Weaknesses

Exhibit 4 summarizes the advantages and disadvantages of forecasting using econometric models, leading indicators, and checklists.

Exhibit 4: Economic Forecasting Approaches: Strengths and Weaknesses	
Strengths	**Weaknesses**
Econometric Models Approach	
■ Models can be quite robust, with many factors included to approximate reality.	■ Complex and time-consuming to formulate.
■ New data may be collected and consistently used within models to quickly generate output.	■ Data inputs not easy to forecast.
	■ Relationships not static. Model may be mis-specified.
■ Delivers quantitative estimates of impact of changes in exogenous variables.	■ May give false sense of precision.
■ Imposes discipline/consistency on analysis.	■ Rarely forecasts turning points well.
Leading Indicator–Based Approach	
■ Usually intuitive and simple in construction.	■ History subject to frequent revision.
■ Focuses primarily on identifying turning points.	• "Current" data not reliable as input for historical analysis.
■ May be available from third parties. Easy to track.	• Overfitted in-sample. Likely overstates forecast accuracy.
	■ Can provide false signals.
	■ May provide little more than binary (no/yes) directional guidance.
Checklist Approach	
■ Limited complexity.	■ Subjective. Arbitrary. Judgmental.
■ Flexible.	■ Time-consuming.
• Structural changes easily incorporated.	■ Manual process limits depth of analysis. No clear mechanism for combining disparate information.
• Items easily added/dropped.	
• Can draw on any information, from any source, as desired.	■ Imposes no consistency of analysis across items or at different points in time. May allow use of biased and/or inconsistent views, theories, assumptions.
■ Breadth: Can include virtually any topics, perspectives, theories, and assumptions.	

EXAMPLE 9

Approaches to Forecasting

Sara Izek and Adam Berke are members of the asset allocation committee at Cycle Point Advisors, which emphasizes the business cycle within its tactical asset allocation process. Berke has developed a time series model of the business cycle that uses a published LEI series as a key input. He presents forecasts based on the model at each asset allocation meeting. Izek is eclectic in her approach, preferring to sample research from a wide variety of sources each month and then focus on whatever perspectives and results seem most interesting. She usually brings a stack of charts she has copied to the asset allocation meeting.

Questions

1. Which of the main forecasting approaches (or combination of approaches) best describe(s) each analyst's own practice?

   Guideline Answer:

   Berke uses the econometric modeling approach in conjunction with the LEI approach. Izek's practice is essentially a checklist approach.

2. What strength(s) are likely to have appealed to each analyst?

   Guideline Answer:

   Berke is probably attracted to the quantitative output provided by a model, the consistency and discipline it imposes on the process, and the ability to generate explicit forecasts. He may have included the LEI in the model because it is designed to capture cyclical turning points or simply because doing so improves the model's statistical fit of the model.

   Izek is probably drawn to the flexibility of the checklist approach with respect to what is included/excluded and how to evaluate the information.

3. What weaknesses might each analyst be overlooking?

   Guideline Answer:

   Berke may be overlooking potential mis-specification of his model, which is apt to make his forecasts systematically inaccurate (i.e., biased). He may also be failing to recognize the likely magnitude of the forecast errors that will be present even if the model is unbiased (i.e., overestimating the precision of the forecasts). By using the historical LEI series as an input to the model, he may be incorporating look-ahead bias into the model.

   Izek is likely overlooking the subjective, judgmental, and idiosyncratic nature of her approach. Her practice of basing her "checklist" on what seems most interesting in other analysts' current research makes her process especially vulnerable to inconsistency and cognitive biases.

6

BUSINESS CYCLE ANALYSIS, PHASES OF THE BUSINESS CYCLE AND MARKET EXPECTATIONS AND THE BUSINESS CYCLE

> ☐ | discuss how business cycles affect short- and long-term expectations

The trend rate of economic growth provides a vital anchor for setting very long-run investment expectations, which in turn provide a starting point for developing projections over short- to intermediate-term horizons. Virtually by definition, deviations from trend wash out in the long run, making information about the current economic and market environment of limited value over very long horizons. Over short to intermediate horizons, however, such information can be very important. From a macroeconomic perspective, the most useful such information typically pertains to fluctuations associated with the **business cycle**.

It is useful to think of fluctuations in economic activity as a superposition of many cycles varying in frequency from very short (days) to very long (decades), each with stochastic amplitude. The business cycle is not a specific, well-defined cycle. It is the result of many intermediate frequency cycles that jointly generate most of the variation in aggregate economic activity (i.e., GDP) around the trend. This fact explains why historical business cycles have varied in both duration and intensity—each was a different realization of a range of underlying stochastic cycles. It also helps to explain why it is difficult to project turning points in real time.

BUSINESS CYCLE PEAKS AND TROUGHS

The best-known record of business cycle peaks and troughs is published for the United States by the National Bureau of Economic research (NBER). According to NBER, the United States has experienced 34 complete business cycles since 1854, averaging 59 months from peak to peak. The longest cycle was 146 months, the shortest only 17 months. Fifty percent of the cycles lasted between 38 and 69 months. On average, the cycle's contraction phase (peak to trough) lasted 17 months, whereas the expansion phase (trough to peak) lasted 42 months.

At a fundamental level, the business cycle arises in response to the interaction of uncertainty, expectational errors, and rigidities that prevent instantaneous adjustment to unexpected events. It reflects decisions that

a. are made based on imperfect information and/or analysis with the expectation of future benefits,

b. require significant current resources and/or time to implement, and

c. are difficult and/or costly to reverse.

Such decisions are, broadly defined, investment decisions. Much of the uncertainty that sustains the cycle is endogenous to the system. Competitors, suppliers, employers, creditors, customers, and policymakers do not behave as expected. Prices and quantities adjust more or less than expected. Other sources of uncertainty are more exogenous. Technological breakthroughs threaten to disrupt whole industries and/or create new ones. Fracking, gene sequencing, e-commerce, "big data," digital advertising, cybersecurity, 3-D printing, the internet of things, and driverless cars are among those now playing out. Weather patterns affect agriculture, construction, and transportation. Natural disasters devastate local economies. Political and geopolitical shifts favor some entities and disadvantage others. And, of course, shocks in one part of the global economy are often transmitted to other parts of the world through trade relations, financial markets, and the prices of goods and services.

Numerous variables can be used to monitor the business cycle. Among them are GDP growth, industrial production (IP), employment/unemployment, purchasing managers indexes, orders for durable goods, the output gap (the difference between GDP estimated as if the economy were on its trend growth path and the actual value of GDP), and the leading indicator indexes discussed earlier.

Phases of the Business Cycle

There are various ways to delineate phases of the business cycle. The most obvious is to divide it into two primary segments (the expansion and the contraction) with two key turning points at which growth changes sign (the peak and the trough). These two periods are fairly easy to identify, at least in retrospect. Subdividing the cycle more finely is more ambiguous, even in retrospect, because it requires identifying more nuanced changes such as acceleration or deceleration of growth without a change in direction. Nonetheless, it is useful to divide the cycle into several phases distinguished through both economic and financial market characteristics. For the purpose of setting expectations for capital markets, we use five phases of the business cycle here: initial recovery, early expansion, late expansion, slowdown, and contraction. The first four occur within the overall expansion.

1. Initial recovery. This period is usually a short phase of a few months beginning at the trough of the cycle in which the economy picks up, business confidence rises, stimulative policies are still in place, the negative output gap is large, and inflation is typically decelerating. Recovery is often supported by an upturn in spending on housing and consumer durables.

   Capital market effects: Short-term rates and government bond yields are low. Bond yields may continue to decline in anticipation of further disinflation but are likely to be bottoming. Stock markets may rise briskly as fears of a longer recession (or even a depression) dissipate. Cyclical assets—and riskier assets, such as small stocks, higher-yield corporate bonds, and emerging market equities and bonds—attract investors and typically perform well.

2. Early expansion. The economy is gaining some momentum, unemployment starts to fall but the output gap remains negative, consumers borrow and spend, and businesses step up production and investment. Profits typically rise rapidly. Demand for housing and consumer durables is strong.

   Capital market effects: Short rates are moving up as the central bank starts to withdraw stimulus put in place during the recession. Longer-maturity bond yields are likely to be stable or rising slightly. The yield curve is flattening. Stocks trend upward.

3. Late expansion. The output gap has closed, and the economy is increasingly in danger of overheating. A boom mentality prevails. Unemployment is low, profits are strong, both wages and inflation are rising, and capacity pressures boost investment spending. Debt coverage ratios may deteriorate as balance sheets expand and interest rates rise. The central bank may aim for a "soft landing" while fiscal balances improve.

   Capital market effects: Interest rates are typically rising as monetary policy becomes restrictive. Bond yields are usually rising, more slowly than short rates, so the yield curve continues to flatten. Private sector borrowing puts pressure on credit markets. Stock markets often rise but may be volatile as nervous investors endeavor to detect signs of looming deceleration. Cyclical assets may underperform while inflation hedges such as commodities outperform.

4. Slowdown. The economy is slowing and approaching the eventual peak, usually in response to rising interest rates, fewer viable investment projects, and accumulated debt. It is especially vulnerable to a shock at this juncture. Business confidence wavers. Inflation often continues to rise as firms raise prices in an attempt to stay ahead of rising costs imposed by other firms doing the same.

    Capital market effects: Short-term interest rates are high, perhaps still rising, but likely to peak. Government bond yields top out at the first clear sign of a slowing economy and may then decline sharply. The yield curve may invert, especially if the central bank continues to exert upward pressure on short rates. Credit spreads, especially for weaker credits generally widen. The stock market may fall, with interest-sensitive stocks such as utilities and "quality" stocks with stable earnings performing best.

5. Contraction. Recessions typically last 12 to 18 months. Investment spending, broadly defined, typically leads the contraction. Firms cut production sharply. Once the recession is confirmed, the central bank eases monetary policy. Profits drop sharply. Tightening credit magnifies downward pressure on the economy. Recessions are often punctuated by major bankruptcies, incidents of uncovered fraud, exposure of aggressive accounting practices, or a financial crisis. Unemployment can rise quickly, impairing household financial positions.

    Capital market effects: Short-term interest rates drop during this phase, as do bond yields. The yield curve steepens substantially. The stock market declines in the earlier stages of the contraction but usually starts to rise in the later stages, well before the recovery emerges. Credit spreads typically widen and remain elevated until signs of a trough emerge and it becomes apparent that firms will be able to roll over near-term debt maturities.

Exhibit 5 summarizes the fives phases of the business cycle, together with their impact on capital markets.

Exhibit 5: The Five Phases of the Business Cycle

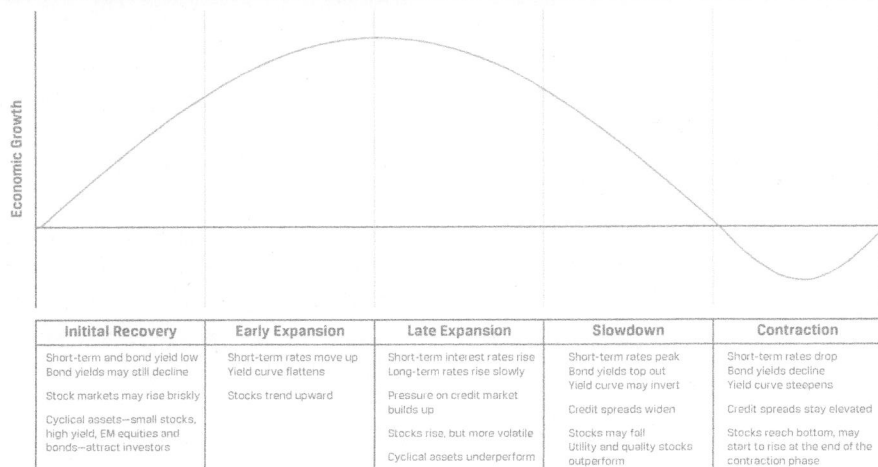

Initial Recovery	Early Expansion	Late Expansion	Slowdown	Contraction
Short-term and bond yield low	Short-term rates move up	Short-term interest rates rise	Short-term rates peak	Short-term rates drop
Bond yields may still decline	Yield curve flattens	Long-term rates rise slowly	Bond yields top out	Bond yields decline
			Yield curve may invert	Yield curve steepens
Stock markets may rise briskly	Stocks trend upward	Pressure on credit market builds up	Credit spreads widen	Credit spreads stay elevated
Cyclical assets—small stocks, high yield, EM equities and bonds—attract investors		Stocks rise, but more volatile	Stocks may fall	Stocks reach bottom, may start to rise at the end of the contraction phase
		Cyclical assets underperform	Utility and quality stocks outperform	

Market Expectations and the Business Cycle

This description of a typical business cycle may suggest that forming capital market expectations for short and intermediate horizons should be relatively straightforward. If an investor can identify the current phase of the cycle and correctly predict when the next phase will begin, is it not easy to make money? Unfortunately, it is not that simple.

First, the phases of the business cycle vary in length and amplitude. Recessions can be steep, and downturns (such as in the 1930s and in 2007–2009) can be frightening. On the other hand, recessions also can be short lived, with only a small decline in output and only a modest rise in unemployment. Sometimes, the weakest phase of the cycle does not even involve a recession but merely a period of slower economic growth or a "growth recession." Similarly, expansions vary in length and intensity.

Second, it is not always easy to distinguish between cyclical forces and secular forces acting on the economy and the markets. The prolonged recovery following the 2007–2009 global financial crisis is a prime example. Interest rates and inflation went far lower and remained extraordinarily low far longer than virtually anyone would have predicted based on a purely cyclical view.

Third, although the connection between the real economy and capital market returns is strong, it is subject to substantial uncertainty. Capital market prices reflect a composite of investors' expectations and attitudes toward risk with respect to all future horizons. How, when, and by how much the markets respond to the business cycle are as uncertain as the cycle itself—perhaps more so.

What does all of this variation and uncertainty imply for setting capital market projections? First, as with virtually any investment information, business cycle analysis generates a noisy signal with respect to prospective opportunities. Second, the signal is likely to be most reliable (a higher "signal-to-noise" ratio), and hence most valuable, over horizons within the range of likely expansion and contraction phases—perhaps one to three years. Returns over substantially shorter horizons are likely to be driven primarily by market reactions to more transitory developments, undermining the cycle's predictive value. On the other hand, as the forecast horizon extends beyond this range, it becomes increasingly likely that one or more turning points will occur within the horizon, implying returns that increasingly reflect averaging over the cycle.

EXAMPLE 10

Cycles, Horizons, and Expectations

Lee Kim uses a statistical model that divides the business cycle into two "regimes": expansion and contraction. The expected (continuously compounded) return on equities is +2% per month during expansions and –2% per month during contractions. Consistent with NBER's historical record (see earlier sidebar), the probabilities of transitioning between regimes imply that expansions last 39 months on average, whereas contractions average 20 months. Correspondingly, over the long run, the economy expands roughly two-thirds of the time and contracts one-third of the time. Hence, the long-term expected equity return is $0.67\% = [(2\% \times 2/3) + (-2\% \times 1/3)]$ per month, or 8% per year. Kim's model indicates that the economy recently transitioned into contraction. For the upcoming asset allocation committee meeting, he will prepare equity return forecasts for horizons of 3 months, 1 year, 5 years, and 10 years.

1. Explain how you would expect the choice of time horizon to affect Kim's projections.

   Guideline Answer:

   The longer the horizon, the more likely that one or more transitions will occur between contraction and expansion; more generally, the more likely it is that the horizon spans more than one business cycle phase or even more than one full cycle. As a result, the longer the horizon, the more Kim's forecast should reflect averaging over periods of expansion and contraction and the closer it will be to the "information-less" average of 8% per year.

   Over the next three months, it is highly likely that the economy will remain in contraction, so Kim's forecast for that period should be very close to –2% per month [cumulatively –6%]. Because contractions last 20 months on average in the model, Kim's forecast for a one-year horizon should reflect only a modestly higher probability of having transitioned to expansion at some point within the period. So, his forecast might be –18% (an average of –1.5% per month) instead of –24% (–2% per month). Over a five-year horizon, it is very likely that the economy will have spent time in both contraction and expansion. As a result, Kim's forecast will put significant weight on each phase. Because the economy starts in contraction (i.e., the starting point is not random), the weight on that phase will probably be somewhat higher than its long-term frequency of 1/3, say 0.40. This assumption implies a forecast of 4.8% per year [$= 12 \times [(0.6 \times 2\%) + (0.4 \times -2\%)]$]. Over a 10-year horizon, the frequency of expansion and contraction months is likely to be very close to the 2-to-1 long-run ratio. So, Kim's forecast should be very close to 8% per year.

7   INFLATION AND DEFLATION: TRENDS AND RELATIONS TO THE BUSINESS CYCLE

> ☐ | explain the relationship of inflation to the business cycle and the implications of inflation for cash, bonds, equity, and real estate returns

Until the early 20th century, the money supply was largely dictated by the supply of specie—gold and/or silver used in coins and to back bank deposits. Periods of both inflation and deflation were common. Today, currencies are backed by the credibility of governments and central banks rather than specie, and people expect the prices of goods and services to trend upward. Persistent deflation is rare. Expectation of an upward trend in prices reflects recognition of an asymmetry in a central bank's so-called "reaction function." It is generally accepted that a central bank's policy tools are more effective in slowing economic activity than in accelerating sluggish activity. Hence, central banks may tend to be more aggressive in combating downward pressure on demand than in reining in strong demand. In addition, it is widely believed that outright deflation damages the economy because it undermines:

- debt-financed investments. Servicing and repayment of nominally fixed debt becomes more onerous as nominal income flows and the nominal value of real assets both decline; and

- the power of central banks. In a deflationary environment, interest rates fall to levels close to (or even below) zero. When interest rates are already very low, the central bank has less leeway to stimulate the economy by lowering interest rates.

In contrast, moderate inflation is generally considered to impose only modest costs on the economy. Both the differential effectiveness of policy and the differential costs of inflation versus deflation suggest that central banks will, implicitly or explicitly, target positive inflation, and investors set their expectations accordingly. The result is that asset prices in general and bond yields in particular generally build in compensation for a positive average inflation rate.

Inflation is procyclical, accelerating in the later stages of the business cycle when the output gap has closed and decelerating when, during a recession or the early years afterward, there is a large output gap, which puts downward pressure on wages and prices. If the central bank's target is credible, the average rate of inflation over the cycle should be near the target.

Because the cyclical pattern of inflation is well known, inflation expectations will also be procyclical. It is important, however, to differentiate inflation expectations by horizon. Very long-term inflation expectations should be virtually unaffected by cyclical fluctuations provided investors maintain confidence in the central bank's target. Short horizon expectations will tend to have about the same amplitude as actual inflation. Inflation, and therefore inflation expectations, over intermediate horizons will be a blend of the different phases of the current and subsequent cycles. Hence, the amplitude of expectations will decline with horizon—again, provided investors do not lose confidence in the central bank's target.

The pattern just described implies a "horizon structure" of inflation expectations that is countercyclical—upward sloping at the trough of the business cycle and inverted at the peak. Because inflation expectations are an important component of bond yields, this countercyclical pattern is one of the reasons that the yield curve's slope is countercyclical.[12]

To assess the effect of inflation on asset classes, we must consider both the cash flows and the discount rates. We consider "cash," nominal bonds, stocks, and real estate.

- *Cash:* In this context, cash is taken to mean short-term interest-bearing instruments, not currency or zero-interest deposits. As long as short-term interest rates adjust with expected inflation, cash is essentially a zero-duration, inflation-protected asset that earns a floating real rate. Inflation above or below expectation contributes to temporary fluctuations in the realized real return. Because central banks aim to stabilize actual and expected inflation, they tend to make the real rate on cash procyclical around a long-term level consistent with their target inflation rate. Hence, cash is relatively attractive (unattractive) in a rising (declining) rate environment. Deflation may make cash particularly attractive if a zero-lower-bound is binding on the nominal interest rate. Otherwise deflation is simply a component of the required short-term real rate.

- *Bonds:* Because the cash flows are fixed in nominal terms, the effect of inflation is transmitted solely through the discount rates (i.e., the yield curve). Rising (falling) inflation induces capital losses (gains) as the expected inflation component of yields rises (falls). If inflation remains within the expected cyclical range, shorter-term yields rise/fall more than longer yields but have less price impact as a result of shorter duration. If, however,

---

12 As will be discussed later, compensation for taking duration risk (the "term premium") is procyclical. As a result, an inverted "horizon structure" of expected inflation does not necessarily imply an inverted yield curve.

inflation moves out of the expected range, longer-term yields may rise/fall more sharply as investors reassess the likelihood of a change in the long-run average level of inflation. Persistent deflation benefits the highest-quality bonds because it increases the purchasing power of the cash flows, but it is likely to impair the creditworthiness of lower-quality debt.

- *Stocks:* As long as inflation stays within the expected cyclical range, there should be little effect on stocks because both expected future cash flows (earnings and dividends) and associated discount rates rise/fall in line with the horizon structure of inflation expectations. Signs that inflation is moving out of the expected range, however, indicate a potential threat. Unexpectedly high and/or rapidly rising inflation could mean that the central bank needs to act to slow the economy, whereas very low and/or falling inflation (possibly deflation) threatens a recession and a decline in asset prices. Within the stock market, higher inflation benefits firms that are able to pass along rising costs, whereas deflation is especially detrimental for asset-intensive, commodity-producing, and/or highly leveraged firms.

- *Real estate:* Short- to intermediate-term nominal cash flows are generally dictated by existing leases, with the speed of adjustment depending on the type of real estate asset held. As long as inflation remains within the expected range, renewal of leases will likely generate rental income rising with expected inflation, accompanied by stable asset values. Higher-than-expected inflation is likely to coincide with high demand for real estate, expectations that rental income will rise even faster than general inflation, and rising property values. The impact may be quite idiosyncratic, however, depending on the length of leases, the existing supply of similar properties, and the likelihood of new supply hitting the market when leases come up for renewal. On the other hand, unexpectedly low inflation (or deflation) will put downward pressure on expected rental income and property values, especially for less-than-prime properties, which may have to cut rents sharply to avoid rising vacancies.

EXAMPLE 11

Inflation

1. Kesia Jabari believes the quantitative easing undertaken by major central banks in the wake of the global financial crisis is finally about to induce a surge in inflation. She believes that without extraordinary policy actions from the central banks, the inflation rate will ultimately rise to the upper end of central banks' tolerance ranges at the peak of the current business cycle.

   Assuming Jabari is correct, discuss the likely implications for floating-rate instruments ("cash"), bonds, stocks, and real estate if:

   a. the market shares Jabari's view, or

   b. once inflation begins to rise, the market doubts that the central banks will be able to contain it.

   Guideline Answer:

   a. If the market agrees with Jabari, then the relationship of inflation and the asset classes to the business cycle should be fairly normal. Short-term rates and bond yields will rise with inflation expectations. The yield curve should flatten because long-term inflation expectations should remain well anchored. Floating-rate instruments (cash) will be relatively attractive, and intermediate maturities ("the belly of the curve") will be the most vulnerable. In general, the rise in inflation should not have much independent impact on stocks or real estate because both cash flows and discount rates will be expected to rise. Firms with pricing power and real estate with relatively short lease-renewal cycles are set to perform best.

b. If the market doubts that central banks can contain inflation within previously perceived tolerances, then long-run inflation expectations will rise and the yield curve may steepen rather than flatten, at least initially. Floating-rate instruments will still be relatively attractive, but now it is the longest maturities that will be the most vulnerable. Stocks are likely to suffer because the market expects central banks to be aggressive in fighting inflation. Real estate with long-term leases and little long-term, fixed-rate debt will suffer. Real estate with substantial long-term, fixed-rate debt should do relatively well, especially high-quality properties with little new supply nearby, which are likely to avoid significant vacancies even in a recession.

In the interest of completeness, we should note a caveat before leaving the topic of inflation. The preceding discussion implicitly assumes that the short-run aggregate supply curve is upward sloping and that the business cycle is primarily driven by fluctuations in aggregate demand. Together, these assumptions imply that inflation is pro-cyclical. Although globalization may have reduced the sensitivity of domestic prices to domestic output, it seems unlikely that domestic output/growth no longer matters. Thus, the aggregate supply curve may be *flatter* but is unlikely to be *flat*. With regard to what drives the cycle, if aggregate supply shocks predominate, then inflation will tend to be *counter*cyclical, reflecting alternating periods of "stagflation" and disinflationary boom. The 1970s oil crisis is a prime example. This pattern is more likely to be the exception rather than the rule, however.

ANALYSIS OF MONETARY AND FISCAL POLICIES 8

☐ | discuss the effects of monetary and fiscal policy on business cycles

Actual and anticipated actions by monetary and fiscal authorities affect the decisions and actions of all other participants in the economy and the markets. As a result, it is somewhat difficult to isolate their role(s) from our broader discussion. Indeed, the foregoing sections have made numerous references to these policies. Nonetheless it is worthwhile to focus directly on these policies from the perspective of setting capital market expectations.

Monetary policy is often used as a mechanism for intervention in the business cycle. Indeed, this use is inherent in the mandates of most central banks to maintain price stability and/or growth consistent with the economy's potential. Each central bank interprets its mandate somewhat differently, sets its own operational objectives and guidelines, and selects its own mix of the tools (e.g., policy rates and liquidity provision) at its disposal. The common theme is that central banks virtually always aim to moderate the cyclical behavior of growth and inflation, in both directions. Thus, monetary policy aims to be countercyclical. The impact of monetary policy, however, is famously subject to "long and variable lags," as well as substantial uncertainty. As a result, a central bank's ability to fine-tune the economy is limited, and there is always risk that policy measures will exacerbate rather than moderate the business cycle. This risk is greatest at the top of the cycle, when the central bank may overestimate the economy's momentum and/or underestimate the effects of restrictive policies. In such situations, monetary policy may trigger a contraction that it cannot immediately counteract. In contrast, expansionary monetary policy rarely, if ever, suffices to turn a contraction into a strong recovery. This asymmetry is captured in a classic analogy: Expansionary policy is like "pushing" on a string, whereas restrictive policy is like "pulling" on a string.

Fiscal policy (government spending and taxation) can also be used to counteract cyclical fluctuations in the economy. Aside from extreme situations, however—such as the Great Depression of the 1930s and recovery from the 2007–2009 global financial crisis—fiscal policy typically addresses objectives other than regulating short-term growth, for at least two main reasons. First, in all but the most authoritarian regimes, the fiscal decision-making process is too lengthy to make timely adjustments to aggregate spending and taxation aimed at short-term objectives. Second, frequent changes of a meaningful magnitude would be disruptive to the ongoing process of providing and funding government services.

Notwithstanding these considerations, fiscal policy often does play a role in mitigating cyclical fluctuations. Progressive tax regimes imply that the effective tax rate on the private sector is pro-cyclical—rising as the economy expands and falling as the economy contracts. Similarly, means-based transfer payments vary inversely with the economy, helping to mitigate fluctuations in disposable income for the most vulnerable households. The effect of these so-called automatic stabilizers should not be overlooked in setting expectations for the economy and the markets.

From the perspective of an investment analyst focused on establishing expectations for broad asset classes, having a handle on monetary policy is mission-critical with respect to cyclical patterns. Under normal conditions, fiscal adjustments are important but likely to be secondary considerations. The reverse is likely with respect to assessing the long run. Of course, if a major change in fiscal stance is contemplated or has been implemented, the impact warrants significant attention with respect to all horizons. The major overhaul of the US tax code (the Tax Cuts and Jobs Act) at the end of 2017 is a good example of these points. Among the main provisions of this tax code change was a corporate tax rate reduction from 35% to 21% and a one-time reduced tax rate for US corporations' foreign earnings if these earnings held in off-shore cash accounts are repatriated to on-shore accounts. These were significant changes with an impact on how US-based global firms handled their foreign earnings. It almost certainly provided a short-term stimulus, especially with respect to capital expenditures. But it was not a short-term policy adjustment. It was the most significant change to the tax code in decades, a major structural change that may affect the path of both the economy and the markets for many years.

Monetary Policy

Central banks can, and do, carry out their mandates somewhat differently. In general, they seek to mitigate extremes in inflation and/or growth via countercyclical policy measures. As a generic illustration of how this might work, we briefly review the **Taylor rule**. In the current context, it can be viewed as a tool for assessing a central bank's stance and a guide to predicting how that stance is likely to evolve.

In essence, the Taylor rule links a central bank's target short-term nominal interest rate to the expected growth rate of the economy and inflation, relative to trend growth and the central bank's inflation target.

$$i^* = r_{\text{neutral}} + \pi_e + 0.5(\hat{Y}_e - \hat{Y}_{\text{trend}}) + 0.5(\pi_e - \pi_{\text{target}})$$

where

i^* = target nominal policy rate

r_{neutral} = real policy rate that would be targeted if growth is expected to be at trend and inflation on target

π_e, π_{target} = respectively, the expected and target inflation rates

$\hat{Y}_e$, $\hat{Y}_{\text{trend}}$ = respectively, the expected and trend real GDP growth rates

The rule can be re-expressed in terms of the real, inflation-adjusted target rate by moving the expected inflation rate to the left-hand side of the equation.

$$i^* - \pi_e = r_{\text{neutral}} + 0.5(\hat{Y}_e - \hat{Y}_{\text{trend}}) + 0.5(\pi_e - \pi_{\text{target}})$$

From this rearrangement, we see that the real, inflation-adjusted policy rate deviates from neutral by one-half the amount by which growth and inflation deviate from their respective targets. As an example, suppose the neutral real policy rate is 2.25%, the target inflation rate is 2%, and trend growth is estimated to be 2.5%. If growth is expected to be 3.5% and inflation is expected to be 3%, the Taylor rule would call for a 6.25% nominal policy rate:

2.25% + 3% + 0.5 (3.5% − 2.5%) + 0.5 (3.0% − 2.0%) = 6.25%.

With expected inflation at 3%, this calculation corresponds to a 3.25% real policy rate.

Even if a central bank were to set its policy rate according to the Taylor rule, there could still be substantial judgment left in the process. None of the inputs to the rule are objectively observable. To make the rule operational, policymakers and their staffs have to specify how the requisite expectations will be generated, and by whom. Whose estimate of trend growth is to be used? What is the appropriate neutral real policy rate? Over what horizon(s) do the expectations apply? Models could be developed to answer all these questions, but there would be judgments to be made in doing so. The upshot for the investment analyst is that monetary policy cannot be reduced to a simple equation. The Taylor rule, or some customized variant, provides a good framework for analyzing the thrust and likely evolution of monetary policy, but the analyst must pay careful attention to situational signals from the central bank. This is why, for example, the investment community literally scrutinizes every word in the Federal Reserve's post-meeting statements and speeches by officials, looking for any hint of a change in the Fed's own interpretation of the environment.

EXAMPLE 12

Policies and the Business Cycle

Albert Grant, CFA, is an institutional portfolio strategist at Camford Advisors. After a period of trend growth, inflation at the central bank's target, and neutral monetary policy, the economy has been hit by a substantial deflationary shock.

1. How are monetary and fiscal policies likely to respond to the shock?

   Camford's economics department estimates that growth is now 1% below trend and inflation is 2% below the central bank's target. Camford's chief investment officer (CIO) has asked Grant to put together a projection of the likely path of policy rates for the next five years.

Guideline Answer:

A countercyclical response can be expected from both monetary and fiscal policy. Assuming the central bank uses a policy rate target as its primary tool, it will cut that rate. On the fiscal side, there may be no explicit expansionary policy action (tax cut or spending increase), but automatic stabilizers built into tax and transfer programs can be expected to cushion the shock's impact on private sector disposable incomes.

2. If Grant believes the central bank will respond in accordance with the Taylor Rule, what other information will he need in order to project the path of policy rates?

Guideline Answer:

Grant will need to know what values the central bank uses for the neutral real rate, trend growth rate, and inflation target. He will also need to know how the central bank forms its expectations of growth and inflation. Finally, he will need to know how growth and inflation are likely to evolve, including how they will be affected by the path of policy rates.

3. What pattern should Grant expect for growth, inflation, and market interest rates if the central bank does *not* respond to the shock?

Guideline Answer:

The deflationary shock is very likely to induce a contractionary phase of the business cycle, putting additional downward pressure on growth and inflation. Short-term market interest rates will be dragged downward by weak demand and inflation. Risky asset prices are likely to fall sharply. A deep and/or protracted recession may be required before conditions conducive to recovery are in place. Grant should therefore expect a deep "U-shaped" path for growth, inflation, and short-term rates.

4. Assuming the central bank does respond and that its reaction function is well approximated by the Taylor Rule, how will this alter Grant's expectations regarding the paths of growth, inflation, and short-term rates over the next five years?

Guideline Answer:

If the central bank responds as expected, it will push short-term rates down farther and faster than they would otherwise fall in an effort to mitigate the downward momentum of growth and inflation. If the central bank correctly calibrates its policy, growth and inflation should decline less, bottom out sooner, and recover more quickly toward trend growth and the target inflation level, respectively, than in the absence of a policy response. Whereas the central bank is virtually certain to drive short rates down farther and faster, it may be inclined to let the market dictate the pace at which rates eventually rise. That is, it may simply "accommodate" the need for higher rates rather than risk unduly restraining the recovery once it is established.

WHAT HAPPENS WHEN INTEREST RATES ARE ZERO OR NEGATIVE? AND IMPLICATIONS OF NEGATIVE RATES FOR CAPITAL MARKET EXPECTATIONS

9

☐ | discuss the effects of monetary and fiscal policy on business cycles

Prior to the 2007–2009 global financial crisis, it was generally accepted that central banks could not successfully implement negative interest rate policies. Belief in a "zero lower bound" on policy rates assumed that individuals would choose to hold currency (coins and notes) if faced with earning a negative interest rate on short-term instruments, including deposits. The move toward holding currency would drain deposits and reserves from the banking system, causing bank balance sheets to shrink. The resulting credit contraction would put upward pressure on interest rates, thwarting the central bank's attempt to maintain negative rates. The contraction of credit would likely also put additional downward pressure on economic growth, thereby reinforcing the need for stimulative policies.

This line of reasoning raised questions about the effectiveness of traditional monetary policy when the economy is so weak that economic growth fails to respond to (nominal) interest rates approaching zero. Following the global financial crisis, as well as after the COVID-19 pandemic began, central banks faced with this situation pursued less conventional measures.

One important measure was quantitative easing, in which central banks committed to large-scale, ongoing purchases of high-quality domestic fixed-income securities. These purchases were funded by creating an equally large quantity of bank reserves in the form of central bank deposits. As a result of QE, central bank balance sheets and bank reserves grew significantly and sovereign bond yields fell. QE was pursued by (among others) the US Federal Reserve, the European Central Bank, the Bank of Japan, and the Bank of England.

Conventional reasoning suggests that QE should have resulted in the desired growth in nominal spending. In theory, banks could use the increased reserves to extend loans, and low interest rates would stimulate businesses and households to borrow. The borrowing was expected to fund capital expenditure by businesses as well as current consumption and purchases of durables (e.g., houses and cars) by households, thereby stimulating the economy. With interest rates low, investors were expected to bid up the prices of stocks and real estate. Although asset prices did increase and businesses that could issue bonds borrowed heavily, proceeds were more often used to fund dividends and stock buybacks rather than capital expenditures. At the same time, household spending ability was significantly curtailed by the legacy of the global financial crisis.

Whether or not QE was effective remains subject to debate. To achieve desired levels of economic growth, central banks tried the previously unthinkable: targeting negative interest rates. The central banks of Denmark, Sweden, Japan, Switzerland, and the euro area were among those that adopted negative policy rates. Contrary to the notion of a "zero lower bound," negative policy rates proved to be sustainable. As of November 2021, 23% of the 1,744 bonds in the Bloomberg Global Aggregate Treasuries Index had negative nominal yield to maturity. These bonds represent 27% of the index's market value. The issuers of such bonds are governments in the eurozone, as well as Switzerland, Denmark, Sweden, and Japan.

The move into currency did not occur as expected because the scale and speed of transactions inherent in modern economies cannot be supported using physical cash as the primary method of exchange.[13] Trillions of dollars change hands daily to facilitate trade in goods, services, and financial instruments, and these transactions cannot be accomplished using physical cash. Bank deposits and bank reserves held at the central bank, rather than as vault cash, have an implicit yield or convenience value that cash does not. As long as this value exceeds the explicit cost of holding those deposits—in the form of a negative interest rate—there is no incentive to convert deposits into cash. In such circumstances, negative policy rates may be achievable and sustainable.

In theory, using negative nominal rates to stimulate an economy should work similarly to using low but still positive rates. Businesses and consumers are encouraged to hold fewer deposits for transaction purposes; investors are encouraged to seek higher expected returns on other assets; consumers are encouraged to save less and/or borrow more against future income; businesses are encouraged to invest in profitable projects; and banks are encouraged to use their reserves in support of larger loan books. All of this is expected to stimulate economic growth.

For consumers, investors, businesses, and banks to behave as described, however, each must believe they will be adequately rewarded for taking the inherent risks. In a negative interest rate environment, these entities are likely to have greater levels of uncertainty as to whether they will be adequately compensated for risks taken, and therefore they may not act as desired by monetary policy makers. As a result, the effectiveness of expansionary monetary policy is more tenuous at low and negative interest rate levels than at higher interest rate levels.

Implications of Negative Interest Rates for Capital Market Expectations

Long-run capital market expectations typically take the level of the "risk-free rate" as a baseline to which various risk premiums are added to arrive at long-run expected returns for risky assets such as long-term bonds and equities. The implicit assumption is that the risk-free rate is at its long-term equilibrium level. When short-term rates are negative, the long-run equilibrium short-term rate can be used as the baseline rate in these models instead of the observed negative rate. This rate can be estimated using the neutral policy rate ($r_{neutral}$) in the Taylor rule (or more generally in the central bank's presumed reaction function), adjusted for a modest spread between policy rates and default-free rates available to investors.

In forming capital market expectations for shorter time horizons, analysts and investors must consider the expected path of interest rates. Paths should be considered that, on average, converge to the long-run equilibrium rate estimate. With negative policy rates in place, this approach means a negative starting point. In theory, many possible scenarios, each appropriately weighted by its likelihood, should be considered. In practice, it may suffice to consider only a few scenarios. Because shorter horizons provide less opportunity for the impact of events to average out, the shorter the forecast horizon, the more important it is to consider deviations from the most likely path.

Negative policy rates are expected to produce asset class returns similar to those occurring in the contraction and early recovery phases of a "more normal" business/policy cycle. Although such historical periods may provide a reasonable starting point

---

13 It should also be noted that banks were reluctant to directly impose negative rates on their retail and commercial deposit customers. In general, rates on these accounts remained non-negative. Thus, the aggregate incentive to move into cash was mitigated somewhat. Various fees (e.g., for overdraft protection) and conditions imposed on the accounts (e.g., compensating balance requirements), however, may still have resulted in a net cost for deposit customers.

in formulating appropriate scenarios, it is important to note that negative rate periods may indicate severe distress in the economy and thus involve greater uncertainty regarding the timing and strength of recovery.

Key considerations when forming capital market expectations in a negative interest rate environment include the following:

- Historical data are less likely to be reliable.

  - Useful data may exist on only a few historical business cycles, which may not include instances of negative rates. In addition, fundamental structural/institutional changes in markets and the economy may have occurred since this data was generated.

  - Quantitative models, especially statistical models, tend to break down in situations that differ from those on which they were estimated/calibrated.

  - Forecasting must account for differences between the current environment and historical averages. Historical averages, which average out differences across phases of the cycle, will be even less reliable than usual.

- The effects of other monetary policy measures occurring simultaneously (e.g., quantitative easing) may distort market relationships such as the shape of the yield curve or the performance of specific sectors.

Incorporating uncertain dynamics, including negative interest rates, into capital market expectations over finite horizons is much more difficult than projecting long-term average levels. The challenge arises from the fact that asset prices depend not only on investor expectations regarding longer term "equilibrium" levels but also on the path taken to get there.

THE MONETARY AND FISCAL POLICY MIX AND THE SHAPE OF THE YIELD CURVE AND THE BUSINESS CYCLE

10

<table>
<tr><td>☐</td><td>discuss the effects of monetary and fiscal policy on business cycles</td></tr>
<tr><td>☐</td><td>interpret the shape of the yield curve as an economic predictor and discuss the relationship between the yield curve and fiscal and monetary policy</td></tr>
</table>

Fiscal policy is inherently political. Central banks ultimately derive their powers from governments, but most strive to be, or at least appear to be, independent of the political process in order to maintain credibility. As a result, to the extent that monetary and fiscal policy are coordinated, it is usually the case that the central bank takes the expected fiscal stance as given in formulating its own policy and disdains guidance from politicians regarding its policy.

The mix of monetary and fiscal policies has its most apparent impact on the level of interest rates and the shape of the yield curve. We first consider the effect of persistently loose or tight policies on the average level of rates. All else the same, loose fiscal policies (large deficits) increase the level of *real* interest rates because the domestic private sector must be induced to save more/investing less and/or additional capital must be attracted from abroad. Conversely, tight fiscal policies reduce real rates. Persistently loose monetary policy generally results in higher actual and expected inflation. Attempts by the central bank to hold down nominal rates will prove self-defeating, ultimately resulting in higher rather than lower nominal interest rates.[14] Conversely, persistently tight monetary policy ultimately reduces actual and expected inflation resulting in lower, rather than higher, nominal rates. Exhibit 6 summarizes the impact of persistent policy mixes on the level of real and nominal rates. In each case, the impact on real rates and on expected inflation is clear. Two cases involve a mix of loose and tight policy. In these cases, the combined impact could be higher or lower nominal rates. Nominal rates are labelled as "mid" level for these cases.

Exhibit 6: Effect of Persistent Policy Mix on the Average Level of Rates

		Fiscal Policy	
		Loose	**Tight**
Monetary Policy	**Loose**	High Real Rates + High Expected Inflation = High Nominal Rates	Low Real Rates + High Expected Inflation = Mid Nominal Rates
	Tight	High Real Rates + Low Expected Inflation = Mid Nominal Rates	Low Real Rates + Low Expected Inflation = Low Nominal Rates

The second impact of policy is on the slope of the yield curve. The slope of the term structure of (default-free) interest rates depends primarily on (1) the expected future path of short-term rates and (2) a risk premium required to compensate for the greater price volatility inherent in longer-maturity bonds. The maturity premium explains why the term structure is normally upward sloping. Changes in the curve's slope—flattening and steepening—are primarily driven by the evolution of short rate expectations, which are mainly driven by the business cycle and policies. This dynamic was described in an earlier discussion on business cycles. Exhibit 7 summarizes the main points regarding the evolution of rates, policy, and the yield curve.

Exhibit 7: Rates, Policy, and the Yield Curve over the Business Cycle

Cycle Phase	Monetary Policy & Automatic Stabilizers	Money Market Rates	Bond Yields and the Yield Curve
Initial recovery	Stimulative stance. Transitioning to tightening mode.	Low/bottoming. Increases expected over progressively shorter horizons.	Long rates bottoming. Shortest yields begin to rise first. Curve is steep.
Early expansion	Withdrawing stimulus	Moving up. Pace may be expected to accelerate.	Yields rising. Possibly stable at longest maturities. Curve is flattening. Front section of yield curve steepening, back half likely flattening.

---

14 This was one of the crucial insights expesented in Friedman (1968).

Cycle Phase	Monetary Policy & Automatic Stabilizers	Money Market Rates	Bond Yields and the Yield Curve
Late expansion	Becoming restrictive	Above average and rising. Expectations tempered by eventual peak/decline.	Rising. Pace slows. Curve flattening from longest maturities inward.
Slowdown	Tight. Tax revenues may surge as accumulated capital gains are realized.	Approaching/reaching peak.	Peak. May then decline sharply. Curve flat to inverted.
Contraction	Progressively more stimulative. Aiming to counteract downward momentum.	Declining.	Declining. Curve steepening. Likely steepest on cusp of Initial Recovery phase.

Exhibit 8 illustrates the yield curve slope measured by the difference between the 10-year and three-month Treasury yield in the context of real GDP growth.

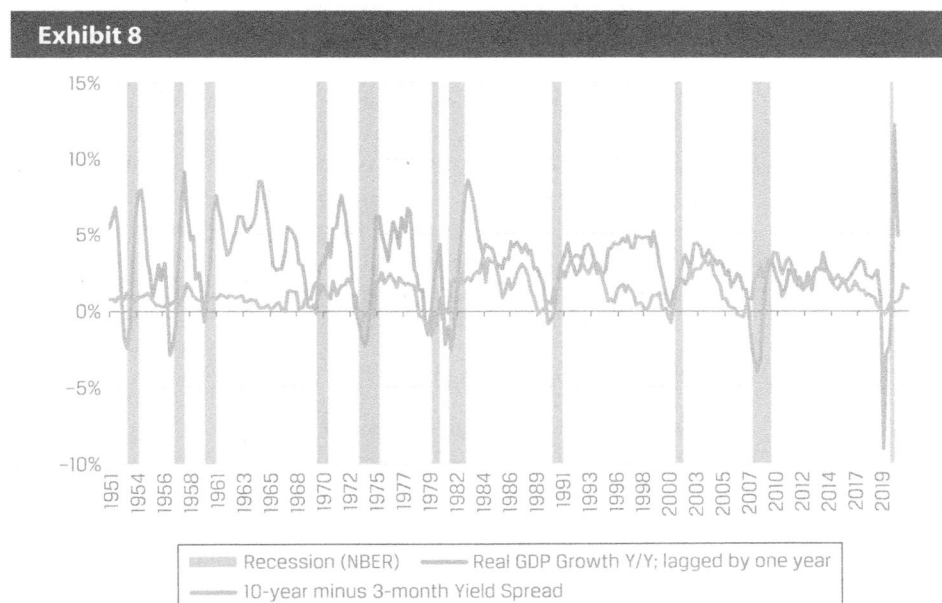

Exhibit 8

Legend: Recession (NBER) — Real GDP Growth Y/Y; lagged by one year — 10-year minus 3-month Yield Spread

Sources: Bloomberg; NBER.

There is a third factor related to monetary and fiscal policy that may, or may not, be significant with respect to the shape of the yield curve and the effectiveness of policy: the relative supply of (government) bonds at various maturities. Does it matter what maturities the government issues in order to fund deficits? Does it matter what maturities the central bank chooses to buy/sell in its open market operations or its quantitative easing? There is no clear answer. The issue became important, however, in the wake of the global financial crisis for at least two reasons.

First, although it is now apparent that there is no clear lower bound on nominal interest rates, the effectiveness of conventional interest rate policies at very low rate levels remains in question. In particular, the central bank's ability to influence long-term rates may be even more tenuous than usual. Second, governments have run, and continue to run, large deficits while quantitative easing by major central banks has caused them to accumulate massive holdings of government debt (and other securities), which they may ultimately need or want to sell. If relative supply of debt along the yield curve really matters, then how governments fund their deficits in the future and how the central banks manage the maturity of their holdings could have significant implications for the yield curve and the broader financial markets.

It is difficult to draw firm conclusions with respect to maturity management. The existing evidence in conjunction with broader observation of markets, however, suggests the following: Sufficiently large purchases/sales at different maturities are likely to have a meaningful effect on the curve while they are occurring, but the effect is unlikely to be sustained for long once the buy/sell operation ends. To put it another way, a sufficiently large *flow* of supply may have a noticeable impact on relative yields, but discrete changes in the quantity of each maturity outstanding are much less likely to have a lasting impact. Government bonds are very liquid, and investors can and do move up and down the yield curve to exploit even very small yield differentials. Having said that, an important caveat pertaining to very long maturities is appropriate. Pension funds and other entities with very long-dated liabilities need correspondingly very long-maturity assets. Severely limiting the available supply of those assets would undoubtedly drive down their yield. Low yields at the very long end of the UK yield curve have been attributed to this effect at various times.

As a final comment on the interaction of monetary and fiscal policy, we acknowledge the potential for politicization of the central bank. If the level of government debt is high relative to the economy (GDP), and especially if it is also rising because of large fiscal deficits, there is a risk that the central bank may be coerced into inflating away the real value of the debt with very accommodative monetary policy. The risk that this dynamic *may* subsequently occur is almost certain to steepen the yield curve. If it *does* occur, such an event is likely to lead to an inflationary spiral, as higher inflation leads to higher nominal rates, which lead to faster accumulation of debt, which call forth even more accommodative monetary policy, and so on.

The Shape of the Yield Curve and the Business Cycle

The shape of the yield curve is frequently cited as a predictor of economic growth and as an indicator of where the economy is in the business cycle. Both casual observation and formal econometric analysis support its usefulness (an extensive bibliography is available at www.newyorkfed.org). The underlying rationale was summarized earlier in Exhibit 7. In simplest terms, the curve tends to be steep at the bottom of the cycle, flatten during the expansion until it is very flat or even inverted at the peak, and re-steepen during the subsequent contraction. Because expectations with respect to the path of short-term rates are the primary determinant of the curve's shape, the shape of the curve contains information about how market participants perceive the state and likely evolution of the economy as well as the impact they expect policymakers to have on that path. Thus, the empirical link between the shape of the yield curve and subsequent growth passes the test set out earlier for a good model—there is a solid rationale for believing it should be predictive. One must, of course, be aware that very few macroeconomic variables are truly exogenous and very few endogenous variables are completely unaffected by the past. "A" (shape of the yield curve) may predict "B" (growth next period), but it may also be the case that "B" predicts "A" in the period after that. The point is that the analyst should be aware of the fact that both the shape of the yield curve and economic growth (i.e., the business cycle) are endogenous within the economy. This is not to suggest throwing out a useful relationship but merely a reminder to interpret results with care.

EXAMPLE 13

The Business Cycle and the Yield Curve

Camford's quantitative analysis team helped Albert Grant incorporate the central bank's reaction function into a reduced-form model of growth and inflation. With this model, he will be able to project the path of short-term rates in the wake of the deflationary shock described in Example 12. Camford's CIO has now asked him to extend the analysis to project the path of bond yields as well.

1. What will Grant need in order to project the path of bond yields?

   Guideline Answer:

   Grant will need a model linking bond yields to the policy rate. In essence, he needs a model of the yield curve.

2. Even before he can undertake the formal analysis, a large client asks Grant to explain the likely implications for the yield curve. What can he say?

   Guideline Answer:

   Following the deflationary shock, the economy is very likely to enter into the contraction phase of the business cycle. The central bank will be cutting the policy rate, perhaps sharply. Long-term yields could drop even faster initially as the market anticipates that policy, but then the curve will steepen as the central bank cuts rates because long-maturity yields will incorporate the expectation of short-term rates rising again once the economy gains sufficient traction. The curve will likely reach its steepest point near the trough of the policy cycle and then gradually flatten as the economy gains strength and the central bank begins to tighten policy.

INTERNATIONAL INTERACTIONS

11

☐ | identify and interpret macroeconomic, interest rate, and exchange rate linkages between economies

In general, the dependence of any particular country on international interactions is a function of its relative size and its degree of specialization. Large countries with diverse economies, such as the so-called G–7 (the United States, United Kingdom, Germany, France, Italy, Japan, and Canada), tend to be less influenced by developments elsewhere than smaller economies, such as Chile, whose output depends significantly on a few commodities like copper. Nonetheless, increasing globalization of trade, capital flows, and direct investment in recent decades has increased the importance of international interactions for nearly all countries.

Macroeconomic Linkages

Macroeconomic linkages between countries are expressed through their respective current and capital accounts. The current account reflects net exports of goods and services, net investment income flows, and unilateral transfers. The capital account, which for the purposes of this discussion also includes what is known as the financial account, reflects net investment flows for Foreign Direct Investment (FDI)—purchase and sale of productive assets across borders—and Portfolio Investment (PI) flows involving transactions in financial assets. By construction, if a country has a surplus on current account, it must have a matching deficit on capital account, or vice versa. Anything that affects one account must induce an equal and opposite change in the other account.

A nation's current and capital accounts are linked to the broader economy by the fact that net exports, virtually always the most significant component of the current account, contributes directly to aggregate demand for the nation's output. National income accounting also implies the following important relationship among net exports $(X - M)$, saving (S), investment (I), and the government surplus $(T - G)$:

$$(X - M) = (S - I) + (T - G).$$

Net exports always equal net private saving (the excess of domestic private saving over investment spending) plus the government surplus. Anything that changes net exports must also change net private saving, the government surplus, or both. Conversely, changes in either of these will be transmitted to the rest of the world through the current account. Of course, because the current account and capital accounts are mirror images, we can reverse all the signs in the foregoing equation and make corresponding statements about the capital account. A surplus on capital account is how a nation funds an excess of investment and government spending over domestic saving plus taxes.

There are four primary mechanisms by which the current and capital accounts are kept in balance: changes in income (GDP), relative prices, interest rates and asset prices, and exchange rates. Strictly speaking, all of these tools can play a role in both the real economy (the current account and FDI) and the financial markets, and they are determined simultaneously. However, markets do not all move at the same pace. In particular, investment markets adjust much more quickly than the real economy. In the short run, interest rates, exchange rates, and financial asset prices must adjust to keep the capital account in balance with the more slowly evolving current account. Meanwhile, the current account, in conjunction with real output and the relative prices of goods and services, tends to reflect secular trends and the pace of the business cycle.

EXAMPLE 14

International Macroeconomic Linkages

A large, diversified economy recently instituted a substantial tax cut, primarily aimed at reducing business taxes. Some provisions of the new law were designed to stem the tide of domestic firms moving production facilities abroad and encourage an increase in corporate investment in the domestic economy. There was no reduction in government spending. Prior to the tax cut, the country had both a current account deficit and a government deficit.

1. What impact is this tax cut likely to have on:

    a. the country's current account balance?

    b. the country's capital account balance?

    c. growth in other countries?

d. the current and capital accounts of other countries?

Guideline Answer:

a. The deficit on current account will almost certainly increase. The government deficit will increase which, all else the same, will result in a one-for-one increase in the current account deficit. If the tax cut works as intended, domestic investment will increase, reducing net private saving and further increasing the current account deficit. Private saving will increase as a result of rising income (GDP), which will diminish the impact on the current account somewhat. Unless saving increases by the full amount of the tax cut plus the increase in investment spending, however, the net effect will be an increase in the current account deficit. In principle, this increase could be thwarted by movements in the financial markets that make it impossible to fund it, but this is unlikely.

b. Because the current account deficit will increase, the country's capital account surplus must increase by the same amount. In effect, the tax cut will be funded primarily by borrowing from abroad and/or selling assets to non-domestic investors. Part of the adjustment is likely to come from a reduction in FDI by domestic firms (i.e., purchases of productive assets abroad) provided the new tax provisions work as intended.

c. Growth in other countries is likely to increase as the tax cut stimulates demand for their exports and that increase in turn generates additional demand within their domestic economies.

d. In the aggregate, other countries must already be running current account surpluses and capital account deficits matching the balances of the country that has cut taxes. Their aggregate current account surplus and capital account deficit will increase by the same amount as the increase in current account deficit and capital account surplus of the tax-cutting country.

2. What adjustments is the tax cut likely to induce in the financial markets?

Guideline Answer:

The country must attract additional capital flows from abroad. This endeavor is likely to be facilitated, at least in part, by the expectation of rising after-tax profits resulting from the business taxes. Equity values should therefore rise. The adjustment may also require interest rates and bond yields to rise relative to the rest of the world. The impact on the exchange rate is less clear. Because the current account and the capital account represent exactly offsetting flows, there is no *a priori* change in demand for the currency. The net impact will be determined by what investors *expect* to happen. (See the following section for a discussion of exchange rate linkages.)

Interest Rate/Exchange Rate Linkages

One of the linkages of greatest concern to investors involves interest rates and exchange rates. The two are inextricably linked. This fact is perhaps most evident in the proposition that a country cannot simultaneously

- allow unrestricted capital flows;
- maintain a fixed exchange rate; and

- pursue an independent monetary policy.

The essence of this proposition is that if the central bank attempts to push interest rates down (up), capital will flow out (in), putting downward (upward) pressure on the exchange rate, forcing the bank to buy (sell) its own currency, and thereby reversing the expansionary (contractionary) policy. Carrying this argument to its logical conclusion suggests that, with perfect capital mobility and a fixed exchange rate, "the" interest rate must be the same in countries whose currencies are pegged to each other.

Can we extend this proposition to encompass the whole (default-free) yield curve? Yes, but in doing so, we have to be somewhat more precise. Under what conditions would two markets share a yield curve? First, there must be unrestricted capital mobility between the markets ensuring that risk-adjusted expected returns will be equalized. The second condition is more difficult: The exchange rate between the currencies must be credibly fixed *forever*.[15] That is, investors must believe there is no risk that the currencies will exchange at a different rate in the future. Otherwise, yield differentials will emerge, giving rise to differential risk and return expectations in the two markets and allowing each market to trade on its own fundamentals. Thus, it is the lack of credibly fixed exchange rates that allows (default-free) yield curves, and hence bond returns, to be less than perfectly correlated across markets.

If a currency is linked to another without full credibility, then bond yields in the weaker currency are nearly always higher. This has been true even in the eurozone where, technically, separate currencies no longer exist—Greece, Italy, and Spain have always traded at meaningful, but varying, spreads over Germany and France. As long as there is no imminent risk of a devaluation, spreads at the very shortest maturities should be comparatively narrow. As demonstrated by the Greek exit ("Grexit") crisis, however, the situation changes sharply when the market perceives an imminent threat of devaluation (or a withdrawal from the common currency). Spreads then widen throughout the curve, but especially at the shortest maturities, and the curve will almost certainly invert. Why? Because in the event of a devaluation, yields in the devaluing currency will decline sharply (as the currency-risk premium collapses), generating much larger capital gains on longer-term bonds and thereby mitigating more of the currency loss.

When the exchange rate is allowed to float, the link between interest rates and exchange rates is primarily expectational. To equalize risk-adjusted expected returns across markets, interest rates must generally be higher (lower) in a currency that is expected to depreciate (appreciate). Ironically, this dynamic can lead to seemingly perverse situations in which the exchange rate "overshoots" in one direction to generate the expectation of movement in the opposite direction. The expectational linkage among exchange rates, interest rates, and asset prices is covered in detail at a later stage.

Capital mobility alone is clearly insufficient to eliminate differences in *nominal* interest rates and bond yields across countries. To a greater or lesser extent, each market responds to its own fundamentals, including policies. But what about *real* yields? We need to look at this question from two perspectives: the financial markets and the real economy.

An investor cares about the real return that she expects to earn *in her own currency*. In terms of a non-domestic asset, what matters is the *nominal* return and the change in the exchange rate. Even if non-domestic interest rates remain unchanged, the real return earned by the investor will not equal the non-domestic real interest rate unless purchasing power parity (PPP) holds over the investor's horizon. The empirical evidence overwhelmingly indicates that PPP does not hold over relevant

---

15 These conditions are necessary and sufficient for permanent convergence. See Chapter 10 of Stewart, Piros, and Heisler (forthcoming 2019) for a full exposition.

investment horizons. Hence, we cannot rely on the simplistic notion that real interest rate differentials represent exploitable opportunities and should be eliminated by portfolio investment flows.

The preceding point is somewhat subtle and should not be construed to mean that real interest rate differentials are irrelevant for cross-market investment decisions. On the contrary, they can, but do not always, point to the likelihood of favorable *nominal* yield and exchange rate movements. The investor needs to assess non-domestic real rates from that perspective.

Ultimately, real interest rates must be consistent with the real saving and investment decisions that drive economic growth and the productivity of capital. As discussed earlier, saving and investment decisions are linked across countries through their current accounts. "Excess" saving in one country funds "excess" investment in another. In essence, there is a global market in which capital flows to where it is expected to be most productive. Although real rates around the world need not be equal, they are linked through the requirement that global savings must always equal global investment. Hence, they will tend to move together. As an example, the widespread low level of real interest rates that persisted in the aftermath of the global financial crisis was widely attributed to a very high level of global saving—primarily in Asia—and an unusually low level of capital investment in many developed markets, notably the United States.

SUMMARY

This is the first of two readings on how investment professionals should address the setting of capital market expectations. The reading began with a general framework for developing capital market expectations followed by a review of various challenges and pitfalls that analysts may encounter in the forecasting process. The remainder of the reading focused on the use of macroeconomic analysis in setting expectations. The following are the main points covered in the reading:

- Capital market expectations are essential inputs for strategic as well as tactical asset allocation.

- The ultimate objective is a set of projections with which to make informed investment decisions, specifically asset allocation decisions.

- Undue emphasis should not be placed on the accuracy of projections for individual asset classes. Internal consistency across asset classes (cross-sectional consistency) and over various time horizons (intertemporal consistency) are far more important objectives.

- The process of capital market expectations setting involves the following steps:

  1. Specify the set of expectations that are needed, including the time horizon(s) to which they apply.

  2. Research the historical record.

  3. Specify the method(s) and/or model(s) that will be used and their information requirements.

  4. Determine the best sources for information needs.

  5. Interpret the current investment environment using the selected data and methods, applying experience and judgment.

  6. Provide the set of expectations and document the conclusions.

  7. Monitor outcomes, compare to forecasts, and provide feedback.

■ Among the challenges in setting capital market expectations are:

- *limitations of economic data* including lack of timeliness as well as changing definitions and calculations;

- *data measurement errors and biases* including transcription errors, survivorship bias, and appraisal (smoothed) data;

- *limitations of historical estimates* including lack of precision, nonstationarity, asynchronous observations, and distributional considerations such as fat tails and skewness;

- ex post *risk as a biased risk measure* such as when historical returns reflect expectations of a low-probability catastrophe that did not occur or capture a low-probability event that did happen to occur;

- *bias in methods* including data-mining and time-period biases;

- *failure to account for conditioning information*;

- *misinterpretation of correlations*;

- *psychological biases* including anchoring, status quo, confirmation, over-confidence, prudence, and availability biases.

- *model uncertainty*.

■ Losing sight of the connection between investment outcomes and the economy is a fundamental, and potentially costly, mistake in setting capital market expectations.

■ Some growth trend changes are driven by slowly evolving and easily observable factors that are easy to forecast. Trend changes arising from exogenous shocks are impossible to forecast and difficult to identify, assess, and quantify until the change is well established.

■ Among the most important sources of shocks are policy changes, new products and technologies, geopolitics, natural disasters, natural resources/ critical inputs, and financial crises.

■ An economy's aggregate trend growth rate reflects growth in labor inputs and growth in labor productivity. Extrapolating past trends in these components can provide a reasonable initial estimate of the future growth trend, which can be adjusted based on observable information. Less developed economies may require more significant adjustments because they are likely to be undergoing more rapid structural changes.

■ The average level of real (nominal) default-free bond yields is linked to the trend rate of real (nominal) growth. The trend rate of growth provides an important anchor for estimating bond returns over horizons long enough for this reversion to prevail over cyclical and short-term forces.

■ The trend growth rate provides an anchor for long-run equity appreciation. In the very long run, the aggregate value of equity must grow at a rate very close to the rate of GDP growth.

■ There are three main approaches to economic forecasting:

- *Econometric models*: structural and reduced-form statistical models of key variables generate quantitative estimates, impose discipline on forecasts, may be robust enough to approximate reality, and can readily forecast the impact of exogenous variables or shocks. However, they tend to be complex, time-consuming to formulate, and potentially mis-specified, and they rarely forecast turning points well.

- *Indicators*: variables that lead, lag, or coincide with turns in the economy. This approach is the simplest, requiring only a limited number of published statistics. It can generate false signals, however, and is vulnerable to revisions that may overfit past data at the expense of the reliability of out-of-sample forecasts.
- *Checklist(s)*: subjective integration of information deemed relevant by the analyst. This approach is the most flexible but also the most subjective. It readily adapts to a changing environment, but ongoing collection and assessment of information make it time-consuming and also limit the depth and consistency of the analysis.

- The business cycle is the result of many intermediate frequency cycles that jointly generate most of the variation in aggregate economic activity. This explains why historical business cycles have varied in both duration and intensity and why it is difficult to project turning points in real time.

- The business cycle reflects decisions that (a) are made based on imperfect information and/or analysis with the expectation of future benefits, (b) require significant current resources and/or time to implement, and (c) are difficult and/or costly to reverse. Such decisions are, broadly defined, investment decisions.

- A typical business cycle has a number of phases. We split the cycle into five phases with the following capital market implications:

  - Initial Recovery. Short-term interest rates and bond yields are low. Bond yields are likely to bottom. Stock markets may rise strongly. Cyclical/riskier assets such as small stocks, high-yield bonds, and emerging market securities perform well.

  - Early Expansion. Short rates are moving up. Longer-maturity bond yields are stable or rising slightly. Stocks are trending up.

  - Late Expansion. Interest rates rise, and the yield curve flattens. Stock markets often rise but may be volatile. Cyclical assets may underperform while inflation hedges outperform.

  - Slowdown. Short-term interest rates are at or nearing a peak. Government bond yields peak and may then decline sharply. The yield curve may invert. Credit spreads widen, especially for weaker credits. Stocks may fall. Interest-sensitive stocks and "quality" stocks with stable earnings perform best.

  - Contraction. Interest rates and bond yields drop. The yield curve steepens. The stock market drops initially but usually starts to rise well before the recovery emerges. Credit spreads widen and remain elevated until clear signs of a cycle trough emerge.

- At least three factors complicate translation of business cycle information into capital market expectations and profitable investment decisions. First, the phases of the cycle vary in length and amplitude. Second, it is not always easy to distinguish between cyclical forces and secular forces acting on the economy and the markets. Third, how, when, and by how much the markets respond to the business cycle is as uncertain as the cycle itself—perhaps more so.

- Business cycle information is likely to be most reliable/valuable in setting capital market expectations over horizons within the range of likely expansion and contraction phases. Transitory developments cloud shorter-term forecasts, whereas significantly longer horizons likely cover portions of multiple cycle phases. Information about the current cyclical state of the economy has no predictive value over very long horizons.

- Monetary policy is often used as a mechanism for intervention in the business cycle. This mechanism is inherent in the mandates of most central banks to maintain price stability and/or growth consistent with potential.

- Monetary policy aims to be countercyclical, but the ability to fine-tune the economy is limited and policy measures may exacerbate rather than moderate the business cycle. This risk is greatest at the top of the cycle when the central bank may overestimate the economy's momentum and/or underestimate the potency of restrictive policies.

- Fiscal policy—government spending and taxation—can be used to counteract cyclical fluctuations in the economy. Aside from extreme situations, however, fiscal policy typically addresses objectives other than regulating short-term growth. So-called automatic stabilizers do play an important role in mitigating cyclical fluctuations.

- The Taylor Rule is a useful tool for assessing a central bank's stance and for predicting how that stance is likely to evolve.

- The expectation that central banks could not implement negative policy rates proved to be unfounded in the aftermath of the 2007–2009 global financial crisis. Because major central banks combined negative policy rates with other extraordinary measures (notably quantitative easing), however, the effectiveness of the negative rate policy is unclear. The effectiveness of quantitative easing is also unclear.

- Negative interest rates, and the environment that gives rise to them, make the task of setting capital market expectations even more complex. Among the issues that arise are the following:

  - It is difficult to justify negative rates as a "risk-free rate" to which risk premiums can be added to establish long-term "equilibrium" asset class returns.
  - Historical data and quantitative models are even less likely to be reliable.
  - Market relationships (e.g., the yield curve) are likely to be distorted by other concurrent policy measures.

- The mix of monetary and fiscal policies has its most apparent effect on the average level of interest rates and inflation. Persistently loose (tight) fiscal policy increases (reduces) the average level of real interest rates. Persistently loose (tight) monetary policy increases (reduces) the average levels of actual and expected inflation. The impact on nominal rates is ambiguous if one policy is persistently tight and the other persistently loose.

- Changes in the slope of the yield curve are driven primarily by the evolution of short rate expectations, which are driven mainly by the business cycle and policies. The slope of the curve may also be affected by debt management.

- The slope of the yield curve is useful as a predictor of economic growth and as an indicator of where the economy is in the business cycle.

- Macroeconomic linkages between countries are expressed through their respective current and capital accounts.

- There are four primary mechanisms by which the current and capital accounts are kept in balance: changes in income (GDP), relative prices, interest rates and asset prices, and exchange rates.

- In the short run, interest rates, exchange rates, and financial asset prices must adjust to keep the capital account in balance with the more slowly evolving current account. The current account, in conjunction with real output and the relative prices of goods and services, tends to reflect secular trends and the pace of the business cycle.

- Interest rates and currency exchange rates are inextricably linked. This relationship is evident in the fact that a country cannot simultaneously allow unfettered capital flows, maintain a fixed exchange rate, and pursue an independent monetary policy.

- Two countries will share a default-free yield curve if (and only if) there is perfect capital mobility and the exchange rate is credibly fixed *forever*. It is the lack of credibly fixed exchange rates that allows (default-free) yield curves, and hence bond returns, to be less than perfectly correlated across markets.

- With floating exchange rates, the link between interest rates and exchange rates is primarily expectational. To equalize risk-adjusted expected returns across markets, interest rates must be higher (lower) in a currency that is expected to depreciate (appreciate). This dynamic can lead to the exchange rate "overshooting" in one direction to generate the expectation of movement in the opposite direction.

- An investor cares about the real return that he or she expects to earn *in his or her owncurrency*. In terms of a foreign asset, what matters is the *nominal* return and the change in the exchange rate.

- Although real interest rates around the world need not be equal, they are linked through the requirement that global savings must always equal global investment. Hence, they will tend to move together.

REFERENCES

Brinson, Gary, Randolph Hood, and Gilbert Beebower. 1986. "Determinants of Portfolio Performance." *Financial Analysts Journal* 42 (4): 39–44. 10.2469/faj.v42.n4.39

Buttiglione, Luigi, Philip R. Lane, Lucrezia Reichlin, and Vincent Reinhart. 2014. Deleveraging? What Deleveraging? International Center for Monetary and Banking Studies.

Friedman, Milton. 1968. "The Role of Monetary Policy." *American Economic Review* 58 (1): 1–17.

Ibbotson, Roger, Paul Kaplan. 2000. "Does Asset Allocation Policy Explain 40, 90, or 100 Percent of Performance?" *Financial Analysts Journal* 56 (1): 26–33. 10.2469/faj.v56.n1.2327

Klement, Joachim. 2015. "What's Growth Got to Do With It? Equity Returns and Economic Growth." *Journal of Investing* 24 (2): 74–78. 10.3905/joi.2015.24.2.074

Marcelo, Jose Luis Miralles, Luis Miralles Quiros Jose, Jose Luis Martins. 2013. "The Role of Country and Industry Factors During Volatile Times." *Journal of International Financial Markets, Institutions and Money* 26:273–90. 10.1016/j.intfin.2013.06.005

McQueen, Grant, Steven Thorley. 1999. "Mining Fools Gold." *Financial Analysts Journal* 55 (2): 61–72. 10.2469/faj.v55.n2.2261

Rapaport, Alfred, Michael Mauboussin. 2001. Expectations Investing: Reading Stock Prices for Better Returns. Boston: Harvard Business School Press.

Stewart, Scott D., Christopher D. Piros, and Jeffrey C. Heisler. 2019, Forthcoming. Portfolio Management: Theory and Practice. Hoboken, NJ: John Wiley & Sons.

PRACTICE PROBLEMS

The following information relates to questions 1-2

Jennifer Wuyan is an investment strategist responsible for developing long-term capital market expectations for an investment firm that invests in domestic equities. She presents a report to the firm's investment committee describing the statistical model used to formulate capital market expectations, which is based on a dividend discount method. In the report, she notes that in developing the model, she researched the historical data seeking to identify the relevant variables and determined the best source of data for the model. She also notes her interpretation of the current economic and market environment.

1. Explain what additional step(s) Wuyan should have taken in the process of setting capital market expectations.

   Wuyan reports that after repeatedly searching the most recent 10 years of data, she eventually identified variables that had a statistically significant relationship with equity returns. Wuyan used these variables to forecast equity returns. She documented, in a separate section of the report, a high correlation between nominal GDP and equity returns. Based on this noted high correlation, Wuyan concludes that nominal GDP predicts equity returns. Based on her statistical results, Wuyan expects equities to underperform over the next 12 months and recommends that the firm underweight equities.

   Commenting on the report, John Tommanson, an investment adviser for the firm, suggests extending the starting point of the historical data back another 20 years to obtain more robust statistical results. Doing so would enable the analysis to include different economic and central bank policy environments. Tommanson is reluctant to underweight equities for his clients, citing the strong performance of equities over the last quarter, and believes the most recent quarterly data should be weighted more heavily in setting capital market expectations.

2. Discuss how *each* of the following forecasting challenges evident in Wuyan's report and in Tommanson's comments affects the setting of capital market expectations:

   i.   Status quo bias

   ii. Data-mining bias

   iii. Risk of regime change

   iv. Misinterpretation of correlation

The following information relates to questions 3-5

Jan Cambo is chief market strategist at a US asset management firm. While preparing a report for the upcoming investment committee meeting, Cambo updates her long-term forecast for US equity returns. As an input into her forecasting model, she uses the following long-term annualized forecasts from the firm's chief economist:

- Labor input will grow 0.5%.
- Labor productivity will grow 1.3%.
- Inflation will be 2.2%.
- Dividend yield will be 2.8%.

Based on these forecasts, Cambo predicts a long-term 9.0% annual equity return in the US market. Her forecast assumes no change in the share of profits in the economy, and she expects some contribution to equity returns from a change in the price-to-earnings ratio (P/E).

3. Calculate the implied contribution to Cambo's US equity return forecast from the expected change in the P/E.

   At the investment committee meeting, the firm's chief economist predicts that the economy will enter the late expansion phase of the business cycle in the next 12 months.

4. **Discuss**, based on the chief economist's prediction, the implications for the following:

   i.   Bond yields

   ii. Equity returns

   iii. Short-term interest rates

5. Cambo compares her business cycle forecasting approach to the approach used by the chief economist. Cambo bases her equity market forecast on a time-series model using a composite index of leading indicators as the key input, whereas the chief economist uses a detailed econometric model to generate his economic forecasts.

   Discuss strengths and weaknesses of the economic forecasting approaches used by Cambo and the chief economist.

	Cambo's Forecasting Approach	Chief Economist's Forecasting Approach
Strengths		
Weaknesses		

The following information relates to questions 6-13

Neshie Wakuluk is an investment strategist who develops capital market expectations for an investment firm that invests across asset classes and global markets. Wakuluk started her career when the global markets were experiencing significant volatility and poor returns; as a result, she is now careful to base her conclusions on objective evidence and analytical procedures to mitigate any potential biases.

Wakuluk's approach to economic forecasting utilizes a structural model in conjunction with a diffusion index to determine the current phase of a country's business cycle. This approach has produced successful predictions in the past, thus Wakuluk has high confidence in the predictions. Wakuluk also determines whether any adjustments need to be made to her initial estimates of the respective aggregate economic growth trends based on historical rates of growth for Countries X and Y (both developed markets) and Country Z (a developing market). Exhibit 1 summarizes Wakuluk's predictions:

Exhibit 1: Prediction for Current Phase of the Business Cycle		
Country X	**Country Y**	**Country Z**
Initial Recovery	Contraction	Late Upswing

Wakuluk assumes short-term interest rates adjust with expected inflation and are procyclical. Wakuluk reviews the historical short-term interest rate trends for each country, which further confirms her predictions shown in Exhibit 1.

Wakuluk decides to focus on Country Y to determine the path of nominal interest rates, the potential economic response of Country Y's economy to this path, and the timing for when Country Y's economy may move into the next business cycle. Wakuluk makes the following observations:

Observation 1   Monetary policy has been persistently loose for Country Y, while fiscal policies have been persistently tight.

Observation 2   Country Y is expected to significantly increase transfer payments and introduce a more progressive tax regime.

Observation 3   The current yield curve for Country Y suggests that the business cycle is in the slowdown phase, with bond yields starting to reflect contractionary conditions.

6. Wakuluk *most likely* seeks to mitigate which of the following biases in developing capital market forecasts?

   A. Availability

   B. Time period

   C. Survivorship

7. Wakuluk's approach to economic forecasting:

   A. is flexible and limited in complexity.

   B. can give a false sense of precision and provide false signals.

   C. imposes no consistency of analysis across items or at different points in time.

8. Wakuluk is *most likely* to make significant adjustments to her estimate of the future growth trend for which of the following countries?

   A. Country Y only

   B. Country Z only

   C. Countries Y and Z

9. Based on Exhibit 1 and Wakuluk's assumptions about short-term rates and expected inflation, short-term rates in Country X are *most likely* to be:

    A. low and bottoming.

    B. approaching a peak.

    C. above average and rising.

10. Based on Exhibit 1, what capital market effect is Country Z *most likely* to experience in the short-term?

    A. Cyclical assets attract investors.

    B. Monetary policy becomes restrictive.

    C. The yield curve steepens substantially.

11. Based on Observation 1, fiscal and monetary policies in Country Y will *most likely* lead to:

    A. low nominal rates.

    B. high nominal rates.

    C. either high or low nominal rates.

12. Based on Observation 2, what impact will the policy changes have on the trend rate of growth for Country Y?

    A. Negative

    B. Neutral

    C. Positive

13. Based on Observation 3, Wakuluk *most likely* expects Country Y's yield curve in the near term to:

    A. invert.

    B. flatten.

    C. steepen.

The following information relates to questions 14-16

Robert Hadpret is the chief economist at Agree Partners, an asset management firm located in the developed country of Eastland. He has prepared an economic report on Eastland for the firm's asset allocation committee. Hadpret notes that the composite index of leading economic indicators has declined for three consecutive months and that the yield curve has inverted. Private sector borrowing is also projected to decline. Based on these recent events, Hadpret predicts an economic contraction and forecasts lower inflation and possibly deflation over the next 12 months.

Helen Smitherman, a portfolio manager at Agree, considers Hadpret's economic forecast when determining the tactical allocation for the firm's Balanced Fund (the fund). Smitherman notes that the fund has considerable exposure to real estate, shares of asset-intensive and commodity-producing firms, and high-quality debt. The fund's cash holdings are at cyclical lows.

14. **Discuss** the implications of Hadpret's inflation forecast on the expected returns of the fund's holdings of:

    i.   cash.

    ii.   bonds.

    iii. equities.

    iv.   real estate.

15. In response to the projected cyclical decline in the Eastland economy and in private sector borrowing over the next year, Hadpret expects a change in the monetary and fiscal policy mix. He forecasts that the Eastland central bank will ease monetary policy. On the fiscal side, Hadpret expects the Eastland government to enact a substantial tax cut. As a result, Hadpret forecasts large government deficits that will be financed by the issuance of long-term government securities.

    Discussthe relationship between the shape of the yield curve and the monetary and fiscal policy mix projected by Hadpret.

16. Currently, Eastland's currency is fixed relative to the currency of the country of Northland, and Eastland maintains policies that allow unrestricted capital flows. Hadpret examines the relationship between interest rates and exchange rates. He considers three possible scenarios for the Eastland economy:

    Scenario 1   Shift in policy restricting capital flows

    Scenario 2   Shift in policy allowing the currency to float

    Scenario 3   Shift in investor belief toward a lack of full credibility that the exchange rate will be fixed forever

    Discuss how interest rate and exchange rate linkages between Eastland and Northland might change under *each* scenario.

    Note: Consider *each* scenario independently.

SOLUTIONS

1. The process of setting capital market expectations (CMEs) involves the following seven steps:

    A. Specify the set of expectations needed, including the time horizon(s) to which they apply.

    B. Research the historical record.

    C. Specify the method(s) and/or model(s) to be used and their information requirements.

    D. Determine the best sources for information needs.

    E. Interpret the current investment environment using the selected data and methods, applying experience and judgment.

    F. Provide the set of expectations needed, documenting conclusions.

    G. Monitor actual outcomes and compare them with expectations, providing feedback to improve the expectation-setting process.

    The first step, which specifies the set of expectations needed, is carried out by the firm. Wuyan, in developing a statistical model based on a dividend discount method, researched the historical data seeking to identify the relevant variables and determined the best source of data for the model. In her report, she also noted her interpretation of the current economic and market environment. To complete the process, Wuyan should complete Steps 6 and 7. Wuyan should provide the set of expectations needed, documenting the conclusions, and include the reasoning and assumptions underlying the projections. Then, she should monitor the actual outcomes and compare them with the expectations, providing feedback to assess and improve the accuracy of the process. The comparison of the capital market expectations estimated by the model against actual results provides a quantitative evaluation of forecast error. The feedback from this step can be used to improve the expectation-setting process.

2. **Discuss** how *each* of the following forecasting challenges evident in Wuyan's report and in Tommanson's comments affects the setting of capital market expectations:

Status quo bias	Tommanson's statement that he is reluctant to underweight equities given the strong performance of equities over the last quarter is an example of status quo bias. His statement that the most recent quarterly data should be weighted more heavily in setting capital market expectations is also an example of this bias. Status quo bias reflects the tendency for forecasts to perpetuate recent observations and for managers to then avoid making changes. Status quo bias can be mitigated by a disciplined effort to avoid anchoring on the status quo.
Data-mining bias	In Wuyan's report, data-mining bias arises from repeatedly searching a data set until a statistically significant pattern emerges. Such a pattern will almost inevitably occur, but the statistical relationship cannot be expected to have predictive value. As a result, the modeling results are unreliable. Irrelevant variables are often included in the forecasting model. As a solution, the analyst should scrutinize the variables selected and provide an economic rationale for each variable selected in the forecasting model. A further test is to examine the forecasting relationship out of sample.

Risk of regime change	The suggestion by Tommanson to extend the data series back increases the risk of the data representing more than one regime. A change in regime is a shift in the technological, political, legal, economic, or regulatory environments. Regime change alters the risk–return relationship since the asset's risk and return characteristics vary with economic and market environments. Analysts can apply statistical techniques that account for the regime change or simply use only part of the whole data series.
Misinterpretation of correlation	Wuyan states that the high correlation between nominal GDP and equity returns implies nominal GDP predicts equity returns. This statement is incorrect since high correlation does not imply causation. In this case, nominal GDP could predict equity returns, equity returns could predict nominal GDP, a third variable could predict both, or the relationship could merely be spurious. Correlation does not allow the analyst to distinguish between these cases. As a result, correlation relationships should not be used in a predictive model without understanding the underlying linkages between the variables.

3. The growth rate in the aggregate market value of equity is expressed as a sum of the following four factors: (1) growth rate of nominal GDP, (2) the change in the share of profits in GDP, (3) the change in P/E, and (4) the dividend yield. The growth rate of nominal GDP is the sum of the growth of real GDP and inflation. The growth rate of real GDP is estimated as the sum of the growth rate in the labor input and the growth rate in labor productivity. Based on the chief economist's estimates, the macroeconomic forecast indicates that nominal GDP will increase by 4.0% (= 0.5% labor input + 1.3% productivity + 2.2% inflation).

Assuming a 2.8% dividend yield and no change in the share of profits in the economy, Cambo's forecast of a 9.0% annual increase in equity returns implies a 2.2% long-term contribution (i.e., 9.0% equity return – 4.0% nominal GDP – 2.8% dividend yield) from an expansion in the P/E.

4.

Discuss, based on the chief economist's prediction, the implications for the following:

Bond yields	In the late expansion phase of the business cycle, bond yields are usually rising but more slowly than short-term interest rates are, so the yield curve flattens. Private sector borrowing puts upward pressure on rates while fiscal balances typically improve.
Equity returns	In the late expansion phase of the business cycle, stocks typically rise but are subject to high volatility as investors become nervous about the restrictive monetary policy and signs of a looming economic slowdown. Cyclical assets may underperform while inflation hedges, such as commodities, outperform.
Short-term interest rates	In the late expansion phase of the business cycle, short-term interest rates are typically rising as monetary policy becomes restrictive because the economy is increasingly in danger of overheating. The central bank may aim for a soft landing.

5.

Discuss strengths and weaknesses of the economic forecasting approaches used by Cambo and the chief economist.

	Cambo's Forecasting Approach	Chief Economist's Forecasting Approach

Strengths	• The leading indicator–based approach is simple since it requires following a limited number of economic/financial variables. • Can focus on individual or composite variables that are readily available and easy to track. • Focuses on identifying/forecasting turning points in the business cycle.	• Econometric models can be quite robust and can examine impact of many potential variables. • New data may be collected and consistently used within models to quickly generate output. • Models are useful for simulating effects of changes in exogenous variables. • Imposes discipline and consistency on the forecaster and challenges modeler to reassess prior view based on model results.
Weaknesses	• Data subject to frequent revisions resulting in "look-ahead" bias. • "Current" data not reliable as input for historical analysis. • Overfitted in sample. Likely overstates forecast accuracy. • Can provide false signals on the economic outlook. • May provide little more than binary directional guidance (no/yes).	• Models are complex and time consuming to formulate. • Requires future forecasts for the exogenous variables, which increases the estimation error for the model. • Model may be mis-specified, and relationships among variables may change over time. • Models may give false sense of precision. • Models perform badly at forecasting turning points.

6. A is correct. Wakuluk started her career when the global markets were experiencing significant volatility and poor returns. She is careful to base her conclusions on objective evidence and analytical procedures to mitigate potential biases, which suggests she is seeking to mitigate an availability bias. Availability bias is the tendency to be overly influenced by events that have left a strong impression and/or for which it is easy to recall an example.

7. B is correct. Wakuluk's approach to economic forecasting utilizes both a structural model (e.g., an econometric model approach) and a diffusion index (e.g., a leading indicator-based approach). However, the two approaches have weaknesses: An econometric model approach may give a false sense of precision, and a leading indicator-based approach can provide false signals. Two strengths of the checklist approach are its flexibility and limited complexity, although one weakness is that it imposes no consistency of analysis across items or at different points in time.

8. B is correct. Country Z is a developing market. Less-developed markets are likely to be undergoing more rapid structural changes, which may require the analyst to make more significant adjustments relative to past trends.

9. A is correct. Country X is predicted to be in the initial recovery phase of the business cycle, which suggests short-term (money market) rates are low or bottoming. Inflation is procyclical. It accelerates in the later stages of the business cycle when the output gap has closed, and it decelerates when a large output gap puts downward pressure on wages and prices, which often happens during a recession or the early years afterward. As long as short-term interest rates adjust with expected inflation, cash is essentially a zero-duration, inflation-protected asset that earns a floating real rate, which is typically procyclical. Wakuluk assumes short-term interest rates adjust with expected inflation and are procyclical. Thus, short-term rates are most likely to be low and bottoming if Country X is in the

initial recovery phase of the business cycle.

10. B is correct. Wakuluk's model predicts that Country Z's business cycle is currently in the late upswing phase. In the late upswing phase, interest rates are typically rising as monetary policy becomes more restrictive. Cyclical assets may underperform, whereas the yield curve is expected to continue to flatten.

11. C is correct. Monetary policy has been persistently loose for Country Y, while fiscal policies have been persistently tight. With this combination of persistently loose and tight policies, the impact could lead to higher or lower nominal rates (typically labeled as mid-nominal rates).

12. C is correct. Country Y is expected to significantly increase transfer payments and introduce a more progressive tax regime. Both of these changes are pro-growth government policies and should have a positive impact on the trend rate of growth for a business cycle that is in slowdown or contraction. Transfer payments help mitigate fluctuations in disposable income for the most vulnerable households, while progressive tax regimes imply that the effective tax rate on the private sector is pro-cyclical (i.e., rising as the economy expands and falling as the economy contracts).

13. C is correct. The current yield curve for Country Y suggests that the business cycle is in the slowdown phase (curve is flat to inverted), with bond yields starting to reflect contractionary conditions (i.e., bond yields are declining). The curve will most likely steepen near term, consistent with the transition to the contractionary phase of the business cycle, and be the steepest on the cusp of the initial recovery phase.

14. **Discuss** the implications of Hadpret's inflation forecast on the expected returns of the fund's holdings of:

Cash	The fund benefits from its cyclically low holdings of cash. With the economy contracting and inflation falling, short-term rates will likely be in a sharp decline. Cash, or short-term interest-bearing instruments, is unattractive in such an environment. However, deflation may make cash particularly attractive if a "zero lower bound" is binding on the nominal interest rate. Otherwise, deflation is simply a component of the required short-term real rate.
Bonds	The fund's holdings of high-quality bonds will benefit from falling inflation or deflation. Falling inflation results in capital gains as the expected inflation component of bond yields falls. Persistent deflation benefits the highest-quality bonds because it increases the purchasing power of their cash flows. It will, however, impair the creditworthiness of lower-quality debt.
Equities	The fund's holdings of asset-intensive and commodity-producing firms will be negatively affected by falling inflation or deflation. Within the equity market, higher inflation benefits firms with the ability to pass along rising costs. In contrast, falling inflation or deflation is especially detrimental for asset-intensive and commodity-producing firms unable to pass along the price increases.
Real Estate	The fund's real estate holdings will be negatively affected by falling inflation or deflation. Falling inflation or deflation will put downward pressure on expected rental income and property values. Especially negatively affected will be sub-prime properties that may have to cut rents sharply to avoid rising vacancies.

15. Hadpret expects that, in response to a forecasted contraction in the Eastland economy, the central bank will ease monetary policy and the government will enact an expansionary fiscal policy. This policy mix has an impact on the shape of the yield curve.

The impact of changes in monetary policy on the yield curve are fairly clear, because changes in the yield curve's slope—its flattening or steepening—are largely determined by the expected movement in short rates. This movement, in turn, is determined by the expected path of monetary policy and the state of the economy. With the central bank easing and the economy contracting, policy rates will be declining and will be expected to decline further as the central bank aims to counteract downward momentum in the economy. Bond yields also decline but by a lesser amount, so the yield curve steepens. The yield curve will typically continue to steepen during the contraction phase as the central bank continues to ease, reaching its steepest point just before the initial recovery phase.

Fiscal policy may affect the shape of the yield curve through the relative supply of bonds at various maturities that the government issues to fund deficits. Unlike the impact of monetary policy, the impact of changes in the supply of securities on the yield curve is unclear. The evidence seems to suggest that sufficiently large purchases/sales at different maturities will have only a temporary impact on yields. As a result, the large government budget deficits forecasted by Hadpret are unlikely to have much of a lasting impact on the yield curve, especially given that private sector borrowing will be falling during the contraction, somewhat offsetting the increase in the supply of government securities.

16. **Discuss** how interest rate and exchange rate linkages between Eastland and Northland might change under *each* scenario. (Note: Consider *each* scenario independently.)

Scenario 1	Eastland currently has a fixed exchange rate with unrestricted capital flows. It is unable to pursue an independent monetary policy, and interest rates will be equal to those in Northland. By restricting capital flows along with a fixed exchange rate, Eastland will be able to run an independent monetary policy with the central bank setting the policy rate. Thus, interest rates can be different in the two countries.
Scenario 2	Eastland currently has a fixed exchange rate pegged to Northland with unrestricted capital flows. Eastland is unable to pursue an independent monetary policy with interest rates in Eastland equal to the interest rates prevailing in Northland (the country to which the currency is pegged). If Eastland allows the exchange rate to float, it will now be able to run an independent monetary policy with interest rates determined in its domestic market. The link between interest rates and exchange rates will now be largely expectational and will depend on the expected future path of the exchange rate. To equalize risk-adjusted returns across countries, interest rates must generally be higher (lower) in the country whose currency is expected to depreciate (appreciate). This dynamic often leads to a situation where the currency overshoots in one direction or the other.
Scenario 3	Eastland and Northland (with currencies pegged to each other) will share the same yield curve if two conditions are met. First, unrestricted capital mobility must occur between them to ensure that risk-adjusted expected returns will be equalized. Second, the exchange rate between the currencies must be credibly fixed forever. Thus, as long as investors believe that there is no risk in the future of a possible currency appreciation or depreciation, Eastland and Northland will share the same yield curve. A shift in investors' belief in the credibility of the fixed exchange rate will likely cause risk and yield differentials to emerge. This situation will cause the (default-free) yield curve to differ between Eastland and Northland.

LEARNING MODULE

2

Capital Market Expectations, Part 2: Forecasting Asset Class Returns

by Christopher D. Piros, PhD, CFA.

Christopher D. Piros, PhD, CFA (USA).

LEARNING OUTCOMES	
Mastery	*The candidate should be able to:*
☐	discuss approaches to setting expectations for fixed-income returns
☐	discuss risks faced by investors in emerging market fixed-income securities and the country risk analysis techniques used to evaluate emerging market economies
☐	discuss approaches to setting expectations for equity investment market returns
☐	discuss risks faced by investors in emerging market equity securities
☐	explain how economic and competitive factors can affect expectations for real estate investment markets and sector returns
☐	discuss major approaches to forecasting exchange rates
☐	discuss methods of forecasting volatility
☐	recommend and justify changes in the component weights of a global investment portfolio based on trends and expected changes in macroeconomic factors

INTRODUCTION

1

This is the second of two readings focusing on capital market expectations. A central theme of both readings is that a disciplined approach to setting expectations will be rewarded. After outlining a framework for developing expectations and reviewing potential pitfalls, the first reading focused on the use of macroeconomic analysis in setting expectations. This reading builds on that foundation and examines setting expectations for specific asset classes—fixed income, equities, real estate, and currencies. Estimation of variance–covariance matrices is covered as well.

Parts of this reading have been adapted from a former Capital Market Expectations reading authored by John P. Calverley, Alan M. Meder, CPA, CFA, Brian D. Singer, CFA, and Renato Staub, PhD.

The reading begins with an overview of the techniques frequently used to develop capital market expectations. The discussion of specific asset classes begins with fixed income in Sections 3 and 4, followed by equities, real estate, and currencies in Sections 5–7. Estimation of variance–covariance structures is addressed in Section 8. Section 9 illustrates the use of macroeconomic analysis to develop and justify adjustments to a global portfolio.

2   OVERVIEW OF TOOLS AND APPROACHES

This section provides a brief overview of the main concepts, approaches, and tools used in professional forecasting of capital market returns. Whereas subsequent sections focus on specific asset classes, the emphasis here is on the commonality of techniques.

The Nature of the Problem

Few investment practitioners are likely to question the notion that investment opportunities change in systematic, but imperfectly predictable, ways over time. Yet the ramifications of that fact are often not explicitly recognized. Forecasting returns is not simply a matter of estimating constant, but unknown, parameters—for example, expected returns, variances, and correlations. Time horizons matter. The previous reading highlighted two aspects of this issue: the need to ensure intertemporal consistency and the relative usefulness of specific information (e.g., the business cycle) over short, intermediate, and long horizons. The choice among forecasting techniques is effectively a choice of the information on which forecasts will be based (in statistical terms, the information on which the forecast is "conditioned") and how that information will be incorporated into the forecasts. The fact that opportunities change over time should, at least in principle, affect strategic investment decisions and how positions respond to changing forecasts.[1]

Although investment opportunities are not constant, virtually all forecasting techniques rely on notions of central tendency, toward which opportunities tend to revert over time. This fact means that although asset prices, risk premiums, volatilities, valuation ratios, and other metrics may exhibit momentum, persistence, and clustering in the short run, over sufficiently long horizons, they tend to converge to levels consistent with economic and financial fundamentals.

What are we trying to forecast? In principle, we are interested in the whole probability distribution of future returns. In practice, however, forecasting expected return is by far the most important consideration, both because it is the dominant driver of most investment decisions and because it is generally more difficult to forecast within practical tolerances than such risk metrics as volatility. Hence, the primary focus here is on expected return. In terms of risk metrics, we limit our attention to variances and covariances.

Approaches to Forecasting

At a very high level, there are essentially three approaches to forecasting: (1) formal tools, (2) surveys, and (3) judgment. Formal tools are established research methods amenable to precise definition and independent replication of results. Surveys involve

---

1 For example, in general, it is not optimal to choose a portfolio on the mean–variance-efficient frontier based on forecasts for the coming period. In addition, the distinction between "strategic" and "tactical" asset allocation is less clear cut since, in general, the optimal allocation evolves with the investor's remaining investment horizon. See Piros (2015) for a non-technical exposition of these issues.

asking a group of experts for their opinions. Judgment can be described as a qualitative synthesis of information derived from various sources and filtered through the lens of experience.

Surveys are probably most useful as a way to gauge consensus views, which can serve as inputs into formal tools and the analyst's own judgment. Judgment is always important. There is ample scope for applying judgment—in particular, economic and psychological insight—to improve forecasts and numbers, including those produced by elaborate quantitative models. In using survey results and applying their own judgment, analysts must be wary of the psychological traps discussed in the Capital Market Expectations Part 1 reading. Beyond these brief observations, however, there is not much new to be said about surveys and judgment.

The formal forecasting tools most commonly used in forecasting capital market returns fall into three broad categories: statistical methods, discounted cash flow models, and risk premium models. The distinctions among these methods will become clear as they are discussed and applied throughout the reading.

Statistical Methods

All the formal tools involve data and statistical analysis to some degree. Methods that are primarily, if not exclusively, statistical impose relatively little structure on the data. As a result, the forecasts inherit the statistical properties of the data with limited, if any, regard for economic or financial reasoning. Three types of statistical methods will be covered in this reading. The first approach is to use well-known sample statistics, such as sample means, variances, and correlations, to describe the distribution of future returns. This is undoubtedly the clearest example of simply taking the data at face value. Unfortunately, sampling error makes some of these statistics—in particular, the sample mean—very imprecise. The second approach, **shrinkage estimation**, involves taking a weighted average of two estimates of the same parameter—one based on historical sample data and the other based on some other source or information, such as the analyst's "prior" knowledge. This "two-estimates-are-better-than-one" approach has the desirable property of reducing forecast errors relative to simple sample statistics. The third method, **time-series estimation**, involves forecasting a variable on the basis of lagged values of the variable being forecast and often lagged values of other selected variables. These models have the benefit of explicitly incorporating dynamics into the forecasting process. However, since they are reduced-form models, they may summarize the historical data well without providing much insight into the underlying drivers of the forecasts.

Discounted Cash Flow

Discounted cash flow (DCF) models express the idea that an asset's value is the present value of its expected cash flows. They are a basic method for establishing the intrinsic value of an asset on the basis of fundamentals and its fair required rate of return. Conversely, they are used to estimate the required rate of return implied by the asset's current price.

Risk Premium Models

The risk premium approach expresses the expected return on a risky asset as the sum of the risk-free rate of interest and one or more risk premiums that compensate investors for the asset's exposure to sources of *priced risk* (risk for which investors demand compensation). There are three main methods for modeling risk premiums: (1) an equilibrium model, such as the CAPM, (2) a factor model, and (3) building blocks. Each of these methods was discussed in earlier readings. Equilibrium models and factor models both impose a structure on how returns are assumed to be generated. Hence, they can be used to generate estimates of (1) expected returns and (2) variances and covariances.

3   FORECASTING FIXED INCOME RETURNS

☐ | discuss approaches to setting expectations for fixed-income returns

There are three main ways to approach forecasting fixed-income returns. The first is discounted cash flow. This method is really the only one that is precise enough to use in support of trades involving individual fixed-income securities. This type of "micro" analysis will not be discussed in detail here since it is covered extensively elsewhere in CFA Program curriculum readings that focus on fixed income. DCF concepts are also useful in forecasting the more aggregated performance needed to support asset allocation decisions. The second approach is the risk premium approach, which is often applied to fixed income, in part because fixed-income premiums are among the building blocks used to estimate expected returns on riskier asset classes, such as equities. The third approach is to include fixed-income asset classes in an equilibrium model. Doing so has the advantage of imposing consistency across asset classes and is especially useful as a first step in applying the Black–Litterman framework, which will be discussed in a later reading.

Applying DCF to Fixed Income

Fixed income is really all about discounted cash flow. This stems from the facts that almost all fixed-income securities have finite maturities and that the (promised) cash flows are known, governed by explicit rules, or can be modeled with a reasonably high degree of accuracy (e.g., mortgage-backed security prepayments). Using modern arbitrage-free models, we can value virtually any fixed-income instrument. The most straightforward and, undoubtedly, most precise way to forecast fixed-income returns is to explicitly value the securities on the basis of the assumed evolution of the critical inputs to the valuation model—for example, the spot yield curve, the term structure of volatilities, and prepayment speeds. A whole distribution of returns can be generated by doing this for a variety of scenarios. As noted previously, this is essentially the only option if we need the "micro" precision of accounting for rolling down the yield curve, changes in the shape of the yield curve, changes in rate volatilities, or changes in the sensitivity of contingent cash flows. But for many purposes—for example, asset allocation—we usually do not need such granularity.

Yield to maturity (YTM)—the single discount rate that equates the present value of a bond's cash flows to its market price—is by far the most commonly quoted metric of valuation and, implicitly, of expected return for bonds. For bond portfolios, the YTM is usually calculated as if it were simply an average of the individual bonds' YTM, which is not exactly accurate but is a reasonable approximation.[2] Forecasting bond returns would be very easy if we could simply equate yield to maturity with expected return. It is not that simple, but YTM does provide a reasonable and readily available first approximation.

Assuming cash flows are received in full and on time, there are two main reasons why realized return may not equal the initial yield to maturity. First, if the investment horizon is shorter than the amount of time until the bond's maturity, any change in interest rate (i.e., the bond's YTM) will generate a capital gain or loss at the horizon. Second, the cash flows may be reinvested at rates above or below the initial YTM.

---

2 Bear in mind that yield to maturity does not account for optionality. However, various yield measures derived from option-adjusted valuation can be viewed as conveying similar information. To keep the present discussion as simple as possible, we ignore the distinction here. If optionality is critical to the forecast, it may be necessary to apply the more granular DCF framework discussed previously.

The longer the horizon, the more sensitive the realized return will be to reinvestment rates. These two issues work in opposite directions: Rising (falling) rates induce capital losses (gains) but increase (decrease) reinvestment income. If the investment horizon equals the (Macaulay) duration of the bond or portfolio, the capital gain/loss and reinvestment effects will roughly offset, leaving the realized return close to the original YTM. This relationship is exact if (a) the yield curve is flat and (b) the change in rates occurs immediately in a single step. In practice, the relationship is only an approximation. Nonetheless, it provides an important insight: *Over horizons shorter than the duration, the capital gain/loss impact will tend to dominate such that rising (declining) rates imply lower (higher) return, whereas over horizons longer than the duration, the reinvestment impact will tend to dominate such that rising (declining) rates imply higher (lower) return.*

Note that the timing of rate changes matters. It will not have much effect, if any, on the capital gain/loss component because that ultimately depends on the beginning and ending values of the bond or portfolio. But it does affect the reinvestment return. The longer the horizon, the more it matters. Hence, for long-term forecasts, we should break the forecast horizon into subperiods corresponding to when we expect the largest rate changes to occur.

EXAMPLE 1

Forecasting Return Based on Yield to Maturity

1. Jesper Bloch works for Discrete Asset Management (DAM) in Zurich. Many of the firm's more risk-averse clients invest in a currency-hedged global government bond strategy that uses cash flows to purchase new issues and seasoned bonds all along the yield curve to maintain a roughly constant maturity and duration profile. The yield to maturity of the portfolio is 1% (compounded annually), and the modified duration is 4.84. DAM's chief investment officer believes global government yields are likely to rise by 200 bps over the next two years as central banks remove extraordinarily ac-commodative policies and inflation surges. Bloch has been asked to project approximate returns for this strategy over horizons of two, five, and seven years. What conclusions is Bloch likely to draw?

Solution:

If yields were not expected to change, the return would be very close to the yield to maturity (1%) over each horizon. The Macaulay duration is 4.89 (= 4.84 × 1.01), so if the yield change occurred immediately, the capital gain/loss and reinvestment impacts on return would roughly balance over five years. Ignoring convexity (which is not given), the capital loss at the end of two years will be approximately 9.68% (= 4.84 × 2%). Assuming yields rise linearly over the initial two-year period, the higher reinvestment rates will boost the cumulative return by approximately 1.0% over two years, so the annual return over two years will be approximately −3.3% [= 1 + (−9.68 + 1.0)/2]. Reinvesting for three more years at the 2.0% higher rate adds anoth-er 6.0% to the cumulative return, so the five-year annual return would be ap-proximately 0.46% [= 3.25 + (1 + 1.0 + 6.0)/5]. With an additional two years of reinvestment income, the seven-year annual return would be about 1.99% [= 1 + (−9.68 + 1.0 + 6.0 + 4.0)/7]. As expected, the capital loss dominated the return over two years, and higher reinvestment rates dominated over seven years. The gradual nature of the yield increase extended the horizon over which the capital gain/loss and reinvestment effects would balance beyond the initial five-year Macaulay duration.

We have extended the DCF approach beyond simply finding the discount rates implied by current market prices (e.g., YTMs), which might be considered the "pure" DCF approach. For other asset classes (e.g., equities), the connection between discount rates and valuations/returns is vague because there is so much uncertainty with respect to the cash flows. For these asset classes, discounted cash flow is essentially a conceptual framework rather than a precise valuation model. In contrast, in fixed income there is a tight connection between discount rates, valuations, and returns. We are, therefore, able to refine the "pure" DCF forecast by incorporating projections of how rates will evolve over the investment horizon. Doing so is particularly useful in formulating short-term forecasts.

The Building Block Approach to Fixed-Income Returns

The building block approach forms an estimate of expected return in terms of required compensation for specific types of risk. The required return for fixed-income asset classes has four components: the one-period default-free rate, the term premium, the credit premium, and the liquidity premium. As the names indicate, the premiums reflect compensation for interest rate risk, duration risk, credit risk, and illiquidity, respectively. Only one of the four components—the short-term default-free rate—is (potentially) observable. For example, the term premium and the credit premium are implicitly embedded in yield spreads, but they are not *equal* to observed yield spreads. Next, we will consider each of these components and summarize applicable empirical regularities.

The Short-term Default-free Rate

In principle, the short-term default-free rate is the rate on the highest-quality, most liquid instrument with a maturity that matches the forecast horizon. In practice, it is usually taken to be a government zero-coupon bill at a maturity that is issued frequently—say, every three months. This rate is virtually always tied closely to the central bank's policy rate and, therefore, mirrors the cyclical dynamics of monetary policy. Secular movements are closely tied to expected inflation levels.

Under normal circumstances, the observed rate is a reasonable base on which to build expected returns for risky assets. In extreme circumstances, however, it may be necessary to adopt a normalized rate. For example, when policy rates or short-term government rates are negative, using the observed rate without adjustment may unduly reduce the required/expected return estimate for risky instruments. An alternative to normalizing the short rate in this circumstance would be to raise the estimate of one or more of the risk premiums on the basis of the notion that the observed negative short rate reflects an elevated willingness to pay for safety or, conversely, elevated required compensation for risk.

Forecast horizons substantially longer than the maturity of the standard short-term instrument call for a different type of adjustment. There are essentially two approaches. The first is to use the yield on a longer zero-coupon bond with a maturity that matches the horizon. In theory, that is the right thing to do. It does, however, call into question the role of the term premium since the longer-term rate will already incorporate the term premium. The second approach is to replace today's observed short-term rate with an estimate of the return that would be generated by rolling the short-term instrument over the forecast horizon; that is, take account of the likely path of short-term rates. This approach does not change the interpretation of the term premium. In addition to helping establish the baseline return to which risk premiums will be added, explicitly projecting the path of short-term rates may help in estimating the term premium.

In many markets, there are futures contracts for short-term instruments. The rates implied by these contracts are frequently interpreted as the market's expected path of short-term rates. As such, they provide an excellent starting point for analysts in formulating their own projections. Some central banks—for example, the US Federal Reserve Board—publish projections of future policy rates that can also serve as a guide for analysts. Quantitative models, such as the Taylor rule, provide another tool.[3]

The Term Premium

The default-free spot rate curve reflects the expected path of short-term rates and the required term premiums for each maturity. It is tempting to think that given a projected path of short-term rates, we can easily deduce the term premiums from the spot curve. We can, of course, derive a set of forward rates in the usual way and subtract the projected short-term rate for each future period. Doing so would give an implied sequence of period-by-period premiums. This may be a useful exercise, but it will not give us what we really want—the expected returns for bonds of different maturities over our forecast horizon. The implication is that although the yield curve contains the information we want and may be useful in forecasting returns, we cannot derive the term premium directly from the curve itself.

A vast amount of academic research has been devoted over many decades to addressing three fundamental questions: Do term premiums exist? If so, are they constant? And if they exist, how are they related to maturity? The evidence indicates that term premiums are positive and increase with maturity, are roughly proportional to duration, and vary over time. The first of these properties implies that term premiums are important. The second allows the analyst to be pragmatic, focusing on a single term premium, which is then scaled by duration. The third property implies that basing estimates on current information is essential.

Ilmanen (2012) argued that there are four main drivers of the term premium for nominal bonds.

- *Level-dependent inflation uncertainty:* Inflation is arguably the main driver of long-run variation in both nominal yields and the term premium. Higher (lower) levels of inflation tend to coincide with greater (less) inflation uncertainty. Hence, nominal yields rise (fall) with inflation because of changes in both expected inflation and the inflation risk component of the term premium.

- *Ability to hedge recession risk:* In theory, assets earn a low (or negative) risk premium if they tend to perform well when the economy is weak. When growth and inflation are primarily driven by aggregate demand, nominal bond returns tend to be negatively correlated with growth and a relatively low term premium is warranted. Conversely, when growth and inflation are primarily driven by aggregate supply, nominal bond returns tend to be positively correlated with growth, necessitating a higher term premium.

- *Supply and demand:* The relative outstanding supply of short-maturity and long-maturity default-free bonds influences the slope of the yield curve.[4] This phenomenon is largely attributable to the term premium since the maturity structure of outstanding debt should have little impact on the expected future path of short-term rates.[5]

---

3 See the Capital Market Expectations Part 1 reading for discussion of the Taylor rule.

4 As discussed in the Capital Market Expectations Part 1 reading, temporary changes in the relative *flow* of bonds to the market may not have a lasting impact on the curve unless they result in a significant, permanent change in the amounts outstanding.

5 Supply/demand effects will be more pronounced if there are reasons for certain investors to prefer or require bonds of specific maturities. This is most likely to occur at the very long end of the curve because the supply of very long-term bonds is typically limited and some institutions must fund very long-term

- *Cyclical effects:* The slope of the yield curve varies substantially over the business cycle: It is steep around the trough of the cycle and flat or even inverted around the peak. Much of this movement reflects changes in the expected path of short-term rates. However, it also reflects countercyclical changes in the term premium.

Although the slope of the yield curve is useful information on which to base forecasts of the term premium, other indicators work as well or better. Exhibit 1 shows correlations with subsequent excess bond returns (7- to 10-year Treasury bond return minus 3-month Treasury bill return) over 1-quarter, 1-year, and 5-year horizons for eight indicators. The indicators are listed in descending order of the (absolute value of the) correlation with one-year returns. The first four are derived from the bond market. The *ex ante* real yield has the strongest relationship over each horizon. Next on the list are the two most complex indicators. The Cochrane and Piazzesi curve factor is a composite measure capturing both the slope and the curvature of the yield curve.[6] The Kim and Wright premium is derived from a three-factor term structure model.[7] The slope of the yield curve is next on the list. Note that it has the weakest relationship over the five-year horizon. The supply indicator—the share of debt with maturity greater than 10 years—has a particularly strong relationship over the longest horizon. Since this variable tends to change gradually over time, it is not surprising that it is more closely related to long-run average returns than it is to shorter-term returns. The three cyclical proxies—the corporate profit-to-GDP ratio, business confidence, and the unemployment rate—are at the bottom of the list since they had the weakest correlation with return over the next year.

Exhibit 1: Correlations with Future Excess Bond Returns, 1962–2009

Current Indicator	Return Horizon		
	1 Quarter	1 Year	5 Years
Ex ante real yield	0.28	0.48	0.69
Cochrane and Piazzesi curve factor	0.24	0.44	0.32
Kim and Wright model premium*	0.25	0.43	0.34
Yield curve slope (10 year – 3 month)	0.21	0.34	0.06
Share of debt > 10 years	0.13	0.28	0.66
Corporate profit/GDP	–0.13	–0.25	–0.52
ISM business confidence	–0.10	–0.20	–0.30
Unemployment rate	0.11	0.18	0.24

* Kim and Wright model results are for 1990–2009.
Source: Ilmanen (2012, Exhibit 3.14).

The Credit Premium

The credit premium is the additional expected return demanded for bearing the risk of default losses—importantly, in addition to compensation for the *expected* level of losses. Both expected default losses and the credit premium are embedded in credit spreads. They cannot be recovered from those spreads unless we impose some structure

---

liabilities. As an example, the long end of the UK curve was severely squeezed in the 1990s.
6 See Cochrane and Piazzesi (2005).
7 See Kim and Wright (2005). The three factors in the theoretical model do not correspond directly with observable variables but may be thought of as proxies for the level, slope, and curvature of the term structure.

(i.e., a model) on default-free rates, default probabilities, and recovery rates. The two main types of models—structural credit models and reduced-form credit models—are described in detail in other readings.[8] In the following discussion, we will focus on the empirical behavior of the credit premium.

An analysis of 150 years of defaults among US non-financial corporate bonds showed that the severity of default losses accounted for only about half of the 1.53% average yield spread.[9] Hence, holders of corporate bonds did, on average, earn a credit premium to bear the risk of default. However, the pattern of actual defaults suggests the premium was earned very unevenly over time. In particular, high and low default rates tended to persist, causing clusters of high and low annual default rates and resultant losses. The study found that the previous year's default rate, stock market return, stock market volatility, and GDP growth rate were predictive of the subsequent year's default rate. However, the aggregate credit spread was not predictive of subsequent defaults. Contemporaneous financial market variables—stock returns, stock volatility, and the riskless rate—were significant in explaining the credit spread, but neither GDP growth nor changes in the default rate helped explain the credit spread. This finding suggests that credit spreads were driven primarily by the credit risk premium and financial market conditions and only secondarily by fundamental changes in the expected level of default losses. Thus, credit spreads do contain information relevant to predicting the credit premium.

Ilmanen (2012) hypothesized that credit spreads and the credit premiums embedded in them are driven by different factors, depending on credit quality. Default rates on top-quality (AAA and AA) bonds are extremely low, so very little of the spread/premium is due to the likelihood of actual default in the absence of a change in credit quality. Instead, the main driver is "downgrade bias"—the fact that a deterioration in credit quality (resulting in a rating downgrade) is much more likely than an improvement in credit quality (leading to an upgrade) and that downgrades induce larger spread changes than upgrades do.[10] Bonds rated A and BBB have moderate default rates. They still do not have a high likelihood of actual default losses, but their prospects are more sensitive to cyclical forces and their spreads/premiums vary more (countercyclically) over the cycle. Default losses are of utmost concern for below-investment-grade bonds. Defaults tend to cluster in times when the economy is in recession. In addition, the default rate and the severity of losses in default tend to rise and fall together. These characteristics imply big losses at the worst times, necessitating substantial compensation for this risk. Not too surprisingly, high-yield spreads/premiums tend to rise ahead of realized default rates.

Exhibit 2 shows three variables that have tended to predict excess returns (over T-bills) for an index of US investment-grade corporate bonds over the next quarter and the next year. Not surprisingly, a high corporate option-adjusted spread is bullish for corporate bond performance because it indicates a large cushion against credit losses—that is, a higher credit premium. A steep Treasury curve is also bullish because, as mentioned earlier, it tends to correspond to the trough of the business cycle when default rates begin to decline. Combining these insights with those from Exhibit 1, the implication is that a steep yield curve predicts both a high term premium and a high

---

8 See the CFA Program curriculum reading "Credit Analysis Models." More in-depth coverage can be found in Jarrow and van Deventer (2015).

9 See Giesecke, Longstaff, Schaefer, and Strebulaev (2011). Default rates were measured as a fraction of the par value of outstanding bonds. The authors did not document actual recovery rates, instead assuming 50% recovery. Hence, the true level of losses could have been somewhat higher or lower.

10 Liquidity relative to government bonds is also an important contributor to yield spreads on very high-quality private sector bonds. By definition, of course, this is really the liquidity premium, rather than part of the credit premium.

credit premium. Higher implied volatility in the equity market was also bullish for corporates, most likely reflecting risk-averse pricing—that is, high risk premiums—across all markets.

Exhibit 2: Correlations with US Investment-Grade Corporate Excess Returns, 1990–2009

	Return Horizon	
Current Indicator	1 Quarter	1 Year
Corporate option-adjusted spread	0.25	0.46
VIX implied equity volatility	0.28	0.39
Yield curve slope (10 year – 2 year)	0.20	0.27

Source: Ilmanen (2012, Exhibit 4.15).

How are credit premiums related to maturity? Aside from situations of imminent default, there is greater risk of default losses the longer one must wait for payment. We might, therefore, expect that longer-maturity corporate bonds would offer higher credit risk premiums. The historical evidence suggests that this has not been the case. Credit premiums tend to be especially generous at the short end of the curve. This may be due to "event risk," in the sense that a default, no matter how unlikely, could still cause a huge proportional loss but there is no way that the bond will pay more than the issuer promised. It may also be due, in part, to illiquidity since many short-maturity bonds are old issues that rarely trade as they gradually approach maturity. As a result, many portfolio managers use a strategy known as a "credit barbell" in which they concentrate credit exposure at short maturities and take interest rate/duration risk via long-maturity government bonds.

The Liquidity Premium

Relatively few bond issues trade actively for more than a few weeks after issuance. Secondary market trading occurs primarily in the most recently issued sovereign bonds, current coupon mortgage-backed securities, and a few of the largest high-quality corporate bonds. The liquidity of other bonds largely depends on the willingness of dealers to hold them in inventory long enough to find a buyer. In general, liquidity tends to be better for bonds that are (a) priced near par/reflective of current market levels, (b) relatively new, (c) from a relatively large issue, (d) from a well-known/frequent issuer, (e) standard/simple in structure, and (f) high quality. These factors tend to reduce the dealer's risk in holding the bond and increase the likelihood of finding a buyer quickly.

As a baseline estimate of the "pure" liquidity premium in a particular market, the analyst can look to the yield spread between fixed-rate, option-free bonds from the highest-quality issuer (virtually always the sovereign) and the next highest-quality large issuer of similar bonds (often a government agency or quasi-agency). Adjustments should then be made for the factors listed previously. In general, the impact of each factor is likely to increase disproportionately as one moves away from baseline attributes. For example, each step lower in credit quality is likely to have a bigger impact on liquidity than that of the preceding step.

EXAMPLE 2

Fixed-Income Building Blocks

Salimah Rahman works for SMECo, a Middle Eastern sovereign wealth fund. Each year, the fund's staff updates its projected returns for the following year on the basis of developments in the preceding year. The fund uses the building block approach in making its fixed-income projections. Rahman has been assigned the task of revising the key building block components for a major European bond market. The following table shows last year's values:

	Description	Value
Risk-free rate	3-month government bill	1.00%
Term premium	5-year duration	0.50%
Credit premium	Baa/BBB corporate	0.90%
Liquidity premium	Government-guaranteed agency	0.15%

Although inflation rose modestly, the central bank cut its policy rate by 50 bps in response to weakening growth. Aggregate corporate profits have remained solid, and after a modest correction, the stock market finished higher for the year. However, defaults on leveraged loans were unexpectedly high this year, and confidence surveys weakened again recently. Equity option volatility spiked mid-year but ended the year somewhat lower. The interest rate futures curve has flattened but remains upward sloping. The 10-year government yield declined only a few basis points, while the yield on comparable government agency bonds remained unchanged and corporate spreads—both nominal and option adjusted—widened.

1. Indicate the developments that are likely to cause Rahman to increase/decrease each of the key building blocks relative to last year.

Guideline answer:

Based on the reduction in policy rates and the flattening of the interest rate futures curve, Rahman is virtually certain to reduce the short-term rate component. Steepening of the yield curve (10-year yield barely responded to the 50 bp rate cut) indicates an increase in both the term premium and the credit premium. Declining confidence also suggests a higher term premium. Widening of credit spreads is also indicative of a higher credit premium. However, the increase in loan defaults suggests that credit losses are likely to be higher next year as well, since defaults tend to cluster. All else the same, this reduces the expected return on corporate bonds/loans. Hence, the credit premium should increase less than would otherwise be implied by the steeper yield curve and wider credit spreads. Modest widening of the government agency spread indicates an increase in the liquidity premium. The resilience of the equity market and the decline in equity option volatility suggest that investors are not demanding a general increase in risk premiums.

4   RISKS IN EMERGING MARKET BONDS

☐ | discuss risks faced by investors in emerging market fixed-income securities and the country risk analysis techniques used to evaluate emerging market economies

Emerging market debt was once nearly synonymous with crisis. The Latin American debt crisis of the 1980s involved bank loans but essentially triggered development of a market for emerging market bonds. In the early 1990s, the Mexican crisis occurred. In the late 1990s, there was the Asian crisis, followed by the Russian crisis, which contributed to the turmoil that sank the giant hedge fund Long-Term Capital Management. There have been other, more isolated, events, such as Argentina's forced restructuring of its debt, but the emerging market bond market has grown, deepened, and matured. What started with only a few government issuers borrowing in hard currencies (from their perspective foreign, but widely used, currencies) has grown into a market in which corporations as well as governments issue in their local currencies and in hard currencies. The discussion here applies not just to emerging markets but also to what are known as "frontier" markets (when they are treated separately or as a subset of emerging markets).

Investing in emerging market debt involves all the same risks as investing in developed country debt, such as interest rate movements, currency movements, and potential defaults. In addition, it poses risks that are, although not entirely absent, less significant in developed markets. These risks fall roughly into two categories: (1) economic and (2) political and legal. A slightly different breakdown would be "ability to pay" and "willingness to pay."

Before discussing these country risks, note that some countries that are labeled as emerging markets may in fact be healthy, prosperous economies with strong fundamentals. Likewise, the political and legal issues discussed in this section may or may not apply to any particular country. Furthermore, these risks will, in general, apply in varying degrees across countries. Emerging markets are widely recognized as a very heterogeneous group. It is up to the analyst to assess which considerations are relevant to a particular investment decision.

Economic Risks/Ability to Pay

Emerging market economies as a whole have characteristics that make them potentially more vulnerable to distress and hence less likely to be able to pay their debts on time or in full, such as the following:

- Greater concentration of wealth and income; less diverse tax base
- Greater dependence on specific industries, especially cyclical industries, such as commodities and agriculture; low potential for pricing power in world markets
- Restrictions on trade, capital flows, and currency conversion
- Poor fiscal controls and monetary discipline
- Less educated and less skilled work force; poor or limited physical infrastructure; lower level of industrialization and technological sophistication
- Reliance on foreign borrowing, often in hard currencies not their own
- Small/less sophisticated financial markets and institutions

- Susceptibility to capital flight; perceived vulnerability contributing to actual vulnerability

Although history is at best an imperfect guide to the future, the analyst should examine a country's track record on critical issues. Have there been crises in the past? If so, how were they handled/resolved? Has the sovereign defaulted? Is there restructured debt? How have authorities responded to fiscal challenges? Is there inflation or currency instability?

The analyst should, of course, examine the health of the macroeconomy in some detail. A few indicative guidelines can be helpful. If there is one ratio that is most closely watched, it is the ratio of the fiscal deficit to GDP. Most emerging countries have deficits and perpetually struggle to reduce them. A persistent ratio above 4% is likely a cause for concern. A debt-to-GDP ratio exceeding 70%–80%, perhaps of only mild concern for a developed market, is a sign of vulnerability for an emerging market. A persistent annual real growth rate less than 4% suggests that an emerging market is catching up with more advanced economies only slowly, if at all, and per capita income might even be falling—a potential source of political stress. Persistent current account deficits greater than 4% of GDP probably indicate lack of competitiveness. Foreign debt greater than 50% of GDP or greater than 200% of current account receipts is also a sign of danger. Finally, foreign exchange reserves less than 100% of short-term debt is risky, whereas a ratio greater than 200% is ample. It must be emphasized that the numbers given here are merely suggestive of levels that may indicate a need for further scrutiny.

When all else fails, a country may need to call on external support mechanisms. Hence, the analyst should consider whether the country has access to support from the International Monetary Fund (IMF), the World Bank, or other international agencies.

Political and Legal Risks/Willingness to Pay

Investors in emerging market debt may be unable to enforce their claims or recover their investments. Weak property rights laws and weak enforcement of contract laws are clearly of concern in this regard. Inability to enforce seniority structures within private sector claims is one important example. The principle of sovereign immunity makes it very difficult to force a sovereign borrower to pay its debts. Confiscation of property, nationalization of companies, and corruption are also relevant hazards. Coalition governments may also pose political instability problems. Meanwhile, the imposition of capital controls or restrictions on currency conversion may make it difficult, or even impossible, to repatriate capital.

As with economic risks, history may provide some guidance with respect to the severity of political and legal risks. The following are some pertinent questions: Is there a history of nationalization, expropriation, or other violations of property rights? How have international disputes been resolved and under which legal jurisdiction? Has the integrity of the judicial system and process been questioned? Are political institutions stable? Are they recognized as legitimate and subject to reasonable checks and balances? Has the transfer of power been peaceful, orderly, and lawful? Does the political process give rise to fragile coalitions that collapse whenever events strain the initial compromises with respect to policy?

EXAMPLE 3

Emerging Market Bonds

1. Belvia has big aspirations. Although still a poor country, it has been growing rapidly, averaging 6% real and 10% nominal growth for the last five years. At the beginning of this period of growth, a centrist coalition gained a narrow majority over the authoritarian, fiscally irresponsible, anti-investor, anti-business party that had been in power for decades. The government has removed the old barriers to trade, including the signing of a regional free-trade agreement, and removed capital controls. Much of its growth has been fueled by investment in its dominant industry—natural resources—financed by debt and foreign direct investment flows. These policies have been popular with the business community, as has the relaxation of regulations affecting key constituencies. Meanwhile, to ensure that prosperity flows rapidly to the people, the government has allowed redistributive social payments to grow even faster than GDP, resulting in a large and rising fiscal deficit (5% of GDP this year, projected to be 7% in two years). The current account deficit is 8% of GDP. Despite the large current account deficit, the local currency has appreciated significantly since it was allowed to float two years ago. The government has just announced that it will issue a large 10-year local currency bond under Belvian law—the first issue of its kind in many years.

   Despite a very strong relationship with the bank marketing the bond, Peter Valt has decided not to invest in it. When pressed for his reasoning, what risks is he likely to identify?

Solution:

There are several significant risks and warning signs. Coalition governments are often unstable, and the most likely alternative would appear to be a return to the previously dominant party that lacks fiscal discipline. That regime is likely to undo the recent pro-growth policies and might even disavow the debt, including this new bond. The bond will be governed by Belvian law, which, combined with the principle of sovereign immunity, will make it very difficult for foreigners to enforce their claims. In addition, the relaxation of regulations affecting key constituencies hints strongly at corruption and possibly at payoffs within the current regime. With respect to the economy, fiscal discipline remains poor, there is heavy reliance on a single industry, and the current account deficit is almost certainly unsustainable (e.g., over the 10-year life of this bond). In addition, the currency is very likely to be overvalued, which will both make it very difficult to broaden global competitiveness beyond natural resources and increase the investor's risk of substantial currency losses.

FORECASTING EQUITY RETURNS

☐ | discuss approaches to setting expectations for equity investment market returns

☐ | discuss risks faced by investors in emerging market equity securities

The task of forecasting equity market returns is often the central focus of setting capital market expectations. In this section, we discuss applying each of the major methodologies to equities.

Historical Statistics Approach to Equity Returns

Exhibit 3 shows the mean real return for each market portfolio centered within a 95% confidence interval. Results are also shown for a world portfolio, a world ex-US portfolio, and Europe. The portfolios are ordered from left to right on the basis of the mean return.

The means range from a low of 5.0% for Austria to a high of 9.4% in South Africa. Note that both of these values lie within the confidence interval for every country. From a statistical perspective, there is really no difference among these markets in terms of mean real return. This illustrates the fact that sample averages, even derived from seemingly long histories, are very imprecise estimates unless the volatility of the data is small relative to the mean. Clearly that is not the case for equity returns. Nonetheless, sample means are frequently cited without regard to the quality of information they convey.

Exhibit 3: Historical Mean Returns with Confidence Intervals by Country, 1900–2017

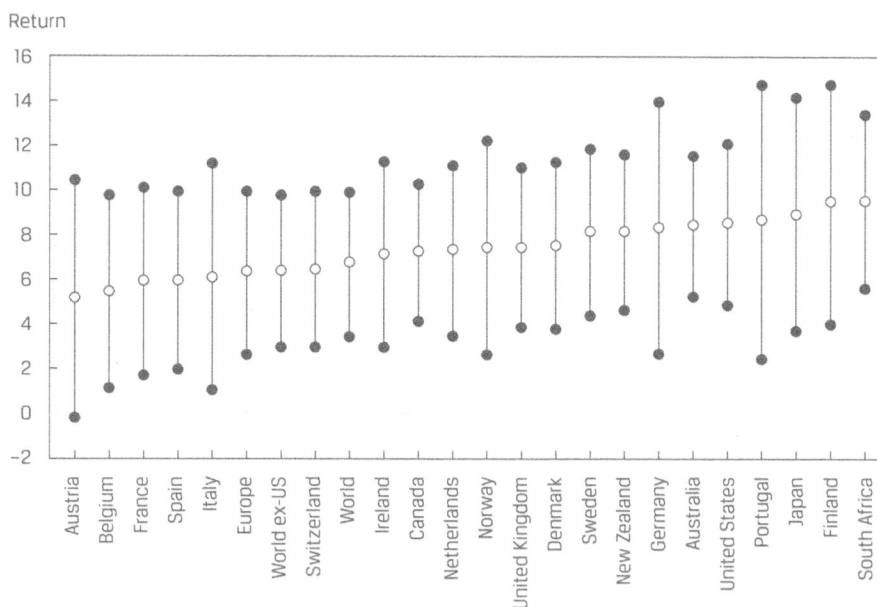

As indicated in Section 2, shrinkage estimators can often provide more reliable estimates by combining the sample mean with a second estimate of the mean return. However, the application of a common shrinkage estimator confirms that there is no basis for believing that the true expected returns for the countries in Exhibit 3 are different.

DCF Approach to Equity Returns

Analysts have frequently used the Gordon (constant) growth model form of the dividend discount model, solved for the required rate of return, to formulate the long-term expected return of equity markets. Although this model is quite simple, it has a big advantage over using historical stock returns to project future returns. The vast majority of the "noise" in historical stock returns comes from fluctuations in the price-to-earnings ratio (P/E) and the ratio of earnings to GDP. Since the amount of earnings appears in the numerator of one ratio and the denominator of the other, the impact of these ratios tends to cancel out over time, leaving the relationship between equity market appreciation and GDP growth much more stable. And GDP growth itself, especially the real growth component, is much less volatile and hence relatively predictable.[11] As an illustration, Exhibit 4 shows historical volatilities (defined as the standard deviation of percentage changes) for the S&P 500 Index return, P/E, the earnings-to-GDP ratio, real US GDP growth, and inflation for 1946–2016. The Gordon growth model allows us to take advantage of this relative stability by linking long-term equity appreciation to a more stable foundation—economic growth.

Exhibit 4: Historical Comparison of Standard Deviations in the United States, 1946–2020

S&P 500	P/E	Earnings/GDP	Real GDP Growth	Inflation
16.09	21.75	31.1	2.4	2.8

Note: Standard deviation of % changes

In the United States and other major markets, share repurchases have become an important way for companies to distribute cash to shareholders. Grinold and Kroner (2002) provided a restatement of the Gordon growth model that takes explicit account of repurchases. Their model also provides a means for analysts to incorporate expectations of valuation levels through the familiar price-to-earnings ratio. The **Grinold–Kroner model**[12] is

$$E\left(R_e\right) \approx \frac{D}{P} + (\%\Delta E - \%\Delta S) + \%\Delta P/E, \tag{1}$$

where $E(R_e)$ is the expected equity return, D/P is the dividend yield, $\%\Delta E$ is the expected percentage change in total earnings, $\%\Delta S$ is the expected percentage change in shares outstanding, and $\%\Delta P/E$ is the expected percentage change in the price-to-earnings ratio. The term in parentheses, $(\%\Delta E - \%\Delta S)$, is the growth rate of earnings per share. Net share repurchases $(\%\Delta S < 0)$ imply that earnings per share grows faster than total earnings.

With a minor rearrangement of the equation, the expected return can be divided into three components:

■ Expected cash flow ("income") return: $D/P - \%\Delta S$

---

11 See the previous reading for a discussion of projecting trend growth.
12 See Grinold and Kroner (2002) for a derivation. The model is shown here in a slightly modified form.

- Expected nominal earnings growth return: $\%\Delta E$
- Expected repricing return: $\%\Delta P/E$

The expected nominal earnings growth return and the expected repricing return constitute the expected capital gains.

In principle, the Grinold–Kroner model assumes an infinite horizon. In practice, the analyst typically needs to make projections for finite horizons, perhaps several horizons. In applying the model, the analyst needs to be aware of the implications of constant growth rate assumptions over different horizons. Failure to tailor growth rates to the horizon can easily lead to implausible results. As an example, suppose the P/E is currently 16.0 and the analyst believes that it will revert to a level of 20 and be stable thereafter. The P/E growth rates for various horizons that are consistent with this view are 4.56% for 5 years, 2.26% for 10 years, 0.75% for 30 years, and an arbitrarily small positive number for a truly long-term horizon. Treating, say, the 2.26% 10-year number as if it is appropriate for the "long run" would imply an ever-rising P/E rather than convergence to a plausible long-run valuation. The only very long-run assumptions that are consistent with economically plausible relationships are $\%\Delta E =$ Nominal GDP growth, $\%\Delta S = 0$, and $\%\Delta P/E = 0$. The longer the (finite) horizon, the less the analyst's projection should deviate from these values.

EXAMPLE 4

Forecasting the Equity Return Using the Grinold–Kroner Model

Cynthia Casey uses the Grinold–Kroner model in forecasting developed market equity returns. Casey makes the following forecasts:

- a 2.25% dividend yield on Canadian equities, based on the S&P/TSE Composite Index;
- a 1% rate of net share repurchases for Canadian equities;
- a long-term corporate earnings growth rate of 6% per year, based on a 1 percentage point (pp) premium for corporate earnings growth over her expected Canadian (nominal) GDP growth rate of 5%; and
- an expansion rate for P/E multiples of 0.25% per year.

1. Based on the information given, what expected rate of return on Canadian equities is implied by Casey's assumptions?

Solution:

The expected rate of return on Canadian equities based on Casey's assumptions would be 9.5%, calculated as

$$E(R_e) \approx 2.25\% + [6.0\% - (-1.0\%)] + 0.25\% = 9.5\%.$$

2. Are Casey's assumptions plausible for the long run and for a 10-year horizon?

Solution:

Casey's assumptions are not plausible for the very long run. The assumption that earnings will grow 1% faster than GDP implies one of two things: either an ever-rising ratio of economy-wide earnings to GDP or the earnings accruing to businesses not included in the index (e.g., private firms) continually shrinking relative to GDP. Neither is likely to persist indefinitely. Similarly, perpetual share repurchases would eventually eliminate all shares, whereas a perpetually rising P/E would lead to an arbitrarily high price per Canadian dollar of earnings per share. Based on Casey's economic growth forecast, a more reasonable long-run expected return would be 7.25% = 2.25% + 5.0%.

Casey's assumptions are plausible for a 10-year horizon. Over 10 years, the ratio of earnings to GDP would rise by roughly $10.5\% = (1.01)^{10} - 1$, shares outstanding would shrink by roughly $9.6\% = 1 - (0.99)^{10}$, and the P/E would rise by about $2.5\% = (1.0025)^{10} - 1$.

Most of the inputs to the Grinold–Kroner model are fairly readily available. Economic growth forecasts can easily be found in investment research publications, reports from such agencies as the IMF, the World Bank, and the OECD, and likely from the analyst firm's own economists. Data on the rate of share repurchases are less straightforward but are likely to be tracked by sell-side firms and occasionally mentioned in research publications. The big question is how to gauge valuation of the market in order to project changes in the P/E.

The fundamental valuation metrics used in practice typically take the form of a ratio of price to some fundamental flow variable—such as earnings, cash flow, or sales—with seemingly endless variations in how the measures are defined and calculated. Whatever the metric, the implicit assumption is that it has a well-defined long-run mean value to which it will revert. In statistical terms, it is a stationary random variable. Extensive empirical evidence indicates that these valuation measures are poor predictors of short-term performance. Over multi-year horizons, however, there is a reasonably strong tendency for extreme values to be corrected. Thus, these metrics do provide guidance for projecting intermediate-term movements in valuation.

Gauging what is or is not an extreme value is complicated by the fact that all the fundamental flow variables as well as stock prices are heavily influenced by the business cycle. One method of dealing with this issue is to "cyclically adjust" the valuation measure. The most widely known metric is the cyclically adjusted P/E (CAPE). For this measure, the current price level is divided by the average level of earnings for the last 10 years (adjusted for inflation), rather than by the most current earnings. The idea is to average away cyclical variation in earnings and provide a more reliable base against which to assess the current market price.

Risk Premium Approaches to Equity Returns

The Grinold–Kroner model and similar models are sometimes said to reflect the "supply" of equity returns since they outline the sources of return. In contrast, risk premiums reflect "demand" for returns.

Defining and Forecasting the Equity Premium

The term "equity premium" is most frequently used to describe the amount by which the expected return on equities exceeds the riskless rate ("equity versus bills"). However, the same term is sometimes used to refer to the amount by which the expected return on equities exceeds the expected return on default-free bonds ("equity versus bonds"). From the discussion of fixed-income building blocks in Sections 3 and 4, we know that the difference between these two definitions is the term premium built into the expected return on default-free bonds. The equity-versus-bonds premium reflects an incremental/building block approach to developing expected equity returns, whereas the equity-versus-bills premium reflects a single composite premium for the risk of equity investment.

Exhibit 5 shows historical averages for both of these equity premium concepts by country for the period 1900–2020.[13] For each country, the bottom portion of the column is the realized term premium (i.e., bonds minus bills) and the top segment is the realized equity-versus-bonds premium. The whole column represents the equity-versus-bills premium. The equity-versus-bills premiums range from 3.0% to 6.3%, the equity-versus-bonds premiums range from 1.8% to 5.2%, and the term premiums range from −0.6% to 2.9%.

Exhibit 5: Worldwide Annualized Bonds vs. Bills and Equity vs. Bonds Premium (%), 1900–2020

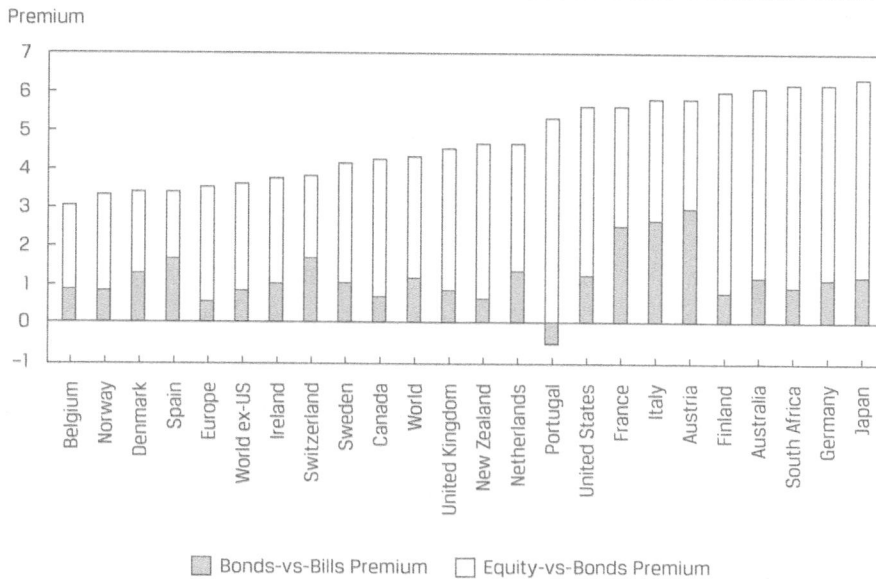

Notes: Germany excludes 1922–1923. Austria excludes 1921–1922. Returns are shown in percentages.

Source: Dimson et al. (2021, Chapter 2, Tables 8 and 9).

As with the mean equity returns in Exhibit 3, these historical premiums are subject to substantial estimation error. Statistically, there is no meaningful difference among them. Thus, the long-run cross section of returns/premiums provides virtually no reliable information with which to differentiate among countries.

Since equity returns are much more volatile than returns on either bills or bonds, forecasting either definition of the equity premium is just as difficult as projecting the absolute level of equity returns. That is, simply shifting to focus on risk premiums provides little, if any, specific insight with which to improve forecasts. The analyst must, therefore, use the other modes of analysis discussed here to forecast equity returns/premiums.

An Equilibrium Approach

There are various global/international extensions of the familiar capital asset pricing model (CAPM). We will discuss a version proposed by Singer and Terhaar (1997) that is intended to capture the impact of incomplete integration of global markets.

---

13 These premiums reflect geometric returns. Therefore, the equity-vs-bills premium is the sum of the term premium and the equity-vs-bonds premium. Premiums using arithmetic returns are systematically higher and are not additive.

The Singer–Terhaar model is actually a combination of two underlying CAPM models. The first assumes that all global markets and asset classes are fully integrated. The full integration assumption allows the use of a single global market portfolio to determine equity-versus-bills risk premiums for all assets. The second underlying CAPM assumes complete segmentation of markets such that each asset class in each country is priced without regard to any other country/asset class. For example, the markets for German equities and German bonds are completely segmented. Clearly, this is a very extreme assumption.

Recall the basic CAPM pricing relationship:

$$RP_i = \beta_{i,M}RP_M, \tag{2}$$

where $RP_i = [E(R_i) - R_F]$ is the risk premium on the ith asset, RP_M is the risk premium on the market portfolio, R_F is the risk-free rate, and $\beta_{i,M}$—asset i's sensitivity to the market portfolio—is given by

$$\beta_{i,M} = \frac{\text{Cov}\,(R_i, R_M)}{\text{Var}\,(R_M)} = \rho_{i,M}\left(\frac{\sigma_i}{\sigma_M}\right). \tag{3}$$

Standard deviations are denoted by σ, and ρ denotes correlation.

Under the assumption of full integration, every asset is priced relative to the global capitalization-weighted market portfolio. Using Equations 2 and 3 and denoting the global market portfolio by "GM," the first component of the Singer–Terhaar model is

$$RP_i^G = \beta_{i,GM}RP_{GM} = \rho_{i,GM}\sigma_i\left(\frac{RP_{GM}}{\sigma_{GM}}\right). \tag{4}$$

A superscript "G" has been added on the asset's risk premium to indicate that it reflects the global equilibrium. The term in parentheses on the far right is the Sharpe ratio for the global market portfolio, the risk premium per unit of global market risk.

Now consider the case of completely segmented markets. In this case, the risk premium for each asset will be determined in isolation without regard to other markets or opportunities for diversification. The risk premium will be whatever is required to induce investors with access to that market/asset to hold the existing supply. In terms of the CAPM framework, this implies treating each asset as its own "market portfolio." Formally, we can simply set β equal to 1 and ρ equal to 1 in the previous equations since each asset is perfectly correlated with itself. Using a superscript "S" to denote the segmented market equilibrium and replacing the global market portfolio with asset i itself in Equation 4, the segmented market equilibrium risk premium for asset i is

$$RP_i^S = 1 \times RP_i^S = 1 \times \sigma_i\left(\frac{RP_i^S}{\sigma_i}\right). \tag{5}$$

This is the second component of the Singer–Terhaar model. Note that the first equality in Equation 5 is an identity; it conveys no information. It reflects the fact that in a completely segmented market, the required risk premium could take any value. The second equality is more useful because it breaks the risk premium into two parts: the risk of the asset (σ_i) and the Sharpe ratio (i.e., compensation per unit of risk) in the segmented market.[14]

The final Singer–Terhaar risk premium estimate for asset i is a weighted average of the two component estimates

$$RP_i = \varphi RP_i^G + (1 - \varphi) RP_i^S. \tag{6}$$

---

14 A somewhat more complex model would allow for integration of asset classes within each country. Doing so would entail incorporating local market portfolios and allowing assets to be less than perfectly correlated with those portfolios. Equation (5) would then look exactly like equation (4) with the local segmented market portfolio replacing the global market portfolio ("GM").

To implement the model, the analyst must supply values for the Sharpe ratios in the globally integrated market and the asset's segmented market; the degree to which the asset is globally integrated, denoted by φ; the asset's volatility; and the asset's β with respect to the global market portfolio. A pragmatic approach to specifying the Sharpe ratios for each asset under complete integration is to assume that compensation for non-diversifiable risk (i.e., "market risk") is the same in every market. That is, assume all the Sharpe ratios equal the global Sharpe ratio.

In practice, the analyst must make a judgment about the degree of integration/segmentation—that is, the value of φ in the Singer–Terhaar model. With that in mind, some representative values that can serve as starting points for refinement can be helpful. Developed market equities and bonds are highly integrated, so a range of 0.75–0.90 would be reasonable for φ. Emerging markets are noticeably less integrated, especially during stressful periods, and there are likely to be greater differences among these markets, so a range of 0.50–0.75 would be reasonable for emerging market equities and bonds. Real estate market integration is increasing but remains far behind developed market financial assets, perhaps on par with emerging market stocks and bonds overall. In general, relative real estate market integration is likely to reflect the relative integration of the associated financial markets. Commodities for which there are actively traded, high-volume futures contracts should be on the higher end of the integration scale.

To illustrate the Singer–Terhaar model, suppose that an investor has developed the following projections for German shares and bonds.

	German Shares	German Bonds
Volatility (σ_i)	17.0%	7.0%
Correlation with global market ($\rho_{i,M}$)	0.70	0.50
Degree of integration (φ)	0.85	0.85
Segmented market Sharpe ratio $\left(RP_i^S/\sigma_i\right)$	0.35	0.25

The risk-free rate is 1.0%, and the investor's estimate of the global Sharpe ratio is 0.30. Note that the investor expects compensation for undiversifiable risk to be higher in the German stock market and lower in the German bond market under full segmentation. The following are the fully integrated risk premiums for each of the assets (from Equation 4):

Equities: $0.70 \times 17.0\% \times 0.30 = 3.57\%$.

Bonds: $0.50 \times 7.0\% \times 0.30 = 1.05\%$.

The following are the fully segmented risk premiums (from Equation 5):

Equities: $17.0\% \times 0.35 = 5.95\%$.

Bonds: $7.0\% \times 0.25 = 1.75\%$.

Based on 85% integration (φ = 0.85), the final risk estimates (from Equation 6) would be as follows:

Equities: $(0.85 \times 3.57\%) + (1 - 0.85) \times 5.95\% = 3.93\%$.

Bonds: $(0.85 \times 1.05\%) + (1 - 0.85) \times 1.75\% = 1.16\%$.

Adding in the risk-free rate, the expected returns for German shares and bonds would be 4.93% and 2.16%, respectively.

Virtually all equilibrium models implicitly assume perfectly liquid markets. Thus, the analyst should assess the actual liquidity of each asset class and add appropriate liquidity premiums. Although market segmentation and market liquidity are conceptually distinct, in practice they are likely to be related. Highly integrated markets are likely to be relatively liquid, and illiquidity is one reason that a market may remain segmented.

EXAMPLE 5

Using the Singer–Terhaar Model

1. Stacy Adkins believes the equity market in one of the emerging markets that she models has become more fully integrated with the global market. As a result, she expects it to be more highly correlated with the global market. However, she thinks its overall volatility will decline. Her old and new estimates are as follows:

	Previous Data	New Data
Volatility (σ_i)	22.0%	18.0%
Correlation with global market ($\rho_{i,M}$)	0.50	0.70
Degree of integration (ϕ)	0.55	0.75
Sharpe ratio (global and segmented markets)	0.30	0.30

If she uses the Singer–Terhaar model, what will the net impact of these changes be on her risk premium estimate for this market?

Solution:

The segmented market risk premium will decline from 6.6% (calculated as 22.0% × 0.30 = 6.6%) to 5.4% (= 18% × 0.30). The fully integrated risk premium will increase from 3.30% (= 0.50 × 22.0% × 0.30) to 3.78% (= 0.70 × 18.0% × 0.30). The weighted average premium will decline from 4.79% [= (0.55 × 3.30%) + (0.45 × 6.60%)] to 4.19% [= (0.75 × 3.78%) + (0.25 × 5.40%)], so the net effect is a decline of 60 bps.

Risks in Emerging Market Equities

Most of the issues underlying the risks of emerging market (and "frontier market" if they are classified as such) bonds also present risks for emerging market equities: more fragile economies, lower degree of informational efficiency, less stable political and policy frameworks, and weaker legal protections. However, the risks take somewhat different forms because of the different nature of equity and debt claims. Again, note that emerging markets are a very heterogeneous group. The political, legal, and economic issues that are often associated with emerging markets may not, in fact, apply to a particular market or country being analyzed.

There has been a debate about the relative importance of "country" versus "industry" risk factors in global equity markets for over 40 years. The empirical evidence has been summarized quite accurately as "vast and contradictory."[15] Both matter, but on the whole, country effects still tend to be more important than (global) industry

---

15 Marcelo, Quirós, and Martins (2013).

effects. This is particularly true for emerging markets. Emerging markets are generally less fully integrated into the global economy and the global markets. Hence, local economic and market factors exert greater influence on risk and return in these markets than in developed markets.

Political, legal, and regulatory weaknesses—in the form of weak standards and/or weak enforcement—affect emerging market equity investors in various ways. The standards of corporate governance may allow interested parties to manipulate the capital structure of companies and to misuse business assets. Accounting standards may allow management and other insiders to hide or misstate important information. Weak disclosure rules may also impede transparency and favor insiders. Inadequate property rights laws, lack of enforcement, and weak checks and balances on governmental actions may permit seizure of property, nationalization of companies, and prejudicial and unpredictable regulatory actions.

Whereas the emerging market debt investor needs to focus on ability and willingness to pay specific obligations, emerging market equity investors need to focus on variety of risks beyond the traditional credit and counterparty risks, especially in times of macroeconomic and political distress.

EXAMPLE 6

Emerging Market Equity Risks

Bill Dwight has been discussing investment opportunities in Belvia with his colleague, Peter Valt (see Example 3). He is aware that Valt declined to buy the recently issued government bond, but he believes the country's equities may be attractive. He notes the rapid growth, substantial investment spending, free trade agreement, deregulation, and strong capital inflows as factors favoring a strong equity market. In addition, solid global growth has been boosting demand for Belvia's natural resources. Roughly half of the public equity market is represented by companies in the natural resources sector. The other half is a reasonably diversified mix of other industries. Many of these firms remain closely held, having floated a minority stake on the local exchange in the last few years. Listed firms are required to have published two years of financial statements conforming to standards set by the Belvia Public Accounting Board, which is made up of the heads of the three largest domestic accounting firms. With the help of a local broker, Dwight has identified a diversified basket of stocks that he intends to buy.

Discuss the risks Dwight might be overlooking.

Guideline answer:

Dwight might be overlooking several risks. He is almost certainly underestimating the vulnerability of the local economy and the vulnerability of the equity market to local developments. The economy's rapid growth is being driven by a large and growing fiscal deficit, in particular, rapidly rising redistributive social payments, and investment spending financed by foreign capital. Appreciation of the currency has made industries other than natural resources less competitive, so the free trade agreement provides little support for the economy. When the government is forced to tighten fiscal policy or capital flows shrink, the domestic economy is likely to be hit hard. Political risk is also a concern. A return to the prior regime is likely to result in a less pro-growth, less business-friendly environment, which would most likely result in attempts by foreign investors to repatriate their capital. Dwight should also have serious concerns about corporate governance, given that most listed companies are closely held, with dominant shareholders posing expropriation risk. He should also be concerned about transparency (e.g., limited history available) and accounting standards (local standards set by the auditing firms themselves).

---

6   FORECASTING REAL ESTATE RETURNS

☐ | explain how economic and competitive factors can affect expectations for real estate investment markets and sector returns

Real estate is inherently quite different from equities, bonds, and cash. It is a physical asset rather than a financial asset. It is heterogeneous, indivisible, and immobile. It is a factor of production, like capital equipment and labor, and as such, it directly produces a return in the form of services. Its services can be sold but can be used/consumed only in one location. Owning and operating real estate involves operating and maintenance costs. All these factors contribute to making real estate illiquid and costly to transfer. The characteristics just described apply to direct investment in real estate (raw land, which does not produce income, is an exception). We will address the investment characteristics of equity REITs versus direct real estate, but unless otherwise stated, the focus is on directly held, unlevered, income-producing real estate.

Historical Real Estate Returns

The heterogeneity, indivisibility, immobility, and illiquidity of real estate pose a severe problem for historical analysis. Individual properties trade infrequently and erratically in time, so there is little chance of getting a sequence of simultaneous, periodic (say, quarterly) transaction prices for a cross section of properties. Even in mor e developed real estate markets, there is a tendence for market transactions to occur predominantly in properties with lower to moderate historical price growth. As a result, real estate owners/investors must rely heavily on appraisals, rather than transactions, in valuing properties. Owing to infrequent transactions and the heterogeneity of properties, these appraisals tend to reflect slowly moving averages of past market conditions. As a result, returns calculated from appraisals represent weighted averages of (unobservable) "true" returns—returns that would have been observed if there had been transaction prices—in previous periods. This averaging does not, in general, bias the mean return. It does, however, significantly distort estimates of volatility and correlations. The published return series is too smooth; that is, the usual sample volatility substantially understates the true volatility of returns. Meanwhile, by disguising the timing of response to market information, the smoothing tends to understate the strength of contemporaneous correlation with other market variables and spuriously induce a lead/lag structure of correlations.

In order to undertake any meaningful analysis of real estate as an asset class, the analyst must first deal with this data issue. It has become standard to "unsmooth" appraisal-based returns using a time-series model. Such techniques, which also apply to private equity funds, private debt funds, and hedge funds, are briefly described in a later section.

Real Estate Cycles

Real estate is subject to cycles that both drive and are driven by the business cycle. Real estate is a major factor of production in the economy. Virtually every business requires it. Every household consumes "housing services." Demand for the services provided by real estate rises and falls with the pace of economic activity. The supply of real estate is vast but essentially fixed at any point in time.[16] As a result, there is a strong cyclical pattern to property values, rents, and occupancy rates. The extent to which this pattern is observable depends on the type of real estate. As emphasized previously, changes in property values are obscured by the appraisal process, although indications can be gleaned from transactions as they occur. The extent to which actual rents and occupancy rates fully reflect the balance of supply and demand depends primarily on the type of property and the quality of the property. High-quality properties with long leases will tend to have little turnover, so fluctuations in actual rents and occupancy rates are likely to be relatively small. In contrast, demand for low-quality properties is likely to be more sensitive to the economy, leading to more substantial swings in occupancy and possibly rents as well. Properties with short leases will see rents adjust more completely to current supply/demand imbalances. Room rates and occupancy at low-quality hotels will tend to be the most volatile.

Fluctuations in the balance of supply and demand set up a classic boom–bust cycle in real estate. First, the boom: Perceptions of rising demand, property values, lease rates, and occupancy induce development of new properties. This investment spending helps drive and/or sustain economic activity, which, in turn, reinforces the perceived profitability of building new capacity. Then, the bust: Inevitably, optimistic projections lead to overbuilding and declining property values, lease rates, and occupancy. Since property has a very long life and is immobile, leases are typically for multiple years and staggered across tenants. In addition, since moving is costly for tenants, it may take many months or years for the excess supply to be absorbed.

A study by Clayton, Fabozzi, Gilberto, Gordon, Hudson-Wilson, Hughes, Liang, MacKinnon, and Mansour (2011) suggested that the US commercial real estate crash following the global financial crisis was the first to have been driven by the capital markets rather than by a boom–bust cycle in real estate fundamentals.[17] The catalyst was not overbuilding, Clayton et al. argued, but rather excess leverage and investment in more speculative types of properties. Consistent with that hypothesis, both the collapse in property prices and the subsequent recovery were unusually rapid. The authors attributed the accelerated response to underlying conditions to appraisers responding more vigorously to signals from the REIT and commercial mortgage-backed security markets. It remains to be seen whether this phenomenon will persist in less extreme circumstances.

Capitalization Rates

The capitalization (cap) rate, defined as net operating income (NOI) in the current period divided by the property value, is the standard valuation metric for commercial real estate. It is analogous to EBITDA as a percentage of EV (reciprocal of EV/EBITDA valuation multiple) for a typical corporate issuer. It is not, strictly speaking, a cash

---

16 Yau, Schneeweis, Szado, Robinson, and Weiss (2018) found that real estate represents from one-third to as much as two-thirds of global wealth.

17 Data from the Investment Property Databank indicate that commercial property values dropped by 21.8% globally and US property values decreased by 33.2% in 2008–2009. Other countries suffered steep losses as well, notably Ireland (55.5%) and Spain (20.1%).

flow yield because a portion of operating income may be reinvested in the property.[18] As with any equity, an estimate of the long-run expected/required rate of return can be derived from this ratio by assuming a constant growth rate for NOI—that is, by applying the Gordon growth model.

$$E(R_{re}) = \text{Cap rate} + \text{NOI growth rate.} \tag{7}$$

The long-run, steady-state NOI growth rate for commercial real estate as a whole should be reasonably close to the growth rate of GDP. The observation that over a 30-year period UK nominal rental income grew about 6.5% per annum, roughly 2.5% in real terms,[19] is consistent with this relationship.

Over finite horizons, it is appropriate to adjust this equation to reflect the anticipated rate of change in the cap rate.

$$E(R_{re}) = \text{Cap rate} + \text{NOI growth rate} - \%\Delta\text{Cap rate.} \tag{8}$$

This equation is analogous to the Grinold–Kroner model for equities, except there is no term for share buybacks. The growth rate of NOI could, of course, be split into a real component and inflation.

Exhibit 6 shows private market cap rates as of 30 June 2021 for US commercial properties differentiated by type, location, and quality. The rates range from 34.7% for industrial properties to 6.8% for retail. The relatively high cap rate for retail reflects the investors' perception that of short-term risks related to in-person shopping during the COVID-19 pandemic and longer-term risks related to ecommerce continuing to take market share from in-store retail.

Exhibit 6: Private Market Cap Rates (%) as of 30 June 2021			
Property Type	**Average**	**Higher Risk**	**Lower Risk**
Hotels	53.0	Limited Service 7.7	Full Service 7.1
Health Care	4.86	Skilled Nursing 9.5	Medical Office 5.7
Retail Malls	6.8	Low Productivity 8.8	High Productivity 5.0
Industrial	3.74		
Office	5.0	Secondary Cities 6.6	Gateway Cities 4.7
Apartments	4.55		

Source: CenterSquare Investment Management (2018).

In-store share losses to ecommerce is especially intense for lower-productivity (less profitable) locations. Cap rates for high- and low-productivity shopping malls began to diverge even before the global financial crisis. In 2006, the difference in cap rates was 1.2 percentage points; by 2018, it was 3.2 percentage points.[20]

Cap rates reflect long-term discount rates. As such, we should expect them to rise and fall with the general level of long-term interest rates, which tends to make them pro-cyclical. However, they are also sensitive to credit spreads and the availability of credit. Peyton (2009) found that the spread between cap rates and the 10-year Treasury yield is positively related to the option-adjusted spread on three- to five-year B-rated corporate bonds and negatively related to ratios of household and non-financial-sector

---

18 Ilmanen (2012) indicated that the difference between cap rates and cash flow yields may be on the order of 3 percentage points. Although significant reinvestment of NOI reduces the cash flow yield, it should increase the growth rate of NOI if the investment is productive.

19 Based on data from Investment Property Databank Limited.

20 CenterSquare Investment Management (2018). These are cap rates implied by REIT pricing, which is why the 2018 differential does not exactly match the private market figures given in Exhibit 6.

debt to GDP. The countercyclical nature of credit spreads mitigates the cyclicality of cap rates. The debt ratios are effectively proxies for the availability of debt financing for leveraged investment in real estate. Since real estate transactions typically involve substantial leverage, greater availability of debt financing is likely to translate into a lower required liquidity premium component of expected real estate returns. Not surprisingly, higher vacancy rates induce higher cap rates.

The Risk Premium Perspective on Real Estate Expected Return

As a very long-lived asset, real estate is quite sensitive to the level of long-term rates; that is, it has a high effective duration. Indeed, this is often the one and only characteristic mentioned in broad assessments of the likely performance of real estate as an asset class. Hence, real estate must earn a significant term premium. Income-earning properties are exposed to the credit risk of the tenants. In essence, a fixed-term lease with a stable stream of payments is like a corporate bond issued by the tenant secured with physical assets. The landlord must, therefore, demand a credit premium commensurate with what his or her average tenant would have to pay to issue such debt. Real estate must also earn a significant equity risk premium (relative to corporate debt) since the owner bears the full brunt of fluctuations in property values as well as uncertainty with respect to rent growth, lease rollover/termination, and vacancies. The most volatile component of return arises, of course, from changes in property values. As noted previously, these values are strongly pro-cyclical, which implies the need for a significant equity risk premium. Combining the bond-like components (term premium plus credit premium) with a stock-like component implies a risk premium somewhere between those of corporate bonds and equities.

Liquidity is an especially important risk for direct real estate ownership. There are two main ways to view illiquidity. For publicly traded equities and bonds, the question is not whether one can sell the security quickly but, rather, at what price. For real estate, however, it may be better to think of illiquidity as a total inability to sell the asset except at randomly spaced points in time. From this perspective, the degree of liquidity depends on the average frequency of these trading opportunities. By adopting this perspective, one can ask how large the liquidity premium must be to induce investors to hold an asset with a given level of liquidity. Ang, Papanikolaou, and Westerfield (2014) analyzed this question. Their results suggest liquidity premiums on the order of 0.60% for quarterly average liquidity, 0.90% for annual liquidity, and 2%, 4%, and 6% for liquidity on average every 2, 5, and 10 years, respectively.[21] All things considered, a liquidity premium of 2%–4% would seem reasonable for commercial real estate.

Real Estate in Equilibrium

Real estate can be incorporated into an equilibrium framework (such as the Singer–Terhaar model). Indeed, doing so might be deemed a necessity given the importance of real estate in global wealth. There are, however, a few important considerations. First, the impact of smoothing must have been removed from the risk/return data and metrics used for real estate. Otherwise, inclusion of real estate will distort the results for all asset classes. Second, it is important to recognize the implicit assumption of fully liquid assets in equilibrium models. Adjusting the equilibrium for illiquidity—that is, adding a liquidity premium—is especially important for real estate and other private

---

21 See Table 3 in Ang et al. (2014). The numbers cited here reflect an assumption of zero correlation between the investor's liquid and illiquid assets.

assets. Third, although real estate investors increasingly venture outside their home markets, real estate is still location specific and may, therefore, be more closely related to local, as opposed to global, economic/market factors than are financial claims.

Public vs. Private Real Estate

Many institutional investors and some ultra-wealthy individuals are able to assemble diversified portfolios of direct real estate holdings. Investors with smaller portfolios must typically choose between limited, undiversified direct real estate holdings or obtaining real estate exposure through financial instruments, such as REIT shares. Assessing whether these alternatives—direct real estate and REITs—have similar investment characteristics is difficult because of return smoothing, heterogeneity of properties, and variations in leverage.

A careful analysis of this issue requires (1) transaction-based returns for unlevered direct real estate holdings, (2) firm-by-firm deleveraging of REIT returns based on their individual balance sheets over time, and (3) carefully constructing direct real estate and REIT portfolios with matching property characteristics. Exhibit 7 shows the results of such an analysis.

Exhibit 7: Direct Real Estate vs. REITs: Four Property Types, 1994–2012

	Mean Return (%)			Standard Deviation (%)		
	Direct Real Estate	REITs		Direct Real Estate	REITs	
		Unlevered	Levered		Unlevered	Levered
Aggregate	8.80	9.29		11.09	9.71	
Apartment	9.49	9.08	11.77	11.42	9.50	20.69
Office	8.43	9.37	10.49	10.97	10.58	23.78
Industrial	9.00	9.02	9.57	11.14	11.65	23.46
Retail	8.96	9.90	12.04	11.54	10.03	23.73

Source: Ling and Naranjo (2015, Table 1).

Deleveraging the REITs substantially reduces both their mean returns and their volatilities. The volatilities are roughly cut in half. Clearly, the deleveraged REIT returns are much more similar to the direct real estate returns than are the levered REIT returns. In the aggregate, REITs outperformed direct real estate by 49 bps per year with lower volatility. Looking at specific property types, REITs had higher returns and lower volatility in two categories—office and retail. Industrial REITs had essentially the same return as directly owned industrial properties but with higher volatility. Apartment REITs lagged the direct market but with significantly lower volatility.

Exhibit 7 certainly shows some interesting differences. The pattern of unlevered REIT returns by property type is not the same as for direct real estate. Retail REITs had the highest return, and industrial REITs had the lowest. Among directly owned properties, apartments had the highest return and offices the lowest. A similar mismatch appears with respect to volatilities.

Overall, this study tends to support the general conclusion reached by most comparisons: Public and private commercial real estate are different. The extent of the difference is less clear. It does appear that once we account for differences in leverage, REIT investors are not sacrificing performance to obtain the liquidity afforded by publicly traded shares. Perhaps REIT investors are able to capture a significant portion of the liquidity risk premium garnered by direct investors (because the REIT is a direct investor) as well as benefit from professional management.

What about the diversification benefits of real estate as an asset class? REITs are traded securities, and that fact shows up in their much higher short-term correlation with equities. In contrast, direct real estate is often touted as a good diversifier based on the notion that it is not very highly correlated with equities. As noted previously, the smoothed nature of most published real estate returns is a major contributor to the appearance of low correlation with financial assets, including with REITs. Once that is corrected, however, the correlation is higher, even over reasonably short horizons, such as a quarter or a year. Importantly, REITs are more highly correlated with direct real estate and less highly correlated with equities over multi-year horizons.[22] Thus, although REITs tend to act like "stocks" in the short run, they act like "real estate" in the longer run. From a strategic asset allocation perspective, REITs and direct real estate are more comparable than conventional metrics suggest.

Long-Term Housing Returns

Savills World Research (2016) estimated that residential real estate accounts for 75% of the total value of developed properties globally. Most individuals' homes are their primary, perhaps only, real estate investment. A relatively new database provides a global perspective on the long-term performance of residential real estate (housing), equities, and bonds.[23] The database covers 145 years (1870–2015) and 16 countries.

Jordà, Knoll, Kuvshinov, Schularick, and Taylor (2017) found that residential real estate was the best performing asset class over the entire sample period, with a higher real return and much lower volatility than equities. However, performance characteristics differed before and after World War II:

- Residential real estate had a higher (lower) real return than equities before (after) World War II.

- Residential real estate had a higher real return than equities in every country except Switzerland, the United Kingdom, and the United States over 1950–1980 but a lower return than equities in every country for 1980–2015.

- Residential real estate and equities had similar patterns—that is, a strong correlation—prior to the war but a low correlation after the war.

- Equity returns became increasingly correlated across countries after the war, but residential real estate returns are essentially uncorrelated across countries.

Exhibit 8 shows the real returns for equities and residential real estate in each country since 1950.

---

22 Stefek and Suryanarayanan (2012).
23 The database was developed for and is described in Jordà, Knoll, Kuvshinov, Schularick, and Taylor (2017).

Exhibit 8: Real Equity and Housing Returns by Country, 1950–2015

Real Housing Return

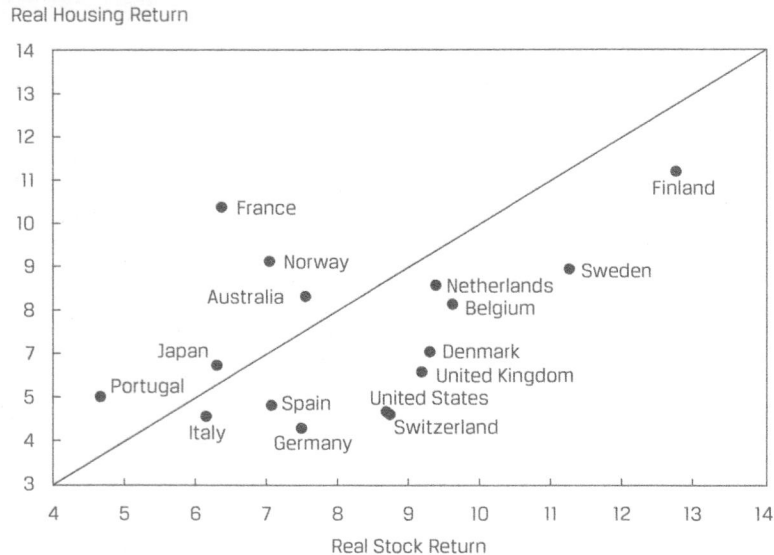

Note: Annual percentage returns are shown.

Source: Jordà et al. (2017).

EXAMPLE 7

Assessing Real Estate Investments

Tammi Sinclair, an analyst at a large retirement fund, recently attended investor presentations by three private real estate firms looking to fund new projects. Office Growth Partners specializes in building and owning low-cost, standardized office space for firms seeking to place sales representatives in the most rapidly growing small population areas across the region. Mega-Box Properties builds and owns large, custom-designed distribution facilities for multinational makers of brand-name products. The facilities are strategically located near major global transportation hubs. Exclusive Elegance Inc. develops and then manages some of the world's most luxurious, sought-after residential buildings in prime locations. It never breaks ground on a new property until at least 85% of the units have been sold and, to date, has never failed to sell out before construction is complete.

Identify important characteristics of each business that Sinclair will need to consider in establishing a required rate of return for each potential investment.

Guideline answer:

Office Growth Partners (OGP) is likely to be a very high-risk investment. It essentially chases hot markets, it builds generic office space, and its typical tenants (opportunistic sales forces) are apt to opt out as soon as the market cools. All these aspects suggest that its business is very exposed to a boom-and-bust cycle. It is likely to end up owning properties with persistently high vacancy rates and high turnover. Hence, Sinclair will likely require a rather high expected return on an investment in OGP.

Mega-Box's business should be fairly stable. The distribution centers are strategically located and designed to meet the needs of the tenant, which suggests long-term leases and low turnover will benefit both Mega-Box and the tenant firms. The average credit quality of the tenants—multinational makers of brand-name products—is likely to be solid and disciplined by the public bond and loan markets. All things considered, Sinclair should probably require a significantly lower expected return on an investment in Mega-Box than in OGP.

Exclusive Elegance appears to be even lower risk. First, it deals only in the very highest-quality, most sought-after properties in prime locations. These should be relatively immune to cyclical fluctuations. Second, it does not retain ownership of the properties, so it does not bear the equity/ownership risks. Third, it is fairly conservative in the riskiest portion of its business—developing new properties. However, Sinclair will need to investigate its record with respect to completing development projects within budget, maintaining properties, and delivering top-quality service to residents.

FORECASTING EXCHANGE RATES   7

☐ | discuss major approaches to forecasting exchange rates

Forecasting exchange rates is generally acknowledged to be especially difficult—so difficult that many asset managers either passively accept the impact of currency movements on their portfolio returns or routinely hedge out the currency exposure even if doing so is costly.

To get a sense for why exchange rates are so difficult to forecast, it is useful to distinguish between "money" and the currency in which it is denominated. Like equities and bonds, money is an asset denominated in a currency. Currencies are the units of account in which the prices of everything else—goods, services, real assets, financial assets, liabilities, flows, and balances—are quoted. An exchange rate movement changes the values of everything denominated in one currency relative to everything denominated in every other currency. That is a very powerful force. It works in the other direction as well. Anything that affects quantities, prices, or values within one currency relative to those in another will exert some degree of pressure on exchange rates. Perhaps even more importantly, anything that changes *expectations* of prices, quantities, or values within any currency can change expectations about the future path of currencies, causing an immediate reaction in exchange rates as people adjust their exposures.

Of course, currencies are not abstract accounting ledgers. They are inherently tied to governments, financial systems, legal systems, and geographies. The laws, regulations, customs, and conventions within and between these systems also influence exchange rates, especially when exchange rates are used as instruments or targets of policy. The consequence of all these aspects is that there is very little firm ground on which to stand for analysts trying to forecast exchange rates. The best we can hope to do is to identify the forces that are likely to be exerting the most powerful influences and assess their relative strength. On a related note, it is not possible to identify mutually exclusive approaches to exchange rate forecasting that are each complete enough to stand alone. Hence, the perspectives discussed in this section should be viewed as complementary rather than as alternatives.

Focus on Goods and Services, Trade, and the Current Account

There are three primary ways in which trade in goods and services can influence the exchange rate. The first is directly through flows. The second is through quasi-arbitrage of prices. The third is through competitiveness and sustainability.

Trade Flows

Trade flows do not, in general, exert a significant impact on contemporaneous exchange rate movements, provided they can be financed. Although gross trade flows may be large, net flows (exports minus imports) are typically much smaller relative to the economy and relative to actual and potential financial flows. If trade-related flows through the foreign exchange market become large relative to financing/investment flows, it is likely that a crisis is emerging.

Purchasing Power Parity

Purchasing power parity (PPP) is based on the notion that the prices of goods and services should change at the same rate regardless of currency denomination.[24] Thus, *the expected percentage change in the exchange rate should be equal to the difference in expected inflation rates.* If we define the *real exchange rate* as the ratio of price levels converted to a common currency, then PPP says that *the expected change in the real exchange rate should be zero.*

The mechanism underlying PPP is a quasi-arbitrage. Free and competitive trade should force alignment of the prices of similar products after conversion to a common currency. This is a very powerful force. It works, but it is slow and incomplete. As a result, the evidence indicates that PPP is a poor predictor of exchange rates over short to intermediate horizons but is a better guide to currency movements over progressively longer multi-year horizons.[25]

There are numerous reasons for deviations from PPP. The starting point matters. Relative PPP implicitly assumes that prices and exchange rates are already well aligned. If not, it will take time before the PPP relationship re-emerges. Not all goods are traded, and virtually every country imposes some trade barriers. PPP completely ignores the impact of capital flows, which often exert much more acute pressure on exchange rates over significant periods of time. Finally, economic developments may necessitate changes in the country's terms of trade; that is, contrary to PPP, the real exchange rate may need to change over time.

The impact of relative purchasing power on exchange rates tends to be most evident when inflation differentials are large, persistent, and driven primarily by monetary conditions. Under these conditions, PPP may describe exchange rate movements reasonably well over all but the shortest horizons. Indeed, the well-known "monetary approach" to exchange rates essentially boils down to two assumptions: (1) PPP holds, and (2) inflation is determined by the money supply.

Competitiveness and Sustainability of the Current Account

It is axiomatic that in the absence of capital flows prices, quantities, and exchange rates would have to adjust so that trade is always balanced. Since the prices of goods and services, production levels, and spending decisions tend to adjust only gradually, the onus of adjustment would fall primarily on exchange rates. Allowing for capital flows mitigates this pressure on exchange rates. The fact remains, however, that imposition

---

24 This version of PPP is usually referred to as "relative PPP" to distinguish it from a stricter notion called "absolute PPP." Absolute PPP is an important concept but is not useful for practical forecasting. See previous CFA Program currency readings for a broader discussion of PPP concepts.

25 See, for example, Abuaf and Jorion (1990); Exhibit 2 in "Currency Exchange Rates: Understanding Equilibrium Value" provides a useful visual illustration of PPP over different horizons.

of restrictions on capital flows will increase the sensitivity of exchange rates to the trade balance or, more generally, the current account balance.[26] This is not usually a major consideration for large, developed economies with sophisticated financial markets but can be important in small or developing economies.

Aside from the issue of restrictions on capital mobility, the extent to which the current account balance influences the exchange rate depends primarily on whether it is likely to be persistent and, if so, whether it can be sustained. These issues, in turn, depend mainly on the size of the imbalance and its source. Small current account balances—say, less than 2% of GDP—are likely to be sustainable for many years and hence would exert little influence on exchange rates. Similarly, larger imbalances that are expected to be transitory may not generate a significant, lasting impact on currencies.

The current account balance equals the difference between national saving and investment.[27] A current account surplus indicates that household saving plus business profits and the government surplus/deficit exceeds domestic investment spending. A current account deficit reflects the opposite. A current account deficit that reflects strong, profitable investment spending is more likely to be sustainable than a deficit reflecting high household spending (low saving), low business profits, or substantial government deficits because it is likely to attract the required capital inflow for as long as attractive investment opportunities persist. A large current account surplus may not be very sustainable either because it poses a sustainability problem for deficit countries or because the surplus country becomes unwilling to maintain such a high level of aggregate saving.

Whether an imbalance is likely to persist in the absence of terms-of-trade adjustments largely depends on whether the imbalance is structural. Structural imbalances arise from (1) persistent fiscal imbalances; (2) preferences, demographics, and institutional characteristics affecting saving decisions; (3) abundance or lack of important resources; (4) availability/absence of profitable investment opportunities associated with growth, capital deepening, and innovation; and, of course, (5) the prevailing terms of trade. Temporary imbalances mainly arise from business cycles (at home and abroad) and associated policy actions.

If a change in the (nominal) exchange rate is to bring about a necessary change in the current account balance, it will have to induce changes in spending patterns, consumption/saving decisions, and production/investment decisions. These adjustments typically occur slowly and are often resisted by decision makers who hope they can be avoided. Rapid adjustment of the exchange rate may also be resisted because people only gradually adjust their expectations of its ultimate level. Hence, both the exchange rate and current account adjustments are likely to be gradual.

Focus on Capital Flows

Since the current account and the capital account must always balance and the drivers of the current account tend to adjust only gradually, virtually all of the short-term adjustment and much of the intermediate-term adjustment must occur in the capital account. Asset prices, interest rates, and exchange rates are all part of the equilibrating mechanism. Since a change in the exchange rate simultaneously affects the relative values of all assets denominated in different currencies, we should expect significant pressure to be exerted on the exchange rate whenever an adjustment of capital flows is required.

---

26 The Mundell–Fleming model of monetary and fiscal policy effects on the exchange rate with high/low capital mobility provides an important illustration of this point. See the CFA Program reading "Currency Exchange Rates: Understanding Equilibrium Value."

27 See Chapter 4 of Piros and Pinto (2013) for discussion of balance of payments accounting.

Implications of Capital Mobility

Capital seeks the highest risk-adjusted expected return. The investments available in each currency can be viewed as a portfolio. Designating one as domestic (d) and one as foreign (f), in a world of perfect capital mobility the exchange rate (expressed as domestic currency per foreign currency unit) will be driven to the point at which the expected percentage change in the exchange rate equals the "excess" risk-adjusted expected return on the domestic portfolio over the foreign portfolio. This idea can be expressed concretely using a building block approach to expected returns.

$$E(\%\Delta S_{d/f})$$
$$= (r^d - r^f) + (\text{Term}^d - \text{Term}^f) + (\text{Credit}^d - \text{Credit}^f) + (\text{Equity}^d - \text{Equity}^f) + (\text{Liquid}^d - \text{Liquid}^f).$$

$$(9)$$

The expected change in the exchange rate ($\%\Delta S_{d/f}$) will reflect the differences in the nominal short-term interest rates (r), term premiums (Term), credit premiums (Credit), equity premiums (Equity), and liquidity premiums (Liquid) in the two markets. The components of this equation can be associated with the expected return on various segments of the portfolio: the money market (first term), government bonds (first and second), corporate bonds (first–third), publicly traded equities (first–fourth), and private assets (all terms), including direct investment in plant and equipment.

As an example, suppose the domestic market has a 1% higher short-term rate, a 0.25% lower term premium, a 0.50% higher credit premium, and the same equity and liquidity premiums as the foreign market. Equation 9 implies that the domestic currency must be expected to depreciate by 1.25% (= 1% – 0.25% + 0.5%)—that is, $E(\%\Delta S_{d/f})$ = 1.25%—to equalize risk-adjusted expected returns.

It may seem counterintuitive that the domestic currency should be expected to depreciate if its portfolio offers a higher risk-adjusted expected return. The puzzle is resolved by the key phrase "driven to the point . . . " in this subsection's opening paragraph. In theory, the exchange rate will instantly move ("jump") to a level where the currency with higher (lower) risk-adjusted expected return will be so strong (weak) that it will be expected to depreciate (appreciate) going forward. This is known as the *overshooting* mechanism, introduced by Dornbusch (1976). In reality, the move will not be instantaneous, but it may occur very quickly if there is a consensus about the relative attractiveness of assets denominated in each currency. Of course, asset prices will also be adjusting.

The overshooting mechanism suggests that there are likely to be three phases in response to relative improvement in investment opportunities. First, the exchange rate will appreciate ($S_{d/f}$ will decline) as capital flows toward the more attractive market. The more vigorous the flow, the faster and greater the appreciation of the domestic currency and the more the flow will also drive up asset prices in that market. Second, in the intermediate term, there will be a period of consolidation as investors begin to question the extended level of the exchange rate and to form expectations of a reversal. Third, in the longer run, there will be a retracement of some or all of the exchange rate move depending on the extent to which underlying opportunities have been equalized by asset price adjustments. This is the phase that is reflected in Equation 9.

Importantly, these three phases imply that the relationship between currency appreciation/depreciation and apparent investment incentives will not always be in the same direction. This fact is especially important with respect to interest rate differentials since they are directly observable. At some times, higher–interest rate currencies appreciate; at other times, they depreciate.

Uncovered Interest Rate Parity and Hot Money Flows

Uncovered interest rate parity (UIP) asserts that the expected percentage change in the exchange rate should be equal to the nominal interest rate differential. That is, only the first term in Equation 9 matters. The implicit assumption is that the response to short-term interest rate differentials will be so strong that it overwhelms all other considerations.

Contrary to UIP, the empirical evidence consistently shows that *carry trades*—borrowing in low-rate currencies and lending in high-rate currencies—earn meaningful profits on average. For example, Burnside, Eichenbaum, Kleshchelski, and Rebelo (2011) found that from February 1976 to July 2009, a strategy of rolling carry trades involving portfolios of high- and low-rate currencies returned 4.31% per annum after transaction costs versus the US dollar and 2.88% per annum versus the British pound.

The profitability of carry trades is usually ascribed to a risk premium, which is clearly consistent with the idea that the risk premiums in Equation 9 matter. The empirical results may also be capturing primarily the overshooting phase of the response to interest rate differentials. In any case, carry trades tend to be profitable on average, and UIP does not hold up well as a predictor of exchange rates.

Vigorous flows of capital in response to interest rate differentials are often referred to as *hot moneyflows*. Hot money flows are problematic for central banks. First, they limit the central bank's ability to run an effective monetary policy. This is the key message of the Mundell–Fleming model with respect to monetary policy in economies characterized by the free flow of capital. Second, a flood of readily available short-term financing may encourage firms to fund longer-term needs with short-term money, setting the stage for a crisis when the financing dries up. Third, the nearly inevitable overshooting of the exchange rate is likely to disrupt non-financial businesses. These issues are generally most acute for emerging markets since their economies and financial markets tend to be more fragile. Central banks often try to combat hot money flows by intervening in the currency market to offset the exchange rate impact of the flows. They may also attempt to *sterilize* the impact on domestic liquidity by selling government securities to limit the growth of bank reserves or maintain a target level of interest rates. If the hot money is flowing *out* rather than *in*, the central bank would do the opposite: sell foreign currency (thereby draining domestic liquidity) to limit/ avoid depreciation of the domestic currency and buy government securities (thereby providing liquidity) to sterilize the impact on bank reserves and interest rates. In either case, if intervention is not effective or sufficient, capital controls may be imposed.

Portfolio Balance, Portfolio Composition, and Sustainability Issues

The earlier discussion on the implications of capital mobility implicitly introduced a portfolio balance perspective. Each country/currency has a unique portfolio of assets that makes up part of the global "market portfolio." Exchange rates provide an across-the-board mechanism for adjusting the relative sizes of these portfolios to match investors' desire to hold them. We will look at this from three angles: tactical allocations, strategic/secular allocations, and the implications of wealth transfer.

The relative sizes of different currency portfolios within the global market portfolio do not, in general, change significantly over short to intermediate horizons. Hence, investors do not need to be induced to make changes in their long-term allocations. However, they are likely to want to make tactical allocation changes in response to evolving opportunities—notably, those related to the relative strength of various economies and related policy measures. Overall, capital is likely to flow into the currencies of countries in the strongest phases of the business cycle. The attraction should be especially strong if the economic expansion is led by robust investment in real, productive assets (e.g., plant and equipment) since that can be expected to generate a new stream of long-run profits.

In the long run, the relative size of each currency portfolio depends primarily on relative trend growth rates and current account balances. Rapid economic growth is almost certain to be accompanied by an expanding share of the global market portfolio being denominated in the associated currency. Thus, investors will have to be induced to increase their strategic allocations to assets in that country/currency. All else the same, this would tend to weaken that currency—partially offsetting the increase in the currency's share of the global portfolio—and upward pressure on risk premiums in that market. However, there are several mitigating factors.

- *With growth comes wealth accumulation:* The share of global wealth owned by domestic investors will be rising along with the supply of assets denominated in their currency. Since investors generally exhibit a strong *home country bias* for domestic assets, domestic investors are likely to willingly absorb a large portion of the newly created assets.

- *Productivity-driven growth:* If high growth reflects strong productivity gains, both foreign and domestic investors are likely to willingly fund it with both financial flows and foreign direct investment.

- *Small initial weight in global portfolios:* Countries with exceptionally high trend growth rates are typically relatively small, have previously restricted foreign access to their local-currency financial markets, and/ or have previously funded external deficits in major currencies (not their own). Almost by definition, these are emerging and frontier markets. Any of these factors would suggest greater capacity to increase the share of local-currency-denominated assets in global portfolios without undermining the currency.

Large, persistent current account deficits funded in local currency will also put downward pressure on the exchange rate over time as investors are required to shift strategic allocations toward that currency. Again, there are mitigating considerations.

- *The source of the deficit matters:* As discussed previously, current account deficits arising from strong investment spending are relatively easy to finance as long as they are expected to be sufficiently profitable. Deficits due to a low saving rate or weak fiscal discipline are much more problematic.

- *Special status of reserve currencies:* A few currencies—notably, the US dollar—have a special status because the bulk of official reserves are held in these currencies, the associated sovereign debt issuer is viewed as a safe haven, major commodities (e.g., oil) are priced in these currencies, and international trade transactions are often settled in them. A small current account deficit in a reserve-currency country is welcome because it helps provide liquidity to the global financial system. Historically, however, reserve currency status has not proven to be permanent.

Current account surpluses/deficits reflect a transfer of wealth from the deficit country to the surplus country. In an ideal world of fully integrated markets, perfect capital mobility, homogeneous expectations, and identical preferences,[28] a transfer of wealth would have virtually no impact on asset prices or exchange rates because everyone would be happy with the same portfolio composition. This is not the case in practice. To pick just one example, as long as investors have a home country bias, the transfer of wealth will increase the demand for the current-account-surplus country's assets and currency and decrease demand for those of the deficit country.

---

28 Note that these are essentially the assumptions underlying the standard CAPM.

Does the composition of a particular currency's portfolio matter? A look back at Equation 9 suggests that it should matter to some degree. For the most part, however, we would expect asset price adjustments (changes in interest rates and risk premiums) to eliminate most of the pressure that might otherwise be exerted on the exchange rate. Nonetheless, some types of flows and holdings are often considered to be more or less supportive of the currency. Foreign direct investment flows are generally considered to be the most favorable because they indicate a long-term commitment and they contribute directly to the productivity/profitability of the economy. Similarly, investments in private real estate and private equity represent long-term capital committed to the market, although they may or may not represent the creation of new real assets. Public equity would likely be considered the next most supportive of the currency. Although it is less permanent than private investments, it is still a residual claim on the profitability of the economy that does not have to be repaid. Debt has to be serviced and must either be repaid or refinanced, potentially triggering a crisis. Hence, a high and rising ratio of debt to GDP gives rise to *debt sustainability* concerns with respect to the economy. This issue could apply to private sector debt. But it is usually associated with fiscal deficits because the government is typically the largest single borrower; typically borrows to fund consumption and transfers, rather than productive investment; and may be borrowing in excess of what can be serviced without a significant increase in taxes. Finally, as noted previously with respect to hot money flows, large or rapid accumulation of short-term borrowing is usually viewed as a clear warning sign for the currency.

EXAMPLE 8

Currency Forecasts

1. After many years of running moderately high current account deficits (2%–4% of GDP) but doing little infrastructure investment, Atlandia plans to increase the yearly government deficit by 3% of GDP and maintain that level of deficit for the next 10 years, devoting the increase to infrastructure spending. The deficits will be financed with local-currency government debt. Pete Stevens, CFA, is faced with the task of assessing the impact of this announcement on the Atlandian currency. After talking with members of the economics department at his firm, he has established the following baseline assumptions:

    -   All else the same, current account deficits will persistently exceed 6% of GDP while the program is in place. Setting aside any lasting impact of the policy/spending, the current account deficit will then fall back to 3% of GDP provided the economy has remained competitive.

    -   Pressure on wages will boost inflation to 1.5% above the global inflation rate. Because of limitations on factor substitutability, costs in the traded good sector will rise disproportionately.

    -   Expectations of faster growth will raise the equity premium.

    -   The central bank will likely tighten policy—that is, raise rates.

Questions:

1. What would purchasing power parity imply about the exchange rate?
2. What are the implications for competitiveness for the currency?
3. What is the likely short-term impact of capital flows on the exchange rate?

4. What does the overshooting mechanism imply about the path of the exchange rate over time? How does this fit with the answers to Questions 1–3?

5. What does a sustainability perspective imply?

Solutions:

1. Purchasing power parity would imply that the Atlandian currency will depreciate by 1.5% per year. The exchange rate, quoted in domestic (Atlandian) units per foreign unit as in Equation 9, will rise by a factor of $1.015^{10} = 1.1605$, corresponding to a 13.83% (= $1 - 1/1.1605$) decline in the value of the domestic currency.[29]

2. Since costs in the traded sector will rise faster than inflation, the exchange rate would need to depreciate faster than PPP implies in order to maintain competitiveness. Thus, to remain competitive and re-establish a 3% current account deficit after 10 years, the *real* exchange rate needs to depreciate.

3. Both the increase in short-term rates and the increase in the equity premium are likely to induce strong short-term capital inflows even before the current account deficit actually increases. This should put significant pressure on the Atlandian currency to appreciate (i.e., the $S_{d/f}$ exchange rate will decline if the Atlandian currency is defined as the domestic currency). The initial impact may be offset to some extent by flows out of government bonds as investors push yields up in anticipation of increasing supply, but as bonds are repriced to offer a higher expected return (a higher term premium), it will reinforce the upward pressure on the exchange rate.

4. The overshooting mechanism would imply that the initial appreciation of the Atlandian currency discussed previously will extend to a level from which the currency is then expected to depreciate at a pace that equalizes risk-adjusted expected returns across markets and maintains equality between the current and capital accounts. The initial appreciation of the currency in this scenario is clearly inconsistent with PPP, but the subsequent longer-term depreciation phase (from a stronger level) is likely to bring the exchange rate into reasonable alignment with PPP and competitiveness considerations in the long run.

5. It is highly unlikely that a current account deficit in excess of 6% of GDP is sustainable for 10 years. It would entail an increase in net foreign liabilities equaling 60% (= 6% × 10) of GDP. Servicing that additional obligation would add, say, 2%–3% of GDP to the current account deficit forever. Adding that to the baseline projection of 3% would mean that the current account deficit would remain in the 5%–6% range even after the infrastructure spending ended, so net foreign liabilities would still be accumulating rapidly. Closing that gap will require a very large increase in net national saving: 5%–6% of annual GDP *in addition to* the 3% reduction in infrastructure spending when the program ends. Standard macroeconomic analysis implies that such an adjustment would require some combination of a very deep recession and a very large depreciation in the real value of the

---

29 Note that a slightly different number is obtained if the 1.5% rate is applied directly to the foreign currency value of the Atlandian currency (i.e., the exchange rate expressed as foreign units per domestic unit). That calculation would give a cumulative depreciation of 14.03% (= $1 - 0.985^{10}$). The difference arises because (1/1.015) is not exactly equal to 0.985.

Atlandian currency (i.e., the real $S_{d/f}$ exchange rate must increase sharply). As soon as investors recognize this, a crisis is almost certain to occur. Bond yields would increase sharply, and equity prices and the currency will fall substantially.

FORECASTING VOLATILITY

8

☐ │ discuss methods of forecasting volatility

In some applications, the analyst is concerned with forecasting the variance for only a single asset. More often, however, the analyst needs to forecast the variance–covariance matrix for several, perhaps many, assets in order to analyze the risk of portfolios. Estimating a single variance that is believed to be constant is straightforward: The familiar sample variance is unbiased and its precision can be enhanced by using higher-frequency data. The analyst's task becomes more complicated if the variance is not believed to be constant or the analyst needs to forecast a variance–covariance (VCV) matrix. These issues are addressed in this section. In addition, we elaborate on de-smoothing real estate and other returns.

Estimating a Constant VCV Matrix with Sample Statistics

The simplest and most heavily used method for estimating constant variances and covariances is to use the corresponding sample statistic—variance or covariance—computed from historical return data. These elements are then assembled into a VCV matrix. There are two main problems with this method, both related to sample size. First, given the short to intermediate sample periods typical in finance, the method cannot be used to estimate the VCV matrix for large numbers of assets. If the number of assets exceeds the number of historical observations, then some portfolios will erroneously appear to be riskless. Second, given typical sample sizes, this method is subject to substantial sampling error. A useful rule of thumb that addresses both of these issues is that the number of observations should be at least 10 times the number of assets in order for the sample VCV matrix to be deemed reliable. In addition, since each element is estimated without regard to any of the others, this method does not address the issue of imposing cross-sectional consistency.

VCV Matrices from Multi-Factor Models

Factor models have become the standard method of imposing structure on the VCV matrix of asset returns. From this perspective, their main advantage is that the number of assets can be very large relative to the number of observations. The key to making this work is that the covariances are fully determined by exposures to a small number of common factors whereas each variance includes an asset-specific component.

In a model with K common factors, the return on the ith asset is given by

$$r_i = \alpha_i + \sum_{k=1}^{K} \beta_{ik} F_k + \varepsilon_i, \tag{10}$$

where α_i is a constant intercept, β_{ik} is the asset's sensitivity to the kth factor, F_k is the kth common factor return, and ε_i is a stochastic term with a mean of zero that is unique to the ith asset. In general, the factors will be correlated. Given the model, the variance of the ith asset is

$$\sigma_i^2 = \sum_{m=1}^{K}\sum_{n=1}^{K}\beta_{im}\beta_{in}\rho_{mn} + v_i^2 \tag{11}$$

where ρ_{mn} is the covariance between the mth and nth factors and v_i^2 is the variance of the unique component of the ith asset's return. The covariance between the ith and jth assets is

$$\sigma_{ij} = \sum_{m=1}^{K}\sum_{n=1}^{K}\beta_{im}\beta_{jn}\rho_{mn} \tag{12}$$

As long as none of the factors are redundant and none of the asset returns are completely determined by the factors (so $v_i^2 \neq 0$), there will not be any portfolios that erroneously appear to be riskless. That is, we will not encounter the first problem mentioned in Section 8, with respect to using sample statistics.

Imposing structure with a factor model makes the VCV matrix much simpler. With N assets, there are $[N(N-1)/2]$ distinct covariance elements in the VCV matrix. For example, if $N = 100$, there are 4,950 distinct covariances to be estimated. The factor model reduces this problem to estimating $[N \times K]$ factor sensitivities plus $[K(K+1)/2]$ elements of the factor VCV matrix, Ω. With $N = 100$ and $K = 5$, this would mean "only" 500 sensitivities and 15 elements of the factor VCV matrix—almost a 90% reduction in items to estimate. (Of course, we also need to estimate the asset-specific variance terms, v_i^2, in order to get the N variances, σ_i^2.) If the factors are chosen well, the factor-based VCV matrix will contain substantially less estimation error than the sample VCV matrix does.

A well-specified factor model can also improve cross-sectional consistency. To illustrate, suppose we somehow know that the true covariance of any asset i with any asset j is proportional to asset i's covariance with any third asset, k, so

$$\frac{\sigma_{ij}}{\sigma_{ik}} = \text{Constant} \tag{13}$$

for any assets i, j, and k. We would want our estimates to come as close as possible to satisfying this relationship. Sample covariances computed from any given sample of returns will not, in general, do so. However, using Equation 12 with only one factor (i.e., $K = 1$) shows that the covariances from a single-factor model will satisfy

$$\frac{\sigma_{ij}}{\sigma_{ik}} = \frac{\beta_j}{\beta_k} \tag{14}$$

for all assets i, j, and k. Thus, in this simple example, a single-factor model imposes exactly the right cross-sectional structure.

The benefits obtained by imposing a factor structure—handling large numbers of assets, a reduced number of parameters to be estimated, imposition of cross-sectional structure, and a potentially substantial reduction of estimation error—come at a cost. In contrast to the simple example just discussed, in general, the factor model will almost certainly be mis-specified. The structure it imposes will not be exactly right. As a result, the factor-based VCV matrix is *biased*; that is, the expected value is not equal to the true (unobservable) VCV matrix of the returns. To put it differently, the matrix is not correct even "on average." The matrix is also *inconsistent*; that is, it does not converge to the true matrix as the sample size gets arbitrarily large. In contrast, the sample VCV matrix is unbiased and consistent. Thus, when we use a factor-based matrix instead of the sample VCV matrix, we are choosing to estimate something that is "not quite right" with relative precision rather than the "right thing" with a lot of noise. The point is that although factor models are very useful, they are not a panacea.

Shrinkage Estimation of VCV Matrices

As with shrinkage estimation in general, the idea here is to combine the information in the sample data, the sample VCV matrix, with an alternative estimate, the target VCV matrix—which reflects assumed "prior" knowledge of the structure of the true VCV matrix—and thereby mitigate the impact of estimation error on the final matrix. Each element (variance or covariance) of the final shrinkage estimate of the VCV matrix is simply a weighted average of the corresponding elements of the sample VCV matrix and the target VCV matrix. The same weights are used for all elements of the matrix. The analyst must determine how much weight to put on the target matrix (the "prior" knowledge) and how much weight to put on the sample data (the sample VCV matrix).

Aside from a technical condition that rules out the appearance of riskless portfolios, virtually any choice of target VCV matrix will increase (or at least not decrease) the efficiency of the estimates versus the sample VCV matrix. "Efficiency" in this context means a smaller mean-squared error (MSE), which is equal to an estimator's variance plus the square of its bias. Although the shrinkage estimator is biased, its MSE will in general be smaller than the MSE of the (unbiased) sample VCV matrix. The more plausible (and presumably less biased) the selected target matrix, the greater the improvement will be. A factor-model-based VCV matrix would be a reasonable candidate for the target.

EXAMPLE 9

Estimating the VCV Matrix

---

1. Isa Berkitz is an analyst at Barnsby & Culp (B&C), a recently formed multi-family office. Berkitz has been asked to propose the method for estimating the variance–covariance matrix to be used in B&C's asset allocation process for all clients. After examining the existing client portfolios and talking with the clients and portfolio managers, Berkitz concludes that in order to support B&C's strategic and tactical allocation needs, the VCV matrix will need to include 25 asset classes. For many of these classes, she will be able to obtain less than 10 years of monthly return data. Berkitz has decided to incorporate both the sample statistics and factor-model approaches using shrinkage estimation.

   Explain the strengths and weaknesses of the two basic approaches and why Berkitz would choose to combine them using the shrinkage framework.

Solution:

The VCV matrix based on sample statistics is correct on average (it is unbiased) and convergences to the true VCV matrix as the sample size gets arbitrarily large (it is "consistent"). The sample VCV method cannot be used if the number of assets exceeds the number of observations, which is not an issue in this case. However, it is subject to large sampling errors unless the number of observations is large relative to the number of assets. A 10-to-1 rule of thumb would suggest that Berkitz needs more than 250 observations (20+ years of monthly data) in order for the sample VCV matrix to give her reliable estimates, but she has at most 120 observations. In addition, the sample VCV matrix does not impose any cross-sectional consistency on the estimates. A factor-model-based VCV matrix can be used even if the number of assets exceeds the number of observations. It can substantially reduce the number of unique parameters to be estimated, it imposes cross-sectional structure, and it can substantially reduce estimation errors. However, unless the structure imposed by the factor model is exactly correct, the VCV matrix will not be correct on average (it will be biased). Shrinkage estimation—a weighted average of the sample VCV and factor-based VCV matrices—will increase (or at least not decrease) the efficiency of the estimates. In effect, the shrinkage estimator captures the benefits of each underlying methodology and mitigates their respective limitations.

Estimating Volatility from Smoothed Returns

The available return data for such asset classes as private real estate, private equity, and hedge funds generally reflect smoothing of unobservable underlying "true" returns. The smoothing dampens the volatility of the observed data and distorts correlations with other assets. Thus, the raw data tend to understate the risk and overstate the diversification benefits of these asset classes. Failure to adjust for the impact of smoothing will almost certainly lead to distorted portfolio analysis and hence poor asset allocation decisions.

The basic idea is that the observed returns are a weighted average of current and past true, unobservable returns. One of the simplest and most widely used models implies that the current observed return, R_t, is a weighted average of the current true return, r_t, and the previous observed return:

$$R_t = (1 - \lambda)r_t + \lambda R_{t-1},\tag{15}$$

where $0 < \lambda < 1$. From this equation, it can be shown that

$$\text{var}(r) = \left(\frac{1+\lambda}{1-\lambda}\right)\text{var}(R) > \text{var}(R).\tag{16}$$

As an example, if $\lambda = 0.8$, then the true variance, $\text{var}(r)$, of the asset is 9 times the variance of the observed data. Equivalently, the standard deviation is 3 times larger.

This model cannot be estimated directly because the true return, r_t, is not observable. To get around this problem, the analyst assumes a relationship between the unobservable return and one or more observable variables. For private real estate, a natural choice might be a REIT index, whereas for private equity, an index of similar publicly traded equities could be used.

EXAMPLE 10

Estimating Volatility from Smoothed Data

While developing the VCV matrix for B&C, Isa Berkitz noted that the volatilities for several asset classes—notably, real estate and private equity categories—calculated directly from available return data appear to be very low. The data are from reputable sources, but Berkitz is skeptical because similar publicly traded classes—for example, REITs and small-cap equities—exhibit much higher volatilities. What is the likely cause of the issue?

Guideline answer:

The very low volatilities are very likely due to smoothing within the reported private asset returns. That is, the observed data reflect a weighted average of current and past true returns. For real estate, this smoothing arises primarily because the underlying property values used to calculate "current" returns are based primarily on backward-looking appraisals rather than concurrent transactions.

Time-Varying Volatility: ARCH Models

The discussion up to this point has focused on estimating variances and covariances under the assumption that their true values do not change over time. It is well known, however, that financial asset returns tend to exhibit **volatility clustering**, evidenced by periods of high and low volatility. A class of models known collectively as autoregressive conditional heteroskedasticity (ARCH) models has been developed to address these time-varying volatilities.[30]

One of the simplest and most heavily used forms of this broad class of models specifies that the variance in period t is given by

$$\sigma_t^2 = \gamma + \alpha \sigma_{t-1}^2 + \beta \eta_t^2$$
$$= \gamma + (\alpha + \beta) \sigma_{t-1}^2 + \beta \left(\eta_t^2 - \sigma_{t-1}^2 \right), \tag{17}$$

where α, β, and γ are non-negative parameters such that $(\alpha + \beta) < 1$. The term η_t is the unexpected component of return in period t; that is, it is a random variable with a mean of zero conditional on information at time $(t - 1)$. Rearranging the equation as in the second line shows that $\left(\eta_t^2 - \sigma_{t-1}^2 \right)$ can be interpreted as the "shock" to the variance in period t. Thus, the variance in period t depends on the variance in period $(t - 1)$ plus a shock. The parameter β controls how much of the current "shock" feeds into the variance. In the extreme, if $\beta = 0$, then variance would be deterministic. The quantity $(\alpha + \beta)$ determines the extent to which the variance in future periods is influenced by the current level of volatility. The higher $(\alpha + \beta)$ is, the more the variance "remembers" what happened in the past and the more it "clusters" at high or low levels. The unconditional expected value of the variance is $[\gamma/(1 - \alpha - \beta)]$.

As an example, assume that $\gamma = 0.000002$, $\alpha = 0.9$, and $\beta = 0.08$ and that we are estimating daily equity volatility. Given these parameters, the unconditional expected value of the variance is 0.0001, implying that the daily standard deviation is 1% (0.01). Suppose the estimated variance at time $(t - 1)$ was 0.0004 (= 0.02^2) and the return in period t was 3% above expectations ($\eta_t = 0.03$). Then the variance in period t would be

$$\sigma_t^2 = 0.000002 + (0.9 \times 0.0004) + (0.08 \times 0.03^2) = 0.000434,$$

which is equivalent to a standard deviation of 2.0833%. Without the shock to the variance (i.e., with $\eta_t^2 = \sigma_{t-1}^2 = 0.0004$), the standard deviation would have been 1.9849%. Even without the shock, the volatility would have remained well above its long-run mean of 1.0%. Including the shock, the volatility actually increased. Note that the impact on volatility would have been the same if the return had been 3% *below* expectations rather than above expectations.

The ARCH methodology can be extended to multiple assets—that is, to estimation of a VCV matrix. The most straightforward extensions tend to be limited to only a few assets since the number of parameters rises very rapidly. However, Engle (2002) developed a class of models with the potential to handle large matrices with relatively few parameters.

EXAMPLE 11

ARCH

Sam Akai has noticed that daily returns for a variety of asset classes tend to exhibit periods of high and low volatility but the volatility does seem to revert toward a fairly stable average level over time. Many market participants capture this tendency by estimating volatilities using a 60-day moving window. Akai

---

30 Chapter 12 of Campbell, Lo, and MacKinlay (1997) provides an excellent, detailed explanation of these models. The present discussion draws on that book.

notes that this method implicitly assumes volatility is constant within each 60-day window but somehow not constant from one day to the next. He has heard that ARCH models can explicitly incorporate time variation and capture the observed clustering pattern.

Explain the models to him.

Guideline answer:

The key idea is to model variance as a linear time-series process in which the current volatility depends on its own recent history or recent shocks. The shocks to volatility arise from unexpectedly large or small returns. In one of the simplest ARCH models, the current variance depends only on the variance in the previous period and the unexpected component of the current return (squared). Provided the coefficients are positive and not "too large," the variance will exhibit the properties Akai has observed: periods of time at high/low levels relative to a well-defined average level.

9   ADJUSTING A GLOBAL PORTFOLIO

☐   recommend and justify changes in the component weights of a global investment portfolio based on trends and expected changes in macroeconomic factors

The coverage of capital market expectations has provided an intensive examination of topics with which analysts need to be familiar in order to establish capital market expectations for client portfolios. This section brings some of this material together to illustrate how analysts can develop and justify recommendations for adjusting a portfolio. The discussion that follows is selective in the range of assets and scenarios it considers. It focuses on connecting expectations to the portfolio and is about "direction of change" rather than the details of specific forecasts.

Macro-Based Recommendations

Suppose we start with a fairly generic portfolio of global equities and bonds (we assume no other asset classes are included or considered) and we are asked to recommend changes based primarily on macroeconomic considerations. Further assume that the portfolio reflects a reasonable strategic allocation for our clients. Hence, we do not need to make any wholesale changes and can focus on incremental improvements based on assessment of current opportunities. To be specific, we limit our potential recommendations to the following:

- Change the overall allocations to equities and bonds.
- Reallocate equities/bonds between countries.
- Adjust the average credit quality of our bond portfolios.
- Adjust duration and positioning on the yield curves.
- Adjust our exposures to currencies.

To approach the task systematically, we begin with a checklist of questions.

1. Have there been significant changes in the drivers of trend growth, globally or in particular countries?

2. Are any of the markets becoming more/less globally integrated?

3. Where does each country stand within its business cycle? Are they synchronized?

4. Are monetary and fiscal policies consistent with long-term stability and the phases of the business cycle?

5. Are current account balances trending and sustainable?

6. Are any currencies under pressure to adjust or trending? Have capital flows driven any currencies to extended levels? Have any of the economies become uncompetitive/super-competitive because of currency movements?

There are certainly many more questions we could ask. In practice, the analyst will need to look into the details. But these questions suffice for our illustration. We will examine each in turn. It must be noted, however, that they are inherently interrelated.

Trend Growth

All else the same, an increase in trend growth favors equities because it implies more rapid long-run earnings growth. Faster growth due to productivity is especially beneficial. In contrast, higher trend growth generally results in somewhat higher real interest rates, a negative for currently outstanding bonds. Identifiable changes in trend growth that have not already been fully factored into asset prices are most likely to have arisen from a shock (e.g., new technology). A global change would provide a basis for adjusting the overall equity/bond allocation. Country-specific or regional changes provide a basis for reallocation within equities toward the markets experiencing enhanced growth prospects that have not already been reflected in market prices.

Global Integration

All else the same, the Singer–Terhaar model implies that when a market becomes more globally integrated, its required return should decline. As prices adjust to a lower required return, the market should deliver an even higher return than was previously expected or required by the market. Therefore, expected increases in integration provide a rationale for adjusting allocations toward those markets and reductions in markets that are already highly integrated. Doing so will typically entail a shift from developed markets to emerging markets.

Phases of the Business Cycle

The best time to buy equities is generally when the economy is approaching the trough of the business cycle. Valuation multiples and expected earnings growth rates are low and set to rise. The Grinold–Kroner model could be used to formalize a recommendation to buy equities. At this stage of the cycle, the term premium is high (the yield curve is steep) and the credit premium is high (credit spreads are wide). However, (short-term) interest rates are likely to start rising soon and the yield curve can be expected to flatten again as the economy gains strength. All else the same, the overall allocation to bonds will need to be reduced to facilitate the increased allocation to equities. Within the bond portfolio, overall duration should be reduced, positions with intermediate maturities should be reduced in favor of shorter maturities (and perhaps a small amount of longer maturities) to establish a "barbell" posture with the desired duration, and exposure to credit should be increased (a "down in quality" trade). The opposite recommendations would apply when the analyst judges that the economy is at or near the peak of the cycle.

To the extent that business cycles are synchronized across markets, this same prescription would apply to the overall portfolio. It is likely, however, that some markets will be out of phase—leading or lagging other markets—by enough to warrant reallocations between markets. In this case, the recommendation would be to reallocate equities from (to) markets nearest the peak (trough) of their respective cycles and to do the opposite within the bond portfolio with corresponding adjustments to duration, yield curve positioning, and credit exposure within each market.

Monetary and Fiscal Policies

Investors devote substantial energy dissecting every nuance of monetary and fiscal policy. If policymakers are doing what we would expect them to be doing at any particular stage of the business cycle—for example, moderate countercyclical actions and attending to longer-term objectives, such as controlling inflation and maintaining fiscal discipline—their activities may already be reflected in asset prices. In addition, the analyst should have factored expected policy actions into the assessment of trend growth and business cycles.

Significant opportunities to add value by reallocating the portfolio are more likely to arise from structural policy changes (e.g., a shift from interest rate targeting to money growth targeting, quantitative easing, and restructuring of the tax code) or evidence that the response to policy measures is not within the range of outcomes that policymakers would have expected (e.g., if massive quantitative easing induced little inflation response). Structural policy changes are clearly intentional and the impact on the economy and the markets is likely to be consistent with standard macroeconomic analysis, so the investment recommendations will follow from the implications for growth trends and business cycles. Almost by definition, standard modes of analysis may be ineffective if policy measures have not induced the expected responses. In this case, the analyst's challenge is to determine what, why, and how underlying linkages have changed and identify the value-added opportunities.

Current Account Balances

Current account balances ultimately reflect national saving and investment decisions, including the fiscal budget. Current accounts must, of course, net out across countries. In the short run, this is brought about in large measure by the fact that household saving and corporate profits (business saving) are effectively residuals whereas consumption and capital expenditures are more explicitly planned. Hence, purely cyclical fluctuations in the current account are just part of the business cycle. Longer-term trends in the current account require adjustments to induce deliberate changes in saving/investment decisions. A rising current account deficit will tend to put upward pressure on real required returns (downward pressure on asset prices) in order to induce a higher saving rate in the deficit country (to mitigate the widening deficit) and to attract the increased flow of capital from abroad required to fund the deficit. An expanding current account surplus will, in general, require the opposite in order to reduce "excess" saving. This suggests that the analyst should consider reallocation of portfolio assets from countries with secularly rising current account deficits to those with secularly rising current account surpluses (or narrowing deficits).

Capital Accounts and Currencies

Setting aside very high inflation situations in which purchasing power parity may be important even in the short term, currencies are primarily influenced by capital flows. When investors perceive that the portfolio of assets denominated in a particular currency offers a higher risk-adjusted expected return than is available in other currencies, the initial surge of capital tends to drive the exchange rate higher, often to a level from which it is more likely to depreciate rather than continue to appreciate. At that point, the underlying assets may remain attractive in their native currency but not in conjunction with the currency exposure. An analyst recommending reallocation of a portfolio toward assets denominated in a particular currency must, therefore, assess whether the attractiveness of the assets has already caused an "overshoot" in the currency or whether a case can be made that there is meaningful appreciation yet to come. In the former case, the analyst needs to consider whether the assets remain attractive after taking account of the cost of currency hedging.

There is one final question that needs to be addressed for all asset classes and currencies. The previous discussion alluded to it, but it is important enough to be asked directly: *What is already reflected in asset prices?* There is no avoiding the fact that valuations matter.

Quantifying the Views

Although the analyst may not be required to quantify the views underlying his or her recommendations, we can very briefly sketch a process that may be used for doing so using some of the tools discussed in earlier sections.

Step 1   Use appropriate techniques to estimate the VCV matrix for all asset classes.

Step 2   Use the Singer–Terhaar model and the estimated VCV matrix to determine equilibrium expected returns for all asset classes.

Step 3   Use the Grinold–Kroner model to estimate returns for equity markets based on assessments of economic growth, earnings growth, valuation multiples, dividends, and net share repurchases.

Step 4   Use the building block approach to estimate expected returns for bond classes based primarily on cyclical and policy considerations.

Step 5   Establish directional views on currencies relative to the portfolio's base currency based on the perceived attractiveness of assets and the likelihood of having overshot sustainable levels. Set modest rates of expected appreciation/depreciation.

Step 6   Incorporate a currency component into expected returns for equities and bonds.

Step 7   Use the Black–Litterman framework (described in a later reading) to combine equilibrium expected returns from Step 2 with the expected returns determined in Steps 3–6.

SUMMARY

The following are the main points covered in the reading.

- The choice among forecasting techniques is effectively a choice of the information on which forecasts will be conditioned and how that information will be incorporated into the forecasts.

- The formal forecasting tools most commonly used in forecasting capital market returns fall into three broad categories: statistical methods, discounted cash flow models, and risk premium models.

- Sample statistics, especially the sample mean, are subject to substantial estimation error.

- Shrinkage estimation combines two estimates (or sets of estimates) into a more precise estimate.

- Time-series estimators, which explicitly incorporate dynamics, may summarize historical data well without providing insight into the underlying drivers of forecasts.

- Discounted cash flow models are used to estimate the required return implied by an asset's current price.

- The risk premium approach expresses expected return as the sum of the risk-free rate of interest and one or more risk premiums.

- There are three methods for modeling risk premiums: equilibrium models, such as the CAPM; factor models; and building blocks.

- The DCF method is the only one that is precise enough to use in support of trades involving individual fixed-income securities.

- There are three main methods for developing expected returns for fixed-income asset classes: DCF, building blocks, and inclusion in an equilibrium model.

- As a forecast of bond return, YTM, the most commonly quoted metric, can be improved by incorporating the impact of yield changes on reinvestment of cash flows and valuation at the investment horizon.

- The building blocks for fixed-income expected returns are the short-term default-free rate, the term premium, the credit premium, and the liquidity premium.

- Term premiums are roughly proportional to duration, whereas credit premiums tend to be larger at the short end of the curve.

- Both term premiums and credit premiums are positively related to the slope of the yield curve.

- Credit spreads reflect both the credit premium (i.e., additional expected return) and expected losses due to default.

- A baseline estimate of the liquidity premium can be based on the yield spread between the highest-quality issuer in a market (usually the sovereign) and the next highest-quality large issuer (often a government agency).

- Emerging market debt exposes investors to heightened risk with respect to both ability to pay and willingness to pay, which can be associated with the economy and political/legal weaknesses, respectively.

- The Grinold–Kroner model decomposes the expected return on equities into three components: (1) expected cash flow return, composed of the dividend yield minus the rate of change in shares outstanding, (2) expected return due to nominal earnings growth, and (3) expected repricing return, reflecting the rate of change in the P/E.

- Forecasting the equity premium directly is just as difficult as projecting the absolute level of equity returns, so the building block approach provides little, if any, specific insight with which to improve equity return forecasts.

- The Singer–Terhaar version of the international capital asset pricing model combines a global CAPM equilibrium that assumes full market integration with expected returns for each asset class based on complete segmentation.

- Emerging market equities expose investors to the same underlying risks as emerging market debt does: more fragile economies, less stable political and policy frameworks, and weaker legal protections.

- Emerging market investors need to pay particular attention to the ways in which the value of their ownership claims might be expropriated. Among the areas of concern are standards of corporate governance, accounting and disclosure standards, property rights laws, and checks and balances on governmental actions.

- Historical return data for real estate is subject to substantial smoothing, which biases standard volatility estimates downward and distorts correlations with other asset classes. Meaningful analysis of real estate as an asset class requires explicit handling of this data issue.

- Real estate is subject to boom–bust cycles that both drive and are driven by the business cycle.

- The cap rate, defined as net operating income in the current period divided by the property value, is the standard valuation metric for commercial real estate.

- A model similar to the Grinold–Kroner model can be applied to estimate the expected return on real estate:

$E(R_{re})$ = Cap rate + NOI growth rate − %ΔCap rate.

- There is a clear pattern of higher cap rates for riskier property types, lower-quality properties, and less attractive locations.

- Real estate expected returns contain all the standard building block risk premiums:

  - Term premium: As a very long-lived asset with relatively stable cash flows, income-producing real estate has a high duration.

  - Credit premium: A fixed-term lease is like a corporate bond issued by the leaseholder and secured by the property.

  - Equity premium: Owners bear the risk of property value fluctuations, as well as risk associated with rent growth, lease renewal, and vacancies.

  - Liquidity premium: Real estate trades infrequently and is costly to transact.

- Currency exchange rates are especially difficult to forecast because they are tied to governments, financial systems, legal systems, and geographies. Forecasting exchange rates requires identification and assessment of the forces that are likely to exert the most influence.

- Provided they can be financed, trade flows do not usually exert a significant impact on exchange rates. International capital flows are typically larger and more volatile than trade-financing flows.

- PPP is a poor predictor of exchange rate movements over short to intermediate horizons but is a better guide to currency movements over progressively longer multi-year horizons.

- The extent to which the current account balance influences the exchange rate depends primarily on whether it is likely to be persistent and, if so, whether it can be sustained.

- Capital seeks the highest risk-adjusted expected return. In a world of perfect capital mobility, in the long run, the exchange rate will be driven to the point at which the expected percentage change equals the "excess" risk-adjusted expected return on the portfolio of assets denominated in the domestic currency over that of the portfolio of assets denominated in the foreign currency. However, in the short run, there can be an exchange rate overshoot in the opposite direction as hot money chases higher returns.

- Carry trades are profitable on average, which is contrary to the predictions of uncovered interest rate parity.
- Each country/currency has a unique portfolio of assets that makes up part of the global "market portfolio." Exchange rates provide an across-the-board mechanism for adjusting the relative sizes of these portfolios to match investors' desire to hold them.
- The portfolio balance perspective implies that exchange rates adjust in response to changes in the relative sizes and compositions of the aggregate portfolios denominated in each currency.
- The sample variance–covariance matrix is an unbiased estimate of the true VCV structure; that is, it will be correct on average.
- There are two main problems with using the sample VCV matrix as an estimate/forecast of the true VCV matrix: It cannot be used for large numbers of asset classes, and it is subject to substantial sampling error.
- Linear factor models impose structure on the VCV matrix that allows them to handle very large numbers of asset classes. The drawback is that the VCV matrix is biased and inconsistent unless the assumed structure is true.
- Shrinkage estimation of the VCV matrix is a weighted average of the sample VCV matrix and a target VCV matrix that reflects assumed "prior" knowledge of the true VCV structure.
- Failure to adjust for the impact of smoothing in observed return data for real estate and other private assets will almost certainly lead to distorted portfolio analysis and hence poor asset allocation decisions.
- Financial asset returns exhibit volatility clustering, evidenced by periods of high and low volatilities. ARCH models were developed to address these time-varying volatilities.
- One of the simplest and most used ARCH models represents today's variance as a linear combination of yesterday's variance and a new "shock" to volatility. With appropriate parameter values, the model exhibits the volatility clustering characteristic of financial asset returns.

REFERENCES

Abuaf, Niso, Philippe Jorion. 1990. "Purchasing Power Parity in the Long Run." *Journal of Finance* (March): 157–74. 10.1111/j.1540-6261.1990.tb05085.x

Ang, Andrew, Dimitris Papanikolaou, and Mark M. Westerfield. 2014. "Portfolio Choice with Illiquid Assets." *Management Science* 6 (11). 10.1287/mnsc.2014.1986

Burnside, Craig, Martin Eichenbaum, Isaac Kleshchelski, and Sergio Rebelo. 2011. "Do Peso Problems Explain the Returns to the Carry Trade?" *Review of Financial Studies* 24 (3): 853–91. 10.1093/rfs/hhq138

Clayton, Jim, Frank J. Fabozzi, S. Michael Gilberto, Jacques N. Gordon, Susan Hudson-Wilson, William Hughes, Youguo Liang, Greg MacKinnon, and Asieh Mansour. 2011. "The Changing Face of Real Estate Investment Management." Special Real Estate Issue *Journal of Portfolio Management*: 12–23.

Cochrane, John H., Monika Piazzesi. 2005. "Bond Risk Premia." *American Economic Review* (March): 138–60. 10.1257/0002828053828581

Dimson, Elroy, Paul Marsh, and Mike Staunton. 2021. Credit Suisse Global Investment Returns Yearbook 2021. Zurich: Credit Suisse Research Institute.

Dornbusch, R. Dec 1976. "Expectations and Exchange Rate Dynamics." *Journal of Political Economy* 84 (6): 1161–76. 10.1086/260506

Engle, Robert. 2002. "Dynamic Conditional Correlation: A Simple Class of Multivariate Generalized Autoregressive Conditional Heteroskedasticity Models." *Journal of Business & Economic Statistics* (July): 339–50. 10.1198/073500102288618487

Giesecke, Kay, Francis A. Longstaff, Stephen Schaefer, and Ilya Strebulaev. 2011. "Corporate Bond Default Risk: A 150-Year Perspective." *Journal of Financial Economics* 102 (2): 233–50. 10.1016/j.jfineco.2011.01.011

Grinold, Richard, Ken Kroner. 2002. "The Equity Risk Premium: Analyzing the Long-Run Prospects for the Stock Market." *Investment Insights* 5 (3).

Ilmanen, Antti. 2012. Expected Returns on Major Asset Classes. Charlottesville, VA: Research Foundation of CFA Institute.

Jarrow, Robert A., Donald R. van Deventer. 2015. "Credit Analysis Models." In *Fixed Income Analysis*, 3rd ed. CFA Institute Investment Series/Wiley.

Jordà, Òscar, Katharina Knoll, Dmitry Kuvshinov, Moritz Schularick, and Alan M. Taylor. 2017. "The Rate of Return on Everything, 1870–2015." NBER Working Paper No. 24112 (December). 10.3386/w24112

Kim, Don H., Jonathan H. Wright. 2005. "An Arbitrage-Free Three-Factor Term Structure Model and the Recent Behavior of Long-Term Yields and Distant-Horizon Forward Rates." Federal Reserve Board Working Paper 2005-33 (August). 10.2139/ssrn.813267

Ling, David C., Andy Naranjo. 2015. "Returns and Information Transmission Dynamics in Public and Private Real Estate Markets." *Real Estate Economics* 43 (1): 163–208. 10.1111/1540-6229.12069

Peyton, Martha S. 2009. "Capital Markets Impact on Commercial Real Estate Cap Rates: A Practitioner's View." Special Real Estate Issue *Journal of Portfolio Management* 38–49. 10.3905/JPM.2009.35.5.038

Piros, Christopher D. 2015. "Strategic Asset Allocation: Plus ça change, plus c'est la meme chose." *Investments & Wealth Monitor* (March/April): 5–8.

Piros, Christopher D., Jerald E. Pinto. 2013. Economics for Investment Decision Makers Workbook: Micro, Macro, and International Economics. Hoboken, NJ: John Wiley & Sons, Inc.

Savills World Research. 2016. Around the World in Dollars and Cents. London: Savills.

Singer, Brian D., Kevin Terhaar. 1997. Economic Foundations of Capital Market Returns. Charlottesville, VA: Research Foundation of the Institute of Chartered Financial Analysts.

Stefek, Daniel, Raghu Suryanarayanan. 2012. "Private and Public Real Estate: What Is the Link?" *Journal of Alternative Investments* (Winter): 66–75.

Yau, Jot K., Thomas Schneeweis, Edward A. Szado, Thomas R. Robinson, and Lisa R. Weiss. 2018. "Alternative Investments Portfolio Management." CFA Program Level III Curriculum Reading 26.

PRACTICE PROBLEMS

The following information relates to questions 1-2

An investor is considering adding three new securities to her internationally focused fixed income portfolio. She considers the following non-callable securities:

- 1-year government bond
- 10-year government bond
- 10-year BBB rated corporate bond

She plans to invest equally in all three securities being analyzed or will invest in none of them at this time. She will only make the added investment provided that the expected spread/premium of the equally weighted investment is at least 1.5 percent (150bp) over the 1-year government bond. She has gathered the following information:

Risk free interest rate (1-year, incorporating 0.6% inflation expectation)	1.0%
Term premium (10-year vs. 1-year government bond)	1%
10-year BBB credit premium (over 10-year government bond)	75bp
Estimated liquidity premium on 10-year corporate bonds	55bp

Using only the information given, address the following problems using the risk premium approach:

1. Calculate the expected return that an equal-weighted investment in the three securities could provide.

2. Calculate the expected total risk premium of the three securities and determine the investor's probable course of action.

The following information relates to questions 3-10

Richard Martin is chief investment officer for the Trunch Foundation (the foundation), which has a large, globally diversified investment portfolio. Martin meets with the foundation's fixed-income and real estate portfolio managers to review expected return forecasts and potential investments, as well as to consider short-term modifications to asset weights within the total fund strategic asset allocation.

Martin asks the real estate portfolio manager to discuss the performance characteristics of real estate. The real estate portfolio manager makes the following statements:

Statement 1   Adding traded REIT securities to an equity portfolio should substantially improve the portfolio's diversification over the next year.

Statement 2   Traded REIT securities are more highly correlated with direct real estate and less highly correlated with equities over multi-year horizons.

Martin looks over the long-run valuation metrics the manager is using for commercial real estate, shown in Exhibit 1.

Exhibit 1: Commercial Real Estate Valuation Metrics

Cap Rate	GDP Growth Rate
4.70%	4.60%

The real estate team uses an in-house model for private real estate to estimate the true volatility of returns over time. The model assumes that the current observed return equals the weighted average of the current true return and the previous observed return. Because the true return is not observable, the model assumes a relationship between true returns and observable REIT index returns; therefore, it uses REIT index returns as proxies for both the unobservable current true return and the previous observed return.

Martin asks the fixed-income portfolio manager to review the foundation's bond portfolios. The existing aggregate bond portfolio is broadly diversified in domestic and international developed markets. The first segment of the portfolio to be reviewed is the domestic sovereign portfolio. The bond manager notes that there is a market consensus that the domestic yield curve will likely experience a single 20 bp increase in the near term as a result of monetary tightening and then remain relatively flat and stable for the next three years. Martin then reviews duration and yield measures for the short-term domestic sovereign bond portfolio in Exhibit 2.

Exhibit 2: Short-Term Domestic Sovereign Bond Portfolio

Macaulay Duration	Modified Duration	Yield to Maturity
3.00	2.94	2.00%

The discussion turns to the international developed fixed-income market. The foundation invested in bonds issued by Country XYZ, a foreign developed country. XYZ's sovereign yield curve is currently upward sloping, and the yield spread between 2-year and 10-year XYZ bonds is 100 bps.

The fixed-income portfolio manager tells Martin that he is interested in a domestic market corporate bond issued by Zeus Manufacturing Corporation (ZMC). ZMC has just been downgraded two steps by a major credit rating agency. In addition to expected monetary actions that will raise short-term rates, the yield spread between three-year sovereign bonds and the next highest-quality government agency bond widened by 10 bps.

Although the foundation's fixed-income portfolios have focused primarily on developed markets, the portfolio manager presents data in Exhibit 3 on two emerging markets for Martin to consider. Both economies increased exports of their mineral resources over the last decade.

Exhibit 3: Emerging Market Data

Factor	Emerging Republic A	Emerging Republic B
Fiscal deficit/GDP	6.50%	8.20%
Debt/GDP	90.10%	104.20%
Current account deficit	5.20% of GDP	7.10% of GDP
Foreign exchange reserves	90.30% of short-term debt	70.10% of short-term debt

The fixed-income portfolio manager also presents information on a new invest-ment opportunity in an international developed market. The team is considering the bonds of Xdelp, a large energy exploration and production company. Both the domestic and international markets are experiencing synchronized growth in GDP midway between the trough and the peak of the business cycle. The foreign country's government has displayed a disciplined approach to maintaining stable monetary and fiscal policies and has experienced a rising current account surplus and an appreciating currency. It is expected that with the improvements in free cash flow and earnings, the credit rating of the Xdelp bonds will be upgraded. Martin refers to the foundation's asset allocation policy in Exhibit 4 before mak-ing any changes to either the fixed-income or real estate portfolios.

Exhibit 4: Trunch Foundation Strategic Asset Allocation—Select Data

Asset Class	Minimum Weight	Maximum Weight	Actual Weight
Fixed income—Domestic	40.00%	80.00%	43.22%
Fixed income—International	5.00%	10.00%	6.17%
Fixed income—Emerging markets	0.00%	2.00%	0.00%
Alternatives—Real estate	2.00%	6.00%	3.34%

3. Which of the real estate portfolio manager's statements is correct?

   A. Only Statement 1

   B. Only Statement 2

   C. Both Statement 1 and Statement 2

4. Based only on Exhibit 1, the long-run expected return for commercial real estate:

   A. is approximately double the cap rate.

   B. incorporates a cap rate greater than the discount rate.

   C. needs to include the cap rate's anticipated rate of change.

5. Based on the private real estate model developed to estimate return volatility, the true variance is *most likely*:

   A. lower than the variance of the observed data.

   B. approximately equal to the variance of the observed data.

C. greater than the variance of the observed data.

6. Based on Exhibit 2 and the anticipated effects of the monetary policy change, the expected annual return over a three-year investment horizon will *most likely* be:

   A. lower than 2.00%.

   B. approximately equal to 2.00%.

   C. greater than 2.00%.

7. Based on the building block approach to fixed-income returns, the dominant source of the yield spread for Country XYZ is *most likely* the:

   A. term premium.

   B. credit premium.

   C. liquidity premium.

8. Using the building block approach, the required rate of return for the ZMC bond will *most likely*:

   A. increase based on the change in the credit premium.

   B. decrease based on the change in the default-free rate.

   C. decrease based on the change in the liquidity premium.

9. Based only on Exhibit 3, the foundation would *most likely* consider buying bonds issued by:

   A. only Emerging Republic A.

   B. only Emerging Republic B.

   C. neither Emerging Republic A nor Emerging Republic B.

10. Based only on Exhibits 3 and 4 and the information provided by the portfolio managers, the action *most likely* to enhance returns is to:

    A. decrease existing investments in real estate by 2.00%.

    B. initiate a commitment to emerging market debt of 1.00%.

    C. increase the investments in international market bonds by 1.00%.

---

11. Jo Akumba's portfolio is invested in a range of developed markets fixed income securities. She asks her adviser about the possibility of diversifying her investments to include emerging and frontier markets government and corporate fixed income securities. Her adviser makes the following comment regarding risk:

    "All emerging and frontier market fixed income securities pose economic, political and legal risk. Economic risks arise from the fact that emerging market countries have poor fiscal discipline, rely on foreign borrowing, have less diverse tax base and significant dependence on specific industries. They are susceptible to capital flight. Their ability to pay is limited. In addition, weak property rights, weak enforcement of contract laws and political instability pose hazard for emerging markets debt investors."

    Discuss the statement made.

The following information relates to questions 12-14

An Australian investor currently holds a A$240 million equity portfolio. He is considering rebalancing the portfolio based on an assessment of the risk and return prospects facing the Australian economy. Information relating to the Australian investment markets and the economy has been collected in the following table:

10-Year Historical	Current	Capital Market Expectations
Average government bond yield: 2.8%	10-year government bond yield: 2.3%	
Average annual equity return: 4.6%	Year-over-year equity return: −9.4%	
Average annual inflation rate: 2.3%	Year-over-year inflation rate: 2.1%	Expected annual inflation: 2.3%
Equity market P/E (beginning of period): 15×	Current equity market P/E: 14.5×	Expected equity market P/E: 14.0×
Average annual dividend income return: 2.6%		Expected annual income return: 2.4%
Average annual real earnings growth: 6.0%		Expected annual real earnings growth: 5.0%

Using the information in the table, address the following problems:

12. Calculate the historical Australian equity risk premium using the "equity-vs-bonds" premium method.

13. Calculate the expected annual equity return using the Grinold–Kroner model (assume no change in the number of shares outstanding).

14. Using your answer to Part B, calculate the expected annual equity risk premium.

The following information relates to questions 15-16

An analyst is reviewing various asset alternatives and is presented with the following information relating to the broad equity market of Switzerland and various industries within the Swiss market that are of particular investment interest.

Expected risk premium for overall global investable market (GIM) portfolio	3.5%
Expected standard deviation for the GIM portfolio	8.5%
Expected standard deviation for Swiss Healthcare Industry equity investments	12.0%
Expected standard deviation for Swiss Watch Industry equity investments	6.0%
Expected standard deviation for Swiss Consumer Products Industry equity investments	7.5%

Assume that the Swiss market is perfectly integrated with the world markets. Swiss Healthcare has a correlation of 0.7 with the GIM portfolio.

Swiss Watch has a correlation of 0.8 with the GIM portfolio.

Swiss Consumer Products has a correlation of 0.8 with the GIM portfolio.

15. Basing your answers only upon the data presented in the table above and using the international capital asset pricing model—in particular, the Singer–Terhaar approach—estimate the expected risk premium for the following:

   i.   Swiss Health Care Industry

   ii.   Swiss Watch Industry

   iii. Swiss Consumer Products Industry

16. Judge which industry is most attractive from a valuation perspective.

17. Identify risks faced by investors in emerging market equities over and above those that are faced by fixed income investors in such markets.

The following information relates to questions 18-25

Judith Bader is a senior analyst for a company that specializes in managing international developed and emerging markets equities. Next week, Bader must present proposed changes to client portfolios to the Investment Committee, and she is preparing a presentation to support the views underlying her recommendations.

Bader begins by analyzing portfolio risk. She decides to forecast a variance–covariance matrix (VCV) for 20 asset classes, using 10 years of monthly returns and incorporating both the sample statistics and the factor-model methods. To mitigate the impact of estimation error, Bader is considering combining the results of the two methods in an alternative target VCV matrix, using shrinkage estimation.

Bader asks her research assistant to comment on the two approaches and the benefits of applying shrinkage estimation. The assistant makes the following statements:

Statement 1   Shrinkage estimation of VCV matrices will decrease the efficiency of the estimates versus the sample VCV matrix.

Statement 2   Your proposed approach for estimating the VCV matrix will not be reliable because a sample VCV matrix is biased and inconsistent.

Statement 3   A factor-based VCV matrix approach may result in some portfolios that erroneously appear to be riskless if any asset returns can be completely determined by the common factors or some of the factors are redundant.

Bader then uses the Singer–Terhaar model and the final shrinkage-estimated VCV matrix to determine the equilibrium expected equity returns for all international asset classes by country. Three of the markets under consideration are located in Country A (developed market), Country B (emerging market), and Country C (emerging market). Bader projects that in relation to the global market, the equity market in Country A will remain highly integrated, the equity market in Country B will become more segmented, and the equity market in

Country C will become more fully integrated.

Next, Bader applies the Grinold–Kroner model to estimate the expected equity returns for the various markets under consideration. For Country A, Bader assumes a very long-term corporate earnings growth rate of 4% per year (equal to the expected nominal GDP growth rate), a 2% rate of net share repurchases for Country A's equities, and an expansion rate for P/E multiples of 0.5% per year.

In reviewing Countries B and C, Bader's research assistant comments that emerging markets are especially risky owing to issues related to politics, competition, and accounting standards. As an example, Bader and her assistant discuss the risk implications of the following information related to Country B:

- Experiencing declining per capita income

- Expected to continue its persistent current account deficit below 2% of GDP

- Transitioning to International Financial Reporting Standards, with full convergence scheduled to be completed within two years

Bader shifts her focus to currency expectations relative to clients' base currency and summarizes her assumptions in Exhibit 1.

Exhibit 1: Baseline Assumptions for Currency Forecasts

	Country A	Country B	Country C
Historical current account	Persistent current account deficit of 5% of GDP	Persistent current account deficit of 2% of GDP	Persistent current account surplus of 2% of GDP
Expectation for secular trend in current account	Rising current account deficit	Narrowing current account deficit	Rising current account surplus
Long-term inflation expectation relative to global inflation	Expected to rise	Expected to keep pace	Expected to fall
Capital flows	Steady inflows	Hot money flowing out	Hot money flowing in

During a conversation about Exhibit 1, Bader and her research assistant discuss the composition of each country's currency portfolio and the potential for triggering a crisis. Bader notes that some flows and holdings are more or less supportive of the currency, stating that investments in private equity make up the majority of Country A's currency portfolio, investments in public equity make up the majority of Country B's currency portfolio, and investments in public debt make up the majority of Country C's currency portfolio.

18. Which of the following statements made by Bader's research assistant is correct?

    A. Statement 1

    B. Statement 2

    C. Statement 3

19. Based on expectations for changes in integration with the global market, all else being equal, the Singer–Terhaar model implies that Bader should shift capital from Country A to:

    A. only Country B.

B. only Country C.

C. both Countries B and C.

20. Using the Grinold–Kroner model, which of the following assumptions for forecasting Country A's expected equity returns is plausible for the very long run?

   A. Rate of net share repurchases

   B. Corporate earnings growth rate

   C. Expansion rate for P/E multiples

21. Based only on the emerging markets discussion, developments in which of the following areas *most likely* signal increasing risk for Country B's equity market?

   A. Politics

   B. Competitiveness

   C. Accounting standards

22. Based on Bader's expectations for current account secular trends as shown in Exhibit 1, Bader should reallocate capital, all else being equal, from:

   A. Country A to Country C.

   B. Country B to Country A.

   C. Country C to Country A.

23. Based on Bader's inflation expectations as shown in Exhibit 1, purchasing power parity implies that which of the following countries' currencies should depreciate, all else being equal?

   A. Country A

   B. Country B

   C. Country C

24. Based on Exhibit 1, which country's central bank is *most likely* to buy domestic bonds near term to sterilize the impact of money flows on domestic liquidity?

   A. Country A

   B. Country B

   C. Country C

25. Based on the composition of each country's currency portfolio, which country is most vulnerable to a potential crisis?

   A. Country A

   B. Country B

   C. Country C

26. Describe the main issues that arise when conducting historical analysis of real

estate returns.

27. An analyst at a real estate investment management firm seeks to establish expectations for rate of return for properties in the industrial sector over the next year. She has obtained the following information:

Current industrial sector capitalization rate ("cap" rate)	5.7%
Expected cap rate at the end of the period	5.5%
NOI growth rate (real)	1%
Inflation expectation	1.5%

Estimate the expected return from the industrial sector properties based on the data provided.

28. A client has asked his adviser to explain the key considerations in forecasting exchange rates. The adviser's firm uses two broad complementary approaches when setting expectations for exchange rate movements, namely focus on trade in goods and services and, secondly, focus on capital flows. Identify the main considerations that the adviser should explain to the client under the two approaches.

29. Looking independently at each of the economic observations below, indicate the country where an analyst would expect to see a strengthening currency for each observation.

	Country X	Country Y
Expected inflation over next year	2.0%	3.0%
Short-term (1-month) government rate	Decrease	Increase
Expected (forward-looking) GDP growth over next year	2.0%	3.3%
New national laws have been passed that enable foreign direct investment in real estate/financial companies	Yes	No
Current account surplus (deficit)	8%	−1%

30. Fap is a small country whose currency is the Fip. Three years ago, the exchange rate was considered to be reflecting purchasing power parity (PPP). Since then, the country's inflation has exceeded inflation in the other countries by about 5% per annum. The Fip exchange rate, however, remained broadly unchanged. What would you have expected the Fip exchange rate to show if PPP prevailed? Are Fips over or undervalued, according to PPP?

SOLUTIONS

1.

	Risk free interest rate (nominal) (%)	+	Premiums (%)	=	Expected annual fixed-income return (%)
1-year government bond	1	+	0	=	1
10-year government bond	1	+	1	=	2
10-year corporate bond	1	+	1 + 0.75 + 0.55	=	3.3

Estimate of the expected return of an equal-weighted investment in the three securities: (1% + 2% + 3.3%)/3 = 2.1%.

2. The average spread (over 1-year government bond) at issue is [0 + 1 + (1 + 0.75 + 0.55)] = 3.3%/3 = 1.1%.

   As the 1.1% is less than 1.5%, the investor will not make the investment.

3. B is correct. Statement 2 is correct because traded REIT securities are more highly correlated with direct real estate and less highly correlated with equities over multi-year horizons. Thus, although REITs tend to act like stocks in the short run, they act like real estate in the longer run.

   A and C are incorrect because Statement 1 is not correct. Traded REIT securities have relatively high correlations with equity securities over short time horizons, such as one year. The higher correlations suggest that traded REIT securities will not act as a good diversifier for an equity portfolio over a one-year period.

4. A is correct. An estimate of the long-run expected or required return for commercial real estate equals the sum of the capitalization rate (cap rate) plus the growth rate (constant) of net operating income (NOI). An approximation of the steady-state NOI growth rate for commercial real estate is equal to the growth rate in GDP. Thus, from Equation 7 and the information provided in Exhibit 1, $E(R_{re})$ = Cap rate + NOI growth rate = 4.70% + 4.60% = 9.30%, which is approximately double the cap rate.

   B is incorrect because the discount rate (expected or required return) equals the sum of the cap rate and the NOI growth rate. Based on the information in Exhibit 1, the 4.70% cap rate is less than (not greater than) the 9.30% discount rate.

   C is incorrect because the discount rate over finite horizons (not long-run horizons) needs to include the anticipated rate of change in the cap rate. For long-run expected return calculations, the anticipated rate of change in the cap rate is not included.

5. C is correct. The in-house model assumes that the current observed return equals the weighted average of the current true return and the previous observed return. The model uses REIT index returns as proxies for the returns in the model. The smoothed nature of most published (observed) real estate returns is a major contributor to the appearance of low correlation with financial assets. This smoothing dampens the volatility of the observed data and distorts correlations with other assets. Thus, the raw observable data tend to understate the risk and

overstate the diversification benefits of these asset classes. It is generally accepted that the true variance of real estate returns is greater than the variance of the observed data.

6. B is correct. If the investment horizon equals the (Macaulay) duration of the portfolio, the capital loss created by the increase in yields and the reinvestment effects (gains) will roughly offset, leaving the realized return approximately equal to the original yield to maturity. This relationship is exact if (a) the yield curve is flat and (b) the change in rates occurs immediately in a single step. In practice, the relationship is only an approximation. In the case of the domestic sovereign yield curve, the 20 bp increase in rates will likely be offset by the higher reinvestment rate, creating an annual return approximately equal to 2.00%.

7. A is correct. From the building block approach to fixed-income returns, the required return for fixed-income asset classes has four components: the one-period default-free rate, the term premium, the credit premium, and the liquidity premium. Since sovereign bonds are considered the highest-quality bonds, they likely do not have a significant credit premium nor are they likely to have a significant premium for illiquidity. The slope of the yield curve is useful information on which to base forecasts of the term premium. Therefore, the dominant source of the yield spread is most likely the term premium for XYZ's sovereign bond.

8. A is correct. The credit premium is the additional expected return demanded for bearing the risk of default losses. A credit downgrade two steps lower will increase the credit premium and the required rate of return. The change in the default-free rate associated with the monetary tightening will increase (not decrease) the required rate of return. The widening of the spread between the sovereign bond and the next highest-quality government agency security indicates an increase in the liquidity premium, which will increase (not decrease) the required rate of return.

   B is incorrect because the required rate of return would increase (not decrease) based on the change in the default-free rate associated with the monetary tightening.

   C is incorrect because the rate of return would increase (not decrease) based on a change in the liquidity premium. The liquidity premium can be estimated from the yield spread between the highest-quality issuer (typically a sovereign bond) and the next highest-quality large issuer of similar bonds (often a government agency). A widening yield spread indicates an increase in the liquidity premium and required rate of return.

9. C is correct. Emerging market debt requires an analysis of economic and political/legal risks. Based on the macroeconomic factors, the risk of a bond investment in either Republic A or Republic B appears to be high. Thresholds such as the risk guidelines listed in the table below can be used to assess the attractiveness of the two emerging market (EM) opportunities in Republic A and Republic B. Most notably, both republics raise concern based solely on their fiscal deficit-to-GDP ratios greater than 4.00% (Republic A's is 6.50% and Republic B's is 8.20%).

Emerging Market Analysis			
Country Political/Economic Risk	Emerging Market Risk Guidelines	Emerging Republic A	Emerging Republic B
Fiscal deficit/GDP	4.00%	Negative	Negative
Debt/GDP	70.00%	Negative	Negative
Current account deficit	4.00% of GDP	Negative	Negative
Foreign exchange reserves	100.00% of short-term debt	Negative	Negative

Analysis of the economic and political risks associated with the two EM opportunities is suggestive of the need for further scrutiny; therefore, the foundation should not invest in Emerging Republic A or Emerging Republic B based only on the information provided.

10. C is correct. An investment in the bonds of the international energy exploration and production company (Xdelp) looks attractive. The international market benefits from positive macroeconomic fundamentals: point in the business cycle, monetary and fiscal discipline, rising current account surplus, and an appreciating currency. The anticipated credit rating improvement will add to the potential for this to become a profitable investment and enhance returns. An increase in the investments within the international fixed-income segment by 1.00% (existing weight is 6.17%) would take advantage of this opportunity and remain in compliance with the foundation's 5.00%–10.00% strategic asset allocation limits.

    A is incorrect because a decrease in the existing weight of real estate by 2.00% would put the portfolio weight below the minimum threshold of 2.00% (i.e., 3.34% ⊠ 2.00% = 1.34%) of the foundation's strategic asset allocation.

    B is incorrect because the information presented in Exhibit 3 would lead the chief investment officer to avoid the two opportunities in emerging market debt (Emerging Republic A and Emerging Republic B) and not initiate a commitment to emerging market debt of 1.00% (i.e., increase the existing weight above 0.00%).

11. The statement correctly identifies economic, political and legal risk. The adviser has correctly identified some of the characteristics typically associated with emerging and frontier markets that may affect their governments' and corporate borrowers' ability and willingness to pay bondholders. However, the assertion that all emerging and frontier market fixed income securities pose such risk is incorrect, as many countries classified as "emerging" are considered to be healthy and prosperous economies.

12. The historical equity risk premium is 1.8%, calculated as follows:

    Historical equity returns − Historical 10-year government bond yield

    = Historical equity risk premium

    $4.6\% - 2.8\% = 1.8\%$

13. The Grinold–Kroner model states that the expected return on equity is the sum of the expected income return (2.4%), the expected nominal earnings growth return (7.3% = 2.3% from inflation + 5.0% from real earnings growth) and the expected repricing return (−3.45%). The expected change in market valuation of −3.45% is calculated as the percentage change in the P/E level from the current 14.5× to the expected level of 14.0×: $(14 - 14.5)/14.5 = -3.45\%$. Thus, the expected return is $2.4\% + 7.3\% - 3.45\% = 6.25\%$.

14. Using the results from Part B, the expected equity return is 6.25 percent.

    Expected equity return − Current 10-year government bond yield

    = Expected equity risk premium

    $6.25\% - 2.3\% = 3.95\%$.

15. Using the formula $RP_i^G = \rho_{i,GM}\,\sigma_i\left(\frac{RP_{GM}}{\sigma_{GM}}\right)$ we can solve for each expected industry risk premium. The term in brackets is the Sharpe ratio for the GIM, computed as $3.5/8.5 = 0.412$.

    i. $RP_{\text{Healthcare}} = (12)(0.7)(0.412) = 3.46\%$
    ii. $RP_{\text{Watch}} = (6)(0.8)(0.412) = 1.98\%$
    iii. $RP_{\text{Consumer Products}} = (7.5)(0.8)(0.412) = 2.47\%$

16. Based on the above analysis, the Swiss Healthcare Industry would have the highest expected return. However, that expected return reflects compensation for systematic risk. Based on the data provided we cannot conclude which industry is most attractive from a valuation standpoint.

17. In addition to the economic, political and legal risks faced by fixed income investors, equity investors in emerging markets face corporate governance risks. Their ownership claims may be expropriated by corporate insiders, dominant shareholders or the government. Interested parties may misuse the companies' assets. Weak disclosure and accounting standards may result in limited transparency that favors insiders. Weak checks and balances on governmental actions may bring about regulatory uncertainty, seizure of property or nationalization.

18. C is correct. Statement 3 is correct. As long as none of the factors used in a factor-based VCV model are redundant and none of the asset returns are completely determined by the common factors, there will not be any portfolios that erroneously appear to be riskless. Therefore, a factor-based VCV matrix approach may result in some portfolios that erroneously appear to be riskless if any asset returns can be completely determined by the common factors or some of the factors are redundant.

    A is incorrect because shrinkage estimation of VCV matrices will increase the efficiency of the estimates versus the sample VCV matrix, because its mean squared error (MSE) will in general be smaller than the MSE of the (unbiased) sample VCV matrix. Efficiency in this context means a smaller MSE.

    B is incorrect because, although the proposed approach is not reliable, the reason is not that the sample VCV matrix is biased and inconsistent; on the contrary, it is unbiased and consistent. Rather, the estimate of the VCV matrix is not reliable because the number of observations is not at least 10 times the number of assets (i.e., with 10 years of monthly return data, there are only 120 observations, but the rule of thumb suggests there should be at least 200 observations for 20 asset classes).

19. B is correct. Bader expects the equity market in Country C (an emerging market) to become more fully integrated with the global market while Country A (a developed market) remains highly integrated. All else being equal, the Singer–Terhaar model implies that when a market becomes more globally integrated (segmented), its required return should decline (rise). As prices adjust to a lower (higher) required return, the market should deliver an even higher (lower) return than was previously expected or required by the market. Therefore, the allocation to markets that are moving toward integration should be increased. If a market

is moving toward integration, its increased allocation will come at the expense of markets that are already highly integrated. This will typically entail a shift from developed markets to emerging markets.

20. B is correct. Country A's long-term corporate earnings growth rate of 4% per year is equal to the expected nominal GDP growth rate of 4%, which is an economically plausible long-run assumption. The only very long-run assumptions that are consistent with economically plausible relationships are %ΔE = Nominal GDP growth, %ΔS = 0, and %ΔP/E = 0, where %ΔE is the expected nominal earnings growth rate, %ΔS is the expected percentage change in shares outstanding, and %ΔP/E is the expected percentage change in the price-to-earnings ratio.

    A is incorrect because a 2% rate of net share repurchases would eventually eliminate all shares, which is not an economically plausible very long-run assumption. The only very long-run assumptions that are consistent with economically plausible relationships are %ΔE = Nominal GDP growth, %ΔS = 0, and %ΔP/E = 0, where %ΔE is the expected nominal earnings growth rate, %ΔS is the expected percentage change in shares outstanding, and %ΔP/E is the expected percentage change in the price-to-earnings ratio.

    C is incorrect because Country A's perpetually rising P/E would lead to an arbitrarily high price per currency unit of earnings per share. The only very long-run assumptions that are consistent with economically plausible relationships are %ΔE = Nominal GDP growth, %ΔS = 0, %ΔP/E = 0, where %ΔE is the expected nominal earnings growth rate, %ΔS is the expected percentage change in shares outstanding, and %ΔP/E is the expected percentage change in the price-to-earnings ratio.

21. A is correct. Per capita income for Country B has been falling, which is a potential source of political stress.

    B is incorrect because the persistent current account deficit has been below 2% of GDP. Persistent current account deficits greater than 4% of GDP probably indicate a lack of competitiveness.

    C is incorrect because Country B has been transitioning to International Financial Reporting Standards, with full convergence expected within two years, which is a positive development for better accounting standards.

22. A is correct. Bader should reallocate capital from Country A, which is expected to have a secularly rising current account deficit, to Country C, which is expected to have a secularly rising current account surplus. A rising current account deficit will tend to put upward pressure on real required returns and downward pressure on asset prices, whereas a rising current account surplus (or narrowing deficit) will put downward pressure on real required returns and upward pressure on asset prices. Analysts should consider reallocation of portfolio assets from countries with secularly rising current account deficits to those with secularly rising current account surpluses (or narrowing deficits).

23. A is correct. Purchasing power parity implies that the value of Country A's currency will decline. Inflation for Country A is expected to rise relative to global inflation. Purchasing power parity implies that the expected percentage change in Country A's exchange rate should be equal to the difference in expected inflation rates. If Country A's inflation is rising relative to global inflation, then the currency will be expected to depreciate.

    B is incorrect because purchasing power parity implies that the value of Country B's currency will remain stable. Inflation for Country B is expected to keep pace with global inflation. Purchasing power parity implies that the expected percentage change in Country B's exchange rate should be equal to the difference in expected inflation rates. If Country B's inflation is keeping pace with global inflation, then the exchange rate will be expected to stay the same, corresponding to a stable value of Country B's currency.

C is incorrect because purchasing power parity implies that the value of Country C's currency will rise. Inflation for Country C is expected to fall relative to global inflation. Purchasing power parity implies that the expected percentage change in Country C's exchange rate should be equal to the difference in expected inflation rates. If Country C's inflation is falling relative to global inflation, then the currency will be expected to appreciate.

24. B is correct. Hot money is flowing out of Country B; thus, Country B's central bank is the most likely to sell foreign currency (thereby draining domestic liquidity) to limit/avoid depreciation of the domestic currency and buy government securities (thereby providing liquidity) to sterilize the impact on bank reserves and interest rates.

    A is incorrect because Country A is not experiencing hot money flows and, therefore, would not need to sterilize the impact of money flows on domestic liquidity.

    C is incorrect because hot money is flowing into Country C; thus, Country C's central bank is most likely to sell government securities to limit the growth of bank reserves and/or maintain a target level of interest rates.

25. C is correct. Public debt makes up the majority of Country C's currency portfolio, which is the least supportive flow (or holding) to a currency. Public debt is less supportive because it has to be serviced and must be either repaid or refinanced, potentially triggering a crisis. Some types of flows and holdings are considered to be more or less supportive of the currency. Investments in private equity represent long-term capital committed to the market and are most supportive of the currency. Public equity would likely be considered the next most supportive of the currency. Debt investments are the least supportive of the currency.

26. Properties trade infrequently so there is no data on simultaneous periodic transaction prices for a selection of properties. Analysis therefore relies on appraisals. Secondly, each property is different, it is said to be heterogenous. The returns calculated from appraisals represent weighted averages of unobservable returns. Published return series is too smooth and the sample volatility understates the true volatility of returns. It also distorts estimates of correlations.

27. The expected change in the cap rate from 5.7% to 5.5% represents a (5.5% − 5.7%)/5.7% = 3.5% decrease.

    Using the expression $E(R_{re})$ = CapRate + NOI growth rate − %ΔCapRate = 5.7% + (1% + 1.5%) − (−3.5%) = 11.7%.

    Note: As the cap rate is expected to decrease, property values are expected to increase, hence the cap rate change contributes to the expected return.

28. Under the first approach analysts focus on flows of export and imports to establish what the net trade flows are and how large they are relative to the economy and other, potentially larger financing and investment flows. The approach also considers differences between domestic and foreign inflation rates that relate to the concept of purchasing power parity. Under PPP, the expected percentage change in the exchange rate should equal the difference between inflation rates. The approach also considers the sustainability of current account imbalances, reflecting the difference between national saving and investment.

    Under the second approach the analysis focuses on capital flows and the degree of capital mobility. It assumes that capital seeks the highest risk-adjusted return. The expected changes in the exchange rate will reflect the differences in the respective countries' assets' characteristics such as relative short-term interest rates, term, credit, equity and liquidity premiums. The approach also considers hot money flows and the fact that exchange rates provide an across the board mechanism for adjusting the relative sizes of each country's portfolio of assets.

29.

	Country X	Country Y
Expected inflation over next year	2.0%	3.0%
Short-term (1-month) government rate	Decrease	Increase
Expected (forward-looking) GDP growth over next year	2.0%	3.3%
New national laws have been passed that enable foreign direct investment in real estate/financial companies	Yes	No
Current account surplus (deficit)	8%	−1%

Note: The shaded cells represent the comparatively stronger measure, where an analyst could expect to see a strengthening currency based on the factor being independently reviewed.

30. According to PPP, to offset the effect of the higher inflation in Fap, the Fip should have depreciated against the other currencies by approximately the difference between Fap inflation and that in the other countries.

According to PPP, Fip is overvalued.

3

Overview of Asset Allocation

by William W. Jennings, PhD, CFA, and Eugene L. Podkaminer, CFA.

William W. Jennings, PhD, CFA, is at the US Air Force Academy (USA). Eugene L. Podkaminer, CFA, is at Franklin Templeton Investments (USA).

LEARNING OUTCOMES

Mastery	The candidate should be able to:
☐	describe elements of effective investment governance and investment governance considerations in asset allocation
☐	formulate an economic balance sheet for a client and interpret its implications for asset allocation
☐	compare the investment objectives of asset-only, liability-relative, and goals-based asset allocation approaches
☐	contrast concepts of risk relevant to asset-only, liability-relative, and goals-based asset allocation approaches
☐	explain how asset classes are used to represent exposures to systematic risk and discuss criteria for asset class specification
☐	explain the use of risk factors in asset allocation and their relation to traditional asset class–based approaches
☐	recommend and justify an asset allocation based on an investor's objectives and constraints
☐	describe the use of the global market portfolio as a baseline portfolio in asset allocation
☐	discuss strategic implementation choices in asset allocation, including passive/active choices and vehicles for implementing passive and active mandates
☐	discuss strategic considerations in rebalancing asset allocations

INTRODUCTION

1

☐	describe elements of effective investment governance and investment governance considerations in asset allocation

Asset owners are concerned with accumulating and maintaining the wealth needed to meet their needs and aspirations. In that endeavor, investment portfolios—including individuals' portfolios and institutional funds—play important roles. Asset allocation is a strategic—and often a first or early—decision in portfolio construction. Because it holds that position, it is widely accepted as important and meriting careful attention. Among the questions addressed in this reading are the following:

- What is a sound governance context for making asset allocation decisions?
- How broad a picture should an adviser have of an asset owner's assets and liabilities in recommending an asset allocation?
- How can an asset owner's objectives and sensitivities to risk be represented in asset allocation?
- What are the broad approaches available in developing an asset allocation recommendation, and when might one approach be more or less appropriate than another?
- What are the top-level decisions that need to be made in implementing a chosen asset allocation?
- How may asset allocations be rebalanced as asset prices change?

The strategic asset allocation decision determines return levels[1] in which allocations are invested, irrespective of the degree of active management. Because of its strategic importance, the investment committee, at the highest level of the governance hierarchy, typically retains approval of the strategic asset allocation decision. Often a proposal is developed only after a formal asset allocation study that incorporates obligations, objectives, and constraints; simulates possible investment outcomes over an agreed-on investment horizon; and evaluates the risk and return characteristics of the possible allocation strategies.

In providing an overview of asset allocation, this reading's focus is the alignment of asset allocation with the asset owner's investment objectives, constraints, and overall financial condition. This is the first reading in several sequences of readings that address, respectively, asset allocation and portfolio management of equities, fixed income, and alternative investments. Asset allocation is also linked to other facets of portfolio management, including risk management and behavioral finance. As coverage of asset allocation progresses in the sequence of readings, various connections to these topics, covered in detail in other areas of the curriculum, will be made.[2]

In the asset allocation sequence, the role of this reading is the "big picture." It also offers definitions that will provide a coordinated treatment of many later topics in portfolio management. The second reading provides the basic "how" of developing an asset allocation, and the third reading explores various common, real-world complexities in developing an asset allocation.

This reading is organized as follows: Section 1 explains the importance of asset allocation in investment management. Section 2 addresses the investment governance context in which asset allocation decisions are made. Section 3 considers asset allocation from the comprehensive perspective offered by the asset owner's economic balance sheet. Sections 4 and 5 distinguish three broad approaches to asset allocation and explain how they differ in investment objective and risk. In Sections 6–9, these three approaches are discussed at a high level in relation to three cases. Section 10

---

1 See Ibbotson and Kaplan (2000, p. 30) and Xiong, Ibbotson, and Chen (2010). The conclusion for the aggregate follows from the premise that active management is a zero-sum game overall (Sharpe 1991).
2 Among these readings, see Blanchett, Cordell, Finke, and Idzorek (2016) concerning human capital and longevity and other risks and Pompian (2011a and 2011b) and Pompian, McLean, and Byrne (2011) concerning behavioral finance.

provides a top-level orientation to how a chosen asset allocation may be implemented, providing a set of definitions that underlie subsequent readings. Section 11 discusses rebalancing considerations.

Asset Allocation: Importance in Investment Management

Exhibit 1 places asset allocation in a stylized model of the investment management process viewed as an integrated set of activities aimed at attaining investor objectives.

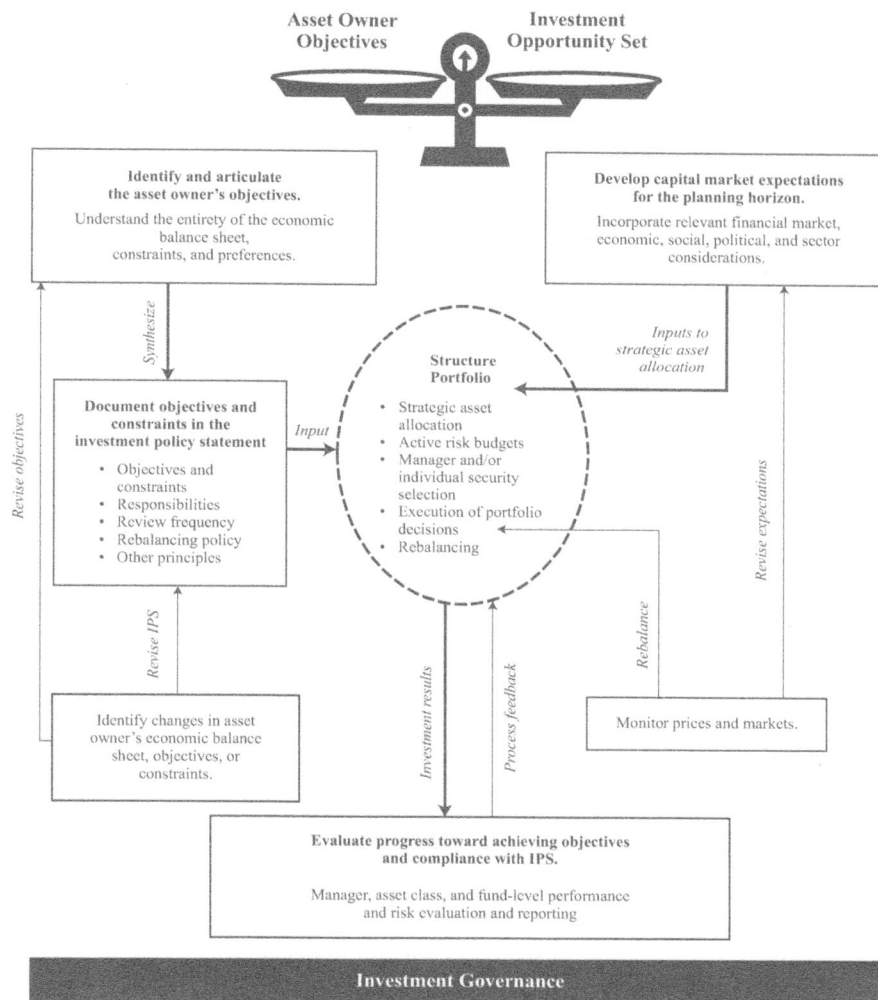

Exhibit 1: The Portfolio Management Process

Exhibit 1 shows that an investment process that is in the asset owner's best interest rests on a foundation of good investment governance, which includes the assignment of decision-making responsibilities to qualified individuals and oversight of processes. The balance at the top of the chart suggests that the portfolio management process must reconcile (balance) investor objectives (on the left) with the possibilities offered by the investment opportunity set (on the right).

The investment process shows a sequence of activities that begins with understanding the asset owner's entire circumstance; objectives, including any constraints; and preferences. These factors, in conjunction with capital market inputs,[3] form the basis for asset allocation as a first step in portfolio construction and give a structure within which other decisions—such as the decision to invest passively or actively—take place. In the flow chart, thick lines show initial flows (or relations of logic) and thin lines show feedback flows.

Asset allocation is widely considered to be the most important decision in the investment process. The strategic asset allocation decision completely determines return levels[4] in which allocations are invested passively and also in the aggregate of all investors, irrespective of the degree of active management.

In providing an overview of asset allocation, this reading's focus is the alignment of asset allocation with the asset owner's investment objectives, constraints, and overall financial condition. The presentation begins with an introduction to the investment governance context of asset allocation. It then moves to present the economic balance sheet as the financial context for asset allocation itself.

2   INVESTMENT GOVERNANCE BACKGROUND

☐ | describe elements of effective investment governance and investment governance considerations in asset allocation

Investment governance represents the organization of decision-making responsibilities and oversight activities. Effective investment governance ensures that assets are invested to achieve the asset owner's investment objectives within the asset owner's risk tolerance and constraints, and in compliance with all applicable laws and regulations. In addition, effective governance ensures that decisions are made by individuals or groups with the necessary skills and capacity.

Investment performance depends on asset allocation *and* its implementation. Sound investment governance practices seek to align asset allocation and implementation to achieve the asset owner's stated goals.

Investment governance structures are relevant to both institutional and individual investors. Because such structures are often formalized and articulated in detail for defined benefit pension plans, we will build our discussion using a pension plan governance framework. Elements of pension plan governance that are not directly related to the management of plan assets—plan design, funding policy, and communications to participants—are not discussed in this reading. Instead, we focus on those aspects of governance that directly affect the asset allocation decision.

Governance Structures

Governance and management are two separate but related functions. Both are directed toward achieving the same end. But governance focuses on clarifying the mission, creating a plan, and reviewing progress toward achieving long- and short-term objectives,

---

3 The set of potential inputs to portfolio construction shown in Exhibit 1 is not exhaustive. For example, for investors delegating asset management, investment managers' performance records are relevant.
4 See Ibbotson and Kaplan (2000, p.30) and Xiong, Ibbotson, Idzorek, and Chen (2010). The conclusion for the aggregate follows from the premise that active management is a zero-sum game overall (Sharpe 1991).

whereas management efforts are geared to outcomes—the execution of the plan to achieve the agreed-on goals and objectives. A common governance structure in an institutional investor context will have three levels within the governance hierarchy:

- governing investment committee
- investment staff
- third-party resources

The investment committee may be a committee of the board of directors, or the board of directors may have delegated its oversight responsibilities to an internal investment committee made up of staff. Investment staff may be large, with full in-house asset management capabilities, or small—for example, two to five investment staff responsible for overseeing external investment managers and consultants. It may even be part time—a treasurer or chief financial officer with many other, competing responsibilities. The term "third-party resources" is used to describe a range of professional resources—investment managers, investment consultants, custodians, and actuaries, for example.

Although there are many governance models in use, most effective models share six common elements. Effective governance models perform the following tasks:

1. Articulate the long- and short-term objectives of the investment program.
2. Allocate decision rights and responsibilities among the functional units in the governance hierarchy effectively, taking account of their knowledge, capacity, time, and position in the governance hierarchy.
3. Specify processes for developing and approving the investment policy statement that will govern the day-to-day operations of the investment program.
4. Specify processes for developing and approving the program's strategic asset allocation.
5. Establish a reporting framework to monitor the program's progress toward the agreed-on goals and objectives.
6. Periodically undertake a governance audit.

In the sections that follow, we will discuss selected elements from this list.

Articulating Investment Objectives

Articulating long- and short-term objectives for an investor first requires an understanding of purpose—that is, what the investor is trying to achieve. Below are examples of simple investment objective statements that can be clearly tied to purposes:

- *Defined benefit pension fund.* The investment objective of the fund is to ensure that plan assets are sufficient to meet current and future pension liabilities.
- *Endowment fund.* The investment objective of the endowment is to earn a rate of return in excess of the return required to fund, after accounting for inflation, ongoing distributions consistent with the endowment's mission.
- *Individual investor.* The investment objective is to provide for retirement at the investor's desired retirement age, family needs, and bequests, subject to stated risk tolerance and investment constraints.

A return requirement is often considered the essence of an investment objective statement, but for that portion of the objective statement to be properly understood requires additional context, including the obligations the assets are expected to fund, the nature of cash flows into and out of the fund, and the asset owner's willingness and ability to withstand interim changes in portfolio value. The ultimate goal is to find the best risk/return trade-off consistent with the asset owner's resource constraints and risk tolerance.

As an example of how the overall context can affect decision making, the pension fund may be an active plan, with new participants added as they are hired, or it may be "frozen" (no additional benefits are being accrued by participants in the plan). The status of the plan, considered in conjunction with its funded ratio (the ratio of pension assets to pension liabilities), has a bearing on future contributions and benefit payments. The company offering the pension benefit may operate in a highly cyclical industry, where revenues ebb and flow over the course of the economic cycle. In this case, the plan sponsor may prefer a more conservative asset allocation to minimize the year-to-year fluctuations in its pension contribution.

The nature of inflows and outflows for an endowment fund can be quite different from those of a pension fund. An endowment fund may be used to support scholarships, capital improvements, or university operating expenses. The fund sponsor has some degree of control over the outflows from the fund but very little control over the timing and amounts of contributions to the fund because the contributions are typically coming from external donors.

These cash inflow and outflow characteristics must be considered when establishing the goals and objectives of the fund.

A third, inter-related aspect of defining the sponsor's goals and objectives is determining and communicating risk tolerance. There are multiple dimensions of risk to be considered: liquidity risk, volatility, risk of loss, and risk of abandoning a chosen course of action at the wrong time.

Effective investment governance requires consideration of the liquidity needs of the fund and the liquidity characteristics of the fund's investments. For example, too large an allocation to relatively illiquid assets, such as real estate or private equity, might impair the ability to make payouts in times of market stress.

A high risk/high expected return asset allocation is likely to lead to wider swings in interim valuations. Any minimum thresholds for funded status that, if breached, would trigger an adverse event, such as higher pension insurance premiums, must be considered in the asset allocation decision.

For individual investors, the risk of substantial losses may be unacceptable for a variety of financial and psychological reasons. When such losses occur after retirement, lost capital cannot be replaced with future earnings.

Asset owners have their own unique return requirements and risk sensitivities. Managing an investment program without a clear understanding of long- and short-term objectives is similar to navigating without a map: Arriving at the correct destination on time and intact is not compatible with leaving much to chance.

Allocation of Rights and Responsibilities

The rights and responsibilities necessary to execute the investment program are generally determined at the highest level of investment governance. The allocation of those rights and responsibilities among the governance units is likely to vary depending on the size of the investment program; the knowledge, skills, and abilities of the internal staff; and the amount of time staff can devote to the investment program if they have other, competing responsibilities. Above all, good governance requires that decisions be delegated to those best qualified to make an informed decision.

The resources available to an organization will affect the scope and complexity of the investment program and the allocation of rights and responsibilities. A small investment program may result in having a narrower opportunity set because of either asset size (too small to diversify across the range of asset classes and investment managers) or staffing constraints (insufficient asset size to justify a dedicated internal staff). Complex strategies may be beyond the reach of entities that have chosen not to develop investment expertise internally or whose oversight committee lacks individuals with sufficient investment understanding. Organizations willing to invest in attracting, developing, and retaining staff resources and in developing strong internal control processes, including risk management systems, are better able to adopt more complex investment programs. The largest investors, however, may find their size creates governance issues: Manager capacity constraints might lead to so many managers that it challenges the investor's oversight capacity.

Allocation of rights and responsibilities across the governance hierarchy is a key element in the success of an investment program. Effective governance requires that the individuals charged with any given decision have the required *knowledge* and expertise to thoroughly evaluate the alternative courses of action and the *capacity* to take on the ongoing responsibility of those decisions, and they must be able to execute those decisions in a timely fashion. (Individual investors engaging a private wealth manager are delegating these expertise, capacity, and execution responsibilities.)

Exhibit 2 presents a systematic way of allocating among governance units the primary duties and responsibilities of running an investment program.

Exhibit 2: Allocation of Rights and Responsibilities

Investment Activity	Investment Committee	Investment Staff	Third-Party Resource
Mission	Craft and approve	n/a	n/a
Investment policy statement	Approve	Draft	Consultants provide input
Asset allocation policy	Approve with input from staff and consultants	Draft with input from consultants	Consultants provide input
Investment manager and other service provider selection	Delegate to investment staff; approval authority retained for certain service providers	Research, evaluation, and selection of investment managers and service providers	Consultants provide input
Portfolio construction (individual asset selection)	Delegate to outside managers, or to staff if sufficient internal resources	Execution if assets are managed in-house	Execution by independent investment manager
Monitoring asset prices & portfolio rebalancing	Delegate to staff within confines of the investment policy statement	Assure that the sum of all sub-portfolios equals the desired overall portfolio positioning; approve and execute rebalancing	Consultants and custodian provide input
Risk management	Approve principles and conduct oversight	Create risk management infrastructure and design reporting	Investment manager manages portfolio within established risk guidelines; consultants may provide input and support
Investment manager monitoring	Oversight	Ongoing assessment of managers	Consultants and custodian provide input
Performance evaluation and reporting	Oversight	Evaluate manager's continued suitability for assigned role; analyze sources of portfolio return	Consultants and custodian provide input
Governance audit	Commission and assess	Responds and corrects	Investment Committee contracts with an independent third party for the audit

The available knowledge and expertise at each level of the hierarchy, the resource capacity of the decision makers, and the ability to act on a timely basis all influence the allocation of these rights and responsibilities.

Investment Policy Statement

The investment policy statement (IPS) is the foundation of an effective investment program. A well-crafted IPS can serve as a blueprint for ongoing fund management and assures stakeholders that program assets are managed with the appropriate care and diligence.

Often, the IPS itself will be a foundation document that is revised slowly over time, whereas information relating to more variable aspects of the program—the asset allocation policy and guidelines for individual investment managers—will be contained in a more easily modified appendix.

Asset Allocation and Rebalancing Policy

Because of its strategic importance, the investment committee, at the highest level of the governance hierarchy, typically retains approval of the strategic asset allocation decision. A proposal is often developed only after a formal asset allocation study that incorporates obligations, objectives, and constraints; simulates possible investment outcomes over an agreed-on investment horizon; and evaluates the risk and return characteristics of the possible allocation strategies.

Governance considerations inform not only the overall strategic asset allocation decision but also rebalancing decisions. The IPS should contain at least general orienting information relevant to rebalancing. In an institutional setting, rebalancing policy might be the responsibility of the investment committee, organizational staff, or the external consultant. Likewise, individual investors might specify that they have delegated rebalancing authority to their investment adviser. Specification of rebalancing responsibilities is good governance.

Reporting Framework

The reporting framework in a well-run investment program should be designed in a manner that enables the overseers to evaluate quickly and clearly how well the investment program is progressing toward the agreed-on goals and objectives. The reporting should be clear and concise, accurately answering the following three questions:

- Where are we now?
- Where are we relative to the goals and objectives?
- What value has been added or subtracted by management decisions?

Key elements of a reporting framework should address performance evaluation, compliance with investment guidelines, and progress toward achieving the stated goals and objectives.

- Benchmarking is necessary for performance measurement, attribution, and evaluation. Effective benchmarking allows the investment committee to evaluate staff and external managers. Two separate levels of benchmarks are appropriate: one that measures the success of the investment managers relative to the purpose for which they were hired and another to measure the gap between the policy portfolio and the portfolio as actually implemented.

- Management reporting, typically prepared by staff with input from consultants and custodians, provides responsible parties with the information necessary to understand which parts of the portfolio are performing ahead of or behind the plan and why, as well as whether assets are being managed in accordance with investment guidelines.

- Governance reporting, which addresses strengths and weaknesses in program execution, should be structured in such a way that regular committee meetings can efficiently address any concerns. Although a crisis might necessitate calling an extraordinary meeting, good governance structures minimize this need.

The Governance Audit

The purpose of the governance audit is to ensure that the established policies, procedures, and governance structures are effective. The audit should be performed by an independent third party. The governance auditor examines the fund's governing documents, assesses the capacity of the organization to execute effectively within the confines of those governing documents, and evaluates the existing portfolio for its "efficiency" given the governance constraints.

Effective investment governance ensures the durability or survivability of the investment program. An investment program must be able to survive unexpected market turmoil, and good investment governance makes certain that the consequences of such turmoil are considered before it is experienced. Good governance seeks to avoid **decision-reversal risk**—the risk of reversing a chosen course of action at exactly the wrong time, the point of maximum loss. Good investment governance also considers the effect of investment committee member and staff turnover on the durability of the investment program. Orientation sessions for new committee members and proper documentation of investment beliefs, policies, and decisions enhance the likelihood that the chosen course of action will be given sufficient time to succeed. New staff or investment committee members should be able to perceive easily the design and intent of the investment program and be able to continue to execute it. Similarly, good investment governance prevents key person risk—overreliance on any one staff member or long-term, illiquid investments dependent on a staff member.

Good governance works to assure accountability. O'Barr and Conley (1992, p.21), who studied investment management organizations using anthropological techniques, found that blame avoidance (not accepting personal responsibility when appropriate to do so) is a common feature of institutional investors. Good governance works to prevent such behavior.

EXAMPLE 1

Investment Governance: Hypothetical Case 1

In January 2016, the Caflandia Office Workers Union Pension (COWUP) made the following announcement:

"COWUP will fully exit all hedge funds and funds of funds. Assets currently amounting to 15% of its investment program are involved. Although hedge funds are a viable strategy for some, when judged against their complexity and cost, hedge fund investment is no longer warranted for COWUP."

One week later, a financial news service reported the following:

"The COWUP decision on hedge funds was precipitated by an allegation of wrongdoing by a senior executive with hedge fund selection responsibilities in COWUP's alternative investments strategy group."

1. Considering only the first statement, state what facts would be relevant in evaluating whether the decision to exit hedge funds was consistent with effective investment governance.

Solution:

The knowledge, capacity, and time available within COWUP to have an effective hedge fund investment program would need to be assessed against the stated concern for complexity and cost. The investment purpose served by hedge funds in COWUP's investment program before it exited them needs to be analyzed.

2. Considering both statements, identify deficiencies in COWUP's investment governance.

Solution:

The second statement raises these concerns about the decision described in the first statement:

- Hiring and oversight of COWUP executives may have been inadequate.
- The initial COWUP information release was incomplete and possibly misleading. Public communications appear not to have received adequate oversight.
- Divesting hedge funds may be a reaction to the personnel issue rather than being based on investment considerations.

EXAMPLE 2

Investment Governance: Hypothetical Case 2

1. The imaginary country of Caflandia has a sovereign wealth fund with assets of CAF$40 billion. A governance audit includes the following:

   "The professional chief investment officer (CIO) reports to a nine-member appointed investment committee board of directors headed by an executive director. Investment staff members draft asset allocation policy in conjunction with consultants and make recommendation to the investment committee; the investment committee reviews and approves policy and any changes in policy, including the strategic asset allocation. The investment committee makes manager structure, conducts manager analysis, and makes manager selection decisions. The CIO has built a staff organization, which includes heads for each major asset class. In examining decisions over the last five years, we have noted several instances in which political or non-economic considerations appear to have influenced the investment program, including the selection of local private equity investments. Generally, the board spends much of its time debating individual manager strategies for inclusion in the portfolio and in evaluating investment managers' performance with comparatively little time devoted to asset allocation or risk management."

   Based on this information and that in Exhibit 2, identify sound and questionable governance practices in the management of the Caflandia sovereign wealth fund.

Solution:

Sound practices: The allocation of responsibilities for asset allocation between investment staff and the investment committee is sound practice. Staff investment expertise should be reflected in the process of asset allocation policy and analysis. The investment committee assumes final responsibility for choices and decisions, which is appropriate given its position in receiving information from all parts of the organization and from all interested parties.

Questionable practices: The investment committee's level of involvement in individual manager selection and evaluation is probably too deep. Exhibit 2 indicates that these functions more effectively reside with staff. Individual manager selection is an implementation and execution decision designed to achieve strategic decisions made by the investment committee and is typically not a strategic decision itself. Manager evaluation has substantial data analysis and technical elements that can be efficiently provided by staff experts and consultants. The finding about political/non-economic influences indicates multiple problems. It confirms that the investment manager analysis and selection processes were misplaced. It also suggests that the investment committee has an inadequate set of governance principles or checks and balances as relates to the investment committee itself.

THE ECONOMIC BALANCE SHEET AND ASSET ALLOCATION

3

> ☐ formulate an economic balance sheet for a client and interpret its implications for asset allocation

An accounting balance sheet reflects a point-in-time snapshot of an organization's financial condition and shows the assets, liabilities, and owners' equity recognized by accountants. An **economic balance sheet** includes conventional assets and liabilities (called "financial assets" and "financial liabilities" in this reading) as well as additional assets and liabilities—known as **extended portfolio assets and liabilities**—that are relevant in making asset allocation decisions but do not appear on conventional balance sheets.

For individual investors, extended portfolio assets include human capital (the present value of future earnings), the present value of pension income, and the present value of expected inheritances. Likewise, the present value of future consumption is an extended portfolio liability.

For an institutional investor, extended portfolio assets might include underground mineral resources or the present value of future intellectual property royalties. Extended portfolio liabilities might include the present value of prospective payouts for foundations, whereas grants payable would appear as conventional liabilities.

Theory and, increasingly, practice suggest that asset allocation should consider the full range of assets and liabilities—both the financial portfolio and extended portfolio assets and liabilities—to arrive at an appropriate asset allocation choice. For example, an asset allocation process that considers the extended balance sheet, including the sensitivity of an individual investor's earnings to equity market risk (and that of the industry in which the individual is working), may result in a more appropriate allocation to equities than one that does not.

Life-cycle balanced funds (also known as target date funds) are examples of investments that seek to coordinate asset allocation with human capital. A 2040 life-cycle balanced fund that seeks to provide a retirement investment vehicle appropriate for many individuals retiring in 2040. Exhibit 3 illustrates a typical path for the composition of an individual's economic balance sheet from age 25 through age 65.

Exhibit 3: Human Capital (HC) and Financial Capital (FC) relative to Total Wealth

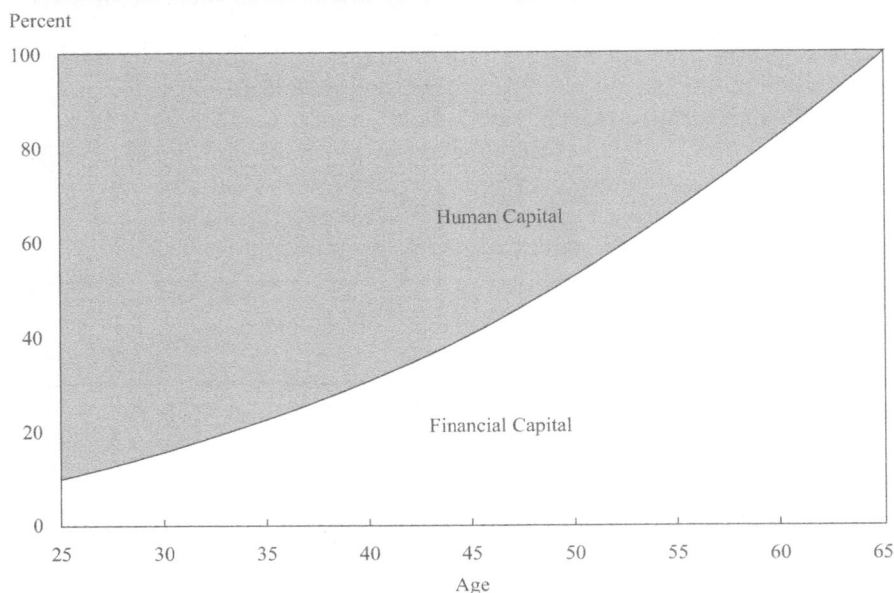

At age 25, with most of the individual's working life ahead of him, human capital dominates the economic balance sheet. As the individual progresses through life, the present value of human capital declines as human capital is transformed into earnings. Earnings saved and invested build financial capital balances. By a retirement age of 65, the conversion of human capital to earnings and financial capital is assumed to be complete.

Life-cycle balanced funds reflect these extended portfolio assets. Research indicates that, on average, human capital is roughly 30% equity-like and 70% bond-like, with significant variation among industries.[5] Making the simplifying assumption that investors have approximately constant risk tolerance through life, their asset allocation for total overall wealth (including human capital and financial capital) should be, in theory, constant over time. In this case, the asset allocation chosen for financial capital should reflect an increasing allocation to bonds as human capital declines to age 65, holding all else constant. Exhibit 4 shows the glide path for the equity/bond allocation chosen by one US mutual fund family. The increasing allocation to bonds is consistent with the view that human capital has preponderant bond-like characteristics.

5 See Blanchett and Straehl (2015) and Blanchett and Straehl (2017).

Exhibit 4: Glide Path of Target Date Investment Funds in One Family		
Assumed Age	Equity Allocation	Bond Allocation
25	85%	15%
35	82	18
45	77	23
55	63	37
65	49	51

Source: Based on data in Idzorek, Stempien, and Voris (2013).

Although estimating human capital is quite complex, including human capital and other extended portfolio assets and economic liabilities in asset allocation decisions is good practice.[6]

EXAMPLE 3

The Economic Balance Sheet of Auldberg University Endowment

- *Name*: Auldberg University Endowment (AUE)
- *Narrative*: AUE was established in 1852 in Caflandia and largely serves the tiny province of Auldberg. AUE supports about one-sixth of Auldberg University's CAF$60 million operating budget; real estate income and provincial subsidies provide the remainder and have been relatively stable. The endowment has historically had a portfolio limited to domestic equities, bonds, and real estate holdings; that policy is under current review. Auldberg University itself (not the endowment) has a CAF$350 million investment in domestic commercial real estate assets, including office buildings and industrial parks, much of it near the campus. AUE employs a well-qualified staff with substantial diverse experience in equities, fixed income, and real estate.
- *Assets*: Endowment assets include CAF$100 million in domestic equities, CAF$60 million in domestic government debt, and CAF$40 million in Class B office real estate. The present value of expected future contributions (from real estate and provincial subsidies) is estimated to be CAF$400 million.
- *Liabilities*: These include CAF$10 million in short-term borrowings and CAF$35 million in mortgage debt related to real estate investments. Although it has no specific legal requirement, AUE has a policy to distribute to the university 5% of 36-month moving average net assets. In effect, the endowment supports $10 million of Auldberg University's annual operating budget. The present value of expected future support is CAF$450 million.

---

6 Human capital is non-tradable, cannot be hedged, is subject to unspecified future taxes, and is a function of an individual's mortality. Human capital is technically defined as the net present value of an investor's future expected labor income weighted by the probability of surviving to each future age (see Ibbotson, Milevsky, Chen, and Zhu 2007). Thus, the present value of future earnings and pensions should be valued with mortality-weighted probabilities of receiving future cash flows, not the present value over life expectancy. There is meaningful extra value from the low-odds event of extreme longevity, which has an important portfolio implication in that individual investors can outlive their financial portfolios but not lifetime annuity payments.

1. Prepare an economic balance sheet for AUE.

Solution:

The economic balance sheet for the endowment (given in the following table) does not include the real estate owned by Auldberg University. The economic net worth is found as a plug item (600 − 10 − 35 − 450 = 105).

AUE Economic Balance Sheet (in CAF$ millions) 31 December 20x6			
Assets		**Liabilities and Economic Net Worth**	
Financial Assets		*Financial Liabilities*	
Domestic equities	100	Short-term borrowing	10
Domestic fixed income	60	Mortgage debt	35
Class B office real estate	40		
Extended Assets		*Extended Liabilities*	
Present value of expected future contributions to AUE	400	Present value of expected future support	450
		Economic Net Worth	
		Economic net worth (Economic assets − Economic liabilities)	105
Total	600		600

2. Describe elements in Auldberg University's investments that might affect AUE's asset allocation choices.

Solution:

AUE's Class B real estate investments' value and income are likely to be stressed during the same economic circumstances as the university's own real estate investments. In such periods, the university may look to the endowment for increased operating support and AUE may not be well positioned to meet that need. Thus, the AUE's real estate investment is actually less diversifying than it may appear and the allocation to it may need to be re-examined. Similar considerations apply to AUE's holdings in equities in relation to Auldberg University's.

4   APPROACHES TO ASSET ALLOCATION

☐   compare the investment objectives of asset-only, liability-relative, and goals-based asset allocation approaches

☐   contrast concepts of risk relevant to asset-only, liability-relative, and goals-based asset allocation approaches

We can identify three broad approaches to asset allocation: (1) **asset-only**, (2) **liability-relative**, and (3) **goals-based**. These are decision-making frameworks that take account of or emphasize different aspects of the investment problem.

Asset-only approaches to asset allocation focus solely on the asset side of the investor's balance sheet. Liabilities are not explicitly modeled. Mean–variance optimization (MVO) is the most familiar and deeply studied asset-only approach. MVO considers only the expected returns, risks, and correlations of the asset classes in the opportunity set. In contrast, liability-relative and goals-based approaches explicitly account for the liabilities side of the economic balance sheet, dedicating assets to meet, respectively, legal liabilities and quasi-liabilities (other needs that are not strictly liabilities but are treated as such) or goals.

Liability-relative approaches to asset allocation choose an asset allocation in relation to the objective of funding liabilities. The phrase "funding of liabilities" means to provide for the money to pay liabilities when they come due. An example is surplus optimization: mean–variance optimization applied to surplus (defined as the value of the investor's assets minus the present value of the investor's liabilities). In modeling, liabilities might be represented by a short position in a bond or series of bonds matched to the present value and duration of the liabilities. Another approach involves constructing a liability-hedging portfolio focused on funding liabilities and, for any remaining balance of assets, a risky-asset portfolio (so called because it is risky or riskier in relation to liabilities—often also called a "return-seeking portfolio" because it explicitly seeks return above and beyond the liability benchmark). **Liability-driven investing** (LDI) is an investment industry term that generally encompasses asset allocation that is focused on funding an investor's liabilities. Related fixed-income techniques are covered in the fixed-income sequence under liability-based mandates.

All approaches to asset allocation can be said to address goals. In investment practice and literature, however, the term "goals based" has come be widely associated with a particular type of approach to asset allocation and investing.

Goals-based approaches to asset allocation, as discussed here, are used primarily for individuals and families, involve specifying asset allocations for sub-portfolios, each of which is aligned to specified goals ranging from supporting lifestyle needs to aspirational. Each goal is associated with regular, irregular, or bulleted cash flows; a distinct time horizon; and a risk tolerance level expressed as a required probability of achieving the goal.[7] For example, a middle-aged individual might specify a goal of maintaining his current lifestyle and require a high level of confidence that this goal will be attained. That same individual might express a goal of leaving a bequest to his alma mater. This would be a very long-term goal and might have a low required probability. Each goal is assigned to its own sub-portfolio, and an asset allocation strategy specific to that sub-portfolio is derived. The sum of all sub-portfolio asset allocations results in an overall strategic asset allocation for the total portfolio. **Goals-based investing** (GBI) is an investment industry term that encompasses the asset allocation focused on addressing an investor's goals.

INSTITUTIONS AND GOALS-BASED ASSET ALLOCATION

Asset segmentation as practiced by some life insurers has some similarities to goals-based investing. Asset segmentation involves notionally or actually segmenting general account assets into sub-portfolios associated with specific lines of business or blocks of liabilities. On one hand, such an approach may be distinguished from goals-based asset allocation for individual investors in being motivated by competitive concerns (to facilitate offering competitive crediting rates on groups of contracts) rather than behavioral ones. On the other hand,

---

7 See Shefrin and Statman (2000) and Brunel (2015).

Fraser and Jennings (2006) described a behaviorally motivated goals-based approach to asset allocation for foundations and endowments. Following their approach, components of an overall appropriate mean–variance optimal portfolio are allocated to time-based sub-portfolios such that uncomfortably novel or risky positions for the entity's governing body are made acceptable by being placed in longer-term sub-portfolios.

Although any asset allocation approach that considers the liabilities side of the economic balance sheet might be termed "liability relative," there are several important distinctions between liabilities for an institutional investor and goals for an individual investor. These distinctions have meaningful implications for asset allocation:[8]

- Liabilities of institutional investors are legal obligations or debts, whereas goals, such as meeting lifestyle or aspirational objectives, are not. Failing to meet them does not trigger similar consequences.

- Whereas institutional liabilities, such as life insurer obligations or pension benefit obligations, are uniform in nature (all of a single type), an individual's goals may be many and varied.

- Liabilities of institutional investors of a given type (e.g., the pension benefits owed to retirees) are often numerous and so, through averaging, may often be forecast with confidence. In contrast, individual goals are not subject to the law of large numbers and averaging. Contrast an estimate of expected death benefits payable for a group of life insurance policies against an individual's uncertainty about the resources needed in retirement: For a 65-year-old individual, the number of remaining years of life is very uncertain, but insurers can estimate the average for a group of 65-year-olds with some precision.

LIABILITY-RELATIVE AND GOALS-BASED APPROACHES TO INVESTING

Various perspectives exist concerning the relationship between liability-relative and goals-based approaches to investing. Professor Lionel Martellini summarizes one perspective in the following three statements:[9]

1. Goals-based investing is related to a new paradigm that advocates more granular and investor-centric investment solutions.

2. This new investment solutions paradigm translates into goals-based investing (GBI) approaches in individual money management, in which investors' problems can be summarized in terms of their goals, and it translates into liability-driven investing (LDI) approaches in institutional money management, where the investors' liability is treated as a proxy for their goal.

3. GBI and LDI are therefore related, but each of these approaches has its own specific characteristics. For example, GBI implies the capacity to help individual investors identify a hierarchical list of goals, with a distinction between different types of goals (affordable versus non affordable, essential versus aspirational, etc.) for which no exact counterpart exists in institutional money management.

---

8 See Rudd and Siegel (2013), which recognizes goals-based planning as a distinct approach. This discussion draws on Brunel (2015).
9 Communication of 3 June 2016, used with permission.

Relevant Objectives

All three of the asset allocation approaches listed here seek to make optimal use of the amount of risk that the asset owner is comfortable bearing to achieve stated investment objectives, although they generally define risk differently. Exhibit 5 summarizes typical objectives.

Exhibit 5: Asset Allocation Approaches: Investment Objective			
Asset Allocation Approach	Relation to Economic Balance Sheet	Typical Objective	Typical Uses and Asset Owner Types
Asset only	Does not explicitly model liabilities or goals	Maximize Sharpe ratio for acceptable level of volatility	Liabilities or goals not defined and/or simplicity is important ■ Some foundations, endowments ■ Sovereign wealth funds ■ Individual investors
Liability relative	Models legal and quasi-liabilities	Fund liabilities and invest excess assets for growth	Penalty for not meeting liabilities high ■ Banks ■ Defined benefit pensions ■ Insurers
Goals based	Models goals	Achieve goals with specified required probabilities of success	Individual investors

In a mean–variance asset-only approach, the objective is to maximize expected portfolio return per unit of portfolio volatility over some time horizon, consistent with the investor's tolerance for risk and consistent with any constraints stated in the IPS. A portfolio's Sharpe ratio is a characteristic metric for evaluating portfolios in an asset-only mean–variance approach.

The basic objective of a liability-relative asset allocation approach is to ensure payment of liabilities when they are due.

A goals-based approach is similar to a liability-relative approach in that it also seeks to ensure that there are sufficient assets to meet the desired payouts. In goals-based approaches, however, goals are generally associated with individual sub-portfolios, and an asset allocation is designed for each sub-portfolio that reflects the time horizon and required probability of success such that the sum of the sub-portfolios addresses the totality of goals satisfactorily.

Relevant Risk Concepts

Asset-only approaches focus on asset class risk and effective combinations of asset classes. The baseline asset-only approach, mean–variance optimization, uses volatility (standard deviation) of portfolio return as a primary measure of risk, which is a function of component asset class volatilities and the correlations of asset class returns. A mean–variance asset allocation can also incorporate other risk sensitivities, including risk relative to benchmarks and downside risk. Risk relative to benchmarks is usually measured by tracking risk (tracking error). Downside risk can be represented in various ways, including semi-variance, peak-to-trough maximum drawdown, and measures that focus on the extreme (tail) segment of the downside, such as value at risk.

Mean–variance results, although often the starting point for understanding portfolio risk, are regularly augmented by Monte Carlo simulation. By providing information about how an asset allocation performs when one or more variables are changed—for example, to values representing conditions of financial market stress—simulation helps complete the picture of risk, including downside and tail risk. Insights from simulation can then be incorporated as refinements to the asset allocation.

Liability-relative approaches focus on the risk of having insufficient assets to pay obligations when due, which is a kind of shortfall risk. Other risk concerns include the volatility of contributions needed to fund liabilities. Risk in a liability-relative context is generally underpinned by the differences between asset and liability characteristics (e.g., their relative size, their interest rate sensitivity, their sensitivity to inflation).

Goals-based approaches are concerned with the risk of failing to achieve goals.[10] The risk limits can be quantified as the maximum acceptable probability of not achieving a goal.[11] The plural in "liabilities" and "goals" underscores that these risks are generally related to multiple future points in time. Overall portfolio risk is thus the weighted sum of the risks associated with each goal.

Generally, a given statistical risk measure may be relevant in any of the three approaches. For example, standard deviation can be used to assess overall portfolio volatility in asset-only approaches, and it may be used to measure surplus volatility (the volatility of the difference between the values of assets and liabilities) or the volatility of the funded ratio (the ratio of the values of assets and liabilities) in liability-relative asset allocation.

5   MODELING ASSET CLASS RISK

☐   explain how asset classes are used to represent exposures to systematic risk and discuss criteria for asset class specification

☐   explain the use of risk factors in asset allocation and their relation to traditional asset class–based approaches

Asset classes are one of the most widely used investment concepts but are often interpreted in distinct ways. Greer (1997) defines an asset class as "a set of assets that bear some fundamental economic similarities to each other, and that have characteristics that make them distinct from other assets that are not part of that class." He specifies three "super classes" of assets:

- *Capital assets.* An ongoing source of something of value (such as interest or dividends); capital assets can be valued by net present value.

- *Consumable/transformable assets.* Assets, such as commodities, that can be consumed or transformed, as part of the production process, into something else of economic value, but which do not yield an ongoing stream of value.

- *Store of value assets.* Neither income generating nor valuable as a consumable or an economic input; examples include currencies and art, whose economic value is realized through sale or exchange.

---

10 See Das, Markowitz, Scheid, and Statman (2010), who call goals "mental accounts."
11 See Brunel (2015).

EXAMPLE 4

Asset Classes (1)

Classify the following investments based on Greer's (1997) framework, or explain how they *do not* fit in the framework:

1. Precious metals

   Precious metals are a store of value asset except in certain industrial applications (e.g., palladium and platinum in the manufacture of catalytic converters).

2. Petroleum

   Petroleum is a consumable/transformable asset; it can be consumed to generate power or provide fuel for transport.

3. Hedge funds

   Hedge funds do not fit into Greer's (1997) super class framework; a hedge fund strategy invests in underlying asset classes.

4. Timberland

   Timberland is a capital asset or consumable/transformable asset. It is a capital asset in the sense that timber can be harvested and replanted cyclically to generate a stream of cash flows; it is a consumable asset in that timber can be used to produce building materials/ packaging or paper.

5. Inflation-linked fixed-income securities

   Inflation-linked fixed-income securities is a capital asset because cash flows can be determined based on the characteristics of the security.

6. Volatility

   Volatility does not fit; it is a measurable investment characteristic. Because equity volatility is the underlying for various derivative contracts and an investable risk premium may be associated with it, it is mentioned by some as an asset.

Greer (1997) approaches the classification of asset classes in an abstract or generic sense. The next question is how to specify asset classes to support the purposes of strategic asset allocation.[12] For example, if a manager lumps together very different investments, such as distressed credit and Treasury securities, into an asset class called "fixed income," asset allocation becomes less effective in diversifying and controlling risk. Furthermore, the investor needs a logical framework for distinguishing an asset class from an investment strategy. The following are five criteria that will help in effectively *specifying asset classes for the purpose of asset allocation*:[13]

1. *Assets within an asset class should be relatively homogeneous.* Assets within an asset class should have similar attributes. In the example just given, defining equities to include both real estate and common stock would result in a non-homogeneous asset class.

---

12 See Kritzman (1999).

13 As opposed to criteria for asset class definition in an absolute sense.

2. *Asset classes should be mutually exclusive.* Overlapping asset classes will reduce the effectiveness of strategic asset allocation in controlling risk and could introduce problems in developing asset class return expectations. For example, if one asset class for a US investor is domestic common equities, then world equities ex-US is more appropriate as another asset class rather than global equities, which include US equities.

3. *Asset classes should be diversifying.* For risk control purposes, an included asset class should not have extremely high expected correlations with other asset classes or with a linear combination of other asset classes. Otherwise, the included asset class will be effectively redundant in a portfolio because it will duplicate risk exposures already present. In general, a pairwise correlation above 0.95 is undesirable (given a sufficient number of observations to have confidence in the correlation estimate).

4. *The asset classes as a group should make up a preponderance of world investable wealth.* From the perspective of portfolio theory, selecting an asset allocation from a group of asset classes satisfying this criterion should tend to increase expected return for a given level of risk. Furthermore, the inclusion of more markets expands the opportunities for applying active investment strategies, assuming the decision to invest actively has been made. However, such factors as regulatory restrictions on investments and government-imposed limitations on investment by foreigners may limit the asset classes an investor can invest in.

5. *Asset classes selected for investment should have the capacity to absorb a meaningful proportion of an investor's portfolio.* Liquidity and transaction costs are both significant considerations. If liquidity and expected transaction costs for an investment of a size meaningful for an investor are unfavorable, an asset class may not be practically suitable for investment.

Note that Criteria 1 through 3 strictly focus on assets themselves, while Criterion 5, and to some extent Criterion 4, involve potential investor-specific considerations.

ASSET CLASSES SHOULD BE DIVERSIFYING

Pairwise asset class correlations are often useful information and are readily obtained. However, in evaluating an investment's value as a diversifier at the portfolio level, it is important to consider an asset in relation to all other assets as a group rather than in a one-by-one (pairwise) fashion. It is possible to reach limited or incorrect conclusions by solely considering pairwise correlations. To give an example, denote the returns to three assets by X, Y, and Z, respectively. Suppose that $Z = aX + bY$; a and b are constants, not both equal to zero. Asset Z is an exact weighted combination of X and Y and so has no value as a diversifier added to a portfolio consisting of assets X and Y. Yet, if the correlation between X and Y is −0.5, it can be shown that Z has a correlation of just 0.5 with X as well as with Y.

Examining return series' correlations during times of financial market stress can provide practically valuable insight into potential diversification benefits beyond typical correlations that average all market conditions.

In current professional practice, the listing of asset classes often includes the following:

- *Global public equity*—composed of developed, emerging, and sometimes frontier markets and large-, mid-, and small-cap asset classes; sometimes treated as several sub-asset classes (e.g., domestic and non-domestic).

- *Global private equity*—includes venture capital, growth capital, and leveraged buyouts (investment in special situations and distressed securities often occurs within private equity structures too).

- *Global fixed income*—composed of developed and emerging market debt and further divided into sovereign, investment-grade, and high-yield sub-asset classes, and sometimes inflation-linked bonds (unless included in real assets; see the following bullet). Cash and short-duration securities can be included here.

- *Real assets*—includes assets that provide sensitivity to inflation, such as private real estate equity, private infrastructure, and commodities. Sometimes, global inflation-linked bonds are included as a real asset rather than fixed income because of their sensitivity to inflation.

EMERGING MARKET EQUITIES AND FIXED INCOME

Investment practice distinguishes between developed and emerging market equities and fixed income within global equities. The distinction is based on practical differences in investment characteristics, which can be related to typical market differences including the following:

- diversification potential, which is related to the degree to which investment factors driving market returns in developed and emerging markets are not identical (a topic known as "market integration");

- perceived level of informational efficiency; and

- corporate governance, regulation, taxation, and currency convertibility.

As of mid-2016, emerging markets represent approximately 10% of world equity value based on MSCI indices.[14] In fixed income, investment opportunities have expanded as governments and corporations domiciled in emerging markets have increasingly issued debt in their own currency. Markets in local currency inflation-indexed emerging market sovereign debt have become more common.[15]

"Asset classes" are, by definition, groupings of assets. Investment vehicles, such as hedge funds, that apply strategies to asset classes and/or individual investments with the objective of earning a return to investment skill or providing attractive risk characteristics may be treated as a category called "strategies" or "diversifying strategies." When that is the case, this category is assigned a percentage allocation of assets, similar to a true asset class. Economically, asset classes contrast with "strategies" by offering, in general, an inherent, non-skill-based *ex ante* expected return premium.[16]

Effective portfolio optimization and construction may be hindered by excessive asset class granularity. Consider Exhibit 6.

---

14 MSCI uses three broad definitions to sort countries into developed, emerging, and frontier: 1) economic development, 2) size and liquidity requirements, and 3) market accessibility criteria (see the MSCI Market Classification Framework at www.msci.com/market-classification).

15 For a discussion of their potential benefits, see Burger, Warnock, and Warnock (2012), Perry (2011), and Swinkels (2012). Kozhemiakin (2011) discusses how emerging market bonds can facilitate broader representation than an equity-only portfolio because some countries (e.g., Argentina) have small equity markets but larger bond markets.

16 See Idzorek and Kowara (2013), p.20.

Exhibit 6: Examples of Asset Classes and Sub-Asset Classes

Asset Class Level
Few common risk factors result in model correlations.

Equity	Debt

Sub-Asset Class Level
Many common risk factors result in substantially positive correlations.

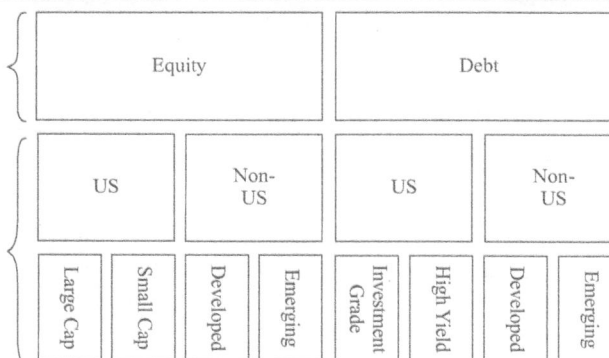

US	Non-US	US	Non-US

Large Cap	Small Cap	Developed	Emerging	Investment Grade	High Yield	Developed	Emerging

As more and more sub-asset classes are defined, they become less distinctive. In particular, the sources of risk for more broadly defined asset classes are generally better distinguished than those for narrowly defined subgroups. For example, the overlap in the sources of risk of US large-cap equity and US small-cap equity would be greater than the overlap between US and non-US equity. Using broadly defined asset classes with fewer risk source overlaps in optimization is consistent with achieving a diversified portfolio. Additionally, historical data for broadly defined asset classes may be more readily available or more reliable. The question of how much to allocate to equity versus fixed income versus other assets is far more important in strategic asset allocation than *precisely* how much to allocate to the various sub-classes of equity and fixed income. However, when the investor moves from the strategic asset allocation phase to policy implementation, sub-asset class choices become relevant.

EXAMPLE 5

Asset Classes (2)

1. Discuss a specification of asset classes that distinguishes between "domestic intermediate-duration fixed income" and "domestic long-duration fixed income." Contrast potential relevance in asset-only and liability-relative contexts.

Solution:

These two groups share key risk factors, such as interest rate and credit risk. For achieving diversification in asset risk—for example, in an asset-only context—asset allocation using domestic fixed income, which includes intermediate and long duration, should be effective and simple. Subsequently, allocation within domestic fixed income could address other considerations, such as interest rate views. When investing in relation to liabilities, distinctions by duration could be of first-order importance and the specification could be relevant.

Any asset allocation, by whatever means arrived at, is expressed ultimately in terms of money allocations to assets. Traditionally—and still in common practice—asset allocation uses asset classes as the unit of analysis. Thus, mean–variance optimization based on four asset classes (e.g., global public equity, global private equity, global fixed income, and real assets) would be based on expected return, return volatility, and return correlation estimates for these asset classes. (The development of such capital market assumptions is the subject of another reading.) Factor-based approaches, discussed in more detail later, do not use asset classes as the basis for portfolio construction. Technically, the set of achievable investment outcomes cannot be enlarged simply by developing an asset allocation by a different means (for instance, using asset classes as the unit of analysis), all else being equal, such as constraints against short selling (non-negativity constraints).[17] Put another way, adopting a factor-based asset allocation approach does not, by default, lead to superior investment outcomes.

There are allocation methods that focus on assigning investments to the investor's desired exposures to specified risk factors. These methods are premised on the observation that asset classes often exhibit some overlaps in sources of risk, as illustrated in Exhibit 7.[18]

Exhibit 7: Common Factor Exposures across Asset Classes

US Equity

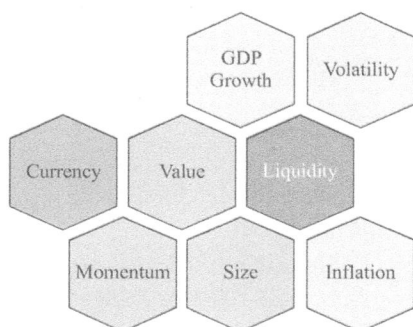

US Corporate Bonds

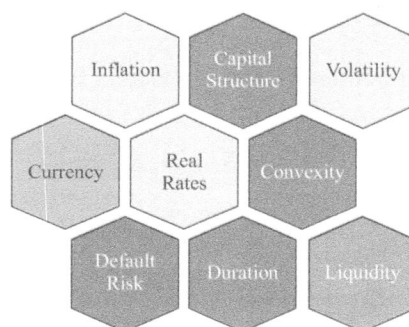

The overlaps seen in Exhibit 7 help explain the correlation of equity and credit assets. Modeling using asset classes as the unit of analysis tends to obscure the portfolio's sensitivity to overlapping risk factors, such as inflation risk in this example. As a result, controlling risk exposures may be problematic. Multifactor risk models, which have a history of use in individual asset selection, have been brought to bear on the issue of controlling systematic risk exposures in asset allocation.

In broad terms, when using factors as the units of analysis, we begin with specifying risk factors and the desired exposure to each factor. Asset classes can be described with respect to their sensitivities to each of the factors. Factors, however, are not directly investable. On that basis, asset class portfolios that isolate exposure to the risk factor are constructed; these factor portfolios involve both long and short positions. A choice of risk exposures in factor space can be mapped back to asset class space for implementation. Uses of multifactor risk models in asset allocation have been labeled "factor-based asset allocation" in contrast to "asset class-based asset allocation," which uses asset classes directly as the unit of analysis.

FACTOR REPRESENTATION

Although risk factors can be thought of as the basic building blocks of investments, most are not directly investable. In this context, risk factors are associated with expected return premiums. Long and short positions in assets (spread

---

17 Stated more formally and demonstrated in Idzorek and Kowara (2013).
18 See Podkaminer (2013).

positions) may be needed to isolate the respective risks and associated expected return premiums. Other risk factors may be accessed through derivatives. The following are a few examples of how risk factor exposures can be achieved.

- *Inflation.* Going long nominal Treasuries and short inflation-linked bonds isolates the inflation component.
- *Real interest rates.* Inflation-linked bonds provide a proxy for real interest rates.
- *US volatility.* VIX (Chicago Board Options Exchange Volatility Index) futures provide a proxy for implied volatility.
- *Credit spread.* Going long high-quality credit and short Treasuries/government bonds isolates credit exposure.
- *Duration.* Going long 10+ year Treasuries and short 1–3 year Treasuries isolates the duration exposure being targeted.

FACTOR MODELS IN ASSET ALLOCATION

The interest in using factors for asset allocation stems from a number of considerations, including the following:

- The desire to shape the asset allocation based on goals and objectives that cannot be expressed by asset classes (such as matching liability characteristics in a liability-relative approach).
- An intense focus on portfolio risk in all of its various dimensions, helped along by availability of commercial factor-based risk measurement and management tools.
- The acknowledgment that many highly correlated so-called asset classes are better defined as parts of the same high-level asset class. For example, domestic and foreign equity may be better seen as subclasses of global public equity.
- The realization that equity risk can be the dominant risk exposure even in a seemingly well-diversified portfolio.

6   STRATEGIC ASSET ALLOCATION

☐ | recommend and justify an asset allocation based on an investor's objectives and constraints

An asset allocation that arises in long-term investment planning is often called the "strategic asset allocation" or "policy portfolio": It is an asset allocation that is expected to be effective in achieving an asset owner's investment objectives, given his or her investment constraints and risk tolerance, as documented in the investment policy statement.

A theoretical underpinning for quantitative approaches to asset allocation is utility theory, which uses a utility function as a mathematical representation of preferences that incorporates the investor's risk aversion. According to utility theory, the optimal asset allocation is the one that is expected to provide the highest utility to the investor at the investor's investment time horizon. The optimization program, in broad terms, is

$$\underset{\substack{\text{Maximize} \\ \text{by choice of asset class weights } w_i}}{} E[U(W_T)] = f\begin{pmatrix} W_0, \ w_i, \\ \text{asset class return distributions,} \\ \text{degree of risk aversion} \end{pmatrix}$$

$$\text{subject to} \sum_{i=1}^{n} w_i = 1 \text{ and any other constraints on } w_i$$

The first line is the objective function, and the second line consists of constraints on asset class weights; other constraints besides those on weights can also be incorporated (for example, specified levels of bond duration or portfolio yield may be targeted). With W_0 and W_T (the values of wealth today and at time horizon T, respectively) the investor's problem is to select the asset allocation that maximizes the expected utility of ending wealth, $E[U(W_T)]$, subject to the constraints that asset class weights sum to 1 and that weights observe any limits the investor places on them. Beginning wealth, asset class weights, and asset class returns imply a distribution of values for ending wealth, and the utility function assigns a value to each of them; by weighting these values by their probability of occurrence, an expected utility for the asset allocation is determined.

An expected utility framework underlies many, but not all, quantitative approaches to asset allocation. A widely used group in asset allocation consists of power utility functions,[19] which exhibit the analytically convenient characteristic that risk aversion does not depend on the level of wealth. Power utility can be approximated by mean–variance utility, which underlies mean–variance optimization.

OPTIMAL CHOICE IN THE SIMPLEST CASE

The simplest asset allocation decision problem involves one risky asset and one risk-free asset. Let λ, μ, r_f, and σ^2 represent, respectively, the investor's degree of risk aversion, the risk asset's expected return, the risk-free interest rate, and the variance of return. With mean–variance utility, the optimal allocation to the risky asset, w^*, can be shown to equal

$$w^* = \frac{1}{\lambda}\left(\frac{\mu - r_f}{\sigma^2}\right)$$

The allocation to the risky asset is inversely proportional to the investor's risk aversion and directly proportional to the risk asset's expected return per unit of risk (represented by return variance).[20]

---

19 Power utility has the form

$$U = \frac{w_T^{1-\lambda}}{1-\lambda},$$

where $\lambda > 0$ is the parameter of risk aversion (if $\lambda \to 0$, the investor is risk neutral).
20 See Ang (2014), Chapter 4, for further analysis.

Selection of a strategic asset allocation generally involves the following steps:[21]

1. Determine and quantify the investor's objectives. What is the pool of assets meant for (e.g., paying future benefit payments, contributing to a university's budget, securing ample assets for retirement)? What is the investor trying to achieve? What liabilities or needs or goals need to be recognized (explicitly or implicitly)? How should objectives be modeled?

2. Determine the investor's risk tolerance and how risk should be expressed and measured. What is the investor's overall tolerance for risk and specific risk sensitivities? How should these be quantified in the process of developing an appropriate asset allocation (risk measures, factor models)?

3. Determine the investment horizon(s). What are the appropriate planning horizons to use for asset allocation; that is, over what horizon(s) should the objectives and risk tolerance be evaluated?

4. Determine other constraints and the requirements they impose on asset allocation choices. What is the tax status of the investor? Should assets be managed with consideration given to ESG issues? Are there any legal and regulatory factors that need to be considered? Are any political sensitivities relevant? Are there any other constraints that the investor has imposed in the IPS and other communications?

5. Determine the approach to asset allocation that is most suitable for the investor.

6. Specify asset classes, and develop a set of capital market expectations for the specified asset classes.

7. Develop a range of potential asset allocation choices for consideration. These choices are often developed through optimization exercises. Specifics depend on the approach taken to asset allocation.

8. Test the robustness of the potential choices. This testing often involves conducting simulations to evaluate potential results in relation to investment objectives and risk tolerance over appropriate planning horizon(s) for the different asset allocations developed in Step 7. The sensitivity of the outcomes to changes in capital market expectations is also tested.

9. Iterate back to Step 7 until an appropriate and agreed-on asset allocation is constructed.

Subsequent readings on asset allocation in practice will address the "how." The following sections give an indication of thematic considerations. We use investors with specific characteristics to illustrate the several approaches distinguished: sovereign wealth fund for asset-only allocation; a frozen corporate DB plan for liability-relative allocation; and an ultra-high-net-worth family for goals-based allocation. In practice, any type of investor could approach asset allocation with varying degrees of focus on modeling and integrating liabilities-side balance sheet considerations. How these cases are analyzed in this reading should not be viewed as specifying normative limits of application for various asset allocation approaches. For example, a liability-relative perspective has wide potential relevance for institutional investors because it has the potential to incorporate all information on the economic balance sheet. Investment advisers to high-net-worth investors may choose to use any of the approaches.

---

21 Arjan Berkelaar, CFA, contributed to this formulation of steps.

STRATEGIC ASSET ALLOCATION: ASSET ONLY

☐ recommend and justify an asset allocation based on an investor's objectives and constraints

☐ describe the use of the global market portfolio as a baseline portfolio in asset allocation

Asset-only allocation is based on the principle of selecting portfolios that make efficient use of asset risk. The focus here is mean–variance optimization, the mainstay among such approaches. Given a set of asset classes and assumptions concerning their expected returns, volatilities, and correlations, this approach traces out an efficient frontier that consists of portfolios that are expected to offer the greatest return at each level of portfolio return volatility. The Sharpe ratio is a key descriptor of an asset allocation: If a portfolio is efficient, it has the highest Sharpe ratio among portfolios with the same volatility of return.

An example of an investor that might use an asset-only approach is the (hypothetical) Government Petroleum Fund of Caflandia (GPFC) introduced next.

INVESTOR CASE FACTS: GPFC, A SOVEREIGN WEALTH FUND

- *Name*: Government Petroleum Fund of Caflandia (GPFC)
- *Narrative*: The imaginary emerging country of Caflandia has established a sovereign wealth fund to capture revenue from its abundant petroleum reserves. The government's goal in setting up the fund is to promote a fair sharing of the benefits between current and future generations (intergenerational equity) from the export of the country's petroleum resources. Caflandia's equity market represents 0.50% of global equity market capitalization. Economists estimate that distributions in the interest of intergenerational equity may need to begin in 20 years. Future distribution policy is undetermined.
- *Tax status*: Non-taxable.
- *Financial assets and financial liabilities*: Financial assets are CAF$40 billion at market value, making GPFC among the largest investors in Caflandia. GPFC has no borrowings.
- *Extended assets and liabilities*: Cash inflows from petroleum exports are assumed to grow at inflation + 1% for the next 15 years and may change depending on reserves and global commodity demand. The present value of expected future income from state-owned reserves is estimated to be CAF$60 billion. Future spending needs are positively correlated with consumer inflation and population growth. In Exhibit 8, the amount for the present value (PV) of future spending, which GPFC has not yet determined, is merely a placeholder to balance assets and liabilities; as a result, no equity is shown.

Exhibit 8: GPFC Economic Balance Sheet (in CAF$ billions) 31 December 20x6

Assets		Liabilities and Economic Net Worth	
Financial Assets		*Financial Liabilities*	
Investments (includes cash, equities, fixed income, and other investments)	40		
Extended Assets		*Extended Liabilities*	
PV of expected future income	60	PV of future spending	100
		Economic Net Worth	
		Economic net worth	0
Total	100		100

For GPFC, the amount and timing of funds needed for future distributions to Caflandia citizens are, as yet, unclear. GPFC can currently focus on asset risk and its efficient use to grow assets within the limits of the fund's risk tolerance. In addition to considering expected return in relation to volatility in selecting an asset allocation, GPFC might include such considerations as the following:

- diversification across global asset classes (possibly quantified as a constraint on the proportion allocated to any given asset classes);
- correlations with the petroleum sources of income to GPFC;
- the potential positive correlation of future spending with inflation and population growth in Caflandia;
- long investment horizon (as a long-term investor, GPFC may be well positioned to earn any return premium that may be associated with the relatively illiquid asset classes); and
- return outcomes in severe financial market downturns.

Suppose GPFC quantifies its risk tolerance in traditional mean–variance terms as willingness to bear portfolio volatility of up to 17% per year. This risk tolerance is partly based on GPFC's unwillingness to allow the fund to fall below 90% funded. GPFC's current strategic asset allocation, along with several alternatives that have been developed by its staff during an asset allocation review, are shown in Exhibit 9. The category "Diversifying strategies" consists of a diversified allocation to hedge funds.

Exhibit 9: GPFC Strategic Asset Allocation Decision[22]

		Asset Allocation		
		Proposed		
	Current	A	B	C
Investment				
Equities				
Domestic	50%	40%	45%	30%
Global ex-domestic		10%	20%	25%
Bonds				
Nominal	30%	30%	20%	10%
Inflation linked				10%
Real estate	20%	10%	15%	10%
Diversifying strategies		10%		15%
Portfolio statistics				
Expected arithmetic return	8.50%	8.25%	8.88%	8.20%
Volatility (standard deviation)	15.57%	14.24%	16.63%	14.06%
Sharpe ratio	0.353	0.369	0.353	0.370
One-year 5% VaR	−17.11%	−15.18%	−18.48%	−14.93%

Notes: The government bond rate is 3%. The acceptable level of volatility is ≤ 17% per year. The value at risk (VaR) is stated as a percent of the initial portfolio value over one year (e.g., −16% means a decline of 16%).

GPFC decides it is willing to tolerate a 5% chance of losing 22% or more of portfolio value in a given year. This risk is evaluated by examining the one-year 5% VaR of potential asset allocations.

Let us examine GPFC's decision. The current asset allocation and the alternatives developed by staff all satisfy the GPFC's tolerance for volatility and VaR limit. The staff's alternatives appear to represent incremental, rather than large-scale, changes from the current strategic asset allocation. We do not know whether capital market assumptions have changed since the current strategic asset allocation was approved.

Mix A, compared with the current asset allocation, diversifies the equity allocation to include non-domestic (global ex-domestic) equities and spreads the current allocation to real estate over real estate and diversifying strategies. Given GPFC's long investment horizon and absence of liquidity needs, an allocation to diversifying strategies at 10% should not present liquidity concerns. Because diversifying strategies are more liquid than private real estate, the overall liquidity profile of the fund improves. It is important to note that given the illiquid nature of real estate, it could take considerable time to reallocate from real estate to diversifying strategies. Mix A has a lower volatility (by 133 bps) than the current allocation and slightly lower tail

---

22 The assumed expected returns and return volatilities are (given in that order in parentheses and expressed as decimals, rather than percentages): domestic equities (0.11, 0.25), non-domestic equities (0.09, 0.18), nominal bonds (0.05, 0.10), inflation-linked bonds (0.035, 0.06), real estate (0.075, 0.16), and diversifying strategies (0.07, 0.09). A correlation matrix with hypothetical values and a hypothetical relationship between the allocations and VaR also lies behind the exhibit. Because the purpose here is to illustrate concepts rather than mechanics, inputs are not discussed although they are very important in asset allocation.

risk (the 5% VaR for Mix A is −15%, whereas the 5% VaR for the current asset mix is −17%). Mix A's Sharpe ratio is slightly higher. On the basis of the facts given, Mix A appears to be an incremental improvement on the current asset allocation.

Compared with Mix A and the current asset allocation, Mix B increases the allocation to equities by 15 percentage points and pulls back from the allocation to bonds and, in relation to Mix A, diversifying strategies. Although Mix B has a higher expected return and its VaR is within GPFC's tolerance of 22%, Mix B's lower Sharpe ratio indicates that it makes inefficient use of its additional risk. Mix B does not appear to deserve additional consideration.

Compared with the current asset allocation and Mix A, Mix C's total allocation to equities, at 55%, is higher and the mix is more diversified considering the allocation of 25% non-domestic equities. Mix C's allocation to fixed income is 20% compared with 30% for Mix A and the current asset mix. The remaining fixed-income allocation has been diversified with an exposure to both nominal and inflation-linked bonds. The diversifying strategies allocation is funded by a combination of the reduced weights to fixed income and real estate. The following observations may be made:

- Mix C's increase in equity exposure (compared with the equity exposure of Mix A and the current mix) has merit because more equity-like choices in the asset allocation could be expected to give GPFC more exposure to such a factor as a GDP growth factor (see Exhibit 9); population growth is one driver of GDP.

- Within fixed income, Mix C's allocation to inflation-linked bonds could be expected to hedge the inflation risk inherent in future distributions.

- Mix C has the lowest volatility and the lowest VaR among the asset allocations, although the differences compared with Mix A are very small. Mix C's Sharpe ratio is comparable to (insignificantly higher than) Mix A's.

Based on the facts given, Mix A and Mix C appear to be improvements over the current mix. Mix C may have the edge over Mix A based on the discussion. As a further step in the evaluation process, GPFC may examine the robustness of the forecasted results by changing the capital market assumptions and simulating shocks to such variables as inflation. The discussion of Mix C shows that there are means for potential liability concerns (the probable sensitivity of spending to inflation and population growth) to enter decision making even from a mean–variance optimization perspective.

EXAMPLE 6

Asset-Only Asset Allocation

1. Describe how the Sharpe ratio, considered in isolation, would rank the asset allocation in Exhibit 9.

Solution:

The ranking by Sharpe ratios in isolation is C (3.70), A (3.69), and current and B (both 3.53). Using only the Sharpe ratio, Mix C appears superior to the other choices, but such an approach ignores several important considerations.

2. State a limitation of basing a decision only on the Sharpe ratio addressed in Question 1.

Solution:

The Sharpe ratio, while providing a means to rank choices on the basis of return per unit of volatility, does not capture other characteristics that are likely to be important to the asset owner, such as VaR and funded ratio. Furthermore, the Sharpe ratio by itself cannot confirm that the absolute level of portfolio risk is within the investor's specified range.

3. An assertion is heard in an investment committee discussion that because the Sharpe ratio of diversifying strategies (0.55) is higher than real estate's (0.50), any potential allocation to real estate would be better used in diversifying strategies. Describe why the argument is incomplete.

Solution:

It is true that the higher the Sharpe ratio of an investment, the greater its contribution to the Sharpe ratio of the overall portfolio, *holding all other things equal*. However, that condition is not usually true. Diversification potential in a portfolio (quantified by correlations) may differ. For example, including both diversifying strategies and real estate in an allocation may ultimately decrease portfolio-level risk through favorable correlation characteristics. Also, as in the solution to Question 2, other risk considerations besides volatility may be relevant.

Financial theory suggests that investors should consider the global market-value weighted portfolio as a baseline asset allocation. This portfolio, which sums all investable assets (global stocks, bonds, real estate, and so forth) held by investors, reflects the balancing of supply and demand across world markets. In financial theory, it is the portfolio that minimizes diversifiable risk, which in principle is uncompensated. Because of that characteristic, theory indicates that the global market portfolio should be the available portfolio that makes the most efficient use of the risk budget.[23] Other arguments for using it as a baseline include its position as a reference point for a highly diversified portfolio and the discipline it provides in relation to mitigating any investment biases, such as home-country bias (discussed below).

At a minimum, the global market portfolio serves as a starting point for discussion and ensures that the investor articulates a clear justification for moving away from global capitalization market weights. The global market portfolio is expressed in two phases. The first phase allocates assets in proportion to the global portfolio of stocks, bonds, and real assets. The second phase disaggregates each of these broad asset classes into regional, country, and security weights using capitalization weights. The second phase is typically used within a global equity portfolio where an asset owner will examine the global capitalization market weights and either accept them or alter them. Common tilts (biases) include overweighting the home-country market, value, size (small cap), and emerging markets. For many investors, allocations to foreign fixed income have been adopted more slowly than allocations to foreign equity. Most investors have at least some amount in non-home-country equity.

---

23 According to the two-fund separation theorem, all investors optimally hold a combination of a risk-free asset and an optimal portfolio of all risky assets. This optimal portfolio is the global market value portfolio.

HOME-COUNTRY BIAS

A given for GPFC was that Caflandia's equity markets represent only 0.50% of the value of world equity markets. However, in all asset allocations in Exhibit 9, the share of domestic equity ranged from 50% for the current asset allocation to 30% for Mix C. The favouring of domestic over non-domestic investment relative to global market value weights is called **home-country bias** and is very common. Even relatively small economies feature pension plans, endowments, and other funds, which are disproportionately tilted toward the equity and fixed-income offerings in the domestic market. The same tendency is true for very large markets, such as the United States and the eurozone. By biasing toward the home market, asset owners may not be optimally aligning regional weights with the global market portfolio and are implicitly implementing a market view. Investment explanations for the bias, such as offsetting liabilities that are denominated in the home currency, may be relevant in some cases, however.

For reference, the MSCI All Country World Portfolio (ACWI), a proxy for the public equities portion of the global equity market portfolio, contains the following capitalization weights as of 31 December 2015:

- Developed Europe and the Middle East: 22.8%
- Developed Pacific: 11.7%
- North America: 55.9%
- Emerging markets: 9.6%

Investing in a global market portfolio faces several implementation hurdles. First, estimating the size of each asset class on a global basis is an imprecise exercise given the uneven availability of information on non-publicly traded assets. Second, the practicality of investing proportionately in residential real estate, much of which is held in individual homeowners' hands, has been questioned. Third, private commercial real estate and global private equity assets are not easily carved into pieces of a size that is accessible to most investors. Practically, proxies for the global market portfolio are often based only on traded assets, such as portfolios of exchange-traded funds (ETFs). Furthermore, some investors have implemented alternative weighting schemes, such as GDP weight or equal weight. However, it is a useful discipline to articulate a justification for any deviation from the capitalization-weighted global market portfolio.

8   STRATEGIC ASSET ALLOCATION: LIABILITY RELATIVE

☐ | recommend and justify an asset allocation based on an investor's objectives and constraints

To illustrate the liability-relative approach, we take the defined benefit (DB) pension plan of (hypothetical) GPLE Corporation, with case facts given below.

A FROZEN DB PLAN, GPLE CORPORATION PENSION

- *Name*: GPLE Corporation Pension

- *Narrative*: GPLE is a machine tool manufacturer with a market value of $2 billion. GPLE is the sponsor of a $1.25 billion legacy DB plan, which is now frozen (i.e., no new plan participants and no new benefits accruing for existing plan participants). GPLE Pension has a funded ratio (the ratio of pension assets to liabilities) of 1.15. Thus, the plan is slightly overfunded. Responsibility for the plan's management rests with the firm's treasury department (which also has responsibility for GPLE Corporation treasury operations).

- *Tax status*: Non-taxable.

- *Financial assets and financial liabilities*: Assets amount to $1.25 billion at market values. Given a funded ratio of 1.15, that amount implies that liabilities are valued at about $1.087 billion. Projected distributions to pension beneficiaries have a present value of $1.087 billion at market value.

GPLE does not reflect any extended assets or liabilities; thus, economic net worth is identical to traditional accounting net worth.

Exhibit 10: GPLE Pension Economic Balance Sheet (in US$ billions) 31 December 20x6			
Assets		**Liabilities and Economic Net Worth**	
Financial Assets		*Financial Liabilities*	
Pension assets	1.250	PV of pension liability	1.087
		Economic Net Worth	
		Economic net worth	0.163
Total	1.250		1.250

GPLE, the plan sponsor, receives two asset allocation recommendations. Recommendation A does not explicitly consider GPLE's pension's liabilities but is instead based on an asset-only perspective: the mean–variance efficient frontier given a set of capital market assumptions. A second recommendation, "Recommendation B," does explicitly consider liabilities, incorporating a liability-hedging portfolio based on an analysis of GPLE pension liabilities and a return-seeking portfolio.

In evaluating asset allocation choices, consider the pensioners' and the plan sponsor's interests. Pensioners want to receive the stream of promised benefits with as little risk, or chance of interruption, as possible. Risk increases as the funded ratio declines. When the funded ratio is 1.0, pension assets just cover pension liabilities with no safety buffer. When the funded ratio is less than 1.0, the plan sponsor generally needs to make up the deficit in pension assets by contributions to the plan. For example, with a 10-year investment time horizon and a choice between two asset allocations, the allocation with the lower expected present value of cumulative contributions to Year 10 would generally be preferred by the sponsor, all else being equal. In practice, all else is usually not equal. For example, the alternative with the lower *expected* present value of contributions may involve more risk to the level of contributions in adverse market conditions. For example, the 5% of *worst outcomes* for the present value of cumulative contributions may be more severe for the lower expected contribution alternative. Thus, possible asset allocations generally involve risk trade-offs.[24] Now consider the recommendations.

Recommendation A, based on asset-only analysis, involves a 65% allocation to global equities and a 35% allocation to global fixed income. Assume that this asset allocation is mean–variance efficient and has the highest Sharpe ratio among portfolios that meet the pension's assumed tolerance for asset return volatility. Capital market assumptions indicate that equities have a significantly higher expected return and volatility than fixed income.

Recommendation B, based on a liability-relative approach to asset allocation, involves an allocation of $1.125 billion to a fixed-income portfolio that is very closely matched in interest rate sensitivity to the present value of plan liabilities (and to any other liability factor risk exposures)—the liability hedging portfolio—and a $0.125 allocation to equities (the return-seeking portfolio). This is a proportional allocation of 10% to equities and 90% to fixed income. The equities allocation is believed to provide potential for increasing the size of the buffer between pension assets and liabilities with negligible risk to funded status. Recommendation B lies below the asset-only efficient frontier with a considerably lower expected return vis-à-vis Recommendation A.

What are the arguments for and against each of these recommendations? Recommendation A is expected, given capital market assumptions, to increase the size of the buffer between pension assets and liabilities. But the sponsor does not benefit from increases in the buffer if the current buffer is adequate.[25] However, with a 0.65 × $1.25 billion = $0.8125 allocation to equities and a current buffer of assets of $1.25 billion − $1.087 billion = $0.163 billion, a decline of that amount or more in equity values (a 20% decline) would put the plan into underfunded status (assuming no commensurate changes in the liability). Thus, Recommendation A creates contribution risk for the plan sponsor without a potential upside clearly benefiting either the sponsor or beneficiaries.

For Recommendation B, because the risk characteristics of the $1.125 billion fixed-income portfolio are closely matched with those of the $1.087 billion of pension liabilities with a buffer, the plan sponsor should not face any meaningful risk of needing to make further contributions to the pension. Pensioners expect the plan to be fully funded on an ongoing basis without any reliance on the sponsor's ability to make additional contributions. This is an excellent outcome for both. The pension liabilities are covered (defeased).

The example is highly stylized—the case facts were developed to make points cleanly—but does point to the potential value of managing risk in asset allocation explicitly in relation to liabilities. A typical use of fixed-income assets in liability-relative asset allocation should be noted: Liability-relative approaches to asset allocation tend to give fixed income a larger role than asset-only approaches in such cases as the one examined here because interest rates are a major financial market driver of both liability and bond values. Thus, bonds can be important in hedging liabilities, but equities can be relevant for liability hedging too. With richer case facts, as when liabilities accrue with inflation (not the case in the frozen DB example), equities may have a long-term role in matching the characteristics of liabilities. In underfunded plans, the potential upside of equities would often have greater value for the plan sponsor than in the fully funded case examined.

---

24 Collie and Gannon (2009) explore the contribution risk trade-off considered here in more detail.
25 Real-world complexities, such as DB plan termination to capture a positive surplus or pension risk transfer (annuitization), are beyond the scope of this reading; generally, there are restrictions and penalties involved in such actions, and the point made here is valid.

LIABILITY GLIDE PATHS

If GPLE were underfunded, it might consider establishing a liability glide path. A **liability glide path** is a technique in which the plan sponsor specifies in advance the desired proportion of liability-hedging assets and return-seeking assets and the duration of the liability hedge as funded status changes and contributions are made. The technique is particularly relevant to underfunded pensions. The idea reflects the fact that the optimal asset allocation in general is sensitive to changes in the funded status of the plan. The objective is to increase the funded status by reducing surplus risk over time. Although a higher contribution rate may be necessary to align assets with liabilities, the volatility of contributions should decrease, providing more certainty for cash flow planning purposes and decreasing risk to plan participants. Eventually, GPLE would hope to achieve and maintain a sufficiently high funded ratio so that there would be minimal risk of requiring additional contributions or transferring pension risk to an annuity provider.

The importance of such characteristics as interest rate sensitivity (duration), inflation, and credit risk in constructing a liability-hedging asset portfolio suggests the relevance of risk-factor modeling in liability-relative approaches. A risk factor approach can be extended to the return-seeking portfolio in order to minimize unintentional overlap among common factors across both portfolios—for example, credit. Exploring these topics is outside the scope of the current reading.

The next section addresses an approach to asset allocation related to liability relative in its focus on funding needs.

STRATEGIC ASSET ALLOCATION: GOALS BASED   9

☐ | recommend and justify an asset allocation based on an investor's objectives and constraints

We use the hypothetical Lee family to present some thematic elements of a goals-based approach.

INVESTOR CASE FACTS: THE LEE FAMILY

- *Name*: Ivy and Charles Lee
- *Narrative*: Ivy is a 54-year-old life sciences entrepreneur. Charles is 55 years old and employed as an orthopedic surgeon. They have two unmarried children aged 25 (Deborah) and 18 (David). Deborah has a daughter with physical limitations.
- *Financial assets and financial liabilities*: Portfolio of SGD 25 million with SGD 1 million in margin debt as well as residential real estate of SGD 3 million with $1 million in mortgage debt.
- *Other assets and liabilities*:

  - Pre-retirement earnings are expected to total SGD 16 million in present value terms (human capital).

- David will soon begin studying at a four-year private university; the present value of the expected parental contribution is SGD 250,000.
- The Lees desire to give a gift to a local art museum in five years. In present value terms, the gift is valued at SGD 750,000.
- The Lees want to establish a trust for their granddaughter with a present value of SGD 3 million to be funded at the death of Charles.
- The present value of future consumption expenditures is estimated at SGD 20 million.

Exhibit 11: Lee Family Economic Balance Sheet (in SGD millions) 31 December 2016

Assets		Liabilities and Economic Net Worth	
Financial Assets		*Financial Liabilities*	
Investment portfolio	25	Margin debt	1
Real estate	3	Mortgage	1
Extended Assets		*Extended Liabilities*	
Human capital	16	David's education	0.25
		Museum gift	0.75
		Special needs trust	3
		PV of future consumption	20
		Economic Net Worth	
		Economic net worth (economic assets less economic liabilities)	18
Total	44		44

The financial liabilities shown are legal liabilities. The extended liabilities include funding needs that the Lees want to meet. The balance sheet includes an estimate of the present value of future consumption, which is sometimes called the "consumption liability." The amount shown reflects expected values over their life expectancy given their ages. If they live longer, consumption needs will exceed the SGD 20 million in the case facts and erode the SGD 18 million in equity. If their life span is shorter, SGD 18 million plus whatever they do not consume of the SGD 20 million in PV of future consumption becomes part of their estate. Note that for the Lees, the value of assets exceeds the value of liabilities, resulting in a positive economic net worth (a positive difference between economic assets and economic liabilities); this is analogous to a positive owners' equity on a company's financial balance sheet.

From Exhibit 11, we can identify four goals totaling SGD 24 million in present value terms: a lifestyle goal (assessed as a need for SGD 20 million in present value terms), an education goal (SGD 0.25 million), a charitable goal (SGD 0.75 million), and the special needs trust (SGD 3 million).

The present value of expected future earnings (human capital) at SGD 16 million is less than the lifestyle present value of SGD 20 million, which means that some part of the investment portfolio must fund the Lees' standard of living. It is important to note that although the Lee family has SGD 18 million of economic net worth, most of this comes from the SGD 16 million extended asset of human capital. Specific investment portfolio assets have not yet been dedicated to specific goals.

Goals-based asset allocation builds on several insights from behavioral finance. The approach's characteristic use of sub-portfolios is grounded in the behavioral finance insight that investors tend to ignore money's fungibility[26] and assign specific dollars to specific uses—a phenomenon known as mental accounting. Goals-based asset allocation, as described here, systemizes the fruitful use of mental accounts. This approach may help investors embrace more-optimal portfolios (as defined in an asset-only or asset–liability framework) by adding higher risk assets—that, without context, might frighten the investor—to longer-term, aspirational sub-portfolios while adopting a more conservative allocation for sub-portfolios that address lifestyle preservation.

In Exhibit 11, the Lees' lifestyle goal is split into three components: a component called "lifestyle—minimum" intended to provide protection for the Lees' lifestyle in a disaster scenario, a component called "lifestyle—baseline" to address needs outside of worst cases, and a component called "lifestyle—aspirational" that reflects a desire for a chance at a markedly higher lifestyle. These sum to the present value of future consumption shown in the preceding Exhibit 11. Exhibit 12 describes these qualitatively; a numerical characterization could be very relevant for some advisers, however. By eliciting information on the Lees' perception of the goals' importance, the investment adviser might calibrate the required probabilities of achieving the goals quantitatively. For example, the three lifestyle goals might have 99%, 90%, and 50% assigned probabilities of success, respectively.

Exhibit 12: Lee Family: Required Probability of Meeting Goals and Goal Time Horizons

Goal	Required Probability of Achieving	Time Horizon
Lifestyle—minimum	Extremely high	Short to distant
Lifestyle—baseline	Very high	Short to distant
Lifestyle—aspirational	Moderate	Distant
Education	Very high	Short
Trust	High	Long
Charitable	Moderate	Short

Because the Lees might delay or forego making a gift to the museum if it would affect the trust goal, the trust goal is more urgent for the Lees. Also note that although parts of the Lees' lifestyle goals run the full time horizon spectrum from short to distant, they also have significant current earnings and human capital (which transforms into earnings as time passes). This fact puts the investment portfolio's role in funding the lifestyle goal further into the future.

Goals-based approaches generally set the strategic asset allocation in a bottom-up fashion. The Lees' lifestyle goal might be addressed with three sub-portfolios, with the longest horizon sub-portfolio being less liquid and accepting more risk than the

---

26 "Fungibility" is the property of an asset that a quantity of it may be replaced by another equal quantity in the satisfaction of an obligation. Thus, any 5,000 Japanese yen note can be used to pay a yen obligation of that amount, and the notes can be said to be fungible.

others. Although for the GPLE pension, no risk distinction was made among different parts of the pension liability vis-à-vis asset allocation, such distinctions are made in goals-based asset allocation.

What about the Lees' other goals? Separate sub-portfolios could be assigned to the special needs and charitable goals with asset allocations that reflect the associated time horizons and required probabilities of not attaining these goals. A later reading on asset allocation in practice addresses implementation processes in detail.

TYPES OF GOALS

As goals-based asset allocation has advanced, various classification systems for goals have been proposed. Two of those classification systems are as follows.

Brunel (2012):

- *Personal goals*—to meet current lifestyle requirements and unanticipated financial needs
- *Dynastic goals*—to meet descendants' needs
- *Philanthropic goals*

Chhabra (2005):

- *Personal risk bucket*—to provide protection from a dramatic decrease in lifestyle (i.e., safe-haven investments)
- *Market risk bucket*—to ensure the current lifestyle can be maintained (allocations for average risk-adjusted market returns)
- *Aspirational risk bucket*—to increase wealth substantially (greater than average risk is accepted)

EXAMPLE 7

Goals-Based Asset Allocation

The Lees are presented with the following optimized asset allocations:

Asset Allocation	Cash	Global Bonds	Global Equities	Diversifying Strategies
A	40%	50%	10%	0%
B	10%	30%	45%	15%

Assume that a portfolio of 70% global equities and 30% bonds reflects an appropriate balance of expected return and risk for the Lees with respect to a 10-year time horizon for most moderately important goals. Based on the information given:

Because of her industry connections in the life sciences, Ivy Lee is given the opportunity to be an early-stage venture capital investor in what she assesses is a very promising technology.

1. What goal(s) may be addressed by Allocation A?

Solution:

Allocation A stresses liquidity and stability. It may be appropriate to meet short-term lifestyle and education goals.

2. What goal(s) may be addressed by Allocation B?

Solution:

Allocation B has a greater growth emphasis, although it is somewhat conservative in relation to a 70/30 equity/bond baseline. It may be appropriate for funding the trust because of the goal's long time horizon and the Lees' desire for a high probability of achieving it.

3. What insights does goals-based asset allocation offer on this opportunity?

Solution:

Early-stage venture capital investments are both risky and illiquid; therefore, they belong in the longer-term and more risk-tolerant sub-portfolios. Ivy's decision about how much money she can commit should relate to how much excess capital remains after addressing goals that have a higher priority associated with them. Note that economic balance sheet thinking would stress that the life sciences opportunity is not particularly diversifying to her human capital.

DISCOUNT RATES AND LONGEVITY RISK

Although calculation of assets needed for sub-portfolios is outside the scope of this reading, certain themes can be indicated. Consider a retiree with a life expectancy of 20 years. The retiree has two goals:

- To maintain his current lifestyle upon retirement. This goal has a high required probability of achievement that is evaluated at 95%.

- To gift $1 million to a university in five years. This is viewed as a "desire" rather than a "need" and has a required probability evaluated at 75%.

Suppose that the investor's adviser specifies sub-portfolios as follows:

- for the first decade of lifestyle spending, a 3% expected return;

- for the second decade of lifestyle spending, a 4.6% expected return; and

- for the planned gift to the university, a 5.4% expected return.

Based on an estimate of annual consumption needs and the amount of the gift and given expected returns for the assigned sub-portfolios, the assets to be assigned to each sub-portfolio could be calculated by discounting amounts back to the present using their expected returns. However, this approach does not reflect the asset owner's required probability of achieving a goal. The higher the probability requirement for a future cash need, the greater the amount of assets needed in relation to it. Because of the inverse relation between present value and the discount rate, to reflect a 95% required probability, for example, the discount rates could be set at a lower level so that more assets are assigned to the sub-portfolio, increasing the probability of achieving the goal to the required level of 95% level.

Another consideration in determining the amount needed for future consumption is longevity risk. Life expectancies are median (50th percentile) outcomes. The retiree may outlive his life expectancy. To address longevity risk, the calculation of the present value of liabilities might use a longer life expectancy, such as a 35-year life expectancy instead of his actuarial 20-year expectation.

> Another approach is to transfer the risk to an insurer by purchasing an annuity that begins in 20 years and makes payments to the retiree for as long as he lives. Longevity risk and this kind of deferred annuity (sometimes called a "longevity annuity") are discussed in another curriculum reading on risk management.[27]

There are some drawbacks to the goals-based approach to asset allocation. One is that the sub-portfolios add complexity. Another is that goals may be ambiguous or may change over time. Goals-based approaches to asset allocation raise the question of how sub-portfolios coordinate to constitute an efficient whole. The subject will be taken up in a later reading, but the general finding is that the amount of sub-optimality is small.[28]

10   IMPLEMENTATION CHOICES

☐ | discuss strategic implementation choices in asset allocation, including passive/active choices and vehicles for implementing passive and active mandates

Having established the strategic asset allocation policy, the asset owner must address additional strategic considerations before moving to implementation. One of these is the passive/active choice.

There are two dimensions of passive/active choices. One dimension relates to the management of the strategic asset allocation itself—for example, whether to deviate from it tactically or not. The second dimension relates to passive and active implementation choices in investing the allocation to a given asset class. Each of these are covered in the sections that follow.

In an advisory role, asset managers have an unequivocal responsibility to make implementation and asset selection choices that are initially, and on an ongoing basis, suitable for the client.[29]

Passive/Active Management of Asset Class Weights

Tactical asset allocation (TAA) involves deliberate short-term deviations from the strategic asset allocation. Whereas the strategic asset allocation incorporates an investor's long-term, equilibrium market expectations, tactical asset allocation involves short-term tilts away from the strategic asset mix that reflect short-term views—for example, to exploit perceived deviations from equilibrium.

Tactical asset allocation is active management at the asset class level because it involves intentional deviations from the strategic asset mix to exploit perceived opportunities in capital markets to improve the portfolio's risk–return trade-off. TAA mandates are often specified to keep deviations from the strategic asset allocation within rebalancing ranges or within risk budgets. Tactical asset allocation decisions might be responsive to price momentum, perceived asset class valuation, or the particular stage of the business cycle. A strategy incorporating deviations from the strategic asset allocation that are motivated by longer-term valuation signals or economic views is sometimes distinguished as **dynamic asset allocation** (DAA).

---

27 See Blanchett et al. (2016) for the management of longevity risk. Milevsky (2016) is a further reference.
28 This is addressed technically in Das et al. (2010). See also Brunel (2015).
29 See Standard III (C) in the Standards of Practice Handbook (CFA Institute 2014).

Tactical asset allocation may be limited to tactical changes in domestic stock–bond or stock–bond–cash allocations or may be a more comprehensive multi-asset approach, as in a global tactical asset allocation (GTAA) model. Tactical asset allocation inherently involves market timing as it involves buying and selling in anticipation of short-term changes in market direction; however, TAA usually involves smaller allocation tilts than an invested-or-not-invested market timing strategy.

Tactical asset allocation is a source of risk when calibrated against the strategic asset mix. An informed approach to tactical asset allocation recognizes the trade-off of any potential outperformance against this tracking error. Key barriers to successful tactical asset allocation are monitoring and trading costs. For some investors, higher short-term capital gains taxes will prove a significant obstacle because taxes are an additional trading cost. A program of tactical asset allocation must be evaluated through a cost–benefit lens. The relevant cost comparisons include the expected costs of simply following a rebalancing policy (without deliberate tactical deviations).

Passive/Active Management of Allocations to Asset Classes

In addition to active and passive decisions about the asset class mix, there are active and passive decisions about how to implement the individual allocations within asset classes. An allocation can be managed passively or actively or incorporate both active and passive sub-allocations. For investors who delegate asset management to external firms, these decisions would come under the heading of manager structure,[30] which includes decisions about how capital and active risk are allocated to points on the passive/active spectrum and to individual external managers selected to manage the investor's assets.[31]

With a **passive management** approach, portfolio composition does not react to changes in the investor's capital market expectations or to information on or insights into individual investments. (The word *passive* means *not reacting*.) For example, a portfolio constructed to track the returns of an index of European equities might add or drop a holding in response to a change in the index composition but not in response to changes in the manager's expectations concerning the security's investment value; the market's expectations reflected in market values and index weights are taken as is. Indexing is a common passive approach to investing. (Another example would be buying and holding a fixed portfolio of bonds to maturity.)

In contrast, a portfolio manager for an active management strategy will respond to changing capital market expectations or to investment insights resulting in changes to portfolio composition. The objective of active management is to achieve, after expenses, positive excess risk-adjusted returns relative to a passive benchmark.

The range of implementation choices can be practically viewed as falling along a passive/active spectrum because some strategies use both passive and active elements. In financial theory, the pure model of a passive approach is indexing to a broad market-cap-weighted index of risky assets—in particular, the global market portfolio. This portfolio sums all investments in index components and is macro-consistent in the sense that all investors could hold it, and it is furthermore self-rebalancing to the extent it is based on market-value-weighted indices. A buy-and-hold investment as a proxy for the global market portfolio would represent a theoretical endpoint on the passive/active spectrum. However, consider an investor who indexes an equity allocation to a broad-based value equity style index. The investment could be said to reflect an active decision in tilting an allocation toward value but be passive in implementation because it involves indexing. An even more active approach would

---

30 Manager structure is defined by the number of managers, types of managers, as well as which managers are selected.
31 See, for example, Waring, Whitney, Pirone, and Castille (2000).

be investing the equity allocation with managers who have a value investing approach and attempt to enhance returns through security selection. Those managers would show positive tracking risk relative to the value index in general. Unconstrained active investment would be one that is "go anywhere" or not managed with consideration of any traditional asset class benchmark (i.e., "benchmark agnostic"). The degree of active management has traditionally been quantified by tracking risk and, from a different perspective, by active share.

Indexing is generally the lowest-cost approach to investing. Indexing involves some level of transaction costs because, as securities move in and out of the index, the port-folio holdings must adjust to remain in alignment with the index. Although indexing to a market-cap-weighted index is self-rebalancing, tracking an index based on other weighting schemes requires ongoing transactions to ensure the portfolio remains in alignment with index weights. An example is tracking an equally weighted index: As changes in market prices affect the relative weights of securities in the portfolio over time, the portfolio will need to be rebalanced to restore equal weights. Portfolios tracking fixed-income indices also incur ongoing transaction costs as holdings mature, default, or are called away by their issuers.

Exhibit 13 diagrams the passive/active choice as a continuum rather than binary (0 or 1) characteristic. Tracking risk and active share are widely known quantitative measures of the degree of active management that capture different aspects of it. Each measure is shown as tending to increase from left to right on the spectrum; however, they do not increase (or decrease) in lockstep with each other, in general.

Exhibit 13: Passive/Active Spectrum

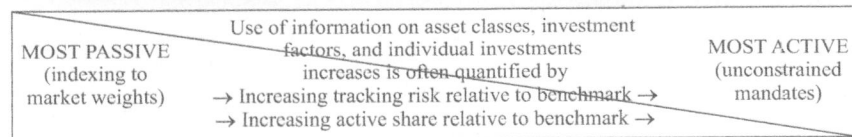

MOST PASSIVE (indexing to market weights)	Use of information on asset classes, investment factors, and individual investments increases is often quantified by → Increasing tracking risk relative to benchmark → → Increasing active share relative to benchmark →	MOST ACTIVE (unconstrained mandates)

Asset class allocations may be managed with different approaches on the spectrum. For example, developed market equities might be implemented purely passively, whereas emerging market bonds might be invested with an unconstrained, index-agnostic approach.

Factors that influence asset owners' decisions on where to invest on the passive/active spectrum include the following:

- *Available investments*. For example, the availability of an investable and representative index as the basis for indexing.

- *Scalability of active strategies being considered*. The prospective value added by an active strategy may begin to decline at some level of invested assets. In addition, participation in it may not be available below some asset level, a consideration for small investors.

- *The feasibility of investing passively while incorporating client-specific con-straints*. For example, an investor's particular ESG investing criteria may not align with existing index products.

- *Beliefs concerning market informational efficiency*. A strong belief in market efficiency for the asset class(es) under consideration would orient the inves-tor away from active management.

- *The trade-off of expected incremental benefits relative to incremental costs and risks of active choices.* Costs of active management include investment management costs, trading costs, and turnover-induced taxes; such costs would have to be judged relative to the lower costs of index alternatives, which vary by asset class.

- *Tax status.* Holding other variables constant, taxable investors would tend to have higher hurdles to profitable active management than tax-exempt investors.[32] For taxable investors who want to hold both passive and active investments, active investments would be held, in general, in available tax-advantaged accounts.

The curriculum readings on equity, fixed-income, and alternative investments will explore many strategies and the nature of any active decisions involved. Investors do need to understand the nature of the active decisions involved in implementing their strategic asset allocations and their appropriateness given the factors described. Exhibit 14 shows qualitatively (rather than precisely) some choices that investors may consider for equity and fixed-income allocations. In the exhibit, non-cap-weighted indexing includes such approaches as equal weighting and quantitative rules-based indexing approaches (discussed further in the equity readings).[33]

Exhibit 14: Placement on the Passive/Active Spectrum: Examples of Possible Choices

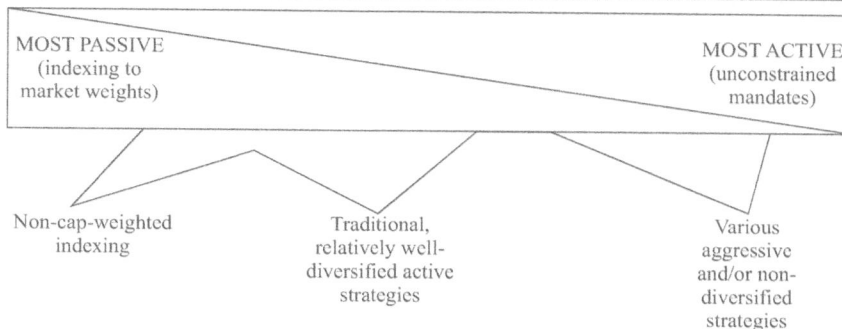

MOST PASSIVE
(indexing to
market weights)

MOST ACTIVE
(unconstrained
mandates)

Non-cap-weighted
indexing

Traditional,
relatively well-
diversified active
strategies

Various
aggressive
and/or non-
diversified
strategies

EXAMPLE 8

Implementation Choices (1)

1. Describe two kinds of passive/active choices faced by investors related to asset allocation.

Solution:

One choice relates to whether to allow active deviations from the strategic asset allocation. Tactical asset allocation and dynamic asset allocation are examples of active management of asset allocations. A second set of choices relates to where to invest allocations to asset classes along the passive/active spectrum.

---

32 See Jeffrey and Arnott (1993).
33 Podkaminer (2015) provides a survey.

2. An equity index is described as "a rules-based, transparent index designed to provide investors with an efficient way to gain exposure to large-cap and small-cap stocks with low total return variability." Compared with the market-cap weighting of the parent index (with the same component securities), the weights in the low-volatility index are proportional to the inverse of return volatility, so that the highest-volatility security receives the lowest weight. Describe the active and passive aspects of a decision to invest an allocation to equities in ETFs tracking such indices.

Solution:

The active element is the decision, relative to the parent index, to overweight securities with low volatility and underweight securities with high volatility. This management of risk is distinct from reducing portfolio volatility by combining a market-cap-weighted index with a risk-free asset proxy because it implies a belief in some risk–return advantage to favoring low-volatility equities on an individual security basis. The passive element is a transparent rules-based implementation of the weighting scheme based on inverse volatilities.

3. Describe how investing in a GDP-weighted global bond index involves both active and passive choices.

Solution:

The passive choice is represented by the overall selection of the universe of global bonds; however, the active choice is represented by the weighting scheme, which is to use GDP rather than capital market weights. This is a tilt toward the real economy and away from fixed-income market values.

EXAMPLE 9

Implementation Choices (2)

Describe characteristic(s) of each of the following investors that are likely to influence the decision to invest passively or actively.

1. Caflandia sovereign wealth fund

For a large investor like the Caflandia sovereign wealth fund (CAF$40 billion), the scalability of active strategies that it may wish to employ may be a consideration. If only a small percentage of portfolio assets can be invested effectively in an active strategy, for example, the potential value added for the overall portfolio may not justify the inherent costs and management time. Although the equities and fixed-income allocations could be invested using passive approaches, investments in the diversifying strategies category are commonly active.

2. GPLE corporate pension

The executives responsible for the GPLE corporate pension also have other, non-investment responsibilities. This is a factor favoring a more passive approach; however, choosing an outsourced chief investment officer or delegated fiduciary consultant to manage active manager selection could facilitate greater use of active investment.

3. The Lee family

The fact that the Lees are taxable investors is a factor generally in favor of passive management for assets not held in tax-advantaged accounts. Active management involves turnover, which gives rise to taxes.

4. Auldberg University Endowment

According to the vignette in Example 3, the Auldberg University Endowment has substantial staff resources in equities, fixed income, and real estate. This fact suggests that passive/active decisions are relatively unconstrained by internal resources. By itself, it does not favor passive or active, but it is a factor that allows active choices to be given full consideration.

Risk Budgeting Perspectives in Asset Allocation and Implementation

Risk budgeting addresses the questions of which types of risks to take and how much of each to take. Risk budgeting provides another view of asset allocation—through a risk lens. Depending on the focus, the risk may be quantified in various ways. For example, a concern for volatility can be quantified as variance or standard deviation of returns, and a concern for tail risk can be quantified as VaR or drawdown. Risk budgets (budgets for risk taking) can be stated in absolute or in relative terms and in money or percent terms. For example, it is possible to state an overall risk budget for a portfolio in terms of volatility of returns, which would be an example of an absolute risk budget stated in percent terms (for example, 20% for portfolio return volatility). Risk budgeting is a tool that may be useful in a variety of contexts and asset allocation approaches.

Some investors may approach asset allocation with an exclusive focus on risk. A risk budgeting approach to asset allocation has been defined as an approach in which the investor specifies how risk (quantified by some measure, such as volatility) is to be distributed across assets in the portfolio, without consideration of the assets' expected returns.[34] An example is aiming for equal expected risk contributions to overall portfolio volatility from all included asset classes as an approach to diversification, which is a risk parity (or equal risk contribution) approach. A subsequent reading in asset allocation addresses this in greater detail.

More directly related to the choice of passive/active implementation are active risk budgets and active risk budgeting. **Active risk budgeting** addresses the question of how much benchmark-relative risk an investor is willing to take in seeking to outperform a benchmark. This approach is risk budgeting stated in benchmark-relative terms. In parallel to the two dimensions of the passive/active decision outlined previously are two levels of active risk budgeting, which can be distinguished as follows:

- At the level of the overall asset allocation, active risk can be defined relative to the strategic asset allocation benchmark. This benchmark may be the strategic asset allocation weights applied to specified (often, broad-based market-cap-weighted) indices.

- At the level of individual asset classes, active risk can be defined relative to the asset class benchmark.

Active risk budgeting at the level of overall asset allocation would be relevant to tactical asset allocation. Active risk budgeting at the level of each asset class is relevant to how the allocation to those asset classes is invested. For example, it can take the form

---

34 See Roncalli (2013).

of expected-alpha versus tracking-error optimization in a manner similar to classic mean–variance optimization. If investment factor risks are the investor's focus, risk budgeting can be adapted to have a focus on allocating factor risk exposures instead. Later readings revisit risk budgeting in investing in further detail.

---

11   REBALANCING: STRATEGIC CONSIDERATIONS

☐ │ discuss strategic considerations in rebalancing asset allocations

Rebalancing is the discipline of adjusting portfolio weights to more closely align with the strategic asset allocation. Rebalancing is a key part of the monitoring and feedback step of the portfolio construction, monitoring, and revision process. An investor's rebalancing policy is generally documented in the IPS.

Even in the absence of changing investor circumstances, a revised economic outlook, or tactical asset allocation views, normal changes in asset prices cause the portfolio asset mix to deviate from target weights. Industry practice defines "rebalancing" as portfolio adjustments triggered by such price changes. Other portfolio adjustments, even systematic ones, are not rebalancing.

Ordinary price changes cause the assets with a high forecast return to grow faster than the portfolio as a whole. Because high-return assets are typically also higher risk, in the absence of rebalancing, overall portfolio risk rises. The mix of risks within the portfolio becomes more concentrated as well. Systematic rebalancing maintains the original strategic risk exposures. The discipline of rebalancing serves to control portfolio risks that have become different from what the investor originally intended.

Consider the example from the internet bubble (1995–2001) in Exhibit 15. The example assumes a 60/40 stock/bond portfolio, in which stocks are represented by the large-cap US growth stocks that characterized the internet bubble. In Panel B, the left-hand scale and upper two lines show month-by-month total portfolio *values* with and without monthly rebalancing ("wealth rebalanced" and "wealth unrebalanced," respectively). The right-hand scale and lower two lines show month-by-month portfolio *risk* as represented by the 5th percentile drawdown (in a VaR model) with and without monthly rebalancing ("risk rebalanced" and "risk unrebalanced," respectively).

Exhibit 15: Rebalancing

Panel A. Asset Mix

Percent

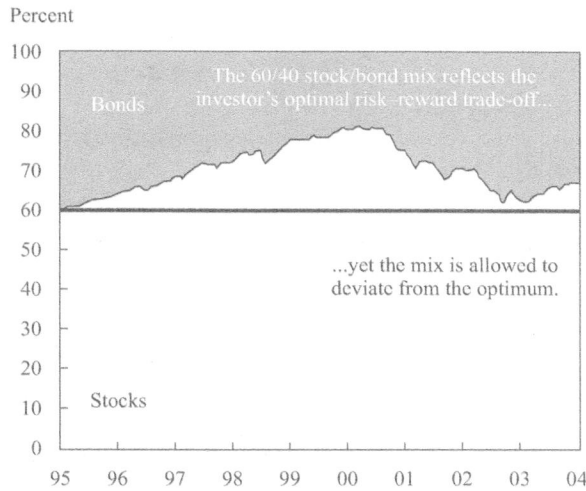

The 60/40 stock/bond mix reflects the investor's optimal risk–reward trade-off…

Bonds

…yet the mix is allowed to deviate from the optimum.

Stocks

Panel B. Portfolio Value and Risk

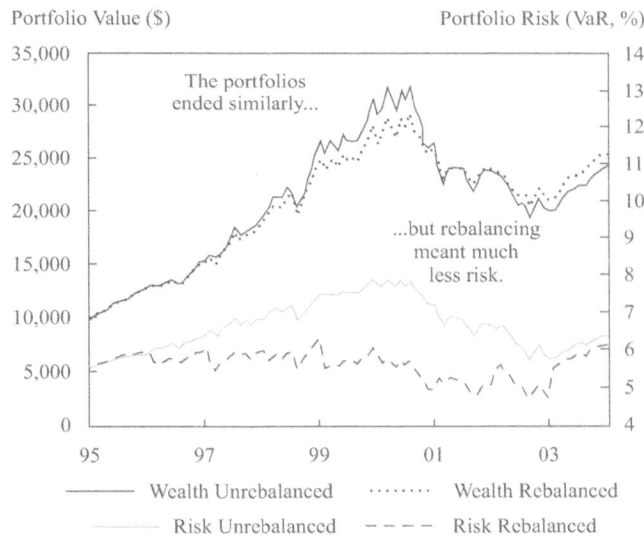

Portfolio Value ($)   Portfolio Risk (VaR, %)

The portfolios ended similarly…

…but rebalancing meant much less risk.

——— Wealth Unrebalanced   ········· Wealth Rebalanced

——— Risk Unrebalanced   – – – – Risk Rebalanced

Note: The data are a 60/40 mix of the S&P 500 Growth Index and the Barclays Capital Aggregate Bond Index.

Because rebalancing is countercyclical, it is fundamentally a contrarian investment approach.[35] Behavioral finance tells us that such contrarianism will be uncomfortable; no one likes to sell the most recently best-performing part of the portfolio to buy the worst. Thus, rebalancing is a *discipline* of adjusting the portfolio to better align with the strategic asset allocation in both connotations of discipline—the sense of a typical practice and the sense of a strengthening regime.

---

35 A quantitative interpretation of rebalancing, given by Ang (2014), is that the return to rebalancing is selling out of the money puts and calls.

A Framework for Rebalancing

The actual mechanics of rebalancing are more complex than they first appear. A number of questions arise: How often should the portfolio be rebalanced? What levels of imbalance are worth tolerating? Should the portfolio be rebalanced to the edge of the policy range or to some other point? These non-trivial questions represent the key strategic decisions in rebalancing.

The simplest approach to rebalancing is **calendar rebalancing**, which involves rebalancing a portfolio to target weights on a periodic basis—for example, monthly, quarterly, semiannually, or annually. The choice of rebalancing frequency may be linked to the schedule of portfolio reviews. Although simple, rebalancing points are arbitrary and have other disadvantages.

Percent-range rebalancing permits tighter control of the asset mix compared with calendar rebalancing. Percent-range approach involves setting rebalancing thresholds or trigger points, stated as a percentage of the portfolio's value, around target values. For example, if the target allocation to an asset class is 50% of portfolio value, **trigger points** at 45% and 55% of portfolio value define a 10 percentage point **rebalancing range** (or corridor) for the value of that asset class. The rebalancing range creates a no-trade region. The portfolio is rebalanced when an asset class's weight first passes through one of its trigger points. Focusing on percent-range rebalancing, the following questions are relevant:

- How frequently is the portfolio valued?
- What size deviation triggers rebalancing?
- Is the deviation from the target allocation fully or partially corrected?

How frequently is the portfolio valued? The percent-range discipline requires monitoring portfolio values for breaches of a trigger point at an agreed-on frequency; the more frequent the monitoring, the greater the precision in implementation. Such monitoring may be scheduled daily, weekly, monthly, quarterly, or annually. A number of considerations—including governance resources and asset custodian resources—can affect valuation frequency. For many investors, monthly or quarterly evaluation efficiently balances the costs and benefits of rebalancing.

What size deviation triggers rebalancing? Trigger points take into account such factors as traditional practice, transaction costs, asset class volatility, volatility of the balance of the portfolio, correlation of the asset class with the balance of the portfolio, and risk tolerance.[36]

Before the rise of modern multi-asset portfolios, the stock/bond split broadly characterized the asset allocation and a traditional ±x% rebalancing band was common. These fixed ranges would apply no matter the size or volatility of the allocation target. For example, both a 40% domestic equity allocation and a 15% real asset allocation might have ±5% rebalancing ranges. Alternatively, proportional bands reflect the size of the target weight. For example, a 60% target asset class might have a ±6% band, whereas a 5% allocation would have a ±0.5% band. Proportional bands might also be set to reflect the relative volatility of the asset classes. A final approach is the use of cost–benefit analysis to set ranges.

Is the deviation from the target allocation fully or partially corrected? Once the portfolio is evaluated and an unacceptably large deviation found, the investor must determine rebalancing trade size, as well as the timeline for implementing the rebalancing. In practice, three main approaches are used: rebalance back to target weights, rebalance to range edge, or rebalance halfway between the range-edge trigger point and the target weight.

---

36 See Masters (2003) for details on these factors apart from traditional factors.

Strategic Considerations in Rebalancing

The four-part rebalancing framework just described highlights important questions to address in setting rebalancing policy. Strategic considerations generally include the following, all else being equal:

- Higher transaction costs for an asset class imply wider rebalancing ranges.
- More risk-averse investors will have tighter rebalancing ranges.
- Less correlated assets also have tighter rebalancing ranges.
- Beliefs in momentum favor wider rebalancing ranges, whereas mean reversion encourages tighter ranges.
- Illiquid investments complicate rebalancing.
- Derivatives create the possibility of synthetic rebalancing.
- Taxes, which are a cost, discourage rebalancing and encourage asymmetric and wider rebalancing ranges.

Asset class volatility is also a consideration in the size of rebalancing ranges.

A cost–benefit approach to rebalancing sets ranges, taking transaction costs, risk aversion, asset class risks, and asset class correlations into consideration. For example, an asset that is more highly correlated with the rest of the portfolio than another would merit a wider rebalancing range, all else equal, because it would be closer to being a substitute for the balance of the portfolio; thus, larger deviations would have less impact on portfolio risk.

EXAMPLE 10

Different Rebalancing Ranges

1. The table shows a simple four-asset strategic mix along with rebalancing ranges created under different approaches. The width of the rebalancing range under the proportional range approach is 0.20 of the strategic target.

   State a reason that could explain why the international equity range is wider than the domestic equity range using the cost–benefit approach.

Asset Class	Strategic Target	Fixed Width Ranges	Proportional Ranges (±1,000 bps)	Cost–Benefit Ranges
Domestic equity	40%	35%–45%	36%–44%	35%–45%
International equity	25%	20%–30%	22½%–27½%	19%–31%
Emerging markets	15%	10%–20%	13½%–16½%	12%–18%
Fixed income	20%	15%–25%	18%–22%	19%–21%

Solution:

Higher transaction costs for international equity compared with domestic equity could explain the wider range for international equity compared with domestic equity under the cost–benefit approach. Another potential explanation relates to the possibility that international equity has a higher correlation with the balance of the portfolio (i.e., the portfolio excluding international equity) than does domestic equity (i.e., with the portfolio excluding domestic equity). If that is the case then, all else being equal, a wider band would be justified for international equity.

Investors' perspectives on capital markets can affect their approach to rebalancing. A belief in momentum and trend following, for example, encourages wider rebalancing ranges. In contrast, a belief in mean reversion encourages stricter adherence to rebalancing, including tighter ranges.

Illiquid assets complicate rebalancing. Relatively illiquid investments, such as hedge funds, private equity, or direct real estate, cannot be readily traded without substantial trading costs and/or delays. Accordingly, illiquid investments are commonly assigned wide rebalancing ranges. However, rebalancing of an illiquid asset may be affected indirectly when a highly correlated liquid asset can be traded or when exposure can be adjusted by means of positions in derivatives. For example, public equity could be reduced to offset an overweight in private equity. Rebalancing by means of highly correlated liquid assets and derivatives, however, involves some imprecision and basis risk.

This insight about liquidity is an instance where thinking ahead about rebalancing can affect the strategic asset allocation. It is one reason that allocations to illiquid assets are often smaller than if trading were possible.

Factor-based asset allocation, liability-relative investing, and goals-based investing, each a valid approach to asset allocation, can give rise to different rebalancing considerations. Factor exposures and liability hedges require monitoring (and rebalancing) the factors weights and surplus duration in addition to asset class weights. Goals-based investing in private wealth management may require both asset class rebalancing and moving funds between different goal sub-portfolios.

Tax considerations also complicate rebalancing. Rebalancing typically realizes capital gains and losses, which are taxable events in many jurisdictions. For private wealth managers, any rebalancing benefit must be compared with the tax cost. Taxes, as a cost, are much larger than other transaction costs, which often leads to wider rebalancing ranges in taxable portfolios than in tax-exempt portfolios. Because loss harvesting generates tax savings and realizing gains triggers taxes, rebalancing ranges in taxable accounts may also be asymmetric. (For example, a 25% target asset class might have an allowable range of 24%–28%, which is −1% to +3%.)

Modern cost–benefit approaches to rebalancing suggest considering derivatives as a rebalancing tool. Derivatives can often be used to rebalance synthetically at much lower transaction costs than the costs of using the underlying stocks and bonds. Using a derivatives overlay also avoids disrupting the underlying separate accounts in a multi-manager implementation of the strategic asset allocation. Tax considerations are also relevant; it may be more cost effective to reduce an exposure using a derivatives overlay than to sell the underlying asset and incur the capital gains tax liability. Lastly, trading a few derivatives may be quicker and easier than hundreds of underlying securities. Of course, using derivatives may require a higher level of risk oversight, but then risk control is the main rationale for rebalancing.

Estimates of the benefits of rebalancing vary. Many portfolios are statistically indistinguishable from each other, suggesting that much rebalancing is unnecessary. In contrast, Willenbrock (2011) demonstrates that even zero-return assets can, in theory, generate positive returns through rebalancing, which is a demonstrable (and surprising) benefit. Whatever the return estimate for the value added from rebalancing, the key takeaway is that rebalancing is chiefly about risk control, not return enhancement.

SUMMARY

This reading has introduced the subject of asset allocation. Among the points made are the following:

- Effective investment governance ensures that decisions are made by individuals or groups with the necessary skills and capacity and involves articulating the long- and short-term objectives of the investment program; effectively allocating decision rights and responsibilities among the functional units in the governance hierarchy; taking account of their knowledge, capacity, time, and position on the governance hierarchy; specifying processes for developing and approving the investment policy statement, which will govern the day-to-day operation of the investment program; specifying processes for developing and approving the program's strategic asset allocation; establishing a reporting framework to monitor the program's progress toward the agreed-on goals and objectives; and periodically undertaking a governance audit.

- The economic balance sheet includes non-financial assets and liabilities that can be relevant for choosing the best asset allocation for an investor's financial portfolio.

- The investment objectives of asset-only asset allocation approaches focus on the asset side of the economic balance sheet; approaches with a liability-relative orientation focus on funding liabilities; and goals-based approaches focus on achieving financial goals.

- The risk concepts relevant to asset-only asset allocation approaches focus on asset risk; those of liability-relative asset allocation focus on risk in relation to paying liabilities; and a goals-based approach focuses on the probabilities of not achieving financial goals.

- Asset classes are the traditional units of analysis in asset allocation and reflect systematic risks with varying degrees of overlap.

- Assets within an asset class should be relatively homogeneous; asset classes should be mutually exclusive; asset classes should be diversifying; asset classes as a group should make up a preponderance of the world's investable wealth; asset classes selected for investment should have the capacity to absorb a meaningful proportion of an investor's portfolio.

- Risk factors are associated with non-diversifiable (i.e., systematic) risk and are associated with an expected return premium. The price of an asset and/or asset class may reflect more than one risk factor, and complicated spread positions may be necessary to identify and isolate particular risk factors. Their use as units of analysis in asset allocation is driven by considerations of controlling systematic risk exposures.

- The global market portfolio represents a highly diversified asset allocation that can serve as a baseline asset allocation in an asset-only approach.

- There are two dimensions of passive/active choices. One dimension relates to the management of the strategic asset allocation itself—for example, whether to deviate from it tactically or not. The second dimension relates to passive and active implementation choices in investing the allocation to a given asset class. Tactical and dynamic asset allocation relate to the first dimension; active and passive choices for implementing allocations to asset classes relate to the second dimension.

- Risk budgeting addresses the question of which types of risks to take and how much of each to take. Active risk budgeting addresses the question of how much benchmark-relative risk an investor is willing to take. At the level of the overall asset allocation, active risk can be defined relative to the strategic asset allocation benchmark. At the level of individual asset classes, active risk can be defined relative to the benchmark proxy.

- Rebalancing is the discipline of adjusting portfolio weights to more closely align with the strategic asset allocation. Rebalancing approaches include calendar-based and range-based rebalancing. Calendar-based rebalancing rebalances the portfolio to target weights on a periodic basis. Range-based rebalancing sets rebalancing thresholds or trigger points around target weights. The ranges may be fixed width, percentage based, or volatility based. Range-based rebalancing permits tighter control of the asset mix compared with calendar rebalancing.

- Strategic considerations in rebalancing include transaction costs, risk aversion, correlations among asset classes, volatility, and beliefs concerning momentum, taxation, and asset class liquidity.

REFERENCES

Ang, Andrew. 2014. Asset Management: A Systematic Approach to Factor Investing. New York: Oxford University Press.

Blanchett, David M., Philip U. Straehl. 2015. "No Portfolio is an Island." *Financial Analysts Journal*, vol. 71, no. 3 (May/June): 15–33. 10.2469/faj.v71.n3.5

Blanchett, David M., Philip U. Straehl. 2017. "Portfolio Implications of Job-Specific Human Capital Risk." *Journal of Asset Management*, vol. 18, no. 1:1–15.

Blanchett, David M., David M. Cordell, Michael S. Finke, and Thomas Idzorek. 2016. "Risk Management for Individuals." CFA Institute.

Brunel, Jean L.P. 2012. "Goals-Based Wealth Management in Practice." Conference Proceedings Quarterly, vol. 29, no. 1 (March): 57–65.

Brunel, Jean L.P. 2015. Goals-Based Wealth Management: An Integrated and Practical Approach to Changing the Structure of Wealth Advisory Practices. Hoboken, NJ: John Wiley.

Burger, John D., Francis E. Warnock, and Veronica Cacdac Warnock. 2012. "Emerging Local Currency Bond Markets." *Financial Analysts Journal*, vol. 68, no. 4 (July/August): 73–93. 10.2469/faj.v68.n4.4

CFA Institute. Standards of Practice Handbook, 11th edition. 2014. CFA Institute.

Chhabra, Ashvin. 2005. "Beyond Markowitz: A Comprehensive Wealth Allocation Framework for Individual Investors." *Journal of Wealth Management*, vol. 7, no. 4 (Spring): 8–34. 10.3905/jwm.2005.470606

Collie, Bob, James A. Gannon. 2009. "Liability-Responsive Asset Allocation: A Dynamic Approach to Pension Plan Management." Russell Investments Insights (April).

Das, Sanjiv, Harry Markowitz, Jonathan Scheid, and Meir Statman. 2010. "Portfolio Optimization with Mental Accounts." *Journal of Financial and Quantitative Analysis*, vol. 45, no. 2 (April): 311–334. 10.1017/S0022109010000141

Fraser, Steve P., William W. Jennings. 2006. "Behavioral Asset Allocation for Foundations and Endowments." *Journal of Wealth Management*, vol. 9, no. 3 (Winter): 38–50. 10.3905/jwm.2006.661431

Greer, Robert J. 1997. "What is an Asset Class, Anyway?" *Journal of Portfolio Management*, vol. 23, no. 2 (Winter): 86–91. 10.3905/jpm.23.2.86

Ibbotson, Roger G., Paul D. Kaplan. 2000. "Does Asset Allocation Policy Explain 40, 90, or 100 Percent of Performance?" *Financial Analysts Journal*, vol. 56, no. 1 (January/February): 26–33. 10.2469/faj.v56.n1.2327

Ibbotson, Roger G., Moshe A. Milevsky, Peng Chen, and Kevin X. Zhu. 2007. Lifetime Financial Advice: Human Capital, Asset Allocation, and Insurance. Charlottesville, VA: CFA Institute Research Foundation.

Idzorek, Thomas M., Maciej Kowara. 2013. "Factor-Based Asset Allocation versus Asset-Class-Based Asset Allocation." *Financial Analysts Journal*, vol. 69, no. 3 (May/June): 19–29. 10.2469/faj.v69.n3.7

Idzorek, Thomas, Jeremy Stempien, and Nathan Voris. 2013. "Bait and Switch: Glide Path Instability." *Journal of Investing*, vol. 22, no. 1 (Spring): 74–82. 10.3905/joi.2013.22.1.074

Jeffrey, Robert H., Robert D. Arnott. 1993. "Is Your Alpha Big Enough to Cover Its Taxes?" *Journal of Portfolio Management*, vol. 19, no. 3 (Spring): 15–25. 10.3905/jpm.1993.710867

Kozhemiakin, Alexander. 2011. "Emerging Markets Local Currency Debt: Capitalizing on Improved Sovereign Fundamentals." BNY Mellon Asset Management.

Kritzman, Mark. 1999. "Toward Defining an Asset Class." *Journal of Alternative Investments*, vol. 2, no. 1 (Summer): 79–82. 10.3905/jai.1999.318919

Masters, Seth J. 2003. "Rebalancing." *Journal of Portfolio Management*, vol. 29, no. 3 (Spring): 52–57. 10.3905/jpm.2003.319883

Milevsky, Moshe A. 2016. "It's Time to Retire Ruin (Probabilities)." *Financial Analysts Journal*, vol. 72, no. 2 (March/April): 8–12. 10.2469/faj.v72.n2.4

Perry, William. 2011. "The Case For Emerging Market Corporates." *Journal of Indexes*, vol. 14, no. 5 (September/October): 10–17.

Podkaminer, Eugene. 2013. "Risk Factors as Building Blocks for Portfolio Diversification: The Chemistry of Asset Allocation." CFA Institute Investment Risk and Performance papers (January).

Podkaminer, Eugene. 2015. "The Education of Beta: Can Alternative Indexes Make Your Portfolio Smarter?" *Journal of Investing*, vol. 24, no. 2 (Summer): 7–34. 10.3905/joi.2015.24.2.007

Pompian, Michael M. 2011a. "The Behavioral Biases of Individuals." CFA Institute.

Pompian, Michael M. 2011b. "The Behavioral Finance Perspective." CFA Institute.

Pompian, Michael, Colin McLean, Alistair Byrne. 2011. "Behavioral Finance and Investment Processes." CFA Institute.

Roncalli, Thierry. 2013. Introduction to Risk Parity and Budgeting. New York: CRC Press.

Rudd, Andrew, Laurence B. Siegel. 2013. "Using an Economic Balance Sheet for Financial Planning." *Journal of Wealth Management*, vol. 16, no. 2 (Fall): 15–23. 10.3905/jwm.2013.16.2.015

Shefrin, H., M. Statman. 2000. "Behavioral Portfolio Theory." *Journal of Financial and Quantitative Analysis*, vol. 35, no. 2 (June): 127–151. 10.2307/2676187

Swinkels, Laurens. 2012. "Emerging Market Inflation-Linked Bonds." *Financial Analysts Journal*, vol. 68, no. 5 (September/October): 38–56. 10.2469/faj.v68.n5.2

Waring, M. Barton, Duane Whitney, John Pirone, and Charles Castille. 2000. "Optimizing Manager Structure and Budgeting Manager Risk." *Journal of Portfolio Management*, vol. 26, no. 3 (Spring): 90–104. 10.3905/jpm.2000.319719

Willenbrock, Scott. 2011. "Diversification Return, Portfolio Rebalancing, and the Commodity Return Puzzle." *Financial Analysts Journal*, vol. 67, no. 4 (July/August): 42–49. 10.2469/faj.v67.n4.1

PRACTICE PROBLEMS

The following information relates to questions 1-8

Meg and Cramer Law, a married couple aged 42 and 44, respectively, are meeting with their new investment adviser, Daniel Raye. The Laws have worked their entire careers at Whorton Solutions (WS), a multinational technology company. The Laws have two teenage children who will soon begin college.

Raye reviews the Laws' current financial position. The Laws have an investment portfolio consisting of $800,000 in equities and $450,000 in fixed-income instruments. Raye notes that 80% of the equity portfolio consists of shares of WS. The Laws also own real estate valued at $400,000, with $225,000 in mortgage debt. Raye estimates the Laws' pre-retirement earnings from WS have a total present value of $1,025,000. He estimates the Laws' future expected consumption expenditures have a total present value of $750,000.

The Laws express a very strong desire to fund their children's college education expenses, which have an estimated present value of $275,000. The Laws also plan to fund an endowment at their alma mater in 20 years, which has an estimated present value of $500,000. The Laws tell Raye they want a high probability of success funding the endowment. Raye uses this information to prepare an economic balance sheet for the Laws.

In reviewing a financial plan written by the Laws' previous adviser, Raye notices the following asset class specifications.

Equity:	US equities
Debt:	Global investment-grade corporate bonds and real estate
Derivatives:	Primarily large-capitalization foreign equities

The previous adviser's report notes the asset class returns on equity and derivatives are highly correlated. The report also notes the asset class returns on debt have a low correlation with equity and derivative returns.

Raye is concerned that the asset allocation approach followed by the Laws' previous financial adviser resulted in an overlap in risk factors among asset classes for the portfolio. Raye plans to address this by examining the portfolio's sensitivity to various risk factors, such as inflation, liquidity, and volatility, to determine the desired exposure to each factor.

Raye concludes that a portfolio of 75% global equities and 25% bonds reflects an appropriate balance of expected return and risk for the Laws with respect to a 20-year time horizon for most moderately important goals. Raye recommends the Laws follow a goals-based approach to asset allocation and offers three possible portfolios for the Laws to consider. Selected data on the three portfolios are presented in Exhibit 1.

Exhibit 1: Proposed Portfolio Allocations for the Law Family

	Cash	Fixed Income	Global Equities	Diversifying Strategies*
Portfolio 1	35%	55%	10%	0%
Portfolio 2	10%	15%	65%	10%
Portfolio 3	10%	30%	40%	20%

* Diversifying strategies consists of hedge funds

Raye uses a cost–benefit approach to rebalancing and recommends that global equities have a wider rebalancing range than the other asset classes.

1. Using the economic balance sheet approach, the Laws' economic net worth is *closest* to:

   A. $925,000.

   B. $1,425,000.

   C. $1,675,000.

2. Using an economic balance sheet, which of the Laws' current financial assets is *most* concerning from an asset allocation perspective?

   A. Equities

   B. Real estate

   C. Fixed income

3. Raye believes the previous adviser's specification for debt is incorrect given that, for purposes of asset allocation, asset classes should be:

   A. diversifying.

   B. mutually exclusive.

   C. relatively homogeneous.

4. Raye believes the previous adviser's asset class specifications for equity and derivatives are inappropriate given that, for purposes of asset allocation, asset classes should be:

   A. diversifying.

   B. mutually exclusive.

   C. relatively homogeneous.

5. To address his concern regarding the previous adviser's asset allocation approach, Raye should assess the Laws' portfolio using:

   A. a homogeneous and mutually exclusive asset class–based risk analysis.

   B. a multifactor risk model to control systematic risk factors in asset allocation.

   C. an asset class–based asset allocation approach to construct a diversified portfolio.

6. Based on Exhibit 1, which portfolio *best* meets the Laws' education goal for their children?

   A. Portfolio 1

   B. Portfolio 2

   C. Portfolio 3

7. Based on Exhibit 1, which portfolio *best* meets the Laws' goal to fund an endowment for their alma mater?

   A. Portfolio 1

   B. Portfolio 2

   C. Portfolio 3

8. Raye's approach to rebalancing global equities is consistent with:

   A. the Laws' being risk averse.

   B. global equities' having higher transaction costs than other asset classes.

   C. global equities' having lower correlations with other asset classes.

SOLUTIONS

1. A is correct. The Laws' economic net worth is closest to $925,000. An economic balance sheet includes conventional financial assets and liabilities, as well as extended portfolio assets and liabilities that are relevant in making asset allocation decisions. The economic balance sheet for the Law family is shown in the following exhibit.

Assets		Liabilities and Economic Net Worth	
Financial Assets		*Financial Liabilities*	
Fixed income	450,000	Mortgage debt	225,000
Real estate	400,000		
Equity	800,000		
Extended Assets		*Extended Liabilities*	
Human capital	1,025,000	Children's education	275,000
		Endowment funding	500,000
		Present value of consumption	750,000
Total Economic Assets	2,675,000	*Total Economic Liabilities*	1,750,000
		Economic Net Worth	925,000

Economic net worth is equal to total economic assets minus total economic liabilities ($2,675,000 − $1,750,000 = $925,000).

2. A is correct. The Laws' equity portfolio is heavily concentrated in WS stock (80% of the equity portfolio), and both Laws work at WS. Should WS encounter difficult economic circumstances, the investment value of WS stock and the Laws' human capital are both likely to be adversely affected. Thus, their investment in WS should be reviewed and their equity portfolio diversified further.

3. C is correct. In order to effectively specify asset classes for the purpose of asset allocation, assets within an asset class should be relatively homogeneous and have similar attributes. The previous adviser's specification of the debt asset class includes global investment-grade corporate bonds and real estate. This definition results in a non-homogeneous asset class.

4. A is correct. For risk control purposes, an asset class should be diversifying and should not have extremely high expected correlations with other classes. Because the returns to the equity and the derivatives asset classes are noted as being highly correlated, inclusion of both asset classes will result in duplication of risk exposures. Including both asset classes is not diversifying to the asset allocation.

5. B is correct. Raye believes the Laws' previous financial adviser followed an asset allocation approach that resulted in an overlap in risk factors among asset classes. A multifactor risk model approach can be used to address potential risk factor overlaps. Risk factor approaches to asset allocation focus on assigning investments to the investor's desired exposures to specified risk factors. These methods are premised on the observation that asset classes often exhibit some overlaps in

sources of risk.

6. A is correct. Portfolio 1 best meets the Laws' education goal for their children. The estimated present value of the Laws' expected education expense is $275,000. Given that the children will be starting college soon, and the Laws have a very strong desire to achieve this goal, Portfolio 1, which stresses liquidity and stability, is most appropriate to meet the Laws' short-term education goal.

7. B is correct. Portfolio 2 best meets the Laws' goal to fund an endowment for their alma mater in 20 years. In present value terms, the gift is valued at $500,000, with the Laws desiring a high probability of achieving this goal. Although slightly more conservative than the 75/25 global equity/bond mix, Portfolio 2 has a greater growth emphasis compared with Portfolios 1 and 3. Therefore, Portfolio 2 is best for funding the endowment at their alma mater given the goal's long-term horizon and the Laws' desire for a high probability of achieving it.

8. B is correct. Using the cost–benefit approach, higher transaction costs for an asset class imply wider rebalancing ranges. Raye's recommendation for a wider rebalancing range for global equities is consistent with the presence of higher transaction costs for global equities.

LEARNING MODULE

4

Principles of Asset Allocation

by Jean L.P. Brunel, CFA, Thomas M. Idzorek, CFA, and John M. Mulvey, PhD.

Jean L.P. Brunel, CFA, is at Brunel Associates LLC (USA). Thomas M. Idzorek, CFA, is at Morningstar (USA). John M. Mulvey, PhD, is at the Bendheim Center for Finance at Princeton University (USA).

LEARNING OUTCOMES

Mastery	The candidate should be able to:
☐	describe and evaluate the use of mean–variance optimization in asset allocation
☐	recommend and justify an asset allocation using mean–variance optimization
☐	interpret and evaluate an asset allocation in relation to an investor's economic balance sheet
☐	recommend and justify an asset allocation based on the global market portfolio
☐	discuss the use of Monte Carlo simulation and scenario analysis to evaluate the robustness of an asset allocation
☐	discuss asset class liquidity considerations in asset allocation
☐	explain absolute and relative risk budgets and their use in determining and implementing an asset allocation
☐	describe how client needs and preferences regarding investment risks can be incorporated into asset allocation
☐	describe the use of investment factors in constructing and analyzing an asset allocation
☐	describe and evaluate characteristics of liabilities that are relevant to asset allocation
☐	discuss approaches to liability-relative asset allocation
☐	recommend and justify a liability-relative asset allocation
☐	recommend and justify an asset allocation using a goals-based approach
☐	describe and evaluate heuristic and other approaches to asset allocation
☐	discuss factors affecting rebalancing policy

1   INTRODUCTION

Determining a strategic asset allocation is arguably the most important aspect of the investment process. This reading builds on the "Introduction to Asset Allocation" reading and focuses on several of the primary frameworks for developing an asset allocation, including asset-only mean–variance optimization, various liability-relative asset allocation techniques, and goals-based investing. Additionally, it touches on various other asset allocation techniques used by practitioners, as well as important related topics, such as rebalancing.

The process of creating a diversified, multi-asset class portfolio typically involves two separate steps. The first step is the asset allocation decision, which can refer to both the process and the result of determining long-term (strategic) exposures to the available asset classes (or risk factors) that make up the investor's opportunity set. Asset allocation is the first and primary step in translating the client's circumstances, objectives, and constraints into an appropriate portfolio (or, for some approaches, multiple portfolios) for achieving the client's goals within the client's tolerance for risk. The second step in creating a diversified, multi-asset-class portfolio involves implementation decisions that determine the specific investments (individual securities, pooled investment vehicles, and separate accounts) that will be used to implement the targeted allocations.

Although it is possible to carry out the asset allocation process and the implementation process simultaneously, in practice, these two steps are often separated for two reasons. First, the frameworks for simultaneously determining an asset allocation and its implementation are often complex. Second, in practice, many investors prefer to revisit their strategic asset allocation policy somewhat infrequently (e.g., annually or less frequently) in a dedicated asset allocation study, while most of these same investors prefer to revisit/monitor implementation vehicles (actual investments) far more frequently (e.g., monthly or quarterly).

Sections 2–9 cover the traditional mean–variance optimization (MVO) approach to asset allocation. We apply this approach in what is referred to as an "asset-only" setting, in which the goal is to create the most efficient mixes of asset classes in the absence of any liabilities. We highlight key criticisms of mean–variance optimization and methods used to address them. This section also covers risk budgeting in relation to asset allocation, factor-based asset allocation, and asset allocation with illiquid assets. The observation that almost all portfolios exist to help pay for what can be characterized as a "liability" leads to the next subject.

Sections 10–14 introduce liability-relative asset allocation—including a straightforward extension of mean–variance optimization known as surplus optimization. Surplus optimization is an economic balance sheet approach extended to the liability side of the balance sheet that finds the most efficient asset class mixes in the presence of liabilities. Liability-relative optimization is simultaneously concerned with the return of the assets, the change in value of the liabilities, and how assets and liabilities interact to determine the overall value or health of the total portfolio.

Sections 15–18 cover an increasingly popular approach to asset allocation called goals-based asset allocation. Conceptually, goals-based approaches are similar to liability-relative asset allocation in viewing risk in relation to specific needs or objectives associated with different time horizons and degrees of urgency.

Section 19 introduces some informal (heuristic) ways that asset allocations have been determined and other approaches to asset allocation that emphasize specific objectives.

Section 20 addresses the factors affecting choices that are made in developing specific policies relating to rebalancing to the strategic asset allocation. Factors discussed include transaction costs, correlations, volatility, and risk aversion[1]

ASSET-ONLY ASSET ALLOCATIONS AND MEAN–VARIANCE OPTIMIZATION

2

☐	describe and evaluate the use of mean–variance optimization in asset allocation
☐	recommend and justify an asset allocation using mean–variance optimization
☐	interpret and evaluate an asset allocation in relation to an investor's economic balance sheet
☐	recommend and justify an asset allocation based on the global market portfolio

In this section, we discuss several of the primary techniques and considerations involved in developing strategic asset allocations, leaving the issue of considering the liabilities to Sections 10–14 and the issue of tailoring the strategic asset allocation to meet specific goals to Sections 15–18.

We start by introducing mean–variance optimization, beginning with unconstrained optimization, prior to moving on to the more common mean–variance optimization problem in which the weights, in addition to summing to 1, are constrained to be positive (no shorting allowed). We present a detailed example, along with several variations, highlighting some of the important considerations in this approach. We also identify several criticisms of mean–variance optimization and the major ways these criticisms have been addressed in practice.

Mean–Variance Optimization: Overview

Mean–variance optimization (MVO), as introduced by Markowitz (1952, 1959), is perhaps the most common approach used in practice to develop and set asset allocation policy. Widely used on its own, MVO is also often the basis for more sophisticated approaches that overcome some of the limitations or weaknesses of MVO.

Markowitz recognized that whenever the returns of two assets are not perfectly correlated, the assets can be combined to form a portfolio whose risk (as measured by standard deviation or variance) is less than the weighted-average risk of the assets themselves. An additional and equally important observation is that as one adds assets to the portfolio, one should focus not on the individual risk characteristics of the additional assets but rather on those assets' effect on the risk characteristics of the entire portfolio. Mean–variance optimization provides us with a framework for determining how much to allocate to each asset in order to maximize the *expected* return of the portfolio for an *expected* level of risk. In this sense, mean–variance optimization is a risk-budgeting tool that helps investors to spend their risk budget—the amount of risk they are willing to assume—wisely. We emphasize the word "expected" because the inputs to mean–variance optimization are necessarily forward-looking estimates, and the resulting portfolios reflect the quality of the inputs.

---

1 In this reading, "volatility" is often used synonymously with "standard deviation."

Mean–variance optimization requires three sets of inputs: returns, risks (standard deviations), and pair-wise correlations for the assets in the opportunity set. The objective function is often expressed as follows:

$$U_m = E\left(R_m\right) - 0.005\lambda\sigma_m^2 \tag{1}$$

where

U_m = the investor's utility for asset mix (allocation) m

R_m = the return for asset mix m

λ = the investor's risk aversion coefficient

σ_m^2 = the expected variance of return for asset mix m

The risk aversion coefficient (λ) characterizes the investor's risk–return trade-off; in this context, it is the rate at which an investor will forgo expected return for less variance. The value of 0.005 in Equation 1 is based on the assumption that $E(R_m)$ and σ_m are expressed as percentages rather than as decimals. (In using Equation 1, omit % signs.) If those quantities were expressed as decimals, the 0.005 would change to 0.5. For example, if $E(R_m)$ = 0.10, λ = 2, and σ = 0.20 (variance is 0.04), then U_m is 0.06, or 6% [= 0.10 – 0.5(2)(0.04)]. In this case, U_m can be interpreted as a certainty-equivalent return—that is, the utility value of the risky return offered by the asset mix, stated in terms of the risk-free return that the investor would value equally. In Equation 1, 0.005 merely scales the second term appropriately.

In words, the objective function says that the value of an asset mix for an investor is equal to the expected return of the asset mix minus a penalty that is equal to one-half of the expected variance of the asset mix scaled by the investor's risk aversion coefficient. Optimization involves selecting the asset mix with the highest such value (certainty equivalent). Smaller risk aversion coefficients result in relatively small penalties for risk, leading to aggressive asset mixes. Conversely, larger risk aversion coefficients result in relatively large penalties for risk, leading to conservative asset mixes. A value of λ = 0 corresponds to a risk-neutral investor because it implies indifference to volatility. Most investors' risk aversion is consistent with λ between 1 and 10.[2] Empirically, λ = 4 can be taken to represent a moderately risk-averse investor, although the specific value is sensitive to the opportunity set in question and to market volatility.

In the absence of constraints, there is a closed-form solution that calculates, for a given set of inputs, the single set of weights (allocation) to the assets in the opportunity set that maximizes the investor's utility. Typically, this single set of weights is relatively extreme, with very large long and short positions in each asset class. Except in the special case in which the expected returns are derived using the reverse-optimization process of Sharpe (1974), the expected-utility-maximizing weights will not add up to 100%. We elaborate on reverse optimization in Section 19.

In most real-world applications, asset allocation weights must add up to 100%, reflecting a fully invested, non-leveraged portfolio. From an optimization perspective, when seeking the asset allocation weights that maximize the investor's utility, one must constrain the asset allocation weights to sum to 1 (100%). This constraint that weights sum to 100% is referred to as the "budget constraint" or "unity constraint." The inclusion of this constraint, or any other constraint, moves us from a problem that has a closed-form solution to a problem that must be solved numerically using optimization techniques.

In contrast to the single solution (single set of weights) that is often associated with unconstrained optimization (one could create an efficient frontier using unconstrained weights, but it is seldom done in practice), Markowitz's mean–variance

---

2 See Ang (2014, p. 44).

optimization paradigm is most often identified with an efficient frontier that plots all potential efficient asset mixes subject to some common constraints. In addition to a typical budget constraint that the weights must sum to 1 (100% in percentage terms), the next most common constraint allows only positive weights or allocations (i.e., no negative or short positions).

Efficient asset mixes are combinations of the assets in the opportunity set that maximize expected return per unit of expected risk or, alternatively (and equivalently), minimize expected risk for a given level of expected return. To find all possible efficient mixes that collectively form the efficient frontier, *conceptually* the optimizer iterates through all the possible values of the risk aversion coefficient (λ) and for each value finds the combination of assets that maximizes expected utility. We have used the word *conceptually* because there are different techniques for carrying out the optimization that may vary slightly from our description, even though the solution (efficient frontier and efficient mixes) is the same. The efficient mix at the far left of the frontier with the lowest risk is referred to as the global minimum variance portfolio, while the portfolio at the far right of the frontier is the maximum expected return portfolio. In the absence of constraints beyond the budget and non-negativity constraints, the maximum expected return portfolio consists of a 100% allocation to the single asset with the highest expected return (which is not necessarily the asset with the highest level of risk).

RISK AVERSION

Unfortunately, it is extremely difficult to precisely estimate a given investor's risk aversion coefficient (λ). Best practices suggest that when estimating risk aversion (or, conversely, risk tolerance), one should examine both the investor's *preference* for risk (willingness to take risk) and the investor's *capacity* for taking risk. Risk preference is a subjective measure and typically focuses on how an investor feels about and potentially reacts to the ups and downs of portfolio value. The level of return an investor hopes to earn can influence the investor's willingness to take risk, but investors must be realistic when setting such objectives. Risk capacity is an objective measure of the investor's ability to tolerate portfolio losses and the potential decrease in future consumption associated with those losses.[3] The psychometric literature has developed validated questionnaires, such as that of Grable and Joo (2004), to approximately locate an investor's risk preference, although this result then needs to be blended with risk capacity to determine risk tolerance. For individuals, risk capacity is affected by factors such as net worth, income, the size of an emergency fund in relation to consumption needs, and the rate at which the individual saves out of gross income, according to the practice of financial planners noted in Grable (2008).

With this guidance in mind, we move forward with a relatively global opportunity set, in this case defined from the point of view of an investor from the United Kingdom with an approximate 10-year time horizon. The analysis is carried out in British pounds (GBP), and none of the currency exposure is hedged. Exhibit 1 identifies 12 asset classes within the universe of available investments and a set of plausible forward-looking capital market assumptions: expected returns, standard deviations, and correlations. The reading on capital market expectations covers how such inputs may be developed.[4] In the exhibit, three significant digits at most are shown, but the subsequent analysis is based on full precision.

---

3 *Risk preference* and *risk capacity* are sometimes referred to as the willingness and the ability to take risk, respectively.
4 The standard deviations and correlations in Exhibit 1 are based on historical numbers, while expected returns come from reverse optimization (described later).

TIME HORIZON

Mean–variance optimization is a "single-period" framework in which the single period could be a week, a month, a year, or some other time period. When working in a "strategic" setting, many practitioners typically find it most intuitive to work with annual capital market assumptions, even though the investment time horizon could be considerably longer (e.g., 10 years). If the strategic asset allocation will not be re-evaluated within a long time frame, capital market assumptions should reflect the average annual distributions of returns expected over the entire investment time horizon. In most cases, investors revisit the strategic asset allocation decision more frequently, such as annually or every three years, rerunning the analysis and making adjustments to the asset allocation; thus, the annual capital market assumption often reflects the expectations associated with the evaluation horizon (e.g., one year or three years).

Exhibit 1: Hypothetical UK-Based Investor's Opportunity Set with Expected Returns, Standard Deviations, and Correlations

Panel A: Expected Returns and Standard Deviations

Asset Class	Expected Return (%)	Standard Deviation (%)
UK large cap	6.6	14.8
UK mid cap	6.9	16.7
UK small cap	7.1	19.6
US equities	7.8	15.7
Europe ex UK equities	8.6	19.6
Asia Pacific ex Japan equities	8.5	20.9
Japan equities	6.4	15.2
Emerging market equities	9.0	23.0
Global REITs	9.0	22.5
Global ex UK bonds	4.0	10.4
UK bonds	2.9	6.1
Cash	2.5	0.7

Panel B: Correlations

	UK Large Cap	UK Mid Cap	UK Small Cap	US Equities	Europe ex UK Equities	Asia Pacific ex Japan Equities	Japan Equities	Emerging Market Equities	Global REITs	Global ex UK Bonds	UK Bonds	Cash
UK large cap	1.00	0.86	0.79	0.76	0.88	0.82	0.55	0.78	0.64	−0.12	−0.12	−0.06
UK mid cap	0.86	1.00	0.95	0.76	0.84	0.75	0.51	0.74	0.67	−0.16	−0.10	−0.17
UK small cap	0.79	0.95	1.00	0.67	0.79	0.70	0.49	0.71	0.61	−0.22	−0.15	−0.17
US equities	0.76	0.76	0.67	1.00	0.81	0.72	0.62	0.69	0.77	0.14	0.00	−0.12
Europe ex UK equities	0.88	0.84	0.79	0.81	1.00	0.82	0.60	0.80	0.72	0.04	−0.04	−0.03

	UK Large Cap	UK Mid Cap	UK Small Cap	US Equities	Europe ex UK Equities	Asia Pacific ex Japan Equities	Japan Equities	Emerging Market Equities	Global REITs	Global ex UK Bonds	UK Bonds	Cash
Asia Pacific ex Japan equities	0.82	0.75	0.70	0.72	0.82	1.00	0.54	0.94	0.67	0.00	−0.02	0.02
Japan equities	0.55	0.51	0.49	0.62	0.60	0.54	1.00	0.56	0.52	0.18	0.07	−0.01
Emerging market equities	0.78	0.74	0.71	0.69	0.80	0.94	0.56	1.00	0.62	−0.02	−0.03	0.04
Global REITs	0.64	0.67	0.61	0.77	0.72	0.67	0.52	0.62	1.00	0.16	0.18	−0.15
Global ex UK bonds	−0.12	−0.16	−0.22	0.14	0.04	0.00	0.18	−0.02	0.16	1.00	0.62	0.24
UK bonds	−0.12	−0.10	−0.15	0.00	−0.04	−0.02	0.07	−0.03	0.18	0.62	1.00	0.07
Cash	−0.06	−0.17	−0.17	−0.12	−0.03	0.02	−0.01	0.04	−0.15	0.24	0.07	1.00

The classification of asset classes in the universe of available investments may vary according to local practices. For example, in the United States and some other larger markets, it is common to classify equities by market capitalization, whereas the practice of classifying equities by valuation ("growth" versus "value") is less common outside of the United States. Similarly, with regard to fixed income, some asset allocators may classify bonds based on various attributes—nominal versus inflation linked, corporate versus government issued, investment grade versus non-investment grade (high yield)—and/or by maturity/duration (short, intermediate, and long). By means of the non-negativity constraint and using a reverse-optimization procedure (to be explained later) based on asset class market values to generate expected return estimates, we control the typically high sensitivity of the composition of efficient portfolios to expected return estimates (discussed further in Sections 19 and 20). Without such precautions, we would often find that efficient portfolios are highly concentrated in a subset of the available asset classes.

Running this set of capital market assumptions through a mean–variance optimizer with the traditional non-negativity and unity constraints produces the efficient frontier depicted in Exhibit 2. We have augmented this efficient frontier with some non-traditional information that will assist with the understanding of some key concepts related to the efficient frontier. A risk-free return of 2.5% is used in calculating the reserve-optimized expected returns as well as the Sharpe ratios in Exhibit 2.

Exhibit 2: Efficient Frontier—Base Case

Expected Return (%)
Slope, Sharpe Ratio, Utility

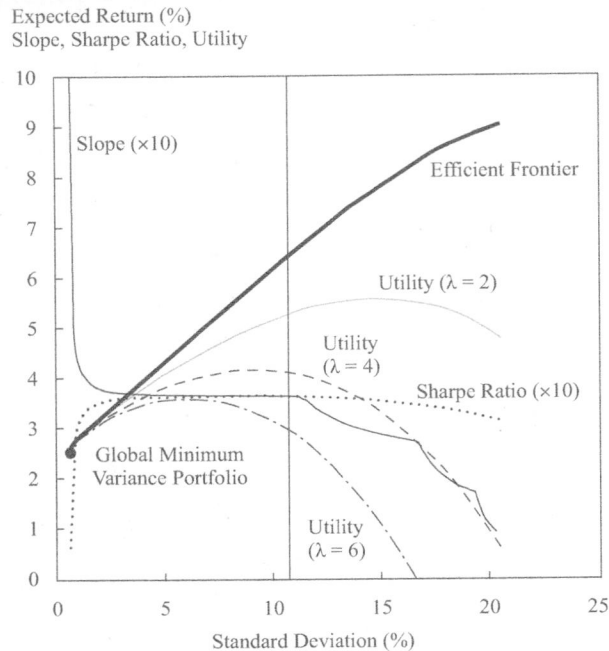

The slope of the efficient frontier is greatest at the far left of the efficient frontier, at the point representing the global minimum variance portfolio. Slope represents the rate at which expected return increases per increase in risk. As one moves to the right, in the direction of increasing risk, the slope decreases; it is lowest at the point representing the maximum return portfolio. Thus, as one moves from left to right along the efficient frontier, the investor takes on larger and larger amounts of risk for smaller and smaller increases in expected return. The "kinks" in the line representing the slope (times 10) of the efficient frontier correspond to portfolios (known as corner portfolios) in which an asset either enters or leaves the efficient mix.

For most investors, at the far left of the efficient frontier, the increases in expected return associated with small increases in expected risk represent a desirable trade-off. The risk aversion coefficient identifies the specific point on the efficient frontier at which the investor refuses to take on additional risk because he or she feels the associated increase in expected return is not high enough to compensate for the increase in risk. Of course, each investor makes this trade-off differently.

For this particular efficient frontier, the three expected utility curves plot the solution to Equation 1 for three different risk aversion coefficients: 2.0, 4.0, and 6.0, respectively.[5] For a given risk aversion coefficient, the appropriate efficient mix from the efficient frontier is simply the mix in which expected utility is highest (i.e., maximized). As illustrated in Exhibit 2, a lower risk aversion coefficient leads to a riskier (higher) point on the efficient frontier, while a higher risk aversion coefficient leads to a more conservative (lower) point on the efficient frontier.

The vertical line (at volatility of 10.88%) identifies the asset mix with the highest Sharpe ratio; it intersects the Sharpe ratio line at a value of 3.7 (an unscaled value of 0.37). This portfolio is also represented by the intersection of the slope line and the Sharpe ratio line.

---

5 Numbers have been rounded to increase readability.

Exhibit 3 is an efficient frontier asset allocation area graph. Each vertical cross section identifies the asset allocation at a point along the efficient frontier; thus, the vertical cross section at the far left, with nearly 100% cash, is the asset allocation of the minimum variance portfolio, and the vertical cross section at the far right, with 45% in emerging markets and 55% in global REITs, is the optimal asset allocation for a standard deviation of 20.5%, the highest level of portfolio volatility shown. In this example, cash is treated as a risky asset; although its return volatility is very low, because it is less than perfectly correlated with the other asset classes, mixing it with small amounts of other asset classes reduces risk further. The vertical line identifies the asset mix with the highest Sharpe ratio and corresponds to the similar line shown on the original efficient frontier graph (Exhibit 2). The asset allocation mixes are well diversified for most of the first half of the efficient frontier, and in fact, for a large portion of the efficient frontier, all 12 asset classes in our opportunity set receive a positive allocation.[6]

Exhibit 3: Efficient Frontier Asset Allocation Area Graph—Base Case

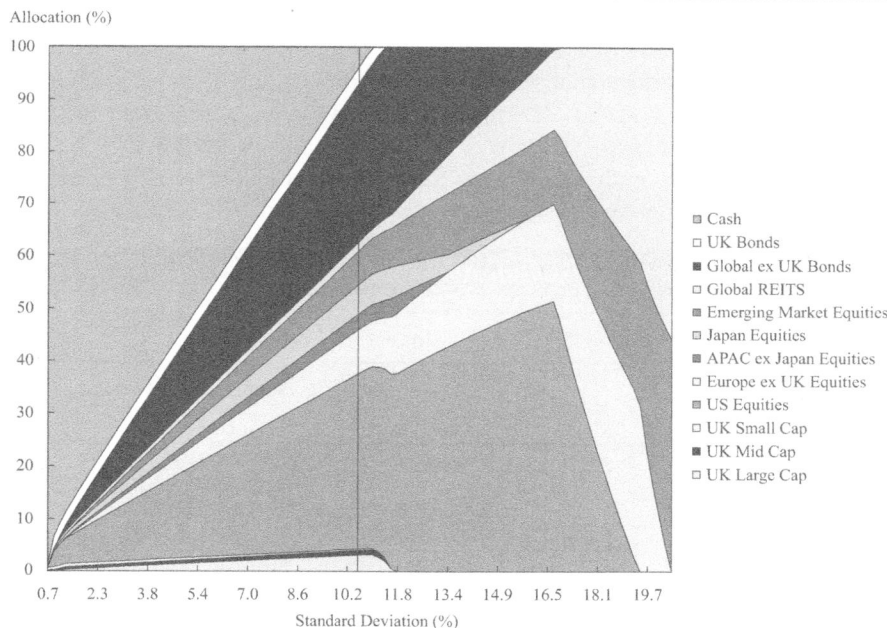

The investment characteristics of potential asset mixes based on mean–variance theory are often further investigated by means of Monte Carlo simulation, as discussed in Section 3. Several observations from theory and practice are relevant to narrowing the choices.

Equation 1 indicates that the basic approach to asset allocation involves estimating the investor's risk aversion parameter and then finding the efficient mix that maximizes expected utility. When the risk aversion coefficient has not been estimated, the investor may be able to identify the maximum tolerable level of portfolio return volatility. If

---

6 Studying Exhibit 3 closely, one notices distinct regime shifts where the rate at which allocations are made to asset classes changes so that a line segment with a different slope begins. These regime shifts occur at what are called *corner portfolios*. The efficient mixes between two adjacent corner portfolios are simply linear combinations of those portfolios. The efficient frontier asset allocation area graph helps to clarify this result. More formally, corner portfolios are points on the efficient frontier at which an asset class either enters or leaves the efficient mix or a constraint either becomes binding or is no longer binding.

that level is 10% per annum, for example, only the part of the efficient frontier associated with volatility less than or equal to 10% is relevant. This approach is justifiable because for a given efficient frontier, every value of the risk aversion coefficient can be associated with a value of volatility that identifies the best point on the efficient frontier for the investor; the investor may also have experience with thinking in terms of volatility. In addition, when the investor has a numerical return objective, he or she can further narrow the range of potential efficient mixes by identifying the efficient portfolios expected to meet that return objective. For example, if the return objective is 5%, one can select the asset allocation with a 5% expected return.

Example 1 illustrates the use of Equation 1 and shows the adaptability of MVO by introducing the choice problem in the context of an investor who also has a shortfall risk concern.

EXAMPLE 1

Mean–Variance-Efficient Portfolio Choice 1

An investment adviser is counseling Aimée Goddard, a client who recently inherited €1,200,000 and who has above-average risk tolerance ($\lambda = 2$). Because Goddard is young and one of her goals is to fund a comfortable retirement, she wants to earn returns that will outpace inflation in the long term. Goddard expects to liquidate €60,000 of the inherited portfolio in 12 months to fund the down payment on a house. She states that it is important for her to be able to take out the €60,000 without invading the initial capital of €1,200,000. Exhibit 4 shows three alternative strategic asset allocations.

Exhibit 4: Strategic Asset Allocation Choices for Goddard

	Investor's Forecasts	
Asset Allocation	Expected Return	Standard Deviation of Return
A	10.00%	20%
B	7.00	10
C	5.25	5

Note: In addressing 2, calculate the minimum return, R_L, that needs to be achieved to meet the investor's objective not to invade capital, using the expression ratio $[E(R_P) - R_L]/\sigma_P$, which reflects the probability of exceeding the minimum given a normal return distribution assumption in a safety-first approach.[7]

1. Based only on Goddard's risk-adjusted expected returns for the asset allocations, which asset allocation would she prefer?

Solution:

Using Equation 1,

---

[7] See the Level I CFA Program reading "Common Probability Distributions" for coverage of Roy's safety-first criterion.

$$U_m = E(R_m) - 0.005\lambda\,\sigma_m^2$$
$$= E(R_m) - 0.005\,(2)\,\sigma_m^2$$
$$= E(R_m) - 0.01\,\sigma_m^2$$

So Goddard's utility for Asset Allocations A, B, and C are as follows:

$$U_A = E(R_A) - 0.01\sigma_A^2$$

$$= 10.0 - 0.01(20)^2$$

$$= 10.0 - 4.0$$

$$= 6.0 \text{ or } 6.0\%$$

$$U_B = E(R_B) - 0.01\sigma_B^2$$

$$= 7.0 - 0.01(10)^2$$

$$= 7.0 - 1.0$$

$$= 6.0 \text{ or } 6.0\%$$

$$U_C = E(R_C) - 0.01\sigma_C^2$$

$$= 5.25 - 0.01(5)^2$$

$$= 5.25 - 0.25$$

$$= 5.0 \text{ or } 5.0\%$$

Goddard would be indifferent between A and B based only on their common perceived certainty-equivalent return of 6%.

2. Recommend and justify a strategic asset allocation for Goddard.

Solution:

Because €60,000/€1,200,000 is 5.0%, for any return less than 5.0%, Goddard will need to invade principal when she liquidates €60,000. So 5% is a threshold return level.

To decide which of the three allocations is best for Goddard, we calculate the ratio $[E(R_P) - R_L]/\sigma_P$:

Allocation A   (10% − 5%)/20% = 0.25

Allocation B   (7% − 5%)/10% = 0.20

Allocation C   (5.25% − 5%)/5% = 0.05

Both Allocations A and B have the same expected utility, but Allocation A has a higher probability of meeting the threshold 5% return than Allocation B. Therefore, A would be the recommended strategic asset allocation.

There are several different approaches to determining an allocation to cash and cash equivalents, such as government bills. Exhibit 1 included cash among the assets for which we conducted an optimization to trace out an efficient frontier. The return to cash over a short time horizon is essentially certain in nominal terms. One approach to asset allocation separates out cash and cash equivalents as a (nominally) risk-free asset and calculates an efficient frontier of risky assets. Alternatively, a ray from the risk-free rate (a point on the return axis) tangent to the risky-asset efficient frontier (with cash excluded) then defines a linear efficient frontier. The efficient frontier then consists of combinations of the risk-free asset with the tangency portfolio (which has the highest Sharpe ratio among portfolios on the risky-asset efficient frontier).

A number of standard finance models (including Tobin two-fund separation) adopt this treatment of cash. According to two-fund separation, if investors can borrow or lend at the risk-free rate, they will choose the tangency portfolio for the risky-asset holdings and borrow at the risk-free rate to leverage the position in that portfolio to achieve a higher expected return, or they will split money between the tangency portfolio and the risk-free asset to reach a position with lower risk and lower expected return than that represented by the tangency portfolio. Since over horizons that are longer than the maturity of a money market instrument, the return earned would not be known, another approach that is well established in practice and reflected in Exhibit 1 is to include cash in the optimization. The amount of cash indicated by an optimization may be adjusted in light of short-term liquidity needs; for example, some financial advisers advocate that individuals hold an amount of cash equivalent to six months of expenses. All of these approaches are reasonable alternatives in practice.

Although we will treat cash as a risky asset in the following discussions, in Example 2, we stop to show the application of the alternative approach based on distinguishing a risk-free asset.

EXAMPLE 2

A Strategic Asset Allocation Based on Distinguishing a Nominal Risk-Free Asset

The Caflandia Foundation for the Fine Arts (CFFA) is a hypothetical charitable organization established to provide funding to Caflandia museums for their art acquisition programs.

CFFA's overall investment objective is to maintain its portfolio's real purchasing power after distributions. CFFA targets a 4% annual distribution of assets. CFFA has the following current specific investment policies.

Return objective

CFFA's assets shall be invested with the objective of earning an average nominal 6.5% annual return. This level reflects a spending rate of 4%, an expected inflation rate of 2%, and a 40 bp cost of earning investment returns. The calculation is $(1.04)(1.02)(1.004) - 1 = 0.065$, or 6.5%.

Risk considerations

CFFA's assets shall be invested to minimize the level of standard deviation of return subject to satisfying the expected return objective.

The investment office of CFFA distinguishes a nominally risk-free asset. As of the date of the optimization, the risk-free rate is determined to be 2.2%.

Exhibit 5 gives key outputs from a mean–variance optimization in which asset class weights are constrained to be non-negative.

Exhibit 5: Corner Portfolios Defining the Risky-Asset Efficient Frontier

Portfolio Number	Expected Nominal Returns	Standard Deviation	Sharpe Ratio
1	9.50%	18.00%	0.406
2	8.90	15.98	0.419

Portfolio Number	Expected Nominal Returns	Standard Deviation	Sharpe Ratio
3	8.61	15.20	0.422
4	7.24	11.65	0.433
5	5.61	7.89	0.432
6	5.49	7.65	0.430
7	3.61	5.39	0.262

The portfolios shown are corner portfolios (see footnote 6), which as a group define the risky-asset efficient frontier in the sense that any portfolio on the frontier is a combination of the two corner portfolios that bracket it in terms of expected return.

1. Based only on the facts given, determine the most appropriate strategic asset allocation for CFFA given its stated investment policies.

Solution:

An 85%/15% combination of Portfolio 4 and the risk-free asset is the most appropriate asset allocation. This combination has the required 6.5% expected return with the minimum level of risk. Stated another way, this combination defines the efficient portfolio at a 6.5% level of expected return based on the linear efficient frontier created by the introduction of a risk-free asset.

Note that Portfolio 4 has the highest Sharpe ratio and is the tangency portfolio. With an expected return of 7.24%, it can be combined with the risk-free asset, with a return of 2.2%, to achieve an expected return of 6.5%:

$$6.50 = 7.24w + 2.2(1 - w)$$

$$w = 0.853$$

Placing about 85% of assets in Portfolio 4 and 15% in the risk-free asset achieves an efficient portfolio with expected return of 6.5 with a volatility of 0.853(11.65) = 9.94%. (The risk-free asset has no return volatility by assumption and, also by assumption, zero correlation with any risky portfolio return.) This portfolio lies on a linear efficient frontier formed by a ray from the risk-free rate to the tangency portfolio and can be shown to have the same Sharpe ratio as the tangency portfolio, 0.433. The combination of Portfolio 4 with Portfolio 5 to achieve a 6.5% expected return would have a lower Sharpe ratio and would not lie on the efficient frontier.

Asset allocation decisions have traditionally been made considering only the investor's investment portfolio (and financial liabilities) and not the total picture that includes human capital and other non-traded assets (and liabilities), which are missing in a traditional balance sheet. Taking such extended assets and liabilities into account can lead to improved asset allocation decisions, however.

Depending on the nature of an individual's career, human capital can provide relatively stable cash flows similar to bond payments. At the other extreme, the cash flows from human capital can be much more volatile and uncertain, reflecting a lumpy, commission-based pay structure or perhaps a career in a seasonal business. For many individuals working in stable job markets, the cash flows associated with their human capital are somewhat like those of an inflation-linked bond, relatively consistent and tending to increase with inflation. If human capital is a relatively large component of the individual's total economic worth, accounting for this type of hidden asset in an asset allocation setting is extremely important and would presumably increase the individual's capacity to take on risk.

Let us look at a hypothetical example. Emma Beel is a 45-year-old tenured university professor in London. Capital market assumptions are as before (see Exhibit 1). Beel has GBP 1,500,000 in liquid financial assets, largely due to a best-selling book. Her employment as a tenured university professor is viewed as very secure and produces cash flows that resemble those of a very large, inflation-adjusted, long-duration bond portfolio. The net present value of her human capital is estimated at GBP 500,000. Beel inherited her grandmother's home on the edge of the city, valued at GBP 750,000. The results of a risk tolerance questionnaire that considers both risk preference and risk capacity suggest that Beel should have an asset allocation involving moderate risk. Furthermore, given our earlier assumption that the collective market risk aversion coefficient is 4.0, we assume that the risk aversion coefficient of a moderately risk-averse investor is approximately 4.0, from a total wealth perspective.

To account for Beel's human capital and residential real estate, these two asset classes were modeled and added to the optimization. Beel's human capital of GBP 500,000 was modeled as 70% UK long-duration inflation-linked bonds, 15% UK corporate bonds, and 15% UK equities.[8] Residential real estate was modeled based on a de-smoothed residential property index for London. (We will leave the complexities of modeling liabilities to Sections 10–14.) Beel's assets include those shown in Exhibit 6.

Exhibit 6: Emma Beel's Assets

Asset	Value (GBP)	Percentage
Liquid financial assets	1,500,000	54.55
UK residential real estate	750,000	27.27
Human capital	500,000	18.18
	2,750,000	100

Beel's UK residential real estate (representing the London house) and human capital were added to the optimization opportunity set. Additionally, working under the assumption that Beel's house and human capital are non-tradable assets, the optimizer was forced to allocate 27.27% or more to UK residential real estate and 18.18% to human capital and then determined the optimal asset allocation based on a risk aversion coefficient of 4. Beel's expected utility is maximized by an efficient asset allocation with volatility of approximately 8.2%. Exhibit 7 displays the resulting asset allocation area graph.

---

8 These weights were used to create the return composite representing Beel's human capital that was used in the asset allocation optimization.

Exhibit 7: Efficient Frontier Asset Allocation Area Graph—Balance Sheet Approach

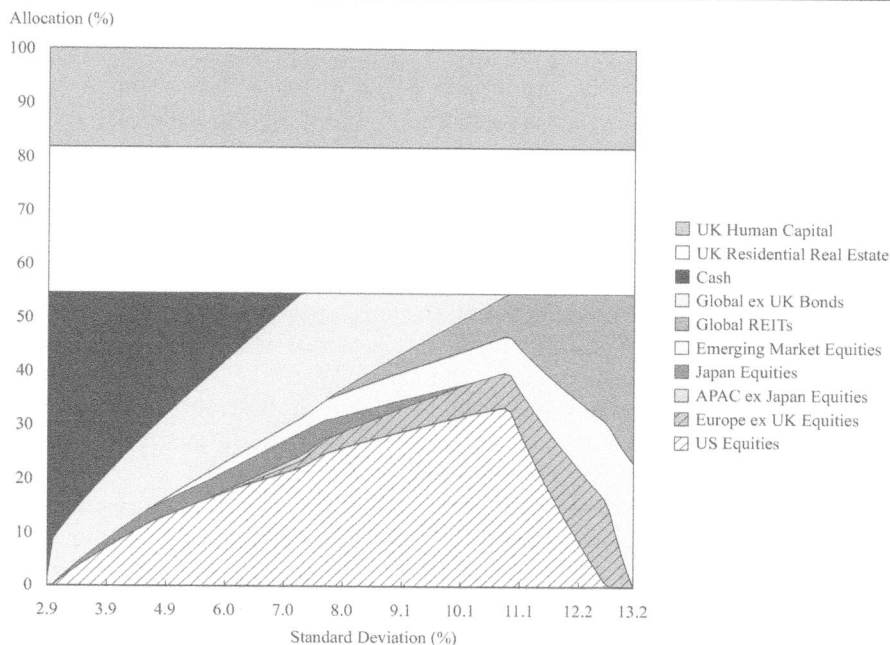

Looking past the constrained allocations to human capital and UK residential real estate, the remaining allocations associated with Beel's liquid financial assets do not include UK equities or UK fixed income. Each of these three asset classes is relatively highly correlated with either UK residential real estate or UK human capital.[9]

MONTE CARLO SIMULATION

3

<table>
<tr><td>☐</td><td>discuss the use of Monte Carlo simulation and scenario analysis to evaluate the robustness of an asset allocation</td></tr>
<tr><td>☐</td><td>recommend and justify an asset allocation using mean–variance optimization</td></tr>
</table>

Monte Carlo simulation complements MVO by addressing the limitations of MVO as a single-period framework. Additionally, in the case in which the investor's risk tolerance is either unknown or in need of further validation, Monte Carlo simulation can help paint a realistic picture of potential future outcomes, including the likelihood of meeting various goals, the distribution of the portfolio's expected value through time, and potential maximum drawdowns. Simulation also provides a tool for investigating the effects of trading/rebalancing costs and taxes and the interaction of evolving financial markets with asset allocation. It is important to note that not all Monte Carlo simulation tools are the same: They vary significantly in their ability

---

9 For additional information on applying a total balance sheet approach, see, for example, Blanchett and Straehl (2015) or Rudd and Siegel (2013).

to model non-normal multivariate returns, serial and cross-correlations, tax rates, distribution requirements, an evolving asset allocation schedule (target-date glide path), non-traditional investments (e.g., annuities), and human capital (based on age, geography, education, and/or occupation).

Using Monte Carlo simulation, an investment adviser can effectively grapple with a range of practical issues that are difficult or impossible to formulate analytically. Consider rebalancing to a strategic asset allocation for a taxable investor. We can readily calculate the impact of taxes during a single time period. Also, in a single-period setting, as assumed by MVO, rebalancing is irrelevant. In the multi-period world of most investment problems, however, the portfolio will predictably be rebalanced, triggering the realization of capital gains and losses. Given a specific rebalancing rule, different strategic asset allocations will result in different patterns of tax payments (and different transaction costs too). Formulating the multi-period problem mathematically would be a daunting challenge. We could more easily incorporate the interaction between rebalancing and taxes in a Monte Carlo simulation.

We will examine a simple multi-period problem to illustrate the use of Monte Carlo simulation, evaluating the range of outcomes for wealth that may result from a strategic asset allocation (and not incorporating taxes).

The value of wealth at the terminal point of an investor's time horizon is a possible criterion for choosing among asset allocations. Future wealth incorporates the interaction of risk and return. The need for Monte Carlo simulation in evaluating an asset allocation depends on whether there are cash flows into or out of the portfolio over time. For a given asset allocation with no cash flows, the sequence of returns is irrelevant; ending wealth will be path independent (unaffected by the sequence or path of returns through time). With cash flows, the sequence is also irrelevant if simulated returns are independent, identically distributed random variables. We could find expected terminal wealth and percentiles of terminal wealth analytically.[10] Investors save/deposit money in and spend money out of their portfolios; thus, in the more typical case, terminal wealth is path dependent (the sequence of returns matters) because of the interaction of cash flows and returns. When terminal wealth is path dependent, an analytical approach is not feasible but Monte Carlo simulation is. Example 3 applies Monte Carlo simulation to evaluate the strategic asset allocation of an investor who regularly withdraws from the portfolio.

EXAMPLE 3

Monte Carlo Simulation for a Retirement Portfolio with a Proposed Asset Allocation

Malala Ali, a resident of the hypothetical country of Caflandia, has sought the advice of an investment adviser concerning her retirement portfolio. At the end of 2017, she is 65 years old and holds a portfolio valued at CAF$1 million. Ali would like to withdraw CAF$40,000 a year to supplement the corporate pension she has begun to receive. Given her health and family history, Ali believes she should plan for a retirement lasting 25 years. She is also concerned about passing along a portion of her portfolio to the families of her three children; she hopes that at least the portfolio's current real value can go to them. Consulting with her adviser, Ali has expressed this desire quantitatively: She wants the median value of her bequest to her children to be no less than her portfolio's current value of CAF$1 million in real terms. The median is the 50th percentile outcome.

---

10 Making a plausible statistical assumption, such as a lognormal distribution, for ending wealth.

The asset allocation of her retirement portfolio is currently 50/50 Caflandia equities/Caflandia intermediate-term government bonds. Ali and her adviser have decided on the following set of capital market expectations (Exhibit 8):

Exhibit 8: Caflandia Capital Market Expectations

	Investor's Forecasts	
Asset Class	Expected Return	Standard Deviation of Return
Caflandia equities	9.4%	20.4%
Caflandia bonds	5.6%	4.1%
Inflation	2.6%	

The predicted correlation between returns of Caflandia equities and Caflandia intermediate-term government bonds is 0.15.

With the current asset allocation, the expected nominal return on Ali's retirement portfolio is 7.5% with a standard deviation of 11%. Exhibit 9 gives the results of the Monte Carlo simulation.[11] In Exhibit 9, the lowest curve represents, at various ages, levels of real wealth at or below which the 10% of worst real wealth outcomes lie (i.e., the 10th percentile for real wealth); curves above that represent, respectively, 25th, 50th, 75th, and 90th percentiles for real wealth.

Exhibit 9: Monte Carlo Simulation of Ending Real Wealth with Annual Cash Outflows

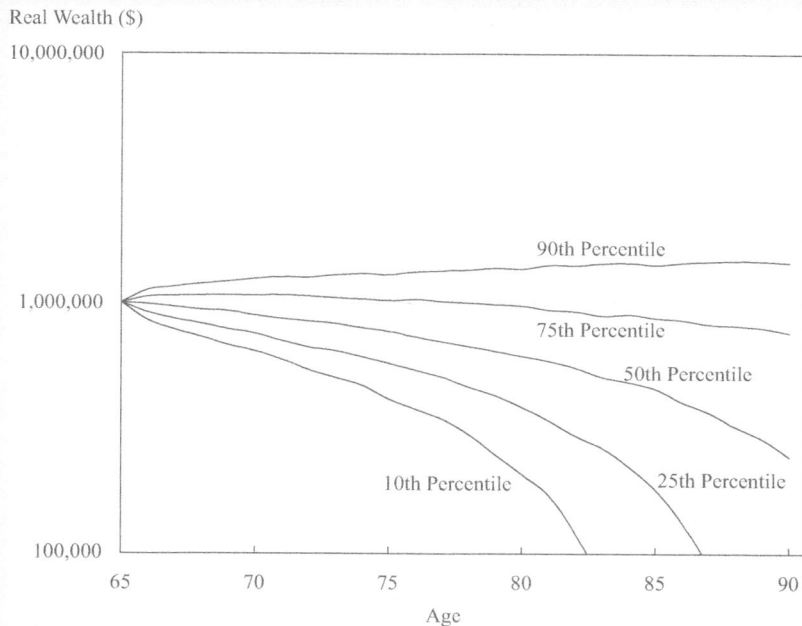

Based on the information given, address the following:

---

11 Note that the y-axis in this exhibit is specified using a logarithmic scale. The quantity CAF$1 million is the same distance from CAF$100,000 as CAF$10 million is from CAF$1 million because CAF$1 million is 10 times CAF$100,000, just as CAF$10 million is 10 times CAF$1 million. CAF$100,000 is 10^5, and CAF $1 million is 10^6. In Exhibit 9, a distance halfway between the CAF$100,000 and CAF$1 million hatch marks is $10^{5.5}$ = CAF$316,228.

1. Justify the presentation of ending wealth in terms of real rather than nominal wealth in Exhibit 9.

Solution:

Ali wants the median real value of her bequest to her children to be "no less than her portfolio's current value of CAF$1 million." We need to state future amounts in terms of today's values (i.e., in real dollars) to assess the purchasing power of those amounts relative to CAF$1 million today. Exhibit 9 thus gives the results of the Monte Carlo simulation in real dollar terms. The median real wealth at age 90 is clearly well below the target ending wealth of real CAF$1 million.

2. Is the current asset allocation expected to satisfy Ali's investment objectives?

Solution:

From Exhibit 9, we see that the median terminal (at age 90) value of the retirement portfolio in real dollars is less than the stated bequest goal of CAF$1 million. Therefore, the most likely bequest is less than the amount Ali has said she wants. The current asset allocation is not expected to satisfy all her investment objectives. Although one potential lever would be to invest more aggressively, given Ali's age and risk tolerance, this approach seems imprudent. An adviser may need to counsel that the desired size of the bequest may be unrealistic given Ali's desired income to support her expenditures. Ali will likely need to make a relatively tough choice between her living standard (spending less) and her desire to leave a CAF$1 million bequest in real terms. A third alternative would be to delay retirement, which may or may not be feasible.

4   CRITICISMS OF MEAN–VARIANCE OPTIMIZATION

☐ | describe and evaluate the use of mean–variance optimization in asset allocation

With this initial understanding of mean–variance optimization, we can now elaborate on some of the most common criticisms of it. The following criticisms and the ways they have been addressed motivate the balance of the coverage of MVO:

1. The outputs (asset allocations) are highly sensitive to small changes in the inputs.
2. The asset allocations tend to be highly concentrated in a subset of the available asset classes.
3. Many investors are concerned about more than the mean and variance of returns, the focus of MVO.
4. Although the asset allocations may appear diversified across assets, the sources of risk may not be diversified.
5. Most portfolios exist to pay for a liability or consumption series, and MVO allocations are not directly connected to what influences the value of the liability or the consumption series.

6. MVO is a single-period framework that does not take account of trading/rebalancing costs and taxes.

In the rest of Sections 2–9, we look at various approaches to addressing criticisms 1 and 2, giving some attention also to criticisms 3 and 4. Sections 10–18 present approaches to addressing criticism 5. "Asset Allocation with Real World Constraints" addresses some aspects of criticism 6.

It is important to understand that the first criticism above is not unique to MVO. Any optimization model that uses forward-looking quantities as inputs faces similar consequences of treating input values as capable of being determined with certainty. Sensitivity to errors in inputs is a problem that cannot be fully solved because it is inherent in the structure of optimization models that use as inputs forecasts of uncertain quantities.

To illustrate the importance of the quality of inputs, the sensitivity of asset weights in efficient portfolios to small changes in inputs, and the propensity of mean–variance optimization to allocate to a relatively small subset of the available asset classes, we made changes to the expected return of two asset classes in our base-case UK-centric opportunity set in Exhibit 1. We increased the expected return of Asia Pacific ex Japan equities from 8.5% to 9.0% and decreased the expected return of Europe ex UK equities from 8.6% to 8.1% (both changes are approximately 50 bps). We left all of the other inputs unchanged and reran the optimization. The efficient frontier as depicted in mean–variance space appears virtually unchanged (not shown); however, the efficient asset mixes of this new efficient frontier are dramatically different. Exhibit 10 displays the efficient frontier asset allocation area graph based on the slightly changed capital market assumptions. Notice the dramatic difference between Exhibit 10 and Exhibit 3. The small change in return assumptions has driven UK large cap, Europe ex-UK equities, and emerging market equities out of the efficient mixes, and the efficient mixes are now highly concentrated in a smaller subset of the available asset classes. Given that the expected returns of UK large cap and emerging market equities were unchanged, their disappearance from the efficient frontier is not intuitive.

Exhibit 10: Efficient Frontier Asset Allocation Area Graph—Changed Expected Returns

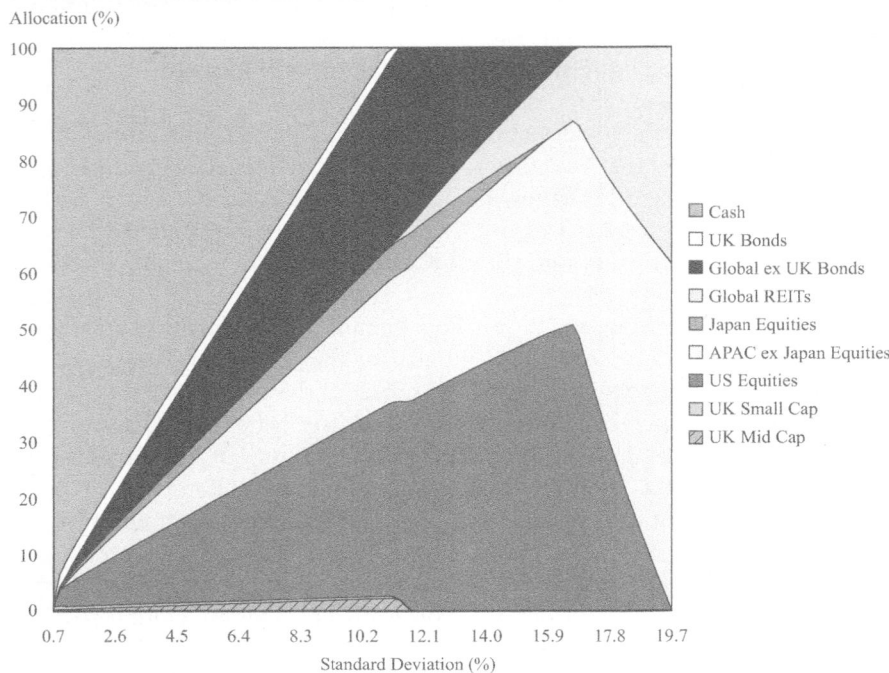

To aid with the comparison of Exhibit 10 with Exhibit 3, we identified three specific efficient asset allocation mixes and compared the version based on the ad hoc modification of expected returns to that of the base case. This comparison is shown in Exhibit 11.

Exhibit 11: Comparison of Select Efficient Asset Allocations—Ad Hoc Return Modification Allocations vs. Base-Case Allocations

	Modified 25/75	Base Case 25/75	Difference	Modified 50/50	Base Case 50/50	Difference	Modified 75/25	Base Case 75/25	Difference
UK large cap	0.0%	1.2%	−1.2%	0.0%	2.5%	−2.5%	0.0%	0.0%	0.0%
UK mid cap	0.8%	0.6%	0.3%	1.7%	0.8%	0.9%	0.0%	0.0%	0.0%
UK small cap	0.5%	0.5%	−0.1%	0.4%	0.4%	0.0%	0.0%	0.0%	0.0%
US equities	13.7%	13.8%	−0.1%	26.6%	26.8%	−0.2%	40.1%	40.5%	−0.4%
Europe ex UK equities	0.0%	2.7%	−2.7%	0.0%	6.5%	−6.5%	0.0%	13.2%	−13.2%
Asia Pacific ex Japan equities	7.5%	1.0%	6.5%	16.6%	2.3%	14.2%	26.8%	1.5%	25.3%
Japan equities	2.2%	2.3%	−0.1%	4.5%	4.5%	0.0%	4.4%	4.3%	0.1%
Emerging market equities	0.0%	2.0%	−2.0%	0.0%	4.9%	−4.9%	0.0%	10.0%	−10.0%
Global REITs	0.3%	0.9%	−0.6%	0.2%	1.4%	−1.3%	3.8%	5.6%	−1.8%

	Modified 25/75	Base Case 25/75	Difference	Modified 50/50	Base Case 50/50	Difference	Modified 75/25	Base Case 75/25	Difference
Global ex UK bonds	10.9%	10.6%	0.3%	24.7%	23.9%	0.7%	25.0%	25.0%	0.0%
UK bonds	2.5%	2.7%	−0.2%	2.4%	3.0%	−0.6%	0.0%	0.0%	0.0%
Cash	61.6%	61.7%	−0.1%	22.9%	23.1%	−0.1%	0.0%	0.0%	0.0%
Subtotal equities	25.0%	25.0%		50.0%	50.0%		75.0%	75.0%	
Subtotal fixed income	75.0%	75.0%		50.0%	50.0%		25.0%	25.0%	

ADDRESSING THE CRITICISMS OF MEAN–VARIANCE OPTIMIZATION

5

☐ | describe and evaluate the use of mean–variance optimization in asset allocation

In this section, we explore several methods for overcoming some of the potential short-comings of mean–variance optimization. Techniques that address the first two criticisms mostly take three approaches: improving the quality of inputs, constraining the optimization, and treating the efficient frontier as a statistical construct. These approaches are treated in the following three subsections.

In MVO, the composition of efficient portfolios is typically more sensitive to expected return estimates than it is to estimates of volatilities and correlations. Furthermore, expected returns are generally more difficult to estimate accurately than are volatilities and correlations. Thus, in addressing the first criticism of MVO—that outputs are highly sensitive to small changes in inputs—the reading will focus on expected return inputs. However, volatility and correlation inputs are also sources of potential error.

Reverse Optimization

Reverse optimization is a powerful tool that helps explain the implied returns associated with any portfolio. It can be used to estimate expected returns for use in a forward-looking optimization. MVO solves for optimal asset weights based on expected returns, covariances, and a risk aversion coefficient. Based on predetermined inputs, an optimizer solves for the optimal asset allocation weights. As the name implies, *reverse* optimization works in the opposite direction. Reverse optimization takes as its inputs a set of asset allocation weights *that are assumed to be optimal* and, with the additional inputs of covariances and the risk aversion coefficient, solves for expected returns. These reverse-optimized returns are sometimes referred to as implied or imputed returns.

When using reverse optimization to estimate a set of expected returns for use in a forward-looking optimization, the most common set of starting weights is the observed market-capitalization value of the assets or asset classes that form the opportunity set. The market capitalization of a given asset or asset classes should reflect the collective information of market participants. In representing the world market portfolio, the use of non-overlapping asset classes representing the majority of the world's investable assets is most consistent with theory.

Some practitioners will find the link between reverse optimization and CAPM equilibrium elegant, while others will see it as a shortcoming. For those who truly object to the use of market-capitalization weights in estimating inputs, the mechanics of reverse optimization can work with any set of starting weights—such as those of an existing policy portfolio, the average asset allocation policy of a peer group, or a fundamental weighting scheme. For those with more minor objections, we will shortly introduce the Black–Litterman model, which allows the expression of alternative forecasts or views.

In order to apply reverse optimization, one must create a working version of the all-inclusive market portfolio based on the constituents of the opportunity set. The market size or capitalization for most of the traditional stock and bond asset classes can be easily inferred from the various indexes that are used as asset class proxies. Many broad market-capitalization-weighted indexes report that they comprise over 95% of the securities, by market capitalization, of the asset classes they are attempting to represent. Exhibit 12 lists approximate values and weights for the 12 asset classes in our opportunity set, uses the weights associated with the asset classes to form a working version of the global market portfolio, and then uses the beta of each asset relative to our working version of the global market portfolio to infer what expected returns would be if all assets were priced by the CAPM according to their market beta. We assume a risk-free rate of 2.5% and a global market risk premium of 4%. Note that expected returns are rounded to one decimal place from the more precise values shown later (in Exhibit 13); expected returns cannot in every case be exactly reproduced based on Exhibit 12 alone because of the approximations mentioned. Also, notice in the final row of Exhibit 12 that the weighted average return and beta of the assets are 6.5% and 1, respectively.

Exhibit 12: Reverse-Optimization Example (Market Capitalization in £ billions)

Asset Class	Mkt Cap	Weight	Return $E[R_i]$		Risk-Free Rate r_f		Beta $\beta_{i,mkt}$	Market Risk Premium
UK large cap	£1,354.06	3.2%	6.62%	=	2.5%	+	1.03	(4%)
UK mid cap	£369.61	0.9%	6.92%	=	2.5%	+	1.11	(4%)
UK small cap	£108.24	0.3%	7.07%	=	2.5%	+	1.14	(4%)
US equities	£14,411.66	34.4%	7.84%	=	2.5%	+	1.33	(4%)
Europe ex UK equities	£3,640.48	8.7%	8.63%	=	2.5%	+	1.53	(4%)
Asia Pacific ex Japan equities	£1,304.81	3.1%	8.51%	=	2.5%	+	1.50	(4%)
Japan equities	£2,747.63	6.6%	6.43%	=	2.5%	+	0.98	(4%)
Emerging market equities	£2,448.60	5.9%	8.94%	=	2.5%	+	1.61	(4%)
Global REITs	£732.65	1.8%	9.04%	=	2.5%	+	1.64	(4%)
Global ex UK bonds	£13,318.58	31.8%	4.05%	=	2.5%	+	0.39	(4%)
UK bonds	£1,320.71	3.2%	2.95%	=	2.5%	+	0.112	(4%)
Cash	£83.00	0.2%	2.50%	=	2.5%	+	0.00	(4%)
	£41,840.04	100.0%	6.50%				1	

Notes: For the Mkt Cap and Weight columns, the final row is the simple sum. For the Return and Beta columns, the final row is the weighted average.

Looking back at our original asset allocation area graph (Exhibit 3), the reason for the well-behaved and well-diversified asset allocation mixes is now clear. By using reverse optimization, we are consistently relating assets' expected returns to their systematic risk. If there isn't a consistent relationship between the expected return and systematic risk, the optimizer will see this inconsistency as an opportunity and seek to take advantage of the more attractive attributes. This effect was clearly visible in our second asset allocation area graph after we altered the expected returns of Asia Pacific ex Japan equities and Europe ex UK equities.

As alluded to earlier, some practitioners find that the reverse-optimization process leads to a nice starting point, but they often have alternative forecasts or views regarding the expected return of one or more of the asset classes that differ from the returns implied by reverse optimization based on market-capitalization weights. One example of having views that differ from the reverse-optimized returns has already been illustrated, when we altered the returns of Asia Pacific ex Japan equities and Europe ex UK equities by approximately 50 bps. Unfortunately, due to the sensitivity of mean–variance optimization to small changes in inputs, directly altering the expected returns caused relatively extreme and unintuitive changes in the resulting asset allocations. If one has strong views on expected returns that differ from the reverse-optimized returns, an alternative or additional approach is needed; the next section presents one alternative.

Black–Litterman Model

A complementary addition to reverse optimization is the Black–Litterman model, created by Fischer Black and Robert Litterman (see Black and Litterman 1990, 1991, 1992). Although the Black–Litterman model is often characterized as an asset allocation model, it is really a model for deriving a set of expected returns that can be used in an unconstrained or constrained optimization setting. The Black–Litterman model starts with excess returns (in excess of the risk-free rate) produced from reverse optimization and then provides a technique for altering reverse-optimized expected returns in such a way that they reflect an investor's own distinctive views yet still behave well in an optimizer.

The Black–Litterman model has helped make the mean–variance optimization framework more useful. It enables investors to combine their unique forecasts of expected returns with reverse-optimized returns in an elegant manner. When coupled with a mean–variance or related framework, the resulting Black–Litterman expected returns often lead to well-diversified asset allocations by improving the consistency between each asset class's expected return and its contribution to systematic risk. These asset allocations are grounded in economic reality—via the market capitalization of the assets typically used in the reverse-optimization process—but still reflect the information contained in the investor's unique forecasts (or views) of expected return.

The mathematical details of the Black–Litterman model are beyond the scope of this reading, but many practitioners have access to asset allocation software that includes the Black–Litterman model.[12] To assist with an intuitive understanding of the model and to show the model's ability to blend new information (views) with reverse-optimized returns, we present an example based on the earlier views regarding the expected returns of Asia Pacific ex Japan equities and Europe ex UK equities. The Black–Litterman model has two methods for accepting views: one in which an absolute return forecast is associated with a given asset class and one in which the return differential of an asset (or group of assets) is expressed relative to another asset

---

12 For those interested in the mathematical details of the Black–Litterman model, see Idzorek (2007); a pre-publication version is available here: http://corporate.morningstar.com/ib/documents/Methodology Documents/IBBAssociates/BlackLitterman.pdf).

(or group of assets). Using the relative view format of the Black–Litterman model, we expressed the view that we believe Asia Pacific ex Japan equities will outperform Europe ex UK equities by 100 bps. We placed this view into the Black–Litterman model, which blends reverse-optimized returns with such views to create a new, mixed estimate.

Exhibit 13 compares the Black–Litterman model returns to the original reverse-optimized returns (as in Exhibit 12 but showing returns to the second decimal place based on calculations with full precision). The model accounts for the correlations of the assets with each other, and as one might expect, all of the returns change slightly (the change in return on cash was extremely small).

Exhibit 13: Comparison of Black–Litterman and Reverse-Optimized Returns

Asset Class	Reverse-Optimized Returns	Black–Litterman Returns	Difference
UK large cap	6.62%	6.60%	−0.02%
UK mid cap	6.92	6.87	−0.05
UK small cap	7.08	7.03	−0.05
US equities	7.81	7.76	−0.05
Europe ex UK equities	8.62	8.44	−0.18
Asia Pacific ex Japan equities	8.53	8.90	0.37
Japan equities	6.39	6.37	−0.02
Emerging market equities	8.96	9.30	0.33
Global REITs	9.02	9.00	−0.01
Global ex UK bonds	4.03	4.00	−0.03
UK bonds	2.94	2.95	0.01
Cash	2.50	2.50	0.00

Next, we created another efficient frontier asset allocation area graph based on these new returns from the Black–Litterman model, as shown in Exhibit 14. The allocations look relatively similar to those depicted in Exhibit 3. However, if you compare the allocations to Asia Pacific ex Japan equities and Europe ex UK equities to their allocations in the original efficient frontier asset allocation graph, you will notice that allocations to Asia Pacific ex Japan equities have increased across the frontier and allocations to Europe ex UK equities have decreased across the frontier with very little impact on the other asset allocations.

Exhibit 14: Efficient Frontier Asset Allocation Area Graph, Black–Litterman Returns

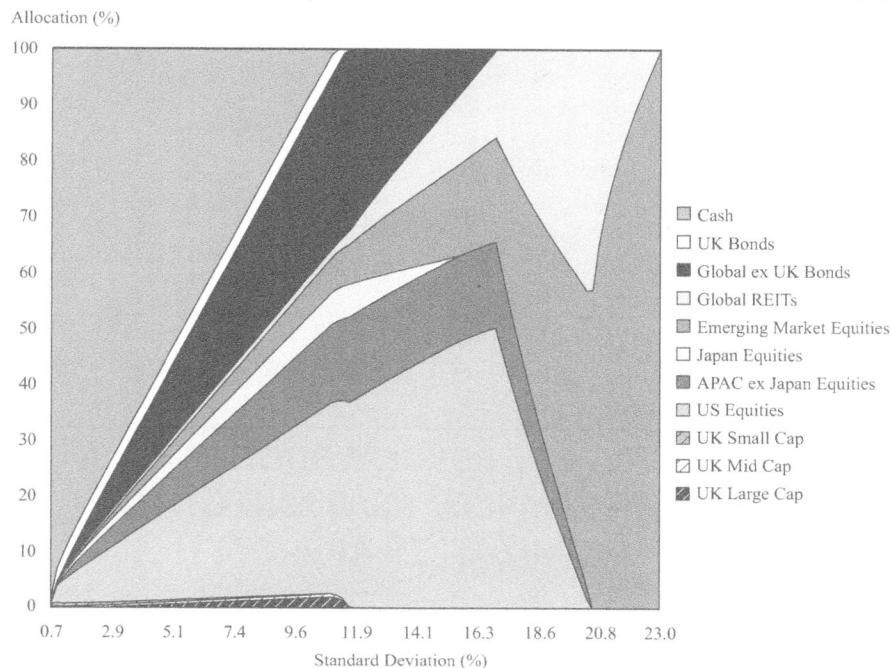

Allocation (%)

Legend:
- Cash
- UK Bonds
- Global ex UK Bonds
- Global REITs
- Emerging Market Equities
- Japan Equities
- APAC ex Japan Equities
- US Equities
- UK Small Cap
- UK Mid Cap
- UK Large Cap

Standard Deviation (%)

As before, to aid in the comparison of Exhibit 14 (Black–Litterman allocations) with Exhibit 3 (the base-case allocations), we identified three specific mixes in Exhibit 14 and compared those efficient asset allocation mixes based on the expected returns from the Black–Litterman model to those of the base case. The results are shown in Exhibit 15.

Exhibit 15: Comparison of Select Efficient Asset Allocations, Black–Litterman Allocations vs. Base-Case Allocations

	Modified 25/75	Base Case 25/75	Difference	Modified 50/50	Base Case 50/50	Difference	Modified 75/25	Base Case 75/25	Difference
UK large cap	0.4%	1.2%	−0.8%	1.4%	2.5%	−1.1%	0.0%	0.0%	0.0%
UK mid cap	0.4	0.6	−0.2	0.5	0.8	−0.3	0.0	0.0	0.0
UK small cap	0.4	0.5	−0.1	0.2	0.4	−0.2	0.0	0.0	0.0
US equities	13.8	13.8	0.0	26.8	26.8	0.0	40.0	40.5	−0.5
Europe ex UK equities	0.0	2.7	−2.7	0.0	6.5	−6.5	0.0	13.2	−13.2
Asia Pacific ex Japan equities	5.2	1.0	4.2	10.8	2.3	8.5	15.4	1.5	14.0
Japan equities	2.2	2.3	0.0	4.5	4.5	0.0	4.2	4.3	−0.1
Emerging market equities	1.8	2.0	−0.1	4.6	4.9	−0.2	9.8	10.0	−0.1
Global REITs	0.8	0.9	−0.1	1.3	1.4	−0.2	5.5	5.6	−0.1

	Modified 25/75	Base Case 25/75	Difference	Modified 50/50	Base Case 50/50	Difference	Modified 75/25	Base Case 75/25	Difference
Global ex UK bonds	10.3	10.6	−0.2	23.6	23.9	−0.3	25.0	25.0	0.0
UK bonds	3.1	2.7	0.3	3.5	3.0	0.5	0.0	0.0	0.0
Cash	61.6	61.7	−0.1	22.9	23.1	−0.1	0.0	0.0	0.0
Subtotal equities	25.0%	25.0%		50.0%	50.0%		75.0%	75.0%	
Subtotal fixed income	75.0%	75.0%		50.0%	50.0%		25.0%	25.0%	

6   ADDING CONSTRAINTS BEYOND BUDGET CONSTRAINTS, RESAMPLED MVO AND OTHER NON-NORMAL OPTIMIZATION APPROACHES

When running an optimization, in addition to the typical budget constraint and the non-negativity constraint, one can impose additional constraints. There are two primary reasons practitioners typically apply additional constraints: (1) to incorporate real-world constraints into the optimization problem and (2) to help overcome some of the potential shortcomings of mean–variance optimization elaborated above (input quality, input sensitivity, and highly concentrated allocations).

Most commercial optimizers accommodate a wide range of constraints. Typical constraints include the following:

1. Specify a set allocation to a specific asset—for example, 30% to real estate or 45% to human capital. This kind of constraint is typically used when one wants to include a non-tradable asset in the asset allocation decision and optimize around the non-tradable asset.

2. Specify an asset allocation range for an asset—for example, the emerging market allocation must be between 5% and 20%. This specification could be used to accommodate a constraint created by an investment policy, or it might reflect the user's desire to control the output of the optimization.

3. Specify an upper limit, due to liquidity considerations, on an alternative asset class, such as private equity or hedge funds.

4. Specify the relative allocation of two or more assets—for example, the allocation to emerging market equities must be less than the allocation to developed equities.

5. In a liability-relative (or surplus) optimization setting, one can constrain the optimizer to hold one or more assets representing the systematic characteristics of the liability short. (We elaborate on this scenario in Sections 10–14.)

In general, good constraints are those that model the actual circumstances/context in which one is attempting to set asset allocation policy. In contrast, constraints that are simply intended to control the output of a mean–variance optimization should be used cautiously. A perceived need to add constraints to control the MVO output would suggest a need to revisit one's inputs. If a very large number of constraints are imposed, one is no longer optimizing but rather specifying an asset allocation through a series of binding constraints.

Resampled Mean–Variance Optimization

Another technique used by asset allocators is called resampled mean–variance optimization (or sometimes "resampling" for short).[13] Resampled mean–variance optimization combines Markowitz's mean–variance optimization framework with Monte Carlo simulation and, all else equal, leads to more-diversified asset allocations. In contrast to reverse optimization, the Black–Litterman model, and constraints, resampled mean–variance optimization is an attempt to build a better optimizer that recognizes that forward-looking inputs are inherently subject to error.

Resampling uses Monte Carlo simulation to estimate a large number of potential capital market assumptions for mean–variance optimization and, eventually, for the resampled frontier. Conceptually, resampling is a large-scale sensitivity analysis in which hundreds or perhaps thousands of variations on baseline capital market assumptions lead to an equal number of mean–variance optimization frontiers based on the Monte Carlo–generated capital market assumptions. These intermediate frontiers are referred to as simulated frontiers. The resulting asset allocations, or portfolio weights, from these simulated frontiers are saved and averaged (using a variety of methods). To draw the resampled frontier, the averaged asset allocations are coupled with the starting capital market assumptions.

To illustrate how resampling can be used with other techniques, we conducted a resampled mean–variance optimization using the Black–Litterman returns from Exhibit 10, above. Exhibit 16 provides the asset allocation area graph from this optimization. Notice that the resulting asset allocations are smoother than in any of the previous asset allocation area graphs. Additionally, relative to Exhibit 15, based on the same inputs, the smallest allocations have increased in size while the largest allocations have decreased somewhat.

---

13 The current embodiments of resampling grew out of the work of Jobson and Korkie (1980, 1981); Jorion (1992); DiBartolomeo (1993); and Michaud (1998).

Exhibit 16: Efficient Frontier Asset Allocation Area Graph, Black–Litterman Returns with Resampling

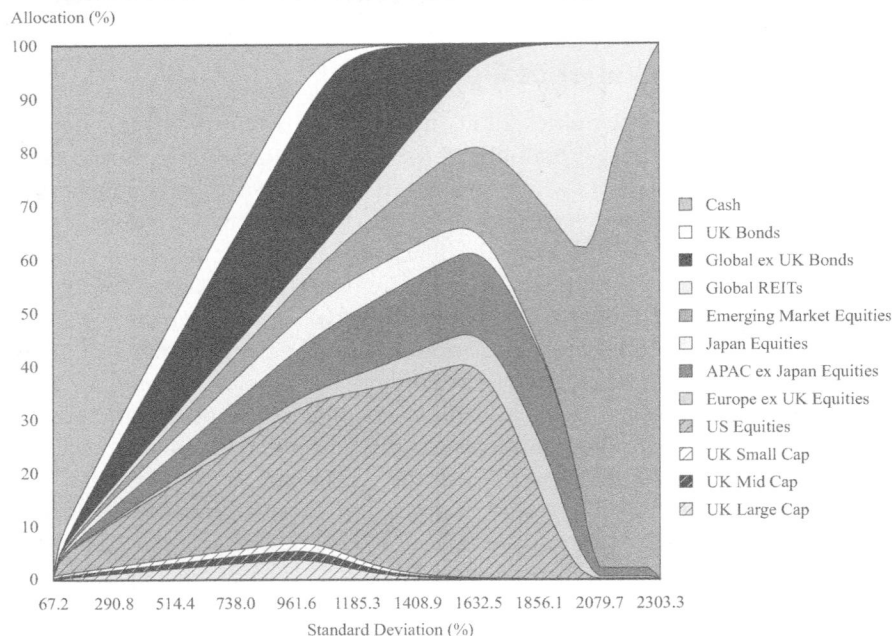

The asset allocations from resampling as depicted in Exhibit 16 are appealing. Criticisms include the following: (1) Some frontiers have concave "bumps" where expected return decreases as expected risk increases; (2) the "riskier" asset allocations are over-diversified; (3) the asset allocations inherit the estimation errors in the original inputs; and (4) the approach lacks a foundation in theory.[14]

Other Non-Normal Optimization Approaches

From our list of shortcomings/criticisms of mean–variance optimization, the third is that investor preferences may go beyond the first two moments (mean and variance) of a portfolio's return distribution. The third and fourth moments are, respectively, skewness and kurtosis. Skewness measures the degree to which return distributions are asymmetrical, and kurtosis measures the thickness of the distributions' tails (i.e., how frequently extreme events occur). A normal distribution is fully explained by the first two moments because the skewness and (excess) kurtosis of the normal distribution are both zero.

Returning to the discussion of Equation 1, the mean–variance optimization program involves maximizing expected utility, which is equal to expected return minus a penalty for risk, where risk is measured as variance (standard deviation). Unfortunately, variance or standard deviation is an incomplete measure of risk when returns are not normally distributed. By studying historical return distributions for the major asset classes and comparing those historical distributions to normal distributions, one will quickly see that, historically, asset class returns are not normally distributed. In fact, empirically extreme returns seem to occur approximately 10 times more often than the normal distribution would suggest. Coupling this finding with the asymmetrical risk preferences observed in investors—whereby the pain of a loss is approximately

---

14 For more details, see Scherer (2002).

twice as significant as the joy from an equivalent gain (according to Prospect theory)—has led to more complex utility functions and optimizers that expressly account for non-normal returns and asymmetric risk preference.[15] A number of variations of these more sophisticated optimization techniques have been put forth, making them challenging to cover. In general, most of them consider the non-normal return distribution characteristics and use a more sophisticated definition of risk, such as conditional value-at-risk. We view these as important advancements in the toolkit available to practitioners.

Exhibit 17 summarizes selected extensions of quantitative asset allocation approaches outside the sphere of traditional mean–variance optimization.

Exhibit 17: Selected Non-Mean–Variance Developments

Key Non-Normal Frameworks	Research/Recommended Reading
Mean–semivariance optimization	Markowitz (1959)
Mean–conditional value-at-risk optimization	Goldberg, Hayes, and Mahmoud (2013) Rockafellar and Uryasev (2000) Xiong and Idzorek (2011)
Mean–variance-skewness optimization	Briec, Kerstens, and Jokung (2007) Harvey, Liechty, Liechty, and Müller (2010)
Mean–variance-skewness-kurtosis optimization	Athayde and Flôres (2003) Beardsley, Field, and Xiao (2012)

Long-Term versus Short-Term Inputs

Strategic asset allocation is often described as "long term," while tactical asset allocation involves short-term movements away from the strategic asset allocation. In this context, "long term" is often defined as 10 or perhaps 20 or more years, yet in practice, very few asset allocators revisit their strategic asset allocation this infrequently. Many asset allocators update their strategic asset allocation annually, which makes it a bit more challenging to distinguish between strategic and tactical asset allocations. This frequent revisiting of the asset allocation policy brings up important questions about the time horizon associated with the inputs. In general, long-term (10-plus-year) capital market assumptions that ignore current market conditions, such as valuation levels, the business cycle, and interest rates, are often thought of as *unconditional* inputs. Unconditional inputs focus on the average capital market assumptions over the 10-plus-year time horizon. In contrast, shorter-term capital market assumptions that explicitly attempt to incorporate current market conditions (i.e., that are "conditioned" on them) are conditional inputs. For example, a practitioner who believes that the market is overvalued and that as a result we are entering a period of low returns, high volatility, and high correlations might prefer to use conditional inputs that reflect these beliefs.[16]

---

15 For more on prospect theory, see Kahneman and Tversky (1979) and Tversky and Kahneman (1992).
16 Relatedly, Chow, Jacquier, Kritzman, and Lowry (1999) showed a procedure for blending the optimal portfolios for periods of normal and high return volatility. The approach accounts for the tendency of asset returns to be more highly correlated during times of high volatility.

EXAMPLE 4

Problems in Mean–Variance Optimization

In a presentation to US-based investment clients on asset allocation, the results of two asset allocation exercises are shown, as presented in Exhibit 18.

Exhibit 18: Asset Allocation Choices

Panel A: Area Graph 1

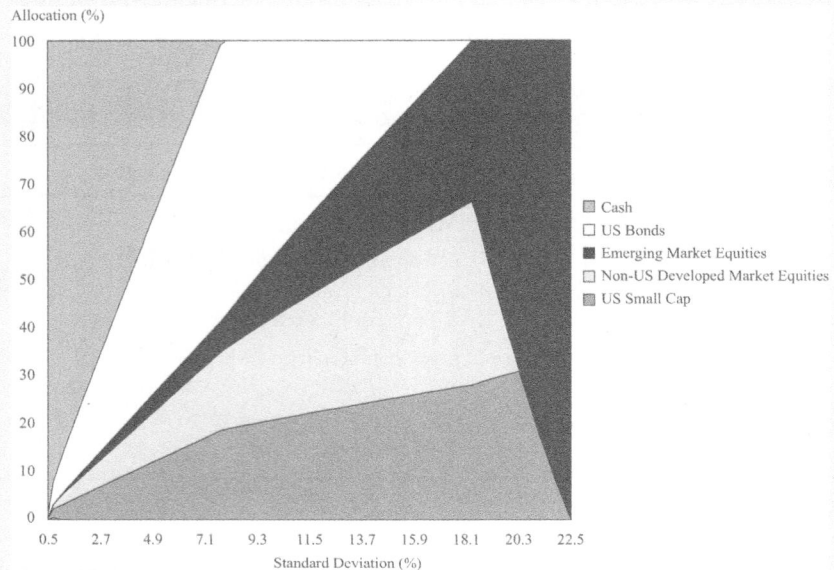

Panel B: Area Graph 2

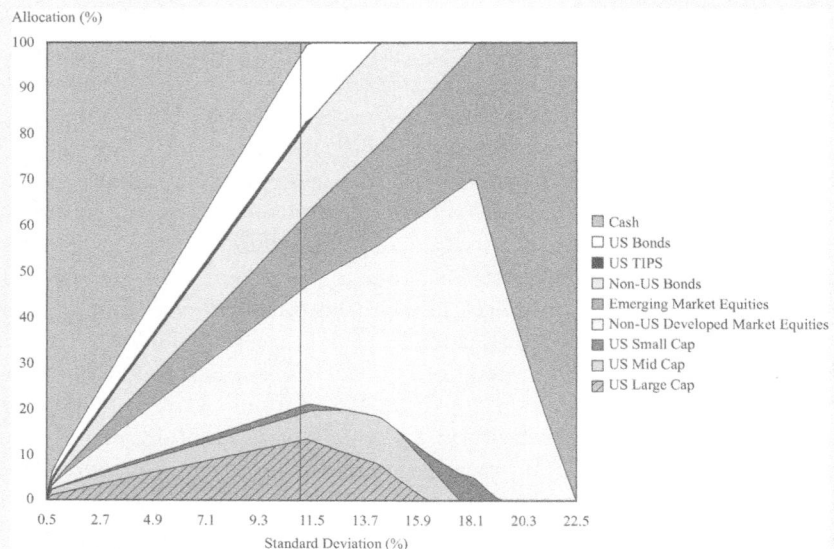

1. Based on Panel A, address the following:

    A. Based on mean–variance analysis, what is the asset allocation that would most likely be selected by a risk-neutral investor?

    B. Based only on the information that can be inferred from Panel A, discuss the investment characteristics of non-US developed market equity (NUSD) in efficient portfolios.

C. Critique the efficient asset mixes represented in Panel A.

Solution to 1A:

For a risk-neutral investor, the optimal asset allocation is 100% invested in emerging market equities. For a risk-neutral investor ($\lambda = 0$), expected utility is simply equal to expected return. The efficient asset allocation that maximizes expected return is the one with the highest level of volatility, as indicated on the x-axis. Panel A shows that that asset allocation consists entirely of emerging market equities.

Solution to 1B:

The weights of NUSD as the efficient frontier moves from its minimum to its maximum risk point suggest NUSD's investment characteristics. This asset class is neither the lowest-volatility asset (which can be inferred to be cash) nor the highest-volatility asset (which is emerging market equity). At the point of the peak of NUSD, when the weight in NUSD is about to begin its decline in higher-risk efficient portfolios, US bonds drop out of the efficient frontier. Further, NUSD leaves the efficient frontier portfolio at a point at which US small cap reaches its highest weight. These observations suggest that NUSD provided diversification benefits in portfolios including US bonds—a relatively low correlation with US bonds can be inferred—that are lost at this point on the efficient frontier. Beyond a volatility level of 20.3%, representing a corner portfolio, NUSD drops out of the efficient frontier.

Solution to 1C:

Of the nine asset classes in the investor's defined opportunity set, five at most are represented by portfolios on the efficient frontier. Thus, a criticism of the efficient frontier associated with Panel A is that the efficient portfolios are highly concentrated in a subset of the available asset classes, which likely reflects the input sensitivity of MVO.

2. Compare the asset allocations shown in Panel A with the corresponding asset allocations shown in Panel B. (Include a comparison of the panels at the level of risk indicated by the line in Panel B.)

Solution to 2:

The efficient asset mixes in Panels A and B cover a similar risk range: The risk levels of the two minimum-variance portfolios are similar, and the risk levels of the two maximum-return portfolios are similar. Over most of the range of volatility, however, the efficient frontier associated with Panel B is better diversified. For example, at the line in Panel B, representing a moderate level of volatility likely relevant to many investors, the efficient portfolio contains nine asset classes rather than four, as in Panel A. At that point, for example, the allocation to fixed income is spread over US bonds, non-US bonds, and US TIPS in Panel B, as opposed to just US bonds in Panel A.

3.

A. Identify three techniques that the asset allocations in Panel B might have incorporated to improve the characteristics relative to those of Panel A.

B. Discuss how the techniques described in your answer to 3A address the high input sensitivity of MVO.

Solution to 3A:

To achieve the better-diversified efficient frontier shown in Panel B, several methods might have been used, including reverse optimization, the Black–Litterman model, and constrained asset class weights.

Solution to 3B:

Reverse optimization and the Black–Litterman model address the issue of MVO's sensitivity to small differences in expected return estimates by anchoring expected returns to those implied by the asset class weights of a proxy for the global market portfolio. The Black–Litterman framework provides a disciplined way to tilt the expected return inputs in the direction of the investor's own views. These approaches address the problem by improving the balance between risk and return that is implicit in the inputs.

A very direct approach to the problem can be taken by placing constraints on weights in the optimization to force an asset class to appear in a constrained efficient frontier within some desired range of values. For example, non-US bonds did not appear in any efficient portfolio in Panel A. The investor could specify that the weight on non-US bonds be strictly positive. Another approach would be to place a maximum on the weight in US bonds to make the optimizer spread the fixed-income allocation over other fixed-income assets besides US bonds.

7   ALLOCATING TO LESS LIQUID ASSET CLASSES

> discuss asset class liquidity considerations in asset allocation

Large institutional investors have the ability to invest in less liquid asset classes, such as direct real estate, infrastructure, and private equity. These less liquid asset classes represent unique challenges to many of the common asset allocation techniques, such as mean–variance optimization.

For traditional, highly liquid asset classes, such as publicly listed equities and bonds, almost all of the major index providers have indexes that do an outstanding job of representing the performance characteristics of the asset class (and its various sub–asset classes). For example, over any reasonably long time period, the risk and return characteristics of a given asset class are nearly identical across the major global equity indexes and the correlations between the returns of the indexes are close to 1. Additionally, in most cases, there are passive, low-cost investment vehicles that allow investors to capture the performance of the asset class with very little tracking error.

CASH, THE RISK-FREE ASSET, AND LIQUIDITY NEEDS

The so called "risk-free asset" has a special and somewhat tricky spot in the world of finance. Asset allocators typically use indexes for either 30-day or 90-day government bills to represent the characteristics associated with holding cash, which they may or may not treat as the risk-free asset. The volatility associated with these total return indexes is extremely low, but it isn't zero. An alternative to using a cash index as a proxy for the risk-free asset is to use a government bond with a duration/maturity that matches the time horizon of the investor. Some asset allocators like to include cash or another asset that could be considered a risk-free asset in the optimization and to allow the optimizer to determine how to mix it with the other asset classes included in the optimization. Other asset allocators prefer to exclude the risk-free asset from the optimization and allow real-world needs, such as liquidity needs, to determine how much to allocate to cash-like assets.

Illiquid assets may offer an expected return premium as compensation for illiquidity as well as diversification benefits. Determining an appropriate allocation to these assets is associated with various challenges, however. Common illiquid asset classes cannot be readily diversified to eliminate idiosyncratic risk, so representing an overall asset class performance is problematic. Furthermore, for less liquid asset classes, such as direct real estate, infrastructure, and private equity, there are, in general, far fewer indexes that attempt to represent aggregate performance. If one were to compare the performance characteristics of multiple indexes representing one of these less liquid asset classes, there would be noticeable risk and return differences, suggesting that it is difficult to accurately measure the risk and return characteristics of these asset classes. Also, due to the illiquid nature of the constituents that make up these asset classes, it is widely believed that the indexes don't accurately reflect their true volatility. In contrast to the more traditional, highly liquid asset classes, there are no low-cost passive investment vehicles that would allow investors to closely track the aggregate performance of these less liquid asset classes.

Thus, the problem is twofold: (1) Due to the lack of accurate indexes, it is more challenging to make capital market assumptions for these less liquid asset classes, and (2) even if there were accurate indexes, there are no low-cost passive investment vehicles to track them.

Compounding the asset allocator's dilemma is the fact that the risk and return characteristics associated with actual investment vehicles, such as direct real estate funds, infrastructure funds, and private equity funds, are typically significantly different from the characteristics of the asset classes themselves. For example, the private equity "asset class" should represent the risk and return characteristics of owning all private equity, just as the MSCI All Country World Index represents the risk and return characteristics of owning all public equity. Purchasing the exchange-traded fund (ETF) that tracks the MSCI All Country World Index completely diversifies public company-specific risk. This scenario is in direct contrast to the typical private equity fund, in which the risk and return characteristics are often dominated by company-specific (idiosyncratic) risk.

In addressing asset allocation involving less liquid asset classes, practical options include the following:

1. Exclude less liquid asset classes (direct real estate, infrastructure, and private equity) from the asset allocation decision and then consider real estate funds, infrastructure funds, and private equity funds as potential implementation vehicles when fulfilling the target strategic asset allocation.

2. Include less liquid asset classes in the asset allocation decision and attempt to model the inputs to represent the *specific risk* characteristics associated with the likely *implementation vehicles.*

3. Include less liquid asset classes in the asset allocation decision and attempt to model the inputs to represent the *highly diversified* characteristics associated with the *true asset classes.*

Related to this last option, some practitioners use listed real estate indexes, listed infrastructure, and public equity indexes that are deemed to have characteristics similar to their private equity counterparts to help estimate the risk of the less liquid asset classes and their correlation with the other asset classes in the opportunity set.

It should be noted that the use of listed alternative indexes often violates the recommendation that asset classes be mutually exclusive—the securities in these indexes are likely also included in indexes representing other asset classes—and thus typically results in higher correlations among different asset classes, which has the negative impact of increasing input sensitivity in most optimization settings.

For investors who do not have access to direct real estate funds, infrastructure funds, and private equity funds—for example, small investors—the most common approach is to use one of the indexes based on listed equities to represent the asset class and then to implement the target allocation with a fund that invests similarly. Thus global REITs might be used to represent (approximately) global real estate.

8   RISK BUDGETING

☐   explain absolute and relative risk budgets and their use in determining and implementing an asset allocation

☐   describe how client needs and preferences regarding investment risks can be incorporated into asset allocation

> [A] risk budget is simply a particular allocation of portfolio risk. An optimal risk budget is simply the allocation of risk such that the first order of conditions for portfolio optimization are satisfied. The risk budgeting process is the process of finding an optimal risk budget.
>
> Kurt Winkelmann (2003, p. 173)

As this quote from Kurt Winkelmann suggests, there are three aspects to risk budgeting:

- The risk budget identifies the total amount of risk and allocates the risk to a portfolio's constituent parts.
- An optimal risk budget allocates risk efficiently.
- The process of finding the optimal risk budget is risk budgeting.

Although its name suggests that risk budgeting is all about risk, risk budgeting is really using risk in relation to seeking return. The goal of risk budgeting is to maximize return per unit of risk—whether overall market risk in an asset allocation setting or active risk in an asset allocation implementation setting.

The ability to determine a position's marginal contribution to portfolio risk is a powerful tool that helps one to better understand the sources of risk. The marginal contribution to a type of risk is the partial derivative of the risk in question (total risk, active risk, or residual risk) with respect to the applicable type of portfolio holding (asset allocation holdings, active holdings, or residual holdings). Knowing a position's marginal contribution to risk allows one to (1) approximate the change in portfolio risk (total risk, active risk, or residual risk) due to a change in an individual holding, (2) determine which positions are optimal, and (3) create a risk budget. *Risk-budgeting tools assist in the optimal use of risk in the pursuit of return.*

Exhibit 19 contains risk-budgeting information for the Sharpe ratio–maximizing asset allocation from our original UK example. The betas are from Exhibit 12. The marginal contribution to total risk (MCTR) identifies the rate at which risk would change with a small (or marginal) change in the current weights. For asset class i, it is calculated as $MCTR_i$ = (Beta of asset class i with respect to portfolio)(Portfolio return volatility). The absolute contribution to total risk (ACTR) for an asset class measures how much it contributes to portfolio return volatility and can be calculated as the weight of the asset class in the portfolio times its marginal contribution to total risk: $ACTR_i = (Weight_i)(MCTR_i)$. Critically, beta takes account not only of the asset's own volatility but also of the asset's correlations with other portfolio assets.

The sum of the ACTR in Exhibit 19 is approximately 10.88%, which is equal to the expected standard deviation of this asset allocation mix. Dividing each ACTR by the total risk of 10.88% gives the percentage of total risk that each position contributes. Finally, an asset allocation is optimal from a risk-budgeting perspective when the ratio of excess return (over the risk-free rate) to MCTR is the same for all assets and matches the Sharpe ratio of the tangency portfolio. So in this case, which is based on reverse-optimized returns, we have an optimal risk budget.

Exhibit 19: Risk-Budgeting Statistics

Asset Class	Weight	MCTR	ACTR	Percent Contribution to Total Standard Deviation	Ratio of Excess Return to MCTR
UK large cap	3.2%	11.19%	0.36%	3.33%	0.368
UK mid cap	0.9	12.02	0.11	0.98	0.368
UK small cap	0.3	12.44	0.03	0.30	0.368
US equities	34.4	14.51	5.00	45.94	0.368
Europe ex UK equities	8.7	16.68	1.45	13.34	0.368
Asia Pacific ex Japan equities	3.1	16.35	0.51	4.69	0.368
Japan equities	6.6	10.69	0.70	6.46	0.368
Emerging market equities	5.9	17.51	1.02	9.42	0.368
Global REITs	1.8	17.79	0.31	2.86	0.368
Global ex UK bonds	31.8	4.21	1.34	12.33	0.368
UK bonds	3.2	1.22	0.04	0.35	0.368
Cash	0.2	0.00	0.00	0.00	0.368
	100.0		10.88	100.00	

For additional clarity, the following are the specific calculations used to derive the calculated values for UK large-cap equities (where we show some quantities with an extra decimal place in order to reproduce the values shown in the exhibit):

- Marginal contribution to risk (MCTR):

Asset beta relative to portfolio × Portfolio standard deviation

$1.0289 \times 10.876 = 11.19\%$

- ACTR:

Asset weight in portfolio × MCTR

$3.2\% \times 11.19\% = 0.36\%$

- Ratio of excess return to MCTR:

(Expected return − Risk-free rate)/MCTR

$(6.62\% - 2.5\%)/11.19\% = 0.368$

EXAMPLE 5

Risk Budgeting in Asset Allocation

1. Describe the objective of risk budgeting in asset allocation.

Solution:

The objective of risk budgeting in asset allocation is to use risk efficiently in the pursuit of return. A risk budget specifies the total amount of risk and how much of that risk should be budgeted for each allocation.

2. Consider two asset classes, A and B. Asset class A has two times the weight of B in the portfolio. Under what condition would B have a larger ACTR than A?

Solution:

Because $\text{ACTR}_i = (\text{Weight}_i)(\text{Beta with respect to portfolio})_i(\text{Portfolio return volatility})$, the beta of B would have to be more than twice as large as the beta of A for B to contribute more to portfolio risk than A.

3. When is an asset allocation optimal from a risk-budgeting perspective?

Solution:

An asset allocation is optimal when the ratio of excess return (over the risk-free rate) to MCTR is the same for all assets.

---

9   FACTOR-BASED ASSET ALLOCATION

☐ | describe the use of investment factors in constructing and analyzing an asset allocation

Until now, we have primarily focused on the mechanics of asset allocation optimization as applied to an opportunity set consisting of traditional, non-overlapping asset classes. An alternative approach used by some practitioners is to move away from an opportunity set of *asset classes* to an opportunity set consisting of investment *factors*.

In factor-based asset allocation, the factors in question are typically similar to the fundamental (or structural) factors in widely used multi-factor investment models. Factors are typically based on observed market premiums and anomalies. In addition to the all-important market (equity) exposure, typical factors used in asset allocation include size, valuation, momentum, liquidity, duration (term), credit, and volatility. Most of these factors were identified as return drivers that help to explain returns that were not explained by the CAPM. These factors can be constructed in a number of different ways, but with the exception of the market factor, typically, the factor represents what is referred to as a zero (dollar) investment, or self-financing investment, in which the underperforming attribute is sold short to finance an offsetting long position in the better-performing attribute. For example, the size factor is the combined return from shorting large-cap stocks and going long small-cap stocks (Size factor return = Small-cap stock return − Large-cap stock return). Of course, if large-cap stocks outperform small-cap stocks, the realized size return would be negative. Constructing factors in this manner removes most market exposure from the factors (because of the short positions that offset long positions); as a result, the factors generally have low correlations with the market and with one another.

We next present an example of a factor-based asset allocation optimization. Exhibit 20 shows the list of factors, how they were specified, and their historical returns and standard deviations (in excess of the risk-free rate as proxied by the return on three-month Treasury bills). The exhibit also includes historical statistics for three-month Treasury bills.

Thus far, our optimization examples have taken place in "total return space," where the expected return of each asset has equaled the expected return of the risk-free asset plus the amount of expected return in excess of the risk-free rate. In order to stay in this familiar total return space when optimizing with risk factors, the factor return needs to include the return on the assumed collateral (in this example, cash, represented by three-month Treasury bills). This adjustment is also needed if one plans to include both risk factors and some traditional asset classes in the same optimization, so that the inputs for the risk factors and traditional asset classes are similarly specified. Alternatively, one could move in the opposite direction, subtracting the return of the three-month Treasury bills from asset class returns and then conducting the optimization in excess-return space. One way to think about a self-financing allocation to a risk factor is that in order to invest in the risk factor, one must put up an equivalent amount of collateral that is invested in cash.

Exhibit 20: Factors/Asset Classes, Factor Definitions, and Historical Statistics (US data, January 1979 to March 2016)

Factor/Asset Class	Factor Definition	Compound Annual Factor Return	Standard Deviation	Total Return	Standard Deviation
Treasury bonds	Long-term Treasury bonds			7.77%	5.66%
Market	Total market return – Cash	7.49%	16.56%	12.97	17.33
Size	Small cap – Large cap	0.41	10.15	5.56	10.65
Valuation	Value – Growth	0.68	9.20	5.84	9.76
Credit	Corporate – Treasury	0.70	3.51	5.87	3.84
Duration	Long Treasury bonds – Treasury bills	4.56	11.29	9.91	11.93
Mortgage	Mortgage-backed – Treasury bonds	0.30	3.38	5.45	3.83
Large growth	—	—	—	12.64	19.27
Large value	—	—	—	13.23	16.52
Small growth	—	—	—	12.30	25.59
Small value	—	—	—	14.54	19.84
Mortgage-backed sec.	—	—	—	8.09	6.98
Corporate bonds	—	—	—	8.52	7.52
Treasury bonds	—	—	—	7.77	5.66
Cash	—	—	—	5.13	1.23

Because of space considerations, we have not included the full correlation matrix, but it is worth noting that the average pair-wise correlation of the risk factor–based opportunity set (in excess of the risk-free rate collateral return) is 0.31, whereas that of the asset class–based opportunity set is 0.57. Given the low pair-wise correlations of the risk factors, there has been some debate among practitioners around whether it is better to optimize using asset classes or risk factors. The issue was clarified by Idzorek and Kowara (2013), who demonstrated that in a proper comparison, neither approach is inherently superior. To help illustrate risk factor optimization and to demonstrate that if the two opportunity sets are constructed with access to similar exposures, neither approach has an inherent advantage, we present two side-by-side optimizations. These optimizations are based on the data given in Exhibit 20.

Exhibit 21 contains the two efficient frontiers. As should be expected, given that the opportunity sets provide access to similar exposures, the two historical efficient frontiers are very similar. This result illustrates that when the same range of potential exposures is available in two opportunity sets, the risk and return possibilities are very similar.

Exhibit 21: Efficient Frontiers Based on Historical Capital Market Assumptions (January 1979 to March 2016)

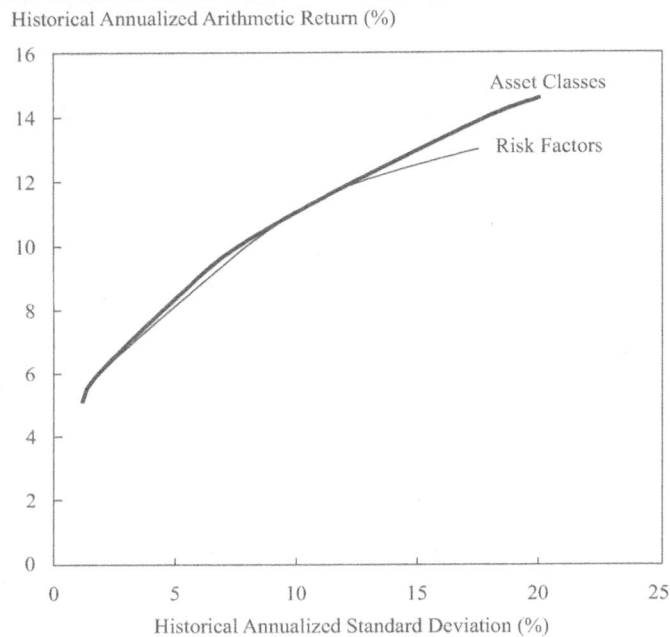

Moving to Exhibit 22, examining the two asset allocation area graphs associated with the two efficient frontiers reveals that the efficient mixes have some relatively clear similarities. For example, in Panel A (risk factors), the combined market, size, and valuation exposures mirror the pattern (allocations) in Panel B (asset classes) of combined large value and small value exposures.

Exhibit 22: Asset Allocation Area Graphs—Risk Factors and Asset Classes

Panel A: Risk Factor Asset Allocation Area Graph

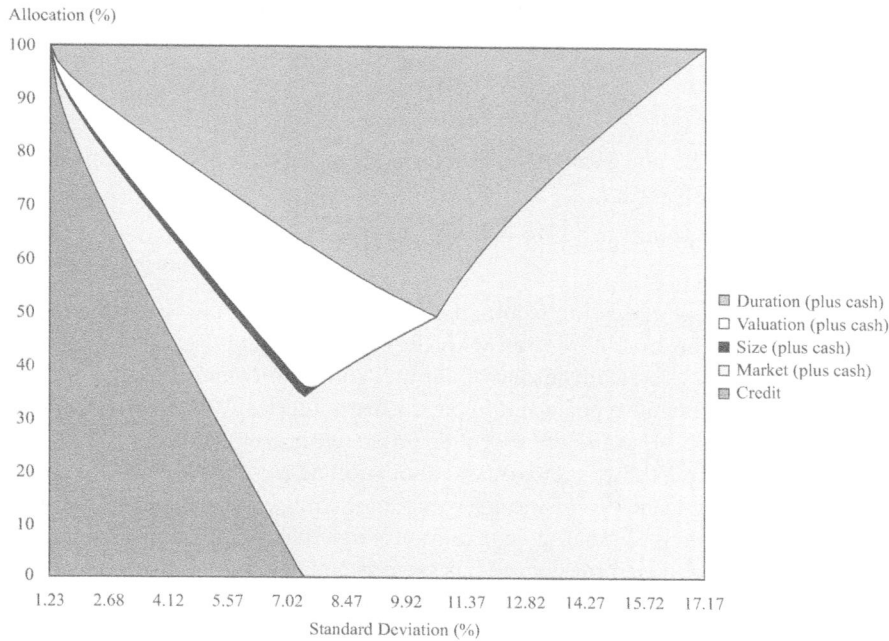

Allocation (%)

Legend:
- Duration (plus cash)
- Valuation (plus cash)
- Size (plus cash)
- Market (plus cash)
- Credit

Standard Deviation (%)

x-axis: 1.23 2.68 4.12 5.57 7.02 8.47 9.92 11.37 12.82 14.27 15.72 17.17

Panel B: Asset Class Asset Allocation Area Graph

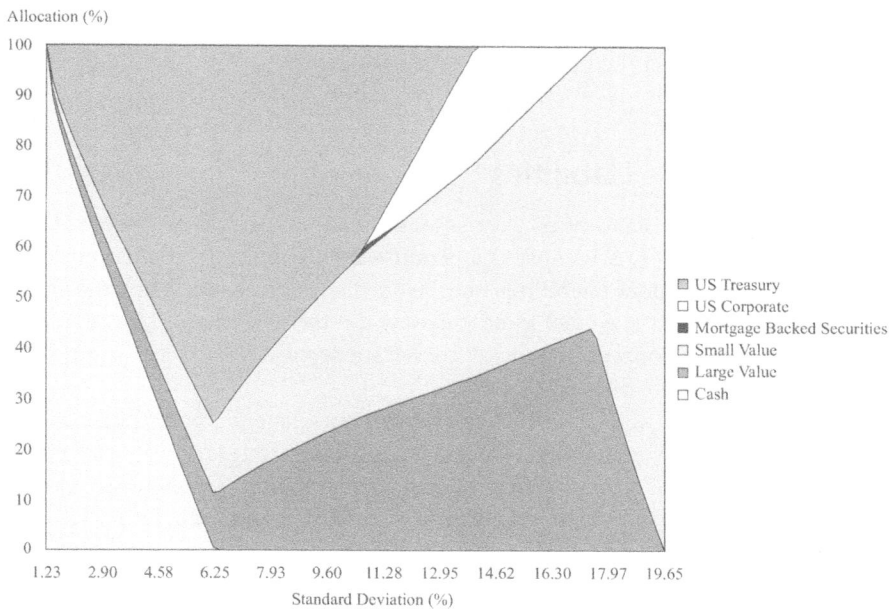

Allocation (%)

Legend:
- US Treasury
- US Corporate
- Mortgage Backed Securities
- Small Value
- Large Value
- Cash

Standard Deviation (%)

x-axis: 1.23 2.90 4.58 6.25 7.93 9.60 11.28 12.95 14.62 16.30 17.97 19.65

Practitioners should choose to carry out asset allocation in the particular space—risk factors or asset classes—in which they are most equipped to make capital market assumptions. Regardless of which space a practitioner prefers, expanding one's opportunity set to include new, weakly correlated risk factors or asset classes should improve the potential risk–return trade-offs.

10   DEVELOPING LIABILITY-RELATIVE ASSET ALLOCATIONS AND CHARACTERIZING THE LIABILITIES

> ☐   describe and evaluate characteristics of liabilities that are relevant to asset allocation
>
> ☐   discuss approaches to liability-relative asset allocation

Liability-relative asset allocation is aimed at the general issue of rendering decisions about asset allocation in conjunction with the investor's liabilities. Liability-relative investors view assets as an inventory of capital, sometimes increased by additions, which is available to achieve goals and to pay future liabilities. What is the chance that an institution's capital is sufficient to cover future cash flow liabilities? This type of question is critical for liability-relative asset allocation because many large institutional investors—for example, banks, insurance companies, and pension plans—possess legal liabilities and operate in regulated environments in which an institution's inability to meet its liabilities with current capital has serious consequences. This concern gives rise to unique risk measures, such as the probability of meeting future cash flow requirements, and the restatement of traditional risk metrics, such as volatility, in relation to liabilities.

Liability-relative methods were developed in an institutional investor context, but these ideas have also been applied to individual investors. This section will focus on institutional investors. A later section addresses a thematically similar approach with behavioral finance roots—goals-based asset allocation.

Characterizing the Liabilities

To be soundly applied, liability-relative asset allocation requires an accurate understanding of the liabilities. A liability is a promise by one party to pay a counterparty based on a prior agreement. Liabilities may be fixed or contingent. When the amounts and timing of payments are fixed in advance by the terms of a contract, the liability is said to be fixed or non-contingent. A corporate bond with a fixed coupon rate is an example.

In many cases relevant to asset allocation, payments depend upon future, uncertain events. In such cases, the liability is a contingent liability.[17] An important example involves the liabilities of a defined benefit (DB) pension plan. The plan sponsor has a legal commitment to pay the beneficiaries of the plan during their retirement years. However, the exact dates of the payments depend on the employees' retirement dates, longevity, and cash payout rules. Insurance companies' liabilities—created by the sale of insurance policies—are also contingent liabilities: The insurance company promises to pay its policyholders a specified amount contingent on the occurrence of a predefined event.

We distinguish legal liabilities from cash payments that are expected to be made in the future and are essential to the mission of an institution but are not legal liabilities. We call these quasi-liabilities. The endowment of a university can fit this category because, in many cases, the endowment contributes a major part of the university's operating budget. The endowment assures its stakeholders that it will continue to

---

17 Note that the term "contingent liability" has a specific definition in accounting. We are using the term more broadly here.

support its essential activities through spending from the endowment capital, and failure to provide such support will often lead to changes in how the endowment is managed. Accordingly, the asset allocation decisions are made in conjunction with the university's spending rules and policies. Asset allocation is just one portion of the investment problem. Although we do not explicitly discuss them here, as suggested in Sections 2–9, the spending needs of an individual represent another type of quasi-liability. Exhibit 23 summarizes the characteristics of liabilities that can affect asset allocation.

Exhibit 23: Characteristics of Liabilities That Can Affect Asset Allocation

1. Fixed versus contingent cash flows
2. Legal versus quasi-liabilities
3. Duration and convexity of liability cash flows
4. Value of liabilities as compared with the size of the sponsoring organization
5. Factors driving future liability cash flows (inflation, economic conditions, interest rates, risk premium)
6. Timing considerations, such as longevity risk
7. Regulations affecting liability cash flow calculations

The above liability characteristics are relevant to liability-relative asset allocation in various ways. For example, they affect the choice of appropriate discount rate(s) to establish the present value of the liabilities and thus the degree to which assets are adequate in relation to those liabilities. Liability characteristics determine the composition of the liability-matching portfolio and that portfolio's basis risk with respect to the liabilities. (Basis risk in this context quantifies the degree of mismatch between the hedging portfolio and the liabilities.)

We will discuss the following case study in detail. It involves a frozen pension plan for LOWTECH, a hypothetical US company. The company has decided to close its defined benefit pension plan and switch to a defined contribution plan. The DB plan has the fixed liabilities (accumulated benefit obligations) shown in Exhibit 24.

Exhibit 24: Projected Liability Cash Flows for Company LOWTECH (US$ billions)

		PV(Liabilities)	
Beginning of Year	Cash Outflow (Liability)	4% Discount Rate	2% Discount Rate
2015	—	$2.261	$3.039
2016	$0.100	2.352	3.10
2017	0.102	2.342	3.06
2018	0.104	2.329	3.02
2019	0.106	2.314	2.97
2020	0.108	2.297	2.92
2021	0.110	2.276	2.87
2022	0.113	2.252	2.82
2023	0.115	2.225	2.76

| | | PV(Liabilities) | |
Beginning of Year	Cash Outflow (Liability)	4% Discount Rate	2% Discount Rate
2024	0.117	2.195	2.69
2025	0.120	2.161	2.63
2026	0.122	2.123	2.56
2027	0.124	2.081	2.49
2028	0.127	2.035	2.41
2029	0.129	1.984	2.33
2030	0.132	1.929	2.24
2031	0.135	1.869	2.15
2032	0.137	1.804	2.06
2033	0.140	1.733	1.96
2034	0.143	1.657	1.86
2035	0.146	1.575	1.75
2036	0.149	1.486	1.63
2037	0.152	1.391	1.52
2038	0.155	1.289	1.39
2039	0.158	1.180	1.26
2040	0.161	1.063	1.13
2041	0.164	0.938	0.98
2042	0.167	0.805	0.84
2043	0.171	0.663	0.68
2044	0.174	0.512	0.52
2045	0.178	0.352	0.36
2046	0.181	0.181	0.181

In the Cash Outflow (Liability) column, the assumption is made that payments for a given year are made at the beginning of the year (in the exhibit, outflows have a positive sign). As of the beginning of 2015, the present value of these liabilities, given a 4% discount rate for high-quality corporate bonds (required in the United States by the Pension Protection Act of 2006, which applies to private DB pension plans), is US$2.261 billion. The current market value of the assets is assumed to equal US$2.5 billion, for a surplus of US$0.239 billion. On the other hand, if the discount rate is equal to the long-term government bond rate at 2% (required before the 2006 US legislation), the surplus becomes a deficit at −$0.539 billion. In many cases, regulations set the appropriate discount rates; these rates have an impact on the determination of surplus or deficit and thus on future contribution rules.

Like other institutions with legal liabilities, the LOWTECH company must analyze its legal future cash flows under its DB pension system and evaluate them in conjunction with the current market value of its assets on an annual basis. The following steps of the valuation exercise for a DB pension plan occur on a fixed annual date:

1. Calculate the market value of assets.
2. Project liability cash flows (via actuarial principles and rules).
3. Determine an appropriate discount rate for liability cash flows.
4. Compute the present value of liabilities, the surplus value, and the funding ratio.

Surplus = Market value (assets) − Present value (liabilities).

The surplus for the LOWTECH company is US$2.500 billion − US$2.261 billion = US$0.239 billion, given the 4% discount rate assumption.

The funding ratio is another significant measure: Funding ratio = Market value (assets)/Present value (liabilities). We say that an investor is fully funded if the investor's funding ratio equals 1 (or the surplus is 0). A state of overfunding occurs when the funding ratio is greater than 1, and a state of underfunding takes place when the funding ratio is less than 1. Based on a discount rate of 4%, the funding ratio for LOWTECH = US$2.5 billion/US$2.261 billion = 1.1057, so that the company is about 10.6% overfunded.

The surplus value and the funding ratio are highly dependent upon the discount rate assumption. For example, if the discount rate is equal to 2.0% (close to the 10-year US Treasury bond rate in early 2016), the surplus drops to −US$0.539 billion and the funding ratio equals 0.8226. The company's status changes from overfunded to underfunded. The choice of discount rate is generally set by regulations and tradition. Rate assumptions are different across industries, countries, and domains. From the standpoint of economic theory, if the liability cash flows can be hedged perfectly by a set of market-priced assets, the discount rate can be determined by reference to the discount rate for the assets. For example, if the pension plan liabilities are fixed (without any uncertainty), the discount rate should be the risk-free rate with reference to the duration of the liability cash flows—for example, a five-year zero-coupon bond yield for a liability with a (modified) duration of 5. In other cases, it can be difficult to find a fully hedged portfolio because an ongoing DB pension plan's liabilities will depend upon future economic growth and inflation, which are clearly uncertain. Even a frozen pension plan can possess uncertainty due to the changing longevity of the retirees over the long-term future.

APPROACHES TO LIABILITY-RELATIVE ASSET ALLOCATION: SURPLUS OPTIMIZATION

11

☐ | describe and evaluate characteristics of liabilities that are relevant to asset allocation

☐ | discuss approaches to liability-relative asset allocation

☐ | recommend and justify a liability-relative asset allocation

Various approaches to liability-relative asset allocation exist. These methods are influenced by tradition, regulations, and the ability of the stakeholders to understand and extend portfolio models that come from the asset-only domain.

There are several guiding principles. The first is to gain an understanding of the make-up of the investor's liabilities and especially the factors that affect the amount and timing of the cash outflows. Given this understanding, the present value of the liabilities is calculated, along with the surplus and funding ratio. These measures are used to track the results of ongoing investment and funding policies and for other tasks. Next come the decisions regarding the asset allocation taking account of the liabilities. There are a number of ways to proceed. We will discuss three major approaches:

- *Surplus optimization.* This approach involves applying mean–variance optimization (MVO) to an efficient frontier based on the volatility of the surplus ("surplus volatility," or "surplus risk") as the measure of risk. Surplus optimization is thus an extension of MVO based on asset volatility.[18] Depending on context, surplus risk may be stated in money or percentage terms ("surplus return volatility" is then another, more precise term for this measure).

- *Hedging/return-seeking portfolios approach.* This approach involves separating assets into two groups: a hedging portfolio and a return-seeking portfolio. The reading also refers to this as the two-portfolio approach. The concept of allocating assets to two distinct portfolios can be applied for various funding ratios, but the reading distinguishes as the basic approach the case in which there is a positive surplus available to allocate to the return-seeking portfolio.

- *Integrated asset–liability approach.* For some institutional investors, such as banks and insurance companies and long–short hedge funds, asset and liability decisions can be integrated and jointly optimized.

We cover these three approaches in turn.

Surplus Optimization

Surplus optimization involves adapting asset-only mean–variance optimization by substituting surplus return for asset return over any given time horizon. The quadratic optimization program involves choosing the asset allocation (mix) that maximizes expected surplus return net of a penalty for surplus return volatility at the chosen time horizon. The objective function is

$$U_m^{LR} = E\left(R_{s,m}\right) - 0.005\lambda\sigma^2\left(R_{s,m}\right) \tag{2}$$

where U_m^{LR} is the surplus objective function's expected value for a particular asset mix m; $E(R_{s,m})$ is the expected surplus return for asset mix m, with surplus return defined as (Change in asset value – Change in liability value)/(Initial asset value); and the parameter λ (lambda) indicates the investor's risk aversion. The more risk averse the investor, the greater the penalty for surplus return volatility. Note that the change in liability value (liability return) measures the time value of money for the liabilities plus any expected changes in the discount rate and future cash flows over the planning horizon.

This surplus efficient frontier approach is a straightforward extension of the asset-only portfolio model. Surplus optimization assumes that the relationship between the value of liabilities and the value of assets can be approximated through a correlation coefficient. Surplus optimization exploits natural hedges that may exist between assets and liabilities as a result of their systematic risk characteristics.

The following steps describe the surplus optimization approach:

1. Select asset categories and determine the planning horizon. One year is often chosen for the planning exercise, although funding status analysis is based on an analysis of all cash flows.

2. Estimate expected returns and volatilities for the asset categories and estimate liability returns (expanded matrix).

3. Determine any constraints on the investment mix.

4. Estimate the expanded correlation matrix (asset categories and liabilities) and the volatilities.[19]

---

18 Among the papers that discuss the surplus optimization model are Leibowitz and Henriksson (1988); Mulvey (1989, 1994); Sharpe and Tint (1990); Elton and Gruber (1992).
19 A covariance matrix is computed by combining the correlation matrix and the volatilities.

5. Compute the surplus efficient frontier and compare it with the asset-only efficient frontier.

6. Select a recommended portfolio mix.

Exhibit 25 lists LOWTECH's asset categories and current allocation for a one-year planning horizon. The current allocation for other asset categories, such as cash, is zero. LOWTECH has been following an asset-only approach but has decided to adopt a liability-relative approach. The company is exploring several liability-relative approaches. With respect to surplus optimization, the trustees want to maintain surplus return volatility at a level that tightly controls the risk that the plan will become under-funded, and they would like to keep volatility of surplus below US$0.25 billion (10%).

Exhibit 25: Asset Categories and Current Allocation for LOWTECH

	Private Equity	Real Estate	Hedge Funds	Real Assets	US Equities	Non-US Equities (Developed Markets)	Non-US Equities (Emerging Markets)	US Corporate Bonds
Allocation	20.0%	12.0%	18.0%	7.0%	15.0%	12.0%	8.0%	8.0%

The second step is to estimate future expected asset and liability returns, the expected present value of liabilities, and the volatility of both assets and PV(liabilities). The capital market projections can be made in several ways—based on historical data, economic analysis, or expert judgment, for example. The plan sponsor and its advisers are responsible for employing one or a blend of these approaches. Exhibit 26 shows the plan sponsor's capital market assumptions over a three- to five-year horizon. Note the inclusion of the present value of liabilities in Exhibit 26.

Exhibit 26: LOWTECH's Capital Market Assumptions: Expected Annual Compound Returns and Volatilities

	Private Equity	Real Estate	Hedge Funds	Real Assets	US Equities	Non-US Equities (Developed Markets)	Emerging Markets	US Corporate Bonds	Cash	PV (Liabilities)
Expected returns	8.50%	7.50%	7.00%	6.00%	7.50%	7.20%	7.80%	4.90%	1.00%	4.90%
Volatilities	14.20%	9.80%	7.70%	6.10%	18.00%	19.50%	26.30%	5.60%	1.00%	5.60%

Typically, in the third step, the investor imposes constraints on the composition of the asset mix, including policy and legal limits on the amount of capital invested in individual assets or asset categories (e.g., a constraint that an allocation to equities must not exceed 50%). In our example, we simply constrain portfolio weights to be non-negative and to sum to 1.

The fourth step is to estimate the correlation matrix and volatilities. We assume that the liabilities have the same expected returns and volatilities as US corporate bonds; thus, the expanded matrix has a column and a row for liabilities with values equal to the corporate bond values. For simplicity, the investor may employ historical performance. Exhibit 27 shows the correlation matrix of asset categories based on historical quarterly returns. Recall that we assume that liability returns (changes in liabilities) are driven by changes in the returns of US corporate bonds. An alternative approach is to deploy a set of underlying factors that drive the returns of the assets.

Factors include changes in nominal and real interest rates, changes in economic activity (such as employment levels), and risk premiums. This type of factor investment model can be applied in an asset-only or a liability-relative asset allocation context.

Exhibit 27: Correlation Matrix of Returns

	Private Equity	Real Estate	Hedge Funds	Real Assets	US Equities	Non-US Equities (Developed Markets)	Non-US Equities (Emerging Markets)	US Corporate Bonds	Cash	PV (Liabilities)
Private equity	1	0.41	0.57	0.32	0.67	0.59	0.49	−0.27	0	−0.27
Real estate	0.41	1	0.45	0.41	0.31	0.33	0.17	−0.08	0	−0.08
Hedge funds	0.57	0.45	1	0.11	0.68	0.61	0.54	−0.23	0	−0.23
Real assets	0.32	0.41	0.11	1	0.04	0.06	−0.06	0.34	0	0.34
US equities	0.67	0.31	0.68	0.04	1	0.88	0.73	−0.38	0	−0.38
Non-US equities (developed)	0.59	0.33	0.61	0.06	0.88	1	0.81	−0.39	0	−0.39
Non-US equities (emerging)	0.49	0.17	0.54	−0.06	0.73	0.81	1	−0.44	0	−0.44
US corporate bonds	−0.27	−0.08	−0.23	0.34	−0.38	−0.39	−0.44	1	0	1
Cash	0	0	0	0	0	0	0	0	1	0
PV(liabilities)	−0.27	−0.08	−0.23	0.34	−0.38	−0.39	−0.44	1	0	1

Exhibit 28 shows a surplus efficient frontier that results from the optimization program based on the inputs from Exhibit 26 and Exhibit 27. Surplus risk (i.e., volatility of surplus) in money terms (US$ billions) is on the x-axis, and expected surplus in money terms (US$ billions) is on the y-axis. By presenting the efficient frontier in money terms, we can associate the level of risk with the level of plan surplus, US$0.329 billion. Like the asset-only efficient frontier, the surplus efficient frontier has a concave shape.

Exhibit 28: Surplus Efficient Frontier

Total Surplus ($, billions)

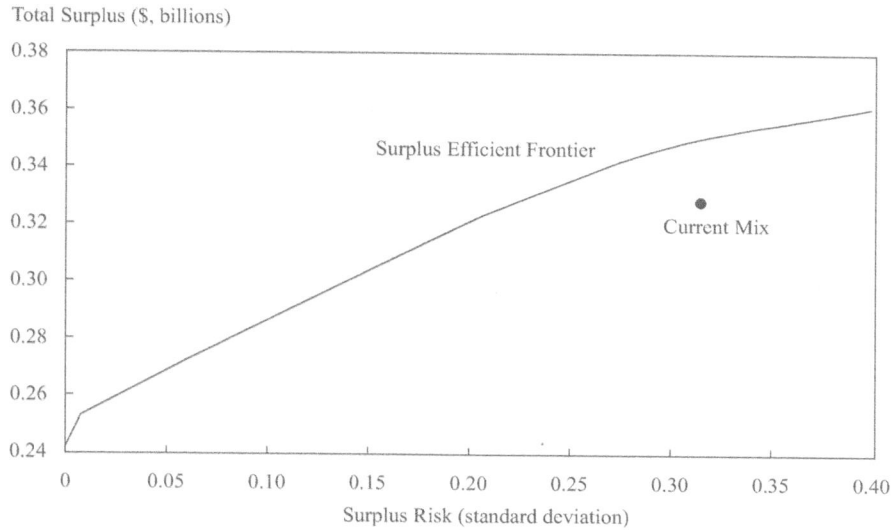

Surplus Risk (standard deviation)

The first observation is that the current mix in Exhibit 28 lies below the surplus efficient frontier and is thus suboptimal.[20] We can attain the same expected total surplus as that of the current mix at a lower level of surplus volatility by choosing the portfolio on the efficient frontier at the current mix's level of expected total surplus. Another observation is that by uncovering the implications of asset mixes for surplus and surplus volatility, this approach allows the deliberate choice of an asset allocation in terms of the tolerable level of risk in relation to liabilities. It may be the case, for example, that neither the surplus volatility of the current mix nor that of the efficient mix with equal expected surplus is the appropriate level of surplus risk for the pension.

The surplus efficient frontier in Exhibit 28 shows efficient reward–risk combinations but does not indicate the asset class composition of the combinations. Exhibit 29 shows the asset class weights for surplus efficient portfolios.

---

20 The current mix can also be shown to lie below the asset-only mean–variance frontier.

Exhibit 29: Surplus Efficient Frontier Asset Allocation Area Graph

Allocation (%)

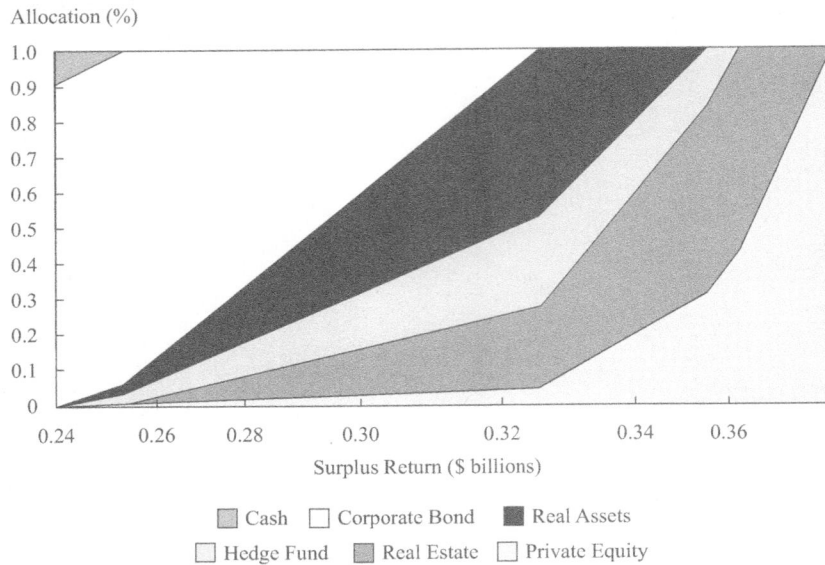

Surplus Return ($ billions)

☐ Cash   ☐ Corporate Bond   ■ Real Assets
☐ Hedge Fund   ■ Real Estate   ☐ Private Equity

Exhibit 30, showing weights for portfolios on the usual *asset-only* efficient frontier based on the same capital market assumptions reflected in Exhibit 29, makes the point that efficient portfolios from the two perspectives are meaningfully different.[21]

Exhibit 30: Asset-Only Efficient Frontier Asset Allocation Area Graph

Allocation (%)

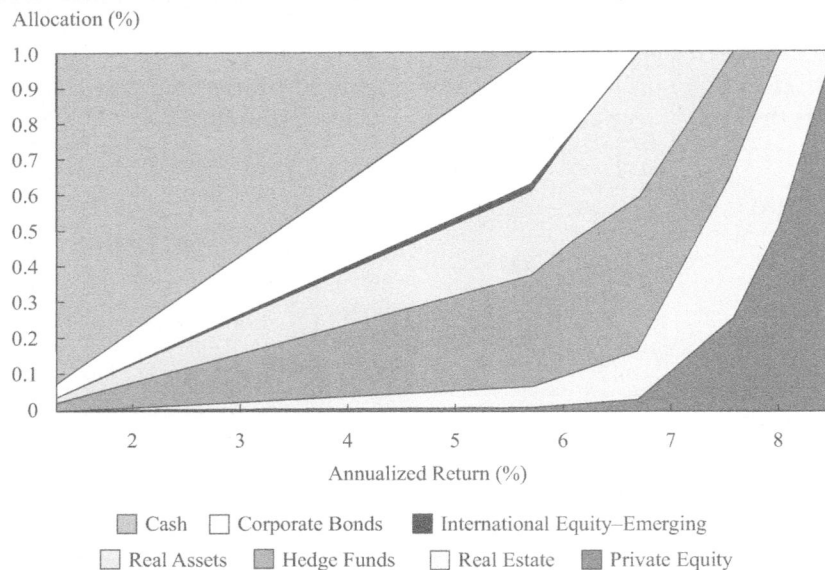

Annualized Return (%)

☐ Cash   ☐ Corporate Bonds   ■ International Equity–Emerging
☐ Real Assets   ■ Hedge Funds   ☐ Real Estate   ■ Private Equity

21 In Exhibit 30, the annualized percentage returns can be equated to monetary surplus returns by multiplying by the asset value, US$2.5 billion.

The asset mixes are very different on the conservative side of the two frontiers. The most conservative mix for the surplus efficient frontier (in Exhibit 29) consists mostly of the US corporate bond index (the hedging asset) because it results in the lowest volatility of surplus over the one-year horizon. Bonds are positively correlated with changes in the present value of the frozen liability cash flows (because the liabilities indicate negative cash flows). In contrast, the most conservative mix for the asset-only efficient frontier (in Exhibit 30) consists chiefly of cash. As long as there is a hedging asset and adequate asset value, the investor can achieve a very low volatility of surplus, and for conservative investors, the asset value at the horizon will be uncertain but the surplus will be constant (or as constant as possible).

The two asset mixes (asset-only and surplus) become similar as the degree of risk aversion decreases, and they are identical for the most aggressive portfolio (private equity). Bonds disappear from the frontier about halfway between the most conservative and the most aggressive mixes, as shown in Exhibit 29 and Exhibit 30.

To summarize, the current asset mix is moderately aggressive and below the surplus efficient frontier. Thus, a mean–variance improvement is possible: either higher expected surplus with the same surplus risk or lower surplus risk for the same expected surplus. The current portfolio is also poorly hedged with regard to surplus volatility; the hedging asset (long bonds in this case) has a low commitment.

The LOWTECH plan has been frozen, and the investment committee is interested in lowering the volatility of the surplus. Accordingly, it seems appropriate to choose an asset allocation toward the left-hand side of the surplus efficient frontier. For instance, a surplus efficient portfolio with about 60% bonds and the remainder in other assets (as can be approximately identified from Exhibit 29) will drop surplus volatility by about 50%.

In the end, the investment committee for the plan sponsor and its advisers and stakeholders are responsible for rendering the best decision, taking into account all of the above considerations. And as always, the recommendations of a portfolio-modeling exercise are only as good as the input data and assumptions.

MULTI-PERIOD PORTFOLIO MODELS

The traditional mean–variance model assumes that the investor follows a buy-and-hold strategy over the planning horizon. Thus, the portfolio is not rebalanced at intermediate dates. A portfolio investment model requires multiple time periods if rebalancing decisions are to be directly incorporated into the model. Mulvey, Pauling, and Madey (2003) discuss the pros and cons of building and implementing multi-period portfolio models. Applicable to both asset-only and liability-relative asset allocation, multi-period portfolio models are more comprehensive than single-period models but are more complex to implement. These models are generally implemented by means of the integrated asset–liability methods discussed in Section 11.

EXAMPLE 6

Surplus Optimization

1. Explain how surplus optimization solutions differ from mean–variance optimizations based on asset class risk alone.

Solution:

The surplus optimization model considers the impact of asset decisions on the (Market value of assets – Present value of liabilities) at the planning horizon.

2. What is a liability return?

Solution:

Liability returns measure the time value of money for the liabilities plus any expected changes in the discount rate over the planning horizon.

3. Compare the composition of a surplus optimal portfolio at two points on the surplus efficient frontier. In particular, take one point at the lower left of the surplus frontier (surplus return = US$0.26 billion) and the other point higher on the surplus efficient frontier (surplus return = US$0.32 billion). Refer to Exhibit 29. Explain the observed relationship in terms of the use of corporate bonds as the hedging asset for the liabilities.

Solution:

Whereas the portfolio at the US$0.26 billion surplus return point on the efficient frontier has a substantial position in corporate bonds, the efficient mix with US$0.32 billion surplus return does not include them. The observed relationship that the allocation to corporate bonds declines with increasing surplus return can be explained by the positive correlation of bond price with the present value of liabilities. The hedging asset (corporate bonds) is employed to a greater degree at the low end of the surplus efficient frontier.

---

12   APPROACHES TO LIABILITY-RELATIVE ASSET ALLOCATION

☐   describe and evaluate characteristics of liabilities that are relevant to asset allocation

☐   discuss approaches to liability-relative asset allocation

☐   recommend and justify a liability-relative asset allocation

Hedging/Return-Seeking Portfolio Approach

In this approach, the liability-relative asset allocation task is divided into two parts. We distinguish as "basic" the two-portfolio approach in the case in which there is a surplus available to allocate to a return-seeking portfolio and as "variants" the approach as applied when there is not a positive surplus. In the basic case, the first part of the asset allocation task consists of hedging the liabilities through a hedging portfolio. In the second part, the surplus (or some part of it) is allocated to a return-seeking portfolio, which can be managed independently of the hedging portfolio (for example, using mean–variance optimization or another method). An essential issue involves the composition of the hedging portfolio. In some cases, such as the LOWTECH frozen DB pension plan, the hedging portfolio is straightforward to identify. The designated cash flows can be hedged via cash flow matching, duration matching, or immunization (as explained in the fixed-income readings). This hedge will support the future cash flows with little or no risk.

In LOWTECH's application of the basic two-portfolio approach, the small surplus causes the pension plan to invest most of its capital in the hedging portfolio. The hedging portfolio can be approximated by the long-bond indexed investment as a first cut. Thus, given a 4% discount rate, US$2.261 billion is placed in long bonds. The remaining US$0.239 billion is invested in a portfolio of higher expected return assets, such as stocks, real estate, and hedge funds. This approach guarantees that the capital is adequate to pay future liabilities, as long as the hedging portfolio does not experience defaults.

Note that if the discount rate were 2% rather than 4%, the pension plan would be underfunded even if all assets were placed in a hedging portfolio. In such a case, the pension plan sponsor would either develop a strategy to increase the funding ratio so that the liabilities would be eventually paid or apply a variant of the two-portfolio approach. An underfunded plan will require higher contributions from the sponsor than a plan that is fully funded or overfunded.

The basic two-portfolio approach is most appropriate for conservative investors, such as insurance companies, and for overfunded pension plans that wish to reduce or eliminate the risk of not being able to pay future liabilities.

Several variants of the two-portfolio approach are possible. These include a partial hedge, whereby capital allocated to the hedging portfolio is reduced in order to generate higher expected returns, and dynamic versions whereby the investor increases the allotment to the hedging portfolio as the funding ratio increases. The specification of this allotment is often referred to as the liability glide path. These variants do not hedge the liabilities to the full extent possible given the assets and thus are less conservative than the basic approach discussed above. Still, there can be benefits to a partial hedge when the sponsor is able to increase contributions if the funding ratio does not increase in the future to 1 or above.

In the following discussion, we focus on determining the hedging portfolio.

Forming the Hedging Portfolio

The hedging portfolio must include assets whose returns are driven by the same factor(s) that drive the returns of the liabilities. Otherwise, even if the assets and liabilities start with equal values, the assets and liabilities will likely become inconsistent over time. One example involves promises (cash outflows) that are dependent upon future inflation. The hedging portfolio in this situation would often include index-linked (inflation-linked) Treasury bonds, again cash matched to the liabilities or immunized to the degree possible.

If there is an active market for the hedging portfolio (securities) in question, the present value of future cash flows is equal to a market value of the assets contained in the hedging portfolio. In this case, the date of valuation for the assets must be the same as the date of valuation for the liabilities. Absent market values, some form of appraised value is used.

The task of forming the hedging portfolio is complicated by the discount rate assumption and by the need to identify assets that are driven by the same factors that affect the liabilities. For example, if the discount rate is set by reference to a marketable instrument, such as the long government bond index, but the liability cash flows are driven by a factor such as inflation, the hedging task may require the use of instruments beyond nominal bonds (perhaps multiple instruments, such as interest rate swaps, inflation-linked bonds, and real assets). And in many applications, the hedge cannot be fully accomplished due to the nature of the driving factors (e.g., if they are non-marketable factors, such as economic growth).

If the uncertainties in the cash flows are related to non-market factors, such as future salary increases, the discount rate will depend upon regulations and tradition. Clearly, high discount rates lead to high funding ratios and in most cases require lower contributions from the sponsoring organization (at least in the short run). Conversely, lower discount rates give rise to lower funding ratios and thereby higher contributions. In the former case, investors with high discount rates will need to generate higher asset returns to achieve their promises if the pension plan sponsor wishes to avoid future contributions. A more conservative route is to designate a lower discount rate, as is the case in much of Europe and Asia. In all cases, it is the regulator's responsibility to set the guidelines, rules, and penalties involved in determining contribution policy.

Several issues complicate the valuation of liability cash flows. In many situations, investors must satisfy their promises without being able to go to a market and purchase a security with positive cash flows equal in magnitude to the liability cash flows.

At times, uncertain liabilities can be made more certain through the law of large numbers. For example, life insurance companies promise to pay beneficiaries when a policyholder dies. The life insurance company can minimize the risk of unexpected losses by insuring large numbers of individuals. Then, valuation of liabilities will use present value of expected cash flows based on a low (or even zero) risk premium in the discount rate. The field of application of the law of large numbers can be limited. For example, averages do not eliminate longevity risk.

Limitations

The basic two-portfolio approach cannot be directly applied under several circumstances. First, if the funding ratio is less than 1, the investor cannot create a fully hedging portfolio unless there is a sufficiently large positive cash flow (contribution). In this case, the sponsor might increase contributions enough to generate a positive surplus. As an alternative, there are conditional strategies that might help improve the investor's funding ratio, such as the glide path rules.[22]

A second barrier occurs when a true hedging portfolio is unavailable. An example involves losses due to weather-related causes, such as hurricanes or earthquakes. In these cases, the investor might be able to partially hedge the portfolio with instruments that share some of the same risks. The investor has "basis risk" when imperfect hedges are employed. (As an aside, the investor might be able to set up a contract with someone who, for a fee, will take on the liability risk that cannot be hedged. Insurance contracts have this defining characteristic.)

---

22 See Gannon and Collins (2009).

The Hedging/Return-Seeking Portfolios Approach

1. Compare how surplus optimization and the hedging/return-seeking portfolio approach take account of liabilities.

Solution:

The surplus optimization approach links assets and the present value of liabilities through a correlation coefficient. The two-portfolio model does not require this input. Surplus optimization considers the asset allocation problem in one step; the hedging/return-seeking portfolio approach divides asset allocation into two steps.

2. How does funding status affect the use of the basic hedging/return-seeking portfolio approach?

Solution:

Implementation of the basic two-portfolio approach depends on having an overfunded plan. A variant of the two-portfolio approach might be applied, however. Surplus optimization does not require an overfunded status. Both approaches address the present value of liabilities, but in different ways.

Integrated Asset–Liability Approach

The previous two approaches are most appropriate when asset allocation decisions are made after, and relatively independently of, decisions regarding the portfolio of liabilities. However, there are numerous applications of the liability-relative perspective in which the institution must render significant decisions regarding the composition of its liabilities *in conjunction with the asset allocation*. Banks, long–short hedge funds (for which short positions constitute liabilities), insurance companies, and re-insurance companies routinely fall into this situation. Within this category, the liability-relative approaches have several names, including asset–liability management (ALM) for banks and some other investors and dynamic financial analysis (DFA) for insurance companies. These approaches are often implemented in the context of multi-period models. Using the following two cases, we review the major issues.

INTEGRATED ASSET–LIABILITY APPROACH FOR PROPERTY/CASUALTY INSURANCE COMPANIES

A property/casualty insurance company must make asset investment decisions in conjunction with business decisions about the portfolio of insured properties, its liabilities. To that end, asset and liability decisions are frequently integrated in an enterprise risk management system. In fact, the liability portfolio is essential to the company's long-term viability. For example, a particular property/casualty (PC) insurance company might engage (accept) liabilities for catastrophic risks such as earthquakes and hurricanes. In this case, the liabilities depend upon rare events and thus are most difficult to hedge against. Specialized firms calculate insured losses for a chosen set of properties for property/casualty insurance companies, and these firms provide liability cash flows on a probabilistic (scenario) basis. In this way information is gathered about the probability of losses over the planning horizon and the estimated losses for each loss event. An important issue involves the amount of capital needed to support the indicated liabilities. This issue is addressed by evaluating the tail risks, such as the 1% Value-at-Risk or Conditional-Value-at-Risk amount. To reduce this risk, there are major advantages to forming a diversified global portfolio of liabilities and rendering asset allocation decisions in conjunction with the liability portfolio decisions. The hedging portfolio in this case is not well defined. Therefore, it is difficult to hedge liabilities for a book of catastrophic risk policies. Liabilities might be addressed via customized products or by purchasing re-insurance. The assets and liabilities are integrated so that the worst-case events can be analyzed with regard to both sides of the balance sheet.

INTEGRATED ASSET–LIABILITY APPROACH FOR BANKS

Large global banks are often required to analyze their ability to withstand stress scenarios, in accordance with the Basel III framework. These institutions must be able to show that their current capital is adequate to withstand losses in their business units, such as asset trading, in conjunction with increases in liabilities. The chief risk officer evaluates these scenarios by means of integrated asset–liability approaches. The asset and liability decisions are linked in an enterprise manner. Both the portfolio of assets and the portfolio of liabilities have major impacts on the organization's risk. Thus, decisions to take on new products or expand an existing product—thereby generating liabilities—must take into account the associated decisions on the asset side. The integrated asset–liability management system provides a mechanism for discovering the optimal mix of assets and liabilities (products). These applications often employ multi-period models via a set of projected scenarios.

Decisions about asset allocation will affect the amount of business available to a financial intermediary, such as a bank or insurance company. Similarly, decisions about the portfolio of liabilities and concentration risks will feed back to the asset allocation decisions. Accordingly, we can set up a linked portfolio model. In a similar fashion, the performance of the assets of an institution possessing quasi-liabilities, such as a university endowment, will affect the spending rules for the institution. We can reduce worst-case outcomes by adjusting spending during crash periods, for example. Portfolio models linked to liabilities can provide significant information, helping the institution make the best compromise decisions for both the assets and the liabilities under its control. The twin goals are to maximize the growth of surplus over time subject to constraints on worst-case and other risk measures relative to the institution's surplus.

Comparing the Approaches

We have introduced three approaches for addressing asset allocation decisions in the context of liability issues; Exhibit 31 summarizes their characteristics. Each of these approaches has been applied in practice. The surplus optimization approach is a straightforward extension of the traditional (asset-only) mean–variance model. Surplus optimization demonstrates the importance of the hedging asset for risk-averse investors and provides choices for investors who are less risk averse in the asset mixes located on the middle and the right-hand side of the efficient frontier. The assumptions are similar to those of the traditional Markowitz model, where the inputs are expected returns and a covariance matrix. Thus, the assets and liabilities are linked through correlation conditions. The second approach, separating assets into two buckets, has the advantage of simplicity. The basic approach is most appropriate for conservative investors, such as life insurance companies, and for overfunded/fully funded institutional investors that can fully hedge their liabilities. Another advantage of this approach is a focus on the hedging portfolio and its composition. The hedging portfolio can be constructed using a factor model and then linked to the assets via the same factors. Unfortunately, underfunded investors do not have the luxury of fully hedging their liabilities and investing the surplus in the risky portion; they must apply variants of the two-portfolio approach. The third approach, integrating the liability portfolio with the asset portfolio, is the most comprehensive of the three. It requires a formal method for selecting liabilities and for linking the asset performance with changes in the liability values. This approach can be implemented in a factor-based model, linking the assets and liabilities to the underlying driving factors. It has the potential to improve the institution's overall surplus. It does not require the linear correlation assumption and is capable of modeling transaction costs, turnover constraints, and other real-world constraints. The capital required for this approach is often determined by reference to the output of integrated asset–liability systems in banks and property/casualty insurance and re-insurance companies.

Exhibit 31: Characteristics of the Three Liability-Relative Asset Allocation Approaches

Surplus Optimization	Hedging/Return-Seeking Portfolios	Integrated Asset–Liability Portfolios
Simplicity	Simplicity	Increased complexity
Linear correlation	Linear or non-linear correlation	Linear or non-linear correlation
All levels of risk	Conservative level of risk	All levels of risk
Any funded ratio	Positive funded ratio for basic approach	Any funded ratio
Single period	Single period	Multiple periods

EXAMPLE 8

Liability-Relative Asset Allocation: Major Approaches

1. Discuss how the probability of not being able to pay future liabilities when they come due is or is not addressed by each of the major approaches to liability-relative asset allocation.

Solution:

Such issues are best addressed by means of multi-period integrated asset–liability models. Surplus optimization and the two-portfolio approach, being single-period models, have difficulty estimating the probability of meeting future obligations.

2. What are the advantages of the three approaches for investors who are more interested in protecting the surplus than growing their assets? Assume that the investor has a positive surplus.

Solution:

The three liability-relative approaches are appropriate for conservative investors (investors who are more interested in protecting the surplus than growing their assets). All of the three approaches force investors to understand the nature of their liabilities. This type of information can help inform the decision-making process.

13   EXAMINING THE ROBUSTNESS OF ASSET ALLOCATION ALTERNATIVES

☐ | discuss approaches to liability-relative asset allocation

As part of a liability-relative asset allocation study, the institutional investor can evaluate performance over selected events and "simulated" historical time periods. Each of the selected events can be interpreted as a "what if" sensitivity analysis. For example, we might wish to consider the effect of a 100 bp increase in interest rates across all maturities—that is, a parallel shift in the yield curve. This event would have a significant impact on the value of government bonds, clearly. Also, there would be a corresponding positive impact on the present discounted value of liabilities that are discounted at the government bond rate. The effect on other liability-relative asset allocation elements is less direct, and assumptions must be made. Suppose, for example, that the investor must discount at the high-quality corporate rate. In that case, we need to estimate the effect of changing government rates on corporate rates. These designated studies are part of the stress tests required by banking and other regulators.

Another type of event study is the construction of scenarios based on carefully selected historical time periods. For example, we might select late 2008 as a reference point. In such a scenario, we are interested in the changes in the economic factors and the associated changes in the values of the institution's assets and liabilities. What would be the impact on our current (or projected) portfolio—assets and PV(liabilities)—if the conditions seen in late 2008 occurred again?

A more comprehensive method for examining robustness involves setting up a multi-stage simulation analysis. Here, we use scenarios to model uncertainty and replace decisions with "rules." The process begins with a set of scenarios for the underlying driving economic factors. Each scenario designates a path for the asset returns and the liability values at each stage of the planning horizon. The result is a set of probabilistic outcomes for the institutional investor's asset portfolio and the cash flows for its liabilities. In such modeling, one must take care to be consistent between asset returns and corresponding liabilities within a scenario; for example, if interest rates are a common factor driving both asset performance and the PV (liabilities), the interest rate effects should be based on the same assumptions.

Through the scenario analysis, the probability of both good and bad outcomes can be estimated. For example, we can measure the probability that an institutional investor will make a capital contribution in the future. Exhibit 32 shows the decision structure for the simulation of an insurance company over several periods, including modeling of the company's business strategy and the required capital rules.

To evaluate robustness, we can apply the simulation system with different assumptions. For instance, if we change the expected return of US equities, what is the effect on the probability of meeting the liabilities over an extended horizon, such as 10 years? This type of sensitivity analysis is routinely done in conjunction with the modeling exercise.

Exhibit 32: Simulation Analysis

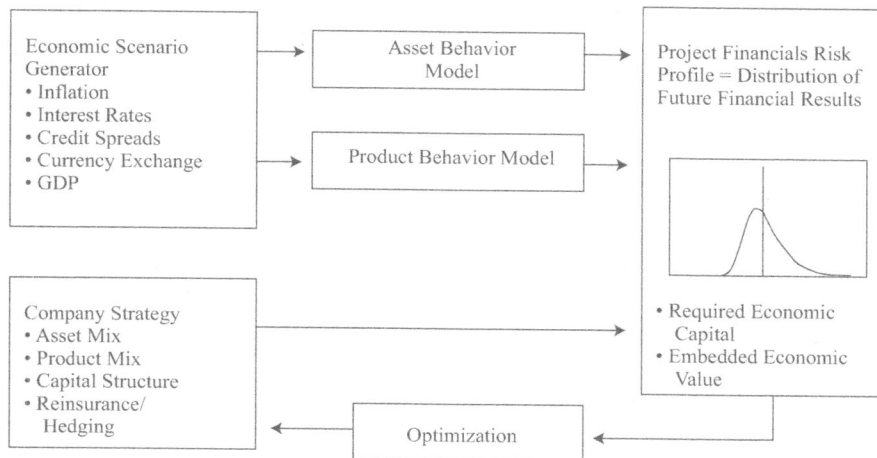

FACTOR MODELING IN LIABILITY-RELATIVE APPROACHES

14

☐ describe the use of investment factors in constructing and analyzing an asset allocation

☐ discuss approaches to liability-relative asset allocation

A factor-based approach for liability-relative asset allocation has gained interest and credibility for several reasons. First, in many applications, the liability cash flows are dependent on multiple uncertainties. The two primary macro factors are future economic conditions and inflation. Many pension payments to beneficiaries will be based on inflation and salary changes over the employees' work span. A fully hedged portfolio cannot be constructed when the liabilities are impacted by these uncertain factors. Recall that a hedged portfolio can be constructed for a frozen plan with fixed liabilities. For ongoing pension schemes, the best that can be done is to add asset categories to the portfolio that are positively correlated with the underlying driving risk factors, such as inflation-linked bonds. A factor-based approach can be implemented with any of the three liability-relative asset allocation methods discussed above.

Robustness and Risk Assessment in Liability-Relative Asset Allocation

1. What types of sensitivity analysis can be evaluated with a multi-period ALM simulation system?

Solution:

To provide estimates of the probability of meeting future obligations and the distribution of outcomes, several types of sensitivity analysis are likely to be performed.

- For example, the expected returns could be increased or decreased to evaluate the impact on future contributions to the plan.

- Likewise, by analyzing historical events, the investor can estimate the size of losses during crash periods and make decisions about the best asset allocation to protect against these worst-case events. Multiple risk measures over time (temporal risk measures) can be readily included in a simulation system.

15   DEVELOPING GOALS-BASED ASSET ALLOCATIONS

☐ | recommend and justify an asset allocation using a goals-based approach

In this section, we review the concept of goals-based asset allocation, focusing first on the rationale behind this different approach and its investment implications. We then discuss the major elements of the process, illustrating them with specific, simplified examples when necessary. We conclude with a discussion of the applicability of the approach and its major shortcomings.

A goals-based asset allocation process disaggregates the investor's portfolio into a number of sub-portfolios, each of which is designed to fund an individual goal (or "mental account") with its own time horizon and required probability of success. The literature behind the development of this approach is very rich. Initially, goals-based wealth management was specifically proposed by a small group of practitioners,[23] each of whom offered his own solution for taking into account the tendency of individuals to classify money into non-fungible mental accounts. Shefrin and Statman (2000) developed the concept of the behavioral portfolio, which can be related to the Maslow (1943) hierarchy of needs. Das, Markowitz, Scheid, and Statman (2010, 2011) showed that traditional and behavioral finance could be viewed as equivalent if one were prepared to change the definition of risk from volatility of returns to the probability of not achieving a goal.[24] The essential point is that optimality requires

---

23 See Brunel (2003, 2005); Nevins (2004); Pompian and Longo (2004); Chhabra (2005).
24 We apologize to these authors for grossly oversimplifying their work, but our aim is to make their insights more readily available without going into excruciating detail.

both a suitably structured portfolio that can meet the given need *and* the correct capital allocation based on an appropriate discount rate, reflecting considerations of time horizon and the required probability of success.

Individuals have needs that are different from those of institutions. The most important difference is that individuals often have multiple goals, each with its own time horizon and its own "urgency," which can be expressed as a specific required probability of success. Exhibit 33 summarizes differences in institutional and individual investor definitions of goals. An individual's goals are not necessarily mutually compatible in two senses: The investor may not be able to address them all given the financial assets available, and there may be internal contradictions among the goals. An alternative process using one set of overall investment objectives—and thus effectively ignoring or "averaging" the different time horizons and required probabilities of success of individual goals—ostensibly loses the granular nature of client goals; as a result, the inherent complexities of the investment problem are less likely to be addressed fully. An approach that breaks the problem into sub-portfolios carries a higher chance of fully addressing an investor's goals, although it may require several iterations to ensure that the investor's portfolio is internally consistent and satisfactory.

Exhibit 33: Institutional and Individual Ways of Defining Goals

	Institutions	Individuals
Goals	Single	Multiple
Time horizon	Single	Multiple
Risk measure	Volatility (return or surplus)	Probability of missing goal
Return determination	Mathematical expectations[a]	Minimum expectations
Risk determination	Top-down/bottom-up	Bottom-up
Tax status	Single, often tax-exempt	Mostly taxable

[a] *"Mathematical expectations" here means the weighted expected return of portfolio components.*

The characteristics of individuals' goals have three major implications for an investment process that attempts to address the characteristics directly:

- The overall portfolio needs to be divided into sub-portfolios to permit each goal to be addressed individually.
- Both taxable and tax-exempt investments are important.
- Probability- and horizon-adjusted expectations (called "minimum expectations" in Exhibit 33) replace the typical use of mathematically expected average returns in determining the appropriate funding cost for the goal (or "discount rate" for future cash flows).

Compared with average return expectations—the median or average return anticipated for a combination of assets that is appropriate to address a goal—minimum expectations reflect a more complex concept. Minimum expectations are defined as the minimum return expected to be earned over the given time horizon with a given minimum required probability of success.

To illustrate, assume that a portfolio associated with a goal has an expected return of 7% with 10% expected volatility and the investor has indicated that the goal is to be met over the next five years with at least 90% confidence. Over the next five years, that portfolio is expected to produce returns of 35% with a volatility of 22.4%.[25] In short, this portfolio is expected to experience an average compound return of only 1.3% per year over five years with a probability of 90%; this result is quite a bit lower than the portfolio's average 7% expected return (see Exhibit 34). Thus, rather than discounting expected cash outflows by 7% to compute the dollar amount needed to defease the goal over that five-year horizon, one must use a considerably lower discount rate and by implication reserve a higher level of capital to meet that goal. Under moderate simplifying assumptions, that computation is valid whether or not return and volatility numbers are pretax or after-tax. Exhibit 34 shows, for the case of a normal distribution of returns, a return level that is expected to be exceeded 90% of the time (the 40% of the probability that lies between the vertical lines plus the 50% to the right of the median).

Exhibit 34: Probability-Weighted Return vs. Expected (= Median) Return

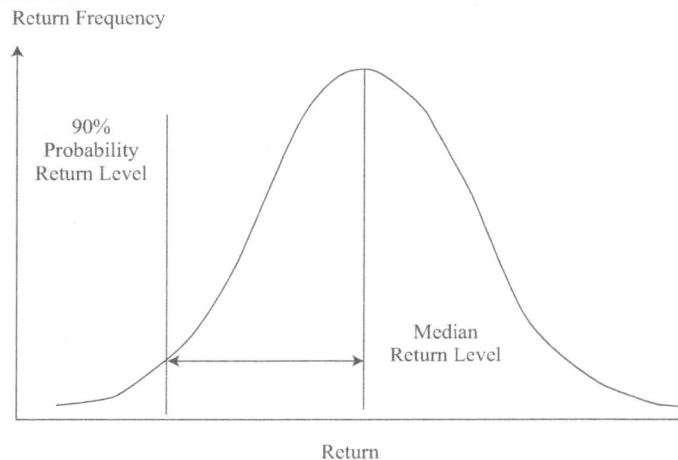

The Goals-Based Asset Allocation Process

Investment advisers taking a goals-based approach to investing client assets may implement this approach in a variety of ways. Exhibit 35 illustrates the major elements of the goals-based asset allocation process described in this reading. Ostensibly, there are two fundamental parts to this process. The first centers on the creation of portfolio modules, while the second involves identifying client goals and matching each of these goals to the appropriate sub-portfolio of a suitable asset size.

---

25 The return is the product of the annual return times the number of years, while the volatility is the product of the annual volatility times the square root of the number of years (under the assumption of independently and identically distributed returns).

Exhibit 35: A Stylized Representation of the Goals-Based Asset Allocation Process

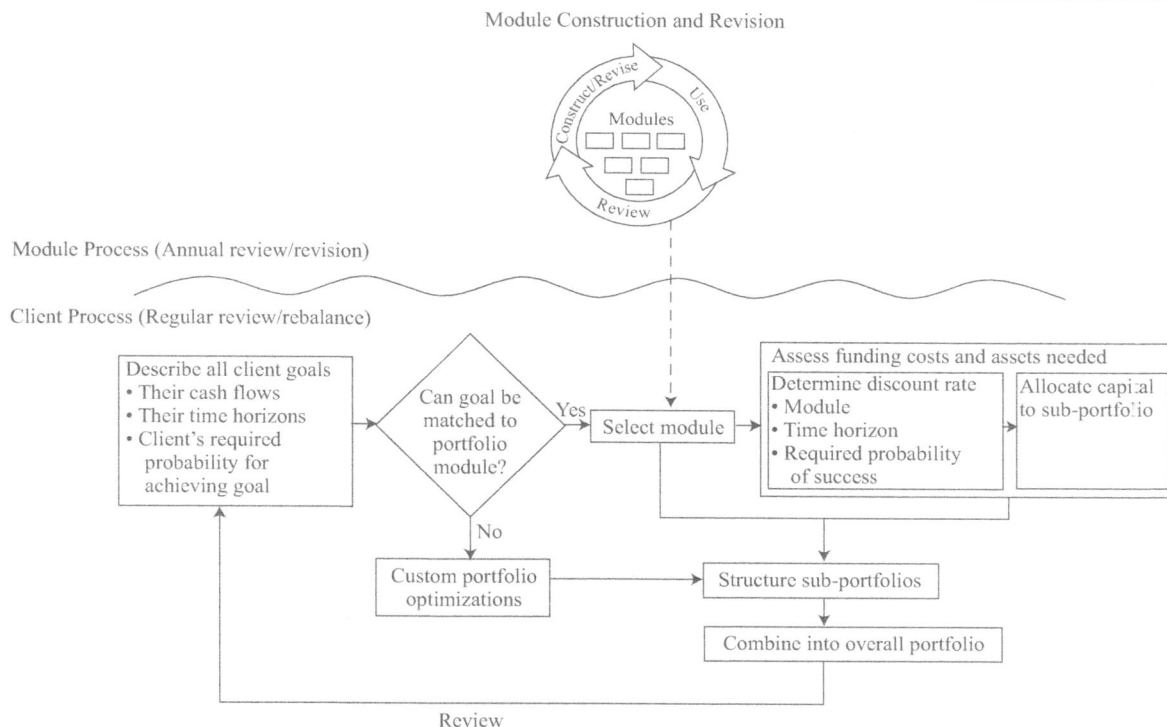

Determining the lowest-cost funding for any given goal requires the formulation of an optimized portfolio that will be used to defease that goal optimally in the sense that risks are not taken for which the investor is not fairly compensated. Note that this process is most often generic and internal to the adviser and his or her firm. The adviser will typically not create a specific sub-portfolio for each goal of each client but rather will select, from a pre-established set, one of a few modules—or model portfolios—that best meet each goal.[26] As discussed above, adjusting the expected return on that portfolio to account for the time horizon and the required probability of success allows one to formulate the relevant discount rate which, when applied to the expected cash flows, will help determine the capital required at the outset. That capital will then be invested in the optimized portfolio asset allocation, where the balance will decline until the end of the horizon, when it runs out.[27] Note that the process is somewhat iterative because individual investors may describe a certain horizon as set when in fact they view it as "the next x years," with the horizon rolling by one year every year. Note also that discounting needs based on probability- and

---

26 See the next paragraph for a discussion of when it makes sense to create specific optimal sub-portfolios.
27 An important reason for the use of a declining-balance portfolio relates to the need for individuals and families to plan for the transfer of assets at death. In order for the income from assets to be used by an individual, these assets must be in the individual's name, or at least in a structure of which he or she is a beneficiary. Such assets would then be a part of the estate of the individual. Using a declining-balance portfolio allows the individual to receive the income—and some of the principal liquidated every year—while still ensuring that the amount of assets kept in the individual's name remains as low as appropriate given the individual's goals. An exception to this scenario would be the case of families whose income needs are so modest in relation to total assets that there is no need to provide income in planning for generational transfers or families that have such large eventual philanthropic intentions that assets kept in some beneficiaries' names are meant to be transferred to charity at death.

horizon-adjusted minimum expectations naturally means that these expectations will be exceeded under "normal circumstances." Thus, it is not unusual for the funding for a goal to seem excessive with the benefit of hindsight.

Although the great majority of advisers will likely create individual client portfolios using model portfolios—precisely, pre-optimized modules—a greater degree of customization is possible. Such customization involves creating specific sub-portfolios for each goal of each client. Indeed, it is conceivable, and mathematically possible, to create an optimal sub-portfolio for each goal. In fact, in practice, one would often proceed in this way when dealing with complex situations and with clients who have highly differentiated needs and constraints.[28] The adviser may find it impossible to use pre-optimized modules if the investment constraints imposed by the client are incompatible with those used in the creation of the module set. These might include, for instance, geographical or credit emphases—or de-emphases—that conflict with the market portfolio concept. Other restrictions might concern base currency, the use of alternative strategies, or the acceptability of illiquid investments, for example. Thus, although it is feasible for advisers to create client-specific modules, this approach can become prohibitively expensive. In short, one would likely use standardized modules for most individuals, except for those whose situation is so complex as to require a fully customized approach.

Many multi-client advisers may prefer to create a set of "goal modules" whose purpose is, collectively, to cover a full range of capital market opportunities and, individually, to represent a series of return–risk trade-offs that are sufficiently differentiated to offer adequate but not excessive choices to meet all the goals they expect their clients to express. These modules should therefore collectively appear to create a form of efficient frontier, though the frontier they depict in fact does not exist because the modules may well be based on substantially different sets of optimization constraints.

The two most significant differences from one module to the next, besides the implied return–risk trade-offs, are liquidity requirements and the eligibility of certain asset classes or strategies. Additionally, while intra–asset class allocation to individual sub–asset classes or strategies may typically be guided by the market portfolio for that asset class, one can conceive of instances where the selection of a specific sub–asset class or strategy is justified, even though the asset class per se may seem inappropriate. For instance, one might agree to hold high-yield bonds in an equity-dominated portfolio because of the equity risk factor exposure inherent in lower-credit fixed income. Conversely, the fixed-income market portfolio might be limited to investment-grade bonds and possibly the base-currency-hedged variant of non-domestic investment-grade bonds. We will return to the construction of these modules in Section 17.

Describing Client Goals

At this point, it is important to note that individual investors do not always consider all goals as being equal and similarly well-formulated in their own minds. Thus, while certain investors will have a well-thought-out set of goals—which may at times not be simultaneously achievable given the financial assets available—others will focus only on a few "urgent" goals and keep other requirements in the background.

Thus, a first step is to distinguish between goals for which anticipated cash flows are available—whether regularly or irregularly timed across the horizon or represented by a bullet payment at some future point—and those we call "labeled goals," for which details are considerably less precise. The term "labeled" here simply means that the individual has certain "investment features" in mind—such as minimal risk, capital

---

28 Note that such an approach, being more complex, is also costlier. It would therefore be more likely to be economically feasible for those advisory clients who also have the ability to pay a higher fee.

preservation, purchasing power preservation, and long-term growth—but has not articulated the actual need that stands behind each label. The individual may already have mentally allocated some portion of his or her assets, in currency or percentage terms, to one or several of these labels. For cash flow–based goals,[29] the time horizon over which the goal is to be met is usually not difficult to ascertain: It is either the period over which cash outflows are expected to be made or the point in time at which a bullet payment is expected. More complex, however, is the issue of the urgency of the goal and thus of the required minimum probability of success.

By working to preserve a human (as opposed to a technical) tone in the advisory conversations, the adviser can serve the client without forcing him or her to come up with a quantified probability of success. The adviser may start with the simple observation that there are two fundamental types of goals: those that one seeks to achieve and those whose consequences one seeks to avoid. Dividing the goals the investor seeks to achieve into "needs, wants, wishes, and dreams" provides the adviser with an initial sense of the urgency of each goal. A need typically must be met and so should command a 90%–99% probability of success, while at the other end of the spectrum, it is an unfortunate fact that we all live with unfulfilled dreams, whose required probabilities of success probably fall below 60%. A parallel—and analogous—structure can be created to deal with goals one seeks to avoid:[30] "nightmares, fears, worries, and concerns," with similar implications in terms of required probabilities of success. In short, while some discussion of probability level may well take place, it can be informed and guided by the use of commonly accepted everyday words that will ensure that the outcome is internally consistent. The adviser avoids the use of jargon, which many clients dislike, and yet is able to provide professional advice.[31]

The simplest way to bring this concept to life is to work with a basic case study. Imagine a family, the Smiths, with financial assets of US$25 million. (For the sake of simplicity, we are assuming that they do not pay taxes and that all assets are owned in a single structure.) The parents are in their mid-fifties, and the household spends about US$500,000 a year. They expect that inflation will average about 2% per year for the foreseeable future. They express four important goals and are concerned that they may not be able to meet all of them:

1. They *need* a 95% chance of being able to maintain their current expenditures over the next five years.

2. They *want* an 85% chance of being able to maintain their current expenditures over the ensuing 25 years, which they see as a reasonable estimate of their joint life expectancy.

3. They *need* a 90% chance of being able to transfer US$10 million to their children in 10 years.

4. They *wish* to have a 75% chance to be able to create a family foundation, which they wish to fund with US$10 million in 20 years.

---

29 Note that all cash flows do not have to be negative (i.e., outflows). One can easily imagine circumstances where certain future inflows are anticipated and yet are not seen, individually, as sufficient to meet the specified goal.

30 Although negative goals may sound surprising, they do exist and play a double role. First, when a negative goal is explicitly stated, it can be "replaced" by a specific positive goal: Avoiding the nightmare of running out of capital, for example, can be turned into the need to meet a certain expense budget. Second, negative goals serve as a useful feedback loop to check the internal consistency of the investor's goal set.

31 Note that the adviser can also identify a series of "secondary" words to help determine whether a need, for instance, means that the required probability of success should be set at 99%, 95%, or 90%. An *indispensable* need could require a 99% probability of being met, while an *urgent* need might require only a 95% probability of success, and a *serious* need a 90% probability.

EXAMPLE 10

Understanding Client Goals

1. A client describes a desire to have a reserve of €2 million for business opportunities that may develop when he retires in five years. What are the important features of this goal?

Solution:

The time horizon is five years. Words such as "desire" in describing a goal, compared with expressions indicating "need," indicate that there is room for "error" in the event that capital markets are not supportive. The portfolio required to meet the goal described as a desire will likely be able to involve a riskier profile. One would want to verify this assumption by comparing the size of that goal compared with the total financial assets available to the client.

2. A 70-year-old client discusses the need to be able to maintain her lifestyle for the balance of her life and wishes to leave US$3 million to be split among her three grandchildren at her death. What are the important features of this situation?

Solution:

The key takeaway is that although the two goals have the same time horizon, the two portfolios designed to defease them will have potentially significantly different risk profiles. The time horizon is approximately 20 years. The first goal relates to maintaining the client's lifestyle and must be defeased with an appropriately structured portfolio. The second goal, relating to the wish to leave some money to grandchildren, will allow more room for risk taking.

---

16   CONSTRUCTING SUB-PORTFOLIOS AND THE OVERALL PORTFOLIO

> ☐ | recommend and justify an asset allocation using a goals-based approach

Having defined the needs of the investor in as much detail as possible, the next step in the process is to identify the amount of money that needs to be allocated to each goal and the asset allocation that will apply to that sum. For most advisers, the process will start with a set of sub-portfolio modules (such as those we briefly discussed in Section 15 and will study in more depth in Section 17). When using a set of pre-optimized modules, the adviser will then need to identify the module best suited to each of the specific goals of the client. That process is always driven by the client's time horizon and required probability of success, and it involves identifying the module that offers the highest possible return given the investor's risk tolerance as characterized by a given required probability of success over a given time horizon.

To illustrate, consider the set of six modules shown in Exhibit 36;[32] these modules result from an optimization process that will be explained later.[33] In the exhibit, the entries for minimum expected return are shown rounded to one decimal place; subsequent calculations for required capital are based on full precision.

Exhibit 36: "Highest Probability- and Horizon-Adjusted Return" Sub-Portfolio Module under Different Horizon and Probability Scenarios

	A	B	C	D	E	F
Portfolio Characteristics						
Expected return	4.3%	5.5%	6.4%	7.2%	8.0%	8.7%
Expected volatility	2.7%	4.5%	6.0%	7.5%	10.0%	12.5%
Annualized Minimum Expectation Returns						
Time Horizon (years)			5			
Required Success						
99%	1.5%	0.9%	0.2%	−0.6%	−2.4%	−4.3%
95	2.3	2.2	2.0	1.7	0.7	−0.5
90	2.7	3.0	3.0	2.9	2.3	1.5
75	3.5	4.2	4.6	4.9	5.0	4.9
Time Horizon (years)			10			
Required Success						
99%	2.3%	2.2%	2.0%	1.7%	0.7%	−0.5%
90	3.2	3.7	4.0	4.1	4.0	3.6
75	3.7	4.6	5.1	5.6	5.9	6.0%
60	4.1	5.2	5.9	6.6	7.2	7.7
Time Horizon (years)			20			
Required Success						
95%	3.3%	3.9%	4.2%	4.4%	4.4%	4.1%
90	3.5	4.3	4.7	5.0	5.2	5.1
85	3.7	4.5	5.0	5.4	5.7	5.8
75	3.9	4.9	5.5	6.0	6.5	6.8
Time Horizon (years)			25			
Required Success						
95%	3.4%	4.1%	4.4%	4.7%	4.7%	4.6%
90	3.6	4.4	4.9	5.2	5.5	5.5
85	3.7	4.6	5.2	5.6	6.0	6.1
75	3.9	4.9	5.6	6.2	6.7	7.0

---

32 The different ranges of required probabilities of success for various time horizons reflect the fact that the differentiation across modules can occur more or less rapidly, reflecting the different ratios of return per unit of risk.

33 Exhibit 38 presents the details of the asset allocation of these modules and the constraints underpinning their optimization.

In Exhibit 36, the top section, on portfolio characteristics, presents the expected return and expected volatility of each module. Below that are four sections, one for each of four time horizons: 5, 10, 20, and 25 years. In a given section, the entries are the returns that are expected for a given required probability of achieving success. For example, at a 10-year horizon and a 90% required probability of success, Modules A, B, C, D, E, and F are expected to return, respectively, 3.2%, 3.7%, 4.0%, 4.1%, 4.0%, and 3.6%. In this case, Module D would be selected to address a goal with this time horizon and required probability of success because its 4.1% expected return is higher than those of all the other modules. Thus, Module D offers the lowest "funding cost" for the given goal. The highest expected return translates to the lowest initially required capital when the expected cash flows associated with the goal are discounted using that expected return.

EXAMPLE 11

Selecting a Module

Address the following module selection problems using Exhibit 36:

1. A client describes a desire to have a reserve of €2 million for business opportunities that may develop when he retires in five years. Assume that the word "desire" points to a wish to which the adviser will ascribe a probability of 75%.

Solution:

The time horizon is five years. Exhibit 36 shows that Module E has the highest expected return (5.0%) over the five-year period and with the assumed 75% required probability of success.

2. A 70-year-old client with a 20-year life expectancy discusses the need to be able to maintain her lifestyle for the balance of her life and wishes to leave US$3 million to be split among her three grandchildren at her death.

Solution:

The time horizon is 20 years. The first goal is a need, while the second is a wish. We assume a required probability of success of 95% for a need and 75% for a wish. Exhibit 36 shows that Module D provides the highest horizon- and required-probability-adjusted return (4.4%) for the first goal. Module F is better suited to the second goal because, even though the second goal has the same time horizon, it involves only a 75% required probability of success; the appropriately adjusted return is 6.8%, markedly the highest, which means the initially required capital is lower.

Returning to the Smiths, let us use that same set of modules to look at their four specific goals. The results of our analysis are presented in Exhibit 37.

1. The first goal is a need, with a five-year time horizon and a 95% required probability of success. Looking at the 95% required probability line in the five-year time horizon section of Exhibit 36, we can see that the module with the highest expected return on a time horizon- and required probability-adjusted basis is Module A and that the appropriately adjusted expected return for that module is 2.3%. Discounting a US$500,000 annual cash flow, inflated by 2% a year from Year 2 onwards, required a US$2,430,000 initial investment. This amount represents 9.7% of the total financial wealth of the Smiths.

2. The second goal is a want, with a 25-year time horizon and an 85% required probability of success. The corresponding line of the table in Exhibit 36 points to Module F and a discount rate of 6.1%. Discounting their current expenses with the same assumption over the 25 years starting in Year 6 with a 6.1% rate points to an initially required capital of US$6,275,000, representing 25.1% of the Smiths' wealth.

3. The third goal is another need, with a 10-year time horizon and a 90% required probability of success. Module D is the best module, and the US$6,691,000 required capital reflects the discounting of a US$10 million payment in 10 years at the 4.1% indicated in Exhibit 36.

4. Finally, the fourth goal is a wish with a 20-year time horizon and a 75% required probability of success. Module F is again the best module, and the discounting of a US$10 million payment 20 years from now at the 6.8% expected return from Exhibit 36 points to a required capital of US$2,683,000 today.

Note that different goals may, in fact, be optimally addressed using the same module; thus, an individual module may be used more than once in the allocation of the individual's overall financial assets. Here, Goals 2 and 4 can both be met with the riskiest of the six modules, although their time horizons differ, as do the required probabilities of success, with Goal 2 being characterized as a want and Goal 4 as a wish.

Exhibit 37: Module Selection and Dollar Allocations (US$ thousands)

	Total Financial Assets				25,000	
	Goals					Overall Asset Allocation
	1	2	3	4	Surplus	
Horizon (years)	5	25	10	20		
Required probability of success	95%	85%	90%	75%	$E(R_t)$	7.2%
Discount rate	2.3%	6.1%	4.1%	6.8%	$\sigma(R_t)$	8.0%
Module	A	F	D	F	C	
Required capital						
In currency	2,430	6,275	6,691	2,683	6,921	25,000
As a % of total	9.7%	25.1%	26.8%	10.7%	27.7%	100.0%

Note also that the Smiths' earlier worry, that they might not be able to meet all their goals, can be addressed easily. Our assumptions suggest that, in fact, they have excess capital representing 27.7% of their total financial wealth. They can either revisit their current goals and bring the timing of payments forward or raise their probability of success. The case suggests that they would rather think of additional goals but will want to give themselves some time to refine their intentions. Their adviser then suggests that a "middle of the road" module be used as a "labeled goal" for that interim period, and they call this module (Module C) "capital preservation."

The Overall Portfolio

Assuming the same six modules, with their detailed composition shown in Exhibit 38, one can then derive the overall asset allocation by aggregating the individual exposures to the various modules. In short, the overall allocation is simply the weighted average exposure to each of the asset classes or strategies within each module, with the weight being the percentage of financial assets allocated to each module. Exhibit 39 presents these computations and the overall asset allocation, which is given in bold in the right-most column. The overall portfolio's expected return and volatility are also shown. In Exhibit 38, liquidity[34] is measured as one minus the ratio of the average number of days that might be needed to liquidate a position to the number of trading days in a year. (Note that the column B values add up to 101 because of rounding.)

Exhibit 38: Asset Allocation of Each Module

	A	B	C	D	E	F
Portfolio Characteristics						
Expected return	4.3%	5.5%	6.4%	7.2%	8.0%	8.7%
Expected volatility	2.7%	4.5%	6.0%	7.5%	10.0%	12.5%
Expected liquidity	100.0%	96.6%	90.0%	86.1%	83.6%	80.0%
Portfolio Allocations						
Cash	80%	26%	3%	1%	1%	1%
Global investment-grade bonds	20	44	45	25	0	0
Global high-yield bonds	0	5	11	25	34	4
Lower-volatility alternatives	0	9	13	0	0	0
Global developed equities	0	9	13	19	34	64
Global emerging equities	0	2	2	3	6	11
Equity-based alternatives	0	0	0	8	0	0
Illiquid global equities	0	0	5	10	15	20
Trading strategy alternatives	0	1	3	6	7	0
Global real estate	0	5	5	3	3	0
Total	100%	100%	100%	100%	100%	100%

---

34 Note that we need to incorporate some estimate of liquidity for all asset classes and strategies to ensure that the client's and the goals' liquidity constraints can be met.

Exhibit 39: Goals-Based Asset Allocation (US$ thousands)

	Total Financial Assets				25,000	
	Goals					**Overall Asset Allocation**
	1	**2**	**3**	**4**	**Surplus**	
Horizon	5	25	10	20		
Required success	95%	85%	90%	75%	$E(R_t)$	7.2%
Discount rate	2.3%	6.1%	4.1%	6.8%	$\sigma(R_t)$	8.0%
Module	**A**	**F**	**D**	**F**	**C**	
Required capital						
In currency	2,430	6,275	6,691	2,683	6,921	25,000
As a % of total	9.7	25.1	26.8	10.7	27.7	100.0
Cash	80%	1%	1%	1%	3%	**9%**
Global investment-grade bonds	20	0	25	0	45	**24**
Global high-yield bonds	0	4	25	4	11	**12**
Lower-volatility alternatives	0	0	0	0	13	**4**
Global developed equities	0	64	19	64	13	**28**
Global emerging equities	0	11	3	11	2	**5**
Equity-based alternatives	0	0	8	0	0	**2**
Illiquid global equities	0	20	10	20	5	**10**
Trading strategy alternatives[a]	0	0	6	0	3	**3**
Global real estate	0	0	3	0	5	**2**
Total	100	100	100	100	100	**100**

[a] *"Trading strategy alternatives" refers to discretionary or systematic trading strategies such as global macro and managed futures.*

REVISITING THE MODULE PROCESS IN DETAIL

17

☐ | recommend and justify an asset allocation using a goals-based approach

Having explained and illustrated the client process in Exhibit 35, we now explore how modules are developed. Creating an appropriate set of optimized modules starts with the formulation of capital market assumptions. Exhibit 40 presents a possible set of forward-looking pretax capital market expectations for expected return, volatility, and liquidity[35] in Panel A and a historical 15-year correlation matrix in Panel B.[36]

Exhibit 40: Example of Capital Market Expectations for a Possible Asset Class Universe

Panel A

	Expected		
	Return	Volatility	Liquidity
Cash	4.0%	3.0%	100%
Global investment-grade bonds	5.5	6.5	100
Global high-yield bonds	7.0	10.0	100
Lower-volatility alternatives	5.5	5.0	65
Global developed equities	8.0	16.0	100
Global emerging equities	9.5	22.0	100
Equity-based alternatives	6.0	8.0	65
Illiquid global equities	11.0	30.0	0
Trading strategy alternatives	6.5	10.0	80
Global real estate	7.0	15.0	100

Panel B

		Global			Global					
	Cash	IG Bonds	HY Bonds	Lower-Volatility Alts	Developed Equities	Emerging Equities	Equity-Based Alts	Trading Strategy Alts	Illiquid Equities	Global Real Estate
Cash	1.00	0.00	−0.12	0.08	−0.06	−0.04	0.02	0.04	−0.26	−0.01
Global investment-grade bonds	0.00	1.00	0.27	0.14	0.28	0.09	0.07	0.16	0.20	0.24
Global high-yield bonds	−0.12	0.27	1.00	0.46	0.70	0.17	0.31	−0.08	0.35	0.28
Lower-volatility alternatives	0.08	0.14	0.46	1.00	0.44	0.61	0.86	0.12	0.65	0.47
Global developed equities	−0.06	0.28	0.70	0.44	1.00	0.17	0.32	−0.03	0.47	0.38
Global emerging equities	−0.04	0.09	0.17	0.61	0.17	1.00	0.72	−0.03	0.67	0.49

---

35 For clients who might invest in traditional asset classes by means of vehicles such as mutual funds or ETFs, these asset classes can be treated as providing virtually instant liquidity. For clients with particularly large asset pools who might use separately managed accounts, the liquidity factor for high-yield or emerging market bonds, small-capitalization equities, and certain real assets might be adjusted downward.
36 For illiquid equities, data availability reduces the time period to seven years. The correlation matrix is based on the 15 years ending with March 2016.

		Global			Global					
	Cash	IG Bonds	HY Bonds	Lower-Volatil-ity Alts	Devel-oped Equities	Emerging Equities	Equity-Based Alts	Trading Strat-egy Alts	Illiquid Equities	Global Real Estate
Equity-based alternatives	0.02	0.07	0.31	0.86	0.32	0.72	**1.00**	0.11	0.72	0.45
Trading strategy alternatives	0.04	0.16	−0.08	0.12	−0.03	−0.03	0.11	**1.00**	−0.09	0.07
Illiquid global equities	−0.26	0.20	0.35	0.65	0.47	0.67	0.72	−0.09	**1.00**	0.88
Global real estate	−0.01	0.24	0.28	0.47	0.38	0.49	0.45	0.07	0.88	**1.00**

Ostensibly, in the real world, the process ought to be associated with a set of after-tax expectations, which usually cannot be limited to broad asset classes or sub-asset classes. Indeed, the tax impact of management processes within individual asset classes or strategies (for instance, index replication, index replication with systematic tax-loss harvesting, broadly diversified portfolios, or concentrated portfolios) requires that each management process within each asset class or strategy be given its own expected return and volatility. We will dispense with that step here for the sake of simplicity, both in absolute terms and with respect to jurisdictional differences.

Exhibit 41 presents a possible set of such modules based on the capital market expectations from Exhibit 40. The optimization uses a mean–variance process and is subject to a variety of constraints that are meant to reflect both market portfolio considerations and reasonable asset class or strategy suitability given the goals that we expect to correspond to various points on the frontier. Note that the frontier is not "efficient" in the traditional sense of the term because the constraints applied to the portfolios differ from one to the next. Three elements within the set of constraints deserve special mention. The first is the need to be concerned with the liquidity of the various strategies: It would make little sense, even if it were appropriate based on other considerations, to include any material exposure to illiquid equities in a declining-balance portfolio expected to "mature" within 10 years, for instance. Any exposure thus selected would be bound to increase through time because portfolio liquidation focuses on more-liquid assets. The second relates to strategies whose return distributions are known not to be "normal." This point applies particularly to a number of alternative strategies that suffer from skew and kurtosis,[37] which a mean–variance optimization process does not take into account (see Section 6). Finally, the constraints contain a measure of drawdown control to alleviate the problems potentially associated with portfolios that, although apparently optimal, appear too risky in overly challenging market circumstances. Drawdown controls are an important element in that they help deal with the often-observed asymmetric tolerance of investors for volatility: upward volatility is much preferred to downward volatility.

---

37 Kat (2003) described the challenge, and Davies, Kat, and Lu (2009) presented a solution that involves the use of mean–variance-skew-kurtosis optimization, which is typically too complex for most real-life circumstances.

Exhibit 41: Six Possible Sub-Portfolio Modules

	A	B	C	D	E	F
Portfolio Characteristics						
Expected return	4.3%	5.5%	6.4%	7.2%	8.0%	8.7%
Expected volatility	2.7	4.5	6.0	7.5	10.0	12.5
Expected liquidity	100.0	96.6	90.0	86.1	83.6	80.0
Portfolio Allocations						
Cash	80%	26%	3%	1%	1%	1%
Global investment-grade bonds	20	44	45	25	0	0
Global high-yield bonds	0	5	11	25	34	4
Lower-volatility alternatives	0	9	13	0	0	0
Global developed equities	0	9	13	19	34	64
Global emerging equities	0	2	2	3	6	11
Equity-based alternatives	0	0	0	8	0	0
Illiquid global equities	0	0	5	10	15	20
Trading strategy alternatives	0	1	3	6	7	0
Global real estate	0	5	5	3	3	0
Total	100%	100%	100%	100%	100%	100%
Constraints						
Maximum volatility	3.0%	4.5%	6.0%	7.5%	10.0%	12.5%
Minimum liquidity	100.0	95.0	90.0	85.0	80.0	70.0
Maximum alternatives	0.0	10.0	20.0	30.0	30.0	30.0
Minimum cash	80.0	20.0	0.3	0.5	0.7	1.0
Maximum HY as a percent of total fixed income	0.0	10.0	20.0	50.0	100.0	100.0
Maximum equity spectrum	0.0	10.0	20.0	40.0	75.0	100.0
Maximum EM as a percent of public equities	15.0	15.0	15.0	15.0	15.0	15.0
Maximum illiquid equities	0.0	0.0	5.0	10.0	15.0	20.0
Maximum trading as a percent of equity spectrum	0.0	10.0	15.0	15.0	20.0	25.0
Maximum real estate	0.0	5.0	10.0	15.0	20.0	25.0
Escrow cash as a percent of illiquid equities	5.0	5.0	5.0	5.0	5.0	5.0
Maximum probability of return < drawdown	1.0	1.5	2.0	2.0	2.5	2.5
Drawdown horizon	3	3	3	3	3	3
Drawdown amount	0.0	−5.0	−7.5	−10.0	−15.0	−20.0

The six sub-portfolios shown in Exhibit 41 satisfy two major design goals: First, they cover a wide spectrum of the investment universe, ranging from a nearly all-cash portfolio (Portfolio A) to an all-equity alternative (Portfolio F). Second, they are sufficiently differentiated to avoid creating distinctions without real differences. These portfolios are graphed in Exhibit 42.

Exhibit 42: Sub-Portfolio Modules Cover a Full Range

Expected Return

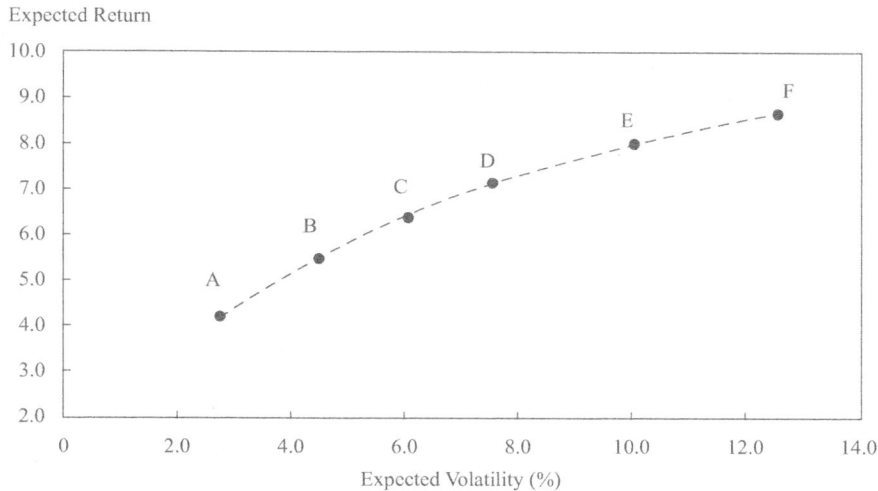

Expected Volatility (%)

Returning to an earlier point about "labeled goals," one can easily imagine "aspirations" to describe each of these modules, ranging from "immediate- to short-term lifestyle" for Module A to "aggressive growth" for Module F. Module B might be labeled "long-term lifestyle," while C and D might represent forms of capital preservation and E a form of "balanced growth."

A final point deserves special emphasis: Modules need to be revisited on a periodic basis. While equilibrium assumptions will likely not change much from one year to the next, the need to identify one's position with respect to a "normal" market cycle can lead to modest changes in forward-looking assumptions. It would indeed be foolish to keep using long-term equilibrium assumptions when it becomes clear that one is closer to a market top than to a market bottom. The question of the suitability of revisions becomes moot when using a systematic approach such as the Black–Litterman model. One may also need to review the continued suitability of constraints, not to mention (when applicable) the fact that the make-up of the market portfolio may change in terms of geography or credit distribution.

ISSUES RELATED TO GOALS-BASED ASSET ALLOCATION

18

☐ | recommend and justify an asset allocation using a goals-based approach

Once set, the goals-based allocation must be regularly reviewed. Two considerations dominate:

1. Goals with an initially fixed time horizon are not necessarily one year closer to maturity after a year. Superficially, one would expect that someone who says that his or her need is to meet lifestyle expenditures over the next five years, for instance, means exactly this. Accordingly, next year, the time horizon should shift down to four years. Yet experience suggests that certain

horizons are "placeholders": One year on, the time horizon remains five years. This is particularly—and understandably—relevant when the horizon reflects the anticipated death of an individual.

2. The preference for upward rather than downward volatility, combined with perceptions that goals may have higher required probabilities of success than is truly the case, leads to portfolios that typically outperform the discount rate used to compute the required initial capital. Thus, one would expect there to be some need for portfolio rebalancing when the assets allocated to certain goals appear excessive, at least in probability- and horizon-adjusted terms. This situation gives rise to important discussions with taxable clients because any form of portfolio rebalancing is inherently more complex and costly in a taxable environment than when taxes do not come into consideration.

Issues Related to Goals-Based Asset Allocation

Although goals-based asset allocation offers an elegant and mathematically sound way to deal with the circumstances of individuals, it is not a panacea. By definition, goals-based asset allocation applies best to individuals who have multiple goals, time horizons, and urgency levels. The classic example of the professional who is just starting to save for retirement and who has no other significant goal (as in the case of Aimée Goddard in Example 1) can be easily be handled with the traditional financial tools discussed in the earlier sections of this reading.[38] However, one should always be cautious to ensure that there is no "hidden" goal that should be brought out and that the apparently "single" retirement goal is not in fact an aggregation of several elements with different levels of urgency, if not also different time horizons. Single-goal circumstances may still be helped by the goals-based asset allocation process when there are sustainability or behavioral questions. In that case, one can look at the single goal as being made up of several similar goals over successive time periods with different required probabilities of success. For instance, one might apply a higher sense of urgency—and thus require a lower risk profile—to contributions made in the first few years, on the ground that adverse market circumstances might negatively affect the willingness of the client to stay with the program. In many ways, this approach can be seen as a conceptual analog to the dollar-cost-averaging investment framework.

Goals-based asset allocation is ideally suited to situations involving multiple goals, time horizons, and urgency levels, whether the assets are large or more modest. In fact, in cases where "human capital" is considered, a multi-goal approach can help investors understand the various trade-offs they face. Ostensibly, the larger the assets, the more complex the nature of the investment problem, the more diverse the list of investment structures, and the more one should expect a client-focused approach to offer useful benefits. However, the ratio of cash outflows to assets under consideration is a more germane issue than the overall size of the asset pool.

---

38 However, an adviser may find it appropriate to help the individual divide the funds he or she believes are needed for retirement into several categories. For instance, there may be some incompressible lifestyle expenditure that represents a minimum required spending level, but there may also be some luxury or at least compressible spending that does not have such a high level of urgency or that applies over a different time frame (say, the early or late years). Thus, one could still describe the problem as involving multiple goals, multiple time horizons, and multiple urgency levels. Then, one could compare the costs associated with the funding of these goals and have the individual weigh potential future satisfaction against the loss of current purchasing power.

Advisers using goals-based wealth management must contend with a considerably higher level of business management complexity. They will naturally expect to have a different policy for each client and potentially more than one policy per client. Thus, managing these portfolios day to day and satisfying the usual regulatory requirement that all clients be treated in an equivalent manner can appear to be a major quandary.

Typically, the solution would involve developing a systematic approach to decision making such that it remains practical for advisers to formulate truly individual policies that reflect their investment insights. Exhibit 43 offers a graphical overview of advisers' activities, divided into those that involve "firm-wide" processes, defined as areas where no real customization is warranted, and those that must remain "client focused." The result is analogous to a customized racing bicycle, whose parts are mass produced but then combined into a truly unique bike custom-designed for the individual racer.

Exhibit 43: Goals-Based Wealth Management Advisory Overview

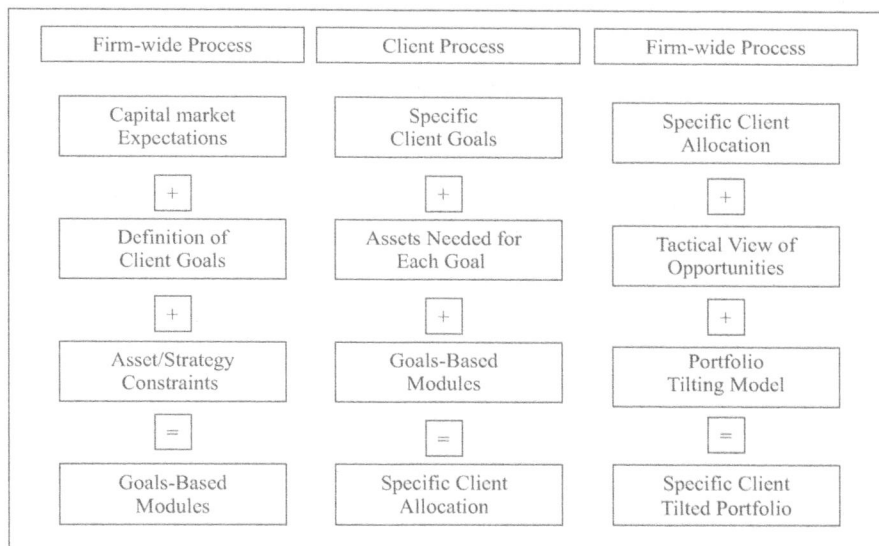

Firm-wide Process	Client Process	Firm-wide Process
Capital market Expectations	Specific Client Goals	Specific Client Allocation
+	+	+
Definition of Client Goals	Assets Needed for Each Goal	Tactical View of Opportunities
+	+	+
Asset/Strategy Constraints	Goals-Based Modules	Portfolio Tilting Model
=	=	=
Goals-Based Modules	Specific Client Allocation	Specific Client Tilted Portfolio

HEURISTICS AND OTHER APPROACHES TO ASSET ALLOCATION

19

☐ | describe and evaluate heuristic and other approaches to asset allocation

In addition to the various asset allocation approaches already covered, a variety of heuristics (rules that provide a reasonable but not necessarily optimal solution) and other techniques deserve mention:

The "120 Minus Your Age" Rule

The phrase "120 minus your age" is a heuristic for inferring a hidden, age-driven risk tolerance coefficient that then leads directly to an age-based stock versus fixed income split: 120 – Age = Percentage allocated to stocks. Thus, a 25-year-old man would allocate 95% of his investment portfolio to stocks. Although we are aware of no theoretic basis for this heuristic—or its older and newer cousins, "100 minus your age" and "125 minus your age," respectively—it results in a linear decrease in equity exposure that seems to fit the general equity glide paths associated with target-date funds, including those that are based on a total balance sheet approach that includes human capital. A number of target-date funds (sometimes called life-cycle or age-based funds) and some target-date index providers report that their glide path (the age-based change in equity exposure) is based on the evolution of an individual's human capital. For example, one set of indexes[39] explicitly targets an investable proxy for the world market portfolio in which the glide path is the result of the evolving relationship of financial capital to human capital.[40]

Exhibit 44 displays the glide paths of the 60 largest target-date fund families in the United States. The retirement year (typically part of the fund's name) on the *x*-axis denotes the year in which the investor is expected to retire, which is almost always assumed to be the year the investor turns 65. Thus, as of 2016, the 2060 allocations correspond to a 21-year-old investor (79% equity, using the heuristic), whereas the 2005 allocation corresponds to a 76-year-old investor (24% equity, using the heuristic).[41] One dashed line represents the equity allocation based on the "100 minus your age" heuristic, while another dashed line represents the "120 minus your age" heuristic. The heuristic lines lack some of the nuances of the various glide path lines, but it would appear that an age-based heuristic leads to asset allocations that are broadly similar to those used by target-date funds.

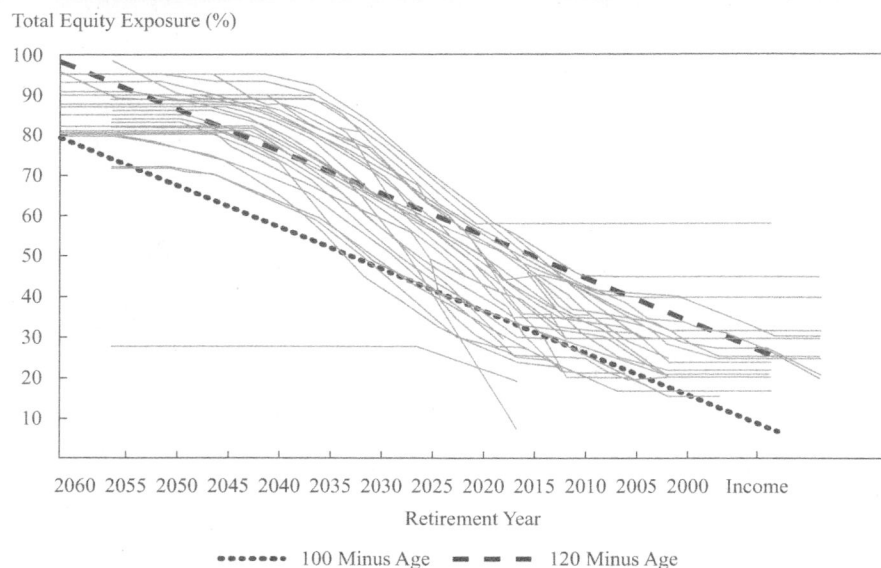

Exhibit 44: Target-Date Funds and Age Heuristics (as of January 2016)

---

39 Morningstar's Lifetime Allocation (target-date) indexes.
40 See Idzorek (2008).
41 Many target-date funds continue to offer a "2005" vintage that would have been marketed/sold to people retiring in 2005.

The 60/40 Stock/Bond Heuristic

Some investors choose to skip the various optimization techniques and simply adopt an asset allocation consisting of 60% equities and 40% fixed income.

The equity allocation is viewed as supplying a long-term growth foundation, and the fixed-income allocation as supplying risk reduction benefits. If the stock and bond allocations are themselves diversified, an overall diversified portfolio should result.

There is some evidence that the global financial asset market portfolio is close to this prototypical 60/40 split. Exhibit 45 displays the estimated market value of eight major components of the market portfolio from 1990 to 2012. In approximately 7 of the 23 years, equities, private equity, and real estate account for slightly more than 60%, while for the rest of the time, the combined percentage is slightly less.

Exhibit 45: Global Market Portfolio, 1990 to 2012

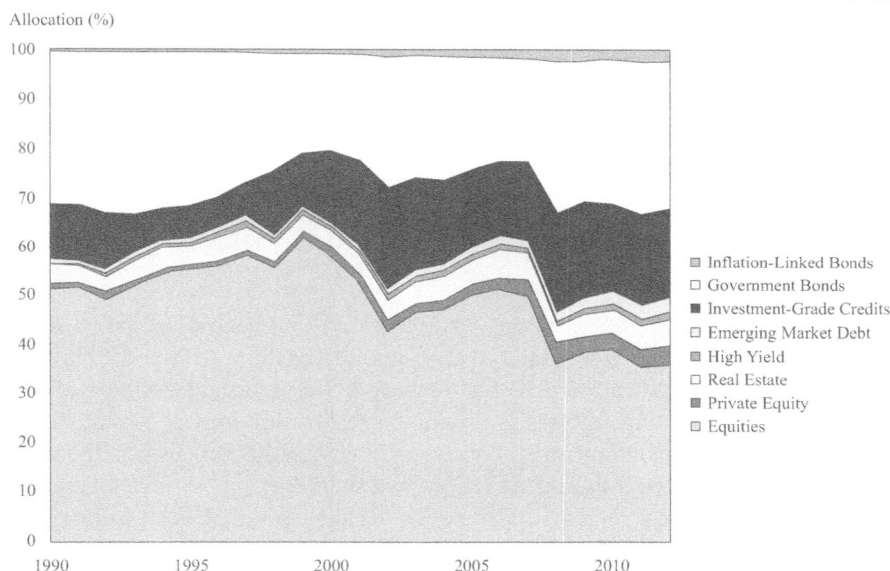

Source: Doeswijk, Lam, and Swinkels (2014).

The Endowment Model

An approach to asset allocation that emphasizes large allocations to non-traditional investments, including equity-oriented investments driven by investment manager skill (e.g., private equities), has come to be known as the endowment model or Yale model. The label "Yale model" reflects the fact that the Yale University Investments Office under David Swensen pioneered the approach in the 1990s; the label "endowment model" reflects the influence of this approach among US university endowments. Swensen (2009) stated that most investors should not pursue the Yale model but should instead embrace a simpler asset allocation implemented with low-cost funds. Besides high allocations to non-traditional assets and a commitment to active management, the approach characteristically seeks to earn illiquidity premiums, which endowments with long time horizons are well positioned to capture. Exhibit 46, showing the Yale endowment asset allocation, makes these points. In the exhibit, "absolute return" indicates investment in event-driven and value-driven strategies.

Exhibit 46: Yale University Endowment Asset Allocation as of June 2014

	Yale University	US Educational Institution Mean
Absolute return	17.4%	23.3%
Domestic equity	3.9	19.3
Fixed income	4.9	9.3
Foreign equity	11.5	22.0
Natural resources	8.2	8.5
Private equity	33.0	10.0
Real estate	17.6	4.2
Cash	3.5	3.5

Source: Yale University (2014, p. 13).

In almost diametrical contrast to the endowment model is the asset allocation approach of Norway's Government Pension Fund Global (Statens pensjonsfond Utland), often called the Norway model.[42] This model's asset allocation is highly committed to passive investment in publicly traded securities (subject to environmental, social, and governance [ESG] concerns), reflecting a belief in the market's informational efficiency. Since 2009, the asset allocation has followed an approximate 60/40 stock/bond mix.

Risk Parity

A risk parity asset allocation is based on the notion that each asset (asset class or risk factor) should contribute equally to the total risk of the portfolio for a portfolio to be well diversified. Recall that in Sections 2–9, we identified various criticisms and potential shortcomings of mean–variance optimization, one of which was that, while the resulting asset allocations may appear diversified across assets, the sources of risk may not be diversified. In the section on risk budgeting, Exhibit 19 contained a risk decomposition of a reverse-optimization-based asset allocation from a United Kingdom–based investor. There, we noted that the overall equity/fixed income split was approximately 54% equities and 46% fixed income, yet of the 10% standard deviation, approximately 74% of the risk came from equities while only 26% came from fixed income.

Risk parity is a relatively controversial approach. Although there are several variants, the most common risk parity approach has the following mathematical form:

$$w_i \times \text{Cov}\left(r_i, r_P\right) = \tfrac{1}{n}\sigma_P^2 \tag{3}$$

where

w_i = the weight of asset i

$\text{Cov}(r_i, r_P)$ = the covariance of asset i with the portfolio

n = the number of assets

σ_P^2 = the variance of the portfolio

In general, there is not a closed-form solution to the problem, and it must be solved using some form of optimization (mathematical programming). Prior to Markowitz's development of mean–variance optimization, which simultaneously considered both risk and return, most asset allocation approaches focused only on return *and*

---

42 See Curtis (2012).

ignoredrisk (or accounted for it in an ad hoc manner). The primary criticism of risk parity is that it makes the opposite mistake: It *ignoresexpected returns*. In general, most of the rules-based risk approaches—such as other forms of volatility weighting, minimum volatility, and target volatility—suffer from this shortcoming.

With risk parity, the contribution to risk is highly dependent on the formation of the opportunity set. For example, if the opportunity set consists of seven equity asset classes and three fixed-income asset classes, intuitively, 70% of risk will come from the equities and 30% of risk will come from fixed income. Conversely, if the opportunity set consists of three equity asset classes and seven fixed-income asset classes, intuitively, 70% of risk will come from fixed income and 30% of risk will come from equities. The point is that practitioners of risk parity must be very cognizant of the formation of their opportunity set.

Exhibit 47 gives a US-centric example consisting of five equity asset classes and three fixed-income asset classes. A constrained optimization routine (weights must sum to 100%) was used to determine the weight to each asset class, such that all asset classes contributed the same amount to total risk. In this case, each asset class contributed 0.8%, resulting in an asset allocation with a total standard deviation of 6.41%. In this example, 5/8 of total risk comes from equity asset classes and 3/8 comes from fixed-income asset classes. Earlier, we explained that reverse optimization can be used to infer the expected return of any set of presumed efficient weights. In Exhibit 47, based on a total market risk premium of 2.13% and a risk-free rate of 3%, we inferred the reverse-optimized total returns (final column). In this case, these seem to be relatively reasonable expected returns.

Exhibit 47: Risk Parity Portfolio Weights and Risk-Budgeting Statistics Based on Reverse-Optimized Returns

Asset Class	Weight	Marginal Contribution to Total Risk (MCTR)	ACTR	Percentage Contribution to Total Standard Deviation	Reverse-Optimized Total Returns
US large-cap equities	7.7%	10.43%	0.80%	12.50%	6.47%
US mid-cap equities	6.1	13.03	0.80	12.50	7.33
US small-cap equities	5.9	13.61	0.80	12.50	7.52
Non-US developed market equities	5.6	14.38	0.80	12.50	7.78
Emerging market equities	4.5	17.74	0.80	12.50	8.89
Non-US bonds	15.5	5.17	0.80	12.50	4.72
US TIPS	23.9	3.36	0.80	12.50	4.12
US bonds	30.8	2.60	0.80	12.50	3.86
Total	100.0%		6.41%	100.00%	5.13%

After deriving a risk parity–based asset allocation, the next step in the process is to borrow (use leverage) or to lend (save a portion of wealth, presumably in cash) so that the overall portfolio corresponds to the investor's risk appetite. Continuing with our example, the market risk premium is 2.13% (above the assumed risk-free rate of 3%) and the market variance is 0.41% (i.e., 6.41% squared); thus, the implied market trade-off of expected return (in excess of the risk-free rate) for risk is 2.13% divided by 0.41%, which equals approximately 5.2. Investors with a greater appetite for risk than the market as a whole would borrow money to lever up the risk parity portfolios, while investors with a lower appetite for risk would invest a portion of their wealth in cash.

Back tests of levered risk parity portfolios have produced promising results, although critics of these back tests argue that they suffer from look-back bias and are very dependent on the ability to use extremely large amounts of leverage at low borrow rates (which may not have been feasible); see, for example, Anderson, Bianchi, and Goldberg (2012). Proponents of risk parity have suggested that the idea of "leverage aversion" contributes to the success of the strategy. Black (1972) suggested that restrictions on leverage and a general aversion to leverage may cause return-seeking investors to pursue higher-returning assets, such as stocks. All else equal, this behavior would reduce the price of bonds, thus allowing the investor to buy bonds at a small discount, hold them to maturity, and realize the full value of the bond. Asness, Frazzini, and Pedersen (2012) have offered this idea as a potential explanation for why a levered (bond-centric) asset allocation might outperform an equity-centric asset allocation with equivalent or similar risk.

The 1/N Rule

One of the simplest asset allocation heuristics involves equally weighting allocations to assets. DeMiguel, Garlappi, and Uppal (2009) define an approach in which $1/N$ of wealth is allocated to each of N assets available for investment at each rebalancing date. Calendar rebalancing to equal weighting at quarterly intervals is one common rebalancing discipline used. By treating all assets as indistinguishable in terms of mean returns, volatility, and correlations, in principle, $1/N$ rule portfolios should be dominated by methods that optimize asset class weights to exploit differences in investment characteristics. In empirical studies comparing approaches, however, the $1/N$ rule has been found to perform considerably better, based on Sharpe ratios and certainty equivalents, than theory might suggest. One possible explanation is that the $1/N$ rule sidesteps problems caused by optimizing when there is estimation error in inputs.

20   PORTFOLIO REBALANCING IN PRACTICE

☐ | discuss factors affecting rebalancing policy

The reading "Introduction to Asset Allocation" provided an introduction to rebalancing, including some detailed comments on strategic considerations. This section aims to present useful additional insight and information.

MEANINGS OF "REBALANCING"

Rebalancing has been defined as the discipline of adjusting portfolio weights to more closely align with the strategic asset allocation. In that sense, rebalancing includes policy regarding the correction of any drift away from strategic asset allocation weights resulting from market price movements and the passage of time for finite-lived assets, such as bonds. In liability-relative asset allocation, adjusting a liability-hedging portfolio to account for changes in net duration exposures from the passage of time, for example, would fall under the rubric of rebalancing.

Some use the term "rebalancing" more expansively, to include the combined effects on asset class weights not only of rebalancing in the above sense but also of active allocation activities. In that sense, rebalancing would include tactical allocations. Although rebalancing policy can be established to accommodate tactical adjustments, tactical asset allocation per se is not covered under "rebalancing" as the term is used here.

Changes in asset allocation weights in response to changes in client circumstances, goals, or other client factors are sometimes also referred to as "rebalancing" (especially if the adjustments are minor). These activities fall under the scope of client monitoring and asset allocation review, as described elsewhere in the CFA curriculum.

An appropriate rebalancing policy involves a weighing of benefits and costs. Benefits depend on the idea that if an investor's strategic asset allocation is optimal, then any divergence in the portfolio from that asset allocation represents an expected utility loss to the investor. Rebalancing benefits the investor by reducing the present value of expected losses from not tracking the optimum. In theory, the basic cost of not rebalancing is this present value of expected utility losses from straying from the optimum.[43]

Apart from the above considerations of trade-offs, disciplined rebalancing has tended to reduce risk while incrementally adding to returns. Several interpretations of this empirical finding have been offered, including the following:

- *Rebalancing earns a diversification return.* The compound growth rate of a portfolio is greater than the weighted average compound growth rates of the component portfolio holdings (given positive expected returns and positive asset weights). Given sufficiently low transaction costs, this effect leads to what has been called a *diversification return* to frequent rebalancing to a well-diversified portfolio.[44]

- *Rebalancing earns a return from being short volatility.* In the case of a portfolio consisting of a risky asset and a risk-free asset, the return to a rebalanced portfolio can be replicated by creating a buy-and-hold position in the portfolio, writing out-of-the-money puts and calls on the risky asset, and investing the premiums in risk-free bonds.[45] As the value of puts and calls is positively related to volatility, such a position is called being short volatility (or being short gamma, by reference to the option Greeks).

Practice appears not to have produced a consensus on the most appropriate rebalancing discipline. Introduction to Asset Allocation defined and discussed calendar rebalancing[46]—sometimes mentioned as common in portfolios managed for individual investors—and percent-range rebalancing. Calendar rebalancing involves lower overhead because of lower monitoring costs. Percent-range rebalancing is a more disciplined risk control policy, however, because it makes rebalancing contingent on market movements. Without weighing costs and benefits in the abstract, Exhibit 48 assumes percent-range rebalancing and summarizes the effects of each of several key factors on the corridor width of an asset class, holding all else equal, except for the factor of the asset class's own volatility.[47] For taxable investors, transactions trigger capital gains in jurisdictions that tax them; therefore, for such investors, higher tax rates on capital gains should also be associated with wider corridors.

---

43 See Leland (2000).

44 See Willenbrock (2011). This phenomenon was called *rebalancing return* by Mulvey and Kim (2009). Luenberger (2013) suggests that the phenomenon could be exploited by a strategy of buying high-volatility assets and rebalancing often, a process he called *volatility pumping.*

45 As shown in Ang (2014, pp. 135–139).

46 Rebalancing a portfolio to target weights on a periodic basis—for example, monthly, quarterly, semi-annually, or annually.

47 See Masters (2003).

Exhibit 48: Factors Affecting the Optimal Corridor Width of an Asset Class		
Factor	**Effect on Optimal Width of Corridor (All Else Equal)**	**Intuition**
Factors Positively Related to Optimal Corridor Width		
Transaction costs	The higher the transaction costs, the wider the optimal corridor.	High transaction costs set a high hurdle for rebalancing benefits to overcome.
Risk tolerance	The higher the risk tolerance, the wider the optimal corridor.	Higher risk tolerance means less sensitivity to divergences from the target allocation.
Correlation with the rest of the portfolio	The higher the correlation, the wider the optimal corridor.	When asset classes move in sync, further divergence from target weights is less likely.
Factors Inversely Related to Optimal Corridor Width		
Volatility of the rest of the portfolio	The higher the volatility, the narrower the optimal corridor.	Higher volatility makes large divergences from the strategic asset allocation more likely.

Among positive factors, the cases of transaction costs and risk tolerance are obvious. Transaction costs can be reduced to the extent that portfolio cash flows can be used to rebalance. The case of correlation is less obvious. Because of correlations, the rebalancing triggers among different asset classes are linked.

Consider correlation in a two–asset class scenario. Suppose one asset class is above its target weight, so the other asset class is below its target weight. A further increase in the value of the overweight asset class implies, on average, a smaller divergence in the asset mix if the asset classes' returns are more highly positively correlated (because the denominator in computing the overweight asset class's weight is the sum of the values of the two asset classes). In a multi-asset-class scenario, all pair-wise asset class correlations would need to be considered, making the interpretation of correlations complex. To expand the application of the two-asset case's intuition, one simplification involves considering the balance of a portfolio to be a single hypothetical asset and computing an asset class's correlation with it.

As indicated in Exhibit 48, the higher the volatility of the rest of the portfolio, excluding the asset class being considered, the more likely a large divergence from the strategic asset allocation becomes. That consideration should point to a narrower optimal corridor, all else being equal.

In the case of an asset class's own volatility, "holding all else equal" is not practically meaningful. If rebalancing did not involve transaction costs, then higher volatility would lead to a narrower corridor, all else equal, for a risk-averse investor.[48] Higher volatility implies that if an asset class is not brought back into the optimal range after a given move away from it, the chance of an even further divergence from optimal is greater. In other words, higher volatility makes large divergence from the strategic asset allocation more likely. However, reducing a corridor's width means more frequent rebalancing and higher transaction costs. Thus, the effect of volatility on optimal corridor width involves a trade-off between controlling transaction costs and controlling risk. Conclusions also depend on the assumptions made about asset price return dynamics.

In practice, corridor width is often specified to be proportionally greater, the higher an asset class's volatility, with a focus on transaction cost control. In *volatility-based rebalancing*, corridor width is set proportionally to the asset class's own volatility. In one variation of *equal probability rebalancing* (McCalla 1997), the manager specifies a corridor for each asset class in terms of a common multiple of the standard deviation of the asset class's returns such that, under a normal probability assumption, each asset class is equally likely to trigger rebalancing.

---

48 As in Masters (2003).

EXAMPLE 12

Tolerance Bands for an Asset Allocation

An investment committee is reviewing the following strategic asset allocation:

Domestic equities 50% ± 5% (i.e., 45% to 55% of portfolio value)

International equities 15% ± 1.5%

Domestic bonds 35% ± 3.5%

The market for the domestic bonds is relatively illiquid. The committee views the above corridors as appropriate *if* each asset class's risk and transaction cost characteristics remain unchanged. The committee now wants to account for differences among the asset classes in setting the corridors.

Evaluate the implications of the following sets of facts for the stated tolerance bands, given an all-else-equal assumption in each case:

1. Tax rates for international equities increase by 10 percentage points.

Solution:

The tolerance band for international equities should increase if the entity is a taxable investor.

2. Transaction costs in international equities increase by 20% relative to domestic equities, but the correlation of international equities with domestic equities and bonds declines. What is the expected effect on the tolerance band for international equities?

Solution:

Increased transaction costs point to widening the tolerance band for international equities, but declining correlations point to narrowing it. The overall effect is indeterminate.

3. The volatility of domestic bonds increases. What is the expected effect on their tolerance band? Assume that domestic bonds are relatively illiquid.

Solution:

Given that the market for domestic bonds is relatively illiquid, the increase in volatility suggests widening the rebalancing band. Containing transaction costs is more important than the expected utility losses from allowing a larger divergence from the strategic asset allocation.

One decision involved in rebalancing policy is whether to adjust asset class holdings to their target proportions, to the limits of the corridors, or to within the corridors but not to target weights. Compared with rebalancing to target weights, rebalancing to the upper or lower limit of the allowed range results in less close alignment with target proportions but lower transaction costs—an especially important consideration in the case of relatively illiquid assets. The choice among alternatives may be influenced by judgmental tactical considerations.

Because one rebalancing decision affects later rebalancing decisions, the optimal rebalancing decisions at different points in time are linked. However, optimal rebalancing in a multi-period, multi-asset case is an unsolved problem.

The analysis of Dybvig (2005) suggests that fixed transaction costs favor rebalancing to the target weights and variable transaction costs favor rebalancing to the nearest corridor border (the interior of the corridor being therefore a "no trade zone"). A number of studies have contrasted rebalancing to target weights and rebalancing to the allowed range based on particular asset classes, time periods, and measures of the benefits of rebalancing. These studies have reached a variety of conclusions, suggesting that no simple, empirically based advice can be provided.

REBALANCING IN A GOALS-BASED APPROACH

The use of probability- and horizon-adjusted discount rates to size the various goal-defeasing sub-portfolios means that portfolios will usually produce returns that are higher than assumed. Thus, as time passes, the dollars allocated to the various sub-portfolios—other than labeled-goal portfolios—may be expected to exceed the actual requirements. For example, in average markets, returns should exceed the conservative requirements of a goal associated with a 90% required probability of success. Sub-portfolios with shorter time horizons for goals with high required probabilities of success will tend to contain relatively low-risk assets, whereas riskier assets may have high allocations in longer-horizon portfolios for goals with lower required probabilities of success. Thus, there is a greater chance that the exposure to lower-risk assets will creep up before one experiences the same for riskier assets. Thus, failing to rebalance the portfolio will gradually move it down the risk axis—and the defined efficient frontier—and thus lead the client to take less risk than he or she can bear.

SUMMARY

This reading has surveyed how appropriate asset allocations can be determined to meet the needs of a variety of investors. Among the major points made have been the following:

- The objective function of asset-only mean–variance optimization is to maximize the expected return of the asset mix minus a penalty that depends on risk aversion and the expected variance of the asset mix.
- Criticisms of MVO include the following:

  - The outputs (asset allocations) are highly sensitive to small changes in the inputs.
  - The asset allocations are highly concentrated in a subset of the available asset classes.
  - Investors are often concerned with characteristics of asset class returns such as skewness and kurtosis that are not accounted for in MVO.
  - While the asset allocations may appear diversified across assets, the sources of risk may not be diversified.
  - MVO allocations may have no direct connection to the factors affecting any liability or consumption streams.
  - MVO is a single-period framework that tends to ignore trading/rebalancing costs and taxes.

- Deriving expected returns by reverse optimization or by reverse optimization tilted toward an investor's views on asset returns (the Black–Litterman model) is one means of addressing the tendency of MVO to produce efficient portfolios that are not well diversified.

- Placing constraints on asset class weights to prevent extremely concentrated portfolios and resampling inputs are other ways of addressing the same concern.

- For some relatively illiquid asset classes, a satisfactory proxy may not be available; including such asset classes in the optimization may therefore be problematic.

- Risk budgeting is a means of making optimal use of risk in the pursuit of return. A risk budget is optimal when the ratio of excess return to marginal contribution to total risk is the same for all assets in the portfolio.

- Characteristics of liabilities that affect asset allocation in liability-relative asset allocation include the following:

  - Fixed versus contingent cash flows

  - Legal versus quasi-liabilities

  - Duration and convexity of liability cash flows

  - Value of liabilities as compared with the size of the sponsoring organization

  - Factors driving future liability cash flows (inflation, economic conditions, interest rates, risk premium)

  - Timing considerations, such longevity risk

  - Regulations affecting liability cash flow calculations

- Approaches to liability-relative asset allocation include surplus optimization, a hedging/return-seeking portfolios approach, and an integrated asset–liability approach.

  - Surplus optimization involves MVO applied to surplus returns.

  - A hedging/return-seeking portfolios approach assigns assets to one of two portfolios. The objective of the hedging portfolio is to hedge the investor's liability stream. Any remaining funds are invested in the return-seeking portfolio.

  - An integrated asset–liability approach integrates and jointly optimizes asset and liability decisions.

- A goals-based asset allocation process combines into an overall portfolio a number of sub-portfolios, each of which is designed to fund an individual goal with its own time horizon and required probability of success.

- In the implementation, there are two fundamental parts to the asset allocation process. The first centers on the creation of portfolio modules, while the second relates to the identification of client goals and the matching of these goals to the appropriate sub-portfolios to which suitable levels of capital are allocated.

- Other approaches to asset allocation include "120 minus your age," 60/40 stocks/bonds, the endowment model, risk parity, and the $1/N$ rule.

- Disciplined rebalancing has tended to reduce risk while incrementally adding to returns. Interpretations of this empirical finding include that rebalancing earns a diversification return, that rebalancing earns a return from being short volatility, and that rebalancing earns a return to supplying liquidity to the market.

- Factors positively related to optimal corridor width include transaction costs, risk tolerance, and an asset class's correlation with the rest of the portfolio. The higher the correlation, the wider the optimal corridor, because when asset classes move in sync, further divergence from target weights is less likely.
- The volatility of the rest of the portfolio (outside of the asset class under consideration) is inversely related to optimal corridor width.
- An asset class's own volatility involves a trade-off between transaction costs and risk control. The width of the optimal tolerance band increases with transaction costs for volatility-based rebalancing.

REFERENCES

Anderson, Robert M., Stephen W. Bianchi, and Lisa R. Goldberg. 2012. "Will My Risk Parity Strategy Outperform?" *Financial Analysts Journal*, vol. 68, no. 6 (November/December): 75–93. 10.2469/faj.v68.n6.7

Ang, Andrew. 2014. *Asset Management*. New York: Oxford University Press.

Asness, Clifford S., Andrea Frazzini, and Lasse H. Pedersen. 2012. "Leverage Aversion and Risk Parity." *Financial Analysts Journal*, vol. 68, no. 1 (January/February): 47–59. 10.2469/faj.v68.n1.1

Athayde, Gustavo M. de, Renato G. Flôres. 2003. "Incorporating Skewness and Kurtosis in Portfolio Optimization: A Multideminsional Efficient Set." In Advances in Portfolio Construction and Implementation, edited by Stephen Satchell and Alan Scowcroft. Oxford, UK: Butterworth–Heinemann.

Beardsley, Xiaoxin W., Brian Field, and Mingqing Xiao. 2012. "Mean–Variance-Skewness-Kurtosis Portfolio Optimization with Return and Liquidity." *Communications in Mathematical Finance*, vol. 1, no. 1: 13–49.

Black, Fischer. 1972. "Capital market equilibrium with restricted borrowing." *Journal of Business*, vol. 45, no. 3: 444–455. 10.1086/295472

Black, Fischer, Robert Litterman. 1990. "Asset Allocation: Combining Investors Views with Market Equilibrium." Fixed Income Research, Goldman, Sachs & Company, September.

Black, Fischer, Robert Litterman. 1991. "Global Asset Allocation with Equities, Bonds, and Currencies." Fixed Income Research, Goldman, Sachs & Company, October.

Black, Fischer, Robert Litterman. 1992. "Global Portfolio Optimization." *Financial Analysts Journal*, vol. 48, no. 5 (September/October): 28–43. 10.2469/faj.v48.n5.28

Blanchett, David M., Philip U. Straehl. 2015. "No Portfolio is an Island." *Financial Analysts Journal*, vol. 71, no. 3 (May/June): 15–33. 10.2469/faj.v71.n3.5

Briec, W., K. Kerstens, O. Jokung. 2007. "Mean–Variance-Skewness Portfolio Performance Gauging: A General Shortage Function and Dual Approach." *Management Science*, vol. 53, no. 1 (January): 135–149. 10.1287/mnsc.1060.0596

Brunel, Jean L.P. 2003. "Revisiting the Asset Allocation Challenge through a Behavioral Finance Lens." *Journal of Wealth Management*, vol. 6, no. 2 (Fall): 10–20. 10.3905/jwm.2003.320479

Brunel, Jean L.P. 2005. "A Behavioral Finance Approach to Strategic Asset Allocation—A Case Study." *Journal of Investment Consulting*, vol. 7, no. 3 (Winter): 61–69.

Chhabra, Ashvin. 2005. "Beyond Markowitz: A Comprehensive Wealth Allocation Framework for Individual Investors." *Journal of Wealth Management*, vol. 7, no. 4 (Spring): 8–34. 10.3905/jwm.2005.470606

Chow, George, Eric Jacquier, Mark Kritzman, Kenneth Lowry. 1999. "Optimal Portfolios in Good Times and Bad." *Financial Analysts Journal*, vol. 55, no. 3 (May/June): 65–73. 10.2469/faj.v55.n3.2273

Curtis, Gregory. 2012. "Yale versus Norway." White Paper 55, Greycourt (September).

Das, Sanjiv, Harry Markowitz, Jonathan Scheid, and Meir Statman. 2010. "Portfolio Optimization with Mental Accounts." *Journal of Financial and Quantitative Analysis*, vol. 45, no. 2 (April): 311–334. 10.1017/S0022109010000141

Das, Sanjiv, Harry Markowitz, Jonathan Scheid, and Meir Statman. 2011. "Portfolios for Investors Who Want to Reach Their Goals While Staying on the Mean–Variance Efficient Frontier." *Journal of Wealth Management*, vol. 14, no. 2 (Fall): 25–31. 10.3905/jwm.2011.14.2.025

Davies, Ryan, Harry M. Kat, and Sa Lu. 2009. "Fund of Hedge Funds Portfolio Selection: A Multiple-Objective Approach." *Journal of Derivatives & Hedge Funds*, vol. 15, no. 2: 91–115. 10.1057/jdhf.2009.1

DeMiguel, V., L. Garlappi, and R. Uppal. 2009. "Optimal versus Naive Diversification: How Inefficient Is the 1/N Portfolio Strategy?" *Review of Financial Studies*, vol. 22, no. 5: 1915–1953. 10.1093/rfs/hhm075

DiBartolomeo, Dan. 1993. "Portfolio Optimization: The Robust Solution." Prudential Securities Quantitative Conference. Available online at http://www.northinfo.com/documents/45.pdf

Doeswijk, Ronald, Trevin Lam, and Laurens Swinkels. 2014. "The Global Multi-Asset Market Portfolio, 1959–2012." *Financial Analysts Journal*, vol. 70, no. 2 (March/April): 26–41. 10.2469/faj.v70.n2.1

Dybvig, Philip H. 2005. "Mean-variance portfolio rebalancing with transaction costs." Working paper, Washington University in Saint Louis.

Elton, Edwin J, Martin J. Gruber. 1992. "Optimal Investment Strategies with Investor Liabilities." *Journal of Banking & Finance*, vol. 16, no. 5: 869–890. 10.1016/0378-4266(92)90030-4

Gannon, James A., Bob Collins. 2009. "Liability-Responsive Asset Allocation." Russell Research Viewpoint.

Goldberg, Lisa R., Michael Y. Hayes, and Ola Mahmoud. 2013. "Minimizing Shortfall." *Quantitative Finance*, vol. 13, no. 10: 1533–1545.

Grable, John E. 2008. "RiskCAT: A Framework for Identifying Maximum Risk Thresholds in Personal Portfolios." *Journal of Financial Planning*, vol. 21, no. 10: 52–62.

Grable, John E., Soo-Hyun Joo. 2004. "Environmental and Biopsychosocial Factors Associated with Financial Risk Tolerance." *Financial Counseling and Planning*, vol. 15, no. 1: 73–88.

Harvey, Campbell R., John C. Liechty, Merrill W. Liechty, and Peter Müller. 2010. "Portfolio Selection with Higher Moments." *Quantitative Finance*, vol. 10, no. 5 (May): 469–485. 10.1080/14697681003756877

Idzorek, Thomas. 2008. "Lifetime Asset Allocations: Methodologies for Target Maturity Funds." Ibbotson Associates Research Report.

Idzorek, Thomas M., Maciej Kowara. 2013. "Factor-Based Asset Allocation vs. Asset-Class-Based Asset Allocation." *Financial Analysts Journal*, vol. 69, no. 3 (May/June): 19–29. 10.2469/faj.v69.n3.7

Jobson, David J., Bob Korkie. 1980. "Estimation for Markowitz Efficient Portfolios." *Journal of the American Statistical Association*, vol. 75, no. 371 (September): 544–554. 10.1080/01621459.1980.10477507

Jobson, David J., Bob Korkie. 1981. "Putting Markowitz Theory to Work." Journal of Portfolio Management, vol. 7, no. 4 (Summer): 70–74. 10.3905/jpm.1981.408816

Jorion, Phillipe. 1992. "Portfolio Optimization in Practice." *Financial Analysts Journal*, vol. 48, no. 1 (January/February): 68–74. 10.2469/faj.v48.n1.68

Kahneman, Daniel, Amos Tversky. 1979. "Prospect Theory: An Analysis of Decision under Risk." *Econometrica*, vol. 47, no. 2: 263–292. 10.2307/1914185

Kat, Harry M. 2003. "10 Things That Investors Should Know about Hedge Funds." *Journal of Wealth Management*, vol. 5, no. 4 (Spring): 72–81. 10.3905/jwm.2003.320466

Leibowitz, Martin L., Roy D. Henriksson. 1988. "Portfolio Optimization Within a Surplus Framework." *Financial Analysts Journal*, vol. 44, no. 2: 43–51. 10.2469/faj.v44.n2.43

Leland, Hayne. 2000. "Optimal Portfolio Implementation with Transaction Costs and Capital Gains Taxes." Working paper, University of California, Berkeley.

Luenberger, David G. 2013. Investment Science, 2nd ed. New York: Oxford University Press.

Markowitz, Harry M. 1952. "Portfolio Selection." *Journal of Finance*, vol. 7, no. 1 (March): 77–91.

Markowitz, Harry M. 1959. Portfolio Selection: Efficient Diversification of Investments. New York: John Wiley & Sons.

Maslow, A. H. 1943. "A Theory of Human Motivation." *Psychological Review*, vol. 50, no. 4: 370–396. 10.1037/h0054346

Masters, Seth J. 2003. "Rebalancing." *Journal of Portfolio Management*, vol. 29, no. 3: 52–57. 10.3905/jpm.2003.319883

McCalla, Douglas B. 1997. "Enhancing the Efficient Frontier with Portfolio Rebalancing." *Journal of Pension Plan Investing*, vol. 1, no. 4: 16–32.

Michaud, Richard O. 1998. Efficient Asset Management. Boston: Harvard Business School Press.

Mulvey, John M. 1989. "A Surplus Optimization Perspective." *Investment Management Review*, vol. 3: 31–39.

Mulvey, John M. 1994. "An Asset-Liability System." *Interfaces*, vol. 24, no. 3: 22–33. 10.1287/inte.24.3.22

Mulvey, J.M., W. Kim. 2009. "Constantly Rebalanced Portfolio—Is Mean Reversion Necessary?" in Rama Cont, ed. Encyclopedia of Quantitative Finance, vol 2, Hoboken, NJ: John Wiley & Sons.

Mulvey, John M., Bill Pauling, and Ron E. Madey. 2003. "Advantages of Multi-Period Portfolio Models." *Journal of Portfolio Management*, vol. 29, no. 2 (Winter): 35–45. 10.3905/jpm.2003.319871

Nevins, Daniel. 2004. "Goal-Based Investing: Integrating Traditional and Behavioral Finance." *Journal of Wealth Management*, vol. 6, no. 4 (Spring): 8–23. 10.3905/jwm.2004.391053

Pompian, Michael M., John B. Longo. 2004. "A New Paradigm for Practical Application of Behavioral Finance." *Journal of Wealth Management*, vol. 7, no. 2 (Fall): 9–15. 10.3905/jwm.2004.434561

Rockafellar, R. Tyrrell, Stanislav Uryasev. 2000. "Optimization of Conditional Value-at-Risk." *Journal of Risk*, vol. 2, no. 3 (Spring): 21–41. 10.21314/JOR.2000.038

Rudd, Andrew, Laurence B. Siegel. 2013. "Using an Economic Balance Sheet for Financial Planning." *Journal of Wealth Management*, vol. 16, no. 2 (Fall): 15–23. 10.3905/jwm.2013.16.2.015

Scherer, Bernd. 2002. "Portfolio Resampling: Review and Critique." *Financial Analysts Journal*, vol. 58, no. 6 (November/December): 98–109.

Sharpe, William. 1974. "Imputing Expected Security Returns from Portfolio Composition." *Journal of Financial and Quantitative Analysis*, vol. 9, no. 3 (June): 463–472. 10.2307/2329873

Sharpe, William, Lawrence G. Tint. 1990. "Liabilities: A New Approach." *Journal of Portfolio Management*, vol. 16, no. 2: 5–10. 10.3905/jpm.1990.409248

Shefrin, H., M. Statman. 2000. "Behavioral Portfolio Theory." *Journal of Financial and Quantitative Analysis*, vol. 35, no. 2: 127–151. 10.2307/2676187

Swensen, D. 2009. Pioneering Portfolio Management: An Unconventional Approach to Institutional Investment, 2nd ed. New York: Free Press.

Tversky, Amos, Daniel Kahneman. 1992. "Advances in prospect theory: Cumulative representation of uncertainty." *Journal of Risk and Uncertainty*, vol. 5, no. 4: 297–323. 10.1007/BF00122574

Willenbrock, Scott. 2011. "Diversification Return, Portfolio Rebalancing, and the Commodity Return Puzzle." *Financial Analysts Journal*, vol. 67, no. 4 (July/August): 42–49. 10.2469/faj.v67.n4.1

Winkelmann, Kurt. 2003. "Developing an Optimal Active Risk Budget," in Modern Investment Management: An Equilibrium Approach Bob Litterman, ed. New York: John Wiley & Sons.

Xiong, James X., Thomas M. Idzorek. 2011. "The Impact of Skewness and Fat Tails on the Asset Allocation Decision." *Financial Analysts Journal*, vol. 67, no. 2 (March/April): 23–35. 10.2469/faj.v67.n2.5

Yale University. 2014. "The Yale Endowment 2014" (http://investments.yale.edu/s/Yale_Endowment_14.pdf).

PRACTICE PROBLEMS

The following information relates to questions 1-8

Megan Beade and Hanna Müller are senior analysts for a large, multi-divisional money management firm. Beade supports the institutional portfolio managers, and Müller does the same for the private wealth portfolio managers.

Beade reviews the asset allocation in Exhibit 1, derived from a mean–variance optimization (MVO) model for an institutional client, noting that details of the MVO are lacking.

Exhibit 1: Asset Allocation and Market Weights (in percent)

Asset Classes	Asset Allocation	Investable Global Market Weights
Cash	0	—
US bonds	30	17
US TIPS	0	3
Non-US bonds	0	22
Emerging market equity	25	5
Non-US developed equity	20	29
US small- and mid-cap equity	25	4
US large-cap equity	0	20

The firm's policy is to rebalance a portfolio when the asset class weight falls outside of a corridor around the target allocation. The width of each corridor is customized for each client and proportional to the target allocation. Beade recommends wider corridor widths for high-risk asset classes, narrower corridor widths for less liquid asset classes, and narrower corridor widths for taxable clients with high capital gains tax rates.

One client sponsors a defined benefit pension plan where the present value of the liabilities is $241 million and the market value of plan assets is $205 million. Beade expects interest rates to rise and both the present value of plan liabilities and the market value of plan assets to decrease by $25 million, changing the pension plan's funding ratio.

Beade uses a surplus optimization approach to liability-relative asset allocation based on the objective function

$$U_m^{LR} = E\left(R_{s,m}\right) - 0.005\lambda\,\sigma^2\left(R_{s,m}\right)$$

where $E(R_{s,m})$ is the expected surplus return for portfolio m, λ is the risk aversion coefficient, and $\sigma^2(R_{s,m})$ is the variance of the surplus return. Beade establishes the expected surplus return and surplus variance for three different asset allocations, shown in Exhibit 2. Given $\lambda = 1.50$, she chooses the optimal asset mix.

Exhibit 2: Expected Surplus Return and Volatility for Three Portfolios

	Return	Standard Deviation
Portfolio 1	13.00%	24%
Portfolio 2	12.00%	18%
Portfolio 3	11.00%	19%

Client Haunani Kealoha has a large fixed obligation due in 10 years. Beade assesses that Kealoha has substantially more funds than are required to meet the fixed obligation. The client wants to earn a competitive risk-adjusted rate of return while maintaining a high level of certainty that there will be sufficient assets to meet the fixed obligation.

In the private wealth area, the firm has designed five subportfolios with differing asset allocations that are used to fund different client goals over a five-year horizon. Exhibit 3 shows the expected returns and volatilities of the subportfolios and the probabilities that the subportfolios will exceed an expected minimum return. Client Luis Rodríguez wants to satisfy two goals. Goal 1 requires a conservative portfolio providing the highest possible minimum return that will be met at least 95% of the time. Goal 2 requires a riskier portfolio that provides the highest minimum return that will be exceeded at least 85% of the time.

Exhibit 3: Characteristics of Subportfolios

Subportfolio	A	B	C	D	E
Expected return, in percent	4.60	5.80	7.00	8.20	9.40
Expected volatility, in percent	3.46	5.51	8.08	10.80	13.59

Required Success Rate	Minimum Expected Return for Success Rate				
99%	1.00	0.07	−1.40	−3.04	−4.74
95%	2.05	1.75	1.06	0.25	−0.60
90%	2.62	2.64	2.37	2.01	1.61
85%	3.00	3.25	3.26	3.19	3.10
75%	3.56	4.14	4.56	4.94	5.30

Müller uses a risk parity asset allocation approach with a client's four–asset class portfolio. The expected return of the domestic bond asset class is the lowest of the asset classes, and the returns of the domestic bond asset class have the lowest covariance with other asset class returns. Müller estimates the weight that should be placed on domestic bonds.

Müller and a client discuss other approaches to asset allocation that are not based on optimization models or goals-based models. Müller makes the following comments to the client:

Comment 1   An advantage of the "120 minus your age" heuristic over the 60/40 stock/bond heuristic is that it incorporates an age-based stock/bond allocation.

Comment 2   The Yale model emphasizes traditional investments and a commitment to active management.

Comment 3   A client's asset allocation using the $1/N$ rule depends on the investment characteristics of each asset class.

1. The asset allocation in Exhibit 1 *most likely* resulted from a mean–variance optimization using:

    A. historical data.

    B. reverse optimization.

    C. Black–Litterman inputs.

2. For clients concerned about rebalancing-related transactions costs, which of Beade's suggested changes in the corridor width of the rebalancing policy is correct? The change with respect to:

    A. high-risk asset classes.

    B. less liquid asset classes.

    C. taxable clients with high capital gains tax rates.

3. Based on Beade's interest rate expectations, the pension plan's funding ratio will:

    A. decrease.

    B. remain unchanged.

    C. increase.

4. Based on Exhibit 2, which portfolio provides the greatest objective function expected value?

    A. Portfolio 1

    B. Portfolio 2

    C. Portfolio 3

5. The asset allocation approach most appropriate for client Kealoha is *best* described as:

    A. a surplus optimization approach.

    B. an integrated asset–liability approach.

    C. a hedging/return-seeking portfolios approach.

6. Based on Exhibit 3, which subportfolios *best* meet the two goals expressed by client Rodríguez?

    A. Subportfolio A for Goal 1 and Subportfolio C for Goal 2

    B. Subportfolio B for Goal 1 and Subportfolio C for Goal 2

    C. Subportfolio E for Goal 1 and Subportfolio A for Goal 2

7. In the risk parity asset allocation approach that Müller uses, the weight that

Müller places on domestic bonds should be:

A. less than 25%.

B. equal to 25%.

C. greater than 25%.

8. Which of Müller's comments about the other approaches to asset allocation is correct?

A. Comment 1

B. Comment 2

C. Comment 3

The following information relates to questions 9-13

Investment adviser Carl Monteo determines client asset allocations using quantitative techniques such as mean–variance optimization (MVO) and risk budgets. Monteo is reviewing the allocations of three clients. Exhibit 1 shows the expected return and standard deviation of returns for three strategic asset allocations that apply to several of Monteo's clients.

Exhibit 1: Strategic Asset Allocation Alternatives

	Adviser's Forecasts	
Asset Allocation	Expected Return (%)	Standard Deviation of Returns (%)
A	10	12.0
B	8	8.0
C	6	2.0

Monteo interviews client Mary Perkins and develops a detailed assessment of her risk preference and capacity for risk, which is needed to apply MVO to asset allocation. Monteo estimates the risk aversion coefficient (λ) for Perkins to be 8 and uses the following utility function to determine a preferred asset allocation for Perkins:

$$U_m = E(R_m) - 0.005\lambda\sigma_m^2$$

Another client, Lars Velky, represents Velky Partners (VP), a large institutional investor with $500 million in investable assets. Velky is interested in adding less liquid asset classes, such as direct real estate, infrastructure, and private equity, to VP's portfolio. Velky and Monteo discuss the considerations involved in applying many of the common asset allocation techniques, such as MVO, to these asset classes. Before making any changes to the portfolio, Monteo asks Velky about his knowledge of risk budgeting. Velky makes the following statements:

Statement 1 An optimum risk budget minimizes total risk.

Statement 2   Risk budgeting decomposes total portfolio risk into its constituent parts.

Statement 3   An asset allocation is optimal from a risk-budgeting perspective when the ratio of excess return to marginal contribution to risk is different for all assets in the portfolio.

Monteo meets with a third client, Jayanta Chaterji, an individual investor. Monteo and Chaterji discuss mean–variance optimization. Chaterji expresses concern about using the output of MVOs for two reasons:

Criticism 1: The asset allocations are highly sensitive to changes in the model inputs.

Criticism 2: The asset allocations tend to be highly dispersed across all available asset classes.

Monteo and Chaterji also discuss other approaches to asset allocation. Chaterji tells Monteo that he understands the factor-based approach to asset allocation to have two key characteristics:

Characteristic 1   The factors commonly used in the factor-based approach generally have low correlations with the market and with each other.

Characteristic 2   The factors commonly used in the factor-based approach are typically different from the fundamental or structural factors used in multifactor models.

Monteo concludes the meeting with Chaterji after sharing his views on the factor-based approach.

9. Based on Exhibit 1 and the risk aversion coefficient, the preferred asset allocation for Perkins is:

   A. Asset Allocation A.

   B. Asset Allocation B.

   C. Asset Allocation C.

10. In their discussion of the asset classes that Velky is interested in adding to the VP portfolio, Monteo should tell Velky that:

    A. these asset classes can be readily diversified to eliminate idiosyncratic risk.

    B. indexes are available for these asset classes that do an outstanding job of representing the performance characteristics of the asset classes.

    C. the risk and return characteristics associated with actual investment vehicles for these asset classes are typically significantly different from the characteristics of the asset classes themselves.

11. Which of Velky's statements about risk budgeting is correct?

    A. Statement 1

    B. Statement 2

    C. Statement 3

12. Which of Chaterji's criticisms of MVO is/are valid?

A. Only Criticism 1

B. Only Criticism 2

C. Both Criticism 1 and Criticism 2

13. Which of the characteristics put forth by Chaterji to describe the factor-based approach is/are correct?

A. Only Characteristic 1

B. Only Characteristic 2

C. Both Characteristic 1 and Characteristic 2

---

14. John Tomb is an investment advisor at an asset management firm. He is developing an asset allocation for James Youngmall, a client of the firm. Tomb considers two possible allocations for Youngmall. Allocation A consists of four asset classes: cash, US bonds, US equities, and global equities. Allocation B includes these same four asset classes, as well as global bonds.

Youngmall has a relatively low risk tolerance with a risk aversion coefficient (λ) of 7. Tomb runs mean–variance optimization (MVO) to maximize the following utility function to determine the preferred allocation for Youngmall:

$$U_m = E(R_m) - 0.005\lambda\sigma_m^2$$

The resulting MVO statistics for the two asset allocations are presented in Exhibit 1.

Exhibit 1: MVO Portfolio Statistics

	Allocation A	Allocation B
Expected return	6.7%	5.9%
Expected standard deviation	11.9%	10.7%

Determine which allocation in Exhibit 1 Tomb should recommend to Youngmall. **Justify** your response.

Determine which allocation in Exhibit 1 Tomb should recommend to Youngmall. (circle one)

Allocation A	Allocation B

Justify your response.

---

15. Walker Patel is a portfolio manager at an investment management firm. After successfully implementing mean–variance optimization (MVO), he wants to apply reverse optimization to his portfolio. For each asset class in the portfolio, Patel obtains market capitalization data, betas computed relative to a global market portfolio, and expected returns. This information, along with the MVO asset allocation results, are presented in Exhibit 1.

Exhibit 1: Asset Class Data and MVO Asset Allocation Results

Asset Class	Market Cap (trillions)	Beta	Expected Returns	MVO Asset Allocation
Cash	$4.2	0.0	2.0%	10%
US bonds	$26.8	0.5	4.5%	20%
US equities	$22.2	1.4	8.6%	35%
Global equities	$27.5	1.7	10.5%	20%
Global bonds	$27.1	0.6	4.7%	15%
Total	$107.8			

The risk-free rate is 2.0%, and the global market risk premium is 5.5%.

Contrast, using the information provided above, the results of a reverse optimization approach with that of the MVO approach for each of the following:

i.   The asset allocation mix

ii.   The values of the expected returns for US equities and global bonds

Justify your response.

16. Viktoria Johansson is newly appointed as manager of ABC Corporation's pension fund. The current market value of the fund's assets is $10 billion, and the present value of the fund's liabilities is $8.5 billion. The fund has historically been managed using an asset-only approach, but Johansson recommends to ABC's board of directors that they adopt a liability-relative approach, specifically the hedging/return-seeking portfolios approach. Johansson assumes that the returns of the fund's liabilities are driven by changes in the returns of index-linked government bonds. Exhibit 1 presents three potential asset allocation choices for the fund.

Exhibit 1: Potential Asset Allocations Choices for ABC Corp's Pension Fund

Asset Class	Allocation 1	Allocation 2	Allocation 3
Cash	15%	5%	0%
Index-linked government bonds	70%	15%	85%
Corporate bonds	0%	30%	5%
Equities	15%	50%	10%
Portfolio Statistics			
Expected return	3.4%	6.2%	3.6%
Expected standard deviation	7.0%	12.0%	8.5%

Determine which asset allocation in Exhibit 1 would be *most appropriate* for Johansson given her recommendation. **Justify** your response.

Determine which asset allocation in Exhibit 1 would be *most appropriate* for Johansson given her recommendation.
(circle one)

| Allocation 1 | Allocation 2 | Allocation 3 |

Justify your response.

The following information relates to questions 17-18

Mike and Kerry Armstrong are a married couple who recently retired with total assets of $8 million. The Armstrongs meet with their financial advisor, Brent Abbott, to discuss three of their financial goals during their retirement.

Goal 1: An 85% chance of purchasing a vacation home for $5 million in five years.

Goal 2: A 99% chance of being able to maintain their current annual expenditures of $100,000 for the next 10 years, assuming annual inflation of 3% from Year 2 onward.

Goal 3: A 75% chance of being able to donate $10 million to charitable foundations in 25 years.

Abbott suggests using a goals-based approach to construct a portfolio. He develops a set of sub-portfolio modules, presented in Exhibit 1. Abbott suggests investing any excess capital in Module A.

Exhibit 1: "Highest Probability- and Horizon-Adjusted Return" Sub-Portfolio Modules under Different Horizon and Probability Scenarios

	A	B	C	D
Portfolio Characteristics				
Expected return	6.5%	7.9%	8.5%	8.8%
Expected volatility	6.0%	7.7%	8.8%	9.7%
Annualized Minimum Expectation Returns				
Time Horizon		**5 Years**		
Required Success				
99%	0.3%	−0.1%	−0.7%	−1.3%
85%	3.7%	4.3%	4.4%	4.3%
75%	4.7%	5.6%	5.8%	5.9%
Time Horizon		**10 Years**		
Required Success				
99%	2.1%	2.2%	2.0%	1.7%
85%	4.5%	5.4%	5.6%	5.6%
75%	5.2%	6.3%	6.6%	6.7%
Time Horizon		**25 Years**		
Required Success				
99%	3.7%	4.3%	4.4%	4.3%
85%	5.3%	6.3%	6.7%	6.8%
75%	5.7%	6.9%	7.3%	7.5%

17. **Select**, for each of Armstrong's three goals, which sub-portfolio module from Exhibit 1 Abbott should choose in constructing a portfolio. **Justify** each selection.

Select, for each of Armstrong's three goals, which sub-portfolio module from Exhibit 1 Abbott should choose in constructing a portfolio.
(circle one module for each goal)

Goal 1	Goal 2	Goal 3
Module A	Module A	Module A
Module B	Module B	Module B
Module C	Module C	Module C
Module D	Module D	Module D

Justify each selection.

18. **Construct** the overall goals-based asset allocation for the Armstrongs given their three goals and Abbott's suggestion for investing any excess capital. **Show** your calculations.

Construct the overall goals-based asset allocation for the Armstrongs given their three goals and Abbott's suggestion for investing any excess capital.
(insert the percentage of the total assets to be invested in each module)

Module A	Module B	Module C	Module D

Show your calculations.

SOLUTIONS

1. A is correct. The allocations in Exhibit 1 are most likely from an MVO model using historical data inputs. MVO tends to result in asset allocations that are concentrated in a subset of the available asset classes. The allocations in Exhibit 1 have heavy concentrations in four of the asset classes and no investment in the other four asset classes, and the weights differ greatly from global market weights. Compared to the use of historical inputs, the Black–Litterman and reverse-optimization models most likely would be less concentrated in a few asset classes and less distant from the global weights.

2. A is correct. Theoretically, higher-risk assets would warrant a narrow corridor because high-risk assets are more likely to stray from the desired strategic asset allocation. However, narrow corridors will likely result in more frequent rebalancing and increased transaction costs, so in practice corridor width is often specified to be proportionally greater the higher the asset class's volatility. Thus, higher-risk assets should have a wider corridor to avoid frequent, costly rebalancing costs. Her other suggestions are not correct. Less-liquid asset classes should have a wider, not narrower, corridor width. Less-liquid assets should have a wider corridor to avoid frequent rebalancing costs. For taxable investors, transactions trigger capital gains in jurisdictions that tax them. For such investors, higher tax rates on capital gains should be associated with wider (not narrower) corridor widths.

3. A is correct. The original funding ratio is the market value of assets divided by the present value of liabilities. This plan's ratio is $205 million/$241 million = 0.8506. When the assets and liabilities both decrease by $25 million, the funding ratio will decrease to $180 million/$216 million = 0.8333.

4. B is correct. The objective function expected value is
    $U_m^{LR} = E(R_{s,m}) - 0.005\lambda\,\sigma^2(R_{s,m})$. λ is equal to 1.5, and the expected value of the objective function is shown in the rightmost column below.

Portfolio	$E(R_s,m)$	$\sigma^2(R_{s,m})$	$U_m^{LR} = E(R_{s,m}) - 0.005(1.5)\sigma^2(R_{s,m})$
1	13.00	576	8.68
2	12.00	324	9.57
3	11.00	361	8.29

Portfolio 2 generates the highest value, or utility, in the objective function.

5. C is correct. The hedging/return-seeking portfolios approach is best for this client. Beade should construct two portfolios, one that includes riskless bonds that will pay off the fixed obligation in 10 years and the other a risky portfolio that earns a competitive risk-adjusted return. This approach is a simple two-step process of hedging the fixed obligation and then investing the balance of the assets in a return-seeking portfolio.

6. A is correct. Goal 1 requires a success rate of at least 95%, and Subportfolio A has the highest minimum expected return (2.05%) meeting this requirement. Goal 2 requires the highest minimum expected return that will be achieved 85% of the time. Subportfolio C meets this requirement (and has a minimum expected return of 3.26%).

7. C is correct. A risk parity asset allocation is based on the notion that each asset class should contribute equally to the total risk of the portfolio. Bonds have the lowest risk level and must contribute 25% of the portfolio's total risk, so bonds must be overweighted (greater than 25%). The equal contribution of each asset class is calculated as:

$$w_i \times \text{Cov}\left(r_i, r_p\right) = \frac{1}{n}\sigma_p^2$$

where

w_i = weight of asset i

$\text{Cov}(r_i, r_p)$ = covariance of asset i with the portfolio

n = number of assets

σ_p^2 = variance of the portfolio

In this example, there are four asset classes, and the variance of the total portfolio is assumed to be 25%; therefore, using a risk parity approach, the allocation to each asset class is expected to contribute $(1/4 \times 25\%) = 6.25\%$ of the total variance. Because bonds have the lowest covariance, they must have a higher relative weight to achieve the same contribution to risk as the other asset classes.

8. A is correct. Comment 1 is correct because the "120 minus your age" rule reduces the equity allocation as the client ages, while the 60/40 rule makes no such adjustment. Comments 2 and 3 are not correct. The Yale model emphasizes investing in alternative assets (such as hedge funds, private equity, and real estate) as opposed to investing in traditional asset classes (such as stock and bonds). The $1/N$ rule allocates an equal weight to each asset without regard to its investment characteristics, treating all assets as indistinguishable in terms of mean returns, volatility, and correlations.

9. C is correct. The risk aversion coefficient (λ) for Mary Perkins is 8. The utility of each asset allocation is calculated as follows:
Asset Allocation A:

$$U_A = 10.0\% - 0.005(8)(12\%)^2$$

$$= 4.24\%$$

Asset Allocation B:

$$U_B = 8.0\% - 0.005(8)(8\%)^2$$

$$= 5.44\%$$

Asset Allocation C:

$$U_C = 6.0\% - 0.005(8)(2\%)^2$$

$$= 5.84\%$$

Therefore, the preferred strategic allocation is Asset Allocation C, which generates the highest utility given Perkins's level of risk aversion.

10. C is correct. Less liquid asset classes—such as direct real estate, infrastructure, and private equity—represent unique challenges when applying many of the common asset allocation techniques. Common illiquid asset classes cannot be readily diversified to eliminate idiosyncratic risk, so representing overall asset class performance is problematic. Furthermore, there are far fewer indexes that

attempt to represent aggregate performance for these less liquid asset classes than indexes of traditional highly liquid asset classes. Finally, the risk and return characteristics associated with actual investment vehicles—such as direct real estate funds, infrastructure funds, and private equity funds—are typically significantly different from the characteristics of the asset classes themselves.

11. B is correct. The goal of risk budgeting is to maximize return per unit of risk. A risk budget identifies the total amount of risk and attributes risk to its constituent parts. An optimum risk budget allocates risk efficiently.

12. A is correct. One common criticism of MVO is that the model outputs, the asset allocations, tend to be highly sensitive to changes in the model. Another common criticism of MVO is that the resulting asset allocations tend to be highly concentrated in a subset of the available asset classes.

13. A is correct. The factors commonly used in the factor-based approach generally have low correlations with the market and with each other. This results from the fact that the factors typically represent what is referred to as a zero (dollar) investment or self-financing investment, in which the underperforming attribute is sold short to finance an offsetting long position in the better-performing attribute. Constructing factors in this manner removes most market exposure from the factors (because of the offsetting short and long positions); as a result, the factors generally have low correlations with the market and with one another. Also, the factors commonly used in the factor-based approach are typically similar to the fundamental or structural factors used in multifactor models.

14.

Determine which allocation in Exhibit 1 Tomb should recommend to Youngmall. (circle one)

Allocation A	Allocation B

Justify your response.

- Tomb should recommend Allocation B.
- The expected utility of Allocation B is 1.89%, which is higher than Allocation A's expected utility of 1.74%.

MVO provides a framework to determine how much to allocate to each asset class or to create the optimal asset mix. The given objective function is:

$$U_m = E\left(R_m\right) - 0.005\lambda\,\sigma_m^2$$

Using the given objective function and the expected returns and expected standard deviations for Allocations A and B, the expected utilities (certainty-equivalent returns) for the two allocations are calculated as:

Allocation A: $6.7\% - 0.005\,(7)\,(11.9\%)^2 = 1.74\%$

Allocation B: $5.9\% - 0.005\,(7)\,(10.7\%)^2 = 1.89\%$

Therefore, Tomb should recommend Allocation B because it results in higher expected utility than Allocation A.

15. **Contrast,** using the information provided above, the results of a reverse optimization approach with that of the MVO approach for each of the following:

    i.   The asset allocation mix

- The asset allocation weights for the reverse optimization method are inputs into the optimization and are determined by the market capitalization weights of the global market portfolio.
- The asset allocation weights for the MVO method are outputs of the optimization with the expected returns, covariances, and a risk aversion coefficient used as inputs.
- The two methods result in significantly different asset allocation mixes.
- In contrast to MVO, the reverse optimization method results in a higher percentage point allocation to global bonds, US bonds, and global equities as well as a lower percentage point allocation to cash and US equities.

The reverse optimization method takes the asset allocation weights as its inputs that are assumed to be optimal. These weights are calculated as the market capitalization weights of a global market portfolio. In contrast, the outputs of an MVO are the asset allocation weights, which are based on (1) expected returns and covariances that are forecasted using historical data and (2) a risk aversion coefficient. The two methods result in significantly different asset allocation mixes. In contrast to MVO, the reverse optimization method results in a 4.9, 5.5, and 10.1 higher percentage point allocation to US bonds, global equities, and global bonds, respectively, and a 6.1 and 14.4 lower percentage point allocation to cash and US equities, respectively.

The asset allocation under the two methods is as follows:

Asset Class	Market Cap (trillions)	Asset Allocation Weights		
		Reverse Optimization	MVO Approach	Difference
Cash	$4.2	3.9%	10%	−6.1%
US bonds	$26.8	24.9%	20%	4.9%
US equities	$22.2	20.6%	35%	−14.4%
Global equities	$27.5	25.5%	20%	5.5%
Global bonds	$27.1	25.1%	15%	10.1%
Total	$107.8	100.0%	100.0%	

ii. The values of the expected returns for US equities and global bonds

- For the reverse optimization approach, the expected returns of asset classes are the outputs of optimization with the market capitalization weights, covariances, and the risk aversion coefficient used as inputs.
- In contrast, for the MVO approach, the expected returns of asset classes are inputs to the optimization, with the expected returns generally estimated using historical data.
- The computed values for the expected returns for global bonds and US equities using the reverse optimization method are 5.3% and 9.7%, respectively.
- In contrast, the expected return estimates used in the MVO approach from Exhibit 1 for global bonds and US equities are 4.7% and 8.6%, respectively.

The output of the reverse optimization method are optimized returns which are viewed as unobserved equilibrium or imputed returns. The equilibrium returns are essentially long-run capital market returns provided by each asset class and are strongly linked to CAPM. In contrast, the expected returns in the MVO approach are generally forecasted based on historical data and are used as inputs along with covariances and the risk aversion coefficient in the optimization. The reverse-optimized returns are calculated using a CAPM approach. The return on an asset class using the CAPM approach is calculated as follows:

Return on Asset Class = Risk-Free Rate + (Beta) (Market Risk Premium)

Therefore, the implied returns for global bonds and US equities are calculated as follows:

Return on Global Bonds = 2.0% + (0.6) (5.5%) = 5.3%

Return on US Equities = 2.0% + (1.4) (5.5%) = 9.7%

The implied equilibrium returns for global bonds and US equities are 5.3% and 9.7%, respectively. These implied returns are above the forecasted returns based on historical data (from Exhibit 1) used as inputs in the MVO approach for global bonds and US equities of 4.7% and 8.6%, respectively.

16.

Determine which asset allocation in Exhibit 1 would be *most appropriate* for Johansson given her recommendation.
(circle one)

Allocation 1	Allocation 2	Allocation 3

Justify your response.

- Allocation 3 is most appropriate.
- To fully hedge the fund's liabilities, 85% ($8.5 billion/$10.0 billion) of the fund's assets would be linked to index-linked government bonds.
- Residual $1.5 billion surplus would be invested into a return-seeking portfolio.

The pension fund currently has a surplus of $1.5 billion ($10.0 billion – $8.5 billion). To adopt a hedging/return-seeking portfolios approach, Johansson would first hedge the liabilities by allocating an amount equal to the present value of the fund's liabilities, $8.5 billion, to a hedging portfolio. The hedging portfolio must include assets whose returns are driven by the same factors that drive the returns of the liabilities, which in this case are the index-linked government bonds.

So, Johansson should allocate 85% ($8.5 billion/$10.0 billion) of the fund's assets to index-linked government bonds. The residual $1.5 billion surplus would then be invested into a return-seeking portfolio. Therefore, Allocation 3 would be the most appropriate asset allocation for the fund because it allocates 85% of the fund's assets to index-linked government bonds and the remainder to a return-seeking portfolio consisting of corporate bonds and equities.

17.

Select, for each of Armstrong's three goals, which sub-portfolio module from Exhibit 1 Abbott should choose in constructing a portfolio.
(circle one module for each goal)

Goal 1	Goal 2	Goal 3
Module A	Module A	Module A
Module B	Module B	Module B
Module C	Module C	Module C
Module D	Module D	Module D

Justify each selection.

- Module C should be chosen for Goal 1, Module B should be chosen for Goal 2, and Module D should be chosen for Goal 3.

- The module that should be selected for each goal is the one that offers the highest return given the time horizon and required probability of success.

The module that should be selected for each goal is the one that offers the highest return given the time horizon and required probability of success. For Goal 1, which has a time horizon of five years and a required probability of success of 85%, Module C should be chosen because its 4.4% expected return is higher than the expected returns of all the other modules. Similarly, for Goal 2, which has a time horizon of 10 years and a required probability of success of 99%, Module B should be chosen because its 2.2% expected return is higher than the expected returns of all the other modules. Finally, for Goal 3, which has a time horizon of 25 years and a required probability of success of 75%, Module D should be chosen because its 7.5% expected return is higher than the expected returns of all the other modules.

18. Guideline Answer:

- The module that should be selected for each goal is the one that offers the highest return given the time horizon and required probability of success.

- Approximately 16.4%, 12.7%, 50.4%, and 20.5% should be invested in Modules A, B, C, and D, respectively.

The appropriate goals-based allocation for the Armstrongs is as follows:

	Goals			
	1	**2**	**3**	**Surplus**
Horizon (years)	5	10	25	
Probability of success	85%	99%	75%	
Selected module	**C**	**B**	**D**	**A**
Discount rate	4.4%	2.2%	7.5%	
Dollars invested (millions)	$4.03	$1.01	$1.64	$1.32
As a % of total	**50.4%**	**12.7%**	**20.5%**	**16.4%**

Supporting calculations:

For Goal 1, which has a time horizon of five years and a required probability of success of 85%, Module C should be chosen because its 4.4% expected return is higher than the expected returns of all the other modules. The present value of Goal 1 is calculated as follows:

N = 5, FV = –5,000,000, I/Y = 4.4%; CPT PV = $4,031,508 (or $4.03 million)

So, approximately 50.4% of the total assets of $8 million (= $4.03 million/$8.00 million) should be allocated to Module C.

For Goal 2, which has a time horizon of 10 years and a required probability of success of 99%, Module B should be chosen because its 2.2% expected return is higher than the expected returns of all the other modules. The present value of Goal 2 is calculated as follows:

$$PV = \frac{\$100,000}{(1.022)^1} + \frac{\$100,000(1.03)^1}{(1.022)^2} + \frac{\$100,000(1.03)^2}{(1.022)^3} + \cdots + \frac{\$100,000(1.03)^9}{(1.022)^{10}}$$

PV = $1,013,670 (or $1.01 million)

So, approximately 12.7% of the total assets of $8 million (= $1.01 million/$8.00 million) should be allocated to Module B.

For Goal 3, which has a time horizon of 25 years and a required probability of success of 75%, Module D should be chosen because its 7.5% expected return is higher than the expected returns of all the other modules. The present value of Goal 3 is calculated as follows:

N = 25, FV = –10,000,000, I/Y = 7.5%; CPT PV = $1,639,791 (or $1.64 million)

So, approximately 20.5% of the total assets of $8 million (= $1.64 million/$8.00 million) should be allocated to Module D.

Finally, the surplus of $1,315,032 (= $8,000,000 – $4,031,508 – $1,013,670 – $1,639,791), representing 16.4% (= $1.32 million/$8.00 million), should be invested in Module A following Abbott's suggestion.

5

Asset Allocation with Real-World Constraints

by Peter Mladina, Brian J. Murphy, CFA, and Mark Ruloff, FSA, EA, CERA.

Peter Mladina is at Northern Trust and UCLA (USA). Brian J. Murphy, CFA, is at Willis Towers Watson (USA). Mark Ruloff, FSA, EA, CERA, is at Aon (USA).

LEARNING OUTCOMES

Mastery	The candidate should be able to:
☐	discuss asset size, liquidity needs, time horizon, and regulatory or other considerations as constraints on asset allocation
☐	discuss tax considerations in asset allocation and rebalancing
☐	recommend and justify revisions to an asset allocation given change(s) in investment objectives and/or constraints
☐	discuss the use of short-term shifts in asset allocation
☐	identify behavioral biases that arise in asset allocation and recommend methods to overcome them

INTRODUCTION

1

This reading illustrates ways in which the asset allocation process must be adapted to accommodate specific asset owner circumstances and constraints. It addresses adaptations to the asset allocation inputs given an asset owner's asset size, liquidity, and time horizon as well as external constraints that may affect the asset allocation choice (Sections 2–5). We also discuss the ways in which taxes influence the asset allocation process for the taxable investor (Sections 6–7). In addition, we discuss the circumstances that should trigger a re-evaluation of the long-term strategic asset allocation (Section 8), when and how an asset owner might want to make short-term shifts in asset allocation (Section 9), and how innate investor behaviors can interfere with successful long-term planning for the investment portfolio (Section 10). Throughout the reading, we illustrate the application of these concepts using a series of hypothetical investors.

2   CONSTRAINTS IN ASSET ALLOCATION AND ASSET SIZE

☐ | discuss asset size, liquidity needs, time horizon, and regulatory or other considerations as constraints on asset allocation

General asset allocation principles assume that all asset owners have equal ability to access the entirety of the investment opportunity set, and that it is merely a matter of finding that combination of asset classes that best meets the wants, needs, and obligations of the asset owner. In practice, however, it is not so simple. An asset owner must consider a number of constraints when modeling and choosing among asset allocation alternatives. Some of the most important are asset size, liquidity needs, taxes, and time horizon. Moreover, regulatory and other external considerations may influence the investment opportunity set or the optimal asset allocation decision.

Asset Size

The size of an asset owner's portfolio has implications for asset allocation. It may limit the opportunity set—the asset classes accessible to the asset owner—by virtue of the scale needed to invest successfully in certain asset classes or by the availability of investment vehicles necessary to implement the asset allocation.

Economies and diseconomies of scale are perhaps the most important factors relevant to understanding asset size as a constraint. The size of an asset owner's investment pool may be too small—or too large—to capture the returns of certain asset classes or strategies efficiently. Asset owners with larger portfolios can generally consider a broader set of asset classes and strategies. On the one hand, they are more likely to have sufficient governance capacity—sophistication and staff resources—to develop the required knowledge base for the more complex asset classes and investment vehicles. They also have sufficient size to build a diversified portfolio of investment strategies, many of which have substantial minimum investment requirements. On the other hand, some asset owners may have portfolios that are *too* large; their desired minimum investment may exhaust the capacity of active external investment managers in certain asset classes and strategies. Although "too large" and "too small" are not rigidly defined, the following example illustrates the difficulty of investing a very large portfolio. Consider an asset owner with an investment portfolio of US$25 billion who is seeking to make a 5% investment in global small-cap stocks:

- The median total market capitalization of the stocks in the S&P Global SmallCap is approximately US$860 million as of November 2021.
- Assume a small-cap manager operates a 50-stock portfolio and is willing to own 3% of the market cap of any one of its portfolio companies. Their average position size would be US$26 million, and an effective level of assets under management (AUM) would be on the order of US$1.3 billion. Beyond that level, the manager may be forced to expand the portfolio beyond 50 stocks or to hold position sizes greater than 3% of a company's market cap, which could then create liquidity issues for the manager.
- Now, our US$25 billion fund is looking to allocate US$1.25 billion to small-cap stocks (US$25 billion × 5%). They want to diversify this allocation across three or four active managers—a reasonable allocation of governance resources in the context of all of the fund's investment activities. The average allocation per manager is approximately US$300 to US$400 million,

which would constitute between 23% and 31% of each manager's AUM. This exposes both the asset owner and the investment manager to an undesirable level of operational risk.

Although many large asset owners have found effective ways to implement a small-cap allocation, this example illustrates some of the issues associated with managing a large asset pool. These include such practical considerations as the number of investment managers that might need to be hired to fulfill an investment allocation and the ability of the asset owner to identify and monitor the required number of managers.

Research has shown that investment managers tend to incur certain disadvantages from increasing scale: Growth in AUM leads to larger trade sizes, incurring greater price impact; capital inflows may cause active investment managers to pursue ideas outside of their core investment theses; and organizational hierarchies may slow down decision making and reduce incentives.[1] Asset *owners*, however, are found to have *increasing* returns to scale, as discussed below.

A study of pension plan size and performance (using data spanning 1990–2008) found that large defined benefit plans outperformed smaller ones by 45–50 basis points per year on a risk-adjusted basis.[2] The gains are derived from a combination of cost savings related to internal management, a greater ability to negotiate fees with external managers, and the ability to support larger allocations to private equity and real estate investments. As fund size increases, the "per participant" costs of a larger governance infrastructure decline and the plan sponsor can allocate resources away from such asset classes as small-cap stocks, which are sensitive to diseconomies of scale, to such other areas as private equity funds or co-investments where they are more likely to realize scale-related benefits.

Whereas owners of large asset pools may achieve these operating efficiencies, scale may also impose obstacles related to the liquidity and trading costs of the underlying asset. Above some size, it becomes difficult to deploy capital effectively in certain active investment strategies. As illustrated in Exhibit 1, owners of very large portfolios may face size constraints in allocating to active equity strategies. The studies referenced earlier noted that these asset owners frequently choose to invest passively in developed equity markets where their size inhibits alpha potential. The asset owner's finite resources can then be allocated instead toward such strategies as private equity, hedge funds, and infrastructure, where their scale and resources provide a competitive advantage.

Exhibit 1: Asset Size and Investor Constraints	
Asset Class	**Investor Constraints by Size**
▪ Cash equivalents and money market funds	No size constraints.
▪ Large-cap developed market equity ▪ Small-cap developed market equity ▪ Emerging market equity	Generally accessible to large and small asset owners, although the very large asset owner may be constrained in the amount of assets allocated to certain active strategies and managers.

---

1 See Stein (2002); Chen, Hong, Huang, and Kubik (2004); and Pollet and Wilson (2008).
2 See Dyck and Pomorski (2011). The median plan in this study was just over US$2 billion. The 25th percentile plan was US$780 million, and the 75th percentile plan was US$6.375 billion.

Asset Class	Investor Constraints by Size
▪ Developed market sovereign bonds ▪ Investment-grade bonds ▪ Non-investment-grade bonds ▪ Private real estate equity	Generally accessible to large and small asset owners, although to achieve prudent diversification, smaller asset owners may need to implement via a commingled vehicle.
Alternative Investments ▪ Hedge funds ▪ Private debt ▪ Private equity ▪ Infrastructure ▪ Timberland and farmland	May be accessible to large and small asset owners, although if offered as private investment vehicles, there may be legal minimum qualifications that exclude smaller asset owners. The ability to successfully invest in these asset classes may also be limited by the asset owner's level of investment understanding/expertise. Prudent diversification may require that smaller asset owners implement via a commingled vehicle, such as a fund of funds, or an ancillary access channel, such as a liquid alternatives vehicle or an alternatives ETF. For very large funds, the allocation may be constrained by the number of funds available.

Even in these strategies, very large asset owners may be constrained by scale. In smaller or less liquid markets, can a large asset owner invest enough that the exposure contributes a material benefit to the broader portfolio? For example, a sovereign wealth fund or large public pension plan may not find enough attractive hedge fund managers to fulfill their desired allocation to hedge funds. True alpha is rare, limiting the opportunity set. Asset owners who find that they have to split their mandate into many smaller pieces may end up with an index-like portfolio but with high active management fees; one manager's active bets may cancel out those of another active manager. A manager mix with no true alpha becomes index-like because the uncompensated, idiosyncratic return variation is diversified away. A much smaller allocation may be achievable, but it may be too small to meaningfully affect the risk and return characteristics of the overall portfolio. More broadly, a very large size makes it more difficult to benefit from opportunistic investments in smaller niche markets or from skilled investment managers who have a small set of unique ideas or concentrated bets. No hard and fast rules exist to determine whether a particular asset owner is too small or too large to effectively access an asset class. Greater governance resources more commonly found among owners of larger asset pools create the capacity to pursue the more complex investment opportunities, but the asset owner may still need to find creative ways to implement the desired allocation. Each asset owner has a unique set of knowledge and constraints that will influence the opportunity set.

Smaller asset owners (typically institutions with less than US$500 million in assets and private wealth investors with less than US$25 million in assets) also find that their opportunity set may be constrained by the size of their investment portfolio. This is primarily a function of the more limited governance infrastructure typical of smaller asset owners: They may be too small to adequately diversify across the range of asset classes and investment managers or may have staffing constraints (insufficient asset size to justify a dedicated internal staff). Complex strategies may be beyond the reach of asset owners that have chosen not to develop investment expertise internally or where the oversight committee lacks individuals with sufficient investment understanding. In some asset classes and strategies, commingled investment vehicles can be used to achieve the needed diversification, provided the governing documents do not prohibit their use.

Access to other asset classes and strategies—private equity, private real estate, hedge funds, and infrastructure—may still be constrained for smaller asset owners. The commingled vehicles through which these strategies are offered typically require high minimum investments. For successful private equity and hedge fund managers, in particular, minimum investments can be in the tens of millions of (US) dollars, even for funds of funds.

Regulatory restrictions can also impose a size constraint. In the United Kingdom, for example, an asset owner in a private investment vehicle must qualify as an elective professional client, meaning they must meet two of the following three conditions:

1. The client has carried out transactions, in significant size, on the relevant market at an average frequency of 10 per quarter over the previous four quarters.

2. The size of the client's financial instrument portfolio exceeds €500,000.

3. The client works or has worked in the financial sector for at least one year in a professional position, which requires knowledge of the transactions or services envisaged.

In the United States, investors must be either accredited or qualified purchasers to invest in many private equity and hedge fund vehicles. To be a qualified purchaser, a natural person must have at least US$5 million in investments, a company must have at least US$25 million in investable assets, and an investment manager must have at least US$25 million under management. In Hong Kong SAR, the Securities and Futures Commission requires that an investor must meet the qualifications of a "Professional Investor" to invest in certain categories of assets. A Professional Investor is generally defined as a trust with total assets of not less than HK$40 million, an individual with a portfolio not less than HK$8 million, or a corporation or partnership with a portfolio not less than HK$8 million or total assets of not less than HK$40 million. The size constraints related to these asset classes suggest that smaller asset owners have real challenges achieving an effective private equity or hedge fund allocation.

Asset size as a constraint is often a more acute issue for individual investors than institutional asset owners. Wealthy families may pool assets through such vehicles as family limited partnerships, investment companies, fund of funds, or other forms of commingled vehicles to hold their assets. These pooled vehicles can then access investment vehicles, asset classes, and strategies that individual family members may not have portfolios large enough to access on their own.

WHERE ASSET SIZE CONSTRAINS INVESTMENT OPPORTUNITY

As of early 2021, the 10 largest sovereign wealth funds globally each exceed US$350 billion in assets. For a fund of this size, a 5% allocation to hedge funds (the average sovereign wealth fund allocation) would imply US$17.5 *billion* to be deployed. The global hedge fund industry manages approximately US$4.3 trillion in total as of the second quarter of 2021. With about 10,000 hedge funds globally, the average asset size of a hedge fund thus would be US$430 million. At the same time, approximately 60% of the funds manage less than US$100 million, and the remaining 40% of the funds have an average size of near US$1 billion. If we assume that the asset owner would want to be no more than 20% of a firm's AUM, we can infer that the average investment might be approximately US$86 million considering the full hedge fund universe or about US$200 million if we limit the choice to larger sized hedge funds. With US$17.5 billion to deploy, the fund would need to invest with nearly 90 (bigger size hedge funds universe) to 200 (total universe) funds to achieve a 5% allocation to hedge funds.

Sources: Sovereign Wealth Fund Institute, BarclayHedge, and Preqin.

EXAMPLE 1

Asset Size Constraints in Asset Allocation

Describe asset size constraints that Aromdee might encounter in implementing this asset allocation. Discuss possible means to address them.

Given the asset size of the fund, formulate a set of questions regarding the feasibility of this recommendation that you would like staff to address at the next Investment Committee meeting.

The new president of the University has stated that he feels the current policy is overly restrictive, and he would like to see a more diversified program that takes advantage of the types of investment strategies used by large endowment programs. Choosing from among the following asset classes, propose a set of asset classes to be considered in the revised asset allocation. Justify your response.

- Cash equivalents and money market funds
- Large-cap developed market equity
- Small-cap developed market equity
- Emerging market equity
- Developed market sovereign bonds
- Investment-grade bonds

- Non-investment-grade bonds
- Private real estate equity
- Hedge funds
- Private debt
- Private equity

1. Akkarat Aromdee is the recently retired President of Alpha Beverage, a producer and distributor of energy drinks throughout Southeast Asia. Upon retiring, the company provided a lump sum retirement payment of THB880,000,000 (equivalent to €20 million), which was rolled over to a tax-deferred individual retirement savings plan. Aside from these assets, Aromdee owns company stock worth about THB70,000,000. The stock is infrequently traded. He has consulted with an investment adviser, and they are reviewing the following asset allocation proposal:

Global equities	40%
Global high-yield bonds	15%
Domestic intermediate bonds	30%
Hedge funds	10%
Private equity	5%

Solution:

With a THB88 million (€2 million) allocation to hedge funds and a THB44 million (€1 million) allocation to private equity funds, Aromdee may encounter restrictions on his eligibility to invest in the private investment vehicles typically used for hedge fund and private equity investment. To the extent he is eligible to invest in hedge funds and/or private equity funds, a fund-of-funds or similar commingled arrangement would be essential to achieving an appropriate level of diversification. Additionally, it is essential that he and his adviser develop the necessary level of expertise to invest in these alternative assets. To achieve a prudent level of diversification, the allocation to global high-yield bonds would most likely need to be accomplished via a commingled investment vehicle.

2. The CAF$40 billion Government Petroleum Fund of Caflandia is overseen by a nine-member Investment Committee. The chief investment officer has a staff with sector heads in global equities, global bonds, real estate, hedge funds, and derivatives. The majority of assets are managed by outside investment managers. The Investment Committee, of which you are a member, approves the asset allocation policy and makes manager selection decisions. Staff has recommended an increase in the private equity allocation from its current 0% to 15%, to be implemented over the next 12 to 36 months. The head of global equities will oversee the implementation of the private equity allocation.

Solution:

Questions regarding the feasibility of the recommendation include the following:

- How many private equity funds do you expect to invest in to achieve the 15% allocation to private equity?
- What is the anticipated average allocation to each fund?
- Are there a sufficient number of high-quality private equity funds willing to accept an allocation of that size?
- What expertise exists at the staff or board level to conduct due diligence on private equity investment funds?
- What resources does the staff have to oversee the increased allocation to private equity?

3. The Courneuve University Endowment has US$250 million in assets. The current allocation is 65% global large-capitalization stocks and 35% high-quality bonds, with a duration target of 5.0 years. The University has adopted a 5% spending policy. University enrollment is stable and expected to remain so. A capital spending initiative of US$100 million for new science buildings in the next three to seven years is being discussed, but it has not yet been approved. The University has no dedicated investment staff and makes limited use of external resources. Investment recommendations are formulated by the University's treasurer and approved by the Investment Committee, composed entirely of external board members.

Solution:

Asset size and limited governance resources are significant constraints on the investment opportunity set available to the Endowment. The asset allocation should emphasize large and liquid investments, such as cash equivalents, developed and emerging market equity, and sovereign and investment-grade bonds. Some small portion of assets, however, could be allocated to commingled investments in real estate, private equity, or hedge funds. Given the University's limited staff resources, it is necessary to ensure that the board members have the level of expertise necessary to select and monitor these more complex asset classes. The Endowment might also consider engaging an outside expert to advise on investment activities in these asset classes.

3   LIQUIDITY

☐   discuss asset size, liquidity needs, time horizon, and regulatory or
       other considerations as constraints on asset allocation

Two dimensions of liquidity must be considered when developing an asset appropriate allocation solution: the liquidity needs of the asset owner and the liquidity characteristics of the asset classes in the opportunity set. Integrating the two dimensions is an essential element of successful investment planning.

The need for liquidity in an investment portfolio will vary greatly by asset owner and by the goals the assets are set aside to achieve. For example, a bank will typically have a very large portfolio supporting its day-to-day operations. That portfolio is likely to experience very high turnover and a very high need for liquidity; therefore, the investment portfolio must hold high-quality, very short-term, and highly liquid assets.

The same bank may have another designated investment pool one level removed from operating assets. Although the liquidity requirements for this portfolio may be lower, the investments most likely feature a high degree of liquidity—a substantial allocation to investment-grade bonds, perhaps with a slight extension of maturity. For its longer-term investment portfolio, the bank may choose to allocate some portion of its portfolio to less liquid investments. The opportunity set for each portfolio will be constrained by applicable banking laws and regulations.

Long-term investors, such as sovereign wealth funds and endowment funds, can generally exploit illiquidity premiums available in such asset classes as private equity, real estate, and infrastructure investments. However, pension plans may be limited in the amount of illiquidity they can absorb. For example, a frozen pension plan may anticipate the possibility of eliminating its pension obligation completely by purchasing a group annuity and relinquishing the responsibility for making pension payments to an insurance company. If there is a significant probability that the company will take this step in the near term, liquidity of plan assets will become a primary concern; and if there is a substantial allocation to illiquid assets, the plan sponsor may be unable to execute the desired annuity purchase transaction.

Liquidity needs must also consider the particular circumstances and financial strength of the asset owner and what resources they may have beyond those held in the investment portfolio. The following examples illustrate this point:

- A university must consider its prospects for future enrollments and the extent to which it relies on tuition to meet operating needs. If the university experiences a significant drop in enrollment, perhaps because of a poor economic environment, or takes on a new capital improvement project, the asset allocation policy for the endowment should reflect the increased probability of higher outflows to support university operations.

- A foundation whose mission supports medical research in a field in which a breakthrough appears imminent may desire a higher level of liquidity to fund critical projects than would a foundation that supports ongoing community efforts.

- An insurance company whose business is predominantly life or auto insurance, where losses are actuarially predictable, can absorb more liquidity risk than a property/casualty reinsurer whose losses are subject to unpredictable events, such as natural disasters.

- A family with several children nearing college-age will have higher liquidity needs than a couple of the same age and circumstances with no children.

When assessing the appropriateness of any given asset class for a given asset owner, it is wise to evaluate potential liquidity needs in the context of an extreme market stress event. The market losses of the 2008–2009 global financial crisis were extreme. Simultaneously, other forces exacerbated investors' distress: Many university endowments were called upon to provide an increased level of operating support; insurers dipped into reserves to offset operating losses; community foundations found their beneficiaries in even greater need of financial support; and some individual investors experienced setbacks that caused them to move, if only temporarily, from being net contributors to net spenders of financial wealth. A successful asset allocation effort will stress the proposed allocation; it will anticipate, where possible, the likely behavior of other facets of the saving/spending equation during times of stress.

It is also important to consider the intersection of asset class and investor liquidity in the context of the asset owner's governance capacity. Although the mission of the organization or trust may allow for a certain level of illiquidity, if those responsible for the oversight of the investment program do not have the mental fortitude or discipline to maintain course through the crisis, illiquid and less liquid investments are unlikely to produce the rewards typically expected of these exposures. Although rates of return may be mean-reverting, wealth is not. Losses resulting from panic selling during times of stress become permanent losses; there are fewer assets left to earn returns in a post-crash recovery.

THE CASE OF VANISHING LIQUIDITY

In the global financial crisis of 2008–2009, many investors learned painful truths about liquidity. When most needed—whether to rebalance or to meet spending obligations—it can evaporate. As investors liquidated their most liquid assets to meet financial obligations (or to raise cash in fear of further market declines), the remaining less liquid assets in their portfolios became an ever-larger percentage of the portfolio. Many investors were forced to sell private partnership interests on the secondary market at steeply discounted prices. Others defaulted on outstanding private fund capital commitments by refusing to honor future obligations.

Similarly, illiquidity became a substantial problem during the Asian currency crisis of 1997–1998 and again with the Russian debt default and Long-Term Capital Management (LTCM) crisis of 1998. In the following paragraphs, we describe several "liquidity crises" that are often used in stress testing asset allocation choices.

The Asian Currency Crisis of 1997

In the spring of 1997, Thailand spent billions to defend the Thai baht against speculative attacks, finally capitulating and devaluing the baht in July 1997. This triggered a series of moves throughout the region to defend currencies against speculators. Ultimately, these efforts were unsuccessful and many countries abandoned the effort and allowed their currencies to float freely. The Philippines, Indonesia, and South Korea abandoned their pegs against the US dollar. On 27 October 1997, rattled by the currency crisis, Asian and European markets declined sharply in advance of the opening of the US markets. The S&P 500 declined nearly 7%, and trading on US stock markets was suspended.

The Russian Debt Default/LTCM Crisis of August 1998

On 17 August 1998, the Russian government defaulted on its short-term debt. This unprecedented default of a sovereign debtor roiled the global bond markets. A global flight-to-quality ensued, which caused credit spreads to widen and liquidity to evaporate. Highly levered investors experienced significant losses. Long-Term

Capital Management, with reported notional exposure of over US$125 billion (a 25-to-1 leverage ratio), exacerbated these price declines as they faced their own liquidity crisis and were forced to liquidate large relative value, distressed, convertible arbitrage, merger arbitrage, and equity positions. Ultimately, the magnitude of the liquidity squeeze for LTCM and the risk of potential disruption to global markets caused the New York branch of the Federal Reserve Bank to orchestrate a disciplined, structured bailout of the LTCM fund.

Financial markets are increasingly linked across borders and asset classes; as a result, changes in liquidity conditions in one country can directly affect liquidity conditions elsewhere. These linkages do improve access to financing and capital markets, but they also show that a liquidity problem in one part of the world can ripple across the globe—increasing volatility, creating higher execution costs for investors, and possibly leading to a reduction in credit availability and a decline in economic activity.

QUANTITATIVE EASING

While the lack of liquidity clearly hurts investors, can too much liquidity in the market place (overliquidity, excess liquidity) also cause problems? Overliquidity in the market, or too much cash, to put it simply, is certainly not an issue for frictionless trade executions. On the other hand, too much liquidity in the market may lead to too high asset valuations as investors are trying to invest their excess liquidity, eroding the expected future returns of various asset classes. Following the Great Financial Crisis, as well as the outbreak of the COVID-19 pandemic, central banks globally pumped extra cash into the economy through the asset purchase/quantitative easing (QE) programs to keep interest rates low and stimulate consumption. The impact of QE (measured by the size of the US Federal Reserve's balance sheet) on equity (S&P 500 Index) valuations and real interest rates (10-year Treasury real yield) are illustrated in Exhibit 2. With the increase of the Federal Reserve's balance sheet in early 2020, the overliquidity fueled a strong rebound of the equity market.

Exhibit 2: Federal Reserve Balance Sheet (QE) and Asset Valuations

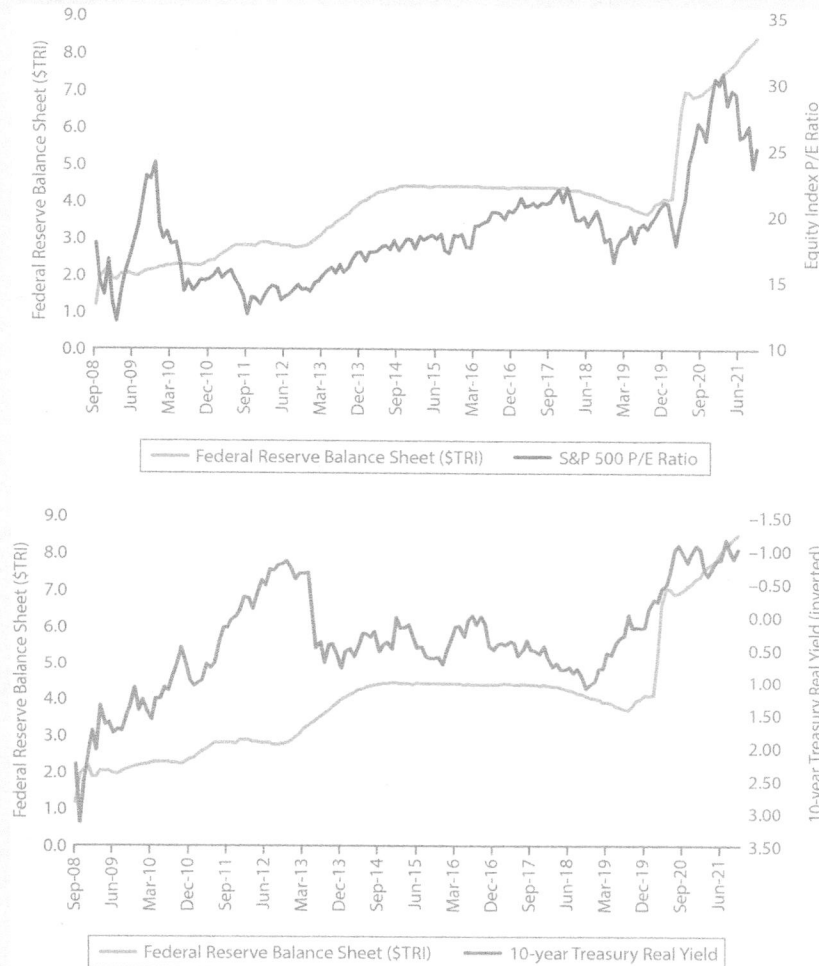

Federal Reserve Balance Sheet ($TRI) — S&P 500 P/E Ratio

Federal Reserve Balance Sheet ($TRI) — 10-year Treasury Real Yield

Similarly, the overliquidity pushed interest rates into the negative territory. Taken together, the impact of overliquidity created an environment that fueled the growth of the equity markets and consumption.

Source: Bloomberg.

EXAMPLE 2

Liquidity Constraints in Asset Allocation

1. The Frentel Furniture Pension Fund has £200 million frozen in a defined benefit pension plan that is 85% funded. The plan has a provision that allows employees to elect a lump sum distribution of their pension benefit at retirement. The company is strong financially and is committed to fully funding the pension obligations over time. However, they also want to minimize cash contributions to the plan. Few governance resources are allocated to

the pension fund, and there is no dedicated staff for pension investment activities. The current asset allocation is as shown:

Global equities	20%
Private equity	10%
Real estate	10%
Infrastructure	5%
Hedge funds	15%
Bonds	40%

The company expects to reduce their employee headcount sometime in the next three to five years, and they are tentatively planning incentives to encourage employees to retire early.

Discuss the appropriateness of the current asset allocation strategy for the pension fund, including benefits and concerns.

Solution:

In addition to the size constraints a £200 million (≈ US$250 million) plan faces when attempting to invest in real estate, private equity, infrastructure, and hedge funds, the likelihood of early retirement incentives and lump-sum distribution requests in the next three to five years indicates a need for increased sensitivity to liquidity concerns. Investments in private equity, infrastructure, and real estate may be unsuitable for the plan given their less liquid nature. Although hedge fund investments would likely be accessible via a commingled vehicle, the liquidity of the commingled vehicle should be evaluated to determine if it is consistent with the liquidity needs of the plan.

---

4   TIME HORIZON

	discuss asset size, liquidity needs, time horizon, and regulatory or other considerations as constraints on asset allocation

An asset owner's time horizon is a critical constraint that must be considered in any asset allocation exercise. A liability to be paid at a given point in the future or a goal to be funded by a specified date each define the asset owner's horizon, thus becoming a basic input to the asset allocation solution. The changing composition of the asset owner's assets and liabilities must also be considered. As time progresses, the character of both *assets* (human capital) and *liabilities* changes.

Changing Human Capital

When asset allocation considers such extended portfolio assets as human capital, the optimal allocation of financial capital can change through time (Bodie, Merton, and Samuelson 1992). Assuming no change in the investor's utility function, as human capital—with its predominately bond-like risk—declines over time, the asset allocation for financial capital would reflect an increasing allocation to bonds. This is a prime example of how time horizon can influence asset allocation.

Changing Character of Liabilities

The changing character of liabilities through time will also affect the asset allocation aligned to fund those liabilities.

As an example, the term structure of liabilities changes as they approach maturity. A pension benefit program is a simple way to illustrate this point. When the employee base is young and retirements are far into the future, the liability can be hedged with long-term bonds. As the employee base ages and prospective retirements are not so far into the future, the liability is more comparable to intermediate- or even short-term bonds. When retirements are imminent, the structure of the liabilities can be characterized as cash-like, and an optimal asset allocation would also have cash-like characteristics.

Similarly, the overall profile of an individual investor's liabilities changes with the progression of time, particularly for investors with finite investment horizons. Nearer-term goals and liabilities move from partially funded to fully funded, while other, longer-term goals and liabilities move progressively closer to funding. As the relative weights of the goals to be funded shift and the time horizon associated with certain goals shortens, the aggregate asset allocation must be adapted if it is to remain aligned with the individual's goals.

Time horizon is also likely to affect the manner in which an investor prioritizes certain goals and liabilities. This will influence the desired risk profile of the assets aligned to fund them. Consider a 75-year-old retired investor with two goals:

1. Fund consumption needs through age 95
2. Fund consumption needs from age 95 through age 105

He most likely assigns a much higher priority to funding goal 1, given the lower probability that he will live beyond age 95.[3] Let's also assume that he has sufficient assets to fund goal 1 and to partially fund goal 2. The higher priority assigned to goal 1 indicates he is less willing to take risk, and this sub-portfolio will be invested more conservatively. Now consider goal 2: Given the low probability of living past 95 and the fact that he does not currently have sufficient assets to fund that goal, the sub-portfolio assigned to goal 2 is likely to have a more growth-oriented asset allocation. The priority of a given goal can change as the investor's time horizon shortens—or lengthens.

Consider the hypothetical investors Ivy and Charles Lee from the reading "Introduction to Asset Allocation." Ivy is a 54-year-old life science entrepreneur. Charles is a 55-year-old orthopedic surgeon. They have two unmarried children aged 25 (Deborah) and 18 (David). Deborah has a daughter with physical limitations. Four goals have been identified for the Lees:

1. Lifestyle/future consumption needs
2. College education for son David, 18 years old
3. Charitable gift to a local art museum in 5 years
4. Special needs trust for their granddaughter, to be funded at the death of Charles

---

3 A 75-year-old US American male has a life expectancy of 11.1 years, per the Social Security Administration's 2014 "Actuarial Life Tables," https://www.ssa.gov/oact/STATS/table4c6_2014.html (Accessed 22 Nov 2018).

The lifestyle/consumption goal is split into three components: required minimum consumption requirements (a worst-case scenario of reduced lifestyle), baseline consumption needs (maintaining current standard of living), and aspirational consumption needs (an improved standard of living). At age 54, the risk preferences assigned to these goals might look something like the following:

Lifestyle Goals	Risk Preference	Asset Allocation	Sub-Portfolio as % of Total*
Required minimum	Conservative	100% bonds and cash	65%
Baseline	Moderate	60% equities/40% bonds	10%
Aspirational	Aggressive	100% equities	4%
College education	Conservative	100% bonds and cash	1%
Charitable gift (aspirational)	Aggressive	100% equities	5%
Special needs trust	Moderate	60% equities/40% bonds	15%
Aggregate portfolio		≈ 25% equities/75% bonds and cash	100%

* *The present value of each goal as a proportion of the total portfolio.*

The asset allocation for the total portfolio aggregates the asset allocations for each of the goal-aligned sub-portfolios, weighted by the present value of each goal. For the Lees, this is an overall asset allocation of about 25% equities and 75% bonds and cash. (Each goal is discounted to its present value by expected return of its respective goal-aligned sub-portfolio.)

Move forward 20 years. The Lees are now in their mid-70s, and their life expectancy is about 12 years. Their son has completed his college education and is successfully established in his own career. The charitable gift has been made. These two goals have been realized. The assets needed to fund the baseline consumption goal are significantly reduced because fewer future consumption years need to be funded. The special needs trust for their granddaughter remains a high priority. Although the Lee's risk preferences for these goals have not changed, the overall asset allocation *will* change because the total portfolio is an aggregated mix of the remaining goal-aligned sub-portfolios, weighted by their current present values:

Lifestyle Goals	Risk Preference	Asset Allocation	Sub-Portfolio as % of Total*
Required minimum	Conservative	100% bonds and cash	54%
Baseline	Moderate	60% equities/40% bonds	9%
Aspirational	Aggressive	100% equities	3%
Special needs trust	Moderate	60% equities/40% bonds	34%
Aggregate portfolio		≈ 30% equities/70% bonds and cash	100%

* *The present value of each goal as a proportion of the total portfolio. The implied assumption is that current assets are sufficient to fund all goals, provided the Lees adopt an aggressive asset allocation strategy for the aspirational and charitable gifting goals. If the value of current assets exceeds the present value of all goals, the Lees would have greater flexibility to adopt a lower risk preference for some or all goals.*

Although for ease of illustration our example assumed the Lee's risk preferences remained the same, this is not likely to be the case in the real world. Required minimum and baseline consumption goals would remain very important; there is less flexibility to withstand losses caused by either reduced earnings potential or lower likelihood of the market regaining lost ground within the shorter horizon. The aspirational lifestyle goal is likely to be a much lower priority, and it may have been eliminated altogether. The special needs trust may have a higher (or lower) priority as the needs of the granddaughter and the ability of her parents to provide for her needs after their death become more evident. The preferred asset allocation for each of these goals will shift over the course of the investor's lifetime.

As an investor's time horizon shifts, both human capital and financial market considerations, along with changes in the investor's priorities, will most likely lead to different asset allocation decisions.

EXAMPLE 3

Time Horizon Constraints in Asset Allocation

1. Akkarat Aromdee, the recently retired President of Alpha Beverage, is 67 years old with a remaining life expectancy of 15 years. Upon his retirement two years ago, he established a charitable foundation and funded it with THB600 million (≈ US$17.3 million). The remaining financial assets, THB350 million (≈ US$10 million), were transferred to a trust that will allow him to draw a lifetime income. The assets are invested 100% in fixed-income securities, consistent with Aromdee's desire for a high level of certainty in meeting his goals. He is a widower with no children. His consumption needs are estimated at THB20 million annually. Assets remaining in the trust at his death will pass to the charities named in the trust.

   While vacationing in Ko Samui, Aromdee met and later married a 45-year-old woman with two teenage children. She has limited financial assets of her own. Upon returning from his honeymoon, Aromdee meets with his investment adviser. He intends to pay the college expenses of his new stepchildren—THB2 million annually for eight years, beginning five years from now. He would also like to ensure that his portfolio can provide a modest lifetime income for his wife after his death.

   Discuss how these changed circumstances are likely to influence Aromdee's asset allocation.

Solution:

At the time Aromdee established the trust, the investment horizon was 15 years and his annual consumption expenditures could easily be funded from the trust. His desire to support his new family introduces two new horizons to be considered: In five years, the trust will begin making annual payments of THB2 million to fund college expenses, and the trust will continue to make distributions to his wife after his death, though at a reduced rate. When the trust needed to support only his consumption requirements, a conservative asset allocation was appropriate. However, the payment of college expenses will reduce his margin of safety and the lengthening of the investment horizon suggests that he should consider adding equity-oriented investments to the asset mix to provide for growth in assets over time.

TIME DIVERSIFICATION OF RISK

In practice, investors often align lower risk/lower return assets with short-term goals and liabilities and higher risk/higher return assets with long-term goals and liabilities. It is generally believed that longer-horizon goals can tolerate the higher volatility associated with higher risk/higher return assets as below average and above average returns even out over time. This is the notion of time diversification.

Mean–variance optimization, typically conducted using a multi-year time horizon, assumes that asset returns follow a random walk; returns in Year X are independent of returns in Year X − 1. Under this baseline assumption, there *is* no reduction in risk with longer time horizons.[4] Although the *probability* of reduced wealth or of a shortfall in funding a goal or liability (based on the mean of the distribution of possible outcomes) may be lower at longer time horizons, the dispersion of possible outcomes widens as the investment horizon expands. Thus, the *magnitude* of potential loss or shortfall can be greater.

Consider the choice of investing US$100,000 in a Global Equity Index ETF with a 7.0% expected return and 15% standard deviation versus a risk-free asset with a 1.5% annual return. The table below compares the return of the risk-free asset over various time horizons, with the range of predicted returns for the S&P 500 Index fund at a 95% confidence interval. Although the *mean* return of the distribution of S&P 500 returns exceeds that of the risk-free asset in each time period (thus the notion that the volatility of higher risk, higher return assets evens out over time), the lower boundary of expected S&P 500 returns is less than the initial investment for all periods less than 10 years! The lower boundary of the S&P 500 outcomes does not exceed the ending wealth of the risk-free investment until the investment horizon is extended to 30 years. If the confidence interval is expanded to 99%, the lower boundary of S&P 500 outcomes falls below the initial investment up until and through 20 years!

	Ending Wealth (US$)		
	S&P 500 95% Confidence Interval		
	Lower Boundary	Upper Boundary	Risk-Free Asset
1 year	77,601	136,399	101,500
5 years	72,815	250,369	107,728
10 years	79,265	452,566	116,054
15 years	91,494	771,352	125,023
20 years	108,876	1,275,182	134,686
30 years	162,543	3,305,454	156,308

Although one-year returns are largely independent, there is some evidence that risky asset returns can display mean-reverting tendencies over intermediate to longer time horizons. An assumption of mean-reverting risky asset returns would support the conventional arguments for funding long-term goals and liabilities with higher risk/higher return assets, and it would also support a reduction in the allocation to these riskier assets as the time horizon shortens.

---

4 See Samuelson (1963) and Samuelson (1969).

REGULATORY AND OTHER EXTERNAL CONSTRAINTS

5

☐ | discuss asset size, liquidity needs, time horizon, and regulatory or other considerations as constraints on asset allocation

Just as an integrated asset/liability approach to asset allocation is likely to result in a different allocation decision than what might have been selected in an asset-only context, external considerations may also influence the asset allocation decision. Local laws and regulations can have a material effect on an investor's asset allocation decisions.

Pension funds, insurance companies, sovereign wealth funds, and endowments and foundations are each subject to externally imposed constraints that are likely to tilt their asset allocation decision away from what may have been selected in a pure asset/liability context.

Insurance Companies

Unlike pension fund or endowment assets—which are legally distinct from the assets of the sponsoring entity—insurance companies' investment activities are an integral part of their day-to-day operations. Although skilled underwriting may be the focus of the firm as the key to profitability, investment returns are often a material contributor to profits or losses. Regulatory requirements and accounting treatment vary from country to country, but insurers are most often highly focused on matching assets to the projected, probabilistic cash flows of the risks they are underwriting. Fixed-income assets, therefore, are typically the largest component of an insurance company's asset base, and investing with skill in this asset class is a key to competitive pricing and success. In some regions, the relevant accounting treatment may be a book value approach, rendering variability in the market pricing of assets to be a secondary consideration as long as an asset does not have to have its book value written down as "other than temporarily impaired" ("OTTI"). Risk considerations for an insurance company include the need for capital to pay policyholder benefits and other factors that directly influence the company's financial strength ratings. Some of the key considerations are risk-based capital measures, yield, liquidity, the potential for forced liquidation of assets to fund negative claims development, and credit ratings.

Additionally, allocations to certain asset classes are often constrained by a regulator. For example, the maximum limit on equity exposure is often 10%, but it ranges as high as 30% in Switzerland and 50% in Mexico. Israel and Korea impose a limit of 15% on real estate investments.[5] Restrictions on non-publicly traded securities might also limit the allocation to such assets as private equity, for example, and there may also be limits on the allocation to high-yield bonds. Insurance regulators generally set a minimum capital level for each insurer based on that insurer's mix of assets, liabilities, and risk. Many countries are moving to Solvency II regulatory standards designed to harmonize risk-based capital requirements for insurance companies across countries.[6] Asset classes are often treated differently for purposes of determining whether an insurer meets risk-based capital requirements.

---

5 https://www.oecd.org/finance/private-pensions/Regulation-of-Insurance-Company-and-Pension-Fund -Investment.pdf (September 2015)--accessed 23 November 2018).
6 Solvency II is an EU legislative program implemented in all 28 member states, including the United Kingdom, in January 2016. It introduces a new, harmonized EU-wide insurance regulatory regime.

Pension Funds

Pension fund asset allocation decisions may be constrained by regulation and influenced by tax rules.[7] Some countries regulate maximum or minimum percentages in certain asset classes. For example, Japanese pension funds must hold a certain minimum percentage of assets in Japanese bonds in order to maintain their tax-exempt status. Canada allows a maximum of 10% of market value invested in any one entity or related entities; Switzerland generally limits real estate investments to 30%; Estonia allows a maximum of 75% of assets invested in public equity with no limit on foreign investments; and Brazil allows a maximum of 70% in public equity with a maximum of 10% in foreign public equity.[8] Ukraine limits bond investments to no more than 40%.

Pension funds are also subject to a wide array of funding, accounting, reporting, and tax constraints that may influence the asset allocation decision. (For example, US public pension funding and public and corporate accounting rules favor equity investments—higher equity allocations support a higher discount rate—and thus lower pension cost. Loss recognition is deferred until later through the smoothing mechanism.) The plan sponsor's appetite for risk is defined in part by these constraints, and the choice among asset allocation alternatives is often influenced by funding and financial statement considerations, such as the anticipated contributions, the volatility of anticipated contributions, or the forecasted pension expense or income under a given asset allocation scenario. The specific constraints vary by jurisdiction, and companies with plans in multiple jurisdictions must satisfy the rules and regulations of each jurisdiction while making sound financial decisions for the organization as a whole.

Exhibit 3 illustrates how funding considerations may affect the asset allocation decision. In this chart, risk is defined as the probability of contributions exceeding some threshold amount. In this case, the risk threshold is specified as the 95th percentile of the present value of contributions—that point on the distribution of possible contributions (using Monte Carlo simulation) where the plan sponsor can be 95% certain that contributions will not exceed that amount.

Assume that an allocation of 70% equities/30% aggregate bonds represents the most efficient portfolio for the plan sponsor's desired level of risk in an asset optimization framework. In Exhibit 3, we can see that the 70% equity/30% aggregate bond mix (Portfolio A) is associated with a present value (PV) of expected contributions of approximately US$51 million (y-axis) and a 95% confidence level that contributions will not exceed approximately US$275 million (x-axis)—Portfolio A in Exhibit 3. If the plan sponsor were to maintain the 70/30 asset mix but shift to longer-duration bonds (from aggregate to long bonds) to better match the duration of liabilities— Portfolio D_1 on Exhibit 3—the PV of expected contributions declines by approximately US$5 million and the 95% confidence threshold improves to approximately US$265 million. In fact, Portfolio D_1 results in nearly the lowest PV of contributions for this plan sponsor. (Note that the vertical axis is ordered from highest contributions at the bottom and lowest contributions at the top, consistent with the notion of lower contributions as a better outcome.)

---

7 Information in this section is based on the OECD "Annual Survey of Investment Regulation of Pension Funds" (2017).
8 Foreign investment is restricted to MERCOSUR countries for equities (other asset classes are more flexible).

Exhibit 3: Efficient Frontiers Where Risk Is Defined as the Risk of Large Contributions

Present Value of Expected Contributions ($ millions)

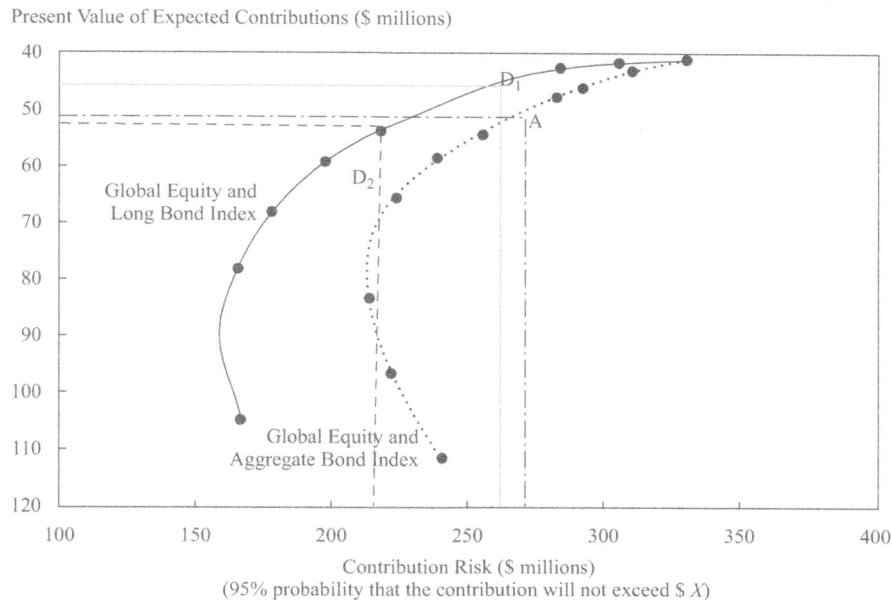

Contribution Risk ($ millions)
(95% probability that the contribution will not exceed $ X)

Now consider Portfolio D_2, 60% equities/40% long bonds. Reducing the equity exposure from 70% to 60% lowers the contribution risk significantly, with only marginally higher expected PV of contributions than Portfolio A. (A lower equity allocation implies a lower expected rate of return, which increases the PV of contributions. However, the lower equity allocation also reduces the probability that less-than-expected returns will lead to unexpectedly large contributions.) The sponsor that wishes to reduce contribution risk substantially is likely to give serious consideration to moving from Portfolio A to Portfolio D_2.

By iterating through various efficient frontiers using different definitions of risk, the sponsor is able to better understand the risk and reward trade-offs of alternative asset allocation choices. The regulatory or tax constraints on minimum and maximum contributions, or on minimum required funded levels, or other values that are important to the plan sponsor, can be factored into the simulations so the sponsor can better understand how these constraints might affect the risk and reward trade-offs.

Endowments and Foundations

Endowments and foundations are often established with the expectation that they will exist in perpetuity and thus can invest with a long investment horizon. In addition, the sponsoring entity often has more flexibility over payments from the fund than does a pension plan sponsor or insurance company. As a result, endowments and foundations generally can adopt a higher-risk asset allocation than other institutions. However, two categories of externally imposed constraints may influence the asset allocation decisions of an endowment or foundation: tax incentives and credit-worthiness considerations.

- *Tax incentives.* Although some endowments and foundations—US public foundations and some Austrian and Asian foundations, for example—are not required to make minimum distributions, many countries provide tax benefits tied to certain minimum spending requirements. For example, a private foundation may be subject to a requirement that it make charitable expenditures equal to at least 5% of the market value of its assets each year or risk losing its tax-favored status. These spending requirements may be relaxed if certain types of socially responsible investments are made, which can, in turn, create a bias toward socially responsible investments for some endowments and foundations, irrespective of their merits in an asset allocation context.

- *Credit considerations.* Although endowments and foundations typically have a very long investment horizon, sometimes external factors may restrict the level of risk-taking in the portfolio. For example, endowment or foundation assets are often used to support the balance sheet and borrowing capabilities of the university or the foundation organization. Lenders often require that the borrower maintain certain minimum balance sheet ratios. Therefore, the asset allocation adopted by the organization will consider the risks of breaking these bond covenants or otherwise negatively affecting the borrowing capabilities of the organization.

As an example, although a hospital foundation fund would normally have a long investment horizon and the ability to invest in less liquid asset classes, it might limit the allocation to illiquid assets in order to support certain liquidity and balance sheet metrics specified by its lender(s).

Sovereign Wealth Funds

Although every sovereign wealth fund (SWF) is unique with respect to its mission and objectives, some broad generalizations can be made with respect to the external constraints that may affect a fund's asset allocation choices. In general, SWFs are government-owned pools of capital invested on behalf of the peoples of their states or countries, investing with a long-term orientation. They are not generally seeking to defease a set of liabilities or known obligations as is common with pension funds and, to a lesser extent, endowment funds.

The governing entities adopt regulations that constrain the opportunity set for asset allocation. For example, the Korean SWF KIC cannot invest in Korean won-denominated domestic assets;[9] and the Norwegian SWF NBIM is not permitted to invest in any alternative asset class other than real estate, which is limited to no more than 7% of assets.[10] Furthermore, as publicly owned entities, SWFs are typically subject to broad public scrutiny and tend to adopt a lower-risk asset allocation than might otherwise be considered appropriate given their long-term investment horizon in order to avoid reputation risk.

In addition to the broad constraints of asset size, liquidity, time horizon, and regulations, there may be cultural or religious factors that also constrain the asset allocation choices. Environmental, social, and governance (ESG) considerations are becoming increasingly important to institutional and individual investors alike. Sharia law, for example, prohibits investment in any business that has links to pork, alcohol, tobacco, pornography, prostitution, gambling, or weaponry, and it constrains investments in most businesses that operate on interest payments (like major Western banks and mortgage providers) and in businesses that transfer risk (such as major Western insurers).[11]

---

9 https://mpra.ub.uni-muenchen.de/44028/1/MPRA_paper_44028.pdf (accessed 23 November 2018) Note: in principle, KIC must invest only in assets denominated in foreign currencies. If KIC manages KRW-denominated assets temporarily for an unavoidable reason, it must be either in the form of bank deposits or passively held public debt.
10 https://www.nbim.no/en/investments/investment-strategy/ (accessed 23 November 2018).
11 Islamic Investment Network (www.islamicinvestmentnetwork.com/sharialaw.php).

ESG goals are not typically modeled during the asset allocation decision process. Instead, these goals may be achieved through the implementation of the asset allocation, or the asset owner may choose to set aside a targeted portion of the assets for these missions. The asset allocation process would treat this "set-aside" in much the same way that a concentrated stock position might be handled: The risk, return, and correlation characteristics of this holding are specified; the "set aside" asset becomes an asset class in the investor's opportunity set; and the asset allocation constraints will designate a certain minimum investment in this asset class.

EXAMPLE 4

External Constraints and Asset Allocation

1. An insurance company has traditionally invested its pension plan using the asset allocation strategy adopted for its insurance assets: The pension assets are 95% invested in high-quality intermediate duration bonds and 5% in global equities. The duration of pension liabilities is approximately 25 years. Until now, the company has always made contributions sufficient to maintain a fully funded status. Although the company has a strong capability to fund the plan adequately and a relatively high tolerance for variability in asset returns, as part of a refinement in corporate strategy, management is now seeking to reduce long-term expected future cash contributions. Management is willing to accept more risk in the asset return, but they would like to limit contribution risk and the risk to the plan's funded status. The Investment Committee is considering three asset allocation proposals for the pension plan:

   A. Maintain the current asset allocation with the same bond portfolio duration.

   B. Increase the equity allocation and lengthen the bond portfolio duration to increase the hedge of the duration risk in the liabilities.

   C. Maintain the current asset allocation of 95% bonds and 5% global equities, but increase the duration of bond investments.

   Discuss the merits of each proposal.

Solution:

Given the intermediate duration bond allocation, Proposal A fails to consider the mismatch between pension assets and liabilities and risks a reduction in the funded status and *increased* contributions if bond yields decline. (If yields decline across the curve, the shorter duration bond portfolio will fail to hedge the increase in liabilities.) To meet the objective of lower future contributions, the asset allocation must include a higher allocation to equities. Proposal B has this higher allocation, and the extension of duration in the bond portfolio in Proposal B reduces balance sheet and surplus risk relative to the pension liabilities. The net effect could be a reduction in short-term contribution risk; moreover, if the greater expected return on equities is realized, it should result in reduced contributions to the plan over the long term. Proposal C improves the hedging of the liabilities, and it may result in a modest improvement in the expected return on assets if the yield curve is upward-sloping. However, the expected return on Proposal C is likely lower than the expected return of Proposal B and is therefore unlikely to achieve the same magnitude of reduction in future cash contributions. Proposal C would be appropriate if the goal was focused on reducing surplus risk rather than reducing long-term contributions.

2. A multinational corporation headquartered in Mexico has acquired a former competitor in the United States. It will maintain both the US pension plan with US$250 million in assets and the Mexican pension plan with MXN$18,600 million in assets (≈ US$1 billion). Both plans are 95% funded and have similar liability profiles. The Mexican pension trust has an asset allocation policy of 30% equities (10% invested in the Mexican equity market and 20% in equity markets outside Mexico), 10% hedge funds, 10% private equity, and 50% bonds. The treasurer has proposed that the company adopt a consistent asset allocation policy across all of the company's pension plans worldwide.

Critique the treasurer's proposal.

Solution:

The treasurer's proposal fails to consider the relative asset size of the two pension plans as well as the likelihood that plans in different jurisdictions may be subject to different funding, regulatory, and financial reporting requirements. The US pension plan may be unable to effectively access certain alternative asset classes, such as private equity, infrastructure, and hedge funds. Although economies of scale may be realized if management of the pension assets is consolidated under one team, the legal and regulatory differences of the markets in which they operate mean that the asset allocation policy must be customized to each plan.

6   ASSET ALLOCATION FOR THE TAXABLE INVESTOR AND AFTER-TAX PORTFOLIO OPTIMIZATION

☐ | discuss tax considerations in asset allocation and rebalancing

Portfolio theory developed in a frictionless world. But in the real world, taxes on income and capital gains can erode the returns achieved by taxable investors. The asset owner who ignores taxes during the asset allocation process is overlooking an economic variable that can materially alter the outcome. Although tax adjustments can be made after the asset allocation has been determined, this is a suboptimal approach because the pre-tax and after-tax risk and return characteristics of each asset class can be materially different.

Some assets are less tax efficient than others because of the character of their returns—the contribution of interest, dividends, and realized or unrealized capital gains to the total return. Interest income is usually taxed in the tax year it is received, and it often faces the highest tax rates. Therefore, assets that generate returns largely comprised of interest income tend to be less tax efficient in many countries.[12] Jurisdictional rules can also affect how the returns of certain assets are taxed. In the United States, for example, the interest income from state and local government bonds is generally

---

12 See Deloitte's tax guides and country highlights: https://dits.deloitte.com/#TaxGuides.

exempt from federal income taxation. As a result, these bonds often constitute a large portion of a US high-net-worth investor's bond allocation. Preferred stocks, often used in lieu of bonds as an income-producing asset, are also eligible for more favorable tax treatment in many jurisdictions, where the income from preferred shares may be taxed at more favorable dividend tax rates.

The tax environment is complex. Different countries have different tax rules and rates, and these rules and rates can change frequently. However, looking across the major economies, there are some high-level commonalities in how investment returns are taxed. Interest income is taxed typically (but not always) at progressively higher income tax rates. Dividend income and capital gains are taxed typically (but not always) at lower tax rates than those applied to interest income and earned income (wages and salaries, for example). Capital losses can be used to offset capital gains (and sometimes income). Generally, interest income incurs the highest tax rate, with dividend income taxed at a lower rate in some countries, and long-term capital gains receive the most favorable tax treatment in many jurisdictions. Once we move beyond these general commonalities, however, the details of tax treatment among countries quickly diverge.

Entities and accounts can be subject to different tax rules. For example, retirement savings accounts may be tax deferred or tax exempt, with implications for the optimal asset allocation solution. These rules provide opportunities for strategic asset *location*—placing less tax-efficient assets in tax-advantaged accounts.

We will provide a general framework for considering taxes in asset allocation. We will not survey global tax regimes or incorporate all potential tax complexities into the asset allocation solution. When considering taxes in asset allocation, the objective is to model material investment-related taxes, thereby providing a closer approximation to economic reality than is represented when ignoring taxes altogether.

For simplicity, we will assume a basic tax regime that represents no single country but includes the key elements of investment-related taxes that are roughly representative of what a typical taxable asset owner in the major developed economies must contend with.

After-Tax Portfolio Optimization

After-tax portfolio optimization requires adjusting each asset class's expected return and risk for expected tax. The expected after-tax return is defined in Equation 1:

$$r_{at} = r_{pt}(1 - t) \tag{1}$$

where

r_{at} = the expected after-tax return

r_{pt} = the expected pre-tax (gross) return

t = the expected tax rate

This can be straightforward for bonds in cases where the expected return is driven by interest income. Take, for example, an investment-grade par bond with a 3% coupon expected to be held to maturity. If interest income is subject to a 40% expected tax rate, the bond has an expected after-tax return of 1.80% [$0.03(1 - 0.40) = 0.018$].

The expected return for equity typically includes both dividend income and price appreciation (capital gains). Equation 2 expands Equation 1 accordingly:

$$r_{at} = p_d r_{pt}(1 - t_d) + p_a r_{pt}(1 - t_{cg}) \tag{2}$$

where

p_d = the proportion of r_{pt} attributed to dividend income

p_a = the proportion of r_{pt} attributed to price appreciation

t_d = the dividend tax rate

t_{cg} = the capital gains tax rate

The treatment of the capital gains portion of equity returns can be more complex. Assuming no dividend income, a stock with an 8% expected pre-tax return that is subject to a 25% capital gains tax rate has an expected after-tax return of 6% [0.08(1 − 0.25) = 0.06]. This is an approximation satisfactory for modeling purposes.[13]

Taxable assets may have existing unrealized capital gains or losses (i.e., the cost basis is below or above market value), which come with embedded tax liabilities (or tax assets). Although there is not a clear consensus on how best to deal with existing unrealized capital gains (losses), many approaches adjust the asset's current market value for the value of the embedded tax liability (asset) to create an after-tax value. Reichenstein (2006) approximates the after-tax value by subtracting the value of the embedded capital gains tax from the market value, as if the asset were sold today. Horan and Al Zaman (2008) assume the asset is sold in the future and discount the tax liability to its present value using the asset's after-tax return as the discount rate. Turvey, Basu, and Verhoeven (2013) argue that the after-tax risk-free rate is the more appropriate discount rate because the embedded tax liability is analogous to an interest-free loan from the government, where the tax liability can be arbitraged away by dynamically investing in the risk-free asset. We will discuss how to incorporate after-tax values into the portfolio optimization process in Section 7, where we address strategies to reduce the impact of taxes.

The ultimate purpose of an asset can be a consideration when modeling tax adjustments. In the preceding material on asset allocation, we discussed goals-based investing. If the purpose of a given pool of assets is to fund consumption in 10 years, then that 10-year holding period may influence the estimated implied annual capital gains tax rate. If the purpose of the specified pool of assets is to fund a future gift of appreciated stock to a tax-exempt charity, then capital gains tax may be ignored altogether. Through this alignment of goals with assets, goals-based investing facilitates more-precise tax adjustments.

Although correlation assumptions need not be adjusted when modeling asset allocation choices for the taxable asset owner (taxes are proportional to return, after-tax co-movements are the same as pre-tax co-movements), taxes do affect the standard deviation assumption for each asset class. The expected after-tax standard deviation is defined in Equation 3:

$$\sigma_{at} = \sigma_{pt}(1 - t) \tag{3}$$

where

σ_{at} = the expected after-tax standard deviation

σ_{pt} = the expected pre-tax standard deviation

Taxes alter the distribution of returns by both reducing the expected mean return and muting the dispersion of returns. Taxes truncate both the high and low ends of the distribution of returns, resulting in lower highs and higher lows. The effect of taxes is intuitive when considering a positive return, but the same economics apply

---

[13] A more precise estimation of the expected after-tax return also takes into account the effect of the holding period on the capital gains tax. For those interested in a more detailed discussion of these issues, see Mladina (2011).

to a negative return: Losses are muted by the same $(1 - t)$ tax adjustment. The investor is not taxed on losses but instead receives the economic benefit of a capital loss, whether realized or not. In many countries, a realized capital loss can offset a current or future realized capital gain. An unrealized capital loss captures the economic benefit of a cost basis that is above the current market value, making a portion of expected future appreciation tax free.

How does the optimal asset allocation along a pre-tax efficient frontier compare with the optimal asset allocation along an after-tax efficient frontier? Let's assume all investment assets are taxable and that cost bases equal current market values. Assume also that interest income is taxed at 40%, and dividend income and capital gains are taxed at 25%.

The asset classes we will consider include investment-grade (IG) bonds, high-yield (HY) bonds, and equity. Exhibit 4 shows the expected pre-tax returns and standard deviations for each asset class as well as the correlation matrix. Note that for ease of illustration, we have assumed that the IG bonds and HY bond returns are comprised of 100% interest income. In practice, some portion of the expected return would be eligible for capital gains tax treatment.

Exhibit 4: Expected Pre-Tax Return and Risk

	Return	Std. Dev.
IG bonds	3.0%	4.0%
HY bonds	5.0%	10.0%
Equity	8.0%	20.0%

Correlations	IG Bonds	HY Bonds	Equity
IG bonds	1.0	0.2	0.0
HY bonds	0.2	1.0	0.7
Equity	0.0	0.7	1.0

Employing mean–variance portfolio optimization with these pre-tax inputs, we obtain the optimal asset allocations in Exhibit 5, which shows the allocations for portfolios P1 (lowest risk), P25, P50 (median risk), P75, and P100 (highest risk)—each on an efficient frontier comprised of 100 portfolios.

Exhibit 5: Optimal Pre-Tax Asset Mixes

	$P1_{pt}$	$P25_{pt}$	$P50_{pt}$	$P75_{pt}$	$P100_{pt}$
IG bonds	93%	52%	25%	0%	0%
HY bonds	5%	18%	26%	33%	0%
Equity	2%	30%	49%	67%	100%

Using Equation 1, Equation 2, and Equation 3, we calculate the expected after-tax returns and standard deviations displayed in Exhibit 6. No adjustments are made to correlations.

Exhibit 6: Expected After-Tax Return and Risk

	Return	Std. Dev.
IG bonds	1.8%	2.4%
HY bonds	3.0%	6.0%
Equity	6.0%	15.0%

Portfolio optimization using these after-tax inputs produces the optimal asset allocations shown in Exhibit 7.

Exhibit 7: Optimal After-Tax Asset Mixes

	$P1_{at}$	$P25_{at}$	$P50_{at}$	$P75_{at}$	$P100_{at}$
IG bonds	92%	60%	38%	16%	0%
HY bonds	7%	7%	7%	7%	0%
Equity	1%	33%	55%	77%	100%

In Exhibit 8, we compare the pre-tax and after-tax efficient frontiers from these previous exhibits. Note that the portfolios at either extreme (P1 and P100) are essentially unchanged after taxes are factored into the assumptions. In portfolios P25, P50, and P75, however, you can see a significant reduction in the allocation to high-yield bonds. This is because of the heavier tax burden imposed on high-yield bonds. Although investment-grade bonds receive the same tax treatment, they are less risky than high-yield bonds and demonstrate a lower correlation with equity, so they continue to play the important role of portfolio risk reduction.

Exhibit 8: Pre-Tax and After-Tax Asset Allocation Comparisons

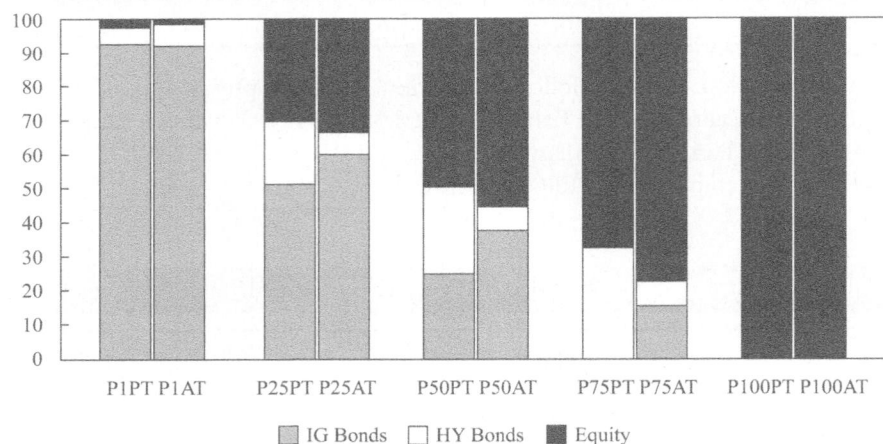

The optimal after-tax asset allocation depends on the interaction of after-tax returns, after-tax risk, and correlations. If an asset class or strategy is tax inefficient, it can still play a diversifying role in an optimal after-tax asset allocation if the asset or strategy offers sufficiently low correlations. After-tax portfolio optimization helps answer that question.

TAXES AND PORTFOLIO REBALANCING

  | discuss tax considerations in asset allocation and rebalancing

Among tax-exempt institutional asset owners, periodic portfolio rebalancing—reallocating assets to return the portfolio to its target strategic asset allocation—is an integral part of sound portfolio management. This is no less true for taxable asset owners, but with the important distinction that more frequent rebalancing exposes the taxable asset owner to realized taxes that could have otherwise been deferred or even avoided. Whereas the tax burden incurred by liquidating assets to fund-required consumption cannot be avoided, rebalancing is discretionary; thus, the taxable asset owner should consider the trade-off between the benefits of tax minimization and the merits of maintaining the targeted asset allocation by rebalancing. The decision to rebalance and incur taxes is driven by each asset owner's unique circumstances.

Because after-tax volatility is less than pre-tax volatility (Equation 3) and asset class correlations remain the same, it takes larger asset class movements to materially alter the risk profile of the taxable portfolio. This suggests that rebalancing ranges for a taxable portfolio can be wider than those of a tax-exempt portfolio with a similar risk profile.

For example, consider a portfolio with a 50% allocation to equity, where equity returns are subject to a 25% tax rate. A tax-exempt investor may establish a target allocation to equities of 50%, with an acceptable range of 40% to 60% (50% plus or minus 10%). A taxable investor with the same target equity allocation can achieve a similar risk constraint with a range of 37% to 63% (50% plus or minus 13%). The equivalent rebalancing range for the taxable investor is derived by adjusting the permitted 10% deviation (up or down) by the tax rate, as shown in Equation 4:

$$R_{at} = R_{pt}/(1 - t) \qquad\qquad (4)$$

where

R_{at} = the after-tax rebalancing range

R_{pt} = the pre-tax rebalancing range

In our example, the 10% rebalancing range for a tax-exempt investor becomes a 13.3% rebalancing range for a taxable investor (when ranges are viewed and monitored from the same gross return perspective):

0.10/(1 − 0.25) = 13.3%

Broader rebalancing ranges for the taxable investor reduce the frequency of trading and, consequently, the amount of taxable gains.

Strategies to Reduce Tax Impact

Additional strategies can be used to reduce taxes, including tax-loss harvesting and choices in the placement of certain types of assets in taxable or tax-exempt accounts (strategic asset location). Tax-loss harvesting is intentionally trading to realize a capital loss, which is then used to offset a current or future realized capital gain in another part of the portfolio, thereby reducing the taxes owned by the investor. It is discussed elsewhere in the curriculum, but we address strategic asset location strategies here.

Strategic asset location refers to placing (or locating) less tax-efficient assets in accounts with more favorable tax treatment, such as retirement savings accounts.

Aggregating assets across accounts with differing tax treatment requires modifying the asset value inputs to the portfolio optimization. Assets held in tax-*exempt* accounts require no tax adjustment to their market values. Assets in tax-*deferred* accounts grow tax free but are taxed upon distribution. Because these assets cannot be distributed (and consumed) without incurring the tax, the tax burden is inseparable from the economic value of the assets. Thus, the after-tax value of assets in a tax-deferred account is defined by Equation 5:

$$v_{at} = v_{pt}(1 - t_i) \tag{5}$$

where

v_{at} = the after-tax value of assets

v_{pt} = the pre-tax market value of assets

t_i = the expected income tax rate upon distribution

In our earlier example, we had three asset classes: investment-grade bonds, high-yield bonds, and equities. If we assume that each of these three asset classes can be held in either of two account types—taxable or tax-deferred—then our optimization uses six different after-tax asset classes (three asset classes times two account types). The three asset classes in taxable accounts use the after-tax return and risk inputs derived earlier. The three asset classes in tax-deferred accounts (which grow tax free) use expected pre-tax return and risk inputs. The optimization adds constraints based on the after-tax value of the assets currently available in each account type and derives the optimal after-tax asset allocation and asset location simultaneously.

As a general rule, the portion of a taxable asset owner's assets that are eligible for lower tax rates and deferred capital gains tax treatment should first be allocated to the investor's taxable accounts. For example, equities should generally be held in taxable accounts, while taxable bonds and high-turnover trading strategies should generally be located in tax-exempt and tax-deferred accounts to the extent possible.

One important exception to this general rule regarding asset location applies to assets held for near-term liquidity needs. Because tax-exempt and tax-deferred accounts may not be immediately accessible without tax penalty, a portion of the bond allocation may be held in taxable accounts if its role is to fund near-term consumption requirements.

EXAMPLE 5

Asset Allocation and the Taxable Investor

Sarah Moreau, 45 years old, is a mid-level manager at a consumer products company. Her investment portfolio consists entirely of tax-deferred retirement savings accounts. Through careful savings and investments, she is on track to accumulate sufficient assets to retire at age 60. Her portfolio is currently allocated as indicated below:

Investment-grade bonds	20%
High-yield bonds	20%
Common stock–dividend income strategy	30%
Common stock–total return (capital gain) strategy	30%
Total portfolio	100%

The common stock–dividend income strategy focuses on income-oriented, high-dividend-paying stocks; the common stock–total return strategy focuses on stocks that represent good, long-term opportunities but pay little to no dividend.

For the purposes of this example, we will assume that the expected long-term return is equivalent between the two strategies. Moreau has a high comfort level with this portfolio and the overall level of risk it entails.

Moreau has recently inherited additional monies, doubling her investable assets. She intends to use this new, taxable portfolio to support causes important to her personally over her lifetime. There is no change in her risk tolerance. She is interviewing prospective investment managers and has asked each to recommend an asset allocation strategy for the new portfolio using the same set of asset classes. She has received the following recommendations:

	Recommendation		
	A	B	C
Investment-grade bonds	20%	40%	30%
High-yield bonds	20%	0%	0%
Common stock–dividend income strategy	30%	30%	0%
Common stock–total return (capital gain) strategy	30%	30%	70%
Total portfolio	100%	100%	100%

1. Which asset allocation is *most* appropriate for the new portfolio? Justify your response.

Solution:

Recommendation C would be the most appropriate asset allocation for the new portfolio. The high-yield bond and common stock–dividend income strategies are tax disadvantaged in a taxable portfolio. (Although investment-grade bonds are also tax disadvantaged, they maintain the role of controlling portfolio risk to maintain Moreau's risk preference.) By shifting this equity-like risk to the total return common stock strategy, Moreau should achieve a greater after-tax return. Given the lower standard deviation characteristics of after-tax equity returns when held in the taxable portfolio, a higher allocation to common stocks may be justified without exceeding Moreau's desired risk level. Recommendations A and B do not consider the negative tax implications of holding the high-yield and/or common stock–dividend income strategies in a taxable portfolio. Recommendation B also fails to consider Moreau's overall risk tolerance: The volatility of the common stock–capital gain strategy is lower when held in a taxable portfolio, thus a higher allocation to this strategy can enhance returns while remaining within Moreau's overall risk tolerance.[14]

2. How should Moreau distribute these investments among her taxable and tax-exempt accounts?

Solution:

If Moreau is willing to think of her investable portfolio as a single portfolio, rather than as independent "retirement" and "important causes" portfolios, she should hold the allocation to high-yield bonds and dividend-paying

---

14 Investment-grade bonds also have lower after-tax volatility. The equivalent risk portfolios in pre-tax and after-tax environments are a function of a complex interaction of after-tax returns, standard deviations, and correlations.

stocks in her tax-exempt retirement portfolio. In addition, subject to the overall volatility of the individual tax-exempt and taxable portfolios, it would be sensible to bear any increased stock risk in the taxable portfolio. A new optimization for *all* of Moreau's assets—using pre-tax and after-tax risk and return assumptions and subject to the constraint that half of the assets are held in a taxable portfolio and half are held in the tax-exempt portfolio—would more precisely allocate investments across portfolio (account) types.

Asset Location for Optimal Tax Efficiency		
	Tax Advantaged Retirement Account	Taxable Account
Investment-grade bonds	X	
High-yield bonds	X	
Common stock–dividend income strategy	X	
Common stock–total return (capital gain) strategy		X

3. You are a member of the Investment Committee for a multinational corporation, responsible for the supervision of two portfolios. Both portfolios were established to fund retirement benefits: One is a tax-exempt defined benefit pension fund, and the other is taxable, holding assets intended to fund non-exempt retirement benefits. The pension fund has a target allocation of 70% equities and 30% fixed income, with a +/– 5% rebalancing range. There is no formal asset allocation policy for the taxable portfolio; it has simply followed the same allocation adopted by the pension portfolio. Because of recent strong equity market returns, both portfolios are now allocated 77% to equities and 23% to bonds. Management expects that the equity markets will continue to produce strong returns in the near term. Staff has offered the following options for rebalancing the portfolios:

Which recommendation is *most* appropriate? Justify your response.

   A. Do not rebalance.

   B. Rebalance both portfolios to the 70% equity/30% fixed-income target allocation.

   C. Rebalance the tax-exempt portfolio to the 70% equity/30% fixed-income target allocation, but expand the rebalancing range for the taxable portfolio.

Solution:

Recommendation C is the most appropriate course of action. Rebalancing of the tax-exempt portfolio is unencumbered by tax considerations, and rebalancing maintains the desired level of risk. The rebalancing range for the taxable portfolio can be wider than that of the tax-exempt portfolio based on the desire to minimize avoidable taxes and the lower volatility of after-tax equity returns. Recommendation A (no rebalancing) does not address the increased level of risk in the tax-exempt portfolio that results from the increase in the stock allocation. Recommendation B would create an unnecessary tax liability for the company, given that the portfolio is still operating in a reasonable range of risk when adjusted for taxes.

INCREASING ALLOCATIONS TO FIXED INCOME IN CORPORATE PENSION PLANS

Increasing allocations to fixed income by defined benefit pension funds worldwide have been driven largely by a desire to better hedge plan liabilities. In some countries, accounting standards discourage de-risking. De-risking, however, is not the only argument in favor of a higher fixed-income allocation.

De-risking

There has been much discussion globally of pension plans "de-risking"—moving toward larger fixed-income allocations to better hedge liabilities, thereby reducing contribution uncertainty. Some countries' accounting rules, however—most notably those in the United States—discourage companies from moving in that direction. Under US GAAP accounting rules, for example, a higher allocation to equities allows the plan sponsor to employ a higher return assumption, thereby reducing pension cost, a non-cash expense that directly affects reported income.

For underfunded pension plans, de-risking leads to higher pension contributions. If a company has a weak core business with a higher-than-average probability of going bankrupt and makes only the minimum required contribution, it might be argued that the asset allocation decision was contrary to the interests of plan participants. If the company were to go bankrupt, the participants would get only the benefits covered by any government guaranty program. Had the company taken equity risk in the plan, there would have been a possibility of closing the funding gap, resulting in higher benefit payments.

Efficient Allocation of Risk

A higher allocation to fixed income—and a lower allocation to equity—might also be driven by corporate governance considerations. Pension investment activities are not a core competency of many companies, especially non-financial companies. Assuming that the company has a limited appetite for risk, shareholders might prefer that management allocate its risk budget to the core business of the company where they are expected to have skill, rather than to the pension fund. The rewards per unit of risk should presumably be greater in the company's core business, and the improved profitability should offset the increase in pension contributions required as a result of the lower equity allocation.

A Holistic Approach to Asset Location

Finally, some have argued that an asset allocation of 100% fixed-income securities can be justified on the premise that the company is acting as an agent for the benefit of all stakeholders, including shareholders and plan participants. This argument centers on tax-efficient asset location. A taxable investor—the shareholder and plan participant—should prefer to take his long-term equity risk in that portion of his overall portfolio where he will receive the benefit of lower capital gains rates rather than in tax-deferred accounts, the proceeds of which will be taxed at income tax rates. Consider a small business owner with US$3 million in total assets. The assets are split between a pension fund of which he is the sole participant (US$1 million) and a taxable portfolio (US$2 million). Assume that the asset allocation that represents his preferred level of risk is 67% equities and 33% fixed income. Where should this individual hold his equity exposure? As discussed, the more favorable tax treatment of equity returns argues for holding the equity exposure in his taxable account, while the investments subject to the higher tax rate should be held in the tax-deferred account—the pension plan. Theoretically, this tax efficiency argument can be extended to pension funds operated by publicly traded companies.[15]

---

8   REVISING THE STRATEGIC ASSET ALLOCATION

> ☐ | recommend and justify revisions to an asset allocation given change(s) in investment objectives and/or constraints

An asset owner's strategic asset allocation is not a static decision. Circumstances often arise that justify revisiting the original decision, either to confirm its appropriateness or to consider a change to the current allocation strategy. It is sound financial practice to periodically re-examine the asset allocation strategy even in the absence of one of the external factors discussed next. Many institutional asset owners typically re-visit the asset allocation policy at least once every five years through a formal asset allocation study, and all asset owners should affirm annually that the asset allocation remains appropriate given their needs and circumstances.

The circumstances that might trigger a special review of the asset allocation policy can generally be classified as relating to a change in *goals*, a change in *constraints*, or a change in *beliefs*. Among the reasons to review the strategic asset allocation are the following:

Goals

- Changes in business conditions affecting the organization supporting the fund and, therefore, expected changes in the cash flows
- A change in the investor's personal circumstances that may alter her risk appetite or risk capacity

Over an individual's lifespan, or throughout the course of an institutional fund's lifespan, it is unlikely that the investment goals and objectives will remain unchanged. An individual may get married, have children, or become disabled, for example, each of which may have implications for the asset allocation strategy.

Significant changes in the core business of an organization supporting or benefiting from the trust might prompt a re-examination of the asset allocation strategy. For example, an automobile manufacturer that has historically generated a significant portion of its revenues from its consumer finance activities may find that technology is disrupting this source of revenue as more online tools become available to car buyers. With greater uncertainty in its revenue stream, company management may move to reduce risk-taking in the pension fund in order to achieve a goal of reducing the variability in year-to-year contributions.

A university may embark on a long-term capital improvement plan that is reliant on the endowment fund for financial support. Or the university may be experiencing declining enrollments and must lean more heavily on the endowment fund to support

---

15 For those interested in a more detailed discussion of this concept, see "The Case against Stock in Public Pension Funds" (Bader and Gold 2007) or the UBS Q-Series article, "Pension Fund Asset Allocation" (Cooper and Bianco 2003).

its ongoing operational expenditures. The source of funds to a sovereign wealth fund may shrink considerably or even evaporate. When any of these, or similar, events occur or are anticipated, the existing asset allocation policy should be re-evaluated.

Constraints

A material change in any one of the constraints mentioned earlier—time horizon, liquidity needs, asset size, or regulatory or other external constraints—is also reason to re-examine the existing asset allocation policy. Some of these changes might include the following:

- Changes in the expected payments from the fund
- A significant cash inflow or unanticipated expenditure
- Changes in regulations governing donations or contributions to the fund
- Changes in time horizon resulting from the adoption of a lump sum distribution option at retirement
- Changes in asset size as a result of the merging of pension plans

Changes in the expected payments from the fund can materially affect the asset allocation strategy. For example, a university reduces its spending policy from 5% to 4% of assets annually; an individual retires early, perhaps for health reasons or an involuntary late-career layoff; or a US corporate pension sponsor reduces or freezes pension benefits because it can no longer afford increasing Pension Benefit Guaranty Corporation[16] premiums. Faced with lower payouts, the university endowment may have greater latitude to invest in less liquid segments of the market. Decisions as to how and where to invest given this greater flexibility should be made within the framework of an asset allocation study to ensure the resulting allocation achieves the optimal trade-off of risk and return.

Similarly, a significant cash inflow has the potential to materially affect the asset allocation strategy. If a university endowment fund with £500 million in assets receives a gift of £100 million, the new monies *could* be invested in parallel with the existing assets, but that fails to consider the increased earning potential of the fund and any spending requirements associated with the donation. Pausing to formally reassess the fund's goals, objectives, constraints, and opportunities through an asset allocation study allows the asset owner to consider more broadly how best to maximize this additional wealth.

A change in regulations may also give rise to a change in asset allocation policy. Examples of regulatory changes that could trigger a re-examination of the asset allocation include the following:

- Regulatory changes in the United States in 2006 mandated a change in the liability discount rate, which resulted in larger pension contributions. With higher required contributions, there was less need to reach for higher investment returns. Many US corporate pension plans began de-risking (adopting an asset allocation strategy focused on hedging the liabilities) to reduce contribution volatility.
- UK tax incentives (30% of social impact investment costs can be deducted from income tax) and relaxed regulations for institutional investors were instituted to encourage socially responsible (impact) investing.

Again, an asset allocation study to objectively evaluate the effect of these changes on the investment opportunity set can help ensure that any new investment strategies adopted are consistent with the fund's overarching goals and objectives.

---

16 The Pension Benefit Guaranty Corporation insures certain US pension plan benefits.

Beliefs

Investment beliefs are a set of guiding principles that govern the asset owner's investment activities. Beliefs are not static, however, and changes in the economic environment and capital market expectations or a change in trustees or committee members are two factors that may lead to an altering of the principles that guide investment activities.[17]

An integral aspect of any asset allocation exercise is the forecasting of expected returns, volatilities, and correlations of the asset classes in the opportunity set. It follows, then, that a material change in the outlook for one or more of the asset classes may heavily influence the asset allocation outcome.

Consider the 2015–2016 environment relative to the environment that prevailed in 1984–2014. The 1984–2014 investing environment was characterized by declining inflation and interest rates (from the extraordinarily high levels of the 1970s and early 1980s); strong global GDP growth, aided by favorable demographics; gains in productivity; and rapid growth in China. Corporate profit growth was extremely robust, reflecting revenue growth from new markets, declining corporate taxes over the period, and improved efficiencies. Despite increased market turbulence, returns on US and Western European equities and bonds during the past 30 years were considerably higher than the long-run trend.

The environment of 2015–2016 was much less favorable for investors. The dramatic decline in inflation and interest rates ended, and labor force expansion and productivity gains stalled, with negative implications for GDP growth. The largest developed-country companies that generated much of the profits of the past 30 years were faced with competitive pressures as emerging-market companies expanded and technology advances changed the competitive landscape. In April 2016, McKinsey Global Institute published a projection of stocks and bonds under two growth scenarios—a slow growth scenario and a moderate growth scenario (Exhibit 9). In neither instance do the expected returns of the next 30 years come close to the returns of the past 30 years.[18] Clearly, an asset allocation developed in 2010 built on return expectations based on the prior 26 years would look materially different than an asset allocation developed using more current, forward-looking return assumptions.

---

17 For an example of an investment belief statement, see www.uss.co.uk/how-uss-invests/investment
-approach/investment-beliefs-and-principles.
18 McKinsey Global Institute, "Diminishing Returns: Why Investors May Need to Lower Their Expectations"
(May 2016).

Exhibit 9: A Major Shift in Underlying Return Assumptions

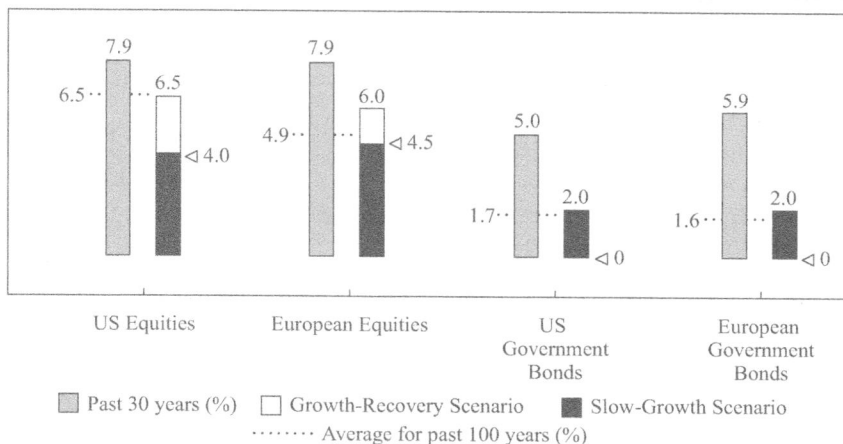

7.9	7.9		
6.5·· ····6.5			5.9
4.9·· ··· 6.0	5.0		
◁ 4.0	◁ 4.5	2.0	2.0
	1.7·· ···· ◁ 0	1.6·· ◁ 0	

US Equities   European Equities   US Government Bonds   European Government Bonds

■ Past 30 years (%)   □ Growth-Recovery Scenario   ■ Slow-Growth Scenario
········ Average for past 100 years (%)

Notes:

Numbers for growth-recovery and slow-growth scenarios reflect the range between the low end of the slow-growth scenario and the high end of the growth-recovery scenario.

European equities: Weighted average real returns based on each year's Geary-Khamis purchasing power parity GDP for 14 countries in Western Europe.

US and European government bonds: Bond duration for United States is primarily 10 years; for Europe, duration varies by country but is typically 20 years.

Source: McKinsey Global Institute (www.mckinsey.com/industries/private-equity-and-principal -investors/our-insights/why-investors-may-need-to-lower-their-sights).

Asset returns and future return expectations shifted widely at the outbreak of the COVID-19 pandemic and during the following period. Unlike in the case of other economic and financial crises, the causes of the pandemic-related turmoil were outside of the economic and financial system; yet, lockdowns and the sudden stop of economic activities led to a recession. The unemployment rate in the United States jumped from 3.5% to 14.7% between February 2021 and April 2021, and the June 2020 annual real GDP growth was −9.1%—extreme numbers not observed since the Great Depression. Equity markets' peak to trough period lasted for about a month: From February through March 2020, the global equity (MSCI ACWI) index fell by 34%, high-yield bonds lost about 21%, and oil prices fell by more than 60%. At the same time, governments and central banks came to the rescue with unprecedented fiscal and monetary stimuli. The 10-year Treasury rate fluctuated around as low as 0.6% in the United States from March through August 2020, and equities posted a very strong recovery for the rest of the year (the MSCI ACWI global equity index was at +70.5% from 23 March 2020 to 31 December 2020).

While short-term market returns resembled a very wild roller coaster in 2020, long-term return expectations did not change that dramatically. Of course, bond return expectations became lower as a result of very low government yield levels due to the monetary stimulus, but it has been a general expectation that corporate earnings would recover as the disruptive impacts of the pandemic decline over time. Since the end of 2021, however, policymakers and market participants have been trying to get a better understanding of the long lasting impacts of the pandemic: Inflation, among others, is one of the most topical issues. The unprecedented fiscal and monetary stimuli, supply chain disruptions, and changes in many people's life style (working from home versus the office) may cause sticky price rises in certain segments of the economy.

Finally, as new advisers or members join the Investment Committee, they bring their own beliefs and biases regarding certain investment activities. Conducting an asset allocation study to educate these new members of the oversight group and introduce them to the investment philosophy and process that has been adopted by the organization will smooth their integration into the governance system and ensure that they have a holistic view of the asset owner's goals and objectives.

In some instances, a change to an asset allocation strategy may reasonably be implemented without a formal asset allocation study. Certain milestones are reasonable points at which to implement a change in the policy, in most instances, reducing the level of risk. (For pension funds, these "milestones" are typically related to changes in the plan's funded status.) Anticipating these milestones by putting an asset allocation policy in place that anticipates these changes allows the investor to respond more quickly to changing circumstances and in a non-reactive and objective manner. This rebalancing policy is frequently referred to as a "glide path." Target-date mutual funds common in retirement investing for individuals are one example of this approach to asset allocation. Exhibit 10 illustrates one fund company's approach to migrating the asset allocation away from equities and towards bonds as retirement approaches.

Exhibit 10: An Asset Allocation Glide Path

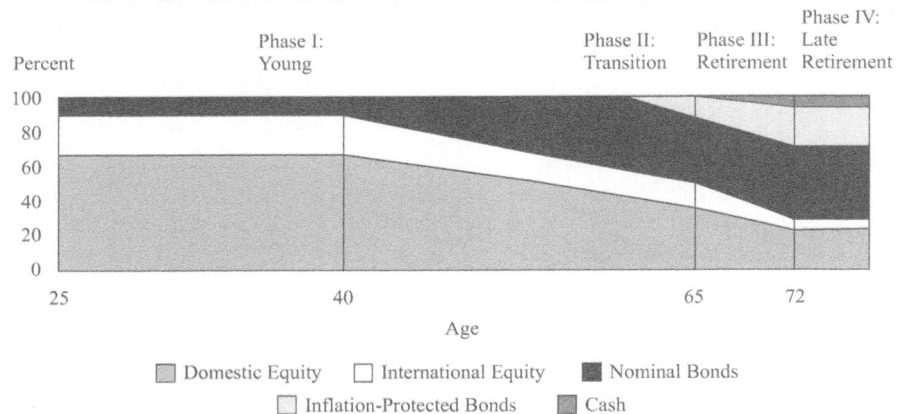

Source: Vanguard, "Target-Date Funds: A Solid Foundation for Retirement Investors" (May 2009): www.vanguard.com/jumppage/targetretirement/TRFCOMM.pdf.

In an institutional framework, the Investment Committee may specify certain funding levels it seeks to achieve. At the start of the period, an underfunded pension plan might adopt a higher equity allocation in an attempt to reduce the underfunding. If this is successful, the plan becomes better funded and there is less of a desire or need to take the higher level of equity risk. A pension fund may quickly implement "pre-programmed" asset allocation changes as the funded status of a pension plan improves. Typically, these planned reallocations are spelled out in an Investment Policy Statement.

EXAMPLE 6

Revising the Strategic Asset Allocation

Auldberg University Endowment Fund (AUE) has assets totaling CAF$200 million. The current asset allocation is as follows:

- CAF$100 million in domestic equities
- CAF$60 million in domestic government debt
- CAF$40 million in Class B office real estate

AUE has historically distributed to the University 5% of the 36-month moving average of net assets, contributing approximately CAF$10 million of Auldberg University's CAF$60 million annual operating budget. Real estate income (from the University's CAF$350 million direct investment in domestic commercial real estate assets, including office buildings and industrial parks, much of it near the campus) and provincial subsidies have been the main source of income to the University. Admission is free to all citizens who qualify academically.

Growth in the Caflandia economy has been fueled by low interest rates, encouraging excess real estate development. There is a strong probability that the economy will soon go into recession, negatively impacting both the property values and the income potential of the University's real estate holdings.

Gizi Horvath, a University alumna, has recently announced an irrevocable CAF$200 million gift to AUE, to be paid in equal installments over the next five years. AUE employs a well-qualified staff with substantial diverse experience in equities, fixed income, and real estate. Staff has recommended that the gift from Ms. Horvath be invested using the same asset allocation policy that the endowment has been following successfully for the past five years. They suggest that the asset allocation policy should be revisited once the final installment has been received.

1. Critique staff's recommendation, and identify the case facts that support your critique.

Solution:

The size of the anticipated contributions will double AUE's assets over the next five years, potentially increasing the opportunity set of asset classes suitable for their investment program. Given that a typical asset allocation study encompasses a long investment horizon—10 years, 20 years, or more—staff should begin to evaluate the opportunities available to them today in *anticipation* of the future cash flows. Given the material change in the economic balance sheet along with changes in the asset size, liquidity, and time horizon constraints, AUE should plan on a regular, more frequent, formal review of the asset allocation policy until the situation stabilizes. The asset allocation study should explore the feasibility of adding new asset classes as well as the ability to improve diversification within existing categories, perhaps by including non-domestic equities and bonds. Furthermore, the forecast economic environment may materially alter the outflows from the fund in support of the University's day-to-day operations. Cash flows from the University's real estate holdings are likely to decline, as are the values of those real estate assets. Given the outlook for real estate, a strong case can be made to limit or reduce the endowment's investment in real estate; moreover, consideration should be given to the effect of declining income from the current real estate investment.

2. The Government Petroleum Fund of Caflandia (GPFC) is operating under the following asset allocation policy, which was developed with a 20-year planning horizon. Target weights and actual weights are given:

	Target Asset Allocation	Current Asset Allocation
Global equities	30%	38%
Global high-yield bonds	10%	15%
Domestic intermediate bonds	30%	25%
Hedge funds	15%	15%
Private equity	15%	7%

When this asset allocation policy was adopted 5 years ago, the petroleum revenues that support the sovereign wealth fund were projected to continue to grow for at least the next 25 years and intergenerational distributions were expected to begin in 20 years. However, since the adoption of this policy, alternate fuel sources have eroded both the price and quantity of oil exports, the economy is undergoing significant restructuring, inflows to the fund have been suspended, and distributions are expected to begin within 5 years.

What are the implications of this change in the liquidity constraints for the current asset allocation policy?

Solution:

GPFC had adopted a long-range asset allocation policy under the expectation of continuing net cash inflows and no immediate liquidity constraints. With the change in circumstances, the need for liquidity in the fund has increased significantly. The current asset allocation policy allocates 40% of the fund's assets to less liquid asset classes—high-yield bonds, hedge funds, and private equity. Although the allocation to private equity has not been fully implemented, the fund is overweight high-yield bonds and at the target weight for hedge funds. These asset classes—or the size of the allocation to these asset classes—may no longer be appropriate for the fund given the change in circumstances.

3. O-Chem Corp has a defined benefit pension plan with US$1.0 billion in assets. The plan is closed, the liabilities are frozen, and the plan is currently 65% funded. The company intends to increase cash contributions to improve the funded status of the plan and then purchase annuities to fully address all of the plan's pension obligations. As part of an asset allocation analysis conducted every five years, the company has recently decided to allocate 80% of assets to liability-matching bonds and the remaining 20% to a mix of global equities and real estate. An existing private equity portfolio is in the midst of being liquidated. This allocation reflects a desired reduction in the level of investment risk.

O-Chem has just announced an ambitious US$15 billion capital investment program to build new plants for refining and production. The CFO informed the Pension Committee that the company will be contributing to the plan only the minimum funding required by regulations for the foreseeable future. It is estimated that achieving fully funded status for the pension plan

under minimum funding requirements and using the current asset allocation approach will take at least 10 years.

What are the implications of this change in funding policy for the pension
plan's asset allocation strategy?

Solution:

The Investment Committee should conduct a new asset allocation study to
address the changes in cash flow forecasts. The lower contributions imply
that the pension plan will need to rely more heavily on investment returns
to reach its funding objectives. A higher allocation to return-seeking assets,
such as public and private equities, is warranted. The company should sus-
pend the current private equity liquidation plan until the new asset allocation study has been completed. A liability-matching bond portfolio is still
appropriate, although less than the current 80% of assets should be allocated
to this portfolio.

SHORT-TERM SHIFTS IN ASSET ALLOCATION

9

☐ | discuss the use of short-term shifts in asset allocation

Strategic asset allocation (SAA), or policy asset allocation, represents long-term
investment policy targets for asset class weights, whereas tactical asset allocation
(TAA) allows short-term deviations from SAA targets.[19] TAA moves might be justified
based on cyclical variations within a secular trend (e.g., stage of business or monetary
cycle) or temporary price dislocations in capital markets. TAA has the objective of
increasing return, or risk-adjusted return, by taking advantage of short-term economic
and financial market conditions that appear more favorable to certain asset classes. In
seeking to capture a short-term return opportunity, TAA decisions move the investor's
risk away from the targeted risk profile. TAA is predicated on a belief that investment returns, in the short run, are predictable. (This contrasts with the random walk
assumption more strongly embedded in most SAA processes.) Using either short-term
views or signals, the investor actively re-weights broad asset classes, sectors, or risk
factor premiums. TAA is not concerned with individual security selection. In other
words, generating alpha through TAA decisions is dependent on successful market or
factor timing rather than security selection. TAA is an asset-only approach. Although
tactical asset allocation shifts must still conform to the risk constraints outlined in
the investment policy statement, they do not expressly consider liabilities (or goals
in goals-based investing).

The SAA policy portfolio is the benchmark against which TAA decisions are measured. Tactical views are developed and bets are sized relative to the asset class targets
of the SAA policy portfolio. The sizes of these bets are typically subject to certain risk
constraints. The most common risk constraint is a pre-established allowable range

---

19 SAA and TAA are distinct from GTAA (global tactical asset allocation), an opportunistic investment
strategy that seeks to take advantage of pricing or valuation anomalies across multiple asset classes, typically
equities, fixed income, and currencies.

around each asset class's policy target. Other risk constraints may include either a predicted tracking error budget versus the SAA or a range of targeted risk (e.g., an allowable range of predicted volatility).

The success of TAA decisions can be evaluated in a number of ways. Three of the most common are

- a comparison of the Sharpe ratio realized under the TAA relative to the Sharpe ratio that would have been realized under the SAA;

- evaluating the information ratio or the *t*-statistic of the average excess return of the TAA portfolio relative to the SAA portfolio; and

- plotting the realized return and risk of the TAA portfolio versus the realized return and risk of portfolios along the SAA's efficient frontier. This approach is particularly useful in assessing the risk-adjusted TAA return. The TAA portfolio may have produced a higher return or a higher Sharpe ratio than the SAA portfolio, but it could be less optimal than other portfolios along the investor's efficient frontier of portfolio choices.

The composition of the portfolio's excess return over the SAA portfolio return can also be examined more closely using attribution analysis, evaluating the specific overweights and underweights that led to the performance differential.

Tactical investment decisions may incur additional costs—higher trading costs and taxes (in the case of taxable investors). Tactical investment decisions can also increase the concentration of risk relative to the policy portfolio. For example, if the tactical decision is to overweight equities, not only is the portfolio risk increased but also the diversification of risk contributions is reduced. This is particularly an issue when the SAA policy portfolio relies on uncorrelated asset classes. These costs should be weighed against the predictability of short-term returns.

There are two broad approaches to TAA. The first is discretionary, which relies on a qualitative interpretation of political, economic, and financial market conditions. The second is systematic, which relies on quantitative signals to capture documented return anomalies that may be inconsistent with market efficiency.

Discretionary TAA

Discretionary TAA is predicated on the existence of manager skill in predicting and timing short-term market moves away from the expected outcome for each asset class that is embedded in the SAA policy portfolio. In practice, discretionary TAA is typically used in an attempt to mitigate or hedge risk in distressed markets while enhancing return in positive return markets (i.e., an asymmetric return distribution).

Short-term forecasts consider a large number of data points that provide relevant information about current and expected political, economic, and financial market conditions that may affect short-term asset class returns. Data points might include valuations, term and credit spreads, central bank policy, GDP growth, earnings expectations, inflation expectations, and leading economic indicators. Price-to-earnings ratios, price-to-book ratios, and the dividend yield are commonly used valuation measures that can be compared to historical averages and across similar assets to inform short-to-intermediate-term tactical shifts. Term spreads provide information about the business cycle, inflation, and potential future interest rates. Credit spreads gauge default risk, borrowing conditions, and liquidity. Other data points are more directly related to current and expected GDP and earnings growth.

Short-term forecasts may also consider economic sentiment indicators. TAA often assumes a close relationship between the economy and capital market returns. Because consumer spending is a major driver of GDP in developed countries, consumer sentiment is a key consideration. Consumer confidence surveys provide insight as to the level of optimism regarding the economy and personal finances.

TAA also considers market sentiment—indicators of the optimism or pessimism of financial market participants. Data points considered in gauging market sentiment include margin borrowing, short interest, and a volatility index.

- Margin borrowing measures give an indication of the current level of bullishness, and the capacity for more or less margin borrowing has implications for future bullishness. Higher prices tend to inspire confidence and spur more buying; similarly, more buying on margin tends to spur higher prices. The aggregate level of margin can be an indicator that bullish sentiment is overdone, although the level of borrowing must be considered in the context of the rate of change in borrowing.

- Short interest measures give an indication of current bearish sentiment and also have implications for future bearishness. Although rising short interest indicates increasing negative sentiment, a high short interest ratio may be an indication of the extreme pessimism that often occurs at market lows.

- The volatility index, commonly known as the fear index, is a measure of market expectations of near-term volatility. VDAX-NEW in Germany, V2X in the United Kingdom, and VIX in the United States each measure the level of expected volatility of their respective indexes as implied by the bid/ask quotations of index options; it rises when put option buying increases and falls when call buying activity increases.

Different approaches to discretionary TAA may include different data points and relationships and also may prioritize and weight those data points differently depending on both the approach and the prevailing market environment. Despite the plethora of data inputs, the interpretation of this information is qualitative at its core.

Systematic TAA

Using signals, systematic TAA attempts to capture asset class level return anomalies that have been shown to have some predictability and persistence. Value and momentum, for example, are factors that have been determined to offer some level of predictability, both among securities within asset classes (for security selection) and at the asset class level (for asset class timing).

The value factor is the return of value stocks over the return of growth stocks. The momentum factor is the return of stocks with higher prior returns over the return of stocks with lower prior returns. Value and momentum (and size) factors have been determined to have some explanatory power regarding the relative returns of equity securities within the equity asset class. Value and momentum phenomena are also present at the asset class level and can be used in making tactical asset allocation decisions across asset classes.

Valuation ratios have been shown to have some explanatory power in predicting variation in future equity returns. Predictive measures for equities include dividend yield, cash flow yield, and Shiller's earnings yield (the inverse of Shiller's P/E[20]). Sometimes these yield measures are defined as the excess of the yield over the local risk-free rate or inflation.[21]

Other asset classes have their own value signals, such as yield and carry in currencies, commodities, and/or fixed income. Carry in currencies uses short-term interest rate differentials to determine which currencies (or currency-denominated assets) to overweight (or own) and which to underweight (or sell short). Carry in commodities compares positive (backwardation) and negative (contango) roll yields to determine which commodities to own or short. And for bonds, yields-to-maturity and term premiums (yields in excess of the local risk-free rate) signal the relative attractiveness of different fixed-income markets.

Asset classes can trend positively or negatively for some time before changing course. Trend following is an investment or trading strategy based on the expectation that asset class (or asset) returns will continue in the same upward or downward trend that they have most recently exhibited.[22] A basic trend signal is the most recent 12-month return: The expectation is that the direction of the most recent 12-month returns can be expected to persist for the next 12 months. Shorter time frames and different weighting schemes can also be used. For example, another trend signal is the moving-average crossover, where the moving average price of a shorter time frame is compared with the moving average price of a longer time frame. This signals an upward (downward) trend when the moving average of the shorter time frame is above (below) the moving average of the longer time frame. Trend signals are widely used in systematic TAA. Asset classes may be ranked or categorized into positive or negative buckets based on their most recent prior 12-month performance and over- or underweighted accordingly. More-complex signals for both momentum/trend signals (such as those that use different lookback periods or momentum signals correlated with earnings momentum) and value/carry are also used.

EXAMPLE 7

Short-Term Shifts in Asset Allocation

Exhibit 11

Asset Class	Asset Allocation	Calendar Year Return
Investment-grade bonds	45%	3.45%
High-yield bonds	5%	−6.07%
Developed markets equity	45%	−0.32%
Emerging markets equity	5%	−14.60%

---

20 A price-to-earnings ratio based on the average inflation-adjusted earnings of the previous 10 years.
21 Return predictability for equity markets is driven by historical mean-reversion, which tends to occur over the intermediate-term. These valuation measures are often used as signals for TAA, but they can also be used to shape return expectations for SAA.
22 Trend following is also called time-series momentum. Cross-sectional momentum describes the relative momentum returns of securities within the same asset class.

Exhibit 12

	Policy Portfolio	Realized Results
12-month return	−0.82%	0.38%
Risk-free rate	0.50%	0.50%
Standard deviation	5.80%	6.20%
Sharpe ratio	−0.23	−0.02

Exhibit 13

Calendar Year Return (%)

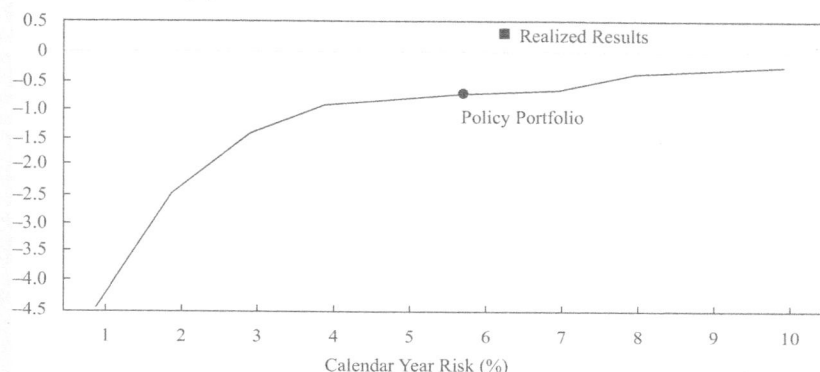

Calendar Year Risk (%)

1. The investment policy for Alpha Beverage Corporation's pension fund allows staff to overweight or underweight asset classes, within pre-established bands, using a TAA model that has been approved by the Investment Committee. The asset allocation policy is reflected in Exhibit 14, and the output of the TAA model is given in Exhibit 15. Using the data presented in Exhibit 14 and Exhibit 15, recommend a TAA strategy for the pension fund and justify your response.

Exhibit 14: Strategic Asset Allocation Policy

SAA Policy	Current Weight	Target Allocation	Upper Policy Limit	Lower Policy Limit
Investment-grade bonds	45%	40%	45%	35%
High-yield bonds	10%	10%	15%	5%
Developed markets equity	35%	40%	45%	35%
Emerging markets equity	10%	10%	15%	5%

Exhibit 15: Trend Signal (the positive or negative trailing 12-month excess return)

	12-Month Return	Risk-Free Return	Excess Return	Signal
Investment-grade bonds	4%	1%	3%	Long
High-yield bonds	−2%	1%	−3%	Short

	12-Month Return	Risk-Free Return	Excess Return	Signal
Developed markets equity	5%	1%	4%	Long
Emerging markets equity	–10%	1%	–11%	Short

Solution:

The TAA decision must be taken in the context of the SAA policy constraints. Thus, although the signals for high-yield bonds and emerging market equities are negative, the minimum permissible weight in each is 5%. Similarly, although the signals for investment-grade bonds and developed markets equities are positive, the maximum permissible weight in each is 45%. Asset classes can be over- or underweighted to the full extent of the policy limits. Based on the trend signals and the policy constraints, the recommended tactical asset allocation is as follows:

- Investment-grade bonds   45% *(overweight by 5%)*
- High-yield bonds   5% *(underweight by 5%)*
- Developed markets equity   45% *(overweight by 5%)*
- Emerging markets equity   5% *(underweight by 5%)*

2. One year later, the Investment Committee for Alpha Beverage Corporation is conducting its year-end review of pension plan performance. Staff has prepared the following exhibits regarding the tactical asset allocation decisions taken during the past year. Assume that all investments are implemented using passively managed index funds. Evaluate the effectiveness of the TAA decisions.

Solution:

The decision to overweight investment grade bonds and underweight emerging markets equity and high-yield bonds was a profitable one. The chosen asset allocation added approximately 120 basis points to portfolio return over the year. Although portfolio risk was elevated relative to the policy portfolio (standard deviation of 6.2% versus 5.8% for the policy portfolio), the portfolio positioning improved the fund's Sharpe ratio relative to allocations they might have selected along the efficient frontier.

A SILVER LINING TO THE 2008–2009 GLOBAL FINANCIAL CRISIS

Prior to 2008, corporate pension plans had begun to shift the fixed-income component of their policy portfolios from an intermediate maturity bond index to a long bond index. Despite the relatively low interest rates at the time, this move was made to better align the plans' assets with the long duration liability payment stream. The fixed-income portfolios were typically benchmarked against a long government and credit index that included both government and corporate bonds. Swaps or STRIPS* were sometimes used to extend duration.

During the global financial crisis that began in 2008, these heavier and longer-duration fixed-income positions performed well relative to equities (the long government and credit index was up 8%, whereas the S&P 500 Index was down 37% in 2008), providing plan sponsors with a level of investment protection that had not been anticipated. Additionally, with its exposure to higher-returning government bonds that benefited from investors' flight to safety, this fixed-income portfolio often outperformed the liabilities. (Recall from the earlier discussion on pension regulation that pension liabilities are typically measured using corporate bond yields. Thus, liabilities rose in the face of declining corporate bond yields while the liability-hedging asset rose even further given its overall higher credit quality.) This was an unintended asset/liability mismatch that had very positive results. Subsequent to this rally in bonds, some plan sponsors made a tactical asset allocation decision—to move out of swaps and government bonds and into physical corporate bonds (non-derivative fixed-income exposure)—locking in the gains and better hedging the liability.

* Treasury STRIPS are fixed-income securities with no interest payments that are sold at a discount to face value and mature at par. STRIPS is an acronym for Separate Trading of Registered Interest and Principal of Securities.

DEALING WITH BEHAVIORAL BIASES IN ASSET ALLOCATION

10

☐ | identify behavioral biases that arise in asset allocation and recommend methods to overcome them

Although global capital markets are competitive pricing engines, human behavior can be less rational than most economic models assume. Behavioral finance—the hybrid study of financial economics and psychology—has documented a number of behavioral biases that commonly arise in investing. The CFA Program reading "The Behavioral Biases of Individuals" discusses 16 common behavioral biases. The biases most relevant in asset allocation include loss aversion, the illusion of control, mental accounting, representativeness bias, framing, and availability bias. An effective investment program will address these decision-making risks through a formal asset allocation process with its own objective framework, governance, and controls. An important first step toward mitigating the negative effects of behavioral biases is simply acknowledging that they exist; just being aware of them can reduce their influence on decision making. It is also possible to incorporate certain behavioral biases into the investment decision-making process to produce better outcomes. This is most commonly practiced in goals-based investing. We will discuss strategies that help deal with these common biases.

Loss Aversion

Loss-aversion bias is an emotional bias in which people tend to strongly prefer avoiding losses as opposed to achieving gains. A number of studies on loss aversion suggest that, psychologically, losses are significantly more powerful than gains. The utility derived from a gain is much lower than the utility given up with an equivalent loss. This behavior is related to the marginal utility of wealth, where each additional dollar of wealth is valued incrementally less with increasing levels of wealth.

A diversified multi-asset class portfolio is generally thought to offer an approximately symmetrical distribution of returns around a positive expected mean return. Financial market theory suggests that a rational investor would think about risk as the dispersion or uncertainty (variance) around the mean (expected) outcome. However, loss aversion suggests the investor assigns a greater weight to the negative outcomes than would be implied by the actual shape of the distribution. Looking at this another way, risk is not measured relative to the expected mean return but rather on an absolute basis, relative to a 0% return. The loss-aversion bias may interfere with an investor's ability to maintain his chosen asset allocation through periods of negative returns.

In goals-based investing, loss-aversion bias can be mitigated by framing risk in terms of shortfall probability or by funding high-priority goals with low-risk assets.

Shortfall probability is the probability that a portfolio will not achieve the return required to meet a stated goal. Where there are well-defined, discrete goals, sub-portfolios can be established for each goal and the asset allocation for that sub-portfolio would use shortfall probability as the definition of risk.

Similarly, by segregating assets into sub-portfolios aligned to goals designated by the client as high-priority and investing those assets in risk-free or low risk assets of similar duration, the adviser mitigates the loss-aversion bias associated with this particular goal—freeing up other assets to take on a more appropriate level of risk. Riskier assets can then be used to fund lower-priority and aspirational goals.

In institutional investing, loss aversion can be seen in the herding behavior among plan sponsors. Adopting an asset allocation not too different from the allocation of one's peers minimizes reputation risk.

Illusion of Control

The illusion of control is a cognitive bias—the tendency to overestimate one's ability to control events. It can be exacerbated by overconfidence, an emotional bias. If investors believe they have more or better information than what is reflected in the market, they have (excessive) confidence in their ability to generate better outcomes. They may perceive *information* in what are random price movements, which may lead to more frequent trading, greater concentration of portfolio positions, or a greater willingness to employ tactical shifts in their asset allocation. The following investor behaviors might be attributed to this illusion of control:

- Alpha-seeking behaviors, such as attempted market timing in the form of extreme tactical asset allocation shifts or all in/all out market calls—the investor who correctly anticipated a market reversal now believes he has superior insight on valuation levels.

- Alpha-seeking behaviors based on a belief of superior resources—the institutional investor who believes her internal resources give her an edge over other investors in active security selection and/or the selection of active investment managers.

- Excessive trading, use of leverage, or short selling—the long/short equity investor who moves from a normal exposure range of 65% long/20% short to 100% long/50% short.

- Reducing, eliminating, or even shorting asset classes that are a significant part of the global market portfolio based on non-consensus return and risk forecasts—the chair of a foundation's investment committee who calls for shortening the duration of the bond portfolio from six years to six months based on insights drawn from his position in the banking industry.

- Retaining a large, concentrated legacy asset that contributes diversifiable risk—the employee who fails to diversify her holding of company stock.

Hindsight bias—the tendency to perceive past investment outcomes as having been predictable—exacerbates the illusion of control.

In the asset allocation process, an investor who believes he or she has better information than others may use estimates of return and risk that produce asset allocation choices that are materially different from the market portfolio. This can result in undiversified portfolios with outsized exposures to just one or two minor asset classes, called extreme corner portfolios. Using such biased risk and return estimates results in a biased asset allocation decision—precisely what an objective asset allocation process seeks to avoid.

The illusion of control can be mitigated by using the global market portfolio as the starting point in developing the asset allocation. Building on the basic principles of CAPM, Markowitz's mean–variance theory, and efficient market theory, the global market portfolio offers a theoretically sound benchmark for asset allocation. Deviations from this baseline portfolio must be thoughtfully considered and rigorously vetted, ensuring the asset allocation process remains objective. A formal asset allocation process that employs long-term return and risk forecasts, optimization constraints anchored around asset class weights in the global market portfolio, and strict policy ranges will significantly mitigate the illusion of control bias in asset allocation.

Mental Accounting

Mental accounting is an information-processing bias in which people treat one sum of money differently from another sum based solely on the mental account the money is assigned to. Investors may separate assets or liabilities into buckets based on subjective criteria. For example, an investor may consider his retirement investment portfolio independent of the portfolio that funds his child's education, even if the combined asset allocation of the two portfolios is sub-optimal. Or an employee with significant exposure to her employer's stock through vested stock options may fail to consider this exposure alongside other assets when establishing a strategic asset allocation.

Goals-based investing incorporates mental accounting directly into the asset allocation solution. Each goal is aligned with a discrete sub-portfolio, and the investor can specify the acceptable level of risk for each goal. Provided each of the sub-portfolios lies along the same efficient frontier, the sum of the sub-portfolios will also be efficient.[23]

Concentrated stock positions also give rise to another common mental accounting issue that affects asset allocation. For example, the primary source of an entrepreneur's wealth may be a concentrated equity position in the publicly traded company he founded. The entrepreneur may prefer to retain a relatively large exposure to this one security within his broader investment portfolio despite the inherent risk. Although there may be rational reasons for this preference—including ownership control, an information advantage, and tax considerations—the desire to retain this riskier exposure is more often the result of a psychological loyalty to the asset that generated his wealth. This mental accounting bias is further reinforced by the endowment effect—the tendency to ascribe more value to an asset already owned rather than another asset one might purchase to replace it.

The concentrated stock/mental accounting bias can be accommodated in goals-based asset allocation by assigning the concentrated stock position to an aspirational goal—one that the client would *like* to achieve but to which he or she is willing to assign a lower probability of success. Whereas lifetime consumption tends to be a high-priority goal requiring a well-diversified portfolio to fund it with confidence, an aspirational

---

23 This condition holds when the asset allocation process is unconstrained. With a long-only constraint, some efficiency is lost but the effect is much less significant than the loss of efficiency from inaccurately specifying risk aversion (which goals-based approaches to asset allocation attempt to mitigate). See Das, Markowitz, Scheid, and Statman (2010) and Das et al. (2011).

goal such as a charitable gift may be an important but much less highly valued goal. It can reasonably be funded with the concentrated stock position. (This could have the additional benefit of avoiding capital gains tax altogether!)

Representativeness Bias

Representativeness, or recency, bias is the tendency to overweight the importance of the most recent observations and information relative to a longer-dated or more comprehensive set of long-term observations and information. Tactical shifts in asset allocation, those undertaken in response to recent returns or news—perhaps shifting the asset allocation toward the highest or lowest allowable ends of the policy ranges—are particularly susceptible to recency bias. Return chasing is a common manifestation of recency bias, and it results in overweighting asset classes with good recent performance.

It is believed that asset prices largely follow a random walk; past prices cannot be used to predict future returns. If this is true, then shifting the asset allocation in response to recent returns, or allowing recent returns to unduly influence the asset class assumptions used in the asset allocation process, will likely lead to sub-optimal results. *If*, however, asset class returns exhibit trending behavior, the recent past *may* contain information relevant to tactical shifts in asset allocation. And if asset class returns are mean-reverting, comparing current valuations to historical norms may signal the potential for a reversal or for above-average future returns.

Recency bias is not uniformly negative. Random walk, trending, and mean-reversion may be simultaneously relevant to the investment decision-making process, although their effect on asset prices will unfold over different time horizons. The strongest defenses against recency bias are an objective asset allocation process and a strong governance framework. It is important that the investor objectively evaluate the motivation underlying the response to recent market events. A formal asset allocation policy with pre-specified allowable ranges will constrain recency bias. A strong governance framework with the appropriate level of expertise and well-documented investment beliefs increases the likelihood that shifts in asset allocation are made objectively and in accordance with those beliefs.

Framing Bias

Framing bias is an information-processing bias in which a person may answer a question differently based solely on the way in which it is asked. One example of framing bias is common in committee-oriented decision-making processes. In instances where one individual frequently speaks first and speaks with great authority, the views of other committee members may be suppressed or biased toward this first position put on the table.

A more nuanced form of framing bias can be found in asset allocation. The investor's choice of an asset allocation may be influenced merely by the manner in which the risk-to-return trade-off is presented.

Risk can mean different things to different investors: volatility, tail risk, the permanent loss of capital, or a failure to meet financial goals. These definitions are all closely related, but the relative importance of each of these aspects can influence the investor's asset allocation choice. Further, the investor's perception of each of these risks can be influenced by the manner in which they are presented—gain and loss potential framed in money terms versus percentages, for example.

Investors are often asked to evaluate portfolio choices using expected return, with standard deviation as the sole measure of risk. Standard deviation measures the dispersion or volatility around the mean (expected) return. Other measures of risk may also be used. Value at risk (VaR) is a loss threshold: "If I choose this asset mix, I can be pretty sure that my losses will not exceed X, most of the time." More formally, VaR is the minimum loss that would be expected a certain percentage of the time over a certain period of time given the assumed market conditions. Conditional value at risk (CVaR) is the probability-weighted average of losses when the VaR threshold is breached. VaR and CVaR both measure downside or tail risk.

Exhibit 16 shows the expected return and risk for five portfolios that span an efficient frontier from P1 (lowest risk) to P100 (highest risk). A normal distribution of returns is assumed; therefore, the portfolio's VaR and CVaR are a direct function of the portfolio's expected return and standard deviation. In this case, standard deviation, VaR, and CVaR measure precisely the same risk but frame that risk differently. Standard deviation presents that risk as volatility, while VaR and CVaR present it as risk of loss. When dealing with a normal distribution, as this example presumes, the 5% VaR threshold is simply the point on the distribution 1.65 standard deviations below the expected mean return.

Exhibit 16: There's More Than One Way to Frame Risk

	P1	P25	P50	P75	P100
Return	3.2%	4.9%	6.0%	7.0%	8.0%
Std. Dev.	3.9%	7.8%	11.9%	15.9%	20.0%
VaR (5%)	−3.2%	−8.0%	−13.6%	−19.3%	−25.0%
CVaR (5%)	−4.8%	−11.2%	−18.5%	−25.8%	−33.2%

When viewing return and volatility alone, many investors may gravitate to P50 with its 6.0% expected return and 11.9% standard deviation. P50 represents the median risk portfolio that appeals to many investors in practice because it balances high-risk and low-risk choices with related diversification benefits. However, loss-aversion bias suggests that some investors who gravitate to the median choice might actually find the −18.5% CVaR of P50 indicative of a level of risk they find very uncomfortable. The CVaR frame intuitively communicates a different perspective of exactly the same risk that is already fully explained by standard deviation—namely, the downside or tail-risk aspects of the standard deviation and mean. With this example, you can see that how risk is framed and presented can affect the asset allocation decision.

The framing effect can be mitigated by presenting the possible asset allocation choices with multiple perspectives on the risk/reward trade-off. The most commonly used risk measure—standard deviation—can be supplemented with additional measures, such as **shortfall probability** (the probability of failing to meet a specific liability or goal)[24] and tail-risk measures (e.g., VaR and CVaR). Historical stress tests and Monte Carlo simulations can also be used to capture and communicate risk in a tangible way. These multiple perspectives of the risk and reward trade-offs among a set of asset allocation choices compel the investor to consider more carefully what outcomes are acceptable or unacceptable.

---

24 Shortfall risk and shortfall probability are often used to refer to the same concept. This author prefers shortfall probability because the measure refers to the probability of shortfall, not the magnitude of the potential shortfall. For example, you may have a low probability of shortfall but the size of the shortfall could be significant. In this case, it could be misleading to say the shortfall risk is low.

Availability Bias

Availability bias is an information-processing bias in which people take a mental shortcut when estimating the probability of an outcome based on how easily the outcome comes to mind. Easily recalled outcomes are often perceived as being more likely than those that are harder to recall or understand. For example, more recent events or events in which the investor has personally been affected are likely to be assigned a higher probability of occurring again, regardless of the objective odds of the event actually occurring. Availability bias in this context is termed the recency effect and is a subset of recency, or representativeness, bias.

As an example, many private equity investors experienced a liquidity squeeze during the financial crisis that began in 2008. Their equity portfolios had suffered large losses, and their private equity investments were illiquid. Worse yet, they were contractually committed to additional capital contributions to those private equity funds. At the same time, their financial obligations continued at the same or an even higher pace. Investors who personally experienced this confluence of negative events are likely to express a strong preference for liquid investments, assigning a higher probability to such an event occurring again than would an investor who had cash available to acquire the private equity interests that were sold at distressed prices.

Familiarity bias stems from availability bias: People tend to favor the familiar over the new or different because of the ease of recalling the familiar. In asset allocation, familiarity bias most commonly results in a **home bias**—a preference for securities listed on the exchanges of one's home country. However, concentrating portfolio exposure in home country securities, particularly if the home country capital markets are small, results in a less diversified, less efficient portfolio. Familiarity bias can be mitigated by using the global market portfolio as the starting point in developing the asset allocation, where deviations from this baseline portfolio must be thoughtfully considered and rigorously vetted.

Familiarity bias may also cause investors to fall into the trap of comparing their investment decisions (and performance) to others', without regard for the appropriateness of those decisions for their own specific facts and circumstances. By avoiding comparison of investment returns or asset allocation decisions with others, an organization is more capable of identifying the asset allocation that is best tailored to their needs.

Investment decision making is subject to a wide range of potential behavioral biases. This is true in both private wealth *and* institutional investing. Employing a formal asset allocation process using the global market portfolio as the starting point for asset allocation modeling is a key component of ensuring the asset allocation decision is as objective as possible.

A strong governance structure, such as that discussed in the overview reading on asset allocation, is a necessary first step to mitigating the effect that these behavioral biases may have on the long-term success of the investment program. Bringing a diverse set of views to the deliberation process brings more tools to the table to solve any problem and leads to better and more informed decision making. A clearly stated mission—a common goal—and a commitment from committee members and other stakeholders to that mission are critically important in constraining the influence of these biases on investment decisions.

EFFECTIVE INVESTMENT GOVERNANCE

Six critical elements of effective investment governance are

1. clearly articulated long- and short-term investment objectives of the investment program;

2. allocation of decision rights and responsibilities among the functional units in the governance hierarchy, taking account of their knowledge, capacity, time, and position in the governance hierarchy;

3. established processes for developing and approving the investment policy statement that will govern the day-to-day operation of the investment program;

4. specified processes for developing and approving the program's strategic asset allocation;

5. a reporting framework to monitor the program's progress toward the agreed-upon goals and objectives; and

6. periodic governance audits.

EXAMPLE 8

Mitigating Behavioral Biases in Asset Allocation

Ivy Lee, the retired founder of a publicly traded company, has two primary goals for her investment assets. The first goal is to fund lifetime consumption expenditures of US$1 million per year for herself and her husband; this is a goal the Lees want to achieve with a high degree of certainty. The second goal is to provide an end-of-life gift to Auldberg University. Ivy has a diversified portfolio of stocks and bonds totaling US$5 million and a sizable position in the stock of the company she founded. The following table summarizes the facts.

Investor Profile	
Annual consumption needs	US$1,000,000
Remaining years of life expectancy	40
Diversified stock holdings	US$3,000,000
Diversified bond holdings	US$2,000,000
Concentrated stock holdings	US$15,000,000
Total portfolio	US$20,000,000

Assume that a 60% equity/40% fixed-income portfolio represents the level of risk Ivy is willing to assume with respect to her consumption goal. This 60/40 portfolio offers an expected return of 6.0%. (For simplicity, this illustration ignores inflation and taxes.)

The present value of the expected consumption expenditures is US$15,949,075. This is the amount needed on hand today, which, if invested in a portfolio of 60% equities and 40% fixed income, would fully fund 40 annual cash distributions of US$1,000,000 each.[25]

The concentrated stock has a highly uncertain expected return and comes with significant idiosyncratic (stock-specific) risk. A preliminary mean–variance optimization using three "asset classes"—stocks, bonds, and the concentrated stock—results in a zero allocation to the concentrated stock position. But Ivy prefers to retain as much concentrated stock as possible because it represents her legacy and she has a strong psychological loyalty to it.

---

25 Assumes cash distributions occur at the beginning of the year and the expected return is the geometric average.

1. Describe the behavioral biases most relevant to developing an asset allocation recommendation for Ivy.

Solution:

Two behavioral biases that the adviser must be aware of in developing an asset allocation recommendation for Ivy are illusion of control and mental accounting. Because Ivy was the founder of the company whose stock comprises 75% of her investment portfolio, she may believe she has more or better information about the return prospects for this portion of the portfolio. The belief that she has superior information may lead to a risk assessment that is not reflective of the true risk in the holding. Using a goals-based approach to asset allocation may help Ivy more fully understand the risks inherent in the concentrated stock position. The riskier, concentrated stock position can be assigned to a lower-priority goal, such as the gift to Auldberg University.

2. Recommend and justify an asset allocation for Ivy given the facts presented above.

Solution:

	Beginning Asset Allocation	**Recommended Asset Allocation**
Diversified stocks	US$3,000,000	US$9,600,000
Diversified bonds	US$2,000,000	US$6,400,000
Funding of lifestyle goal		*US$16,000,000*
Concentrated stock	US$15,000,000	US$4,000,000
Total portfolio	US$20,000,000	US$20,000,000

It is recommended that Ivy fully fund her high-priority lifestyle consumption needs (US$15,949,075) with US$16 million in a diversified portfolio of stocks and bonds. To achieve this, US$11 million of the concentrated stock position should be sold and the proceeds added to the diversified portfolio that supports lifestyle consumption needs. The remaining US$4 million of concentrated stock can be retained to fund the aspirational goal of an end-of-life gift to Auldberg University. In this example, the adviser has employed the mental accounting bias to achieve a suitable outcome: By illustrating the dollar value needed to fund the high-priority lifetime consumption needs goal, the adviser was able to clarify for Ivy the risks in retaining the concentrated stock position. The adviser might also simulate portfolio returns and the associated probability of achieving Ivy's goals using a range of scenarios for the performance of the concentrated stock position. Framing the effect this one holding may have on the likelihood of achieving her goals may help Ivy agree to reduce the position size. Consideration of certain behavioral biases like mental accounting can improve investor outcomes when they are incorporated in an objective decision-making framework.

SUMMARY

- The primary constraints on an asset allocation decision are asset size, liquidity, time horizon, and other external considerations, such as taxes and regulation.

- The size of an asset owner's portfolio may limit the asset classes accessible to the asset owner. An asset owner's portfolio may be too small—or too large—to capture the returns of certain asset classes or strategies efficiently.

- Complex asset classes and investment vehicles require sufficient governance capacity.

- Large-scale asset owners may achieve operating efficiencies, but they may find it difficult to deploy capital effectively in certain active investment strategies given liquidity conditions and trading costs.

- Smaller portfolios may also be constrained by size. They may be too small to adequately diversify across the range of asset classes and investment managers, or they may have staffing constraints that prevent them from monitoring a complex investment program.

- Investors with smaller portfolios may be constrained in their ability to access private equity, private real estate, hedge funds, and infrastructure investments because of the high required minimum investments and regulatory restrictions associated with those asset classes. Wealthy families may pool assets to meet the required minimums.

- The liquidity needs of the asset owner and the liquidity characteristics of the asset classes each influence the available opportunity set.

- Liquidity needs must also take into consideration the financial strength of the investor and resources beyond those held in the investment portfolio.

- When assessing the appropriateness of any given asset class for a given investor, it is important to evaluate potential liquidity needs in the context of an extreme market stress event.

- An investor's time horizon must be considered in any asset allocation exercise. Changes in human capital and the changing character of liabilities are two important time-related constraints of asset allocation.

- External considerations—such as regulations, tax rules, funding, and financing needs—are also likely to influence the asset allocation decision.

- Taxes alter the distribution of returns by both reducing the expected mean return and muting the dispersion of returns. Asset values and asset risk and return inputs to asset allocation should be modified to reflect the tax status of the investor. Correlation assumptions do not need to be adjusted, but taxes do affect the return and the standard deviation assumptions for each asset class.

- Periodic portfolio rebalancing to return the portfolio to its target strategic asset allocation is an integral part of sound portfolio management. Taxable investors must consider the tax implications of rebalancing.

- Rebalancing thresholds may be wider for taxable portfolios because it takes larger asset class movements to materially alter the risk profile of the taxable portfolio.

- Strategic asset location is the placement of less tax-efficient assets in accounts with more-favorable tax treatment.

- An asset owner's strategic asset allocation should be re-examined periodically, even in the absence of a change in the asset owner's circumstances.

- A special review of the asset allocation policy may be triggered by a change in goals, constraints, or beliefs.

- In some situations, a change to an asset allocation strategy may be implemented without a formal asset allocation study. Anticipating key milestones that would alter the asset owner's risk appetite, and implementing pre-established changes to the asset allocation in response, is often referred to as a "glide path."

- Tactical asset allocation (TAA) allows short-term deviations from the strategic asset allocation (SAA) targets and are expected to increase risk-adjusted return. Using either short-term views or signals, the investor actively re-weights broad asset classes, sectors, or risk-factor premiums. The sizes of these deviations from the SAA are often constrained by the Investment Policy Statement.

- The success of TAA decisions is measured against the performance of the SAA policy portfolio by comparing Sharpe ratios, evaluating the information ratio or the t-statistic of the average excess return of the TAA portfolio relative to the SAA portfolio, or plotting outcomes versus the efficient frontier.

- TAA incurs trading and tax costs. Tactical trades can also increase the concentration of risk.

- Discretionary TAA relies on a qualitative interpretation of political, economic, and financial market conditions and is predicated on a belief of persistent manager skill in predicting and timing short-term market moves.

- Systematic TAA relies on quantitative signals to capture documented return anomalies that may be inconsistent with market efficiency.

- The behavioral biases most relevant in asset allocation include loss aversion, the illusion of control, mental accounting, recency bias, framing, and availability bias.

- An effective investment program will address behavioral biases through a formal asset allocation process with its own objective framework, governance, and controls.

- In goals-based investing, loss-aversion bias can be mitigated by framing risk in terms of shortfall probability or by funding high-priority goals with low-risk assets.

- The cognitive bias, illusion of control, and hindsight bias can all be mitigated by using a formal asset allocation process that uses long-term return and risk forecasts, optimization constraints anchored around asset class weights in the global market portfolio, and strict policy ranges.

- Goals-based investing incorporates the mental accounting bias directly into the asset allocation solution by aligning each goal with a discrete sub-portfolio.

- A formal asset allocation policy with pre-specified allowable ranges may constrain recency bias.

- The framing bias effect can be mitigated by presenting the possible asset allocation choices with multiple perspectives on the risk/reward trade-off.

- Familiarity bias, a form of availability bias, most commonly results in an overweight in home country securities and may also cause investors to inappropriately compare their investment decisions (and performance) to other organizations. Familiarity bias can be mitigated by using the global market portfolio as the starting point in developing the asset allocation and by carefully evaluating any potential deviations from this baseline portfolio.

- A strong governance framework with the appropriate level of expertise and well-documented investment beliefs increases the likelihood that shifts in asset allocation are made objectively and in accordance with those beliefs. This will help to mitigate the effect that behavioral biases may have on the long-term success of the investment program.

REFERENCES

Bader, Lawrence N., Jeremy Gold. 2007. "The Case against Stock in Public Pension Funds." *Financial Analysts Journal*, vol. 63, no. 1 (January/February): 55–62. 10.2469/faj.v63.n1.4407

Bodie, Zvi, Robert C. Merton, and William F. Samuelson. 1992. "Labor Supply Flexibility and Portfolio Choice in a Life Cycle Model." *Journal of Economic Dynamics & Control*, vol. 16: 427–449. 10.1016/0165-1889(92)90044-F

Chen, Joseph, Harrison Hong, Ming Huang, and Jeffrey Kubik. 2004. "Does Fund Size Erode Mutual Fund Performance? The Role of Liquidity and Organization." *American Economic Review*, vol. 94, no. 5: 1276–1302. 10.1257/0002828043052277

Cooper, Stephen, David Bianco. 2003. "Q-Series^{TM}: Pension Fund Asset Allocation." UBS Investment Research (September).

Das, Sanjiv, Harry Markowitz, Jonathan Scheid, and Meir Statman. 2010. "Portfolio Optimization with Mental Accounts." *Journal of Financial and Quantitative Analysis*, vol. 45, no. 2: 311–334. 10.1017/S0022109010000141

Das, Sanjiv, Harry Markowitz, Jonathan Scheid, and Meir Statman. 2011. "Portfolios for Investors Who Want to Reach Their Goals While Staying on the Mean–Variance Efficient Frontier." *Journal of Wealth Management*, vol. 14, no. 2 (Fall): 25–31. 10.3905/jwm.2011.14.2.025

Dyck, Alexander, Lukasz Pomorski. 2011. "Is Bigger Better? Size and Performance in Pension Plan Management." Rotman School of Management Working Paper No. 1690724.

Horan, Stephen, Ashraf Al Zaman. 2008. "Tax-Adjusted Portfolio Optimization and Asset Location: Extensions and Synthesis." *Journal of Wealth Management*, vol. 11, no. 3: 56–73. 10.3905/JWM.2008.11.3.056

Kritzman, Mark. 2015. "What Practitioners Need to Know about Time Diversification (corrected March 2015)." *Financial Analysts Journal*, vol. 71, no. 1 (January/February): 29–34. 10.2469/faj.v71.n1.4

Mladina, Peter. 2011. "Portfolio Implications of Triple Net Returns." *Journal of Wealth Management*, vol. 13, no. 4 (Spring): 51–59. 10.3905/jwm.2011.13.4.051

Pollet, Joshua, Mungo Wilson. 2008. "How Does Size Affect Mutual Fund Behavior?" *Journal of Finance*, vol. 63, no. 6 (December): 2941–2969. 10.1111/j.1540-6261.2008.01417.x

Reichenstein, William. 2006. "After-Tax Asset Allocation." *Financial Analysts Journal*, vol. 62, no. 4 (July/August): 14–19. 10.2469/faj.v62.n4.4183

Samuelson, Paul A. 1963. "Risk and Uncertainty: A Fallacy of Large Numbers." *Scientia*, vol. 57, no. 98: 108–113.

Samuelson, Paul A. 1969. "Lifetime Portfolio Selection by Dynamic Stochastic Programming." *Review of Economics and Statistics*, vol. 51, no. 3: 239–246. 10.2307/1926559

Stein, Jeremy. 2002. "Information Production and Capital Allocation: Decentralized versus Hierarchical Firms." *Journal of Finance*, vol. 57, no. 5 (October): 1891–1921. 10.1111/0022-1082.00483

Turvey, Philip, Anup Basu, and Peter Verhoeven. 2013. "Embedded Tax Liabilities and Portfolio Choice." *Journal of Portfolio Management*, vol. 39, no. 3: 93–101. 10.3905/jpm.2013.39.3.093

PRACTICE PROBLEMS

The following information relates to questions 1-7

Elsbeth Quinn and Dean McCall are partners at Camel Asset Management (CAM). Quinn advises high-net-worth individuals, and McCall specializes in retirement plans for institutions.

Quinn meets with Neal and Karina Martin, both age 44. The Martins plan to retire at age 62. Twenty percent of the Martins' $600,000 in financial assets is held in cash and earmarked for funding their daughter Lara's university studies, which begin in one year. Lara's education and their own retirement are the Martins' highest-priority goals. Last week, the Martins learned that Lara was awarded a four-year full scholarship for university. Quinn reviews how the scholarship might affect the Martins' asset allocation strategy.

The Martins have assets in both taxable and tax-deferred accounts. For baseline retirement needs, Quinn recommends that the Martins maintain their current overall 60% equity/40% bonds (± 8% rebalancing range) strategic asset allocation. Quinn calculates that given current financial assets and expected future earnings, the Martins could reduce future retirement savings by 15% and still comfortably retire at 62. The Martins wish to allocate that 15% to a sub-portfolio with the goal of making a charitable gift to their alma mater from their estate. Although the gift is a low-priority goal, the Martins want the sub-portfolio to earn the highest return possible. Quinn promises to recommend an asset allocation strategy for the Martins' aspirational goal.

Next, Quinn discusses taxation of investments with the Martins. Their interest income is taxed at 35%, and capital gains and dividends are taxed at 20%. The Martins want to minimize taxes. Based on personal research, Neal makes the following two statements:

Statement 1   The after-tax return volatility of assets held in taxable accounts will be less than the pre-tax return volatility.

Statement 2   Assets that receive more favorable tax treatment should be held in tax-deferred accounts.

The equity portion of the Martins' portfolios produced an annualized return of 20% for the past three years. As a result, the Martins' equity allocation in both their taxable and tax-deferred portfolios has increased to 71%, with bonds falling to 29%. The Martins want to keep the strategic asset allocation risk levels the same in both types of retirement portfolios. Quinn discusses rebalancing; however, Neal is somewhat reluctant to take money out of stocks, expressing confidence that strong investment returns will continue.

Quinn's CAM associate, McCall, meets with Bruno Snead, the director of the Katt Company Pension Fund (KCPF). The strategic asset allocation for the fund is 65% stocks/35% bonds. Because of favorable returns during the past eight recession-free years, the KCPF is now overfunded. However, there are early signs of the economy weakening. Since Katt Company is in a cyclical industry, the Pension Committee is concerned about future market and economic risk and fears that the high-priority goal of maintaining a fully funded status may be adversely affected. McCall suggests to Snead that the KCPF might benefit from an updated IPS. Following a thorough review, McCall recommends a new IPS and strategic asset allocation.

The proposed IPS revisions include a plan for short-term deviations from strategic asset allocation targets. The goal is to benefit from equity market trends by automatically increasing (decreasing) the allocation to equities by 5% whenever the S&P 500 Index 50-day moving average crosses above (below) the 200-day moving average.

1. Given the change in funding of Lara's education, the Martins' strategic asset allocation would *most likely* decrease exposure to:

   A. cash.

   B. bonds.

   C. equities.

2. The *most* appropriate asset allocation for the Martins' new charitable gift sub-portfolio is:

   A. 40% equities/60% bonds.

   B. 70% equities/30% bonds.

   C. 100% equities/0% bonds.

3. Which of Neal's statements regarding the taxation of investments is correct?

   A. Statement 1 only

   B. Statement 2 only

   C. Both Statement 1 and Statement 2

4. Given the Martins' risk and tax preferences, the taxable portfolio should be rebalanced:

   A. less often than the tax-deferred portfolio.

   B. as often as the tax-deferred portfolio.

   C. more often than the tax-deferred portfolio.

5. During the rebalancing discussion, which behavioral bias does Neal exhibit?

   A. Framing bias

   B. Loss aversion

   C. Representativeness bias

6. Given McCall's IPS recommendation, the *most* appropriate new strategic asset allocation for the KCPF is:

   A. 40% stocks/60% bonds.

   B. 65% stocks/35% bonds.

   C. 75% stocks/25% bonds.

7. The proposal for short-term adjustments to the KCPF asset allocation strategy is

known as:

A. de-risking.

B. systematic tactical asset allocation.

C. discretionary tactical asset allocation.

The following information relates to questions 8-13

Rebecca Mayer is an asset management consultant for institutions and high-net-worth individuals. Mayer meets with Sebastian Capara, the newly appointed Investment Committee chairman for the Kinkardeen University Endowment (KUE), a very large tax-exempt fund.

Capara and Mayer review KUE's current and strategic asset allocations, which are presented in Exhibit 1. Capara informs Mayer that over the last few years, Kinkardeen University has financed its operations primarily from tuition, with minimal need of financial support from KUE. Enrollment at the University has been rising in recent years, and the Board of Trustees expects enrollment growth to continue for the next five years. Consequently, the board expects very modest endowment support to be needed during that time. These expectations led the Investment Committee to approve a decrease in the endowment's annual spending rate starting in the next fiscal year.

Exhibit 1: Kinkardeen University Endowment—Strategic Asset Allocation Policy

Asset Class	Current Weight	Target Allocation	Lower Policy Limit	Upper Policy Limit
Developed markets equity	30%	30%	25%	35%
Emerging markets equity	28%	30%	25%	35%
Investment-grade bonds	15%	20%	15%	25%
Private real estate equity	15%	10%	5%	15%
Infrastructure	12%	10%	5%	15%

As an additional source of alpha, Mayer proposes tactically adjusting KUE's asset-class weights to profit from short-term return opportunities. To confirm his understanding of tactical asset allocation (TAA), Capara tells Mayer the following:

Statement 1   The Sharpe ratio is suitable for measuring the success of TAA relative to SAA.

Statement 2   Discretionary TAA attempts to capture asset-class-level return anomalies that have been shown to have some predictability and persistence.

Statement 3   TAA allows a manager to deviate from the IPS asset-class upper and lower limits if the shift is expected to produce higher expected risk-adjusted returns.

Capara asks Mayer to recommend a TAA strategy based on excess return forecasts for the asset classes in KUE's portfolio, as shown in Exhibit 2.

Exhibit 2: Short-Term Excess Return Forecast

Asset Class	Expected Excess Return
Developed markets equity	2%
Emerging markets equity	5%
Investment-grade bonds	−3%
Private real estate equity	3%
Infrastructure	−1%

Following her consultation with Capara, Mayer meets with Roger Koval, a member of a wealthy family. Although Koval's baseline needs are secured by a family trust, Koval has a personal portfolio to fund his lifestyle goals.

In Koval's country, interest income is taxed at progressively higher income tax rates. Dividend income and long-term capital gains are taxed at lower tax rates relative to interest and earned income. In taxable accounts, realized capital losses can be used to offset current or future realized capital gains. Koval is in a high tax bracket, and his taxable account currently holds, in equal weights, high-yield bonds, investment-grade bonds, and domestic equities focused on long-term capital gains.

Koval asks Mayer about adding new asset classes to the taxable portfolio. Mayer suggests emerging markets equity given its positive short-term excess return forecast. However, Koval tells Mayer he is not interested in adding emerging markets equity to the account because he is convinced it is too risky. Koval justifies this belief by referring to significant losses the family trust suffered during the recent economic crisis.

Mayer also suggests using two mean–variance portfolio optimization scenarios for the taxable account to evaluate potential asset allocations. Mayer recommends running two optimizations: one on a pre-tax basis and another on an after-tax basis.

8. The change in the annual spending rate, in conjunction with the board's expectations regarding future enrollment and the need for endowment support, could justify that KUE's target weight for:

   A. infrastructure be increased.

   B. investment-grade bonds be increased.

   C. private real estate equity be decreased.

9. Which of Capara's statements regarding tactical asset allocation is correct?

   A. Statement 1

   B. Statement 2

    C. Statement 3

10. Based on Exhibits 1 and 2, to attempt to profit from the short-term excess return forecast, Capara should increase KUE's portfolio allocation to:

    A. developed markets equity and decrease its allocation to infrastructure.

    B. emerging markets equity and decrease its allocation to investment-grade bonds.

    C. developed markets equity and increase its allocation to private real estate equity.

11. Given Koval's current portfolio and the tax laws of the country in which he lives, Koval's portfolio would be more tax efficient if he reallocated his taxable account to hold more:

    A. high-yield bonds.

    B. investment-grade bonds.

    C. domestic equities focused on long-term capital gain opportunities.

12. Koval's attitude toward emerging markets equity reflects which of the following behavioral biases?

    A. Hindsight bias

    B. Availability bias

    C. Illusion of control

13. In both of Mayer's optimization scenarios, which of the following model inputs could be used without adjustment?

    A. Expected returns

    B. Correlation of returns

    C. Standard deviations of returns

The following information relates to questions 14-18

Emma Young, a 47-year-old single mother of two daughters, ages 7 and 10, recently sold a business for $5.5 million net of taxes and put the proceeds into a money market account. Her other assets include a tax-deferred retirement account worth $3.0 million, a $500,000 after-tax account designated for her daughters' education, a $400,000 after-tax account for unexpected needs, and her home, which she owns outright.

Her living expenses are fully covered by her job. Young wants to retire in 15 years and to fund her retirement from existing assets. An orphan at eight who experienced childhood financial hardships, she places a high priority on retirement security and wants to avoid losing money in any of her three accounts.

14. **Identify** the behavioral biases Young is *most likely* exhibiting. **Justify** each response.

Bias	Justification
Loss Aversion	
Illusion of Control	
Mental Accounting	
Representative Bias	
Framing Bias	
Availability Bias	

15. A broker proposes to Young three portfolios, shown in Exhibit 1. The broker also provides Young with asset class estimated returns and portfolio standard deviations in Exhibit 2 and Exhibit 3, respectively. The broker notes that there is a $500,000 minimum investment requirement for alternative assets. Finally, because the funds in the money market account are readily investible, the broker suggests using that account only for this initial investment round.

Exhibit 1: Proposed Portfolios

Asset Class	Portfolio 1	Portfolio 2	Portfolio 3
Municipal Bonds	5%	35%	30%
Small-Cap Equities	50%	10%	35%
Large-Cap Equities	35%	50%	35%
Private Equity	10%	5%	0%
Total	100%	100%	100%

Exhibit 2: Asset Class Pre-Tax Returns

Asset Class	Pre-Tax Return
Municipal Bonds	3%
Small-Cap Equities	12%
Large-Cap Equities	10%
Private Equity	25%

Exhibit 3: Portfolio Standard Deviations	
Proposed Portfolio	**Post-Tax Standard Deviation**
Portfolio 1	28.2%
Portfolio 2	16.3%
Portfolio 3	15.5%

Young wants to earn at least 6.0% after tax per year, without taking on additional incremental risk. Young's capital gains and overall tax rate is 25%.

Determine which proposed portfolio *most closely* meets Young's desired objectives. **Justify** your response.

Portfolio 1	Portfolio 2	Portfolio 3

Justify your response.

16. The broker suggests that Young rebalance her $5.5 million money market account and the $3.0 million tax-deferred retirement account periodically in order to maintain their targeted allocations. The broker proposes the same risk profile for the equity positions with two potential target equity allocations and rebalancing ranges for the two accounts as follows:

- Alternative 1: 80% equities +/− 8.0% rebalancing range
- Alternative 2: 75% equities +/− 10.7% rebalancing range

Determine which alternative *best* fits each account. **Justify** each selection.

Account	Alternative	Justify each selection.
$5.5 Million Account	Alternative 1 Alternative 2	
$3.0 Million Account	Alternative 1 Alternative 2	

17. Ten years later, Young is considering an early-retirement package offer. The package would provide continuing salary and benefits for three years. The broker recommends a special review of Young's financial plan to assess potential changes to the existing allocation strategy.

Identify the *primary* reason for the broker's reassessment of Young's circumstances. **Justify** your response.

Change in goals	Change in constraints	Change in beliefs

Justify your response.

18. Young decides to accept the retirement offer. Having very low liquidity needs, she wants to save part of the retirement payout for unforeseen costs that might occur

more than a decade in the future. The broker's view on long term stock market prospects is positive and recommends additional equity investment.

Determine which of Young's accounts (education, retirement, reallocated money market, or unexpected needs) is *best* suited for implementing the broker's recommendation.

Account	Justification
Education	
Reallocated Money Market	
Retirement	
Unexpected Needs	

The following information relates to questions 19-20

Mark DuBord, a financial adviser, works with two university foundations, the Titan State Foundation (Titan) and the Fordhart University Foundation (Fordhart). He meets with each university foundation investment committee annually to review fund objectives and constraints.

Titan's portfolio has a market value of $10 million. After his annual meeting with its investment committee, DuBord notes the following points:

- Titan must spend 3% of its beginning-of-the-year asset value annually to meet legal obligations.
- The investment committee seeks exposure to private equity investments and requests DuBord's review of the Sun-Fin Private Equity Fund as a potential new investment.
- A recent declining trend in enrollment is expected to continue. This is a concern because it has led to a loss of operating revenue from tuition.
- Regulatory sanctions and penalties are likely to result in lower donations over the next five years.

DuBord supervises two junior analysts and instructs one to formulate new allocations for Titan. This analyst proposes the allocation presented in Exhibit 1.

Exhibit 1: Fund Information for Titan

Fund Name	Existing Allocation	Proposed Allocation	Fund Size in Billions (AUM)	Fund Minimum Investment
Global Equity Fund	70%	70%	$25	$500,000
Investment-Grade Bond Fund	27%	17%	$50	$250,000
Sun-Fin Private Equity Fund	0%	10%	$0.40	$1,000,000
Cash Equivalent Fund	3%	3%	$50	$100,000

19. **Discuss** *two* reasons why the proposed asset allocation is inappropriate for Titan.

20. The Fordhart portfolio has a market value of $2 billion. After his annual meeting with its investment committee, DuBord notes the following points:

   - Fordhart must spend 3% of its beginning-of-the-year asset value annually to meet legal obligations.

   - The investment committee seeks exposure to private equity investments and requests that DuBord review the CFQ Private Equity Fund as a potential new investment.

   - Enrollment is strong and growing, leading to increased operating revenues from tuition.

   - A recent legal settlement eliminated an annual obligation of $50 million from the portfolio to support a biodigester used in the university's Center for Renewable Energy.

   DuBord instructs his second junior analyst to formulate new allocations for Fordhart. This analyst proposes the allocation presented in Exhibit 2.

Exhibit 2: Fund Information for Fordhart

Fund Name	Existing Allocation	Proposed Allocation	Fund Size in Billions (AUM)	Fund Minimum Investment
Large-Cap Equity Fund	49%	29%	$50	$250,000
Investment-Grade Bond Fund	49%	59%	$80	$500,000
CFQ Private Equity Fund	0%	10%	$0.5	$5,000,000
Cash Equivalent Fund	2%	2%	$50	$250,000

   Discuss *two* reasons why the proposed asset allocation is inappropriate for Fordhart.

SOLUTIONS

1. A is correct. The changing character of liabilities through time affects the asset allocation to fund those liabilities. The Martins' investment horizon for some of their assets has changed. The amount of liquidity needed for Lara's near-term education has been greatly reduced owing to the receipt of the scholarship. The Martins will likely still have to pay for some university-related expenses; however, a large part of the $120,000 in cash that is earmarked for Lara's expenses can now be allocated to the Martins' long-term goal of early retirement. Retirement is 18 years away, much longer than the one- to five-year horizon for university expenses. Therefore, the Martins' allocation to cash would likely decrease.

2. C is correct. The Martins' sub-portfolio is aspirational and a low priority. Investors are usually willing to take more risk on lower-priority, aspirational portfolios. The charitable gift will be made from their estate, which indicates a long time horizon. In addition, the Martins want the highest return possible. Therefore, the highest allocation to equities is most appropriate.

3. A is correct. Taxes alter the distribution of returns by both reducing the expected mean return and muting the dispersion of returns. The portion of an owner's taxable assets that are eligible for lower tax rates and deferred capital gains tax treatment should first be allocated to the investor's taxable accounts.

4. A is correct. The Martins wish to maintain the same risk level for both retirement accounts based on their strategic asset allocation. However, more frequent rebalancing exposes the taxable asset owner to realized taxes that could have otherwise been deferred or even avoided. Rebalancing is discretionary, and the Martins' also wish to minimize taxes. Because after-tax return volatility is lower than pre-tax return volatility, it takes larger asset-class movements to materially alter the risk profile of a taxable portfolio. This suggests that rebalancing ranges for a taxable portfolio can be wider than those of a tax-exempt/tax-deferred portfolio with a similar risk profile; thus, rebalancing occurs less frequently.

5. C is correct. Representativeness, or recency, bias is the tendency to overweight the importance of the most recent observations and information relative to a longer-dated or more comprehensive set of long-term observations and information. Return chasing is a common result of this bias, and it results in overweighting asset classes with strong recent performance.

6. A is correct. McCall recommends a new IPS. Changes in the economic environment and capital market expectations or changes in the beliefs of committee members are factors that may lead to an altering of the principles that guide investment activities. Because the plan is now overfunded, there is less need to take a higher level of equity risk. The Pension Committee is concerned about the impact of future market and economic risks on the funding status of the plan. Katt Company operates in a cyclical industry and could have difficulty making pension contributions during a recession. Therefore, a substantial reduction in the allocation to stocks and an increase in bonds reduce risk. The 40% stocks/60% bonds alternative increases the allocation to bonds from 35% to 60%. Increasing the fixed-income allocation should moderate plan risk, provide a better hedge for liabilities, and reduce contribution uncertainty.

7. B is correct. Using rules-based, quantitative signals, systematic tactical asset allocation (TAA) attempts to capture asset-class-level return anomalies that have been shown to have some predictability and persistence. Trend signals are widely

used in systematic TAA. A moving-average crossover is a trend signal that indicates an upward (downward) trend when the moving average of the shorter time frame, 50 days, is above (below) the moving average of the longer time frame, 200 days.

8. A is correct. A lower annual spending rate, in addition to the board's expectations of rising enrollment and minimal need for endowment support over the next five years, indicates a decreased need for liquidity. Therefore, KUE could justify an increase in the strategic allocation to less liquid asset classes (such as private real estate equity and infrastructure) and a decrease in the strategic allocation to liquid assets (such as investment-grade bonds).

9. A is correct. The Sharpe ratio is suitable for measuring the success of TAA relative to SAA. Specifically, the success of TAA decisions can be evaluated by comparing the Sharpe ratio realized under the TAA with the Sharpe ratio that would have been realized under the SAA.

10. A is correct. The forecast for expected excess returns is positive for developed markets equity and negative for infrastructure. Therefore, to attempt to profit from the short-term excess return forecast, KUE can overweight developed markets equity and underweight infrastructure. These adjustments to the asset-class weights are within KUE's lower and upper policy limits.

11. C is correct. As a general rule, the portion of a taxable asset owner's assets that are eligible for lower tax rates and deferred capital gains tax treatment should first be allocated to the investor's taxable accounts. Assets that generate returns mainly from interest income tend to be less tax efficient and in Koval's country are taxed at progressively higher rates. Also, the standard deviation (volatility) of after-tax returns is lower when equities are held in a taxable account. Therefore, Koval's taxable account would become more tax efficient if it held more domestic equities focused on long-term capital gain opportunities.

12. B is correct. Availability bias is an information-processing bias in which people take a mental shortcut when estimating the probability of an outcome based on how easily the outcome comes to mind. On the basis of the losses incurred by his family trust during the recent economic crisis, Koval expresses a strong preference for avoiding the emerging markets equity asset class. Such behavior is consistent with availability bias, where investors who personally experience an adverse event are likely to assign a higher probability to such an event occurring again.

13. B is correct. After-tax portfolio optimization requires adjusting each asset class's expected return and risk for expected taxes. The correlation of returns is not affected by taxes and does not require an adjustment when performing after-tax portfolio optimization.

14. Of the six potential behavioral biases, Young is most likely exhibiting three as explained below.

Identify the behavioral biases Young is *most likely* exhibiting. (Circle the correct answers.) **Justify** each response.

Bias	Justification

Loss Aversion	Under loss-aversion bias, people strongly prefer avoiding losses as opposed to achieving gains and they assign a greater weight to potential negative outcomes than positive ones. Young's strong emphasis on retirement security and her desire to avoid losing money indicates that she has a loss-aversion bias. This bias could interfere with her willingness to maintain ideal asset allocations during times of negative returns.
Illusion of Control	
Mental Accounting	Under mental accounting bias, people treat one sum of money differently from another sum based solely on the mental account to which the money is assigned. Young is considering her $3 million tax-deferred retirement account, her $500,000 account for the girls' education, and the $400,000 emergency account separately, rather than seeing them all as a combined investable total. In doing this, she sets herself up for the possibility of sub-optimal allocation.
Representative Bias	
Framing Bias	
Availability Bias	Under availability bias, people take a mental shortcut when estimating the probability of an outcome based on how easily the outcome comes to mind. Easily recalled outcomes are often perceived as being more likely than those that are harder to recall or understand. Young's strong emphasis on retirement security and her desire to avoid losing money both could be driven by her strong memories of her childhood financial hardships.

15.

Determine which proposed portfolio *most closely* meets Young's desired objectives. (Circle one.)

Portfolio 1	Portfolio 2	Portfolio 3

Justify your response.

Portfolio 3 comes closest to meeting Young's desire to earn at least 6% after tax per year without taking on additional incremental risk. Portfolio 3 offers a lower standard deviation than Portfolio 2, as summarized in Exhibit 3, while producing approximately the same return. Portfolio 1 achieves the highest returns but at a much greater level of volatility than Portfolio 3, not satisfying Young's risk criterion.

Given the $500,000 minimum investment requirement for alternative assets, at Young's total portfolio size of $5.5 million, the suggested 5% allocation to private equity in Portfolio 2 results in only a $275,000 exposure, insufficient to invest in private equity. Thus, Portfolio 2, as presented, is not viable, whereas Portfolio 1, with a private equity investment of $550,000, meets the minimum requirement for alternative investments. This minimum investment requirement is not an issue for Portfolio 3 because it has no private equity component.

Asset Class	Portfolio 3	Pre-Tax Return	Post-Tax Return	Resulting Return
Municipal Bonds	30%	3%	3.00%	0.90%
Small-Cap Equities	35%	12%	9.00%	3.15%
Large-Cap Equities	35%	10%	7.50%	2.63%

Asset Class	Portfolio 3	Pre-Tax Return	Post-Tax Return	Resulting Return
Private Equity	0%	25%	18.75%	0.00%
Total	100%			6.68%

16.

Determine which alternative (circle one) *best* fits each account.

Account	Alternative	Justify each selection.
$5.5 Million Account	Alternative 1	The $5.5 million account is after tax. Because after-tax volatility is lower than pre-tax volatility, the rebalancing range for an after-tax account is wider. The range reflected for Alternative 2 is 10.7%, whereas the range for Alternative 1 is 8.0% (to achieve the same risk constraint), reflecting the impact of taxes on the $5.5 million account.
	Alternative 2	In addition, asset sales in the after-tax account result in taxes due. A wider target range allows more price movement before the rebalancing range is exceeded (and a decision must be made to initiate an asset sale, incur associated tax payments, and rebalance back to the target equity allocation). The after-tax account range is calculated by adjusting the pre-tax range for taxes. After-tax rebalancing range = Pre-tax rebalancing range/ (1 − Tax rate). 8.0%/(1 − 0.25) 10.67%
$3.0 Million Account	Alternative 1	The $3.0 million is a tax-deferred retirement account. Because pre-tax volatility is higher than after-tax volatility, the rebalancing range for a pre-tax account is narrower. The range reflected for Alternative 1 is 8.0%, whereas the range for Alternative 2 is 10.7% (to achieve the same risk constraint), reflecting the impact of tax deferral on the $3.0 million account versus the effect of taxes on the $5.5 million account.
	Alternative 2	

17.

Identify the *primary* reason for the broker's reassessment of Young's circumstances. (Circle one.)

Change in goals	Change in constraints	Change in beliefs

| | **Justify** your response. |

A change in constraints relates to material changes in constraints, such as time horizon, liquidity needs, asset size, and regulatory or other external constraints. In this case, Young's circumstances have changed; she is considering accepting the offer and retiring five years sooner than she originally anticipated.
A change in an investor's personal circumstances that may alter her risk appetite or risk capacity is considered to be a change in *goals*. In this circumstance, Young's risk appetite or risk capacity have not changed, whereas the time horizon associated with her goals has.
A change in the investment beliefs or principles guiding an investor's investment activities is considered to be a change in *beliefs*. In this circumstance, Young's guiding principles have not changed.

Young decides to accept the retirement offer. Having very low liquidity needs, she wants to save part of the retirement payout for unforeseen costs that might occur more than a decade in the future. The broker's view on long-term stock market prospects is positive and recommends additional equity investment.

18.

Determine which of Young's accounts is *best* suited for implementing the broker's recommendation. (Circle one.)

Account	Justification
Education	
Reallocated Money Market	As a general rule, the portion of a taxable asset owner's assets that is eligible for lower tax rates and deferred capital gains tax treatment should first be allocated to the investor's taxable accounts. Equities should generally be held in taxable accounts, whereas taxable bonds and high turnover trading strategies should generally be located in tax-exempt and tax-deferred accounts. The reallocated money market account is a taxable account, whereas the retirement account is tax-deferred. The unexpected needs account requires liquidity (in case of unexpected needs), so it is better suited for shorter-term positions. Given the ages of Young's two daughters, now 17 and 20, the education account is most likely currently funding college expenses and will be for the next several years. Accordingly, it needs to be invested in highly liquid assets to cover these costs.
Retirement	
Unexpected Needs	

19. The proposed asset allocation for Titan is not appropriate because:

1. Given the shift in enrollment trends and declining donations resulting from the sanctions, Titan will likely need greater liquidity in the future because of the increased probability of higher outflows to support university operations. The proposed asset allocation shifts Titan's allocation into risky assets (increases the relative equity holdings and decreases the relative bond holdings), which would introduce greater uncertainty as to their future value.

2. Titan is relatively small for the proposed addition of private equity. Access to such an asset class as private equity may be constrained for smaller asset owners, such as Titan, who may lack the related internal investment expertise. Additionally, the Sun-Fin Private Equity Fund minimum investment level is $1 million. This level of investment in private equity would be 10% of

Titan's total portfolio value. Given Titan's declining financial position due to declining enrollments and its resulting potential need for liquidity, private equity at this minimum level of investment is not appropriate for Titan.

20. The proposed asset allocation for Fordhart is inappropriate because:

1. Given the increasing enrollment trends and recent favorable legal settlement, Fordhart will likely require lower liquidity in the future. The proposed allocation shifts Fordhart's portfolio away from risky assets (decreases the relative equity holdings and increases the relative bond holdings).

2. The proposed 10% allocation to private equity creates an overly concentrated position in the underlying investment. A 10% allocation to the CFQ Private Equity Fund is $200 million (10% of Fordhart's $2 billion). The CFQ Private Equity Fund has assets under management (AUM) of $500 million. Hence, Fordhart would own 40% of the entire CFQ Private Equity Fund. This position exposes both Fordhart and the CFQ fund to an undesirable level of operational risk.

Level III Core Glossary

Absolute return benchmark   A minimum target return that an investment manager is expected to beat.

Accrual taxes   Taxes levied and paid on a periodic basis.

Accumulation phase   Phase where the government predominantly contributes to a sovereign wealth pension reserve fund.

Active management   A portfolio management approach that allows risk factor mismatches relative to a benchmark index causing potentially significant return differences between the active portfolio and the underlying benchmark.

Active return   The return on a portfolio minus the return on the portfolio's benchmark.

Active risk   The standard deviation of active returns.

Active risk budgeting   Risk budgeting that concerns active risk (risk relative to a portfolio's benchmark).

Active share   A measure of how similar a portfolio is to its benchmark. A manager who precisely replicates the benchmark will have an active share of zero; a manager with no holdings in common with the benchmark will have an active share of one.

Aggregate wealth   The total value of all assets owned, encompassing personal property, financial assets, real assets, and rights.

Arithmetic attribution   An attribution approach which explains the arithmetic difference between the portfolio return and its benchmark return. The single-period attribution effects sum to the excess return, however, when combining multiple periods, the sub-period attribution effects will not sum to the excess return.

Ask price   The price at which a trader will sell a specified quantity of a security. Also called *ask, offer price,* or *offer.*

Asset-only   With respect to asset allocation, an approach that focuses directly on the characteristics of the assets without explicitly modeling the liabilities.

Authority bias   A behavioral bias which involves groups deferring to a group member that is a subject matter expert or in a position of authority.

Aversion to complexity   A behavioral phenomenon of groups in many professional contexts, in which disproportionate attention is given to trivial issues at the expense of important but harder-to-grasp or contested topics.

Back-fill bias   The distortion in index or peer group data which results when returns are reported to a database only after they are known to be good returns.

Base   With respect to a foreign exchange quotation of the price of one unit of a currency, the currency referred to in "one unit of a currency."

Basis risk   The possibility that the expected value of a derivative differs unexpectedly from that of the underlying.

Bear spread   An option strategy that becomes more valuable when the price of the underlying asset declines, so requires buying one option and writing another with a *lower* exercise price. A put bear spread involves buying a put with a higher exercise price and selling a put with a lower exercise price. A bear spread can also be executed with calls.

Best ask   The offer to sell with the lowest ask price. Also called *best offer* or *inside ask.*

Best bid   The highest bid in the market.

Best offer   The lowest offer (ask price) in the market.

Best-in-class   An ESG implementation approach that seeks to identify the most favorable companies in an industry based on ESG considerations.

Bid price   In a price quotation, the price at which the party making the quotation is willing to buy a specified quantity of an asset or security.

Bid–ask spread   The ask price minus the bid price.

Buffering   Establishing ranges around breakpoints that define whether a stock belongs in one index or another.

Bull spread   An option strategy that becomes more valuable when the price of the underlying asset rises, so requires buying one option and writing another with a *higher* exercise price. A call bull spread involves buying a call with a lower exercise price and selling a call with a higher exercise price. A bull spread can also be executed with puts.

Business cycle   Fluctuations in GDP in relation to long-term trend growth, usually lasting 9-11 years.

Calendar rebalancing   Rebalancing a portfolio to target weights on a periodic basis; for example, monthly, quarterly, semi-annually, or annually.

Calendar spread   A strategy in which one sells an option and buys the same type of option but with different expiration dates, on the same underlying asset and with the same strike. When the investor buys the more distant (near-term) call and sells the near-term (more distant) call, it is a long (short) calendar spread.

Canada model   Characterized by a high allocation to alternatives. Unlike the endowment model, however, the Canada model relies more on internally managed assets. The innovative features of the Canada model are the: a) reference portfolio, b) total portfolio approach, and c) active management.

Capital market expectations (CME)   Expectations concerning the risk and return prospects of asset classes.

Capital sufficiency analysis   The process of evaluating whether a client has sufficient capital resources to achieve their financial goals and objectives; it considers the client's assets, liabilities, income, expenses, risk tolerance, time horizon, and other relevant factors.

Capture ratio   A measure of the manager's gain or loss relative to the gain or loss of the benchmark.

Carhart model   A four factor model used in performance attribution. The four factors are: market (RMRF), size (SMB), value (HML), and momentum (WML).

Carry trade   A trading strategy that involves buying a security and financing it at a rate that is lower than the yield on that security.

Cash flow matching   Immunization approach that attempts to ensure that all future liability payouts are matched precisely by cash flows from bonds or fixed-income derivatives.

Cash-secured put   An option strategy involving the writing of a put option and simultaneously depositing an amount of money equal to the exercise price into a designated account (this strategy is also called a fiduciary put).

Collar   An option position in which the investor is long shares of stock and then buys a put with an exercise price below the current stock price and writes a call with an exercise price above the current stock price. Collars allow a shareholder to acquire downside protection through a protective put but reduce the cash outlay by writing a covered call.

Contingent immunization   Hybrid approach that combines immunization with an active management approach when the asset portfolio's value exceeds the present value of the liability portfolio.

Cost basis   The initial cost of acquiring an investment including expenses incurred to acquire the investment. Also referred to as simply basis.

Covered call   An option strategy in which a long position in an asset is combined with a short position in a call on that asset.

Cross hedge   A hedge involving a hedging instrument that is imperfectly correlated with the asset being hedged; an example is hedging a bond investment with futures on a non-identical bond.

Cross-currency basis swap   A swap in which notional principals are exchanged because the goal of the transaction is to issue at a more favorable funding rate and swap the amount back to the currency of choice.

Cross-sectional consistency   A feature of expectations setting which means that estimates for all classes reflect the same underlying assumptions and are generated with methodologies that reflect or preserve important relationships among the asset classes, such as strong correlations. It is the internal consistency across asset classes.

Currency overlay programs   A currency overlay program is a program to manage a portfolio's currency exposures for the case in which those exposures are managed separately from the management of the portfolio itself.

Custom security-based benchmark   Benchmark that is custom built to accurately reflect the investment discipline of a particular investment manager. Also called a *strategy benchmark* because it reflects a manager's particular strategy.

Decision-reversal risk   The risk of reversing a chosen course of action at the point of maximum loss.

Decumulation phase   Phase where the government predominantly withdraws from a sovereign wealth pension reserve fund.

Deferred taxes   Taxes postponed until some future date.

Defined benefit   A retirement plan in which a plan sponsor commits to paying a specified retirement benefit.

Defined benefit plan   Retirement plan that is funded by the employer that guarantees a retirement benefit based on factors such as years of service, salary, and age.

Defined contribution   A retirement plan in which contributions are defined but the ultimate retirement benefit is not specified or guaranteed by the plan sponsor.

Defined contribution plan   Retirement plan in which the employer, employee, or both contribute to an account in which the employee bears the investment risk.

Delay costs   Implicit trading costs that arise from the inability to complete desired trades immediately. Also called *slippage*.

Delta   The relationship between the option price and the underlying price, which reflects the sensitivity of the price of the option to changes in the price of the underlying. Delta is a good approximation of how an option price will change for a small change in the stock.

Delta hedging   Hedging that involves matching the price response of the position being hedged over a narrow range of prices.

Demand deposits   Accounts that can be drawn upon regularly and without notice. This category includes checking accounts and certain savings accounts that are often accessible through online banks or automated teller machines (ATMs).

Diffusion index   Reflects the proportion of the index's components that are moving in a pattern consistent with the overall index.

Dividend capture   A trading strategy whereby an equity portfolio manager purchases stocks just before their ex-dividend dates, holds these stocks through the ex-dividend date to earn the right to receive the dividend, and subsequently sells the shares.

Domestic asset   An asset that trades in the investor's domestic currency (or home currency).

Domestic currency   The currency of the investor, i.e., the currency in which he or she typically makes consumption purchases, e.g., the Swiss franc for an investor domiciled in Switzerland.

Domestic-currency return   A rate of return stated in domestic currency terms from the perspective of the investor; reflects both the foreign-currency return on an asset as well as percentage movement in the spot exchange rate between the domestic and foreign currencies.

Drawdown   A percentage peak-to-trough reduction in net asset value.

Drawdown duration   The total time from the start of the drawdown until the cumulative drawdown recovers to zero.

Due diligence   Investigation and analysis in support of a recommendation; the failure to exercise due diligence may sometimes result in liability according to various securities laws.

Duration matching   Immunization approach based on the duration of assets and liabilities. Ideally, the liabilities being matched (the liability portfolio) and the portfolio of assets (the bond portfolio) should be affected similarly by a change in interest rates.

Duration times spread   Weighting of spread duration by credit spread in order to incorporate the empirical observation that spread changes for lower-rated bonds tend to be consistent on a percentage, rather than absolute, basis.

Dynamic asset allocation   Dynamic asset allocation is an investment strategy premised on long-term asset allocation but employing short-term, tactical trading to maintain investment allocation targets.

Dynamic hedge   A hedge requiring adjustment as the price of the hedged asset changes.

Econometrics   The application of quantitative modeling and analysis grounded in economic theory to the analysis of economic data.

Economic balance sheet   An extended balance sheet that includes the present values of both lifetime earnings and future consumption.

Economic indicators   Economic statistics provided by government and established private organizations that contain information on an economy's recent past activity or its current or future position in the business cycle.

Effective federal funds (FFE) rate The fed funds rate actually transacted between depository institutions, not the Fed's target federal funds rate.

Effective spread Two times the difference between the execution price and the midpoint of the market quote at the time an order is entered.

Endowment model Characterized by a high allocation to alternative investments (private investments and hedge funds), significant active management, and externally managed assets.

Enhanced indexing approach Maintains a close link to the benchmark but attempts to generate a modest amount of outperformance relative to the benchmark.

Excess return Used in various senses appropriate to context: 1) The difference between the portfolio return and the benchmark return, which may be either positive or negative; 2) The return in excess of the risk-free rate, thus representing the return for bearing risk.

Exhaustive Covering or containing all possible outcomes.

Extended portfolio assets and liabilities Assets and liabilities beyond those shown on a conventional balance sheet that are relevant in making asset allocation decisions; an example of an extended asset is human capital.

Factor-model-based benchmarks Benchmarks constructed by examining a portfolio's sensitivity to a set of factors, such as the return for a broad market index, company earnings growth, industry, or financial leverage.

Family offices Private firms that offer a range of wealth management services tailored specifically for ultra-high-net-worth individuals.

Foreign assets Assets denominated in currencies other than the investor's home currency.

Foreign currency Currency that is not the currency in which an investor makes consumption purchases, e.g., the US dollar from the perspective of a Swiss investor.

Foreign-currency return The return of the foreign asset measured in foreign-currency terms.

Forward rate bias An empirically observed divergence from interest rate parity conditions that active investors seek to benefit from by borrowing in a lower-yield currency and investing in a higher-yield currency.

Funding currencies The low-yield currencies in which borrowing occurs in a carry trade.

Gamma A numerical measure of how sensitive an option's delta (the sensitivity of the derivative's price) is to a change in the value of the underlying.

General account Account holding assets to fund future liabilities from traditional life insurance and fixed annuities, the products in which the insurer bears all the risks—particularly mortality risk and longevity risk.

Gini coefficient A measure of inequality of wealth, or i, that ranges from 0 (perfect equality) to 1 (perfect inequality).

Goals-based With respect to asset allocation or investing, an approach that focuses on achieving an investor's goals (for example, related to supporting lifestyle needs or aspirations) based typically on constructing sub-portfolios aligned with those goals.

Goals-based investing An investment industry term for approaches to investing for individuals and families focused on aligning investments with goals (parallel to liability-driven investing for institutional investors).

Grinold–Kroner model An expression for the expected return on a share as the sum of an expected income return, an expected nominal earnings growth return, and an expected repricing return.

Groupthink A behavioral bias that occurs when a team minimizes conflict and dissent in reaching and maintaining a consensus.

Hedge ratio The proportion of an underlying that will offset the risk associated with a derivative position.

High-net-worth individuals (HNWIs) Individuals with investable assets exceeding a certain minimum level, often as low as USD1 million, but typically more.

High-water mark A measure that reflects the fund's maximum value as of a performance fee payment date net of fees.

Holdings-based attribution A "buy and hold" attribution approach which calculates the return of portfolio and benchmark components based upon the price and foreign exchange rate changes applied to daily snapshots of portfolio holdings.

Holdings-based style analysis A bottom-up style analysis that estimates the risk exposures from the actual securities held in the portfolio at a point in time.

Home bias A preference for securities listed on the exchanges of one's home country.

Home currency See *domestic currency*.

Home-country bias The favoring of domestic over non-domestic investments relative to global market value weights.

Human capital The present value of an individual's future expected labor income.

Impact investing Refers to investments made with the specific intent of generating positive, measurable social and environmental impact alongside a financial return (which differentiates it from philanthropy).

Implementation shortfall (IS) The difference between the return for a notional or paper portfolio, where all transactions are assumed to take place at the manager's decision price, and the portfolio's actual return, which reflects realized transactions, including all fees and costs.

Implied volatility The standard deviation that causes an option pricing model to give the current option price.

Implied volatility surface A three-dimensional plot, for put and call options on the same underlying asset, of days to expiration (x-axis), option strike prices (y-axis), and implied volatilities (z-axis). It simultaneously shows the volatility skew (or smile) and the term structure of implied volatility.

Inflation-linked bonds Debt instruments that link the principal and interest to inflation.

Input uncertainty Uncertainty concerning whether the inputs are correct.

Inside ask See *best ask*.

Inside bid See *best bid*.

Inside spread The spread between the best bid price and the best ask price. Also called the *market bid-ask spread, inside bid-ask spread*, or *market spread*.

Interaction effect The impact of overweighting and underweighting individual securities within sectors that are themselves overweighted or underweighted.

Intertemporal consistency A feature of expectations setting which means that estimates for an asset class over different horizons reflect the same assumptions with respect to the potential paths of returns over time. It is the internal consistency over various time horizons.

Intrinsic value The amount gained (per unit) by an option buyer if an option is exercised at any given point in time. May be referred to as the exercise value of the option.

Investable net worth The sum of liquid assets, such as savings and investment accounts, and less short-term liabilities such as credit card debt.

Investable wealth The sum of liquid assets such as savings and investment accounts.

Investment currencies The high-yielding currencies in a carry trade.

Investment policy statement (IPS) A description of a client's unique investment objectives, risk tolerance, investment time horizon, and other applicable constraints.

Investment style A natural grouping of investment disciplines that has some predictive power in explaining the future dispersion of returns across portfolios.

Key person risk The risk that results from over-reliance on an individual or individuals whose departure would negatively affect an investment manager.

Knock-in/knock-out Features of a vanilla option that is created (or ceases to exist) when the spot exchange rate touches a pre-specified level.

Latency The elapsed time between the occurrence of an event and a subsequent action that depends on that event.

Leading economic indicators Turning points that usually precede those of the overall economy; they are believed to have value for predicting the economy's future state, usually near-term.

Liability driven investing (LDI) model In the LDI model, the primary investment objective is to generate returns sufficient to cover liabilities, with a focus on maximizing expected surplus return (excess return of assets over liabilities) and managing surplus volatility.

Liability glide path A specification of desired proportions of liability-hedging assets and return-seeking assets and the duration of the liability hedge as funded status changes and contributions are made.

Liability-based mandates Mandates managed to match or cover expected liability payments (future cash outflows) with future projected cash inflows.

Liability-driven investing An investment industry term that generally encompasses asset allocation that is focused on funding an investor's liabilities in institutional contexts.

Liability-relative With respect to asset allocation, an approach that focuses directly only on funding liabilities as an investment objective.

Limit order book The book or list of limit orders to buy and sell that pertains to a security.

Limited-life foundations A type of foundation where founders seek to maintain control of spending while they (or their immediate heirs) are still alive.

Longevity risk The risk of exhausting an individual's financial resources before passing away, thereby leaving insufficient capital for living expenses and unmet needs.

Lorenz curve A measure of the cumulative percentage of wealth owned by each percentage of the population.

Macro attribution Attribution at the sponsor level.

Manager peer group See *manager universe*.

Manager universe A broad group of managers with similar investment disciplines. Also called *manager peer group*.

Marginal tax rate The highest rate of tax applied to taxable income.

Market fragmentation Trading the same instrument in multiple venues.

Market impact The effect of the trade on transaction prices. Also called *price impact*.

Micro attribution Attribution at the portfolio manager level.

Midquote price The average, or midpoint, of the prevailing bid and ask prices.

Minimum-variance hedge ratio A mathematical approach to determining the optimal cross hedging ratio.

Mission-related investing Investing aimed at causes promoting positive societal or environmental change.

Model uncertainty Uncertainty as to whether a selected model is correct.

Negative screening An ESG investment approach that consists of excluding investments in certain sectors, companies, or practices in a fund or portfolio based on specific ESG criteria.

Net worth The difference between assets and liabilities.

Non-deliverable forwards Forward contracts that are cash settled (in the non-controlled currency of the currency pair) rather than physically settled (the controlled currency is neither delivered nor received).

Nonstationarity A characteristic of series of data whose properties, such as mean and variance, are not constant through time. When analyzing historical data it means that different parts of a data series reflect different underlying statistical properties.

Norway model Characterized by an almost exclusive reliance on public equities and fixed income (the traditional 60/40 equity/bond model falls under the Norway model), with largely passively managed assets and with very little to no allocation to alternative investments.

Offer price The price at which a counterparty is willing to sell one unit of the base currency.

Opportunity cost The value that investors forgo by choosing a particular course of action; the value of something in its best alternative use.

Optional stock dividends A type of dividend in which shareholders may elect to receive either cash or new shares.

Overbought When a market has trended too far in one direction and is vulnerable to a trend reversal, or correction.

Oversold The opposite of overbought; see *overbought*.

Packeting Splitting stock positions into multiple parts.

Parameter uncertainty Uncertainty arising because a quantitative model's parameters are estimated with error.

Participant-switching life-cycle options Automatically switch DC plan members into a more conservative asset mix as their age increases. There may be several automatic de-risking switches at different age targets.

Participant/cohort option Pools the DC plan member with a cohort that has a similar target retirement date.

Passive management A buy-and-hold approach to investing in which an investor does not make portfolio changes based upon short-term expectations of changing market or security performance.

Percent-range rebalancing An approach to rebalancing that involves setting rebalancing thresholds or trigger points, stated as a percentage of the portfolio's value, around target values.

Performance attribution The process of disaggregating a portfolio's return to determine the drivers of its performance.

Personal assets Nonbusiness, on-investment assets including personal property and real property.

Personal property Property owned by individuals that are not real property and not considered investments.

Planned goals Financial objectives that can be reasonably estimated or quantified at the onset and can be achieved within an expected time horizon.

Position delta The overall or portfolio delta. For example, the position delta of a covered call, consisting of long 100 shares and short one at-the-money call, is +50 (= +100 for the shares and -50 for the short ATM call).

Positive screening An ESG investment approach that consists of including investments in sectors or companies in a fund or portfolio typically based on ESG performance relative to industry peers.

Price improvement When trade execution prices are better than quoted prices.

Private wealth management Financial planning and investment management to help individual investors, particularly high-net-worth individuals (HNWIs) and ultra-high-net-worth individuals (UHNWIs), manage their wealth.

Protective put A strategy of purchasing an underlying asset and purchasing a put on the same asset.

Pure indexing Attempts to replicate a bond index as closely as possible, targeting zero active return and zero active risk.

Put spread A strategy used to reduce the upfront cost of buying a protective put, it involves buying a put option and writing another put option.

Re-base With reference to index construction, to change the time period used as the base of the index.

Realized volatility Historical volatility, the square root of the realized variance of returns, which is a measure of the range of past price outcomes for the underlying asset.

Rebalancing In the context of asset allocation, a discipline for adjusting the portfolio to align with the strategic asset allocation.

Rebalancing range A range of values for asset class weights defined by trigger points above and below target weights, such that if the portfolio value passes through a trigger point, rebalancing occurs. Also known as a corridor.

Rebate rate The portion of the collateral earnings rate that is repaid to the security borrower by the security lender.

Reduced form models Statistical credit models that solve for the probability of default over a specific time period, using observable company-specific and market-based variables.

Regime The governing set of relationships (between variables) that stem from technological, political, legal, and regulatory environments. Changes in such environments or policy stances can be described as changes in regime.

Relative value A concept that describes the selection of the most attractive individual securities to populate the portfolio with, using ranking and comparing.

Repo rate The interest rate on a repurchase agreement.

Repurchase agreements In repurchase agreements, or repos, a security owner agrees to sell a security for a specific cash amount while simultaneously agreeing to repurchase the security at a specified future date (typically one day later) and price.

Reserve portfolio The component of an insurer's general account that is subject to specific regulatory requirements and is intended to ensure the company's ability to meet its policy liabilities. The assets in the reserve portfolio are managed conservatively and must be highly liquid and low risk.

Resistance levels Price points on dealers' order boards where one would expect to see a clustering of offers.

Return attribution A set of techniques used to identify the sources of the excess return of a portfolio against its benchmark.

Returns-based attribution An attribution approach that uses only the total portfolio returns over a period to identify the components of the investment process that have generated the returns. The Brinson–Hood–Beebower approach is a returns-based attribution approach.

Returns-based benchmarks Benchmarks constructed by examining a portfolio's sensitivity to a set of factors, such as the returns for various style indexes (e.g., small-cap value, small-cap growth, large-cap value, and large-cap growth).

Returns-based style analysis A top-down style analysis that involves estimating the sensitivities of a portfolio to security market indexes.

Reverse repos Repurchase agreements from the standpoint of the lender.

Risk attribution The analysis of the sources of risk.

Risk aversion The dislike for risk such that compensation is required in terms of higher expected returns for assuming higher risk.

Risk budgeting The establishment of objectives for individuals, groups, or divisions of an organization that takes into account the allocation of an acceptable level of risk.

Risk capacity The ability to bear financial risk.

Risk premiums Extra returns expected by investors for bearing some specified risk.

Risk reversal A strategy used to profit from the existence of an implied volatility skew and from changes in its shape over time. A combination of long (short) calls and short (long) puts on the same underlying with the same expiration is a long (short) risk reversal.

Risk tolerance The level of risk an investor is willing and able to bear.

Seagull spread An extension of the risk reversal foreign exchange option strategy that limits downside risk.

Securities lending A form of collateralized lending that may be used to generate income for portfolios.

Selective An index construction methodology that targets only those securities with certain characteristics.

Separate accounts Accounts holding assets to fund future liabilities from variable life insurance and variable annuities, the products in which customers make investment decisions from a menu of options and themselves bear investment risk.

Sharpe ratio The ratio of mean excess return to standard deviation (excess return).

Shortfall probability The probability of failing to meet a specific liability or goal.

Shrinkage estimation Estimation that involves taking a weighted average of a historical estimate of a parameter and some other parameter estimate, where the weights reflect the analyst's relative belief in the estimates.

Special dividends Dividends paid by a company that does not pay dividends on a regular schedule, or dividends that supplement regular cash dividends with an extra payment.

Spread duration The change in bond price for a given change in yield spread. Also referred to as OAS duration when the option-adjusted spread (OAS) is the yield measure used.

Static hedge A hedge that is not sensitive to changes in the price of the asset hedged.

Stock lending Securities lending involving the transfer of equities.

Stops   Stop-loss orders involve leaving bids or offers away from the current market price to be filled if the market reaches those levels.

Straddle   An option combination in which one buys *both* puts and calls, with the same exercise price and same expiration date, on the same underlying asset. In contrast to this long straddle, if someone *writes* both options, it is a short straddle.

Strangle   A variation on a straddle in which the put and call have different exercise prices; if the put and call are held long, it is a long strangle; if they are held short, it is a short strangle.

Strategic asset allocation   A long-term strategy that establishes target allocations for various asset classes and aims to optimize the balance between risk and reward by diversifying investments.

Structural models   Models that specify functional relationships among variables based on economic theory. The functional form and parameters of these models are derived from the underlying theory. They may include unobservable parameters.

Support levels   Price points on dealers' order boards where one would expect to see a clustering of bids.

Surplus   The difference between assets and liabilities, analogous to shareholders' equity on a corporate balance sheet.

Surplus portfolio   The component of an insurer's general account that is intended to realize higher expected returns than the reserve portfolio and so can assume some liquidity risk. Surplus portfolio assets are often managed aggressively with exposure to alternative assets.

Survivorship bias   Relates to the inclusion of only current investment funds in a database. As such, the returns of funds that are no longer available in the marketplace (have been liquidated) are excluded from the database. Also see *backfill bias*.

Synthetic long forward position   The combination of a long call and a short put with identical strike price and expiration, traded at the same time on the same underlying.

Synthetic short forward position   The combination of a short call and a long put at the same strike price and maturity (traded at the same time on the same underlying).

Tactical asset allocation   A proactive strategy that adjusts asset class allocations within a portfolio based on short-term market trends, economic conditions, or valuation changes to capitalize on temporary market inefficiencies or opportunities to improve returns or manage risk more effectively.

Tax drag   The negative effect of taxes on an investment's net returns.

Taylor rule   A rule linking a central bank's target short-term interest rate to the rate of growth of the economy and inflation.

Term deposits   Interest-bearing accounts that have a specified maturity date. This category includes savings accounts and certificates of deposit (CDs). Also see *time deposits*.

Term structure of volatility   The plot of implied volatility (y-axis) against option maturity (x-axis) for options with the same strike price on the same underlying. Typically, implied volatility is not constant across different maturities – rather, it is often in contango, meaning that the implied volatilities for longer-term options are higher than for near-term ones.

Thematic investing   An ESG investment approach with a focus on assets relating to ESG factors or themes, such as clean energy, green technology, sustainable agriculture, gender diversity, and affordable housing.

Theta   The change in a derivative instrument for a given small change in calendar time, holding everything else constant. Specifically, the theta calculation assumes nothing changes except calendar time. Theta also reflects the rate at which an option's time value decays.

Threshold-based rebalancing policy   The manager rebalances the portfolio when asset class weights deviate from their target weights by a prespecified percentage regardless of timing and frequency.

Time deposits   Interest-bearing accounts that have a specified maturity date. This category includes savings accounts and certificates of deposit (CDs). Also see *term deposits*.

Time value   The difference between an option's premium and its intrinsic value.

Time-based rebalancing policy   The manager rebalances the portfolio regularly, at a certain given time interval such as quarterly, semi-annually, or annually, regardless of any difference between prevailing asset class weights and target asset class weights.

Time-series estimation   Estimators that are based on lagged values of the variable being forecast; often consist of lagged values of other selected variables.

Total factor productivity   A scale factor that reflects the portion of growth unaccounted for by explicit factor inputs (e.g., capital and labor).

Total return payer   Party responsible for paying the reference obligation cash flows and return to the receiver but that is also compensated by the receiver for any depreciation in the index or default losses incurred by the portfolio.

Total return receiver   Receives both the cash flows from the underlying index and any appreciation in the index over the period in exchange for paying the MRR plus a predetermined spread.

Tracking risk   The standard deviation of the differences between a portfolio's returns and its benchmarks returns. Also called tracking error.

Transactions-based attribution   An attribution approach that captures the impact of intra-day trades and exogenous events such as a significant class action settlement.

Trigger points   In the context of portfolio rebalancing, the endpoints of a rebalancing range (corridor).

Ultra-high-net-worth individuals (UHNWIs)   Individuals with net worth usually exceeding USD30 million or more.

Unplanned goals   Unforeseen financial needs that are difficult to quantify because either the funding need, the timing of the financial need, or both may not be estimated.

Unsmoothing   An adjustment to the reported return series if serial correlation is detected. Various approaches are available to unsmooth a return series.

Variance notional   The notional amount of a variance swap; it equals vega notional divided by two times the volatility strike price [i.e., (vega notional)/(2 × volatility strike)].

Vega   The change in a given derivative instrument for a given small change in volatility, holding everything else constant. A sensitivity measure for options that reflects the effect of volatility.

Vega notional   The trade size for a variance swap, which represents the average profit and loss of the variance swap for a 1% change in volatility from the strike.

Vesting The process of an employee becoming unconditionally entitled to, and an employer becoming obligated to pay, compensation.

Volatility clustering The tendency for large (small) swings in prices to be followed by large (small) swings of random direction.

Volatility skew The skewed plot (of implied volatility (y-axis) against strike price (x-axis) for options on the same underlying with the same expiration) that occurs when the implied volatility increases for OTM puts and decreases for OTM calls, as the strike price moves away from the current price.

Volatility smile The U-shaped plot (of implied volatility (y-axis) against strike price (x-axis) for options on the same underlying with the same expiration) that occurs when the implied volatilities priced into both OTM puts and calls trade at a premium to implied volatilities of ATM options.

Wealth The value of all the assets owned by an individual.

Wealth life cycle Stages of an individual investor's wealth in terms of human capital, financial capital, and economic net worth.

Portfolio Management Pathway Glossary

Accounting defeasement   A way of extinguishing a debt obligation by setting aside sufficient high-quality securities to repay the liability. Also called *in-substance defeasance*.

Active management   A portfolio management approach that allows risk factor mismatches relative to a benchmark index causing potentially significant return differences between the active portfolio and the underlying benchmark.

Active return   The return on a portfolio minus the return on the portfolio's benchmark.

Active risk   The standard deviation of active returns.

Active share   A measure of how similar a portfolio is to its benchmark. A manager who precisely replicates the benchmark will have an active share of zero; a manager with no holdings in common with the benchmark will have an active share of one.

Agency trade   A trade in which the broker is engaged to find the other side of the trade, acting as an agent. In doing so, the broker does not assume any risk for the trade.

Alpha decay   In a trading context, alpha decay is the erosion or deterioration in short term alpha after the investment decision has been made.

Alternative trading systems   Trading venues that function like exchanges but that do not exercise regulatory authority over their subscribers except with respect to the conduct of the subscribers' trading in their trading systems. Also called *electronic communications networks* or *multilateral trading facilities*.

Arrival price   In a trading context, the arrival price is the security price at the time the order was released to the market for execution.

Asset swap spread (ASW)   The spread over MRR on an interest rate swap for the remaining life of the bond that is equivalent to the bond's fixed coupon.

Asset swaps   Convert a bond's fixed coupon to MRR plus (or minus) a spread.

Authorized participants   (APs) A special group of institutional investors who are authorized by the ETF issuer to participate in the creation/redemption process. APs are large broker/dealers, often market makers.

Barbell   A fixed-income investment strategy combining short- and long-term bond positions.

Bear flattening   A decrease in the yield spread between long- and short-term maturities across the yield curve, which is largely driven by a rise in short-term bond yields-to-maturity.

Bear steepening   An increase in the yield spread between long- and short-term maturities across the yield curve, which is largely driven by a rise in long-term bond yields-to-maturity.

Breadth   The number of truly independent decisions made each year.

Bull flattening   A decrease in the yield spread between long- and short-term maturities across the yield curve, which is largely driven by a decline in long-term bond yields-to-maturity.

Bull steepening   An increase in the yield spread between long- and short-term maturities across the yield curve, which is largely driven by a decline in short-term bond yields-to-maturity.

Bullet   A fixed-income investment strategy that focuses on the intermediate term (or "belly") of the yield curve.

Butterfly spread   A measure of yield curve shape or curvature equal to double the intermediate yield-to-maturity less the sum of short- and long-term yields-to-maturity.

Butterfly strategy   A common yield curve shape strategy that combines a long or short bullet position with a barbell portfolio in the opposite direction to capitalize on expected yield curve shape changes.

Carry trade across currencies   A strategy seeking to benefit from a positive interest rate differential across currencies by combining a short position (or borrowing) in a low-yielding currency and a long position (or lending) in a high-yielding currency.

Cash drag   Tracking error caused by temporarily uninvested cash.

CDS curve   Plot of CDS spreads across maturities for a single reference entity or group of reference entities in an index.

Cell approach   See *stratified sampling*.

Closet indexer   A fund that advertises itself as being actively managed but is substantially similar to an index fund in its exposures.

Completion overlay   A type of overlay that addresses an indexed portfolio that has diverged from its proper exposure.

Conditional value at risk   (CVaR) Also known as expected loss The average portfolio loss over a specific time period conditional on that loss exceeding the value at risk (VaR) threshold.

Contingent immunization   Hybrid approach that combines immunization with an active management approach when the asset portfolio's value exceeds the present value of the liability portfolio.

Covered interest rate parity   The relationship among the spot exchange rate, the forward exchange rate, and the interest rates in two currencies that ensures that the return on a hedged (i.e., covered) foreign risk-free investment is the same as the return on a domestic risk-free investment. Also called *interest rate parity*.

Credit cycle   The expansion and contraction of credit over the business cycle, which translates into asset price changes based on default and recovery expectations across maturities and rating categories.

Credit default swap (CDS) basis   Yield spread on a bond, as compared to CDS spread of same tenor.

Credit loss rate   The realized percentage of par value lost to default for a group of bonds equal to the bonds' default rate multiplied by the loss severity.

Credit migration   The change in a bond's credit rating over a certain period.

Credit valuation adjustment (CVA)   The present value of credit risk for a loan, bond, or derivative obligation.

Cross-currency basis swap   A swap in which notional principals are exchanged because the goal of the transaction is to issue at a more favorable funding rate and swap the amount back to the currency of choice.

Currency overlay   A type of overlay that helps hedge the returns of securities held in foreign currency back to the home country's currency.

Decision price   In a trading context, the decision price is the security price at the time the investment decision was made.

Default intensity   POD over a specified time period in a reduced form credit model.

Default risk   See *credit risk*.

Delay cost   The (trading related) cost associated with not submitting the order to the market in a timely manner.

Direct market access   (DMA) Access in which market participants can transact orders directly with the order book of an exchange using a broker's exchange connectivity.

Discount margin   The discount (or required) margin is the yield spread versus the MRR such that the FRN is priced at par on a rate reset date.

Duration Times Spread (DTS)   Weighting of spread duration by credit spread to incorporate the empirical observation that spread changes for lower-rated bonds tend to be consistent on a percentage rather than absolute basis.

Empirical duration   Estimation of the price–yield relationship using historical bond market data in statistical models.

Enhanced indexing strategy   A method investors use to match an underlying market index in which the investor purchases fewer securities than the full set of index constituents but matches primary risk factors reflected in the index.

Evaluated pricing   See *matrix pricing*.

Excess spread   Surplus difference of yield remaining after payments to bondholders are made after expenses are made and losses are covered.

Execution cost   The difference between the (trading related) cost of the real portfolio and the paper portfolio, based on shares and prices transacted.

Expected shortfall   The average loss conditional on exceeding the VaR cutoff; sometimes referred to as *conditional VaR* or *expected tail loss*.

Expected tail loss   See *expected shortfall*.

Forward rate bias   An empirically observed divergence from interest rate parity conditions that active investors seek to benefit from by borrowing in a lower-yield currency and investing in a higher-yield currency.

Full replication approach   When every issue in an index is represented in the portfolio and each portfolio position has approximately the same weight in the fund as in the index.

G-spread   Yield spread in basis points between a bond's yield-to-maturity and that of an actual or interpolated government bond. It represents the return for bearing risks relative to the government bond.

Green bonds   Bonds used in green finance whereby the proceeds are earmarked toward environmental-related products.

Hazard rate   The probability that an event will occur, given that it has not already occurred.

I-spread (interpolated spread)   Yield spread measure using swaps or constant maturity Treasury YTMs as a benchmark.

Immunization   An asset/liability management approach that structures investments in bonds to match (offset) liabilities' weighted-average duration; a type of dedication strategy.

Implementation shortfall   (IS) The difference between the return for a notional or paper portfolio, where all transactions are assumed to take place at the manager's decision price, and the portfolio's actual return, which reflects realized transactions, including all fees and costs.

Incremental VaR (or partial VaR)   The change in the minimum portfolio loss expected to occur over a given time period at a specific confidence level resulting from increasing or decreasing a portfolio position.

Information coefficient   Formally defined as the correlation between forecast return and actual return. In essence, it measures the effectiveness of investment insight.

Key rate duration   Also known as partial duration, is a measure of a bond's sensitivity to a change in the benchmark yield at a specific maturity.

Liquidity budget   The portfolio allocations (or weightings) considered acceptable for the liquidity categories in the liquidity classification schedule (or time-to-cash table).

Liquidity classification schedule   A liquidity management classification (or table) that defines portfolio liquidity "buckets" or categories based on the estimated time necessary to convert assets in that particular category into cash.

Loss severity   Portion of a bond's value (including unpaid interest) an investor loses in the event of default.

Matrix pricing   An estimation process for financial instruments based on the prices of comparable instruments.

Multilateral trading facilities   See *alternative trading systems*.

Negative butterfly   An increase in the butterfly spread due to lower short- and long-term yields-to-maturity and a higher intermediate yield-to-maturity.

OAS duration   The change in bond price for a given change in OAS.

Opportunity cost   The value that investors forgo by choosing a particular course of action; the value of something in its best alternative use.

Option-adjusted spread (OAS)   A generalized constant yield spread over the zero curve that incorporates bond option pricing based on assumed interest rate volatility and may be used for callable, putable, and non-callable bonds.

Options on bond futures contracts   Instruments that involve the right, but not the obligation, to enter into a bond futures contract at a pre-determined strike (bond price) on a future date in exchange for an up-front premium.

Overlay   A derivative position (or derivative positions) used to adjust a pre-existing portfolio closer to its objectives.

Passive investment   In the fixed-income context, it is investment that seeks to mimic the prevailing characteristics of the overall investments available in terms of credit quality, type of borrower, maturity, and duration rather than express a specific market view.

Portfolio overlay   An array of derivative positions managed separately from the securities portfolio to achieve overall intended portfolio characteristics.

Positive butterfly   A decrease in the butterfly spread due to higher short- and long-term yields-to-maturity and a lower intermediate yield-to-maturity.

Present value of distribution of cash flows methodology   Method used to address a portfolio's sensitivity to rate changes along the yield curve. This approach seeks to approximate and match the yield curve risk of an index over discrete time periods.

Principal trade   A trade in which the market maker or dealer becomes a disclosed counterparty and assumes risk for the trade by transacting the security for their own account. Also called *broker risk trades*.

Probability of default   The likelihood that a borrower defaults or fails to meet its obligation to make full and timely payments of principal and interest.

Program trading   A strategy of buying or selling many stocks simultaneously.

Pure indexing   Attempts to replicate a bond index as closely as possible, targeting zero active return and zero active risk.

Quoted margin   Specified spread of a floating rate instrument over a market reference rate or benchmark.

Rebalancing overlay   A type of overlay that addresses a portfolio's need to sell certain constituent securities and buy others.

Reduced form credit models   Credit models that solve for default probability over a specific time period using observable company-specific variables such as financial ratios and macroeconomic variables.

Relative VaR   See *ex ante tracking error*.

Request for quote   (RFQ) A non-binding quote provided by a market maker or dealer to a potential buyer or seller upon request. Commonly used in fixed income markets these quotes are only valid at the time they are provided.

Scenario analysis   A variation of the valuation process combining a base case with alternative outcomes, allowing the incorporation of more favorable or adverse scenarios in the valuation process.

Smart beta   Involves the use of transparent, rules-based strategies as a basis for investment decisions.

Smart order routers   (SOR) Smart systems used to electronically route small orders to the best markets for execution based on order type and prevailing market conditions.

Spread duration   The change in bond price for a given change in yield spread. Also referred to as OAS duration when the option-adjusted spread (OAS) is the yield measure used.

Stratified sampling   A sampling method that guarantees that subpopulations of interest are represented in the sample. Also called *representative sampling* or *cell approach*.

Structural credit models   Credit models that apply market-based variables to estimate the value of an issuer's assets and the volatility of asset value.

Structural risk   Risk that arises from portfolio design, particularly the choice of the portfolio allocations.

Surplus   The difference between assets and liabilities, analogous to shareholders' equity on a corporate balance sheet.

Swaption   This instrument grants a party the right, but not the obligation, to enter into an interest rate swap at a pre-determined strike (fixed swap rate) on a future date in exchange for an up-front premium.

Time-to-cash table   See *liquidity classification schedule*.

Total return swap   A swap in which one party agrees to pay the total return on a security. Often used as a credit derivative, in which the underlying is a bond.

Tracking error   The standard deviation of the differences between a portfolio's returns and its benchmark's returns; a synonym of active risk. Also called *tracking risk*.

Tracking risk   The standard deviation of the differences between a portfolio's returns and its benchmarks returns. Also called tracking error.

Trade urgency   A reference to how quickly or slowly an order is executed over the trading time horizon.

Transfer coefficient   The ability to translate portfolio insights into investment decisions without constraint.

Uncovered interest rate parity   The proposition that the expected return on an uncovered (i.e., unhedged) foreign currency (risk-free) investment should equal the return on a comparable domestic currency investment.

Value at risk (VaR)   The minimum loss that would be expected a certain percentage of the time over a certain period of time given the assumed market conditions.

Yield spread   The difference in yield-to-maturity between a bond and that of a another bond.

Z-score   A reduced-form statistical credit measure that uses company-specific and market-based ratios to create a composite score used to determine whether a firm is likely to default or remain solvent.

Zero-discount margin (Z-DM)   A yield spread calculation for FRNs that incorporates forward MRR.

Zero-volatility spread (Z-spread)   A constant spread which is estimated using the market prices of comparable bonds for issuers of similar credit quality of a bond over the benchmark rate.

Private Markets Pathway Glossary

100/10/1 rule of thumb A VC investor's rule of thumb that demonstrates the high selectivity required, as one may review 100 startup pitches, conduct due diligence on 10 of those reviewed, and select just one for investment.

Acquisition and development loan A loan used to purchase and prepare land for a specific construction use.

Agency cost of equity A principal–agent problem which arises when company managers have more information about a company than public shareholders, limiting the ability to assess performance and take corrective action.

Agreement among lenders A contractual arrangement among lenders in a unitranche debt facility which may reallocate interest and principal payments, priority of claims, or voting rights on covenant or other credit agreement changes.

Angel investors High-net-worth investors who are also often entrepreneurs that provide seed financing to startup companies.

Arbitrage spread The difference between an announced acquisition price and the post-announcement market price, which represents the potential return to a merger arbitrage strategy prior to considering transaction costs.

Asset impairment An adverse change in the market value of an asset that falls below its balance sheet carrying value.

Asset swap Converts a bond's fixed coupon to MRR plus (or minus) a spread using an interest rate swap for the remaining life of the bond.

Asset-based lending Revolving credit facility extended on a secured basis using accounts receivable, inventory, or equipment as collateral.

Bankruptcy Legal proceedings, which vary by jurisdiction, allowing a firm whose liabilities exceed its assets to restructure existing debt obligations or liquidate assets in an orderly manner.

Bond tender offer An offer from a fixed-income issuer to repurchase outstanding loans or bonds.

Brownfield investment Infrastructure investments that involve existing rather than to-be-built facilities, which may involve the privatization or repurposing of existing public assets or an expansion of existing facilities.

Build-operate-transfer (BOT) project Infrastructure project whose construction and development is conducted by private entities sponsored by a public entity and transferred to public control after a finite operating period.

Business development companies A type of closed-end investment vehicle in the United States which are publicly traded and specialize in private debt.

Buyout equity Private equity investment in a mature company with the intent to transform, divest, or acquire businesses and sell the reorganized firm at a higher price to public or private investors.

Capital structure arbitrage An investment approach that combines long or short debt, equity, and/or credit default swap positions to exploit mispricing in a single issuer's obligations.

Capitalization rate A measure of the required rate of return on a property, also known as *cap rate*.

Capitalization table A detailed summary of changes in firm value, fractional ownership dilution, and prices paid by investors or stakeholders over the course of multiple equity rounds typically shown on a fully diluted basis.

Carbon offset Investments that reduce or remove carbon dioxide and other greenhouse gases to compensate for emissions produced elsewhere to achieve reduction or net-zero emission goals.

Carried interest A performance or incentive fee applied to private market fund investments based on returns above a hurdle rate.

Catch-up clause A clause in a limited partner agreement that specifies that a general partner will receive 100% of the distributions above a prespecified hurdle *until* the GP receives the carried interest percentage (such as 20%) of the returns generated and then every excess dollar will be split between the LPs and GP based on the carried interest percentage.

CDS basis Differences in bond and CDS spreads that arise because of bond price differences from par, accrued interest, and varying contract terms.

Change of control A debt clause that requires an issuer to repurchase outstanding bonds at a fixed price at or above par if a new owner acquires a predetermined percentage of voting shares.

Change of control clause Debt provision that requires an issuer to offer to repay outstanding debt if a new owner acquires a predetermined percentage of voting shares.

Change of control provision A restrictive covenant typically included in a high-yield bond indenture that requires the issuer to offer to repurchase outstanding bonds at a fixed price (above par) if a new owner acquires a predetermined percentage of voting shares.

Circulation Zoning requirement mandating provisions for security and emergency access to buildings or facilities.

Clawback provisions Limited partnership agreement provisions that involve returning GP performance fees to LPs in cases where transactions that are initially successful later face losses.

Closed-end funds Funds with a finite life requiring an initial capital commitment with a lockup period and eventual sale of the property or properties for distribution to investors.

Collateralized loan obligations (CLOs) Investment vehicle with exposure to a portfolio of leveraged loans separated into tranches with different cash flow claims and exposure to losses based on a waterfall.

Concession agreement A contractual arrangement under which an entity (also known as a grantor) establishes terms and conditions with a developer or operator (referred to as a concessionaire) to plan, build, operate, finance, and maintain an infrastructure asset for a specific period.

Concessionaire A developer or operator that is provided the right under a concession agreement to charge user fees over an operating period to recover construction, maintenance, and operational costs and compensate investors.

Construction and development (C&D) loan Debt financing for real estate development which is committed prior to project initiation and drawn through a construction phase, accruing interest over time, and typically repaid with a mortgage loan.

Construction and development loan A loan used to provide funds during the building phase of a real estate project.

Continuation funds New private investment funds established by GPs through the sale of existing assets in another limited partnership in GP-led secondary transactions.

Contracts for difference (CfDs) Contracts used as an income stabilization measure under which the difference between a pre-agreed, fixed contractual price (or strike price) for a service or good is exchanged for the current prevailing market price (or so-called reference price).

Contractual subordination Use of contract or intercreditor agreement between senior and subordinated lenders to establish seniority ranking of debt obligations.

Conversion period The period over which a convertible bond may be exchanged for equity at a predetermined price.

Conversion price Predetermined share price at which convertible debt may be fully exchanged for common shares during the conversion period.

Conversion ratio The number of common shares a convertible bond or noteholder may receive in exchange for a specific bond par value.

Conversion value The current contingency feature value derived by comparing a convertible bond's price with its value if a bondholder were to exchange bonds for shares.

Convertible arbitrage A special situations investment approach that involves capitalizing on the perceived mispricing of the underlying risk components of a convertible bond.

Convertible debt A fixed-income instrument which combines the features of debt with equity via a contingent feature, allowing debtholders to exchange their claim for common shares at a predetermined fixed price in the future.

Convertible preferred shares (CPS) A form of preferred stock that may pay a dividend and be converted into common shares at a fixed conversion ratio, or number of common shares received for each preferred share.

Convexity The second order, usually a positive change in the price of a bond for a given change in yield, which can be negative for a callable bond such as a high-yield bond.

Covenant-lite Debt transactions involving a relatively weak set of restrictive covenants imposed on an issuer due to competitive market pressures.

Credit event An occurrence that triggers the settlement of a CDS contract, including failure to make a debt payment, debt restructuring, or a bankruptcy filing.

Credit loss rate The realized percentage of par value lost to default for a group of bonds equal to the bonds' default rate multiplied by the loss severity.

Credit valuation adjustment (CVA) The present value of credit risk for a loan, bond, or derivative obligation.

Data room A repository used to store confidential company documents that may be accessed by potential bidders who sign a non-disclosure agreement.

Debt profile A detailed breakdown of short-term and long-term liabilities by tenor, seniority, and other features, used in a private debt market strategy.

Debt service coverage ratio A ratio in which the net operating income of a real estate investment for a specific period is divided by the amount of debt service to be paid during the same time period.

Debt service reserve account (DSRA) A separate fund established to accumulate the cash flow necessary to meet debt service requirements from which cash is released when debt interest and principal payments are due.

Debt-for-equity exchange An exchange executed by distressed firms in which new shares are issued to debtholders in exchange for the extinguishment of existing debt claims.

Debtor in possession (DIP) A debtor that has filed for Chapter 11 US bankruptcy protection but remains in possession of company assets for the purpose of maintaining operations as a going concern.

Delay option Developers may increase a project's present value by postponing property construction until market conditions improve.

DIP financing Super senior debt financing obtained on a short-term basis to cover ongoing bankruptcy costs and provide funding to maintain operations as a company completes the bankruptcy process.

Direct capitalization approach A property valuation approach that divides a single year's net operating income by the cap rate to estimate a property's value.

Direct co-investment The direct purchase of an ownership stake or private debt investment with the use of one or more partners, one or more of whom may be a private fund manager.

Direct investment The purchase of an ownership stake or debt investment without the use of a partner or an investment intermediary.

Direct lending A type of senior secured leveraged loan privately issued on a floating-rate basis by non-bank lenders, usually to small and medium-sized companies.

Distressed debt Loans or bonds which face a high likelihood of non-payment or bankruptcy.

Distressed debt exchange An exchange of existing bonds for new securities from the same issuer that involve lower par values, longer maturities, and/or fewer protective financial covenants than current outstanding bonds.

Distributed to paid-in (DPI) Also referred to as the cash-on-cash return, this ratio gauges an investor's realized rate of return via the ratio of cumulative distributions to limited partners to the capital invested.

Dividend recapitalization A change in the mix of debt and equity outstanding for an existing corporate issuer which increases leverage via debt-financed dividends or share repurchases to benefit existing shareholders.

Down round Venture capital financing of an early-stage company which takes place at a share price below that of the previous financing round.

Duration The first-order, linear change in a bond's price for a given yield change in yield, which is a negative or inverse relationship.

Effective spread duration Change in a loan or bond price for a given change in yield spread, with the spread typically defined as OAS.

Empirical duration Estimation of the price–yield relationship using historical bond market data in statistical models.

Equity dividend rate A ratio in which a real estate investment's before-tax cash flow (equal to net operating income minus debt service) is divided by the difference between the investment's purchase price and the amount of debt outstanding.

Exit value of equity The expected terminal value of an early-stage firm at the end of a holding period is determined by using the required return on investment or a market multiple if the firm is expected to be profitable.

Export credit agencies (ECAs) Quasi-government entities sponsored by developed market governments to promote the export of domestic goods and services via credit insurance, political risk insurance, or subsidized or guaranteed debt financing.

Fallen angels Formerly investment-grade-rated issuers whose bonds are downgraded to high yield due to credit deterioration.

Feed crops Crops such as grain used as either raw material in food production or as an intermediate good.

Financial buyer An owner seeking to earn investment returns from an existing company without identifying or capitalizing on synergies from a controlling interest.

Financial dislocation A situation in which market prices are misaligned on an absolute or relative basis due to financial market stress, changes in liquidity, market constraints, or other industry- or company-specific factors.

Financial sponsor A private equity buyout fund which purchases a controlling stake in a firm distributed to investors in the form of limited partnerships.

First lien Also known as a priority lien, this investor protection grants a lender the right to take possession of property from a borrower which fails to repay debt.

First-out tranche Senior debt tranche in a unitranche facility which is typically at an interest rate below the blended facility rate and repaid earlier than subordinated debt claims.

Fraudulent conveyance An unlawful transfer of assets by an issuer to a third party to prevent creditors from reaching a borrower's assets, which in some cases may be voided by a court under bankruptcy law.

Free cash flow to the firm (FCFF) Free cash flow to both debt and equity holders composed of after-tax EBITDA plus tax benefits of depreciation less changes in long-term assets and working capital.

Free fall bankruptcy A situation in which an issuer enters the bankruptcy process without a reorganization plan in place.

General partners (GPs) Private fund managers responsible for sourcing and deploying capital from limited partner investors over an investment life cycle and distributing returns to those investors over a finite investment holding period.

Go-shop process Provision in a sale or merger agreement in which the seller solicits bids from potential third-party buyers for a limited period after extending the offer to an initial buyer.

Governance rights Powers extended to preferred or minority shareholders which may include board seats, special voting rights, or the ability to observe board meetings, among others.

GP-led secondary A form of private market sale in which a general partner sells a private asset from an existing portfolio into a new fund.

Grantor Another word for "settlor," who is a person who creates a trust.

Greenfield investment New "to be built" infrastructure projects and assets created to provide a specific essential service or to supply a public good.

Growth equity Private equity investment in a young company with a business model and growing revenue used to reach its total addressable market and reduce concentrated ownership of founders and initial investors.

Growth equity method Valuation approach used for private companies engaging in profitable expansion which incorporates cash flow projections over an investment horizon required to achieve a desired exit valuation and initial capital necessary to reach a targeted investor ROI.

Hard hurdle rate The minimum rate of return in a performance-based fee arrangement in which the GP earns only fees on annual returns that exceed the hurdle rate.

Heavily indebted poor countries (HIPCs) A specific group of developing countries eligible for support from the International Monetary Fund (IMF) and the World Bank.

High-water mark A measure that reflects the fund's maximum value as of a performance fee payment date net of fees.

High-yield bonds Fixed-income securities issued on a fixed-rate basis by sub-investment grade companies, which are typically subordinate to leveraged loans and include call features.

Hurdle rate A predetermined minimum rate of return an investment fund must reach before a GP receives incentive-based compensation.

Incurrence covenants Restrictive debt covenants involving financial metrics which only must be met at the time the issuer seeks to take on additional debt.

Infrastructure Company Classification Standard (TICCS) A standard developed to categorize infrastructure investments based on key characteristics affecting relative risk and return with the input of asset owners and asset managers.

Insolvency A situation in which an issuer's total liabilities exceed the market value of its assets.

Intercreditor agreement Legal contract specifying details of the priority of claims and other key terms governing separate debt claims to the same assets and legal entity.

Intermittent market reference price (IMRP) The UK market reference price for intermittently produced power determined daily based on the prior day's hourly electricity rates.

Internal rate of return (IRR) The uniform discount rate for a series of cash flows over n periods that returns a net present value of zero.

Interval funds Open-end funds with certain constraints that have no predetermined maturity date but include liquidity restrictions, such as limits on the fraction of total assets available for redemption on a periodic basis.

J-curve effect Net income over a multiyear private investment holding period characterized by negative returns in an initial phase, followed by cash flow and income growth toward the end of the holding period.

Land expectation value Value of an acre of bare land in perpetual timberland production.

Last-out tranche Junior debt tranche in a unitranche facility which is at an interest rate above the blended facility rate and repaid after senior debt claims.

LBO model Valuation approach used for buyout equity which uses expected cash flows of a target acquisition, as well as expected capital structure composition and cost, to establish the maximum price that can be paid to a seller while satisfying targeted financing returns.

Leveraged buyout (LBO) Buyout equity transaction that uses a high proportion of debt financing to make a company acquisition.

Leveraged loan Term debt extended to sub-investment-grade borrowers with a floating-rate periodic coupon based on market reference rates plus a spread that usually is secured and involves restrictive covenants.

Leveraged loans Term debt extended to sub-investment grade borrowers with a floating-rate periodic coupon based upon market reference rates plus a spread, which usually are secured and involve restrictive covenants.

Limited partner co-investment Involves the purchase of an ownership stake or private debt investment in a single investment that is managed by a private fund manager or general partner.

Limited partners (LPs) Outside investors in a private market fund who own a fractional interest in a limited, closed-end partnership managed by a general partner based on the investment commitment and other terms set out in a limited partner agreement.

Limited partnership Closed-end form of ownership frequently used in private market funds in which private market fund investors, or limited partners, commit capital that is invested, managed, and distributed by a private market fund manager, or general partner, over an investment holding period.

Liquidation preference payout Predefined distribution of cash proceeds to preferred shareholders made in full before any distributions are made to common shareholders.

Liquidity financing Private debt funds which seek to generate income by investing in a portfolio of short-term obligations in order to maintain a stable net asset value.

Loan to value (LTV) A measure of leverage used by debt investors that equals the loan amount outstanding divided by the project value.

Loan-to-value ratio A ratio in which the amount of debt outstanding on a real estate investment is divided by the current value of the investment.

Lockup agreement A provision requiring a private equity investor to retain a material interest in the shares of a new public company for a predetermined period to protect the interests of institutional investors.

Loss given default (LGD) The amount a debtholder fails to recover if a default occurs, usually expressed as a percentage of par value.

Low Carbon Contracts Company (LCCC) UK government-owned counterparty for qualified low-carbon energy contracts for difference.

Maintenance covenants Restrictive debt covenants requiring an issuer to meet certain financial metrics for each financial reporting period.

Management buyout A private sale to a strategic buyer that includes a company's existing management. The management team commits their own equity capital along with other investors as an incentive to grow the firm's cash flows and value.

Merchant payment scheme Also referred to as a commercial payment scheme, under this structure frequently used for power generation and toll road assets, an operator has the right to collect service or user fees over an operating period but remains exposed to the asset's business risk based on demand and other economic factors.

Merger arbitrage Special situations investments related to business combinations in which investors seek to capitalize on price discrepancies of securities issued by the target company.

Mezzanine debt Debt claims that are serviced after all senior debt claims, but before common shares and other forms of equity in the capital structure.

Mezzanine loan A debt claim that is serviced after all senior debt claims but before common shares and other forms of equity in the capital structure.

Multiple of invested capital A ratio in which the total value of all realized investments and residual asset values (assets that may still be awaiting sale) are divided by capital invested.

Multiple of invested capital (MOIC) Also referred to as the multiple of money or total value to paid-in, this private market performance measure incorporates both the cumulative distributions received and the net asset value of a fund as a proportion of invested capital.

Multiple of money (MOM) Also referred to as the multiple of invested capital or total value to paid-in, this private market return measure incorporates both the cumulative distributions received and the fund's net asset value as a proportion of invested capital.

Net operating income A key property income measure that ignores financing costs and taxes and is measured as NOI = Effective gross income – Operating expenses – Property maintenance allowance.

Non-disclosure agreement A legal contract specifying that any confidential information received by a prospective company buyer is used only to evaluate a possible transaction.

Non-sponsored loans Direct loans to small- or medium-sized firms which lack a controlling financial sponsor and involve greater search, due diligence, and monitoring costs.

Open-end diversified core equity (ODCE) funds Private investment funds that hold portfolios of core income-producing properties.

Open-end funds Funds which allow investors to contribute or withdraw capital freely and have no predetermined end date.

Optimal conversion point The implied equity price at which convertible preferred shareholders are better off exercising their right to convert preferred shares into common shares.

Option-adjusted spread (OAS) A generalized constant yield spread over the zero curve that incorporates bond option pricing based on assumed interest rate volatility and may be used for callable, putable, and non-callable bonds.

Own–lease A farmland investing model more common among financial investors in which an owner or lessor receives fixed rental payments for undeveloped tillable acreage under a multiyear lease agreement from a farm operator lessee who assumes all other business risks.

Own–operate A farmland investing model which involves owning land, buildings, equipment, and other assets as well as operating an agricultural business.

P90 level Probability-weighted measure of the minimum amount of electricity an average wind turbine is 90% likely to produce over an average period given changing weather conditions.

Paid-in capital (PIC) Reflects the proportion of the limited partners' total committed capital that the general partner has so far deployed, following any capital calls, to total committed capital.

Participation rights   Preferred share feature which offers upside gains to investors via similar distributions to those received by common shareholders instead of a conversion to common equity.

Payment in kind (PIK)   Interest paid not in cash, but via accrual, increasing the debt principal outstanding, which is then paid at maturity.

Permanent crops   Agricultural crops planted for many seasons, such as orchards or vineyards, which typically generate a higher return per acre or hectare.

Post-money valuation   A combination of the pre-money valuation and new equity invested.

Pre-money valuation   Estimated current value of a startup company prior to new financing derived using the VC method.

Pre-seed capital   Initial equity capital for a new business, most often sourced from founders and angel investors, which is used to establish the feasibility of a product or market need.

Prepackaged bankruptcy   A detailed business plan and exit strategy with a new capital structure proposal that is formulated and agreed on with major creditors prior to entering the bankruptcy process.

Price step-up   Change in a company's price per share over a series of financings.

Private asset investment life cycle   Refers to the multiyear investment holding period common among private investments that consists of capital commitment, deployment, distribution and exit phases.

Probability of default (POD)   The likelihood that a borrower fails to make full and timely payments of principal and interest according to debt terms, usually expressed in annual percentage terms.

Public market equivalent   A theoretical public market investment in which private fund cash outflows are invested in a public market index while cash inflows are sold from a public market index.

Public–private partnerships (PPPs)   A long-term contractual relationship between the public and private sectors involving a concession agreement or other form of compensation in exchange for delivering an essential service or public good.

Pulpwood   A timber product consisting of lower-quality, small, and often thinned trees that is the primary input for paper products.

Quoted margin (QM)   Spread over the market reference rate for a floating-rate loan established at the time of issuance to compensate investors for issuer credit and liquidity risk.

Ratchet provision   Antidilution provision negotiated by investors in early-stage companies that partially or fully reduces the conversion price of existing options or preferred shares to the price at which new shares are issued in a subsequent financing round.

Real options   Refers to the right but not the obligation to take future action. The existence of such options may affect the value of a real estate investment.

Recurring revenue financing   A form of venture debt in which a private loan is offered to a startup firm with an established subscriber base in the form of a discounted upfront monthly payment of expected subscription revenue in exchange for all monthly subscriber cash flows.

Redemption rights   Grant an investor the right to redeem preferred shares for cash as a form of downside protection against adverse events.

Reduced form models   Statistical credit models that solve for the probability of default over a specific time period, using observable company-specific and market-based variables.

Reference price   The current prevailing market price for a service or good whose difference from a pre-agreed, fixed contractual price (or strike price) determines the settlement amount in a contract for difference.

Request for proposal (RFP)   Standardized document used by public entities to choose parties involved in the development, construction, operation, and financing of infrastructure projects that outlines project details, requirements, and timing, as well as assessment criteria used to award contracts to successful bidders.

Required margin   Also known as discount margin. The market-determined yield spread over or under the market reference rate such that a floating-rate loan is priced at par on a rate reset date following issuance.

Reserve currencies   Freely floating currencies issued by central banks in major developed markets that are widely held by external parties, including central banks.

Residual value to paid-in (RVPI)   A measure of an investor's unrealized return on investment equal to the fund's net asset value as a proportion of the total invested capital.

Retained cash flow (RCF)   Net cash from operating activities less dividends, and often compared to net debt as a measure of financial leverage.

Return on investment (ROI)   A simple performance measure equal to the ratio or multiplier of cash flows received versus those invested that ignores the time value of money and length of an investment holding period.

Revolving credit agreement   The most reliable form of a short-term bank borrowing facility, which can be drawn and repaid based upon working capital needs and in effect for multiple years on either a secured or unsecured basis. Also known as revolvers.

Row crops   Agricultural crops harvested annually and rotated.

Sawtimber   Top-quality timber used for construction lumber, as well as other building products, such as plywood or particleboard.

Scenario analysis   A variation of the valuation process combining a base case with alternative outcomes, allowing the incorporation of more favorable or adverse scenarios in the valuation process.

Second lien   An investor protection which increases the recovery rate in the event of default versus unsecured debt. A second lien loan is secured by an asset with an existing lien and will only be repaid once the first lien creditor receives payment.

Secondaries   Limited partnership stakes in existing mid-cycle private market funds that are purchased and sold among LPs, which in many cases involves the fund GP as an intermediary.

Seed capital   Equity investment(s) used to launch a startup company once it has a proven business idea.

Sensitivity analysis   A form of analysis used to determine the impact of a change in one or more key variables affecting investment returns or valuation.

Sequencing option   Dividing and executing a project in staggered phases rather than all at once, which may increase a project's risk-adjusted return by reducing exposure to market oversupply during the lease-up period.

Series financing   One or more stages of equity investment in young companies which occurs after the firm is established and before it is sold or goes public.

Setback   Zoning requirement mandating provisions for distance to property lines.

Social infrastructure   Infrastructure investments directed toward essential government services, such as education and health care.

Soft hurdle rate   The minimum rate of return in a performance-based fee arrangement in which the entire return is subject to the fee once the hurdle is exceeded.

Sovereign immunity   A principle that limits legal recourse of lenders from forcing a sovereign borrower to declare bankruptcy or liquidate its assets to settle debt claims.

Special purpose entity (SPE)   Also referred to as a special purpose vehicle (SPV), this legal entity is created for a specific economic purpose. In the case of a project SPV, the entity's sole purpose is to facilitate the construction, operation, and financing of an infrastructure asset over its contractual life.

Special situations   An area of private capital investment that targets return by investing in stressed, distressed, or event-driven opportunities.

Specialty financing   Involves forms of non-bank lending to commercial and consumer borrowers such as credit card receivables, leasing, and installment loans.

Sponsored loans   Debt funding in which a private equity firm with a large equity investment in a prospective borrower directly solicits debt investors for the company.

Stabilized NOI   A more permanent level of the property's earnings potential over time, as opposed to the amount of NOI observed during a specific time period that may result from temporary market cycles.

Strategic buyer   An investor seeking to capitalize on synergies by extending the value creation process initiated by a GP, combining a business with another portfolio company, or taking other actions to increase firm value.

Strike price   A pre-agreed, fixed contractual price per period whose difference from the current prevailing market price (or so-called reference price) determines the settlement amount in a contract for difference.

Structural credit risk models   Option-based models of a firm's market value of assets over time versus its fixed obligations used to link an issuer's likelihood of default to its equity price.

Structural subordination   Refers to the positioning of debt, which is issued by a legal entity, typically a holding company, which is separate and therefore one step removed from an operating company, which holds assets pledged under a security agreement to senior secured debtholders.

Stumpage fee   A fee paid to timberland owners by private firms for the right to harvest timber.

Subscription lines   Short-term lines of credit extended to private market funds that are secured by LP investor fund commitments prior to drawdown.

Sum-of-the-parts valuation   A valuation approach that considers the value of a firm's business segments if they are sold separately.

Switching option   The option to choose among alternative projects for a given plot of land or switch economic uses for an existing project, such as a mixed-use facility, which may increase value.

Take-private transaction   Also referred to as a *go-private transaction*, this involves the purchase of a public company by private investors in which the target company's shares are no longer publicly traded.

Technical default   A violation of the terms and conditions of a credit, loan, or bond agreement, such as the breach of a financial covenant.

Tender process   Early bond repayment mechanism in which a voluntary offer is extended to bondholders by an issuer to repurchase outstanding bonds prior to maturity.

Total addressable market   A measure of the industry-wide revenue potential for the company's product or service.

Total value to paid-in (TVPI)   Also referred to as multiple of invested capital or multiple of money, this measure reflects the overall value to the limited partner by incorporating both the cumulative distributions received and the net asset value as a proportion of invested capital. TVPI is the sum of distributed to paid-in and residual value to paid-in.

Turnkey   A type of construction project in which a general contractor agrees to deliver a project on a fully completed basis.

Unitranche debt   A hybrid loan combining senior and subordinated debt in one facility, typically issued to small- or medium-sized corporate borrowers by private debt funds.

VC method   Valuation method for startup companies in which the current value is determined using the expected terminal value of the firm (or exit value of equity) and the required return on investment.

Venture capital   Private equity investment in a startup or early-stage company involving high risk and a high rate of failure.

Venture debt   Unsecured debt from non-bank lenders offered to startup companies, often in anticipation of follow-on equity offerings, which typically involves a loan plus a warrant.

Vintage year   Year in which capital is initially deployed to a specific investment or project or a private market fund, used for benchmarking purposes and to seek diversification over time in a private market allocation.

Voidable preference   A situation in which an issuer grants a preference to one creditor over another in violation of a loan agreement or bond indenture, which may be reversed in bankruptcy court.

Warrant   Debt feature or security granting the right to purchase additional common equity shares issued by the company at a predetermined price for a given period.

Weighted average cost of capital (WACC)   The expected cost of debt and equity weighted by the proportion of each used in a company's capital structure.

Z-score   A reduced-form statistical credit measure that uses company-specific and market-based ratios to create a composite score used to determine whether a firm is likely to default or remain solvent.

Zero-volatility spread (Z-spread)   A constant spread which is estimated using the market prices of comparable bonds for issuers of similar credit quality of a bond over the benchmark rate.

Private Wealth Pathway Glossary

Accumulation The process of saving for retirement.

Accumulation period In a lifetime or period-certain annuity, the accumulation period is the phase during which the annuitant makes regular premium payments to build up the annuity's investment value.

Acquirer's dilemma The process of incorporating a new identity as a wealthy person into the identity that an individual already has from their formative years.

Advanced-life deferred annuity An annuity purchased in later life, providing deferred income initiated by a lump-sum payment.

Agreeableness A personality trait that describes the degree to which a person has a kind and empathic orientation to others.

Allocation effect The impact of overweighting and underweighting sectors relative to the benchmark on the return of the portfolio.

Alternative minimum tax (AMT) A special regime of taxation under which an individual calculates their taxes under two sets of rules—one being the conventional and an alternative one, usually more conservative with respect to deductions and tax credits, which is referred to as AMT. The taxable entity will pay the tax calculated under the method that results in the higher tax amount.

Anchoring A type of cognitive bias that makes individuals focus on the first idea or value they are presented with as a baseline for subsequent evaluations of a decision.

Annuity A decumulation vehicle that requires an upfront payment for a stream of periodic payments.

Anstalt A structure combining the attributes of a company and a foundation that is used in civil law jurisdictions for wealth transfer purposes.

Arithmetic active return The arithmetic difference between the return of the portfolio and the return of its benchmark.

Arm's-length transaction Both buyer and seller act independently without any preexisting relationship that may sway their decision making.

Asset structuring The process of structuring a collection of investments, business interests, or other financial holdings to maximize wealth.

Availability heuristic A type of cognitive bias that makes individuals overweight information that is readily available when making decisions.

Beneficiary A person who has beneficial ownership of trust assets and to whom the trustee is accountable.

Bequest The act of giving or leaving property to a specified person(s) through the provisions of a will.

Centralized portfolio management (CPM) A paradigm of total portfolio construction and investment operation whereby the assets of a single beneficiary are managed by multiple managers, internal or external, who act in a coordinated fashion with the goal of improving the optimality of the investment outcome. The coordination involves trading, information sharing, and aggregation that reduces turnover, taxes, and improves the risk-return profile of the overall portfolio.

Charitable incorporated organizations Legally incorporated entities established for non-profit purposes, like social welfare, education, and environmental protection, under the law of Japan.

Charitable lead trust (CLT) A US philanthropic vehicle that inverts the sequence of benefits provided by a CRT. A CLT focuses on offering an immediate income stream to charitable causes while preserving the remainder of the trust's assets for the donor's heirs.

Charitable remainder trust (CRT) A US philanthropic vehicle that provides an income stream to the donor while committing the remaining assets to a future gift to charity.

Choice overload bias This cognitive bias occurs when an individual feels paralyzed into inaction because of the variety and abundance of options.

Citizenship-based tax systems Tax their citizens regardless of their residential status.

Civil law system The elected legislatures, derived from Roman jurisprudence, that enact laws; the courts interpret and apply these laws to each particular case through their judges.

Cohabitation agreement A legal and financial framework for a relationship between two unmarried adults that defines how assets and debts will be treated during cohabitation and in the event of separation or death.

Common law system A case law system derived from the British legal tradition in which previously adjudicated cases influence pending and future cases.

Community foundation A charitable organization that makes social or educational grants for the benefit of a local community as is typically funded by public donations.

Community property Property acquired by a spouse during a marriage that is owned jointly by both spouses and is divided upon divorce, annulment, or the death of a spouse.

Community property regimes Regimes that treat marital assets as jointly owned and thus divided equally in the event of divorce.

Comprehensive wealth planning Focuses on integrated management of all of a client's financial and business affairs.

Concentrated position A holding that, due to its low tax basis and implicit large potential capital gains or personal association with the client, inhibits the development of an efficient, diversified portfolio.

Confirmation bias A type of cognitive bias that makes individuals view information that confirms beliefs they already hold as more salient.

Conscientiousness A personality trait characterizing the ability to exercise discipline and self-control to achieve goals.

Cost-push inflation Inflation triggered by an increase in the costs of production inputs, such as labor and materials, which leads businesses to raise their prices.

Credit method A method that offsets domestic tax liability with the taxes already paid to a foreign country.

Cross-Border Financial Center A financial hub that specializes in providing financial services, like banking, asset management, or investment opportunities, to clients located in different jurisdictions. Unlike OFCs, the emphasis is not necessarily on tax advantages but on serving diverse geographic markets.

Custodian   A specialized financial institution responsible for safeguarding an investor's financial assets and is not typically involved in asset management activities. The custodian may offer additional services like performance analytics to assist in portfolio evaluation.

Decumulation   The process of spending down savings in retirement.

Deduction method   A method that reduces taxable income by the amount already paid to a foreign government.

Deemed disposition   A tax event upon death, among others, in certain countries, including Canada, which treats property as if it were sold upon death and imposes a capital gains tax on the assets as if they were sold.

Deferred fixed annuity   Provides an annuity payout at a future date, not immediately.

Deferred variable annuities   Annuities that initiates payments at a future date, allowing contributions to an investment account whose performance affects payouts.

Demand-pull inflation   Inflation triggered by increased consumer demand for goods and services, resulting in upward pressure on prices.

Digital Security   Technologies and best practices employed to protect sensitive financial information and digital assets from unauthorized access, data breaches, or cyberattacks. For high-net-worth individuals, robust digital security measures are essential to safeguard not only investment portfolios but also personal data, as these clients are often prime targets for cybercriminals.

Disability   A temporary or permanent impairment that substantially limits an individual's employment, employability, and human capital.

Discretionary financial goals   Non-essential objectives that are desirable but not critical for maintaining one's lifestyle.

Discretionary trust   A trust that provides the trustee discretion in determining what distributions may be made to a beneficiary.

Discretionary wealth   The difference between the sum of explicit and implied assets less the sum of current and implied liabilities.

Disposition effect   A type of cognitive bias that makes individuals unwilling to sell their possessions at a loss.

Donative intent   The making of a transfer without any expectation of anything in exchange.

Donee   The person receiving the gift.

Donor   A person making a lifetime gift.

Donor-advised fund (DAF)   A philanthropic fund that allows donors to make charitable contributions, immediately benefit from tax deductions, and subsequently recommend grants to other qualified charities over time.

Double taxation   Income is taxed twice.

Dynasty trusts   Trusts that can last for multiple generations, perhaps perpetually, usually created in a jurisdiction that has abolished its rule against perpetuities.

Embedded family office (EFO)   A dedicated space within the family business with a small number of staff who handle the financial, legal, and tax matters of the owners.

Endowment effect   A type of cognitive bias that makes individuals value an object more highly if they own it than if they did not.

Endowment life insurance   A hybrid insurance product that combines features of term and whole life insurance, offering a set coverage period after which the policy matures and pays out the cash value to the policy owner if the insured has not died by that time.

Entrepreneurial personality profile   A set of personality traits described in Bill Wagner's book, The Entrepreneur Next Door: Discover the Secrets to Financial Independence, that differentiate entrepreneurs from an average person.

Equivalency determination   The determination by the tax authorities that a donee non-US charity is the equivalent of a US public charity.

Estate   A person's assets at death.

Estate tax   A tax imposed on the value of the estate of a decedent payable by the estate, not the recipient.

Excess return   Used in various senses appropriate to context: 1) The difference between the portfolio return and the benchmark return, which may be either positive or negative; 2) The return in excess of the risk-free rate, thus representing the return for bearing risk.

Exemption method   A method that allows for offsetting taxes; the home country relinquishes its taxation rights on foreign-source income.

Expenditure responsibility   The determination by the tax authorities that a donee non-US charity will use a grant for appropriate purposes as stated in the grant agreement.

External Asset Managers (EAMs)   Independent firms or individuals that manage assets on behalf of a client but use the infrastructure and services of a larger financial institution for trade execution, custody, and other operational needs. EAMs offer a personalized touch and can provide a more boutique experience than traditional asset management services.

Externally managed assets   Financial and investment assets managed by a hired external manager who the client has determined can add more value to than the client themselves.

Extroversion   A personality trait characterizing the degree to which an individual is comfortable in social environments.

Family advisory board   A group of family members and non-family members that assist in setting a strategic direction and establishing priorities for overseeing the family's wealth.

Family constitution   A formal written agreement among family members that sets out the principles, values, and guidelines by which the family will interact with its wealth, including its family business(es), investments, and philanthropic endeavors.

Family council   A select group of family members who act as a representative body that makes decisions on issues concerning family wealth and family business.

Family extended balance sheet   Comprehensively accounts for a client's explicit and implicit financial assets, current and future expected liabilities, and net worth.

Family foundation   A platform for focused philanthropy. It unites family members toward achieving common charitable goals.

Family limited partnership (FLP)   A family limited partnership is a limited partnership created by a family to pool assets. While FLPs have non-tax reasons for their creation, often interests in the FLP can be transferred to family members for estate planning purposes at a valuation discount.

Family mission statement   An aspirational statement that reflects a family's shared values and commitments.

Family office A private wealth management advisory firm serving very wealthy clients.

Fideicomiso A trust-like entity that holds and manages assets for specific purposes, including charitable ones, within certain civil law jurisdictions in Latin America.

Fiduciary standard of care States that an advisor must put their clients' interests above their own over the entire course of a relationship.

Fixed annuity An annuity offering a predetermined, fixed annual income derived from an initial lump-sum investment.

Fixed trust A trust that, by its terms, provides for fixed distributions to a beneficiary.

Fondation An independent legal entity used in European civil law countries for philanthropic activities and charitable grantmaking in which founders benefit from income tax deductions for contributions, and the Fondation typically enjoys tax exempt status.

Forced heirship The regime in civil law jurisdictions that requires disposing of a portion of one's estate to one's spouse and descendants.

Forced inheritance rules Rules that establish a legal obligation to leave a portion of one's estate to certain family members, typically children or descendants.

Framing effects A type of cognitive bias that makes the way in which a choice is presented affect decisions.

Funding ratio The ratio of assets to liabilities.

Funding ratio return The ratio of funding ratio at time t to funding ratio at time $t - 1$.

Generation skipping The process of transferring capital directly to the third generation to avoid a double layer of taxation.

Generation-skipping transfer tax A tax imposed in the United States on transfers that skip a generation, which is intended to impose a tax at each generational level.

Gift tax A tax imposed on the donor of a gift based on the value of the gift.

Goals-based planning Aligns an individual's financial resources with their unique goals and circumstances, with the aim of achieving specific financial objectives.

Golden visas Visas that provide initial residency, work rights, and a path to permanent residency, and potentially citizenship, through significant investments in areas like real estate, government debt, or business ventures.

Grantor Another word for "settlor," who is a person who creates a trust.

Grantor retained annuity trust (GRAT) A trust that provides the grantor with an annuity for a period of years.

Health risk Risk that encompasses both direct and indirect costs stemming from unexpected illness or injury, affecting human capital.

Healthspan The number of years of life from birth to the onset of chronic disease or disability.

Hindsight bias A type of cognitive bias that makes individuals misremember the past in ways that make them appear to have made better and more well-informed choices.

Immediate variable annuities Annuities beginning payments immediately after a lump-sum investment, where payment amounts vary based on underlying investment performance.

Income yield The fixed annual income, expressed as a percentage of the initial annuity investment, that the annuitant receives.

Individualism versus collectivism A Hofstede cultural dimension that considers the degree to which individuals are supposed to look out for themselves versus relying on the community for support and sustenance.

Indulgence versus restraint A Hofstede cultural dimension that refers to society's willingness to accept and encourage the gratification of desires versus discouraging the gratification of desires within a relatively rigid set of norms. Another way of looking at this is the degree of permissiveness within a society.

Inflation-adjusted payments Payments that allow annuitants to counter inflation erosion by choosing payments that adjust for inflation or grow by a fixed percentage, although the latter provides a weaker protection against inflation.

Information ratio The ratio of mean active return to standard deviation (active return).

Inheritance Assets that a person receives as a beneficiary after someone's death.

Inheritance tax A tax imposed on the recipient of an inheritance.

Inheritor's dilemma The combination of financial and emotional challenges faced by individuals inheriting significant wealth. It is marked by the pressure to manage and uphold the legacy responsibly.

Institutional family office (IFO) See Professional family office (PFO).

Intentionally defective grantor trust A trust that is created in the United States whereby the gift is not part of the estate of the grantor, but the grantor continues to pay income tax on the assets in the trust.

Inter vivos trust A trust created during the settlor's lifetime.

Interaction effect The impact of overweighting and underweighting individual securities within sectors that are themselves overweighted or underweighted.

Internally managed assets Businesses in which the individual or family holds controlling or direct ownership, privately owned residential real estate, or other properties that generate value through the client's activities; human capital is an important component of internally managed assets.

Intestacy Dying without a will.

Investor visa A visa that offers temporary residency in exchange for specified investments in local businesses or industries, without guaranteeing a route to full citizenship.

Irrevocable trust A trust that cannot be changed or revoked by the settlor.

Joint life annuity An annuity that covers two annuitants, typically spouses with lifetime payments. Also called *survivor option*.

Joint tenants with right of survivorship (JTWROS) A form of ownership of property in which two or more individuals own the property together, and upon the death of one of the owners, the deceased owner's share automatically passes to the surviving owner(s).

Kinecon group A network of individuals that share both a kinship bond and economic interests.

Liability risk The risk of financial losses due to legal responsibility for property damage or personal injury.

Life annuity with period certain An annuity in which the annuitants are guaranteed a minimum number of payments even if they die prematurely, with any remaining payments going to a designated beneficiary.

Life annuity with return-of-premium An annuity that ensures that if the annuitant passes away before recouping the initial investment, the unpaid principal balance, after subtracting any fees and adjustments, is disbursed to a designated beneficiary.

Life insurance wrappers A type of financial product that allows investors to house a variety of assets, such as equities or hedge funds, within a life insurance policy coverage structure and to benefit from tax advantages on investment income generated by these assets.

Lifespan The number of years of life from birth to death.

Lifetime annuity An annuity in which annuitants can opt to receive payments for their entire lives. Also called *period-certain payments.*

Lifetime gifts Gifts made during lifetime, usually for tax purposes.

Liquidity event Converts heretofore illiquid assets into more liquid assets either in the form of cash or securities.

Liquidity premium The compensation for liquidity risk that increases in proportion to the investment's illiquidity.

Liquidity risk The risk that an investment may not be readily sold at its true value.

Logarithmic active return The natural log of 1+Arithmetic active return.

Long-term versus short-term orientation A Hofstede cultural dimension that refers to the degree to which cultures encourage delayed gratification of material, social, and emotional needs.

Longevity risk The risk of exhausting an individual's financial resources before passing away, thereby leaving insufficient capital for living expenses and unmet needs.

Loss control Strategies implemented to mitigate or prevent a loss.

Loss prevention Strategies implemented to mitigate the likelihood of incurring a loss.

Loss reduction Strategies implemented to mitigate the impact after a loss occurs.

Masculine versus feminine A Hofstede cultural dimension that defines "masculine values" as success, wealth, and personal accomplishment and "feminine values" as those that emphasize caring for others and a holistic quality of life.

Mission-related investing Investing aimed at causes promoting positive societal or environmental change.

Money scripts Function as unconscious "tapes" consisting of beliefs and attitudes about money that are informed and shaped by one's experiences as a child or a young adult.

Multi-family office Unlike a single-family office that serves one affluent family, a multi-family office (MFO) provides comprehensive wealth management services to multiple high-net-worth families. The scale allows for a diversified service offering and potential cost efficiencies.

Multi-partiality A facilitation technique in which the advisor takes the sides of all participants simultaneously, thus giving equal attention to the many identities and experiences of the dialogue participants.

Net New Business Volume The volume of new business across new and existing clients.

Net New Money New sources of revenue obtained within a specific time frame, net of cancellations and other revenue deductions. In private wealth management, it is a key measure of the effectiveness of Relationship Managers and other asset gatherers.

Neuroticism A personality trait characterizing the degree to which a person displays emotional instability.

No contest clause A provision included in an estate plan that disinherits any beneficiary who challenges the plan.

Non-discretionary financial goals Encompass necessary expenses essential for sustaining the current lifestyle.

Non-forfeiture clause Clause allowing policyholders of permanent life insurance to access a portion of their benefits even if they miss premium payments, provided this is done before the policy lapses.

Non-grantor charitable lead trust A charitable lead trust where the donor is not a remainder beneficiary.

Non-participating life insurance Insurance that offers policyholders fixed benefits that remain unaffected by the insurer's profits or performance.

Offshore Financial Centers (OFCs) Jurisdictions that provide financial services to non-residents in a way that is more regulatory-efficient or tax-efficient than the client's home jurisdiction. These centers often attract capital flows seeking tax optimization, asset protection, or enhanced confidentiality.

Offshore trust A trust established in a foreign jurisdiction, often a foreign tax haven.

Openness A personality trait characterizing the willingness to be open to new experiences.

Participating life insurance Insurance that enables policyholders to share in the insurer's profits via potential dividends above the guaranteed value.

PATRIOT Act A US law enacted in 2001 which, among other goals, was aimed at preventing the funding of terrorist activities.

Performance attribution The process of disaggregating a portfolio's return to determine the drivers of its performance.

Permanent life insurance A type of life insurance that remains in force for the insured's entire lifetime, provided the premiums are consistently paid, and offers an accumulated cash value component.

Personal umbrella liability policy Such an insurance offers specified limits and pays claims when the liability limits of the home or auto insurance are reached, thereby providing additional coverage.

Polysemy Refers to the fact that value terms can have multiple meanings to different people.

Postnuptial agreements Contracts signed after marriage that outline the division of assets, debts, and financial obligations in case of divorce or death.

Power distance index A Hofstede cultural dimension that reflects the degree to which a society accepts that power in social groups is distributed unequally.

Prenuptial agreements Contracts signed before marriage that outline the division of assets, debts, and financial obligations in case of divorce or death.

Prepaid variable forward A contract that offers the asset owner an immediate cash payment, without immediate tax consequences, from a sale.

Private grant-making foundation An independent legal entity created for charitable purposes in which the donor funds the foundation and receives a tax deduction, and the foundation must distribute at least 5% of its assets annually towards charitable endeavors.

Private Placement Life Insurance (PPLI) A form of variable universal life insurance that offers more extensive investment choices and greater flexibility compared to traditional life insurance products. Often used by high-net-worth individuals for tax optimization and estate planning, PPLI policies are not publicly available and must be purchased through private placement. The policyholder can customize the asset allocation, which may include a range of investment options often not available in standard life insurance policies.

Probability of ruin The likelihood that an investor will deplete their financial assets before meeting a specific financial obligation or goal, including sustaining spending throughout retirement.

Probate A legal proceeding to confirm the validity of a will.

Professional family office (PFO) An institutionally backed entity that offers comprehensive services to its wealthy clients (also known as an institutional family office [IFO]).

Property or wealth tax Applies to property, real estate, financial, and other assets and is usually assessed annually.

Prudent investor rule The rule of law that governs trust investing.

Publicly supported charitable organizations Charities in the United States receive at least one-third of their support from the public, such as churches, hospitals, museums, and schools.

Qualified charitable distribution An income tax-free gift of up to USD 100,000 made via a required minimum distribution from a US retirement plan.

Related-party, arm's-length transaction A business arrangement between a company and its owners or executives made on terms that are comparable to what would be offered in the open market to unrelated parties under similar circumstances.

Residence rules The time a person can spend in a country without becoming a taxable resident.

Resident An individual or entity subject to tax in a specific country based on such factors as domicile or physical residence.

Revocable trust A trust that can be changed or revoked by the settlor.

Risk acceptance The decision of assuming specific risks and a strategy to mitigate the overall financial exposure based on one's financial capacity.

Risk avoidance The decision of avoiding specific risks and a strategy to mitigate the overall likelihood of significant loss by eliminating certain risks.

Risk mitigation Strategies implemented to mitigate the severity or probability of financial loss.

Risk transfer Strategies implemented to mitigate the impact of specific risks by transferring them to an insurance company.

Robo-Advisers Automated investment platforms that use algorithms to provide financial planning services with minimal human intervention. While they often serve retail clients, they are increasingly being integrated into wealth management offerings for more affluent clients.

Rule against perpetuities A common law rule that requires trusts to terminate or vest within 21 years after the date of death of a group of individuals who were alive when the trust was created or where a fixed date for termination or vesting is required.

Selection effect The impact of overweighting and underweighting individual securities relative to the benchmark on the return of the portfolio.

Separate property The regime in which each spouse can own and control property as an individual, enabling each to dispose of property as they wish.

Separate property regimes Regimes that consider pre-marital or post-marital gifts and inheritances as individual property.

Settlor A person who creates and funds a trust, also sometimes referred to as a grantor.

Shari'a law The law of Islam.

Sharpe ratio The ratio of mean excess return to standard deviation (excess return).

Short sale against the box position A hedging strategy that shorts a security that is held long.

Single-family office (SFO) A corporate structure owned by a single family and dedicated to the management of family assets and the fulfillment of individual and tailored needs of family members.

Single-premium immediate annuity (SPIA) An annuity converting a lump-sum investment into fixed annual income for a predetermined period or lifetime.

Social desirability bias A bias in which individuals give an answer that they believe is more socially acceptable than their genuine and authentic feeling.

Socioemotional wealth (SEW) A methodology to understand how family firms make decisions regarding the disposition of their business. It takes into account the fact that family business owners are often motivated by considerations other than profit.

Source state Jurisdiction where income originates—generally where the related economic activity takes place.

Stamp duties Taxes imposed on the purchase price of assets like shares or real estate.

Stewardship of wealth Refers to the responsible management of one's wealth to ensure a positive, lasting impact. It is typically manifested by wealthy individuals through philanthropy and aligning assets with values to benefit both family and society.

Stiftung A structure similar to an institution or foundation used in civil law jurisdictions for wealth transfer purposes.

Supposedly irrelevant factors (SIFs) A factor that is supposedly irrelevant to a decision being made. In practice, however, some SIFs have an outsized influence on decision making.

Surplus The difference between assets and liabilities, analogous to shareholders' equity on a corporate balance sheet.

Tax avoidance The practice of using legal means to reduce tax liability by conforming to both the spirit and the letter of the tax codes in relevant jurisdictions.

Tax domicile Country where an individual is considered a tax resident.

Tax evasion The illegal act of reducing tax liability by deliberately misreporting or concealing information from tax authorities.

Tax haven A country or independent region with no or very low tax rates for foreign investors.

Tax lot Represents the quantity, cost basis, and date of the security for tax purposes in a particular transaction.

Tax-deferred account Investment and contributions may be made on a pretax basis, and investment returns accumulate on a tax-deferred basis until funds are withdrawn, at which time they are typically taxed at ordinary income.

Tax-exempt account Taxes may or may not be assessed on the initial investment or contribution. Investment returns are typically allowed to grow and the proceeds withdrawn without tax.

Tax-loss harvesting A strategy used by investors to reduce their tax liability in taxable accounts by creating a tax offset, and involves selling securities at a loss to offset capital gains, thereby reducing the net tax liability in that period.

Taxable account The normal tax rules of the jurisdiction apply.

Term life insurance   A type of life insurance that provides coverage for a predetermined period but lacks a cash value component and becomes void if the insured individual either fails to pay the premiums or does not die within the policy term. Also called *temporary life insurance.*

Territorial tax system   A country that taxes income sourced within its borders; also known as source jurisdiction.

Testamentary   A provision in a will.

Testamentary documents   Documents such as a will or testamentary trust that take effect at death.

Testamentary gratuitous transfer   A gift by will.

Testamentary trust   A trust created under a will.

Testator   The person who creates a will.

Tontine   A pooled decumulation vehicle that allows longevity risk to the moderated by averaging.

Transfer tax   The tax imposed on the transfer of assets, including gift tax, estate tax, inheritance tax, and generation-skipping tax.

Treaty shopping   The attempt by a taxpayer to leverage treaty tax advantages without engaging in genuine economic activities in either country.

Trust   A structure whereby legal title to assets is held by one person (a trustee) who holds and manages the assets for the benefit of a third party or parties (the beneficiaries) who are the beneficial owners of the assets.

Trust agreement   The document that sets forth the terms of a trust.

Trustee   A person who has legal title to assets in the trust and who must administer the trust for the benefit of its beneficiaries.

Unanchored inflation expectations   The anticipation of rising inflation rates in the future, subsequently influencing economic decision-making for consumers, manufacturers, and service providers.

Uncertainty avoidance index   A Hofstede cultural dimension that considers the degree to which individuals are comfortable in ambiguous situations and tolerant of risk.

Universal life insurance   A flexible type of permanent life insurance that permits adjustable premiums and offers investment options for the accumulated cash value, remaining in effect as long as premiums are paid.

Virtual family office (VFO)   A legally organized business designed to manage, control, and facilitate both the financial and non-financial wealth and transactions of a family.

Wash sale   An investor sells a security at a loss and buys a very similar or substantially identical stock or security within a given time period before or after the sale.

Wealth transfer tax   Tax when assets are transferred from one owner to another through means other than a direct sale or purchase.

Whole life insurance   A life insurance policy that provides coverage for the insured's entire lifetime, with premiums usually paid annually. See *Permanent life insurance.*

Will   A legal document that becomes effective after a person's death that disposes of that person's property.

Withholding taxes   Imposed by countries for non-resident investors for interest and dividend payments. Depending on the jurisdictions involved, there may be tax treaties between the sending and receiving countries, which will impact the withholding tax rate.

Worldwide tax systems   Jurisdictions that tax all income no matter where it's earned.

Zeroed-out CLAT   A charitable lead annuity trust with an annuity so large that the actuarial remainder value is zero.